HISTORY IN DISPUTE

ADVISORY BOARD

HISTORY IN DISPUTE

Volume 8

World War I:
First Series

Edited by **Dennis Showalter**

A MANLY, INC. BOOK

ST. JAMES PRESS

GALE GROUP

THOMSON LEARNING

Detroit • New York • San Diego • San Francisco
Boston • New Haven, Conn. • Waterville, Maine
London • Munich

HISTORY IN DISPUTE

 ## Volume 8 ▪ World War I, First Series

Matthew J. Bruccoli and Richard Layman, *Editorial directors.*

Karen L. Rood, *Senior editor.*

Anthony J. Scotti Jr., *Series editor.*

James F. Tidd Jr., *Assistant in-house editor.*

Philip B. Dematteis, *Production manager.*

Kathy Lawler Merlette, *Office manager.* Ann M. Cheschi, Amber L. Coker, and Angi Pleasant, *Administrative support.* Ann-Marie Holland, *Accounting.*

Sally R. Evans, *Copyediting supervisor.* Phyllis A. Avant, Brenda Carol Blanton, Melissa D. Hinton, Charles Loughlin, Rebecca Mayo, Nancy E. Smith, Elizabeth Jo Ann Sumner, *Copyediting staff.* Jennie Williamson, *Freelance copyeditor.*

Janet E. Hill, *Layout and graphics supervisor.* Zoe R. Cook, *Lead layout and graphics.* Karla Corley Brown, *Layout and graphics.*

Scott Nemzek, Paul Talbot, *Photography editors.* Jason Paddock, *Photo permissions.* Joseph M. Bruccoli and Zoe R. Cook, *Digital photographic copy work.*

Jason Paddock, *SGML supervisor.* Frank Graham, Linda Dalton Mullinax, and Alex Snead, *SGML staff.*

Marie L. Parker, *Systems manager.*

Kathleen M. Flanagan, *Typesetting supervisor.* Jaime All, Patricia Marie Flanagan, Mark J. McEwan, and Pamela D. Norton, *Typesetting staff.*

Walter W. Ross, *Library researcher.* Jaime All, *Assistant library researcher.* Tucker Taylor, *Circulation department head, Thomas Cooper Library, University of South Carolina.* John Brunswick, *Interlibrary-loan department head.* Virginia W. Weathers, *Reference department head.* Brette Barclay, Marilee Birchfield, Paul Cammarata, Gary Geer, Michael Macan, Tom Marcil, and Sharon Verba, *Reference librarians.*

CONTENTS

About the Series xiii

Preface by Dennis Showalter xv

Chronology xxi

Alienation of Soldiers: Did soldiers who had fought at the front
feel permanently alienated from civilian culture? 1
Yes. The conditions of the fighting and the remoteness of many
theaters combined to establish a barrier of understanding
between those who fought and those who did not.
(Paul Du Quenoy) 2
No. The myth that front-line soldiers were alienated from
homefront society is based on the experience of a small,
vocal group. *(H. B. McCartney)* 6

American Military Independence: Was U.S. insistence on
maintaining military independence a decisive element in the
Allied victory? 10
Yes. Military independence allowed the American forces to
defend Paris successfully in the summer of 1918 and to
spearhead the decisive counteroffensive in September of the
same year. *(Paul Du Quenoy)* 11
No. American troops performed poorly under their own
officers, and the Allied victory can be attributed simply to the
American role in introducing two million fresh troops at a time
when the Central Powers had no more manpower reserves.
(James Corum) 14
No. General Pershing's intransigence concerning the
integration of U.S. troops into existing Allied units cost lives
and time when both were in short supply. *(James J. Cooke)* 18

American Tactics: Was General Pershing's emphasis on open
warfare appropriate for the Western Front? 21
Yes. General Pershing recognized that the war could not be
decided from the trenches. The problem of the American
Expeditionary Force (AEF) was less a failure of strategy than
defective training systems. *(James J. Cooke)* 22
No. The American Expeditionary Force (AEF) went to Europe
with a tactical doctrine unsuitable to the nature of the war
and, as a result, U.S. forces paid a heavy price.
(Mark E. Grotelueschen) 25

Anglo–German Naval Race: Was the naval arms race the central
factor in the growth of Anglo-German antagonism prior to
World War I? 29
Yes. As the premier naval power at the turn of the twentieth
century, Great Britain felt threatened by the growing naval
capabilities and heavy-handed diplomacy of Germany.
(Paul Du Quenoy) 30

No. The German naval threat was almost welcome, as the one
challenge Britain was confident it could defeat. German hostility
was instead the price Britain paid for rapprochement with
her imperial rivals, France and Russia. *(John Abbatiello)* **33**

Arab Uprising: Did the Arab uprising of 1916 contribute significantly
to the military and political developments in the Middle East? **37**
Yes. The Arab revolt gave the Allies political leverage in the
region and established Arab nationalism as a postwar force.
(John Wheatley) **38**
No. The Arab revolt represented a minor military event that was
peripheral to the more significant fighting taking place west of
the Jordan River. *(Edward J. Erickson)* **39**

Austria–Hungary: Did Austria-Hungary's abandonment
of great-power status to concentrate on the Balkans play a
major role in generating the Great War? **43**
Yes. Austria-Hungary in 1914 had become, de facto, another
Balkan power, and it was correspondingly indifferent to the
consequences of its actions in Europe. *(Graydon A. Tunstall)* **44**
No. The policy of Austria-Hungary after the assassination of
Archduke Franz Ferdinand reflected a determination to
maintain the Dual Monarchy's status as a great power, able and
willing to act independently in defense of its own vital interests.
(John Wheatley) **47**

BEF Technology: Did the integration of tanks in the British
Expeditionary Force (BEF) contribute to the Allied victory? **51**
Yes. Armor was the central element of British Expeditionary
Force (BEF) tactics in the final offensives of 1918.
(Robert M. Citino) **52**
No. In the final Allied offensives of 1918 mechanical warfare and
tanks were less significant to victory than traditional technologies,
especially artillery. *(William J. Astore)* **55**

Combat Experience: Did blood lust prolong the war? **59**
Yes. The blood lust exhibited by frontline soldiers throughout the
conflict stopped only with the collapse of the German war effort.
(William R. Forstchen) **60**
No. The ordinary frontline soldier was no more inclined to act
aggressively against the enemy than to adopt a "live and let live"
approach toward him. *(Mary Habeck)* **61**

Culture of the Offensive: Were the war plans of 1914 manifestations
of a "culture of the offensive" at any cost? **66**
Yes. Between 1871 and 1914 European armies moved toward an
intellectualized concept of the offensive as a sovereign recipe for
victory, without regard for the objective analyses of developments
in technology and administration that predicted a prolonged war.
(William R. Forstchen) **67**
No. Many military planners before 1914 envisioned a limited
offensive war of short duration in which the European balance
of power would be maintained. *(Daniel Lee Butcher)* **69**
No. The general commitment to offensive warfare reflected a
careful calculation of prewar armies' perceived strengths,
weaknesses, and potential as well as the similarities
characterizing those armies. *(Robert T. Foley)* **72**

CONTENTS

David Lloyd George: Was David Lloyd George an effective wartime prime minister? 77

Yes. Lloyd George provided strong leadership when Britain was under intense pressure on many fronts. His personal charm and political skills were major assets, and it is unlikely any of his contemporaries could have done better. *(Philip Giltmer)* 78

No. Lloyd George's pursuit of victory at all costs committed Britain to policies that could not be sustained, and the nation's survival depended upon strokes of good fortune. *(Robert McJimsey)* 81

East Africa: Was the 1914–1918 campaign of German general Paul von Lettow-Vorbeck in East Africa a success? 84

Yes. As both a military operation and an example of creating a multiethnic army, Lettow-Vorbeck's campaign was brilliant. *(Michelle Moyd)* 85

No. The demographic and ecological havoc wrought by Lettow-Vorbeck's operations had little impact on the German war effort. *(William J. Astore)*. 87

Eastern Europe: Did German occupation policies in Eastern Europe prefigure those of the Third Reich? 91

Yes. The Nazis, who added genocidal racism to the mix, perpetuated German views of the East and its peoples as fields of conquest and development. *(Lawrence A. Helm)*. 92

No. The German occupation of Eastern Europe was concerned initially with providing administration and security and subsequently with reorganizing the conquered territory along traditional imperialist lines. *(Paul Du Quenoy)* 97

Easterners and Westerners: Was the conflict between Prime Minister David Lloyd George and Chief of Staff Sir William Robertson the result of a basic disagreement on war strategy? 102

Yes. David Lloyd George emphasized military operations in the East while Sir William Robertson advocated continuing the offensive in the West. *(Michael S. Neiberg)* 103

No. David Lloyd George and Sir William Robertson had flexibility in their respective positions, but they were unable to find a way of working together systematically. *(William J. Astore)*. 105

Firepower and Mobility: Was the crucial military problem of World War I an imbalance between firepower and mobility on the battlefield? 109

Yes. By successfully addressing the tactical problem of the "last 300 yards of no man's land," the Allies won the Great War. *(William J. Astore)*. 110

No. The crucial military problem of World War I was that Allied leaders formulated offensive strategies that never accommodated the realities of trench warfare. *(David J. Ulbrich)* 112

Gallipoli: Was the Allied effort on the Gallipoli Peninsula doomed from the start? 117

Yes. Allied planners seriously underestimated Turkish fighting capabilities and defensive preparations. *(Edward J. Erickson)* 118

No. Poor decisions made on the strategic, operational, and tactical levels determined the failure of the Gallipoli campaign. *(Dennis Showalter)*. 121

Gender Roles: Were women excluded from the Great War? 124

Yes. World War I essentially was a masculine activity. *(David J. Ulbrich)* 125

No. The Great War was an experience that both transcended and denied sex-role stereotyping. *(William J. Astore)* 128

CONTENTS

German Commerce Raiders: Were German surface-commerce raiders effective? 132

Yes. Surface raiders exercised continuous pressure on commercial shipping in open waters. *(Sanders Marble)* 133

No. Surface-commerce raiding was obsolescent as early as 1914, having no more than a nuisance value against the British maritime empire. *(David H. Olivier)* 135

German Economic Mobilization: Was the 1916–1917 Hindenburg-Ludendorff program for German economic mobilization a failure? 139

Yes. The mobilization of national resources intended by the program took little account of German economic realities. *(Dennis Showalter)* 140

No. The program eventually did succeed in integrating the army, industry, and labor behind the war effort to a significant degree. *(David N. Spires)* 143

Internal French Politics: Did internal French politics prior to World War I significantly weaken relations between the civil government and the military? 146

Yes. The mutual suspicion and hostility of the years before 1914 endured throughout the conflict and negatively shaped French conduct in the war. *(Michael S. Neiberg)* 147

No. Prewar political animosity dissipated with the need to confront a common challenge and enemy. *(Eugenia C. Kiesling)* 151

Irish Independence: How did the Great War affect the Irish independence movement? 154

The Great War renewed the historical divisions of British intransigence and Irish nationalist factionalism, resulting in the drift of the independence movement into militancy. *(Robert McJimsey)* 155

The Great War afforded the Irish independence movement with an opportunity to strike against Britain while its attention was concentrated on the Continent. *(William Kautt)* 156

By declaring the defense of the rights of small nations among its war aims, Britain lost its moral authority in Ireland and inadvertently strengthened the independence movement there. *(James S. Corum)* 160

Jewish Community: What impact did the war have on the European Jewish community? 163

Physical devastation and a surge in anti-Semitism combined to make the lot of European Jews far worse in 1919 than in 1914. *(Michael S. Neiberg)* 164

By the end of the war Europe was more tolerant of Jews as evidenced by their greater role in political, cultural, and intellectual life. *(Paul Du Quenoy)* 166

Kerensky: Did the Kerensky government make a mistake when it tried to keep Russia in the war? 170

Yes. The decision of the new government antagonized the proponents of the slogan "Peace, Land, Bread!" *(Josh Sanborn)* 171

No. The new government needed all the help it could get, and the promise of generous French and British support made staying in the war a reasonable calculated risk. *(Paul Du Quenoy)* 174

CONTENTS

Lorraine: Was the 1914 German offensive in Lorraine an appropriate response to altered circumstances on the Western Front? 179

Yes. Having defeated the initial French offensive in Lorraine, the Germans were justified in committing reserves t reinforce theirposition. *(Dennis Showalter)*. 180

No. Diverting forces to a secondary theater in the south seriously hampered German efforts in Belgium. *(Paul Du Quenoy)* 182

Lost Generation: Did the Great War create a "lost generation"? 186

Yes. The war did in fact exact a disproportionate physical and psychic toll on Europe's "best and brightest" young men. *(Mary Habeck)* 187

No. The "lost generation" was an invention of the interwar years, a convenient excuse for those who failed to mee the challenges that arose after 1918. *(Adrian Gregory)* 188

New Weapons: Did World War I accelerate the technological development of weaponry? 193

Yes. The synergies of technical development of weaponry during World War I represented a marked change in the conduct of war as well as the attitudes about it. *(William J. Astore)* 194

No. The technological innovations introduced in 1914–1918 were part of a continuum of increasingly improved firepower capabilities. *(William Kautt)*. 197

Organized Religion: Did organized religion support the war efforts of the various nations involved in the Great War? 202

Yes. Many Christian denominations, motivated by patriotism, viewed the struggle as a spiritual test of their respective nations' moral virtue. *(William J. Astore)* 203

No. The churches provided one of the first influential sources of challenge to specific aspects of the war's conduct. *(William Kautt)* 207

Ottoman Empire: Did the collapse of the Ottoman Empire during the war establish the conditions for the rise of the Turkish state afterward? 211

Yes. Conflict with various European nations and internal Arab rebellion reduced the Ottoman Empire to a core Turkish state. *(Michael S. Neiberg)*. 212

No. The achievements of the Ottoman Empire during the war were remarkable, and its weaknesses and handicaps in no way prefigured a Turkish nationalist successor state. *(Edward J. Erickson)* 214

Passchendaele: Should the Passchendaele offensive of 1917 have been called off once it became clear that a breakthrough was impossible?. 218

Yes. Because of the early high casualties and failed initial assaults, the British should have stopped the offensive before the heavy rains began. *(William J. Astore)*. 219

No. A steadily increasing British battlefield superiority legitimated Sir Douglas Haig's belief that the attack was worth pursuing, even under the appalling weather conditions. *(Dennis Showalter)*. . . . 223

Permanent Alliances: Did the system of permanent alliances that arose in Europe after 1871 cause World War I?. 225

Yes. The alliances encouraged belligerence and risk taking by making all the great powers believe they would be supported by their allies in almost any situation. *(Richard L. Dinardo)* 226

No. If any factor shaped diplomacy, it was the perceived weakness of pre-1914 alliance treaties, all of which featured escape clauses and reservations as opposed to affirming mutual support. *(Paul Du Quenoy)*. 228

Plan XVII: Was Plan XVII the blueprint for a French offensive? 232

Yes. Plan XVII was an aggressive military strategy that dictated the need to seize the initiative from the Germans and not allow them time to coordinate a proper defense. *(Robert B. Bruce)* 233

No. Plan XVII made provisions only for the mobilization and concentration of French troops and not their offensive use on the battlefield. *(Eugenia C. Kiesling)* 235

Poison Gas: Was the poison gas used in World War I essentially a nuisance weapon? 239

Yes. Gas was used primarily for harassment, increasing the misery of war and lowering morale. *(David N. Spires)* 240

No. When used properly, in conjunction with small arms fire and artillery barrages, gas was a lethal weapon. *(James Corum)* 241

Schlieffen Plan: Was the Schlieffen Plan of the German General Staff a sound war strategy? 245

Yes. The various directives that made up the German war plan indicate a high level of flexibility and a willingness to respond to events. *(Robert T. Foley)* 246

No. The Schlieffen Plan was predicated on an inexorable progression to an all-or-nothing victory. *(Antulio Echevarria)* 248

No. The Schlieffen Plan seriously underestimated the capabilities of enemy forces and did not take into account their tenacity and rapid deployment. *(John Wheatley)*. 251

Socialists: Did European Socialists give their ultimate loyalty to national governments rather than the universal proletariat during the war? 254

Yes. Socialist parties sustained national war efforts with recruits, votes, and propaganda. *(Paul Du Quenoy)* 255

No. Socialists took advantage of the general war weariness to advance the cause of workers. *(Dennis Showalter)*. 260

Soldiers' Motivations: What motivated soldiers in all armies to fight?. 263

The essential reason why millions of soldiers continued to fight was consent, derived from love of country, hatred of the enemy, and a crusading spirit. *(William J. Astore)* 264

Comradeship and coercion ultimately kept soldiers at their posts. *(David J. Ulbrich)* 267

The Somme: Were the British doomed in the Battle of the Somme (1916) by the decision to seek a decisive breakthrough? 271

Yes. Sir Douglas Haig's decision to seek a decisive breakthrough damaged his army's ability to sustain itself in the later stages of the operation. *(Dennis Showalter)* 272

No. The problems experienced by the British Expeditionary Force (BEF) at the Somme reflected inexperience in planning for such an offensive. *(Albert Palazzo)* 273

Treaty of Versailles: Did the Treaty of Versailles in 1919 provide the framework for a durable peace?........................ 277

Yes. The Versailles settlement was purposely designed to establish lasting international stability. It was no harsher than comparable treaties and was entirely appropriate for the political environment of 1919. *(Michael S. Neiberg)*. 278

No. The Treaty of Versailles was disastrous because it embittered Germany and fostered political radicalism in that country. *(Paul Du Quenoy)*. 281

CONTENTS

Unrestricted Submarine Warfare: Was the German policy of
unrestricted submarine warfare a commitment to total war?........ 287

Yes. By targeting all shipping and sinking vessels without
warning, Germany practiced a form of total war on its
enemies. *(John Abbatiello)*.................................. 288

No. Although the desire to remove Great Britain from the conflict
was great, Germany was incapable of accomplishing
such a task. *(Mark Karau)* 290

War and America: Did the Great War have a positive impact
on the United States?... 295

Yes. The war provided focus for the United States and
introduced the nation to the nature of its responsibilities
as a great power. *(Kristi L. Nichols)* 296

No. World War I highlighted and exacerbated internal ethnic,
social, and economic tensions, while militarizing the country to
a far greater degree than even the Civil War.
(Michael S. Neiberg).. 299

References.. 303

Contributors' Notes... 311

Index... 313

CONTENTS

ABOUT THE SERIES

History in Dispute is an ongoing series designed to present, in an informative and lively pro-con format, different perspectives on major historical events drawn from all time periods and from all parts of the globe. The series was developed in response to requests from librarians and educators for a history-reference source that will help students hone essential critical-thinking skills while serving as a valuable research tool for class assignments.

Individual volumes in the series concentrate on specific themes, eras, or subjects intended to correspond to the way history is studied at the academic level. For example, early volumes cover such topics as the Cold War, American Social and Political Movements, and World War II. Volume subtitles make it easy for users to identify contents at a glance and facilitate searching for specific subjects in library catalogues.

Each volume of *History in Dispute* includes up to fifty entries, centered on the overall theme of that volume and chosen by an advisory board of historians for their relevance to the curriculum. Entries are arranged alphabetically by the name of the event or issue in its most common form. (Thus, in Volume 1, the issue "Was detente

a success?" is presented under the chapter heading "Detente.")

Each entry begins with a brief statement of the opposing points of view on the topic, followed by a short essay summarizing the issue and outlining the controversy. At the heart of the entry, designed to engage students' interest while providing essential information, are the two or more lengthy essays, written specifically for this publication by experts in the field, each presenting one side of the dispute.

In addition to this substantial prose explication, entries also include excerpts from primary-source documents, other useful information typeset in easy-to-locate shaded boxes, detailed entry bibliographies, and photographs or illustrations appropriate to the issue.

Other features of *History in Dispute* volumes include: individual volume introductions by academic experts, tables of contents that identify both the issues and the controversies, chronologies of events, names and credentials of advisers, brief biographies of contributors, thorough volume bibliographies for more information on the topic, and a comprehensive subject index.

PREFACE

By many standards World War I (1914–1918) was limited in time and space. Its outcome depended primarily on events in a single region: Northern France and Flanders, the traditional "cockpit of Europe." Its duration was short in comparison to the quarter century of war that followed the French Revolution of 1789, the generation of strife accompanying the seventeenth-century reign of Louis XIV, or even the Seven Years' War of 1756–1763. Yet, none of these conflicts matched World War I in its sheer intensity and bloodshed: nearly nine million killed with a further estimated twenty-one million wounded worldwide. The unprecedented losses in human life and material resources have earned this conflict another name: the *Great War.*

The central themes of this conflict, the disputes addressed in these two volumes, correspondingly tend to defy binary division. While the historical introduction is presented chronologically, the subjects discussed are presented alphabetically by their titles. The origins of the Great War, for example, have attracted almost as much intellectual attention as the conflict itself. Interpretations can be organized into two general categories: structural and volitional. Each category has two opposing poles. The structural argument stresses Europe's generic vulnerabilities to the catastrophe that overtook it in 1914. In turn, the structural argument can be built around long-term or short-term causes.

Long-term factors include nationalism, militarism, imperialism, and a diplomatic system able to derive no better solution to the problem of international tensions than rival alliance systems that risked turning any conflict into a doomsday machine. These factors also include the domestic tensions generated by industrialism: capitalist economies and the Marxist challenge to them; and, less obviously, the corresponding emergence of an "upper class" of old aristocrats and new bourgeoisie arguably willing to risk war to maintain their position at the top of the social pyramid.

The short-term structural causes of the Great War are not as well-defined but are often described in terms of an arms race that after 1905 escalated to a point where war became a solution of first instance rather than a continuation of policy by other means. Short-term structural causes also encompass the turn-of-the-century rise of a popular press that sold papers by nurturing fear and xenophobia. They incorporate the diplomatic, military, and political systems that in 1914 were controlled by men who followed standard operating procedures all the way into the trenches. Not least, they incorporate Europe's collective failure to address the new set of problems caused by the expulsion of the Ottomans from Europe in the decade prior to 1914. The rapid rise of the Balkan States, with their high levels of military mobilization and their sharp-edged commitments to various forms of nationalism, represented a wild card to which Europe's major players failed to adjust until too late.

In the volitional category the internal dichotomy is between collective and individual responsibility. The "collectivists" depict the outbreak of the war in terms of the body of decisions made in particular time frames by the so-called Great Powers: Germany, Great Britain, France, Russia, and Austria-Hungary. The period under debate can be as short as the summer of 1914 or it can extend as far back as the Franco-German War of 1870–1871. What defines this approach is its definition of the synergies among state policies as crucial to the coming of war, and the implied acceptance of a rational-actor model for behaviors. Governments, in other words, responded to each other's actions and acted according to their perceptions of their best interests at the time, whether those perceptions may have been accurate or prudent. The Great War thus becomes a kind of accident, with a relatively small event setting in motion a chain reaction that drew the great states and their clients into a war that no one wanted, a war that no one expected at that particular time, and a war that proved ultimately lethal to the European order that had sustained its participants.

There is little room in the "collectivist" model for "evil empires"–or even for misguided ones. The opposite pole, however, insists on individual responsibility and finding the state whose behavior finally and irrevocably tipped Europe and the world on the downward slide to war. Between 1919 and 1939, and to a certain degree in the 1950s and 1960s as well, Russia, France, Austria-Hungary, and Great Britain all received the blame in due course. Since the 1960s and the research of Fritz Fischer and his followers, if a particular state is singled out for primary responsibility, that state is likely to be Germany. The charges usually begin with Germany's "incomplete modernization," resulting in an unstable and anomalous social structure. Its ruling classes in turn sought to stabilize their system by enhancing its power in both European and global contexts. In the circumstances of 1914 Germany believed it had a good enough chance of achieving its objectives by force that its generals and statesmen chose to roll the dice. That decision generated responses that insisted Germany must be stopped whatever the long-range costs of resistance.

All the interpretative matrices agree that the catalytic event of the war, the assassination of the Austro-Hungarian heir apparent Franz Ferdinand and his wife on 28 June 1914 by a Balkan nationalist, was not an obviously sufficient cause for the chain of events that sent millions of men to war slightly more than a month later. Recent research has demonstrated that far from generating enthusiasm, the outbreak of hostilities was greeted with a trepidation only partly alleviated by propaganda generated by the self-mobilization of Europe's chattering classes: its journalists, clergymen, and politicians.

One anodyne was the widespread belief that the war would be over in a few weeks. "You will be home before the leaves fall," German emperor William II informed one departing contingent of soldiers. This short-war illusion was not the product of more-humane ways of waging war. It instead reflected the collective judgment of army general staffs that modern technology had rendered battlefields so lethal and war so demanding that states and societies could endure the killing—and the accompanying economic sacrifices—for only a brief time before collapsing into chaos. As a result each army sought to get the initiative, determining the outcome by forcing the pace. The Germans proposed to crush the French and then turn on the Russians while the Russians intended to overrun the Central Powers before German reinforcements could arrive from the West.

The Schlieffen Plan of Germany, Plan XVII of France, and their counterparts also had in common a vitalist emphasis on "will to conquer" that in practice too often ignored the effects of artillery rifles and machine guns on the poorly trained reservists that made up the vast majority of the men hurried to the battlefield. Too often as well the armies of 1914 overlooked logistical factors, expecting mobilized civilians to march and to fight on nearly empty stomachs. The result was a general stagnating of fronts and a hecatomb of dead and maimed: 1.75 million in the West alone by the turn of the year. Not least of the hidden losses was the sacrifice of the peacetime cadres of trained junior officers who had at least some professional background on which to build an understanding of the new circumstances they faced. Their successors, starting nearly from scratch, took two more years to determine how to cope with the demands of mass war.

The establishment of trench systems on what became the Western Front began at small-unit levels. Men on both sides threw away the book by digging in, replacing maneuver with fire, and letting the other side take the risks of attacking. The last spasms of open warfare came in November 1914, as the Germans mounted a series of desperate frontal attacks in northern Belgium. Yet, Chief of Staff Erich von Falkenhayn, who had replaced Helmuth von Moltke the Younger when the initial German drive on Paris fell short, had no clear sense of what should happen if his armies reached open country. Within weeks of the outbreak of the war, offensive operations had been transformed from a means to victory and had become ends in themselves.

In the East lower force-to-space ratios on both sides kept the fronts flexible a few weeks longer. An initial Russian offensive into Prussia was checked at Tannenberg, thrown back in the First Battle of the Masurian Lakes (7–14 September). At the same time, Russian and Austro-Hungarian armies grappled blindly on the open plains of Galicia to the south, and by mid September an outnumbered and exhausted Habsburg army was reeling back toward its own frontiers. The Germans sent a full army into Poland, striking the Russian rear and checking their advance as winter stabilized the front in spite of the generals.

In the winter of 1914 Germany contemplated a shift of strategic emphasis. The Schlieffen Plan had been based on knocking France, and by implication Britain, out of the war in a single round. Now Russia seemed the more vulnerable adversary. Initial Austro-German offensives foundered in the snowdrifts. However, beginning on 2 May 1915, the ground forces of the Central Powers breached the front on a sector forty miles

PREFACE

wide and sent the Russian army reeling backward—to no purpose. The Tsarist government, sustained by Entente promises, refused to consider a separate peace.

In the West the Allies took the offensive, beginning in the last days of the old year with a French offensive in Champagne that was a prototype for dozens of its successors in producing small gains for high costs. The British replicated the experience at Neuve Chapelle in March. The Germans responded by using the first major technical innovation of the war: chlorine gas. After releasing it in clouds to drift across Allied lines with the prevailing winds, the Germans counterattacked around Ypres in April. The Allies held their ground and then mounted a series of ripostes in the second half of the year. Notre Dame de Lorette, Aubers Ridge, Champagne, and Loos—these names were a litany of horror to the fighting men of both sides.

The young soldiers of 1914 were filling graveyards and hospitals and were replaced in French and German ranks by men in their thirties, family men who had never expected to be summoned to this kind of sacrifice. A British army still based on the volunteer principle saw its long-service regulars replaced by a new kind of soldier enlisted for the war's duration in the territorial forces or the "New Armies" of War Minister Horatio Herbert Kitchener. Meanwhile, on both sides of the trenches, the high casualty rates continued.

The Western allies were no further along in breaking through the German defensive systems than they had been a year earlier. The Central Powers had been successful in terms of ground gained against their Russian enemy. They had succeeded as well in overrunning Serbia: a peripheral operation that opened a new theater of operations without compensating gains in men or resources. With Austria-Hungary balanced on the edge of exhaustion and Germany still making slow progress in mobilizing its resources effectively, the Central Powers seemed on the edge of conquering themselves to exhaustion.

By 1915 the Great War's paradoxical nature was becoming clear. It was a conflict that involved the world's resources, yet concentrated in the European matrix. The war's archetypal conditions, indeed, were found in an even more limited sector. Northern France and Belgium were the only regions sufficiently developed to sustain the huge armies; to keep the flow of food, ammunition, and replacements coming; and to provide the infrastructure to keep the struggle from imploding from its own weight. The further away the war moved from its epicenter, the more it resembled more-traditional conflicts, with death rates from disease still exceeding substantially those from combat; with logistical systems still based on animal transpor-

tation; and with modern levels of firepower only occasionally sustainable, after long and painstaking periods of buildup.

The pattern of a global war with a European focus was sustained by the nature of the naval war. Experts had predicted an early engagement as the massive battle fleets of Germany and England clashed for mastery of the North Sea, while their smaller counterparts grappled in the Mediterranean. Instead, the dreadnoughts built at such immense costs swung at anchor, with their occasional sorties timed for mutual avoidance. The "sacred vessels" could not be risked in a combat that might, in Winston Churchill's words, "lose the war in an afternoon."

In that context the Allies benefited, as German commerce was driven from the seas, the few cruisers outside home waters pitilessly hunted down, and the colonies overrun and occupied with the exception of East Africa, where a marginal but effective campaign at least distracted Britain's attention. Despite increasingly effective interdiction operations by an increasingly effective submarine force, the world's ships continued to dock at Entente ports, bringing men from the empires, raw materials, and, increasingly, finished products from the rest of the world.

Allied control of the sea led to efforts at using that control to break the deadlock on land. The first possibility emerged when the Ottoman Empire joined the Central Powers. Britain responded by sending a task force into the Persian Gulf to seize the oil fields around Basra, then launched an ill-supported expedition up the Tigris River toward Baghdad. A more promising opportunity, at least in the mind of First Lord of the Admiralty Churchill, involved using the Allied fleets to force the straits of the Dardanelles and to open a way to Constantinople and a warm-water supply route to Russia. The initial attack failed, partly from poor leadership and partly from underestimating the difficulties involved. The Allies reinforced failure by committing ground troops to some of the worst terrain in Europe, the Gallipoli Peninsula. The operation lasted nine months, cost 250,000 Allied casualties, and ended in an ignominious evacuation.

Another way to create fresh strategic opportunities seemed to lie at the policy level. Italy, an ostensible ally of Germany and Austria-Hungary, had declared its neutrality in 1914. Its leaders called the policy "sacred egotism." Everybody else in Europe knew what Italy was—all that remained was to set a price. The Allies were able to offer the kinds of concessions—territory taken from Austria-Hungary and imperial prospects in the Middle East—impossible for the Central Powers to match. On 24 May 1915 Italy entered the war and launched a massive offensive against the mountain chains that separated it from Austria-Hungary. Two years later its ill-equipped and poorly trained armies were in essentially the same places, having fought eleven battles along the Isonzo River.

The year 1916 was a turning point in Germany's war. Civilian political authority had been steadily declining since 1914, because for previous decades the soldiers had been presumed competent by definition. They would win the wars; the diplomats and politicians would shape the peace. Unfortunately the army, and in particular Falkenhayn, had found it easier to go to war than to win it. His cooperation with Chancellor Theobald von Bethmann Hollweg did not extend far enough to consider a comprehensive rethinking of the Central Powers' strategic position. Instead, Falkenhayn developed plans for an offensive seeking another kind of decision.

Conventional analyses of the German attack on Verdun describe an intention of drawing the numerically inferior French into a killing ground that would systematically erode their forces to a point where collapse or negotiation became the alternatives. More recent scholarship suggests Falkenhayn at least hoped that the careful preparation of the attack, including an unprecedented level of artillery preparation, would in fact produce a decisive breakthrough. The attritional element was his post facto rationalization of the failure of this larger aim.

Whatever Germany's intentions, the result was a four-month death grapple that drew the German as well as the French army into what German soldiers called "the death mill on the Meuse." The French grew increasingly sophisticated in using artillery and machine-gun fire to help hold and recapture positions. Casualties continued to mount, and Verdun began taking on the mythic significance for Germany that the Germans believed it possessed for the French. It became impossible for Falkenhayn to end an increasingly pointless killing machine without endangering his own position. In the end Verdun was shut down by external factors, in particular the British attack on the Somme.

The date of 1 July 1916 is increasingly recognized as one of the seminal ones in British history and mythology. It began with bright promises: Kitchener's New Armies, the best of Britain, spearheading a breakthrough of the German lines that would open the way to final victory. The day ended with sixty thousand British casualties, one-third of them dead, and the front lines essentially unchanged. For another five months Canadians, Australians, and New Zealanders joined men from the British Isles in pushing forward a few yards at a time, over ground so torn by shellfire that autumn rains turned it in many places to swamps.

The death of illusion is what makes the Somme experience so poignant. Those who fought there remembered it as a touchstone, a watershed in their war experience. At home, anticipation gave way to grief as the casualty lists came in. Yet, the Somme was more than its images—and realities—of futile slaughter. From mid 1915, generals and political leaders had discussed the issue of joint Franco-British action—no illusions of an immediate breakthrough but a systemic operation to erode the strength of enemy forces and the morale of the German people. As originally conceived, the plan was for a joint attack on either side of the Somme River. A primary advantage of that sector was its relatively pristine nature. Undestroyed by shellfire, the rolling, open terrain of Picardy offered opportunities for large-scale advances once the frontline defenses were broken.

The earlier German attack on Verdun fundamentally changed the Allies' force structure—but not their intention. The increasing absorption of French resources at Verdun meant instead that the British would be taking over the major burden of the attack. French manpower resources were fully committed and quickly eroding. Britain's New Armies, on the other hand, were only beginning to reach the front. Canadians, Australians, and New Zealanders were also arriving in force—ten divisions of them by mid July.

The British high command was not especially enthusiastic at the prospect of an offensive in Picardy without massive French support. British Expeditionary Force (BEF) commander in chief Sir Douglas Haig preferred Flanders, where the Channel ports offered an immediate strategic objective. Even should the German lines be broken decisively, there was nothing significant behind them. As a consequence, British planning focused increasingly on doing as much damage as possible to the German army. The next question then became how success was best sought: bombardment or surprise? The general immediately responsible for the attack, Sir Henry Rawlinson, favored heavy bombardment and limited objectives: "Bite and hold." Haig had more faith in the prospects of a real breakthrough in the gap to be torn in the German lines.

Nonetheless, the artillery was unable to destroy or to neutralize the German defenses. The infantry, burdened with loads often amounting to more than one-half a soldier's body weight, under orders to advance at a walk, were mowed down in thousands. Yet, the battle continued—or rather, the twelve separate battles awarded as "honors" to the participating regiments. More than four hundred thousand of Haig's men were killed, wounded, or missing. The French, whose participation is often overlooked, had two hundred thousand casualties. Enemy losses were about the same, but the Germans also suffered the erosion of their peacetime-trained cadres. The British, on the other hand, were increasingly recognized as developing a steep learning curve, improving in every aspect from tactics to logistics. Nor was morale as seriously eroded as postwar accounts claimed. Peter Liddle in particular has made a strong case that the BEF's fighting spirit and its determination to persevere were challenged by the Somme experience but survived unbroken and in some ways improved.

Despite the costs of Verdun, the Somme, and the war's other fronts, none of the combatants were sufficiently influenced by their experiences in 1916 to seek seriously to end the conflict. The year 1916 nevertheless marked the end of the first phase of the Great War. Among the belligerents, the diplomatic and military artifices of 1914 had been exploited to their maximums, and found to be wanting. The mobilization of human resources and matériel had been taken to the limits, and produced no positive results.

The consequences of that gridlock are developed in the second half of this essay, published in volume II of *History in Dispute: World War I*. In 1917 and 1918 the Great War was defined by a relentless search for new paradigms. On land the Germans sought to develop new assault tactics for the traditional arms, infantry and artillery. The French and British increasingly turned to all-arms combat teams, including an unexpected innovation: the tank. At sea the Battle of Jutland on 31 May 1916 confirmed a maritime stalemate Germany sought to break by another innovation: unrestricted submarine warfare. Meanwhile, unable to drive Russia from the war by military means, Germany sought a political solution: encouraging already-active forces whose triumph in the Bolshevik Revolution of November 1917 offered promises of a new world order to the increasingly war-weary populations of Europe. Those promises were balanced by a United States that joined the Allies in April 1917 to defend its own interests—but then defined those interests as "making the world safe for democracy." The Fourteen Points of Woodrow Wilson, promising open diplomatic negotiations, boundaries redrawn to meet national aspirations, and an end to the burdens of militarism, resonated not only in Europe but also throughout the world as governments sought to keep their war-exhausted peoples under control in hopes that something—anything—might break the four-year stalemate.

—DENNIS SHOWALTER,
COLORADO COLLEGE, COLORADO SPRINGS

PREFACE

CHRONOLOGY

Boldface type refers to a chapter title.

1914

JUNE: Austrian foreign minister Leopold Berchtold schemes to gain German support for an Austrian-Hungarian-Bulgarian-Turkish alliance to encircle Serbia.

25 JUNE: Austrian archduke Francis "Franz" Ferdinand, nephew of Emperor Francis Joseph, arrives in Bosnia to supervise summer maneuvers by the Hapsburg army.

28 JUNE: Ferdinand and his wife, Sophia Chotek, are shot and killed in Sarajevo, Bosnia, by Gavrilo Princip, a Bosnian Serbian nationalist who is identified as being a member of *Narodna Odbrana* (National Defense) and part of a six-man assassination team.

5 JULY: An Austrian emissary travels to Berlin to inform the Germans that Austria will ask for a guarantee of good conduct from the Serbs or that they will make them face military action. Kaiser William II agrees to support Austria.

7 JULY: Berchtold, who does not believe that the Russians will respond to Austrian aggression in the Balkans, proposes to the Imperial Council of Ministers that Austria mobilize against Serbia. Hungarian prime minister Kálmán Tisza insists that a note be sent first, rather than an ultimatum setting conditions, including the right of Austrian investigators to supervise the investigation of the assassinations.

16 JULY: French president Raymond Poincaré makes a state visit to its ally Russia, which supports Serbia.

23 JULY: The Austrian note, dated to expire on 25 July, arrives in Belgrade. The Serbs reject the demands.

26–27 JULY: Serbia mobilizes its forces; Russia calls up its military reservists.

26–27 JULY: Turkish minister of war Enver Paşa, who had served as the military attache to Germany in 1909–1911, speaks with German diplomats about the possibility of an alliance between their two countries.

28 JULY: Austrian border guards fire on a Serbian patrol that strays across the border. Austria-Hungary declares war on Serbia. Russian military leaders decide to order a formal mobilization of their army, but they are held in check by Tsar Nicholas II.

28 JULY: The Ottoman Empire declares war on Bosnia.

29 JULY: Austrian gunboats on the Danube River bombard Belgrade.

30 JULY: Russia formally mobilizes its troops and orders reservists to report to depots on 31 July. German officials respond by ordering a "State of Danger of War."

AUGUST: Great Britain calls for enlistments, which will become the nucleus of the New Army. These troops will be ready for action by 1915.

1 AUGUST: Germany orders the mobilization of its armies and declares war against Russia.

2 AUGUST: Germany demands that Belgium allow German troops the right to transverse its territory for operations against France. Germany invades Luxembourg.

2 AUGUST: Great Britain mobilizes its naval fleet.

3 AUGUST: Germany formally declares war on France.

4 AUGUST: The German Tenth Army Corps, under the command of Otto von Emmich, invades Belgium and faces resistance at Liège. Civilians, including priests, are killed and the town of Battice is burned. Larger massacres occur during the next three weeks, as German reservist units arrive in the country; the killings are known as the "Rape of Belgium," reports of which stir anti-German sentiment in the United States.

4 AUGUST: President Woodrow Wilson declares that the United States will remain a neutral country.

4 AUGUST: The British navy begins blockading sea traffic to German ports.

5 AUGUST: Great Britain, France, and Russia are officially at war with Germany. Austria declares war on Russia.

5 AUGUST: The German minelayer *Königin Luise* is sunk by the HMS *Amphion* off the coast of eastern England.

6 AUGUST: The HMS *Amphion* hits a mine and sinks in the North Sea.

7 AUGUST: Liège surrenders to the Germans.

7 AUGUST: The French Seventh Corps, ordered forward by General Joseph Joffre, attack Mulhouse in Alsace. The French are beaten back by a German counterattack three days later.

7 AUGUST: HMS *Gloucester* engages the German cruisers *Goeben* and *Breslau* in the Mediterranean Sea, after the cruisers leave the port of Messina in Italy. The German ships had just three days earlier bombarded French-held ports in Algeria, allegedly while flying Russian flags.

8 AUGUST: The British Parliament passes the Defense of the Realm Act, which prohibits spying and the spread of disinformation, and gives the government the right to confiscate factories and property deemed necessary to prosecute the war.

8 AUGUST: British and French African colonial troops invade Togoland, West Africa, and destroy a communications center in the Battle of Kamina, which is over by 26 August. The two countries divide control of the colony between themselves.

8 AUGUST: British forces shell the towns of Bagamoyo and Dar-es-Salaam on the German East African coast.

9 AUGUST: The Germans lose their first submarine, the *U–15,* which is rammed and sunk by the HMS *Birmingham.*

10 AUGUST: Austrian troops invade Poland.

12 AUGUST: Great Britain and France declare war on Austria. Italy asserts its neutrality.

12 AUGUST: Fort Pontisse in Belgium is bombarded by a huge German artillery gun, a Krup 420, which fires two-thousand-pound shells. The garrison surrenders on 13 August, as do the defenders of several other local forts that come under fire from the Germans.

12 AUGUST: The *U–13,* which is probably sunk after striking a mine, goes down in Heligoland Bight.

12–21 AUGUST: Austrian troops cross the Drina River and engage the Serbians in the Battle of the Jadar. The Serbs, however, are successful in pushing the Austrians back.

13 AUGUST: British fighter aircraft of the Royal Flying Corps (RFC) arrive in France.

14 AUGUST: The French First Army, under the command of Auguste Dubail, advances toward the city of Sarrebourg. The Germans stoutly defend against this incursion, but gradually fall back. The twelve-day battle that follows is called the Battle of the Frontiers (Lorraine).

14 AUGUST: The British Expeditionary Force (BEF) disembarks at Boulogne and marches toward Belgium.

15 AUGUST: Fort Loncin, headquarters for Belgian general Gérard Leman, explodes after a German shell hits a munitions magazine. Leman is knocked unconscious in the blast and is captured by the Germans.

15 AUGUST: The Panama Canal is officially opened to traffic, although barges have been regularly traversing the waterway since mid May.

15 AUGUST: The Japanese insist that the Germans leave China.

18 AUGUST: Sarrebourg is captured by the French.

18–19 AUGUST: German forces defeat Belgian opposition in the Battle of Tirlement; German general Heinrich von Kluck leads his troops into Brussels on 20 August.

19 AUGUST: Mulhouse is recaptured by the Germans. Dubail orders a night attack on German positions to restore communications with other French corps along the front.

20 AUGUST: A front-wide counterattack is undertaken by eight German corps, which smash French opposition. The French Seventh Corps is pushed back; only the Twentieth Corps, under the command of Ferdinand Foch, holds firm. The remainder of the French army, which lost more than 140,000 men, retreats behind the Meurthe River by 23 August.

20 AUGUST: Russian troops, under the command of Pavel Rennenkampf, attack the German Eighth Army in East Prussia, forcing it to withdraw to the Vistula River. The German commander is replaced by Generals Paul von Hindenburg and Erich Ludendorff.

22 AUGUST: The French Third Army, which had been advancing into the Ardennes Forest, collapses under a German counterattack. French colonial troops, part of the Fourth Army, are encircled by the German army.

CHRONOLOGY

The Third Colonial Division loses more than eleven thousand soldiers of its fifteen-thousand-man complement. The Third and Fourth Armies are pushed back across the Meuse River by 25 August.

22 AUGUST: Admiral Maximilian Graf von Spee commands the German Far Eastern Squadron in the Pacific Ocean. His fleet bombards Papeete in Tahiti and then heads for South America.

23 AUGUST: German and British soldiers fight for the first time in the war at the Battle of Mons. Approximately seventy thousand British, positioned alongside the French Fifth Corps, are forced to retreat by the German First Army, which is nearly double the size of its opponents.

23 AUGUST: Japan, realizing an opportunity to enlarge its empire at the expense of the heavily engaged Central Powers, declares war against Germany. The Japanese, supported by the British, lay siege to Tsingtao, a German-controlled port on the Chinese coast.

24 AUGUST: Forts in the vicinity of Namur, Belgium, are reduced by German artillery.

25 AUGUST–7 SEPTEMBER: The Germans attack the Allied front established along the Meurthe River, breaking through French defensive lines.

26 AUGUST: British troops, under the command of General Horace Smith-Dorrien, while retreating from their defeat at Mons, fight a defending action at Le Cateau. Nearly eight thousand casualties are suffered by the British. A combined Belgian and French counterattack slows the German advance and allows the weary British troops to withdraw.

26 AUGUST: The German light cruiser *Magdeburg* is beached in the Baltic Sea and the Russians are able to capture its code books and key. These items are sent to England where, along with other materials confiscated from German ships, British intelligence is able to read German naval transmissions.

26–31 AUGUST: The Russian Second Army, under the command of Alexandr Samsonov, enters East Prussian and engages German troops, who are initially forced to retreat. After a change of leadership and the arrival of fresh troops, the Germans surround the Russian army; the Russians are defeated; Samsonov commits suicide (29 August); and the invading force is destroyed or captured. Only one out of every fifteen Russian soldiers of the original 150,000-man force are able to withdraw from the engagement. The Allies censor

information about the battle to avoid a collapse of confidence.

28 AUGUST: British admiral David Beatty leads his fleet of two cruisers and twenty destroyers against a German fleet at Heligoland Bight. The HMS *Arethusa* and *Ariadne* are seriously damaged; the Germans lose the *Mainz* and *Köln,* and their fleet is forced back into port.

29 AUGUST: The French Fifth Army, commanded by Charles Lanrezac, engages the German Second Army. Known as the Battle of Guise, in this engagement the Germans attack during a foggy morning, but a surprise French counterattack throws them back.

29 AUGUST: German Samoa is captured by a New Zealand force of 1,400 men.

30 AUGUST: German troops reach positions just west of Paris, but General Kluck realizes his units have lost contact with other elements of the German army and he stops the advance. The Germans take Ameins.

30 AUGUST: German planes attack Paris.

2 SEPTEMBER: The French government is moved to Bordeaux in the face of a potential assault by the Germans on Paris.

5 SEPTEMBER: The light cruiser HMS *Pathfinder,* the first British warship sunk by a submarine, is torpedoed and sunk off the Firth of Forth by the *U–21.*

5–9 SEPTEMBER: In an effort to protect Paris, the French, led by Joffre, plan an attack on the German Second Army, commanded by Karl von Bülow. The engagement is known as the Battle of the Marne (First Marne). The Germans inadvertently leave their flank exposed after turning their army to the southeast. Beginning on 6 September a combined French and British assault forces the Germans into a retreat across the Aisne River. Reportedly, the overall German commander, Helmuth von Moltke (the Younger), suffers a mental breakdown and is replaced by General Erich von Falkenhayn. The battle effectively ends the German drive to conclude the war quickly.

5–9 SEPTEMBER: The first use of aerial photography by the RFC for military purposes occurs during the Battle of the Marne.

8–17 SEPTEMBER: Austrian and Serbian troops clash at the Battle of Drina, as the Serbs enter Bosnia. The occupation is both short-lived and costly.

9 SEPTEMBER: The Germans shift their troops, which have defeated the Russian Second Army, against Rennenkampf's army at the Battle of Masurian Lakes. The Rus-

sians suffer heavy losses and retire from East Prussia by 14 September.

13 SEPTEMBER: Australian troops capture Bougainville, Solomon Islands.

13 SEPTEMBER: Lemberg (Lvov), Ukraine, is captured by the Russians, who push the Austrians out of the area. Russian troops continue to advance, capturing towns and forts, as they move toward the Carpathian Mountains.

15–18 SEPTEMBER: British and French troops attempt to push the Germans back from their placements along the Aisne River. The Germans are entrenched, however, beginning a pattern of trench warfare that becomes the mainstay of World War I engagements; frontal attacks against the Germans, dug in on the high ground, are repulsed with heavy losses. A strategy of gradual western movement, as each army tries to outflank their opponent, becomes known as "The Race to the Sea."

20 SEPTEMBER: The German cruiser *Königsberg* destroys the cruiser HMS *Pegasus* off Zanzibar. The German raider had captured and scuttled the freighter *City of Winchester,* which was carrying the tea crop for that year from Ceylon, on 6 August.

21 SEPTEMBER: The Australians capture New Guinea from the Germans.

22 SEPTEMBER: Three British cruisers (HMS *Aboukir, Hogue,* and *Cressy*), on patrol in the North Sea, are attacked and sunk by the *U–9,* commanded by Otto Weddigen. More than 1,400 sailors perish. The entire crew of the submarine wins the Iron Cross for their action.

22 SEPTEMBER: Madras, a port on the Indian coast, is shelled by the German cruiser *Emden,* captained by Karl von Müller.

25–29 SEPTEMBER: The French Second Army, commanded by Noel de Castlenau, a leading proponent of offensive war and a participant in the development of the French order of battle called Plan XVII, attacks the German trench lines in the Battle of Albert. The French are stopped short of capturing the town of Albert.

26 SEPTEMBER: The Indian Expeditionary Force arrives in Marseilles.

26–27 SEPTEMBER: Duala (Cameroons) is captured by the British. Germany had been expanding its territorial interests in West Africa, but by February 1916 they are pushed out of the colony.

27 SEPTEMBER: The Russians invade Hungary.

27 SEPTEMBER–10 OCTOBER: British and Belgian forces engage the Germans in the Battle of Artois. The town falls to the BEF.

OCTOBER: Turkish authorities place restrictions on its Armenian population, confiscate their weapons, arrest Armenian leaders, and impose censorship of news about its activities.

1–2 OCTOBER: The French Tenth Army attempts to flank the Germans at the Battle of Arras. They manage to capture and hold Arras, but most of their initial gains are pushed back by the German Sixth Army.

4 OCTOBER: The Austrians begin an offensive into Galicia, forcing the Russians out of the Carpathian Mountains.

6 OCTOBER: The Germans, who want to stop the flow of British troops into the theater of battle, attack Antwerp in an attempt to reach the North Sea. British and Belgian troops provide a stiff defense but are forced to withdraw from the city on 10 October.

7 OCTOBER: The Japanese capture the Marshall Islands.

7 OCTOBER: British pilots from the Royal Naval Air Service (RNAS) destroy a German Zeppelin hanger in Dusseldorf. They try a similar attack on 22 September but are foiled by foggy weather.

11 OCTOBER: The Germans capture Ghent.

11 OCTOBER: The *U–26* sinks the Russian cruiser *Pallada* in the Gulf of Finland, while the *U–9* makes another score, sinking the light cruiser HMS *Hawke* off the coast of Aberdeen.

12 OCTOBER: The Germans advance to Warsaw but are pushed back by Russian counterattacks.

14 OCTOBER: Bruges, in West Flanders, falls to the Germans.

14 OCTOBER: The Canadian Expeditionary Force (CEF) arrives in France.

15–21 OCTOBER: The Austrians move northward against the Russians in the Battle of Warsaw but are forced back.

19 OCTOBER–24 NOVEMBER: The Germans attempt to dislodge the Allies from positions along the Yser River, in order to gain cities along the North Sea, in what becomes known as the Battle of Ypres. British, Belgian, and French troops block a much larger German army.

20 OCTOBER: Just south of Norway, the *U–17* sinks the first merchantman destroyed by a submarine, the British steamer *Glitra.* The crew is allowed to abandon ship before it is sent to the bottom.

27 OCTOBER: The Belgians, as ordered by King Albert I, open their dikes and flood the Yser region.

30 OCTOBER: The German battle cruisers *Goeben* and *Breslau,* flying the colors of the Ottoman Empire, which joins the conflict on the side of the Central Powers on the previous day, bombard Russian ports along the Black Sea. Although they have new names and are officially owned by the Turkish government, the two ships retain their German crews. German and Ottoman control of the Dardanelles constricts the flow of supplies from the Allies to Russia.

31 OCTOBER: The British aircraft carrier HMS *Hermes* is sunk in the English Channel by the *U-27.*

1 NOVEMBER: Admiral Spee's fleet, which is disrupting sea traffic along the South American coast, engages and defeats the British Fourth Cruiser Squadron, commanded by Sir Christopher Cradock, off of Coronel, Chile. HMS cruisers *Monmouth* and *Good Hope* are sunk; Cradock goes down with the *Good Hope.*

2 NOVEMBER: Russia invades Prussia again. Russia declares war on the Ottoman Empire.

2–5 NOVEMBER: An Indian and British invasion force is defeated by the Germans at the Battle of Tanga, in German East Africa.

5 NOVEMBER: Great Britain declares war on Turkey and captures Cyprus.

7 NOVEMBER: British and Indian troops land in Mesopotamia, which is part of the Ottoman Empire. The British hope to protect vital oil supplies and quickly capture Basra.

7 NOVEMBER: Japanese and Allied troops capture Tsingtao.

8 NOVEMBER: Austria invades Serbia.

9 NOVEMBER: The German raider *Emden* is sunk by the Australian cruiser *Sydney* after an engagement off of the Cocos Islands in the Indian Ocean.

10 NOVEMBER: The Russian Army recaptures Przemysl and turns toward Hungary.

11–25 NOVEMBER: German and Russian armies, each alternately reinforced, struggle to gain an upper hand in the Battle of Lõdz. Eventually the Germans push the Russians back and capture Lõdz on 6 December.

14 NOVEMBER: Russian ships engage the *Goeben* in the Black Sea, inflicting serious damage and causing 115 to be killed and 59 wounded aboard the German cruiser.

19 NOVEMBER: In addition to increasing its attacks on Armenian civilians, the Turkish army arrests and kills its Armenian soldiers in mass executions.

21 NOVEMBER: RNAS pilots carry out a successful bombing mission against Friedrichshafen, Germany.

23 NOVEMBER: The *U-18* is captured by British destroyers off Pentland Firth, between the Orkney Islands and Scotland.

2 DECEMBER: Belgrade is captured by the Austrians.

5 DECEMBER: Austrian and Russian armies fight at the Battle of Limanova, outside of Krakow, Poland.

8 DECEMBER: Despite his victory at Coronel, Spee's five-ship fleet is caught near the Falkland Islands and destroyed by the British, commanded by Frederick Sturdee. Low on shells, the Germans also faced a superior British fleet. The Germans lose the *Scharnhorst, Gneisenau, Nürnberg,* and *Leipzig;* only the *Dresden* escapes.

14 DECEMBER: The Turkish battleship *Messudieh* is sunk in the Dardanelles, off Canakkale, by a British submarine.

15 DECEMBER: The Serbians recapture Belgrade from the Austrians.

16 DECEMBER: The Germans bombard Hartlepool, Whitby, and Scarborough, England, killing or wounding more than five hundred civilians.

18 DECEMBER: In an attempt to block German aid to the forces engaged in Arras, Indian troops are sent against the German lines in the Battle of Givenchy. They capture two trenches but are pushed back by German counterattacks. On the following day the Germans retake, then lose, the town to a British counterattack. When the battle is over, the combatants are essentially in the same positions in which they had started, with the exception of having suffered nearly six thousand combined dead.

20 DECEMBER: Former German chancellor Bülow travels to Rome to try to keep the Italians neutral by offering some territorial concessions. A similar mission is sent to Vienna to see if the Austrians will likewise placate the Italians.

21 DECEMBER: Dover, England, is attacked by German seaplanes, although the bombs land in the sea. A more successful bombing run is carried out by the same plane four nights later.

21 DECEMBER: The Ottoman Third Army attacks the Russians in the Caucasus Mountains.

25 DECEMBER: An unofficial truce is established across no-man's land in France. Lasting in some cases for several days, but opposed by the commanders, the truce allows enemy troops to talk with each other, trade food and souvenirs, and play sports during the lull.

25 DECEMBER: British seaplanes, launched from tenders in the North Sea, attack Cuxhaven, a German seaport on the mouth of the Elbe River. The bombing achieves little success, although it boosts the morale of the British.

25 DECEMBER: The French battleship *Jean Bart* is sunk by an Austrian submarine in the Straits of Otranto.

25 DECEMBER: British colonel Ernest Swinton suggests to Secretary of State for War Horatio Kitchener that the British develop a tank.

29 DECEMBER: The Russians counterattack near Kars in northeastern Turkey in the Battle of Sarikamish. The Turkish army is forced to surrender on 2 January 1915; only 20 percent of the nearly one-hundred-thousand-man Turkish army survives, with many of the deaths caused by freezing.

1915

1 JANUARY: The HMS *Formidable* is sunk in the English Channel. More than five hundred sailors lose their lives.

3 JANUARY: Gas-filled artillery shells are fired by the Germans on Russian positions along the Rawka River near Warsaw, Poland. The gas is a nonlethal tear-producing chemical.

10 JANUARY: American women's rights activists and social reformers Jane Addams and Carrie Chapman Catt organize the Woman's Peace Party.

14 JANUARY: South African leader Louis Botha captures Swakopmund on the Orange River and puts down an Afrikaner revolt. By 9 July 1915 Botha has defeated German interests in South West Africa.

15 JANUARY: The French lose a submarine, the *Saphir,* in an attempt to break through the Dardanelles.

24 JANUARY: Beatty commands an English fleet at the Battle of Dogger Bank. The German cruiser *Blücher* is sunk; the HMS *Lion* is damaged.

3 FEBRUARY: Fifteen thousand Turkish troops cross the Sinai Peninsula and attack the Suez Canal, but they are defeated by Allied defenders.

18 FEBRUARY: The German submarine blockade of England begins, though it was officially announced on 4 February.

19 FEBRUARY: Allied naval forces bombard, and also send raiding parties against, Turkish forts in the Dardanelles. These assaults continue into March.

19–20 FEBRUARY: German airships bomb Kings Lynn and Great Yarmouth, in the English province of Norfolk, during a night attack.

9 MARCH: The Austrians agree to cede Trentino to Italy, but only after the war is finished, which angers the Italians.

9–10 MARCH: The Germans attempt to push the Russians out of East Prussia.

10 MARCH: The British carry out their first aerial attack on enemy installations by bombing a rail yard and enemy headquarters in France.

10–15 MARCH: Sixty thousand British and Indian troops assault and take German lines at the Battle of Nueve Chappelle, forcing a wide breach in the front. The British halt their advance, however, and the Germans recover. A counterattack on 12 March results in high casualties for the Germans.

14 MARCH: The *Dresden* is caught and forced to be scuttled by the British fleet about four hundred miles off the coast of Chile, near the Juan Fernandez Islands.

18 MARCH: The *U–29,* with Captain Weddigen aboard, is rammed and sunk off Pentland Firth by HMS *Dreadnought.*

18 MARCH: A combined French and British fleet suffers major damage while trying to open the Dardanelles. Most of the ships are sunk by mines. The French lose the battleship *Bouvet;* the English, the *Irresistible.* Other battleships are damaged and have to retire for repairs.

22 MARCH: Russian troops recapture Przemsyl and move to face the Austrians in the Carpathian Mountains.

28 MARCH: The SS *Falaba,* a passenger ship, is sunk by the *U–28;* an American traveler, Leon Thrasher, is killed in the attack.

2–25 APRIL: A combined Austrian and German force pushes the Russians out of the Carpathian Mountains.

22 APRIL–25 MAY: The Second Battle of Ypres ends in a stalemate. During the engagement the Germans employ poisonous gases (chlorine gas) against enemy troops for the first time. The Allies use wet cloths across their faces to counter the effect of the gas and hold their lines. The Germans lose more than thirty-five thousand men; the Allies, twice that number. The Germans will later employ other gases, including phosgene and mustard, in the war.

25 APRIL: Thirty-five thousand British soldiers and seventeen thousand Anzacs (members of the Australian and New Zealand Army Corps) land at Gallipoli, a peninsula jutting out between the Aegean Sea and the Dardanelles. The Anzacs immediately encounter a Turkish force that pins them down along the coastline. More than two thousand soldiers die on the first day. Within two weeks, while making little advance, the Allies lose one-third of their strength.

26 APRIL: Italian leaders who favor intervention on the side of the Allies gain the upper hand and join a secret pact in London (with England, France, and Russia) that promises to obtain for Italy many territorial and colonial additions should the Allies win.

27 APRIL: The French cruiser *Léon Gambetta* is sunk in the Adriatic Sea by an Austrian submarine performing a submerged night attack. More than six hundred sailors perish.

28 APRIL: Austrian and German troops advance into Galicia.

1 MAY: The *Gulflight* is sunk, and two Americans are killed in a U-boat attack in the Atlantic Ocean.

2 MAY: German and Austro-Hungarian troops attack the Russians in Poland. Centered around the cities of Gorlice and Tarnów, the assault catches the Russians by surprise and forces them to retreat, beginning a four-month withdrawal that costs them nearly two million casualties, control of Poland, valuable military stocks, and removal of their commander, Grand Duke Nicholas.

7 MAY: The Cunard passenger liner *Lusitania*, passing through the Irish Sea, is torpedoed by the *U-20*. The ship sinks with the loss of 1,198 lives, including 128 U.S. citizens. The Germans claim that banned war supplies were being transported to England and had warned passengers before they left New York of the danger of traveling aboard the ship; U.S. sentiment, however, is enraged against the Germans.

9 MAY: The British fail to push German troops off the high ground in the Battle of Aubers Ridge; they lose more than eleven thousand men during the assault.

10 MAY: The Italians agree to a naval convention with Britain and France.

13 MAY: HMS *Goliath* is torpedoed and sunk off Cape Helles, Greece, by a Turkish destroyer. More than five hundred men perish.

13 MAY: President Wilson and Secretary of State William Jennings Bryan send a note of complaint to Germany about the series of U-boat attacks that have resulted in American deaths.

15 MAY: British and Indian troops suffer nearly sixteen thousand casualties in a night attack on German lines at the Battle of Festubert.

23 MAY: Italy declares war on Austria-Hungary. Germany severs diplomatic relations with Italy.

24 MAY: The Allies send a diplomatic note to Turkey, holding it responsible for massacres of Armenian citizens. Since the beginning of the year, hundreds of thousands of Armenians have been arrested, raped, killed, or deported. Many of the people deported are sent to the Syrian desert. Hundreds of Armenian villages and businesses are obliterated. The warning, however, does not stop the atrocities.

25 MAY: The battleship HMS *Triumph* is sunk in the Mediterranean Sea by the *U-21*.

27 MAY: While serving in the Dardanelles, the battleship HMS *Majestic* is sunk by the *U-21*.

31 MAY-1 JUNE: A German zeppelin drops bombs and grenades on London, the first such raid on the capital.

6-7 JUNE: A German zeppelin attacks the English towns of Hull and Grimsby. Twenty-four civilians are killed.

7 JUNE: A zeppelin is shot down over Ghent by a British fighter.

29 JUNE-7 JULY: The Italians and Austrians fight the Battle of the Isonzo (the first of eleven such engagements that bear the same name). The opposing sides pushed each other back and forth across a sixty-mile front in northeastern Italy, seldom more than ten miles in either direction.

4 JULY: The Germans make an official protest to the Turkish government about the atrocities carried out against the Armenian population. Their entreaty is ignored.

9 JULY: German forces in Southwest Africa surrender to Allied forces.

11 JULY: The German raider *Königsberg*, which had been forced to stay in port for eight months, is destroyed by British naval fire, in the Rufiji River in East Africa.

18 JULY-10 AUGUST: The Second Battle of the Isonzo is fought.

21 JULY: President Wilson directs his cabinet to begin preparations for possible participation in the war.

24 JULY: British troops, led by John Nixon, capture Nasiriya in Mesopotamia (modern Iraq) from Turkish forces. The British army moves northward along the Euphrates River.

5 AUGUST: The Germans enter Warsaw, while their allies, the Austrians, capture Ivangorod (Deblen) in eastern Poland.

8 AUGUST: A British landing on the Gallipoli Peninsula, in an attempt to control the Dardanelles, ends a failure in the Battle of Suvla Bay.

12 AUGUST: The first torpedo attack from an airplane occurs when a British seaplane hits a Turkish merchant vessel in the Sea of Marmara.

18 AUGUST: *The New York Times* reports on the Armenian massacres.

19 AUGUST: The White Star liner *Arabic* is sunk off of southern Ireland by the *U-24*. Forty-four people die, including two Americans.

19 AUGUST: British jurist, former ambassador to the United States, and member of the International Court of Justice, Lord James Bryce reports that more than five hundred thousand Armenians have been massacred in Turkey.

30 AUGUST: In order to placate the Americans, the Germans pull back from the policy of unannounced U-boat attacks.

1 SEPTEMBER: The Germans pledge not to attack unarmed passenger ships.

21 SEPTEMBER: British and French troops land in Macedonia.

25–28 SEPTEMBER: As part of a planned strategy to break the German lines in three places, the British engage the Germans at the Battle of Loos. On the first day a British gas attack is blown back upon their own troops, slowing their advance and leading to high casualties against concentrated German machine-gun fire. On the second day several British attacks are repelled, with high casualties. The two concurrent attacks, against Artois and Champagne, also fail and are completed by 8 October. The British suffer more than sixty thousand casualties.

25–28 SEPTEMBER: British and Indian troops, fighting in 120-degree heat, assault Turkish lines and capture the city of Kut-al-Amara. The Turks withdraw and set up defensive lines nearly four hundred miles to the north at Ctesiphon, the site of an ancient city located approximately halfway between Baghdad and Kut.

29 SEPTEMBER: The French take Vimy Ridge.

OCTOBER: Americans raise money to aid Armenian deportees. Reports claim that as many as eight hundred thousand Armenians have been killed. The Germans, defending their Turkish allies, argue that the claims are fabricated. The deportations and murders, however, continue.

3–5 OCTOBER: British and French forces land at Salonika, Greece.

8–9 OCTOBER: The Austrians capture Belgrade.

11 OCTOBER: The Bulgarians invade Serbia.

14 OCTOBER: The Allies declare war on Bulgaria.

18 OCTOBER–3 NOVEMBER: Third Battle of the Isonzo.

10 NOVEMBER–10 DECEMBER: Fourth Battle of the Isonzo.

22 NOVEMBER–3 DECEMBER: Nixon's army, as it advances toward Baghdad, attacks Turkish lines defending Ctesiphon. Although they initially push back the Turks, who lose nearly ten thousand men, the British are forced to withdraw to Kut, as they suffer nearly five thousand casualties, including more than half of one Indian division. Poor planning and inefficient medical preparation hurts British morale and prestige. The Turks bottle up the British at Kut and harass their lines during December.

4 DECEMBER: The *Oskar II,* a ship carrying peace activists from the United States, leaves the port of Hoboken, New Jersey, for a trip to Europe. Financed by American industrialist and peace activist Henry Ford, the group hopes to sponsor a peace conference to end the conflict. The ship arrives in Stockholm and a conference is arranged; however, no representatives from the warring nations attend.

19 DECEMBER: General Douglas Haig is appointed commander of the BEF, replacing John French.

20 DECEMBER: The withdrawal of Allied troops from Gallipoli is completed. The British suffer 33,512 killed, 7,636 missing, and 78,000 wounded, while the Anzacs lose 8,000 killed and 18,000 wounded in the attempt to capture the peninsula.

31 DECEMBER: By this time a Jewish underground in Palestine, called the Nili, is formed to aid the British in the battle against the Turks in the Middle East. The

CHRONOLOGY

British utilize their intelligence and espionage but are wary of their motives.

1916

JANUARY: The British Secret Service Bureau becomes MI5, overseeing counterespionage efforts.

1 JANUARY: Yaunde (Cameroon) is captured from the Germans by Allied forces. By 18 February all German troops in Cameroon have surrendered to the Allies.

6-7 JANUARY: A British relief force, moving up the Euphrates to help embattled troops at Kut, are defeated by the Turks at Sheikh Sa'ad. More than four thousand Allied soldiers are killed. Another attempt to relieve the troops at Kut is defeated on 13 January.

31 JANUARY-1 FEBRUARY: During the night a large force of German airships raid England, but they fall short of hitting their designated target, Liverpool. Nearly four hundred bombs are dropped; seventy civilians are killed.

21 FEBRUARY: The German Fifth Army, led by General Falkenhayn, assaults the fortress at Verdun, an important symbolic marker for the French. The Germans shell the area for nearly a full day prior to their assault. The Battle for Verdun lasts until December 1916.

21 FEBRUARY: The Germans inform the Americans that armed merchantmen can be sunk because they will be considered navy vessels.

25 FEBRUARY: The French fort at Douaumont falls to the Germans. General Philippe Pétain takes over the defense of Verdun.

26 FEBRUARY: The French cruiser *Provence,* sailing off the coast of Kithria Island, Greece, is sunk by the *U-35.*

27 FEBRUARY: President Wilson begins a national tour to promote military preparedness.

9 MARCH: Germany declares war on Portugal.

9 MARCH: A group of Mexican bandits, led by Pancho Villa, cross the United States-Mexico border and raid Columbus, Mexico.

18 MARCH-14 APRIL: The Russian Second Army goes on the offensive east of Vilna (Vilnius), Lithuania, but it loses nearly one hundred thousand men at the Battle of Lake Naroch, which stalls the advance.

24 MARCH: More Americans perish because of the submarine war, this time aboard the French passenger liner *Sussex,* which is sunk in the English Channel.

9-14 APRIL: A five-day barrage, launched by more than 2,500 British artillery pieces, rains down on German positions at Vimy, but it fails to dislodge the enemy. A gas attack, followed by a Canadian advance, allows Allied troops to capture the ridge with few casualties.

29 APRIL: British and Indian forces at Kut surrender to the Turks. More than thirteen thousand men are taken captive in one of the worst defeats suffered by British arms; many prisoners of war are killed by the Turks or die on forced marches. During this battle the defenders are resupplied by air drops from the RFC and the RNAS.

10 MAY: The Germans promise to back off unrestricted submarine warfare.

29 MAY: The French are pushed off Le Mort Homme, a hill overlooking the town of Verdun.

31 MAY: The German High Seas Fleet and British Grand Fleet face each other in the North Sea at the Battle of Jutland. German admiral Reinhard Scheer is tasked with destroying the English fleet, commanded by John Jellicoe. The British had broken German naval codes and knew of their plans. In the following battle, which many historians judge a draw, the British lose the *Indefatigable, Invincible,* and *Queen Mary,* as well as four cruisers and eight destroyers; the Germans lose the *Derfflinger,* four cruisers, and five destroyers, while the *Seydiltz* is badly damaged. The High Seas Fleet retires to port and never again puts to sea to engage the Grand Fleet.

2-13 JUNE: Canadian troops fight at the Battle of Mount Sorrel. The highest ranking Canadian soldier to die in the war, a major general, perishes during the engagement.

3 JUNE: The American Board of Commissioners for Foreign Missions issues a report on the Armenian massacres.

3 JUNE: The U.S. Congress passes the National Defense Act, raising the size of the army to 175,000 men and the National Guard to 450,000 men.

4 JUNE: A large Russian offensive, with more than forty divisions led by Aleksey Alekseyevich Brusilov, invades Galicia and attacks Austro-Hungarian forces, pushing them rearward for approximately sixty miles. The Germans respond by pulling troops away from their assaults on Verdun.

5 JUNE: Lord Kitchener dies at sea near the Orkney Islands, off the northeast coast of Scotland. He is on a mission to confer with

the Russians when his ship, the cruiser *Hampshire,* is sunk by a German U-boat.

7 JUNE: Fort Vaux, which is just three miles outside of Verdun, falls to the Germans.

22 JUNE: The Germans renew their attacks on Verdun, trying to capture two bridges leading to the city, but they do not achieve any success. More than seven hundred thousand men, from both sides, die during the contest to control Verdun.

1 JULY: Originally planned to commence on 29 June, and designed to take pressure off the French at Verdun, the Battle of the Somme begins late because of poor visibility for pilots to direct artillery strikes. British and French divisions attack, with the French achieving a greater level of surprise. British losses are high in the initial assaults; they lose nearly one thousand officers and more than eighteen thousand enlisted men. South African and Australian troops also participate in the battle. On 14 July a surprise German night counterattack recaptures lost territory and seals a gap in their lines. The Battle for the Somme lasts until 19 November. More than 1.2 million men, from both sides, lose their lives in this engagement.

3 JULY: A synchronized propeller/machine gun is introduced on British aircraft.

7 JULY: British forces in Africa capture Tanga from the Germans, as well as gain control of Lake Tanganyika.

30 JULY: Munitions and dynamite stored in barges and railcars are blown up in a freight terminal at Black Tom Island, south of the Statue of Liberty in New York harbor, allegedly by German agents. The shock from the blast is said to be felt as far away as Philadelphia. Facilities at nearby Ellis Island suffer $400,000 in damage.

1 AUGUST: The Italians are heavily involved along the Isonzo Front.

3 AUGUST: British and Turkish forces clash at the Battle of Rumani in Egypt. The Turks make an advance on the Suez Canal, which was blunted by British and Australian troops, who build false trenches and utilize cavalry attacks.

6–9 AUGUST: The Italians take the town of Gorizia from the Austro-Hungarians.

15 AUGUST: Bitlis, a town in eastern Turkey, is captured from the Russians by the Turkish army. The Russians will recapture the town nine days later.

15 AUGUST: Bagamoyo, in German East Africa, falls to the British.

27 AUGUST: Hindenburg and Ludendorff are given command of the German armies.

28 AUGUST: Romania declares war on Austria; Italy declares war on Germany; Germany declares war on Rumania the following day.

2–3 SEPTEMBER: A large zeppelin attack on England results in little damage, but the Germans lose a zeppelin to English aircraft.

4 SEPTEMBER: Dar-es-Salaam falls to the English.

15 SEPTEMBER: Twenty-four British, Canadian, and Scottish tanks are employed during the Battle of the Somme, which is their first such use in combat.

18 SEPTEMBER: Florina, in Macedonia, is captured by the British.

25 SEPTEMBER: The British Fourth Army, including New Zealand troops, attacks German lines around the towns of Morval and Lesbeoufs, France. The army succeeds in taking several miles of trenches.

26–28 SEPTEMBER: Four divisions of British troops attack the strong German entrenchments along Thiepval Ridge. They suffer heavy casualties in the assaults. German soldiers in the trenches reportedly taunt their enemy as they advance.

4 OCTOBER: The Austrians and Germans begin major incursions, which will last until December, into Romania.

8–9 OCTOBER: President Wilson proclaims two "Armenian Relief Days."

10 OCTOBER: The Eighth Battle of the Isonzo is fought.

24 OCTOBER: The French counterattack at Verdun, pushing back the Germans, who are weakened by reductions of their forces because of manpower needs on the Eastern Front. Fort Douaumont is recaptured by the Allies.

26 OCTOBER: A German destroyer raids into the Dover Straits.

5 NOVEMBER: The Germans and Austrians proclaim the creation of the kingdom of Poland. Józef Pilsudski, who led an army of ten thousand Poles against the Russians, is made the head of a military commission but is later imprisoned when he holds back his troops after the Germans refuse to provide assurances of independence.

1–14 NOVEMBER: The Ninth Battle of the Isonzo is fought.

7 NOVEMBER: President Wilson, a Democrat, wins reelection by defeating Republican candidate Charles Evans Hughes.

9–18 NOVEMBER: British forces attempt to dislodge German positions at the Battle of the Ancre, which ends the Somme Offensive. The British capture Beaumont-Hamel.

28 NOVEMBER: German planes attack London for the first time.

1–4 DECEMBER: German and Austrian troops defeat the Romanians at the Battle of the Argesul River. The Romanians lose Bucharest.

7 DECEMBER: David Lloyd George, the former Minister of Munitions and Secretary of State for War, becomes Prime Minister of England, replacing Herbert Asquith. Lloyd George reforms the War Cabinet.

31 DECEMBER: The Russian mystic and confidant of the royals, Grigory Rasputin, is assassinated by Russian noblemen.

1917

8–9 JANUARY: The British forces under Archibold Murray gain control of the Sinai from the Turks. This victory opens the war for further British attacks in the Middle East.

9 JANUARY: The Germans resume unrestricted submarine attacks on all shipping to Great Britain, although this decision is not announced until the last day of the month.

FEBRUARY: The Dutch exotic dancer Margaretha Geertruida "Zelle" MacLeod, better known to history as Mata Hari, is executed by a French firing squad for allegedly spying for the Germans.

3 FEBRUARY: The United States ends diplomatic relations with Germany.

22–24 FEBRUARY: The British force a Turkish withdrawal from Kut.

23–27 FEBRUARY: Food riots break out in Petrograd (formerly St. Petersburg), Russia. Some of the city garrison troops mutiny and burn down government buildings.

1 MARCH: The contents of the Zimmermann telegram are released to the public. This secret diplomatic note from German foreign minister Arthur Zimmermann to the Mexican government, intercepted and decoded by British intelligence, suggests that Mexico might be interested in joining Germany in opposition to the United States, should the Americans join the war on the side of the Allies. Mexico is offered the opportunity to regain territory in the continental United States that it had lost to the Americans. Sentiment in the United States rises against the Germans.

5 MARCH: President Wilson is sworn in for his second term in office. He won reelection largely on his promise to keep the United States out of the war.

11 MARCH: Baghdad is captured by the British.

12 MARCH: President Wilson orders that merchant ships be armed.

13 MARCH: A provisional government, led by Aleksandr Kerensky, is established in Russia.

15 MARCH: Tsar Nicholas II abdicates. He and his family are imprisoned on 21 March.

APRIL: Germany is hit by several work stoppages and strikes by workers upset about food shortages and inflation.

2 APRIL : President Wilson, in a speech to Congress, calls for war against Germany.

6 APRIL: The United States declares war on Germany; the following day the United States declares war against Austria-Hungary.

7 APRIL: The U.S. Navy takes control of all wireless stations in the United States.

9 APRIL: British and Canadian troops, including remnants from the Gallipoli campaign, participate in an assault against the Germans in the Second Battle of Arras. The Canadians distinguish themselves by capturing the Vimy Ridge.

14 APRIL: President Wilson establishes the Committee on Public Information, better known as the Creel Commission (after its chairman, newspaperman George Creel), which utilizes propaganda to increase pro-war sentiment in the United States and also materials to dishearten the enemy. The board even helps change traditional Germanic words in the English language: for example, sauerkraut becomes "liberty cabbage."

16 APRIL: Allied troops under the command of Robert Nivelle attack the Germans, who are entrenched behind the Hindenburg Line, in what becomes known as the Second Battle of the Aisne River or Chemin des Dames offensive. The assaulting troops are slaughtered, raising the ire of French soldiers and citizens; many regiments refuse to engage the enemy.

20–21 APRIL: Turkey ends diplomatic relations with the United States.

20–21 APRIL: The destroyers HMS *Broke* and *Swift* engage a German force of twelve destroyers as they make a raid into the Dover Strait. The *Broke* rams one German ship and hand-to-hand combat follows while the ships are engaged. The British ships are badly damaged, but the Germans lose two destroyers.

24 APRIL: U.S. secretary of the treasury William McAdoo authorizes the Liberty Loan Act to raise money by public subscription to fund wartime activities.

24 APRIL: The first U.S. naval squadron, made up of destroyers, leaves Boston for service in the European theater.

28 APRIL: The Canadians capture the city of Arleux.

MAY: The British institute the convoy system to protect shipping crossing the Atlantic Ocean from German U-boat attacks.

MAY: Wilson establishes the War Industries Board, which controls raw materials and war production, chaired by investor Bernard Baruch. The agency guarantees profits for manufacturers.

15 MAY: General Pétain takes command of the French Army from Nivelle and calms his mutinous army.

15 MAY: British and Italian naval vessels engage in a two-hour fight with Austrian ships in the Straits of Otranto, which connects the Adriatic Sea with the Ionian Sea. The Austrians, who had initiated the engagement by attacking barrage vessels stationed in the straits, suffer some damage to one of their cruisers, which is towed from the battle to a safe port; a British cruiser is badly damaged in a torpedo attack.

18 MAY: The Selective Service Act is passed by the U.S. Congress. Men from the age of twenty-one to thirty years of age are required to register. Nearly 10,000,000 men register, and a lottery selects around 700,000 names in the first draft. By the end of the war more than 2,800,000 men have been inducted.

26 MAY: The British hospital ship *Dover Castle,* carrying wounded from Malta to Gibraltar, is sunk by the *U–67* in the Mediterranean Sea.

5 JUNE: The Germans carry out a daylight air raid on Folkestone in Kent, England.

7 JUNE: British troops, using nineteen massive underground mines detonated beneath the enemy's lines, take a stretch of heights near the town of Messines, which gives them a commanding position against German positions, at a cost of twenty-four thousand casualties.

12–18 JUNE: Tenth Battle of the Isonzo.

13 JUNE: London is the target of another daylight German bombing raid. More than 160 civilians are killed. London, and other parts of England, will be repeatedly attacked in the coming months in similar raids.

15 JUNE: The Espionage Act is passed by the U.S. Congress, outlawing espionage carried out by agents for foreign countries.

26 JUNE: U.S. troops arrive at St. Nazaire, France. The American Expeditionary Force (AEF) is commanded by John Pershing. Only four divisions arrive in France during the year. When African American divisions land, Pershing detaches them to the French, who supply them with arms and helmets and send them into battle.

27 JUNE: The Allies help form a new government in Greece, led by Prime Minister Eleuthérios Venizélos. Greece declares war on Germany.

1 JULY: The Second Brusilov offensive begins as Russians attack Austrian forces in Galicia. The Russians experience good initial results but then are pushed back by Austrian counterattacks by the end of the month.

2 JULY: Pershing asks for a million-man army, later moving the target figure to three million.

11 JULY: Kerensky is named prime minister of Russia.

31 JULY–10 NOVEMBER: The Third Battle of Ypres (also known as the Battle of Passchendaele) is fought. Over extremely soggy and muddy territory, which has been churned up by constant bombardment, the British army charges into machine-gun fire and poisonous gas attacks from hardened defensive positions, and the attackers suffer severe casualties. Some of the troops actually drown in the mud. Canadian troops succeed in taking the town of Passchendaele. A total, from both sides, of nearly five hundred thousand men become casualties.

2 AUGUST: British pilot E. H. Dunning conducts the first landing on a moving aircraft carrier, HMS *Furious,* which is a converted cruiser. Dunning dies five days later attempting to land on the ship.

10 AUGUST: President Wilson issues an executive order creating the Food Administration. The agency, headed by Herbert Hoover, is tasked with assuring supply and conservation of food, supervising transportation, and preventing monopolies and hoarding.

14 AUGUST: China declares war on Germany and Austria-Hungary.

15–16 AUGUST: Mustard gas is used by the Germans against the Canadians, who are attacking Hill 70, north of Lens. The Canadians beat back three days of counterattacks (18–20 August).

16–18 AUGUST: British and Irish troops, weary from several weeks of constant shelling and rainy weather, engage the Germans in heavy fighting at the Battle of Langemarck. The

Allied troops suffer severe losses as soldiers get bogged in the mire and are raked by concentrated enemy fire.

18 AUGUST–20 SEPTEMBER: Italy attacks on the Isonzo-Carso front in the Eleventh Battle of the Isonzo.

23 AUGUST: Racial tension explodes in Texas when approximately one hundred African American troops, stationed at Camp Logan, after being provoked by citizens of Houston, march on the town and open fire on the police station, killing sixteen whites and wounding twelve. Sixty-four men are court-martialed: forty-two are given life sentences and thirteen are condemned to die. The condemned are executed on 11 December.

30 AUGUST: The American Field Service (AFS), an ambulance corps staffed mostly by young American college students who volunteer to serve in Europe, is merged with the U.S. Army. More than 2,500 drivers serve in the AFS; more than 150 perish. Other organizations, including the American Red Cross, supplies drivers. Many of these volunteers become famous later as writers, including John Dos Passos, Ernest Hemingway, W. Somerset Maugham, and E. E. Cummings.

1 SEPTEMBER: The Germans begin an offensive on the Eastern Front and capture Riga, Latvia (3 September).

2–30 SEPTEMBER: German air raids are carried out on London and southeast England.

20 SEPTEMBER: British and Anzac troops in the Second and Fifth Armies engage the Germans in the Battle of Menin Road. The Allied price for capturing roughly five square miles of territory is twenty-one thousand casualties.

26 SEPTEMBER–3 OCTOBER: In an attempt to gain momentum on the victories earned at the Battle of Menin Road, the Allies continue their attack, with much success, against German lines at the Battle of Polygon Wood.

3 OCTOBER: The U.S. Congress passes the War Revenue Act, which increases revenues from $809 million in 1917 to $3.6 billion in 1918.

4 OCTOBER: Anzac troops attack German trenches and pill boxes at Broodseinde and capture more than five thousand enemy soldiers.

14 OCTOBER: Six hundred thirty-nine African American army officers graduate from officer training school and are commissioned at Fort Dodge, Des Moines, Iowa.

15 OCTOBER: The destroyer USS *Cassin* is torpedoed by the *U–105* off the coast of Ireland, but there is only one casualty.

15–18 OCTOBER: German troops defeat the Allies at the battle of Mahiwa. They then begin to invade Portuguese territory in East Africa along the Zambezi River.

24 OCTOBER–12 NOVEMBER: Austrian-German attacks break through Italian defenses, held by the Second Army, at Caporetto, Austria. The Italians, who lose nearly three hundred thousand men, are pushed back to the Piave River.

2 NOVEMBER: British foreign secretary Arthur Balfour issues a declaration that Great Britain will support the establishment of a homeland for Jews in Palestine.

3 NOVEMBER: U.S. troops engage the enemy for the first time in trench warfare along the Rhine-Marne Canal. Three soldiers are killed and eleven are captured.

6 NOVEMBER: Passchendaele is captured by Canadian troops.

6 NOVEMBER: The Bolsheviks, led by Lenin, depose the provisional government in Russia. The new government includes Leon Trotsky as commissar for foreign affairs and Joseph Stalin as commissar for national minorities.

7 NOVEMBER: Gaza is taken by the British from the Turks.

13 NOVEMBER: The U.S. Army Nurses Corps accepts eighteen black nurses on an "experimental" basis.

15 NOVEMBER: Georges Clémenceau again becomes the premier of France.

17 NOVEMBER: Jaffa, northwest of Jerusalem, is captured by the British.

20 NOVEMBER: The British mass more than three hundred tanks to spearhead an infantry attack against German lines. The assault, called the Battle of Cambrai, proves successful and deep breaches are punched through German positions, but the British fail to take advantage of the situation. Aircraft are used to bomb advance positions.

29 NOVEMBER: The U.S. War Department authorizes the creation of the first large all-black unit, the 92nd Division.

6 DECEMBER: U.S. warships join the Allied fleet off the northern coast of Scotland. The destroyer USS *Jacob Jones* is torpedoed and sunk by the *U–53*, east of Start Point, England; sixty-four sailors are killed.

6 DECEMBER: The French munitions transport *Mont Blanc*, after a collision with the Belgian "relief" ship *Imo*, catches fire and explodes in Halifax harbor. The blast causes 1,600 deaths and wounds an additional 9,000 people. An entire Indian village situated up a nearby river is wiped out by a wave caused by the explosion and pieces of the bulkhead are blown several miles inshore.

9 DECEMBER: The British Egyptian Expeditionary Force, led by Edmund Allenby, captures Jerusalem from the Ottoman Empire.

15 DECEMBER: Peace negotiations between Russia and Germany at Brest-Litovsk result in an armistice between the two countries, though the sides clash over terms.

1918

1 JANUARY: The 369th Infantry, the first African American combat unit in France, arrives.

4 JANUARY: The British hospital ship *Rewa* is sunk in the Bristol Channel; three lives are lost.

8 JANUARY: President Wilson announces his Fourteen Points, a plan for establishing a lasting peace in Europe, to a joint session of Congress. His plan calls for open diplomacy among nations, self-determination of nationalities, freedom of the seas, free trade, and a reduction of armaments. Foreign troops are to leave Russia, France, Belgium, Turkey, the Balkans, and several other occupied regions. He also calls for a general association of nations to guarantee the independence and territorial integrity of all countries.

20 JANUARY: After leaving port and sinking two British monitors, the *Goeben* hits several mines and is forced to run aground. The cruiser is later pulled off the shoal and returns to port, but it is out of commission for the rest of the war. The *Breslau* hits five mines and sinks, with the loss of most of its crew, in the Dardanelles.

3 MARCH: The Treaty of Brest-Litovsk is signed by Russia and Central Powers. Russia is out of the war and is forced to cede lands in the Baltic, Poland, and Ukraine to the Germans.

4 MARCH: British marines land at Murmansk, a Russian city on the Barents Sea, beginning an occupation that lasts until 1920. The British fear that the Finns, who were allied with the Germans, might capture large stores of arms in the city. Trotsky also invites the British in, as he hopes to gain arms for his Red Army.

21 MARCH: With Russia out of the war, Ludendorff orders an offensive, featuring 190 divisions, against the Allies in a bid to capture the city of Amiens. The British Fifth

Army is destroyed, but two Australian divisions blunt the German attack.

22 MARCH: The Germans reach the Somme. Péronne is lost; the following day, Albert and Noyon are captured. On 27 March the Germans are checked at the Scarpe River. French counterattacks on the next day hold Germans in the Somme region. The final German offensive is checked east of Villers-Bretonneux on 4–5 April by Australian troops.

26 MARCH: The Allies hold an emergency conference at Doullens to discuss the most recent attack, to plan strategy, and to form an oversight council. General Foch is appointed to coordinate actions of the Allies on the Western Front. Foch convinces Pershing to allow the use of American troops.

APRIL: The assassin Princip dies of tuberculosis at Theresienstadt, Bohemia.

1 APRIL: The Royal Air Force (RAF) is created, along with a women's auxiliary.

2 APRIL: The Germans attack Lys, Arras, and Aisne in a Spring Offensive. Although initially successful, with more than 160,000 casualties suffered, the Germans halt their advance in June.

9 APRIL: The Germans attack in Belgium and capture Bailleul on 15 April; they take Wytschaete and Meteren on 16 April; and Kemmel and Dranoutre on 17 April.

14 APRIL: General Foch is appointed commander in chief of all Allied Armies in France.

15 APRIL: Bailleul is captured by the Germans.

17–19 APRIL: German counterattacks recapture lost ground around Kemmel.

21 APRIL: German fighter ace Manfred von Richthofen, "The Red Baron," credited with downing eighty enemy airplanes, is killed when his aircraft is shot down in action over France.

22–23 APRIL: The British raid Zeebrugge, a coastal city that defends a canal from Bruges to the North Sea, which provides greater access to German U-boats to the North Sea. HMS *Vindictive* lands a raiding party to occupy the Germans, while a submarine torpedoes the locks. Three concrete-filled warships are then sunk in the harbor to block U-boat traffic.

23 APRIL: Heavy German attacks help gain the town of Villers-Bretonneux.

23 APRIL: The U.S.S. *Stewart* attacks a German U-boat off the coast of France. The submarine is under assault by French air and sea

CHRONOLOGY

forces, and the *Stewart* comes alongside and drops depth charges; although initially listed as a kill, the *U–108* survives the attack.

1 MAY: U.S. troops join the front line at Amiens.

7 MAY: The Peace of Bucharest ends hostilities between Central Powers and Romania.

16 MAY: The U.S. Espionage Act is amended to include the outlawing of sedition acts, including prohibitions on anyone who would "wilfully utter, print, write, or publish any disloyal, profane, scurrilous, or abusive language about the form of government of the United States, or the Constitution of the United States, or the military or naval forces of the United States, or the flag."

23 MAY: German artillery shells Paris.

27 MAY–2 JUNE: The Germans attack along the Aisne River.

28 MAY: An Armenian republic is declared.

28 MAY: U.S. troops, under French control, engage in a limited counterattack—their first offensive action—on German positions at Cantigny.

29 MAY: The French are driven back across Aisne, and the Germans capture Soissons.

30 MAY: The Germans reach the Marne River.

31 MAY: The first of three American troop transports is sunk by German submarines. The USS *President Lincoln* is torpedoed six hundred miles off the French coast with the loss of twenty-six. One month later, on 1 July, the USS *Covington* is sunk off Brest, France, with the loss of six. On 5 September the *Mount Vernon* is sunk, with the loss of thirty-six lives, off the coast of France.

2–4 JUNE: U.S. troops stop a German advance at the Battle of Chateau-Thierry.

6–24 JUNE: U.S. Marines, attached to the Second Division of the AEF, attack entrenched German positions in Belleau Wood (11–12 June), northwest of Chateau-Thierry. After nearly two weeks of fighting and nearly eight thousand casualties the Americans succeed in capturing the territory.

9–13 JUNE: The Germans attack toward Compiègne in the Gneisenau offensive.

11 JUNE: The German advance is checked.

15–23 JUNE: The Austro-Hungarians suffer heavy casualties during attacks on the Italians along the Piave River and are forced to withdraw.

27 JUNE: The Canadian hospital ship *Llandovery Castle* is sunk without warning by the *U–86* near Fastnet, with the loss of 234 lives. The ship is sailing from Halifax to Liverpool; the Germans claim that U.S. pilots

and ammunition are being ferried to Europe. The submarine crew also fires upon the lifeboats. Among the dead are fourteen Canadian female nurses. Two of the German officers, but not the captain, who cannot be found, are tried for war crimes and given four-year prison sentences after the war ends.

4 JULY: Anzac and American troops take ground from the Germans at Hamel.

15 JULY: The Second Battle of the Marne begins with a final German attack. More than eighty-five thousand U.S. troops fight alongside French contingents.

16 JULY: Tsar Nicholas and his family are executed by their Bolshevik guards at Yekaterinburg.

18 JULY: A massive Allied counterattack begins southwest of the Marne; by 22 July the Germans are in retreat. The first major American offensive, with around 250,000 troops, attacks German positions at Soissons and pushes the enemy out of the region.

1 AUGUST: The Allied Expeditionary Force lands at Archangel, Russia, and captures the city from its defenders. The army is composed of troops from fourteen allied countries, including the United States. More than eight thousand U.S. troops remain on Russian soil until April 1920.

2 AUGUST: The French retake Soissons.

3 AUGUST: Allied expeditionary soldiers, including Japanese troops, land at Vladivostok.

6–12 AUGUST: A massive Allied attack, supported by more than two thousand artillery guns and two hundred tanks, strikes the Germans along a fifteen-mile front.

8 AUGUST: A British attack, led by five hundred tanks, smashes into German lines along the Somme River. German troops become disillusioned and mutinous during the battle.

9–16 AUGUST: The French advance and capture Lassigny.

17–20 AUGUST: The French drive the Germans from the Aisne Heights.

18 AUGUST: The German retreat from Ancre begins.

21–31 AUGUST: British troops push back German lines in the Second Battle of Bapaume. They recapture Albert on 22 August, Bapaume on 29 August, and Péronne on 30 August. Nearly thirty-five thousand German soldiers are captured.

26 AUGUST–3 SEPTEMBER: British and German troops struggle for the Hindenburg

Line in the Battle of the Scarpe. On 31 August the British capture Bullecourt.

26 AUGUST: The British capture Monchy-le-Preux.

3-9 SEPTEMBER : The Germans are forced to fall back behind the Hindenburg Line.

6 SEPTEMBER: American troops reach the Aisne River.

12-16 SEPTEMBER: A massive U.S. attack, supported by the French and more than 1,400 airplanes, commences on German lines around St. Mihiel. The entire salient quickly collapses, and the Germans are expelled.

14 SEPTEMBER: The Germans retreat to an area between Meuse and Moselle.

19-30 SEPTEMBER: The British begin an offensive in Palestine and Syria. They are aided by an Armenian legion. The Turkish armies are defeated and Damascus is captured on 1 October.

26 SEPTEMBER: The U.S. Coast Guard cutter *Tampa* is sunk in the Bristol Channel, probably by a U-boat attack, with the loss of its complete crew—118 men are killed.

26-29 SEPTEMBER: The U.S. First Army attacks the German Fifth Army in the Argonne Forest. By 16 October the Germans are pushed out of the forest. More than 600,000 U.S. troops participated, losing 117,000 killed or wounded.

26-30 SEPTEMBER: French troops attack German forces in the Champagne region.

26 SEPTEMBER-5 OCTOBER: British troops attack on a thirty-mile front between St. Quentin and the Sensée.

28 SEPTEMBER: British, French, and American divisions attack on the twelve-mile front, cross the St. Quentin Canal, and capture Bellecourt.

29 SEPTEMBER: Bulgaria signs an armistice with the Allies and surrenders the following day.

3 OCTOBER: The Hindenburg Line is crossed by Allied troops.

6-12 OCTOBER : During an offensive movement, the British capture Cambrai (8 October) and Le Cateau (10 October).

7 OCTOBER: Beirut is captured by the British.

9 OCTOBER: The Germans evacuate the Argonne Forest.

14 OCTOBER: Turkey makes diplomatic overtures of peace to the United States.

17 OCTOBER : The Belgians enter Ostend and liberate Zeebrugge and Bruges.

21-31 OCTOBER: American and French troops are involved in fierce fighting against the Germans north of Verdun and along the Meuse River.

24-30 OCTOBER: Italian troops attack and rout the Austro-Hungarians in the Battle of Vittorio Veneto.

25-30 OCTOBER: The Turkish army surrenders to the British in Mesopotamia.

26 OCTOBER: Ludendorff resigns after he disagrees with the German government over the acceptance of President Wilson's ideas for peace.

26 OCTOBER: Aleppo is captured by the British; 125,000 deported Armenians are saved.

27 OCTOBER: Austria-Hungary applies to the United States for an armistice.

28 OCTOBER: The Czechs and Slovaks form the independent country of Czechoslovakia.

29 OCTOBER: Yugoslavia announces its independence.

30 OCTOBER: The Allies sign an armistice with the Ottoman Empire, which reopens the Dardanelles and allows Allied forces onto its territory.

30 OCTOBER: Austria is declared an independent nation and its soldiers seek an armistice with the Allies.

31 OCTOBER: A revolution breaks out in Hungary, leading to its independence as a nation.

1-11 NOVEMBER: A Franco-American attack on Forêt de Bourgogne sparks a rapid advance against the Germans.

1-11 NOVEMBER: The British advance between Sambre and Scheldt.

2 NOVEMBER: The British enter Valenciennes, clear Forêt de Mormal, and by 11 November liberate Avesnes, Maubeuge, and Mons. The Canadians are heavily involved in the capture of Valenciennes.

2 NOVEMBER: German troops begin an invasion of Rhodesia.

2 NOVEMBER: The *Surada* and *Murcia* are the last British merchant ships sunk by U-boats in the war.

3 NOVEMBER: German sailors, fearing they are to be sacrificed in a senseless attack on the enemy, mutiny at Kiel. Some mutinous activity may have been initiated as early as 28 October.

4 NOVEMBER: Hostilities between Austria-Hungary and the Allies come to an end.

4 NOVEMBER: The New Zealand Rifle Brigade scales the sixty-foot ramparts at Le Quesnoy.

6 NOVEMBER: The French enter Rethel and the Americans enter Sedan.

8 NOVEMBER: German peace delegates confer with Marshal Foch near Compiègne, France.

9 NOVEMBER: Revolts breaks out in Berlin.

10 NOVEMBER: Kaiser William II abdicates and flees to Holland. Germany is proclaimed a republic, under the leadership of the socialist Friedrich Ebert.

11 NOVEMBER: A general armistice between the Allies and Germans is signed and hostilities cease.

11 NOVEMBER: Poland is declared an independent, sovereign state. The country was devastated by the war, suffering more than one million casualties and the nearly complete destruction of its infrastructure.

21 NOVEMBER: The German Battle Fleet surrenders to the British off Firth of Forth.

23 NOVEMBER: The Yugoslavian people declare an independent state.

1 DECEMBER: Allied troops enter Germany.

20 DECEMBER: New Zealand troops enter Cologne.

31 DECEMBER: By this time an influenza epidemic works its way around the globe, killing an estimated twenty-two million people (possibly as many as forty million), more than were killed as a result of combat in the war. The first cases in the United States are discovered among returning soldiers at Boston, and during the pandemic even the draft is suspended. More than six hundred thousand Americans die from the disease.

1919

18 JANUARY: Peace talks begin in Paris.

7 FEBRUARY: British delegates to peace talks insist that alleged war criminals be arrested and brought to trial.

14 FEBRUARY: President Wilson presents his plan for the League of Nations, a group of sovereign states who agree to pursue common policies and to submit all differences among themselves to arbitration.

21 JUNE: The German fleet, interned by the Allies in Scapa Flow, is scuttled by its own crews.

28 JUNE: The Treaty of Versailles is signed, and under Article 231 Germany accepts responsibility "for causing all the loss and damage to which the Allied and Associated Governments and their nationals have been subjected as a consequence of the war imposed upon them." Germany loses substantial territory, including Alsace-Lorraine (given to France) and Posen and West Prussia (given to Poland). The region west of the Rhine and 50 kilometers east of it becomes a demilitarized zone. Danzig is declared a free port and the French are allowed to operate the coal mines of the Saar for fifteen years. The German army is limited to a one-hundred-thousand-man force without the support of tanks, heavy artillery, and aircraft; the navy is reduced to a small coastal force. Finally, Germany is required to pay an indemnity to the Allies (estimated in 1921 at $33 billion).

ALIENATION OF SOLDIERS

Did soldiers who had fought at the front feel permanently alienated from civilian culture?

Viewpoint: Yes. The conditions of the fighting and the remoteness of many theaters combined to establish a barrier of understanding between those who fought and those who did not.

Viewpoint: No. The myth that front-line soldiers were alienated from home-front society is based on the experience of a small, vocal group.

Among the persistent images of the Great War is that of an unbridgeable gulf between the home front and the fighting fronts. Accordingly, shock at the comprehensive alienness of the front-line experience combined with the nurturing comradeship of the trenches to create a state of being impossible to describe to civilians blinded by traditional myths of glory and heroism. As the war progressed, the armies became substitute societies, providing nurture, entertainment, family surrogates—even to a degree sexual substitutes, as evidenced by the "transgressive" female impersonators that were such a frequent and popular feature of the British Expeditionary Force (BEF)'s concert parties.

Letters home only deepened the gulf, as men sought both to reassure those left behind and to conceal from themselves the true nature of their own circumstances. Memoirs and fiction alike are replete with narratives of soldiers on leave who felt comprehensively alienated from even their families and returned to their front-line "homes" with something approximating relief.

To a degree, the concept of alienation between home front and fighting front served as a shorthand mythic explanation for the impact of the war on societies that never expected anything like the events of 1914–1918. It served as well to explain the revolutionary phenomena, and the social changes, that shook Europe to its foundations during the 1920s and 1930s. It served, finally, as a trope of identification for a "war generation" that considered itself a product of the trenches, no matter what had been the specific experience of particular individuals.

Recent research, applying the methods of the "new social history," has significantly modified the traditional construction. At the most basic level the Great War featured extensive physical movement between front and home. Men mobilized in the first rush of 1914 were subsequently demobilized or furloughed to work in the factories and on the farms whose products were vital for the war effort. Many of these men were in turn "combed out": returned to the war when the demands of the trenches escalated. Near-universal literacy meant that civilians were kept closely and consistently informed of conditions in the field, and systematic evaluation of the preserved correspondence shows high levels of frankness on both sides. The men at the front were kept well informed by their families of shortages and hardships; the soldiers pulled few punches in describing their experiences.

Another major link between the worlds were the wounded. To keep the forward facilities free for later arrivals, casualties were sent home in unprecedented numbers. Medicine and surgery, moreover, had progressed to points where large numbers of men who would have died of trauma or infection survived—some faceless, others limbless, all reminders that mocked propaganda.

Their counterpoints were the teenage boys, for whom the war was waiting after school, and for whom the summons came earlier and earlier as armies anticipated conscription call-ups to keep their ranks filled. Their common reaction was a desire to experience life before they had to risk it. For the working classes, "deviant behavior" usually amounted to spending their earnings on liquor, cigarettes, and movies instead of bringing their pay home. For the sons of the bourgeoisie, rebellion meant indulging in such things openly instead of clandestinely. Both the challenge to traditional patriarchal/authoritarian order and its roots in the war were, however, clearly understood by all parties involved.

Viewpoint:
Yes. The conditions of the fighting and the remoteness of many theaters combined to establish a barrier of understanding between those who fought and those who did not.

It goes without saying that World War I was in every way a new kind of conflict. One of the striking new phenomena that emerged from the battlefield was the intense sense of alienation from civilian life felt by a generation of traumatized combat soldiers. Famously expressed in the timeless works of such writers as Ernest Hemingway, Erich Maria Remarque, Ernst Jünger, Siegfried Sassoon, John McCrae, Wilfred Owen, and Robert Graves—all World War I soldiers—the persistence of a "front mentality" became a serious challenge to the stability of European societies.

At the most basic level, the unprecedented magnitude of the destructive power of the war left a serious psychological impact on combatants. Unlike the relatively short and "easy" wars that had characterized European military history in the century before 1914, World War I came to involve tens of millions of men in uniform, millions of casualties, and a long and apparently interminable duration. On the Western Front, the bloodiest and most heavily contended theater of the conflict, combat degenerated into a senseless series of frontal assaults and counterassaults on enemy trenches, machine-gun posts, and artillery batteries. The static nature of battles and campaigns abandoned the idealized European tradition of swift and glorious campaigns for ignominious death in a mess of barbed wire and mud.

That several years of exposure to this unimaginable horror would have an impact on the psyches and mentalities of surviving soldiers should be self-evident. Yet, medical science, especially the emerging field of psychology, developed an array of diagnoses relating to the damaged mental condition of soldiers. Although

they were certainly not new to the human condition, shell shock, survivor guilt, combat fatigue, and a general desensitization to violence became mass phenomena for a huge segment of the adult male population of Europe. The enormous human scale of the war created such large numbers of psychologically afflicted men that their alienation could neither be marginalized nor avoided by civilian society.

In a war with wholly unprecedented casualty rates, the very nature of European military organization worked to destroy the fabric that bound soldiers to the home front. For logistical expediency, the recruitment and formation of military units in most countries was defined by localities or regions. "Home regiments," often named for a city, region, province, or even profession, had traditionally been a source of local pride, military prestige, and civilian morale. When more men had to be recruited to replace immense battlefield losses, many governments maintained and emphasized this continuity in peacetime social relationships because they believed it would lead to better morale at the front. The creation of so-called "chums" and "pals" battalions by Lord Horatio Herbert Kitchener, the British Minister of War, explicitly promised the preservation of civilian communities in the ranks of the army as an inducement for young men to enlist. A large number of soldiers of many nationalities, therefore, went off to the destructive war alongside friends, neighbors, classmates, colleagues, and others known to them personally. In a war where units were regularly—and often repeatedly—decimated, however, the traditional policy of unit formation merely forced soldiers to endure battlefield catastrophes compounded by the loss of their former-civilian fellows. The protagonist of Remarque's semi-autobiographical novel *All Quiet on the Western Front* (1929) witnessed the deaths of most of his high school graduating class before he, too, was killed.

The main source of social friction that resulted from the new facts of war was that nothing in the civilian experience could possibly relate to it. Earlier conflicts, or at least those in living memory, had been small enough not to involve millions of troops and short enough to bring them home after relatively brief campaigns. Soldiers had certainly suffered, but their numbers had always been too small to create a measurable impact on broader civilian societies.

Previous European conflicts, moreover, had involved relatively mobile campaigns that often brought armies into direct contact with civilian populations. The stagnation of West European battlefronts early in the struggle created a paradox in which the human scale of the war was infinitely larger than it ever had been before; yet, the direct involvement of civilians was chiefly limited to frontier zones. Surely the Germans occupied Belgium and Poland, but there was no repeat of the bloody Prussian siege of Paris (1870–1871) or of the occupation of that city by the armies of a European coalition after 1815. Napoleon Bonaparte's deep penetration into the Russian heartland of 1812 had no World War I equivalent, despite the impressive success of the German army on the Eastern Front. Russian and French troops never got to Berlin, as they had in 1760 and 1806, respectively, nor did French troops ever reach Vienna, as they had in 1809. As a result, the civilian populations of the major combatant powers remained quite unaffected by the violence of World War I. Material shortages were suffered and small frontier nations such as Belgium and Serbia were subject to cruel occupations, but life for the average British, French, or German civilian rarely intersected with the living hell of the front. It therefore became extremely difficult for civilians to understand or even imagine what conditions were like there. Since the war resulted in a long-term clash between fixed defensive positions, moreover, soldiers of all armies were able to return to their homes and the relative normalcy of civilian life on furloughs. The technological innovation of railroads made this movement easier, even if it had also ironically facilitated the mass concentration of troops. As Remarque's striking description depicts, the transition from trench to hometown and back again was surreal. Ordinary soldiers were able to see their families and neighbors, yet were incapable of sharing with them the details of army life and the daily struggle between life and death. The frustration that Remarque's protagonist felt when the older men of his hometown engaged him in patronizing armchair strategy stands as a seminal example of the disconnect between the pain of those who could not relay and the awkwardness of those who could not relate.

Another important measure of the alienation of World War I combat soldiers is their collective activity after the war. As European nations tried to reintegrate demobilized troops into civilian life, former soldiers often became an important force in social and political destabilization. Throughout Europe the return of men from the front meant high unemployment, long-term financial burdens from caring for wounded and disabled veterans, and the social question of having to deal with a generation of psychologically traumatized young men.

Not all nations dealt with these problems effectively. Britain, it is true, established a comprehensive system of social support for its combat veterans and war-wounded in the 1920s and also benefited from its long-standing traditions of political stability. The continent was not so blessed, however. In France, war veterans took up leading roles in social and political movements that presented philosophical challenges to the Republic and its security. A large number of veterans from across the political spectrum were active in the pacifist movement. Their wartime experiences, which included both traumatic combat and a widespread mutiny in 1917–1918, had been horrible enough to motivate them to work to keep France out of war for all time. The popular novels of combat-veteran writers such as Henry de Montherlant and Louis-Ferdinand Destouches (Louis-Ferdinand Céline) were paeans to pacifism. Almost every French analysis of the domestic determinants of foreign polity in the interwar period takes its popular pacifist movement into account when analyzing the reluctance to confront Germany over peace-treaty violations and aggressive behavior in the 1930s. The pacifism of war veterans was by no means the only factor in the decision of the French government to pursue the appeasement of Nazi Germany, but it was a factor nevertheless.

Equally important was the decision of many veterans to support extreme right-wing groups that were inimical to the survival of the French Republic. Although some have argued that these groups were fascist in nature, the label generally does not seem apt. Nevertheless, it was clear that they opposed democracy and the republican status quo. Colonel François de la Rocque's *Croix de feu* (Cross of Fire), a veteran's organization that had several hundred thousand members by the mid 1930s, advocated the installation of an authoritarian regime. Another group, *Action française* (French Action), which advocated the restoration of a reactionary monarchy, also included many veterans, particularly aristocratic officers and devout Catholics. In addition to those formations, there were several

PHANTOMS

British infantry officer Siegfried Sassoon writes of a convalescence at home:

I couldn't be free from the War; even this hospital ward was full of it, and every day the oppression increased. Outwardly it was a pleasant place to be lazy in. Morning sunshine slanted through the tall windows, brightening the grey-green walls and the forty beds. Daffodils and tulips made spots of color under three red-draped lamps which hung from the ceiling. Some officers lay humped in bed, smoking and reading newspapers; others loafed about in dressing-gowns, going to and from the washing room where they scraped the bristles from their contented faces. A raucous gramophone ground out popular tunes. . . . Before midday no one had enough energy to begin talking war shop, but after that I could always hear scraps of conversation from around the two fireplaces. My eyes were reading one of Lamb's Essays, but my mind was continually distracted by such phrases as "Barrage lifted at the first objective," "shelled us with heavy stuff," "couldn't raise enough decent N.C.O.'s," "first wave got held up by machine-guns," and "bombed them out of a sap."

There were no serious cases in the ward, only flesh wounds and sick. These were the lucky ones, already washed clean of squalor and misery and strain. They were lifting their faces to the sunlight, warming their legs by the fire; but there wasn't much to talk about except the War.

In the evening they played cards at a table opposite my bed; the blinds were drawn, the electric light was on, and a huge fire glowed on walls and ceiling. Glancing irritably up from my book I criticized the faces of the card-players and those who stood watching the game. There was a lean airman in a gray dressing-gown, his narrow whimsical face puffing a cigarette below a turban-like bandage; he'd been brought down by the Germans behind Arras and had spent three days in a bombarded dug-out with Prussians, until our men drove them back and rescued him. The Prussians hadn't treated him badly, he said. . . . Along the ward they were still talking about "counter-attacked from the redoubt," "permanent rank of captain," "never drew any allowances for six weeks," "failed to get through their wire" . . . I was beginning to feel the need for escape from such reminders. My brain was screwed up tight, and when people came to see me I answered their questions excitedly and said things I hadn't intended to say.

From the munition factory across the road, machinery throbbed and droned and crashed like the treading of giants; the noise got on my nerves. I was being worried by bad dreams. More than once I wasn't sure whether I was awake or asleep; the ward was half shadow and half sinking firelight, and the beds were quiet with huddled sleepers. Shapes of mutilated soldiers came crawling across the floor; the floor seemed to be littered with fragments of mangled flesh. Faces glared upward; hands clutched at neck or belly; a livid grinning face with bristly mustache peered at me above the edge of my bed; his hands clawed at the sheets. Some were like the dummy figures used to deceive snipers; others were alive and looked at me reproachfully, as though envying me the warm safety of life which they'd longed for when they shivered in the gloomy dawn, waiting for the whistles to blow and the bombardment to lift . . . A young English private in battle equipment pulled himself painfully toward me and fumbled in his tunic for a letter; as he reached forward to give it to me his head lolled sideways and he collapsed; there was a hole in his jaw and the blood spread across his white face like ink spilt on blotting paper. . . .

Violently awake, I saw the ward without its phantoms. The sleepers were snoring and a nurse in gray and scarlet was coming silently along to make up the fire.

Source: Siegfried Sassoon, Memories of an Infantry Officer *(New York: Coward-McCann, 1930), pp. 238–240.*

ALIENATION OF SOLDIERS

other prominent "leagues" and groupings that were structured along military lines—often involving uniforms, marches, and training—and included many veterans. In the turbulence of interwar French politics these mass organizations were not to be taken lightly. A violent right-wing demonstration in Paris in February 1934 caused the collapse of a democratically elected ministerial government. Two years later a gang of youths connected with the fighting arm of *Action française* nearly murdered the leader of the French Socialist Party and the future Prime Minister, Léon Blum. Several leading right-wing figures supported by this constituency of radical veterans' organizations backed and even accepted positions (albeit usually marginal) in the Vichy regime that governed France after the defeat of 1940.

Nowhere was veteran unrest more prominent than in Germany, however. It did not help that many German soldiers had served in armies that were either victorious (in the East) or still standing deep in enemy territory (in the West) when an armistice that many regarded as a betrayal had brought them home. In the immediate postwar period, many demobilized German soldiers (including Corporal Adolf Hitler) were employed in the so-called *Freikorps* (Free Corps), a paramilitary militia used by the Weimar government to control left-wing civic unrest. After Hitler became leader of the National Socialist German Workers' (Nazi) Party, he organized it along military lines, according to a *Führerprinzip* (leadership principle) that gave him complete control of a hierarchical party structure. Many prominent Nazis, including Hitler, Rudolf Hess, Ernst Röhm, and Hermann Göring, were veterans of World War I but so too were many of their rank-and-file followers, especially early on. The fighting arm of the Nazis, the *Stürmabteilung* (SA, or storm troopers), became a paramilitary force that paraded around in brown shirts and caps and engaged in street brawls with opponents. It grew to be so threatening that even after the Nazis came to power, Hitler himself decided in 1934 to demilitarize it and execute its leaders. In the 1920s many other German combat veterans joined the *Stahlhelm* (steel helmet), a conservative veterans' organization linked to a right-wing political party. Although they remained distinct from the Nazis, in 1933 the party they supported helped Hitler become chancellor by agreeing to govern in coalition with him.

Veterans played an important role in other countries as well. Like its northern neighbor, the new Austrian republic was also destabilized by veterans who could not be integrated into the mainstream political life of the country—a problem enhanced by the defeat and dissolution of the Habsburg Empire and the territorial truncation of the Austrian republic. Many Austrian veterans joined Prince Stahremberg's *Heimwehr* (Home Guard), a paramilitary veterans group similar to the German *Freikorps*, while others joined the indigenous Austrian Nazi movement. Interwar Austrian politics was bedeviled by coup plots, political assassinations, street violence, and finally the coerced union of the country with Nazi Germany in March 1938.

Although Italy had turned up on the winning side of the conflict, it was not satisfied by the peace. Much Italian-populated territory that had been promised to Rome by the Allies as an enticement to enter the war in 1915 was ultimately not turned over. Italy had also suffered serious military defeats, heavy casualties, and economic dislocation as a result of the conflict. Many Italian veterans, frustrated with the peace and traumatized by the fighting, joined the militant Black Shirts, a paramilitary group organized by the fascist leader Benito Mussolini. His seizure of power in October 1922 resulted directly from a threatened "March on Rome" by fifty thousand armed Black Shirts. Without even having to show his strength, Mussolini won appointment as Prime Minister and, eventually, license to establish a dictatorship in Italy.

The tremendous divide between soldier and civilian is no modernist myth. Soldiers felt a widespread alienation from civilian society after prolonged involvement in a war that had been bloodier and more violent than ever before. The gap of understanding between soldier and civilian is well attested in the memoirs, novels, poetry, and other media of the war years and interwar period. Bearing unexpressible grief, feeling deep guilt, having grown accustomed to violence, and facing economic and political disappointment at home, many soldiers became involved in destructive political movements that promised military order and the violent achievement of extreme goals. The destabilization of political life in France, Germany, Austria, Italy, and several smaller countries besides, at least partly inhered in their inability to reintegrate psychologically tortured communities of veterans into civilian life. The failure of the governments of those countries to deal adequately with the needs and sentiments of those soldiers contributed to their eventual undoing.

–PAUL DU QUENOY,
GEORGETOWN UNIVERSITY

ALIENATION OF SOLDIERS

Viewpoint:
No. The myth that front-line soldiers were alienated from homefront society is based on the experience of a small, vocal group.

The traditional view, advocated by many historians, maintains that a gulf of misunderstanding separated the fighting front and the home front during the Great War. It was an idea first popularized by many war novelists and poets in the late 1920s and 1930s. Through their writing, authors, including Siegfried Sassoon, Henri Barbusse, and Erich Maria Remarque, suggested that civilian ignorance of conditions at the front had embittered the ordinary soldier and led to the perpetuation of the war for four long years. These powerful sentiments have contributed to the myth that characterizes the World War I soldier as a disillusioned figure, who, angered by censorship and propaganda at home and unable to find the means to convey the horrors of the trenches to his friends and family, became alienated from civilian society and retreated into his own trench culture to survive the war experience. Elements of this myth remain influential today, surfacing in the work of historians who see World War I as a watershed in the development of modernist cultural trends and providing the framework for the majority of discussions examining propaganda and censorship during the war.

As compelling and familiar as this interpretation may sound, the idea that the front line had an alienating effect on the majority of soldiers is fundamentally flawed. The problem is that the thesis is based on evidence produced by a small group of self-selecting, privileged veterans. Moreover, the negative attitudes displayed toward the home front by this group have been taken at face value, when, in fact, their writing has more significance when viewed as a disillusioned search for the meaning of the war in the disappointing aftermath of peace. In other words, their testimony was more a reaction to the inadequacies of the peace than a true reflection of war experience. While it would, of course, be wrong to discount the testimonies of these privileged few, in using these sources almost exclusively, historians have endowed them with a wider applicability than they deserve.

When a broader range of sources incorporating those derived from the rank and file is viewed, a different picture emerges. Family and friends, in addition to social, religious, and workplace affiliations, continued to play a vital role in the lives of the soldiers of the Great War. Communication between front and home front occurred though a variety of mediums. Letters, war literature, newspaper and film reports, and face-to-face conversations between civilians and soldiers wounded or on leave transmitted information and ideas to and from the trenches, traversing easily the line between front and home front. This communication became the mainstay of many soldiers, helping to keep them engaged with family and community and providing them with material support and emotional solace through the long years of war.

The letter remained the most popular method of maintaining contact with home, and indeed, it was continually noted by military authorities that delays in delivering mail and depriving soldiers of news of home—and the attendant food and clothing parcels—had a dangerously depressive effect on the men. The utility of the letter in transmitting the reality of the trenches to those at home is hotly disputed because of the issue of censorship. The existence of a censorship regime has long been used by historians to support the idea that soldiers were prevented from disclosing their true feelings through fear of punishment or through the black lines of the censor's pencil. The reality appears rather more complex when the dual role of the military censor is examined.

For the British and French authorities it was initially deemed important to keep the troops from communicating information that could be of use to the enemy, but as the war progressed, the censorship system became a valuable tool in monitoring army morale. Army intelligence services were able to scrutinize a proportion of letters that passed through the postal system each day to deduce the thoughts and attitudes of the troops. Military authorities were thus faced with something of a conundrum. On the one hand, they advocated tight control of information leaving the front line, and on the other they required the troops to express themselves freely in order to ascertain the state of their morale. The result was a compromise. While specific information, such as troop movements and casualty figures, was routinely censored, and censorship became more severe leading up to an attack, in many cases the soldiers had ample opportunity to express themselves freely in a letter. Of all the protagonists, the German soldier had been given the most leeway during the early years of the war, as field post was not censored until 1917; while the British authorities helped to facilitate freedom of expression by instituting a system of green envelopes that guaranteed that a soldier's letter would not be censored by his own officer, in line with general practice at the time, but by an unknown official in England.

Alongside the official military censorship, a form of self-censorship also operated amongst soldiers. Some combatants wanted to protect loved ones from the horrors they were suffering, while others did not possess the inclination, or the necessary literary skills, to express themselves adequately. To assume, however, in the manner of historian Paul Fussell, that the experience of the war was indescribable and that soldiers retreated behind formulaic and meaningless expression in their letters is to deny the diversity and vitality of the many thousands of letters that now lie in European archives.

To be sure, each letter would have been crafted for its target audience. Thus, letters to families and friends, particularly those addressed to male civilians, were often the most revealing, describing conditions at the front and the nature and circumstances of the deaths of friends. Expressions of boredom with trench warfare, of the strain of living under constant shellfire, and of course, the pain of privations were all to be found in letters to families.

The soldiers were not totally obsessed by their own lives in the trenches. For them, the real and meaningful life was that which they had left behind on enlistment, and so it was not surprising that the soldiers inquired about the progress of events at home. For the French peasantry, this interest often involved giving advice on the conduct of the harvest or the rearing of livestock. For the urban recruits who populated the British army, letters often centered on the mechanics of an abandoned business or the vagaries of the sometimes unreliable allowances system.

Letters were not restricted to family and friends. Soldiers of the Great War left a network of community and business contacts behind with whom they were anxious to keep in touch. A typical British soldier may have been in contact with his home church, sports team, and former workplace, and many of these institutions produced their own journals, in which letters from the front played a prominent role. As one might expect, these letters were of a less intimate nature than those sent to individuals, but the conditions of the front line were constantly described, if only to prompt the dispatch of a parcel. In contributing to these journals and newsletters, the soldiers helped to determine their content and hence the messages they wished to be transmitted about their experience of the war. In some small way, soldiers were able to remain part of the community they had left behind.

Trench journals, the humorous and often cynical newspapers produced by the soldiers themselves, also helped to propagate messages from the front. Although primarily designed for internal consumption, many were destined for a civilian audience, winging their way to families and workplaces across Europe. In these publications the soldiers retained editorial control and thus the freedom to express their grievances. French and British trench journals were able to rail against authority, both civilian and military, as well as criticize certain sections of the population ranging from war profiteers to journalists and their newspapers.

Criticism directed at newspapers was a consequence of censorship and propaganda.

British soldiers on the Western Front receiving gifts of cigarettes sent by family members and well-wishers, 1916

(from The Illustrated War News, *13 December 1916, page 22, Joseph M. Bruccoli Great War Collection, Thomas Cooper Library, University of South Carolina)*

ALIENATION OF SOLDIERS

The German authorities enforced tight management of the news, even dictating the form and tone to be employed, while the British government relied on self-censoring principles of the newspaper magnates. Censorship was a feature of life in all belligerent states, whether authoritarian or liberal democracies, and their journalists were not averse to pedaling a propagandist line. The French had a word for the contents of their newspapers, which translates simply as "eyewash."

Many of the newspapers, the nationals in particular, were guilty as charged, but the extent to which all information from the front was suppressed or misrepresented is exaggerated. Studies of German, French, and British newspapers have revealed that the degree of censorship exercised varied throughout the war. In Germany the censorship regime depended upon the deputy commanding generals in charge of the twenty-four army-corps districts, while a cursory glance at the British provincial press, with its long casualty lists, letters from the front, and graphic reports of fighting, suggests that the informal agreements between press and government had not been as binding as some historians have claimed.

Civilian populations during the Great War, moreover, were not the unthinking, gullible masses that have been previously portrayed. With letters streaming from the front, they had alternative sources of information against which to test the veracity of what they read. Most people, civilians and soldiers alike, were aware of the extent of the censorship and propaganda permeating their press but were also aware of its necessity in wartime. Despite soldierly skepticism of the content of their newspapers, there was, nevertheless, a constant demand for deliveries to the front. Newspapers provided an escape from reality, and for this reason alone, both soldiers and civilians did not want to consume a diet of unrelieved horror. Some soldiers valued the blatant falsehoods about the success of their side, because it renewed their hope and faith in the ending of the war, and eagerly devoured the domestic news pages as a means of keeping in touch with events at home. Soldiers and civilians may have been reading partial truths about the war, but they were the same partial truths and helped to maintain a shared perspective on the conflict.

Soldiers and civilians not only shared the same newspapers, but also the same forms of popular entertainment. The soldier visited civilian music halls while on leave, and the music, films, art, and literature released on the home front were also accessible at the fighting front. For the Allies, many of these entertainments had some type of patriotic, propagandist message at their core, but far from alienating the troops, these messages served to remind them of home and their motivation for fighting. The Allies were more effective in boosting commitment to the war through these media because they were willing to allow a modicum of the anguish and destruction of war to be featured. German and Austrian entertainment, on the other hand, took a different path, concentrating on escapist themes. Nevertheless, all these cultural activities had one thing in common: they ensured that the home and fighting fronts experienced the same entertainment, which helped in the retention of common cultural and social values throughout the war and guarded against the emergence of a specific trench culture far removed from the civilian sphere.

The real test of a soldier's connection with the civilian world was his ability to reintegrate into civilian society. Throughout the war a steady stream of soldiers returned home briefly on leave, and others reappeared permanently wounded or were recalled for essential war work in heavy industry or mining. Thus, there was no shortage of men who had experienced war to mingle with civilians on the home front.

There is ample evidence to suggest that, far from being alienated from civilian culture, soldiers who returned to civilian life, if only for a few days, and with the absence of censorship, communicated the reality of the trenches freely to those at home. Of course, there were veterans who chose not to discuss their experiences, and many were horrified at the power and greed of the war profiteers, the newspaper magnates, and the politicians, but overall this anger did not stop the men from communicating with the civilians they had known prewar. Indeed, by 1917 soldiers and veterans were seen as the most significant group molding public opinion. The authorities became concerned at the effect that tales of the trenches might have on civilians, as well as the potentially depressive effect on the army of tales of hardship on the home front, which were communicated by soldiers returning from leave. The situation became particularly acute for German authorities after June 1918, when conditions on the home front deteriorated still further and the hope of military success receded. Ultimately, the German home front and its army collapsed at the same time because soldiers and civilians held common views on the conflict and each was essential in supporting the other.

In the aftermath of the Great War it was inevitable that a proportion of soldiers failed to reintegrate into society and felt alienated and betrayed by those for whom they had fought.

Yet, the literary offerings of this minority group of veterans do not provide sufficient evidence to support the notion of a rift between home front and fighting front during the Great War. For the majority of soldiers there was an understandable desire to pick up their lives where they had left off and re-immerse themselves in the everyday activities of those homes and communities they had fought to preserve. That they were able to do so with relative ease suggests that they had maintained their links with home and had remained an integral part of the life of their communities throughout the long years of conflict.

—H. B. MCCARTNEY, KING'S
COLLEGE, LONDON

References

Paul Addison and Angus Calder, eds., *Time to Kill: The Soldier's Experience of War in the West, 1939–1945* (London: Pimlico, 1997).

Maurice Agulhon, *The French Republic, 1879–1992*, translated by Antonia Nevill (Oxford, U.K. & Cambridge, Mass.: Blackwell, 1993).

Stéphane Audoin-Rouzeau, *Men at War, 1914–1918: National Sentiment and Trench Journalism in France during the First World War,* translated by Helen McPhail (Providence, R.I.: Berg, 1992).

Joanna Bourke, *Dismembering the Male: Men's Bodies, Britain and the Great War* (Chicago: University of Chicago Press, 1996).

Hugh Cecil and Peter H. Liddle, eds., *Facing Armageddon: The First World War Experienced* (London: Cooper, 1996).

Roger Chickering and Stig Förster, eds., *Great War, Total War: Combat and Mobilization on the Western Front, 1914–1918* (Washington, D.C.: German Historical Institute, 2000; Cambridge & New York: Cambridge University Press, 2000).

John Dos Passos, *Three Soldiers* (New York: Dovan, 1921).

David Englander, "Soldiering and Identity: Reflections on the Great War," *War in History,* 1 (3) (1994): 300–318.

Paul Fussell, *The Great War and Modern Memory* (New York: Oxford University Press, 1975).

Robert Graves, *Good-bye to All That: An Autobiography* (London: Cape, 1929).

Ernest Hemingway, *A Farewell to Arms* (New York: Scribners, 1929).

John Horne, ed., *State, Society, and Mobilization in Europe During the First World War* (Cambridge & New York: Cambridge University Press, 1997).

John Keegan, *The First World War* (London: Hutchinson, 1998).

Alice Goldfarb Marquis, "Words as Weapons: Propaganda in Britain and Germany during the First World War," *Journal of Contemporary History,* 13 (1978): 467–498.

Erich Maria Remarque, *All Quiet on the Western Front,* translated by A. W. Wheen (Boston: Little, Brown, 1929).

Aviel Roshwald and Richard Stites, eds., *European Culture in the Great War: The Arts, Entertainment, and Propaganda, 1914–1918* (Cambridge & New York: Cambridge University Press, 1999).

Peter Simkins, *Kitchener's Army: The Raising of the New Armies, 1914–16* (Manchester & New York: Manchester University Press, 1988).

Eugen Weber, *The Hollow Years: France in the 1930s* (New York: Norton, 1994).

Jay Winter, *Sites of Memory, Sites of Mourning: The Great War in European Cultural History* (Cambridge & New York: Cambridge University Press, 1995).

AMERICAN MILITARY INDEPENDENCE

Was U.S. insistence on maintaining military independence a decisive element in the Allied victory?

Viewpoint: Yes. Military independence allowed the American forces to defend Paris successfully in the summer of 1918 and to spearhead the decisive counteroffensive in September of the same year.

Viewpoint: No. American troops performed poorly under their own officers, and the Allied victory can be attributed simply to the American role in introducing two million fresh troops at a time when the Central Powers had no more manpower reserves.

Viewpoint: No. General Pershing's intransigence concerning the integration of U.S. troops into existing Allied units cost lives and time when both were in short supply.

The American Expeditionary Force (AEF) was employed more incrementally in World War I than General John Pershing—or anyone else, Allied and American—wanted. The rapid entry of the United States into the war from a position of near-total military unpreparedness meant that until the fall of 1918 the direct American contribution to the war effort was minor. It took almost a year for the U.S. Army to put a single division into the line, and even that formation was largely composed of poorly trained draftees, for all its designation as a "regular army" formation.

That in turn required the British and French to accept on faith—or rather, on Pershing's word—that the United States could deliver combat-ready divisions in time to make a difference. Pershing's approach to doctrine and training, especially his emphasis on rifle marksmanship and open-warfare tactics, has been sharply criticized. AEF levels of training, never impressive, diminished as high casualty rates forced men to the front, men who could often not load their rifles—and according to some accounts, were charged $5 a lesson by their capitalistic comrades in arms. Nevertheless, the Americans learned quickly enough to merit praise from those in the best position to know: the Germans. The AEF compensated for such structural weaknesses as a shortage of Allied officers. It organized a Service of Supply that overlaid French administrative structures. Without trivializing the consequences of the negative synergies of inexperience and improvisation in the AEF, by contrast the U.S. Army in World War II had a year and a half to train before committing division-sized units to battle. In eighteen months the war began and ended for the AEF.

Pershing not only formed an effective army but also used it well. That fact was manifested even in the Argonne campaign, the one most often cited as bringing the AEF nearly to gridlock. Pershing erred by using too many inexperienced divisions unnecessarily in the first wave and against key objectives. In the later stages of the operation, however, even less-experienced divisions performed well, while the administrative chaos of the initial attack was also coming under control. A reasonable case can be made that only the armistice kept Pershing from the kind of semimobile breakthrough-cum-pushback that the Allies were achieving in other sectors. That the war might have ended before the Germans were convinced of their defeat was not the fault of Pershing or his men.

Viewpoint:
Yes. Military independence allowed the American forces to defend Paris successfully in the summer of 1918 and to spearhead the decisive counteroffensive in September of the same year.

The entry of the United States into World War I suggested to many British and French leaders that any commitment of American troops to European battlefields would mean their subordination to the more-experienced military commanders of Britain and France. Indeed, as the war progressed in the years before American involvement, Britain, France, Russia, and their lesser allies had developed an elaborate system of consultation on military matters. Given its limited military experience, the United States was expected to join this structure on a junior footing. When the French commander in chief, Marshal Joseph Joffre, said that he needed "men, men, men," he was referring to foot soldiers that his field commanders and their British counterparts could command in battle, not to independent American commanders who would decide priorities and execute serious decisions. European expectations were disappointed. Under the leadership of General John Pershing, the American Expeditionary Force (AEF) sent to France maintained its independence from European commanders.

There were few reasons why American troops should have been placed under foreign command. Constitutionally, the president of the United States is commander in chief of the armed forces. This position has not been a mere ceremonial privilege that exists on paper, with the actual decision making left to others, as the British monarch's military command authority is. From the first days of American nationhood, its presidents had used the army as an instrument of national policy to defend independence, expand the frontiers westward, to preserve the integrity of the Union, and to rise finally to a major international role. Day-to-day command may have been left to experts, but American presidents are empowered to take, and they usually exercise, broad authority over military affairs and strategic planning. Surrendering this power to foreign generals, and to their political leaders, represented an unacceptable breach of national sovereignty and an unwanted erosion of presidential power. Indeed, the precedent of

preserving direct or de facto control of American armed forces remained a cornerstone of U.S. military policy until President William Clinton placed American troops under nominal United Nations command in Bosnia-Herzegovina in December 1995.

The notion of placing the AEF under European command also contradicted the U.S. precedent of not entering into entangling alliances with foreign powers. Although the United States had long sympathized with Britain and France, entered the war on their side, and has been conventionally regarded as one of several Allied powers, there was never any formal alliance treaty defining it as such. The preferred phrase of the Wilson administration to describe the American position in the conflict was "associated power," implying only that the United States and the Entente powers had a common enemy in Germany, and nothing more.

While the United States had broad strategic reasons for involvement in the war, especially preventing Germany from establishing hegemony over continental Europe, Congress and American public opinion would only countenance armed participation in combat situations directed against the clear enemy. Despite the obvious biases of his administration toward Britain and France, President Woodrow Wilson had only been able to secure a Congressional endorsement for a declaration of war after a series of direct German submarine attacks on American merchant ships. Subordinating American troops to European military command would have meant that they could technically have been used for any purpose that foreign commanders decided. Since British and French political leaders, particularly British prime minister David Lloyd George and French premier Georges Clemenceau, intruded broadly into military and strategic planning, it was probable that they would at least try to use American troops for their own political ends. Conceivably these decisions could have included operations against Austria-Hungary, even though Congress only voted a symbolic declaration of war against it in December 1917, or against Bulgaria and the Ottoman Empire, even though no state of war ever existed between those two countries and the United States. Diverting American forces to fight on those fronts may seem extreme or impractical in retrospect, but it was entirely possible that Britain and France would have tried to pressure the United States to aid them in more places than the Western Front. In the diplomatic maneuvering of the postwar settlement, moreover, the Entente powers suggested that the United States take up an expensive and resource-consuming mandate over distant Armenia after Britain and Italy determined that it would be too costly for them to do so. Keeping American troops under American command ensured that they would only be used in accordance with the predetermined policies and interests of Washington.

Maintaining independent American military command had implications that went far beyond wartime strategic concerns. As is the case in any conflict, the combatant powers of World War I established a preliminary outline of what they wanted to achieve in the peace settlement. A significant function of the American decision to enter the war came from the realization that if a new postwar order were made in the absence of U.S. influence or participation, that order could only be crafted to the detriment of its commercial and strategic interests. President Wilson and his foreign policy advisers had clear evidence that this situation would be the case as early as May 1916, when they learned of clandestine inter-Allied discussions on postwar economic relations. One item on the Allies' agenda was a consideration of the role of American economic strength in world affairs, and the conclusion reached at the conference was that the rising power would have to be contained through aggressive protectionism and a coordination of Entente economic, trade, and financial policies.

This discovery was a source of both surprise and dismay to Wilson, who was even then supplying British and French armies in the field and edging toward war. He could not fail to consider that the dubious postwar plans of the Allies would remain the basis of their approach to peace, even if the United States entered the war on their side. Since the Entente powers could not prevail easily—or possibly at all—without American military help, the president and his advisers feared that the British and French would use any subordination of U.S. troops under their command to minimize the apparent decisiveness of their contribution to the victory. All the while, however, the Americans would be maximizing their battlefield usefulness. British and French planners, in other words, wanted to use the brawn of American manpower to win the war and then exclude the brains of its strategic planners from crafting the peace.

With a few notable exceptions, most British and French generals dismissed the quality and reliability of U.S. troops even before they were sent into combat. When the Americans acquitted themselves bravely and proved their combat effectiveness, the same naysayers argued that the American contribution was only partially effective, or that U.S. units simply had the luck to be engaged against German troops that were already preparing to retreat. In both cases, the implication was that American troops were a marginal asset and that their contribution to victory was not decisive. These assertions are best seen as politically motivated rhetoric. If America did, in fact, make an indisputably large contribution to victory, how could it be denied an equal role in forging the peace? Conversely, if its contribution truly had been marginal, how could it be given an equal role in forging the peace?

Of course the chauvinistic pronouncements of the Allied generals were not true. Two million American troops were in France by the end of the war, taking the field at a time when the British could no longer replace their losses, when much of the French army was still stewing in near-mutinous conditions, and when revolutionary Russia had left the war permanently. Despite their relatively late start in combat, American units played a crucial role in defending the approaches to Paris in the summer of 1918, often attacking or counterattacking while the French units deployed beside them were retreating in confusion. If American troops were unnecessary, how could they also have been critical to the defense of the capital of France? The front-wide offensive of September 1918 was one of the greatest victories of American arms in history. In less than three weeks Pershing and the six hundred thousand American troops under his command broke the stalemate on the Western Front, erased the German gains of 1918, and drove the Germans back beyond positions they had held since 1914. This success was decisive in convincing even the most reticent officers of the German High Command, including its de facto strategic chief, General Erich Ludendorff, that they could not win the war. The potential consequences of further massive American offensive operations were critical in the German decision to ask for an armistice.

If Pershing's armies had been placed under European operational control, their singular contribution to victory would certainly have been much less prominent in the operational history of the war and much more easily obscured by the Entente generals' self-serving and inaccurate deprecation of their role than was actually the case. By keeping American forces independent in 1917–1918, Wilson enjoyed full partnership with the other major Allied leaders at the Paris Peace Conference. While the decline in his health impacted his effectiveness, Wilson's undeniable presence and prestige enabled him to compel the European powers to abandon many of their more extreme goals (such as the dismem-

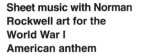

Sheet music with Norman Rockwell art for the World War I American anthem

(Joseph M. Bruccoli Great War Collection, Thomas Cooper Library, University of South Carolina)

berment of the German state) and to accept others that they viewed with clear skepticism (such as the League of Nations). It goes without saying that the prominent position of the United States, ensured by the independence of its military command, decisively prevented the European Allies from containing and marginalizing the international economic and strategic position of the United States after the war.

The political ramifications of surrendering American military independence had the most long-term significance, but apart from these paramount concerns, there were other sound, practical reasons for the United States to keep independent operational control of its armed forces. Despite the Entente commanders' posturing about their superior experience and greater qualifications to lead armies in modern combat, their track record on the Western Front had little to recommend itself to American leaders. By the time the United States entered the war, Britain and France had already suffered millions of casualties. The huge losses often occurred not because their "expert" leaders had no other choice but to accept them but because they were generally unimaginative and often highly detached from the harsh realities of modern mechanized warfare. Even though millions of men had fallen in pointless frontal assaults that won little ground, the same tactics were used over and over again with little modification. Attempts to make infantry attacks more successful through the saturation shelling of enemy positions or the close coordination of infantry advances and artillery barrages were only variations on a theme, and the Germans easily identified and countered them. Innovators who argued that tanks and armored cars would make all the difference—as they did in World War II—only saw their ideas implemented on an experimental scale.

For a new combatant such as America, where both the general public and the legislature had only reluctantly committed themselves to war, the prospect of combat losses on the standard scale for the Western Front would undoubtedly have stretched the tolerance of its citizens. Even as the first U.S. contingents were being organized, American strategists and officers were watching the terrible consequences of the British offensive around the Belgian town of Passchendaele, where 250,000 men fell in a futile three-month campaign that gained only a few miles of useless lowlands. Although the American commanders' expertise was limited to chasing bandits in the Southwest, fighting the decayed Spanish army in 1898, and occupation duty in Latin America and the Phillippines, they still had no reason to believe that their troops would be better off in British or French hands. Indeed, notwithstanding their paucity of recent experience, American officers could see plainly that Europe still placed its faith in defending strategic fortresses and executing frontal infantry attacks on nearly impenetrable positions—concepts that had been discredited in American strategic thinking since their disastrous application in the Civil War (1861–1865).

As it turned out, European claims that American troops and commanders were militarily ingenuous could not hide the British and French military commanders' own sad lack of brilliance and inspiration. Nor did the American lack of experience stop them from successfully defending Paris from the approaching German armies or from playing the leading role in the decisive offensive of September 1918. It is also worth mentioning that the total battlefield casualties of Americans in the entire war were about half the number suffered by the British at Passchendaele alone. Total American combat deaths were two and a half times the number of British soldiers killed on a single day, 1 July 1916—the first day of the Battle of the Somme.

The refusal of the United States to concede authority over its armed forces was necessary for both political and military reasons. Giving over command to British and French commanders would have meant that British and French generals would have been able to use them as an instrument of their national policies while also intruding on an important traditional prerogative of the American presidency. As a result, U.S. troops would almost certainly have been diverted from the goals that their own government had assigned them. They were also likely to have been used for their military power and then denied the proper credit and glory that the United States both deserved as a matter of national honor and needed to assume an equal role at the peace conference. Since the European Allies were already determined to limit American influence in the postwar world, building political capital through military victory was a vital priority that Wilson could not ignore and could not accomplish without insisting on independent military command. Further, American leaders had no logical reason to believe that they could turn over operational command of their armed forces to European officers without needlessly suffering the massive losses that had resulted from almost every other Western Front campaign. Keeping American armed forces under the control of its own commanders was a valuable lesson and remained an important principle of American military policy long after.

–PAUL DU QUENOY,
GEORGETOWN UNIVERSITY

**Viewpoint:
No. American troops performed poorly under their own officers, and the Allied victory can be attributed simply to the American role in introducing two million fresh troops at a time when the Central Powers had no more manpower reserves.**

When the United States entered into World War I on the Allied side it suffered from many disadvantages. First of all, the total strength of the U.S. Army in April 1917 was considerably less than the trained manpower available to Bulgaria. In a war that often swallowed up the lives of tens of thousands of soldiers in a day, the total strength of the U.S. Army and National Guard could have been exhausted in one short battle. Second, the United States, although a great industrial power, did not have the means to

AMERICAN MILITARY INDEPENDENCE

THE AMERICAN FIRST DIVISION IN ACTION

Major Frederick Palmer of the First Division of the American Expeditionary Force (AEF) describes the engagement of his troops at Cantigny on 28 May 1918:

At 6.45 in the early dawn of May 28th, as has happened many times before, the line of figures started up from the earth and began their advance. The formations were the same as those of the practice maneuvers, and the movement was equally precise as it kept to the time-table of the barrage. Each unit was doing its part, the tanks as they nosed their way forward doing theirs. Our shelling of the lower end of the town suddenly ceased; and then our men were seen entering the town exactly on time. Headquarters waited on reports, and they came of prisoners taken, of the further progress of our units—all according to the charts. We had passed through the town; we were mopping it up; and we had reached our objective in front of the town. Our losses to that point were less than a hundred men, with three hundred and fifty prisoners. A small offensive as offensives go, but our own, and our first.

Going over the top in a frontal attack had been almost tame, it was so like practice exercises. The fact that our practice exercises had been so systematically applied, that, indeed, we had done everything in the book, accounted for the perfect success of Cantigny. There was a glad, proud light in the eyes of our wounded. They had been hit in a "real party." Nobody could deny that they were graduate soldiers now. But there was to be the reaction which always comes with limited objectives when you do not advance far enough to draw the enemy's fangs—his guns. Upon the roads along which men must pass to bring up supplies, upon every point where men must work or men or wagons pass, upon the command posts, he turns the wrath of his resentment over the loss of men and ground, and in his rage concentrates most wickedly, most persistently and powerfully upon the infantry which is trying to organize the new front.

The German artillery would show this upstart American division its mistake in thinking that it could hold what it had gained. Eight-inch shells were the favorites in the bombardment of our men, who now had Cantigny at their backs as they dug in, while showers of shrapnel and gas added to the variety of that merciless pounding that kept up for three days. We suffered serious casualties now; but we did not go back, and we took revenge for our casualties in grim use of rifle and machine gun which, with the aid of prompt barrages, repulsed all counter-attacks, until the Germans were convinced of the futility of further efforts.

Later, when I did the usual thing of rising at three in the morning in order to go over our positions at Cantigny, the sector had become settled in its habits though still active. Part of the walls of the chateau which had had a single hit when I first saw it were still standing; all the surrounding village was in ruins almost as complete as if it had been in the Ypres salient.

From the front line I watched the early morning "strafe" of the German guns; the selected points of "hate," here and there along the front receiving a quarter of an hour's attention, while the crushed remains of Cantigny were being subjected to additional pulverization. We held the line, but with cunning men hidden in the earth. You hardly knew of the presence unless you stumbled on them.

Everybody you met at the front had a certain air of proprietorship in the sector; and back at headquarters the thoroughbred veteran chief of staff and all the other officers of that much-schooled First received you with their habitual attitude, which seemed to say, "Any suggestions or criticism? We are always listening—but, understand, please, we are the First Division."

Source: *Charles F. Horne, ed., Source Records of the Great War, volume 6 (Indianapolis: American Legion, 1930), pp. 191–192.*

equip a large army in less than a few years. Third, the small U.S. Army officer corps did not have more than a handful of trained officers capable of leading the large forces needed on the Western Front.

For these reasons, building an independent U.S. Army that could contribute meaningfully to the defeat of Germany was an unrealistic notion from the beginning. From a sound strategic viewpoint, Germany might well win the war before an independent American force could make its way into battle. On the other hand, committing an independent U.S. Army to battle without proper training and preparation might simply result in a massive bloodletting with little to show for it. Every sound military consideration argued in favor of using U.S. manpower to fill the ranks of the Allied armies, who had equipment and trained officers but suffered from a grave shortage of men. However, as the nineteenth-century Prussian military strategist Carl von Clausewitz might have reminded the World War I generals, America simply had to field its own army on the Western Front, no matter how inefficient, in order to meet President Woodrow Wilson's political objective of being the primary player at the peace conference that would shape the postwar world.

When President Wilson committed the United States to war in April 1917, American military preparedness was in even worse shape than the president imagined. Only months before, the Army general staff had been rebuked by Congress because the Army War College, which served as the planning staff for the U.S. Army, had actually drawn up the outline for plans in case of war against Germany. Congress had been outraged that the officers charged with planning for war had actually planned for war! Faced with this attitude, the army had done little prior to the declaration of war to prepare for the task ahead. The U.S. Army of 1917 had about 120,000 regular soldiers, as well as 200,000 National Guard troops. The National Guard, in the long tradition of the American militia, was poorly trained and equipped. The U.S. Army was scattered around the country in small garrisons and had rarely trained in a formation larger than a regiment or brigade. The trouble caused by the Mexican bandit Pancho Villa on the American Southwest border in 1916–1917 was a great benefit to the United States because the army was forced to mobilize a large number of National Guard units and concentrate large forces into provisional divisions on the Mexican border. Yet, in Europe, soldiers were being committed to battle on a much larger scale—in armies and army groups.

The material situation of the U.S. military at the start of the war was nothing short of disastrous. The United States had not a single aircraft suitable for combat over the Western Front. There were few machine guns. The Army had only 544 modern artillery field-pieces, with enough ammunition stockpiled to last about one day at the normal firing rates of the Western Front. America was not even able to equip a mass army properly, as it only had 600,000 modern rifles on hand. However, such material shortages could, and were, to be made up by Britain and France, whose factories had been geared up to produce vast quantities of equipment and munitions by 1917. An even more-troublesome problem that faced America in 1917 was the lack of trained military leaders.

The junior officers of the U.S. Army were as good as officers anywhere. Standards were high, small-unit training was good, and the military academy at West Point provided a rigorous education to most of the regular army officers. No one doubted that America could find some first-rate leadership material among its National Guard officers or could recruit young men of intelligence, courage, and talent to fill the junior leadership ranks of the U.S. Army. The lack of senior leaders troubled the Allied powers. In April 1917 the entire U.S. Army general staff numbered only nineteen officers. While the U.S. Army offered a sound education program for higher officers, only twenty-three men had gone through both the staff college at Ft. Leavenworth, Kansas, and the Army War College at Carlisle Barracks, Pennsylvania. While the United States might be able to recruit and conscript a large army quickly from its population of one hundred million, there were hardly enough officers trained and qualified to fill a division or corps staff—much less provide competent leadership for a large army. Despite every effort, the decision to field a large independent U.S. Army on the Western Front was also a decision to go into battle with weak and untrained military leadership.

While General John Pershing and President Wilson get the blame for most of the strategic decisions made by the United States at the start of World War I, there were several other major players who had an equally significant role in the creation of a large, independent U.S. Army on the Western Front. When the United States declared war on 6 April 1917, Britain and France immediately sent large and high-ranking political/military delegations to the United States to set up a process of Allied strategy. In many cases, strategic direction depends more on personalities and personal relationships than upon logic—and U.S. military strategy in World War I was such a case. The French had the wisdom of sending a delegation headed by a former premier, René Viviani, and including Joseph Joffre, Marshal of France and chief of the French army to late 1916. The British sent a delegation headed by Lord Arthur Balfour, with Major General George Bridges as its military adviser. The two delegations offered opposing strategies to the Americans and, in the end, Gallic charm overcame British logic, and the U.S. military strategy was mapped out.

From the beginning of his visit, Joffre charmed the Americans and, in turn, the Americans greatly admired the modest hero of the Marne. Joffre had been tasked by his government to establish a "general outline of a policy of cooperation between the US and Allied nations." Joffre had a better grasp of political reality than most politicians. At the start of his visit he determined that any scheme to simply fit U.S. forces into the Allied ranks would be politically unacceptable. Even if President Wilson countenanced it (which he would not), the U.S. Congress would not tolerate it. When he met with the U.S. Army chief of staff, General Hugh Scott, on 27 April 1917, Joffre proposed that the United States immediately form a division and send it to France as a symbol of the American contribution to the war. The U.S. unit would initially serve under French command and the French would train and equip other U.S. divisions until there were enough forces to form a full army. The drawback of the plan was the long time it would take for the Americans to have an effect upon the battlefield.

The British proposed an "amalgamation" scheme by which American soldiers, or small U.S. units not larger than a battalion, would be quickly trained and directly incorporated into the British army. With no unit larger than a battalion at the front, the critical lack of trained senior American officers would not be a factor. It made tremendous military sense and it meant that the United States could quickly have a major impact on the war. Yet, this proposal met with a hostile reaction from the senior U.S. military leadership, as well as from President Wilson and Secretary of War Newton Baker. They believed that the U.S. flag had to be prominently displayed on the Western Front—and this decision meant an independent U.S. army. In May 1917 the U.S. Army drew up plans that endorsed Joffre's concept in toto. When General Pershing was appointed as the commander of the American Expeditionary Force (AEF) his instructions from Secretary Baker were quite clear. While U.S. troops might at first serve under British and French command, the U.S. Army would field force under its own flag as soon as possible.

To their credit, the Allied powers, especially the French, put forth an enormous effort to train and equip the American army in World War I. The French worked especially hard to train the U.S. military leadership. Thousands of American officers and noncommissioned officers (NCOs) were trained in specialist courses run by the French army. The French also set up a short general staff course to provide U.S. divisions, corps, and armies with competent staff officers. More than five hundred American officers went through the French staff course before the end of the war. U.S. divisions were trained by experienced French units and instructors before being committed to combat, and the U.S. Army was rapidly equipped with French machine guns, artillery, and airplanes.

The first major engagements of the AEF in June/July 1918 proved that the doubts held by the British and French officers concerning U.S. leadership and the ability to fight effectively were well justified. The Americans were unable to plan, or to coordinate artillery fire and troop movements. In the corps counteroffensive at Soissons, the First and Second U.S. Divisions captured 143 German guns and 6,500 German prisoners of war, but at the appalling cost of 12,200 casualties. The Americans had proven tactically and operationally deficient and had only accomplished the mission through incredible bravery.

Despite the poor performance of the U.S. Army leadership in the summer fighting of 1918, Pershing pressed the Allied high command to field an independent U.S. Army as soon as possible. The war was going against Germany by this time, and the United States was determined to play an independent role on the battlefield. In September 1918 the First U.S. Army took to the field to eliminate a fairly minor German salient at St. Mihiel. In October, the U.S. Army, now with more than 2 million men in France and more arriving daily, was given a long stretch of the front in the Meuse-Argonne.

The Meuse-Argonne offensive of October-November 1918 was the one major U.S. offensive in the war. The Americans were successful in pushing back part of the German line and contributing to the final Allied victory—but at a tremendous cost. While poorly trained American soldiers carried the day with almost suicidal bravery and a willingness to take horrendous losses, the officers and staffs proved unequal to the task of fighting veteran German formations. Planning and logistics were poor, infantry/artillery coordination failed, and American units attacked with methods more suitable for 1914 than 1918. In just a month, the U.S. Army took more than two hundred thousand casualties in a secondary offensive. If the U.S. Army had been under experienced foreign commanders, the losses would certainly have been much lower.

While the U.S. Army performed poorly as an independent army in the 1918 campaigns, it had a decisive effect on the war simply by its arrival. The Germans, faced with two million fresh and highly aggressive American troops, knew that they would be getting no more replacements for their losses. The numbers alone made the German request for an armistice necessary.

–JAMES CORUM, USAF SCHOOL OF
ADVANCED AIRPOWER STUDIES

AMERICAN MILITARY
INDEPENDENCE

**Viewpoint:
No. General Pershing's
intransigence concerning the
integration of U.S. troops into
existing Allied units cost lives
and time when both were in
short supply.**

In 1916 Woodrow Wilson ran for a second term for the presidency of the United States, and one of his most consistent slogans on billboards, celluloid buttons, and the like was "He Kept Us Out Of War." He made promises not to send American troops to fight on the Western Front, or on any front of the European war, for that matter. When World War I broke out in August 1914, Wilson promised that the United States would be the great neutral—the struggle old Europe was of no concern to the New World. There were nagging doubts, however, about the course of the war: it had not been settled by 1917; a Central Powers victory could well submerge democracy in a tide of authoritarianism; and the Imperial German government was becoming more and more difficult to deal with over questions of free navigation of the seas, the use of the submarine, and diplomatic relations with one of the closest U.S. neighbors, Mexico. Then there was Wilson himself—a man Italian premier Vittorio Emanuele Orlando called "a kind-of clergyman." If Wilson listened to such things—in 1916 and early 1917, the most popular song from Tin Pan Alley was "I Didn't Raise My Boy To Be a Soldier"—and if noninterventionists needed a sign from 1600 Pennsylvania Avenue, it came on 9 March 1916 when Wilson named an old friend and a well-known pacifist, Newton Baker, as secretary of war. Wilson had had grave differences with Baker's predecessor, Lindley Garrison, over questions of preparedness, but many thought Baker's arrival was a signal that Wilson would keep the United States out of the Great War.

Most probably, the staunch Presbyterian Wilson had no blinding conversion "on the road to Damascus" in 1917—deep in his heart there was a firm commitment to the concepts of democracy and progressive reform. What would the world look like if indeed Germany and Austria won the war? The final blow to Wilson's neutrality was the declaration by Germany in mid January 1917 that it would begin again a campaign of unrestricted submarine warfare. On 4 April 1917 Wilson went before Congress to ask for a declaration of war; after two days of bitter debate, on 6 April, the United States went to war.

Initially the British and French wanted unlimited access to the industrial potential of America, but there was also a question of manpower. The warring powers were weakened from the great battles sweeping Europe, and America had a vast reservoir of strong, young, unbloodied men. The United States entered the war with a small army, with few trained general-staff officers; its soldiers were scattered from the continental United States to the Caribbean to the Philippine Islands. When the United States staggered onto the world stage during its war with Spain in 1898, the army was unprepared for large-scale operations. The Spanish were even more unready to fight, and the United States emerged from the war as a victor with a new empire and a vast number of military problems that had to be solved. Between the Splendid Little War of 1898 and the entry into World War I there were reforms, but the European view of the U.S. Army was one of a struggling, obstreperous adolescent unfit to fight against the professional might of the German army. If Wilson's America was to have a say in the future of the postwar world—and Wilson was determined that it would—then the contribution in material and in blood would have to assure an equal place at the peace table, a place the old-world politicians could not deny.

If Wilson was a hardheaded, progressive idealist, it then followed that the man to command American forces had to be equally determined in his resolve to see that the U.S. Army came into being and fought under its own flag, with its own commanders, and in its own sector of the European battlefield. The selection for commander went to John Pershing, a graduate of the West Point class of 1888, the most recent and most experienced American field commander. Born in Missouri in 1860, Pershing had achieved a noteworthy record on the frontier, in the war with Spain, in the Philippines, and, most recently, as commander of the 1916–1917 punitive expedition against Francisco "Pancho" Villa in Mexico. A grim-faced man saddened by the loss of his wife and three daughters in a fire in 1915, Pershing was committed to the idea that the American soldier could be the equal of any soldier in the world, given proper training and leadership. He was the product of the turbulent era of the Civil War (1861–1865), an American patriot in a time when devotion to one's country could be worn for all to see.

In 1907 President Theodore Roosevelt promoted then-Captain Pershing over 862 officers to the rank of brigadier general. When Pershing was called to Washington in 1917 he believed he was to be given command of the First Infantry Division. Much to his surprise, he was elevated to Commander-in-Chief, American Expeditionary Forces (AEF) and given the command to go to France, build his army, win, and bring the troops back home. How Pershing did that was his own concern.

The great problem was that there was no real American army to take to France to fight or to assure Wilson his place at the peace table. The British and French preached the need for amalgamation, the integration of American soldiers into their existing, but weary, weakened forces. On the surface amalgamation made sense. The Doughboys, as they were now known, were in fine physical condition and their morale was high, unaffected by three years in the trenches or by such slaughter pens as the Somme (1916) or Verdun (1916). That was not how Wilson or Pershing, however, envisioned the contribution of the United States, nor would the American people, turned almost overnight into a warrior nation, support such a use of their fathers and sons. The newest hit song from Tin Pan Alley was "Over There," and almost everyone from the president to the laborer believed that the new world would rescue the old and show them the ways of progressive democracy. From the first day Pershing and his absurdly small staff arrived in France, it was clear that Pershing had no intention of allowing American soldiers to serve in anything but an American army. The French and British, however, looked around and asked just where this army from the new world was. By Christmas 1917 the AEF consisted of only four combat divisions and a growing number of support troops, a far cry from the hundreds of Allied and enemy divisions deployed along the Western Front. Training and more training, usually by highly competent French and British instructors, were what his men needed to prepare for the day the AEF was hurled at the enemy.

Pershing firmly believed that the trenches had dulled the fighting spirit of the British and French, and only "open" or maneuver warfare would break the stalemate of the Western Front and bring defeat to the German army. The infantryman, supported by artillery and other weapons such as the tank and airplane, was the key to open warfare and to final victory. For Pershing, orthodoxy was the "Cult of the Rifle," and he insisted that soldiers preparing to arrive in France be fully trained in the care and use of the infantryman's basic weapon, the rifle. As Pershing constructed the 28,000-man division, he made certain that it was a combined-arms team with infantry being the largest element. There were, in addition to four 4,000-soldier infantry regiments, an artillery brigade of three regiments; machine-gun battalions; and communications, medical and supply units. It was a first-rate organization for conducting open or maneuver warfare, and it was not a division for static trench

warfare. Normally an aero-observation squadron and a company with one balloon was assigned to each division. Pershing saw that airpower could extend the battlefield further than was ever needed if troops simply remained in the deep, muddy, lethal trenches. When the AEF fought—Pershing made this an article of faith—it would fight in the open, closing with the enemy by means of fire and maneuver.

When would the Americans fight? The British and the French were furious with Pershing, and French premier Georges Clemenceau suggested that perhaps it would be best if Pershing were relieved and sent back to the United States. The American people would not have stood for Pershing's removal, as he had become a hero. In March 1918 the Germans launched a series of offensives, and the Western Front was rocked by five major offensives from March into July. The Allies screamed for American troops as the casualty lists grew alarmingly large. While Pershing reluctantly agreed that infantry and machine-gun units be sent to France, he steadfastly held to the idea that the Americans could only function best when, as a combined-arms team, they served under their own flag and commanders. Some AEF divisions fought during the period of the great German onslaught, and Pershing won a commitment to form the U.S. First Army with its own sector of combat. The first great American offensive was in the St. Mihiel salient, a triangular-based piece of France that the Germans had held since 1914.

For Pershing and the AEF the mission to reduce the St. Mihiel salient had to be accomplished. To this end he committed his best-trained combat divisions to the operation, and the French gave more than one hundred thousand soldiers to supplement the AEF. The Allies—British, French, and Italians—contributed airplanes to the fledgling U.S. Air Services to bring the number of aircraft to more than 1,400. Lieutenant Colonel George Patton, fresh from training with the French, moved his Allied-built tanks into position to begin the campaign on 12 September 1918.

In a driving rainstorm, the St. Mihiel offensive began with spectacular results. Unknown to Pershing and his staff, the Germans had decided to abandon the salient to shorten their lines, but they exacted a price for the American success with well-placed artillery and machine-gun positions. It seemed to Pershing, however, that his insistence on keeping American fighting forces intact and preparing for open warfare was justified. While the best-trained divisions were assaulting the St. Mihiel salient from two sides, the remainder of the AEF was moving into staging areas to launch the Meuse-Argonne Offensive on 26 September 1918. The euphoria that infected Pershing's First Army Headquarters masked the reality—the divisions preparing to attack into the tangle of the Argonne Forest were poorly prepared, with many divisions having been in France only a few weeks and lacking the benefit of seasoning under the tutelage of the Allies. What basically happened was a direct frontal assault against entrenched and determined troops, the German staff having decided to contest every inch of ground. A series of well-prepared defensive infantry positions, expertly supported with artillery and machine guns, awaited the Doughboys, and the result was a bloodbath in which the first attacking divisions could make almost no headway. The offensive ground to a halt until Pershing decided to push forward on 4 October, this time using those old divisions of the AEF that had been in France for some time and were veterans of St. Mihiel.

The First Infantry Division, Pershing's pride, was used up by 11 October, with casualties exceeding 60 to 70 percent in most infantry companies. They had attacked directly into the teeth of the major German line, known as the *Kriemhilde Stellung,* and paid dearly for a little more than a mile of ground. They were relieved by the Forty-Second "Rainbow" Division, which was almost combat ineffective because of battle casualties and disease. To the left of the Rainbows was the Eighty-Second Division, another veteran of the St. Mihiel fight, and in a few days some infantry companies had to be consolidated, commanded by sergeants. While the German lines were breeched and the Doughboys moved toward the Meuse River, the AEF was worn out. Not only were men breaking down as a result of constant battle, poor food, and terrible weather conditions, but their rifles, machine guns, and artillery pieces were also to a point of being combat ineffectual. Despite superhuman efforts the supply trains could not bring needed food and ammunition fast enough. Weeks of battle and cold, rainy weather turned roads into impassible quagmires. Open warfare had boiled down to direct, costly attacks against a well-positioned and expertly led German army. The armistice of 11 November 1918 did not come soon enough.

The AEF, however, did fight; their bravery was well noted, and troop ships were bringing Doughboys by the tens of thousands into France. Pershing went to France with his own agenda, and his intransigence concerning amalgamation left the Allies shorthanded at critical times. His faith in "the Cult of the Rifle" and open warfare cost lives because the AEF was too inexperienced to adjust battlefield techniques quickly enough. The St. Mihiel victory obscured the fact that the AEF, leadership and troops, was not ready to take on the monumental Meuse-Argonne Offensive. As soon as the guns fell silent on the Western Front, President Wilson announced that he would personally come to Europe to help negotiate the peace. On 8 January 1918 Wilson gave his "Fourteen Points" speech, which outlined his views on a just peace based on democracy and self-determination, with no annexations and no harsh indemnities. He ended his speech with a call for the establishment of a League of Nations, an international body that would solve disputes and assure the peace of the world. Frankly, after four years of war, Clemenceau of France, Lloyd George of Britain, and Orlando of Italy were in no mood to agree to such idealism: Germany was defeated and was made to pay for four years of slaughter and destruction. Wilson had his place at the Versailles Conference (1919), but his view of the postwar world did not. To be sure, the Great War was a turning point for the United States, but it did not assure to either Wilson or Pershing the results they wanted.

–JAMES J. COOKE, UNIVERSITY OF MISSISSIPPI

References

Paul F. Braim, *The Test of Battle: The American Expeditionary Forces in the Meuse-Argonne Campaign* (Newark: University of Delaware Press; London: Associated University Presses, 1987).

Robert H. Farrell, *Woodrow Wilson and World War I, 1917–1921* (New York: Harper & Row, 1985).

Martin Gilbert, *The First World War: A Complete History* (New York: Holt, 1994).

John Keegan, *The First World War* (London: Hutchinson, 1998).

Walter LaFeber, *The American Age: Foreign Policy at Home and Abroad,* volume 2, *Since 1896,* second edition (New York: Norton, 1994).

John J. Pershing, *My Experiences in the World War,* two volumes (New York: Stokes, 1931).

John Terraine, *To Win a War: 1918, the Year of Victory* (London: Sidgwick & Jackson, 1978).

David F. Trask, *The AEF and Coalition Warmaking, 1917–1918* (Lawrence: University Press of Kansas, 1993).

Frank E. Vandiver, *Black Jack: The Life and Times of John J. Pershing,* two volumes (College Station: Texas A&M Press, 1977).

AMERICAN TACTICS

Was General Pershing's emphasis on open warfare appropriate for the Western Front?

Viewpoint: Yes. General Pershing recognized that the war could not be decided from the trenches. The problem of the American Expeditionary Force (AEF) was less a failure of strategy than defective training systems.

Viewpoint: No. The American Expeditionary Force (AEF) went to Europe with a tactical doctrine unsuitable to the nature of the war and, as a result, U.S. forces paid a heavy price.

American doctrine in World War I is best described as "mass open warfare." American Expeditionary Force (AEF) commander John Joseph Pershing emphasized the importance of aggressive action by rifle-armed infantry as the key to breaking the stalemate of the Western Front. This alleged "cult of the rifle" has been regularly—perhaps excessively—derided. Pershing believed Americans had "natural" skill as riflemen, but he also asserted the importance of proper training and effective leadership. By October 1918 he was threatening disciplinary action against any commander who failed to use combined-arms tactics against the machine-gun nests that were inflicting heavy casualties on advancing American units. Pershing, moreover, believed marksmanship must be complemented by mass assault. U.S. divisions were twice the size of any on the Western Front, with a binary organization intended to produce staying power. They were structured to crash into German positions and still retain enough vitality to implement the open warfare that Pershing insisted was the precondition of victory.

These doctrinal concepts were not particularly imaginative, but neither were they entirely misconceived. The problems lay in implementation: command, tactics, and administration. In the first area, generals were the least significant AEF problem. Division and corps commanders were sufficiently visible, and Pershing was sufficiently ruthless, that the unfit, inefficient, and ineffective were quickly weeded out. Generals, moreover, were easily replaced. The same could not be said of their staffs. World War I was ultimately a war of management. The U.S. Army of 1917 possessed a system of advanced schools that produced staff officers at least as well qualified as their European counterparts of 1914. Only about four hundred graduates of those schools, however, were available in 1917. The AEF thus lacked professionally trained staff officers.

Regimental-level command posed an even greater challenge than staff appointments. Few of the officers who would command AEF regiments had ever seen 5,000 men in one place. Prior to 1917 none had any experience handling the 3,800 men authorized for the regiments sent to France. The newly promoted majors and captains of the regular army were in the same situation relative to their respective commands. At the lower tactical levels of the AEF, its companies of 250 and platoons of 60 were too large to be commanded effectively in the ways required by Pershing's concept of open-order tactics. The size that generated sustainability diminished flexibility—particularly given the nature of the junior officer corps. Only one-sixth of the 200,000 men commissioned in the U.S. Army during the war had previous service as officers, and a large number of these were National Guardsmen. The rest were drawn from civilian life. A comprehensive system of schools in the United States and France sought to bridge the gap, but about half the candidates failed even the attenuated three-month programs that made "ninety-day wonder" a synonym for a new second lieutenant.

The prewar American noncommissioned officer (NCO) was not a professionalized junior leader like his British or German counterpart. The sergeants and corporals of the regular army tended instead to be ad hoc appointments, gaining stripes and losing them according to lapses of behavior and superiors' whims. For the higher grades, literacy and technical skills were valued above leadership. Like the junior officers, as AEF divisions gained experience, the infantry NCOs were increasingly men their squads and sections would follow in combat, but they tended as well to keep their roots in the ranks, exercising authority in good part by consensus. In an experienced, worked-in unit that system is not necessarily a bad thing. In too many AEF rifle companies, however, it was a case of the myopic leading the blind. Courage untempered by skill in tactics and man management was not enough to implement the AEF doctrine of "open mass warfare" at its small-unit cutting edge.

Viewpoint:
Yes. General Pershing recognized that the war could not be decided from the trenches. The problem of the American Expeditionary Force (AEF) was less a failure of strategy than defective training systems.

Like any other professional officer in the U.S. Army, John Joseph Pershing watched the war in Europe with great interest. When the conflict began in 1914, no one could have envisioned the carnage on the Western Front; terms such as "The Trenches" and "Over the Top" and places such as the Somme, Verdun, and Ypres became well-known to the soldiers who served a state that was officially neutral in the conflict. When President Woodrow Wilson ran for a second term in 1916, he pledged to keep the United States out of the war; by that time Brigadier General Pershing was preparing to lead a punitive expedition into Mexico to chase down Francisco "Pancho" Villa, who had raided into New Mexico. In one year Pershing was out of Mexico and President Wilson was angered by the announcement by Germany that it would begin again a policy of unrestricted submarine warfare. Wilson, despite his pledges, went before Congress and requested a declaration of war against the Central Powers. On 6 April 1917, after bitter debate, Congress voted to declare war and the United States became a belligerent.

The British and French believed that the contribution of the United States could well lie in the vast industrial potential of American industry. The Allied armies, however, had been through three years of horrendous slaughter; the British and French had just about reached the end of their endurance, as far as manpower was concerned. The Germans, too, faced a crisis and were conscripting younger and younger generations of men. War weariness ground down the troops in the trenches and the civilian populations at home. It was obvious that the United States offered a nearly unlimited source of young strong men, which the Allies saw as the answer to their critical shortage of replacements. "Send us the men," they stated, "and we will train them, integrate them into our existing formations, and lead them into battle." That arrangement the politician Wilson and the American people would not agree to. If Wilson was to have any influence on a peace treaty based on national self-determination, democracy, and no indemnities, then there had to be a powerful U.S. Army fighting on the Western Front under American leadership.

To select the proper commander for those forces going to France became a critical matter, and it was decided that the task would fall to fifty-seven-year-old Pershing, considered at that time to be the most experienced field commander in the United States. Born in Missouri in 1860, Pershing graduated from West Point in 1888 and served in the cavalry. A product of Civil War America and the frontier experience, he saw service in the West and in the Spanish-American War (1898). President Theodore Roosevelt promoted him above eight hundred officers to the rank of brigadier general in 1907. His service in the Philippines had been exemplary, and in 1916 he was selected to lead American forces into Mexico. There Pershing used aircraft for reconnaissance and telephones for rapid communication. He was aware of the great changes in warfare in the early twentieth century. Pershing was convinced that the Great War would show that the American army, properly trained and commanded, could be the equal of any in the world. Like many other professional soldiers he was convinced that the trench warfare as being waged on the Western Front was not the way to win a great war.

Pershing carried with him the historical baggage of the American officer corps. The United States had fought in the trenches in the final year of

AMERICAN TACTICS

the Civil War (1861–1865), and a weakened Confederate Army under Robert E. Lee had stalled a numerically superior Federal Army under Ulysses S. Grant at Petersburg, Virginia. Grant knew that to win the war it was necessary to get Lee's army into the open, to maneuver against them, and then bring them to decisive battle. After the Civil War the U.S. Army turned its attention to the great frontier, where small-unit tactics against the Native Americans were necessary. Marksmanship, so sadly lacking on the battlefields of the Civil War, became a near obsession with the army, and the fighting on the frontier and in the Spanish-American War reinforced this need.

Pershing was convinced that an infantryman, proficient with his rifle and bayonet, well supported by artillery, and fighting in the open, could defeat the Germans. Pershing was faced with a serious problem, however. The massive influx of men into the training camps in 1917 placed a great strain on an army with few experienced men to serve as instructors; many of the senior and noncommissioned officers were needed to staff the divisions that were scheduled to depart for France. To overcome this deficiency, Black Jack Pershing obtained an agreement for the British and French to train Americans once they arrived in Europe. The process of seasoning divisions for service on the Western Front would take many months, including at least one month of training in open areas, one month in the trenches in a so-called quiet zone, and another month of actual service under enemy fire. In reality this schedule required more than three months, because it took time for a division to orient itself to being in France and to complete necessary requisitions for food, equipment, and transportation. If the beleaguered French and British believed that they would see a mass of men rushing to the front, they were sadly mistaken.

By the Christmas season of 1917 Pershing had only four twenty-eight-thousand-man divisions in France—the First and Second of the Regular Army and the Twenty-Sixth and Forty-Second of the National Guard. There were American pilots training in Britain and France in Allied aircraft, but plans were made to open a huge U.S. air-training base in Issoudun, France, which by Christmas remained only farmland. The American divisions were forming slowly and the army was simply overwhelmed by the massive task before it. For example, in October and November 1917 the Eighty-Second Division, training at Camp Gordon, Georgia, lost almost every enlisted soldier to transfers mandated by the War Department. In that division the three artillery regiments had no modern guns with which to train.

The Allies became concerned that the American Expeditionary Forces (AEF) would not become a reality for almost a year at the least, and Pershing was under great pressure to integrate his troops into existing British and French formations, but he stood firm, obstinate, and committed against such a policy. Fortunately for the Eighty-Second Division, they finally arrived in France by early June 1918 and had training time with the Allies. Not all divisions had that luxury; some were committed to the opening phase of the Meuse-Argonne Offensive in late September with no training at all, and they paid dearly for it. The concept of the well-trained soldier fighting in maneuver or open warfare was a good one, but the training to produce such a warrior did not meet existing time schedules. An army fights as a team, to be sure, and to do so it takes well-prepared commanders and staff officers to bring all of the combat and logistical elements together. Good leaders in combat are well prepared for their tasks, which means having a solid military education. The great Confederate general Thomas Jonathan "Stonewall" Jackson once said, "staff officers should be useful as well as ornamental."

General Pershing could not have agreed more, but the training of officers in the U.S. Army prior to the outbreak of World War I was limited. Military schools in the United States, such as the General Staff College at Fort Leavenworth, Kansas, needed many months to train those men. Pershing did not have the luxury of time—he needed trained, competent officers quickly. In late November 1917 Pershing opened a General Staff school at Langres, France, with a course of study designed to last for three months of intensive work free of frills, comforts, and distractions. There were short courses for commanders of regiments and brigades, as well as the General Staff course. The main problem for the AEF was a simple one: when a promising staff officer was sent to Langres, he was lost to his division just at the time it was preparing for deadly battle. While the goal of having a well-trained army—the equal of any in the world—was a good one, at times the goal obscured reality. The General Staff school took on a life of its own, and just before the opening of the Meuse-Argonne Offensive many divisions—most of the recently arrived and poorly trained ones—were required to send promising staff officers to Langres. The results were often catastrophic as unit cohesion collapsed and staff coordination broke down. A good example of this situation is the Thirty-Fifth Division, which suffered severe staff, command, and leadership problems in the first few days of the Meuse-Argonne Offensive; its commander, Major General Peter E. Traub, literally wore himself out trying to patch together its staff and fighting units. A good argument can be made that in the long run the staff school added little to the competence of the AEF. Time was simply too short; the AEF was in Europe less than two years and full-scale combat operations lasted only from early September to 11 November 1918.

PERSHING AND OPEN WARFARE

In his memoirs, My Experiences in the World War *(1931), General John Joseph Pershing, commander of the American Expeditionary Force (AEF) in France, commented on the training of his troops:*

Our units then in training were nearly all recruits and many of the officers and non-commissioned officers were easily influenced by the ideas of the French designated to assist us. In order to avoid the effect of the French teaching, it became necessary gradually to take over and direct all instruction ourselves. For the purpose of impressing our own doctrine upon officers, a training program was issued which laid great stress on open warfare methods and offensive action. The following is a pertinent extract from my instructions on this point:

"The above methods to be employed must remain and become distinctly our own. All instruction must contemplate the assumption of a vigorous offensive. This purpose will be emphasized in every phase of training until it becomes a settled habit of thought."

Intimately connected with the question of training for open warfare was the matter of rifle practice. The earliest of my cablegrams on this subject was in August, in which it was urged that thorough instruction in rifle practice should be carried on at home because of the difficulty of giving it in France. . . .

The armies of the Western Front in recent battles that I had witnessed had all but given up the use of the rifle. Machine guns, grenades, Stokes mortars, and one-pounders had become the main reliance of the average Allied soldier. These were all valuable weapons for specific purposes but they could not replace the combination of an efficient soldier and his rifle. Numerous instances were reported in the Allied armies of men chasing an individual enemy throwing grenades at him instead of using the rifle. Such was the effect of association that continuous effort was necessary to counteract this tendency among our own officers and men and inspire them with confidence in the efficacy of rifle fire. Ultimately, we had the satisfaction of hearing the French admit that we were right, both in emphasizing training for open warfare and insisting upon proficiency in the use of the rifle.

My view was that the rifle and bayonet still remained the essential weapons of the infantry, and my cables, stressing the fact that the basic principles of warfare had not changed, were sent in an endeavor to influence the courses of training at home. Unfortunately, however, no fixed policy of instruction in the various arms, under a single authority, was ever carried out there. Unresponsive to my advice, the inclination was to accept the views of French specialists and to limit training to the narrow field of trench warfare. Therefore, in large measure, the fundamentals so thoroughly taught at West Point for a century were more or less neglected. The responsibility for the failure at home to take positive action on my recommendations in such matters must fall upon the War Department General Staff.

Source: *John J. Pershing,* My Experiences in the World War, *volume 1 (New York: Stokes, 1931), pp. 152–154.*

The Allies fully expected that the war would continue well into 1919. Allied planners could not have foreseen the collapse of German internal resolve, the abdication of Kaiser William II, and the decision by German military planners to seek an armistice. The guns of the Western Front fell silent in November, but the military operations continued. Pershing agreed to send an American occupation force into Germany. An armistice was simply that; soldiers were no longer killing each other, but there was no peace—that condition would have to come with a comprehensive treaty. If negotiations failed, the armistice would end and fighting would begin again. American occupation troops moved up to the west bank of the Rhine River, where five experienced divisions began to train in open, or maneuver, warfare. Several divisions were sent into Belgium and Luxembourg to secure supply lines to the troops in Germany. The force, named the Third U.S. Army, was a complete army with all air, communications, medical, and combat elements preparing on enemy ground to begin battle again if the peace treaty failed to become reality. The occupation force fitted in with Pershing's goals.

Was the AEF in 1918 actually equal to other modern armies? Few generals really put their personal stamp on the armies they command; the AEF, nevertheless, was molded in the image of Pershing and reflected his concepts of battle. Pershing correctly believed that World War I could not end in victory if the combatants remained in the hundreds of miles of trenches that slashed the countryside of eastern France. Pershing and his generals believed that the trenches produced a mentality of defensiveness and protection. When the troops finally got out of the trenches, however, Pershing and his commanders learned some serious lessons.

The first American offensive with Pershing in command was the St. Mihiel operation (12–16 September 1918), which was basically a two-pronged assault on a triangular salient that the Germans had held since 1914. For Pershing this battle showed the correctness of the concept of open or maneuver warfare. A massive number of troops, aircraft, artillery, and tanks participated in the assault as the Doughboys left their trenches and cleared the salient within four days. There was a problem, however, in that the German high command, unknown to the Allies, had decided to abandon their positions within the salient, and fought the battle with well-placed machine-gun and artillery positions. Unaware of the German decision to abandon the salient, Pershing was convinced by the results that his strategy was correct; his troops fought the next great battle—the Meuse-Argonne offensive—in the same manner, but this time with terrible results.

After the St. Mihiel operation a euphoria filled Pershing's headquarters, and the planners firmly believed that open warfare was the way to end the war. The Germans, however, had decided to defend every inch of the Argonne Forest; for four years they had prepared the ground with barbed-wire entanglements, obstacles, an excellent trench system, and first-rate artillery positions. Just as important, the Germans placed well-trained and highly motivated troops into those prepared positions. This engagement would be a different situation than that which existed in the St. Mihiel salient. The AEF planners also made a basic mistake in that when the St. Mihiel operation was planned, the oldest, most experienced, and best-trained divisions were designated to do the fighting. The divisions earmarked for the start of the Argonne fight on 26 September were less experienced, and many troops were poorly trained and unprepared for the battle. When the battle began, those units were unable to make any headway, and General Pershing was forced to stop operations and plan for a new phase to begin on 4 October using more experienced troops fresh from St. Mihiel.

Those divisions suffered high casualties, and often "maneuver" boiled down to direct frontal attacks against troops and machine-gun positions, but the AEF moved slowly forward until the armistice was reached. It was good that the respite came in November, because it appeared that the AEF had reached the limit of its combat effectiveness. There was great rejoicing in Europe and the United States when the guns fell silent on the Western Front. After the war Pershing was cited by some critics for his insistence on open or maneuver warfare. The fundamental concept was rooted in the American historical military experience and made sense, but the training time and experience of officers, both at the staff and combat-unit level, was lacking. The European allies had four years of war to develop their officer-training systems and had the time to season those men. This luxury the United States did not have, and, despite Pershing's obstinacy in resisting using American troops under Allied command, there was the need to use the AEF forces in battle. The St. Mihiel and Meuse-Argonne operations were a response to that need, one addressed by an inexperienced but highly motivated American force. The basic concept of open warfare was not incorrect; the problem rested with the collapse of a system stressed by time, inexperience, and a lack of trained officers.

–JAMES J. COOKE,
UNIVERSITY OF MISSISSIPPI

Viewpoint:
No. The American Expeditionary Force (AEF) went to Europe with a tactical doctrine unsuitable to the nature of the war, and, as a result, U.S. forces paid a heavy price.

In the spring of 1914, before the start of the Great War, American combat doctrine mirrored that of most European armies in teaching that speed, movement, and mobility were the keys to warfare. By 1917 European armies were becoming more reliant on massive fire-support from all forms of modern weapons—automatic rifles, machine guns, rifle grenades, rapid-firing field artillery, and as many heavy guns and howitzers as possible. Yet, when the first American soldiers accompanied General John Joseph Pershing to France in June of that year, U.S. doctrine had changed little. American doctrine, as promulgated in the Army *Field Service Regulations,* continued to emphasize the importance of the rifle and bayonet while minimizing the value of firepower by describing machine guns as "emergency weapons" and treating heavy artillery as essentially useless in field engagements. Furthermore, the regulations described modern battles as events more akin to Civil War engagements than the massive campaigns of human and material attrition that were taking place in Europe. Without a doubt, when the U.S. Army entered World War I it possessed an outdated combat doctrine.

Of course, just because the U.S. Army failed to keep its operational concepts current during the years of neutrality did not mean that it could not make rapid changes when faced with the reality of eventual combat in the largest, most technologically advanced war in human history. More than a year elapsed between the declaration of war by the United States and the first American fighting in Europe. If one or more officers of sufficient rank and importance devoted themselves to the task of doctrinal modernization, much improvement could have been made. However, by all accounts, the man most capable of making such changes,

General Pershing, believed wholeheartedly in the prewar army doctrine as elucidated in the existing regulations. Shortly after arriving in Europe, he noted that Allied combat methods not only differed from American doctrine, they often directly contradicted it. On the one hand, while many American officers expected the infantry to work its way across no-man's-land, fight with minimal assistance from the other branches, and continue the attack until the enemy was either crushed or in full flight, French and British attack plans, on the other hand, increasingly expected the infantry to move forward and to occupy only those positions that had been already neutralized by the preliminary and accompanying artillery fire. Pershing criticized these kinds of Allied attacks as being "based upon the cautious advance of infantry with prescribed objectives, where obstacles had been destroyed and resistance largely broken by artillery." In particular, he denounced the typical French infantryman for not relying enough on the "great power" of his own rifle. Pershing expected that an "aggressive offensive based on self-reliant infantry" would eject the Germans from the safety of their trenches and inaugurate a period of "open warfare" in which his sharpshooting American rifleman would excel.

This concept of "open warfare" was the key for Pershing, as it was for most other American officers. The mantra-like references to "open warfare" by officers of all ranks belied the confusion that existed about what such warfare really was and exposed their misunderstanding of the nature of the war in Europe. Pershing claimed that "open warfare" was defined by the lack of a rolling barrage to protect the infantry, while his chief of staff, General James G. Harbord, insisted it would begin when "someone somewhere" simply got out of his trench and attempted to advance. Others described it differently, while General Hunter Liggett, the commander of the American First Army, admitted he had seen no army document that would help division commanders prepare their troops for this nebulous concept. Nevertheless, most American officers thought they understood "open warfare," which evoked images of soldiers in blue and gray facing off in Virginia, or of small units of infantry and cavalry outmaneuvering groups of Native Americans in the Great Plains. For these reasons, based more on tradition and intellectual conviction than on any recent experience or rigorous current analysis, the American Expeditionary Forces (AEF) initially adopted the established army doctrine as laid out in the prewar regulations. It seems that American officers rarely questioned their ability to prevent Germans from using the immense power of fortified positions and heavy firepower that were available all along the Western Front (for example, the Hindenburg Line) to resist the American challenge to fight out in the open.

Only a few American officers resisted the inclination to assume that the prewar doctrine would work on the Western Front. The most vocal of these critics was Colonel Charles P. Summerall, a hard-charging artillery officer. Even before the AEF did any fighting, Summerall announced to both the AEF headquarters staff and the War Department back in Washington that current doctrine would cause American infantry to "suffer great harm and unnecessary losses." Instead of basing American doctrine on the infantryman and his rifle and bayonet, Summerall wanted the AEF to employ unprecedented amounts of heavy firepower so that the infantry needed only to "follow the bar-

rage, mop up the trenches as taken, and consolidate the final objectives." In fact, these concepts were accepted by some of the most-successful operational commanders in the Allied armies. Nevertheless, Summerall's warnings not only went unheeded, but senior officers in the AEF also criticized him severely for his heresy.

American efforts to use the prewar doctrine on the field of battle often had terrible consequences. In the first sustained American offensive effort of the war, when troops of the Second Division attacked German defenders at Belleau Wood in June 1918, the inadequacy of the prewar doctrine should have become clear. The commander of the attacking troops happened to be General Harbord. Throughout three weeks of hard fighting in and around Belleau Wood, Harbord proved to be a true believer in Pershing's attempts to use "self-reliant infantry" in "open warfare." He repeatedly ordered infantry to attack with insufficient, and on more than one occasion, almost nonexistent artillery support. In every case his infantry battalions were mauled by German artillery and machine-gun fire and failed to achieve their objectives.

Were such instances rare, they would be easy to dismiss as isolated acts of incompetence; unfortunately, they were not. Even in the Second Division, one of the best in the AEF, American officers repeatedly ordered their men forward with inadequate fire support, under the supposition that "self-reliant infantry" could handle whatever came up out in the open. Other units, such as the First Division, made the same error, especially at Soissons in July 1918. Even in the final American offensive of the war, in the Meuse-Argonne, the expectations of what "self-reliant" infantry could do probably contributed to the excessively optimistic plans for a ten-mile advance in the first two days, after which the infantry would have to breach the strongest German line without any significant fire support whatsoever. Unable to advance successfully without the support of massive firepower in all phases of the attack, American units suffered horrible casualties, eventually totaling more than one hundred thousand by the end of the campaign. It took Pershing's infantrymen some three weeks to finally reach the line that they were supposed to take in the first forty-eight hours.

Even though the AEF learned to employ massive amounts of firepower at the start of each major offensive, the old prewar ideas consistently surfaced in subsequent stages of American attacks. In many cases American units would initially make impressive advances, but then, instead of stopping to consolidate the ground gained and to methodically prepare for another well-supported attack, the exhausted infantry were ordered to continue the initial advance, without adequate fire support and often in the face of stiffening German resistance. The goal of such aggressive orders, encouraged by the prewar doctrine, was to achieve the much sought after, but never realized, "breakthrough" that Pershing and many other American officers assumed would lead to the war-ending period of "open warfare." The "breakthrough" never really came. Instead, Pershing's "self-reliant" infantry ultimately ran headlong into German machine-gun nests and field artillery that were beyond the range of most American fire support. The results were predictably bloody and terribly unnecessary.

By the end of the war many combat commanders, though not all, had learned to discard the prewar doctrine and fight in a more conservative, firepower-based style. Instead of emphasizing the role and value of the individual rifle and bayonet, they learned to prepare detailed fire-support plans that smothered the enemy with firepower. For them, skill and morale were important, but those attributes were often squandered if not used within a modern, firepower-based combat doctrine. They agreed with Summerall, who insisted that "If we are to be economical with our men, we must be prodigal with guns and ammunition."

The AEF suffered from many of the problems that plague rapidly mobilized forces. Staff work was often inadequate, logistical support was erratic, and most commanders, at all levels, were inexperienced at the tasks they needed to perform on the modern battlefield. All but one of the combat divisions received significantly less training than the AEF High Command originally programmed. All of these internal problems worked against the AEF, often with tragic effect on the battlefield. But to these troubles one must also add the self-inflicted wound of attempting to implement an outdated doctrine, one that was more applicable to fighting human-centered battles with small, mobile units on the Great Plains than waging offensives with huge masses of men and modern weapons on the Western Front.

–MARK E. GROTELUESCHEN,
U.S. AIR FORCE ACADEMY

References

American Battle Monuments Commission, *American Armies and Battlefields in Europe: A History, Guide, and Reference Book* (Washington, D.C.: U.S. Government Printing Office, 1938).

Paul F. Braim, *The Test of Battle: The American Expeditionary Forces in the Meuse-Argonne Campaign* (Newark: University of Delaware Press; London: Associated University Presses, 1987).

Edward M. Coffman, *The War to End All Wars: The American Military Experience in World War I* (New York: Oxford University Press, 1968).

James J. Cooke, *The All-Americans at War: The 82nd Division in the Great War, 1917–1918* (Westport, Conn.: Praeger, 1999).

Cooke, *Pershing and His Generals: Command and Staff in the AEF* (Westport, Conn.: Praeger, 1997).

Mark E. Grotelueschen, *Doctrine Under Trial: American Artillery Employment in World War I* (Westport, Conn.: Greenwood Press, 2001).

James H. Hallas, ed., *Doughboy War: The American Expeditionary Force in World War I* (Boulder, Colo.: Lynne Rienner, 1999).

James G. Harbord, *The American Army in France, 1917–1919* (Boston: Little, Brown, 1936).

Perry D. Jamieson, *Crossing the Deadly Ground: United States Army Tactics, 1865–1899* (Tuscaloosa: University of Alabama Press, 1994).

Douglas V. Johnson II and Rolfe L. Hillman Jr., *Soissons, 1918* (College Station: Texas A&M University Press, 1999).

John J. Pershing, *My Experiences in the World War,* two volumes (New York: Stokes, 1931).

James W. Rainey, "Ambivalent Warfare: The Tactical Doctrine of the AEF in World War I," *Parameters: Journal of the US Army War College,* 13 (September 1983): 34–46.

Charles P. Summerall, "Comments by the Corps Commander upon the Operations of the Fifth Army Corps," undated typescript in 5th Army Corps Historical File, Entry 1118, Record Group 120, National Archives.

Summerall, "Memorandum from Artillery Section of Military Mission to England and France to Adjutant General of the Army, Subject: Organization of Field Artillery," 21 July 1917, in Folder 1, Box 11, CP 10, Charles P. Summerall Papers, The Citadel Archives and Museum.

David F. Trask, *The AEF and Coalition Warmaking, 1917–1918* (Lawrence: University Press of Kansas, 1993).

United States, Department of the Army, Historical Division, *United States Army in the World War, 1917–1919,* seventeen volumes (Washington, D.C.: Government Printing Office, 1948).

United States, War Department, *Field Service Regulations: United States Army, 1914, Corrected to July 31, 1918* (Washington, D.C.: Government Printing Office, 1918).

United States, War Department, *Field Service Regulations: United States Army, 1914 (with changes Nos. 1 to 7)* (Washington, D.C.: Government Printing Office, 1917).

ANGLO-GERMAN NAVAL RACE

Was the naval arms race the central factor in the growth of Anglo-German antagonism prior to World War I?

Viewpoint: Yes. As the premier naval power at the turn of the twentieth century, Great Britain felt threatened by the growing naval capabilities and heavy-handed diplomacy of Germany.

Viewpoint: No. The German naval threat was almost welcome, as the one challenge Britain was confident it could defeat. German hostility was instead the price Britain paid for rapprochement with her imperial rivals, France and Russia.

The Anglo-German naval rivalry preceding World War I had its genesis in the turn-of-the century decision by Imperial Germany to create a battle fleet capable of challenging the British Royal Navy in its home waters: the North Sea and the English Channel. Forty-one battleships, twenty big cruisers, and light forces in proportion—even as theoretical objectives in successive naval bills, these were numbers to stagger a Britain that did not even have a major naval base on its eastern coastline.

Though Germany by 1900 possessed the nucleus of a colonial empire, imperialism as such played at best a minor role in a major shift away from a traditional policy of limiting naval strength to concentrate on the army. Instead, an expanding business and industrial community was eager to secure contracts for warships, and to see those warships used to safeguard and nurture burgeoning German international trade. Bored with stories of the founding of the Reich, the German public demanded new achievements. An unstable government headed by a kaiser, William II, whose ambition to rule was not matched by any talent in that direction, saw the fleet as a "wedge issue" that would mobilize the patriotic middle classes against the Social Democratic and Progressive Left. Finally, a group of naval strategists headed—or fronted—by Admiral Alfred von Tirpitz saw the new navy as a means of impelling Britain to conclude an alliance with the Second Reich. At the very least, this school argued, the emerging High Seas Fleet would be a "risk navy," influencing Britain toward caution in its dealings with Germany.

The British reply took time to take shape, but eventually resulted in a major naval race characterized by the rapid introduction of new ship types, such as the all-big-gun "dreadnought" battleship and the thinly armored battle cruiser; and by the successful effort of Britain to balance the claims of imperial security on a global scale with security from the direct threat now posed by Germany. On one level that was done by the Entente alliances. On another it reflected a fundamental recasting of the British naval-defense profile, which by 1914 was shifting to an emphasis on submarines and flotilla craft for direct defense, while the capital ships supported the empire in distant waters. Ironically, however, of all the enemies Britain faced in the years from 1898 to 1914, the German navy was the only one it was always sure it could defeat—under any circumstances and in any waters.

**Viewpoint:
Yes. As the premier naval power at the turn of the twentieth century, Great Britain felt threatened by the growing naval capabilities and heavy-handed diplomacy of Germany.**

For most of its modern history Great Britain was the preeminent naval power in the world. For centuries the British government identified naval supremacy as its first line of national defense and the most critical element in assuring the security of its empire. When Imperial Germany began to construct its own powerful battle fleet at the turn of the twentieth century, the British government almost immediately viewed Germany as the most direct threat to its position in the world. In the decade or so leading up to World War I, fears of German naval competition colored most aspects of British foreign relations and led Great Britain to adopt an increasingly anti-German stance in international affairs. At the same time, this pronounced mistrust caused German diplomacy much consternation and soured the approach of the Berlin government toward Britain and its interests.

At the height of its imperial ascendancy Britain attached more importance to absolute naval superiority than any country ever had before or ever has since. When Queen Victoria died in 1901, she had reigned over one-quarter of the Earth's land mass and had more than four hundred million subjects. The relatively small British isles controlled domains that were scattered over all six inhabited continents and touched every ocean. In an age of steam and sail the integrity of the empire depended on complete mastery of the seas and a monopolization of sea power. Even more crucially, the British mainland was close enough to Europe to be vulnerable to potential adversaries in the event of a major war. Phillip II of Spain, Napoleon Bonaparte, and Adolf Hitler all made serious plans to land troops on British shores and use their superior ground forces to conquer the country. If the British were to remain unconquerable, their navy had to be strong enough to overwhelm any foreign power that tried to transport its armies to Great Britain.

As Europe entered an age dominated by total war and massive armies, naval defense became all the more imperative for Britain. Unlike the major continental powers, Britain resisted the development of a large, costly, and unpopular standing army. Historically, a strong current in British political thought had argued against the maintenance of any kind of standing army. If Britain knew that its coasts were secure from invasion, an army equal to those of the other great powers was neither necessary nor acceptable. In its imperial age all that was required was a relatively small army of professional (as opposed to conscripted) soldiers who could fight localized conflicts against rebellious colonial peoples or campaigns against indigenous populations targeted for imperial control. As Admiral Sir John Fisher, British First Sea Lord (senior naval commander) before and during World War I, said, "the British army is a projectile launched by the British navy."

The naval mastery that Fisher's comment suggested was, therefore, a crucial element in British national defense. As colonial competition grew in the latter half of the nineteenth century, the British government formalized its naval security requirements in 1889. The strategic outline adopted that year elaborated that British command of the seas could be maintained only if its naval strength exceeded the combined strength of the next two largest sea powers. This concept was a truly ambitious position to maintain. Even the predominant sea power of the United States in the twentieth century was governed by the principle of maintaining a navy that was "second to none," not one that outgunned the next two largest navies in combination.

Yet, when British strategists developed their plan for naval dominance, they were thinking that the major threat, represented by the next two largest navies, would come from two of its most serious colonial competitors, France and Japan. Germany was by no means a naval power until more than a decade after 1889. Although it boasted the most powerful European army after national reunification in 1871, German maritime capabilities were non-existent. Before Kaiser William II's reign, Germany was without serious colonial ambitions. When the great German statesman Otto von Bismarck was asked about colonial aspirations, the Chancellor gestured to a map of Europe and said "this is my Africa." In the British strategic plan of 1889 Germany was not the threat. Prussia, the leading state of the German Empire, had established a naval command only in 1853, more than three centuries after Henry VIII's traditionally commemorated founding of the British navy. For most of the next half century, the Prussian and united German navies floated small surface ships and torpedo boats for limited coastal defense. Between 1872 and William II's ascension to the throne in 1888, the German navy was commanded successively by two army generals who felt degraded by the task and whose imaginations were not stirred by their new venue.

That situation changed with striking suddenness in the next two decades. After 1888, William II's determination to make Germany a major player in world affairs began to alarm British interests. As early as 1895 he provoked a minor diplomatic crisis by suggesting to the Boer President of the Orange Free State that German support might have been at his disposal if he had serious trouble repelling a raid on his territory by British residents of the South African Cape Colony. What lay between Germany and South Africa but six thousand miles of ocean that German forces would have to cross? Four years later Germany used the civil strife occurring between Samoan factions as an excuse to suggest joint Anglo-German action against the American presence on the islands. While the Germans were posturing on the side of the British, it was nevertheless clear that they were interested in expanding their role in another faraway place. German colonial acquisitions in other Pacific islands, in Africa, and on the Kiaochow peninsula of China, together with the German attempt to purchase colonial possessions from the near-bankrupt Portuguese government, alarmed many British strategists about German intentions.

What could the Germans really do in the 1890s? Despite some modest naval construction in the first eight years of the decade, they still had no serious power at sea. Regardless of the frenetic energy of William II's *Weltpolitik* (world policy), the British could remain complacent. Indeed, even as Germany was becoming an active colonial power in the 1890s, France and Russia still presented the greatest threats to British interests. Disputes over the control of Egypt, Equatorial Africa, Persia, and Afghanistan were much more vital to British interests than tiffs over Samoa.

The German government knew that its saber rattling was ineffectual without serious naval-combat capabilities. The timely publication of Alfred Thayer Mahan's groundbreaking work on the decisive role of fleets of battleships, *The Influence of Sea Power Upon History, 1660–1783* (1890), made a strong impression on German strategic thought. In 1898 the newly organized German naval command structure, led by Navy Minister Admiral Alfred Tirpitz (von Tirpitz after he was ennobled in 1900), successfully politicked for a greatly expanded naval-construction budget. In March 1898 the Reichstag approved an appropriations bill that locked the country into an unalterable seven-year budget intended to increase the German battle fleet to nineteen battleships armed and armored on par with the best British warships.

Despite this dramatic development, the British still did not feel threatened enough to take serious notice. It was only with the passage by Germany of the Second Naval Law in July 1900 that tensions mounted. This legislation greatly expanded naval construction and aimed at doubling the projected size of the German surface fleet to thirty-eight, all to be operational by 1920. Astute British observers immediately seized on the growing German threat. As early as 1901 the Earl of Selborne, the First Lord of the Admiralty (the senior civilian office for naval affairs), articulated that new German naval construction represented the aspirations of Berlin to world leadership. The following year he amplified his analysis by labeling the planned German fleet a direct threat to British interests. His deputy, the First Sea Lord Admiral Fisher, openly predicted war with Germany over the naval competition and was even said to have suggested a preemptive strike to destroy German sea power before it could be used in war. Then, in 1907 Sir Eyre Crowe, a senior foreign office official, wrote a memorandum declaring that regardless of the immediate intentions of Germany, its possession of a competing battle fleet was a long-term security risk.

Although Selborne, Fisher, and Crowe could not have known empirically that German naval construction was intended to be a direct challenge, they guessed that fact nevertheless. Admiral Tirpitz's strategic memorandum for the Second Naval Law clearly indicated that he envisaged the German fleet as a direct military instrument to be used against "the greatest sea power." No one who read the memo could have doubted that he was referring to Britain. In Tirpitz's view the German navy was to be a "risk navy." While it was not expected to exceed the British navy in size or power, Tirpitz and other German hawks believed that it would become substantial enough to pose a serious threat to British security. With the Royal Navy scattered throughout the world to defend the entire British Empire, it was conceivable that the concentrated power of the German fleet could defeat the limited forces deployed to defend the British home waters. If the British were able to confront the Germans with their entire fleet, Tirpitz hoped that his navy would inflict enough damage on the Royal Navy to end its supremacy in the long term.

Tirpitz's belligerent policy did not translate into an open confrontation, however. William II and his advisers instead used the implicit threat of the German navy to attempt

to "scare" the British into accommodating their growing ambitions in the world. The son of an English Princess Royal, a grandson of Queen Victoria, a nephew of Edward VII, and a first cousin of George V, the kaiser had naturally close connections to the British monarchy and a natural affinity for things British. Rather than advocating military measures against his mother's country, the kaiser instead believed that Britain and Germany were natural allies with complementary interests. German exuberance in world affairs might be necessary to impress that fact upon the British, but ultimately William hoped to convince them of the logic of forming an alliance or other benevolent relationship with Germany.

Although a recent revisionist argument suggests the Kaiser was right and that British interests would have been best served by accommodation with Germany, his heavy-handed diplomacy could not have repelled the British more. No world hegemony wants to have its actions and policies dictated by a lesser power. In the Anglo-German case this fact was amplified by traditional British resistance to entering into alliances with continental European powers and by its propensity to act decisively when it saw a direct threat to its interests. As the Germans candidly acknowledged (at least internally) and the British quickly realized, German naval construction represented exactly that kind of threat.

William II's diplomacy, however, only worsened the situation. When Germany claimed rights in French Morocco in 1905, the kaiser again demonstrated his determination to play a global role without regard for the interests of other powers. Regardless of his intentions, a German strategic position adjacent to the Straits of Gibraltar posed a potential threat to the most direct route from Britain to Egypt and India. At an international conference held in Algeciras, Spain, in 1906 Britain lined up decisively with other colonial powers against German ambitions in Morocco.

By this time the British government was well on its way to realigning its foreign policy against Germany. In 1904 it had signed an agreement with France, resolving all of the colonial disputes between the two countries, and pledged to engage in joint military action with the French if the interests of both powers were threatened. In 1907 Britain resolved outstanding territorial disputes with Russia. Although neither agreement included an explicit alliance, British diplomacy nevertheless indicated that London was eliminating potential conflict situations with other powers so that it could concentrate on any threat posed by Germany.

British realignment caused consternation in Berlin. The kaiser came to believe that Great Britain was pursuing an explicitly anti-German policy supported by his uncle, Edward VII. Needless to say, the king did not return the kaiser's affinity for his country, and uncle and nephew did not have the best relationship. In 1908 the exasperated William II publicly aired his frustrations with Britain in an interview injudiciously published in the *Daily Telegraph*. In the course of the conversation he expressed surprise with growing British suspicions and said that Britons were "mad, mad as March hares" for thinking he had any aggressive intent. As for the German navy, he remarked that it might be useful in the Far East, that is, against Japan. William's attempt to defuse British concern was a catastrophic failure. In addition to having insulted the British people's sensibility, he had also insulted their intelligence by trying to convince them that the naval development was not meant to be threatening to them when the leaders of both countries knew that it was. While British opinion was inflamed against Germany, the kaiser fulminated against the stubborn refusal of the British to believe in his "good intentions." Three years later a second naval-related diplomatic incident occurred when two German gunboats appeared at the Moroccan coastal town of Agadir, allegedly to defend German commercial interests from a restless native population. Despite German clamoring about the right to defend overseas interests, Britain once again unequivocally backed French presence in Morocco and told the Germans that peace would best be assured if they did, too.

After 1911 the Anglo-German antagonism was an unalterable fact of international politics. German fleet construction, augmented by additional bills that expanded upon the ambitious Second Naval Law of 1900, was taken as a continuing explicit threat to British interests. Britain accelerated naval construction in its turn to keep ahead of German growth. At the same time, the German government, especially the authoritarian kaiser, resented British determination to keep its place as the greatest world power at what Berlin believed to be its own expense. Both sides offered late-hour attempts to defuse the naval arms race and repair relations, but they failed to attract sufficient support. A few doves in the British government, notably the First Lord of the Admiralty, Winston Churchill, and the War Minister, Richard Haldane, failed to impress upon the Germans the urgent need for them to restrain their provocative naval construction and remained alone in their calls for reconciliation. After the death of "the encircler," Edward VII, in 1910, William II thought that his much friendlier relationship with the new king, George V, could cure the problematic relationship between the two countries. Despite the concerted efforts and partial success of the congenial new German ambassador to London, Prince Karl Lichnowsky, tempers in both countries remained uneasy. By 1914 hawkish members of the German government had actually begun to question Lichnowsky's loyalty and patriotism. Although it took the German invasion of neutral Belgium to prompt British entry into the war, the naval arms race set the two powers on a collision course.

—PAUL DU QUENOY,
GEORGETOWN UNIVERSITY

Viewpoint:
No. The German naval threat was almost welcome, as the one challenge Britain was confident it could defeat. German hostility was instead the price Britain paid for rapprochement with her imperial rivals, France and Russia.

The Anglo-German naval race was not the central factor in the growth of Anglo-German antagonism prior to World War I. The race was only a byproduct of a much larger issue—the strategic dilemma of the British in trying to maintain a position of strength in an increasingly industrialized world. As traditional strategic threats evolved and new challengers arose, Britain found itself having to throw out "splendid isolation" and seek a foreign policy that it could rationally and financially support. The naval race—one that Germany could never win—was simply a sideshow.

By the late nineteenth century Britain still maintained the dominance on the oceans that she had earned at Trafalgar in 1805. The British empire spanned the globe and included Canada, Australia, India, vast territories in Africa, and valuable islands in the Caribbean Sea, Mediterranean Sea, and Pacific Ocean. Her navy and merchant marine were the largest in the world and safely protected and carried her commerce. Additionally, the British shipbuilding industry produced most of the steamships in the world.

Until the *Entente Cordiale* of 1904 the primary enemies of Great Britain were France and Russia. France, jealous of the British colonial empire, was a potential threat to the western Mediterranean, African, and Asian trade routes. Countless "invasion scare" warnings filled British newspapers in the 1880s. The Fashoda Incident (1898) demonstrated that France was willing to challenge British control of the Nile. Equally threatening was Czarist Russia, still smarting from her defeat in the Crimean War (1853–1856) and Balkan crises of the latter half of the century. Russia was a threat to eastern Mediterranean trade, the British Indian Empire, and the British commercial position in China. The nightmare scenario for the Royal Navy was a linking of the French Mediterranean Fleet with the Russian Black Sea Flotilla—hence the presence of the powerful and prestigious British Mediterranean Fleet based at Malta. The Two Power Standard, requiring the British Royal Navy to be equal to the next two largest navies combined, was specifically aimed at France and Russia.

TIRPITZ ON NAVAL BALANCE

In his memoirs German navy minister Admiral Alfred von Tirpitz wrote about the balance of power on the seas prior to World War I:

Every warship constructed anywhere in the world except in England was ultimately an advantage for us because it helped to adjust the balance of power at sea. Before the world-war, the omnipotence of England at sea, as well as on land, had not yet been declared sacrosanct. Just as Bulgaria and Roumania for example were able to have, side by side with the great land powers, armies of their own that were of no account in themselves, but which meant a great deal under certain conditions owing to their alliance value, smaller navies were being built side by side with that of Great Britain which were important in the light of the idea of alliance expressed by Bismarck. If any English monopoly of the sea was recognized, then not only the building of any fleet, not only any independent policy, but, I may say, any feeling of freedom on the part of other nations was out of the question. But why did Japan, France, Russia, America, why did Italy and the smaller States build warships?

If it is admitted that it would be useless to enter into competition with the strongest sea-power, there would be no point in any State having a navy. There is no real reason why the interests of the various nations at sea should not be based on a principle of give and take, just as on land. As regards the military side of the question, the strongest power at sea has no greater advantage than the strongest power on land, owing to the unlimited area that it controls. But its omnipotence can be broken by the luck of battle, which plays a more decisive part in a naval engagement than in a land war, and second by means of alliances. . . .Germany acquired an alliance-value with regard to States that were separate from us by the ocean. And as the most compelling factor which had forced upon us the construction of our fleet for the protection of our influence at sea ran parallel with the interests of all other non-English powers who had built fleets, the Government, if it was not going to render worthless the whole building of the fleet, could and must partly extend its aims beyond this new point and partly restrict them.

. . . In our position, one single ally worth mentioning would have been of decisive influence, whether it was Russia or Italy, whose naval armaments could have been constantly strengthened by us in the most opportune manner. Japan's benevolent neutrality would probably have hindered the outbreak of war. A reliably neutral attitude on the part of Russia in the event of an Anglo-German war would have sufficed, in view of the status of our fleet in 1914, to have left our navy free morally and actually for an offensive against England. In order to estimate the strength of the trump card which our fleet put in the hands of an energetic diplomacy at this time, one must remember that in consequence of the concentration of the English forces which we had caused in the North Sea, the English control of the Mediterranean and Far-Eastern waters had practically ceased.

Source: *Alfred von Tirpitz,* My Memoirs, *volume one (New York: Dodd, Mead, 1919), pp. 233–236.*

The strategic situation of Britain was rather grim by 1900. The years of complete superiority in commerce and naval strength that it formerly enjoyed were now gradually slipping away. America, Japan, and other major European powers continued to industrialize, build modern fleets, and expand overseas commerce. The Royal Navy could no longer be strong everywhere and had to rationalize its strategic position by reducing the number of potential foes it might face. Thus, Britain established an alliance with Japan (1902) to counter growing Franco-Russian naval strength in the Orient. Additionally, she abandoned the idea of facing the United States in an armed conflict—economic and social ties were just too strong—and pulled back most of her naval assets from the Western Hemisphere in 1904–1905.

France and Russia, however, still posed an immediate threat to the British position in the world. The Boer War (1899–1902) had shown that "splendid isolation" was now a dangerous game. Instead of attempting to build an alliance against France and Russia—no European power could effectively help Britain in her colonial contests with these rivals—Britain sought a rapprochement. The first breakthrough was with France in 1904. The *Entente Cordiale* acknowledged a French sphere of influence in Morocco and British control of Egypt. Diplomats also reached agreements concerning fishing rights off the Canadian coast and the status of Siam (present-day Thailand) as a buffer between French Indochina (present-day Vietnam) and Burma. The *Entente* gradually strengthened through the crises of the pre–World War I decade, including the Moroccan Crisis of 1905, and led to informal military and naval staff discussions.

It was not until the loss of the Russian fleets during the Russo-Japanese War (1904–1905), closely followed by a revolution in Russia (1905), that conditions favored a rapprochement between Britain and Russia. In 1907 the former rivals signed agreements concerning borders in Afghanistan, Persia (present-day Iran), and Tibet—long-standing areas of contention. Although these agreements were not as "cordial" as those signed between Britain and France, they still served to calm much of the concern over Russian threats to the British empire. The *Triple Entente*—among France, Russia, and Britain—was more of a diplomatic understanding than a formal military alliance, which Germany enjoyed with Austria and Italy just prior to the Great War. But as Paul W. Schroeder summarizes, in an article in *The Outbreak of the First World War: Causes and Responsibilities,* edited by Dwight E. Lee (1975), it is important to note that

> [t]he Triple Entente was a natural development explicable purely in terms of the needs and aims of the three powers—especially Britain. Her friendships with France and Russia were ends in themselves, vital for her imperial interests, and not means of checking Germany, and remained so. Rather than seeking friendly agreements with France and Russia because of the German threat, Britain tended to see Germany as a threat because of the agreements she sought and obtained from France and Russia.

So what of the threat from Germany? After its unification, resulting from the Franco-Prussian War of 1870–1871, Germany challenged the traditional balancing act of the great powers of Europe. Its army had performed brilliantly in the Wars of German Unification (1864–1871); rapid industrial growth, a burgeoning population, and a sufficient agricultural base supported the new nation. Germany now took the stage as a great power in Europe.

Until his fall in 1890 German chancellor Otto von Bismarck skillfully maintained a European balance to contain French attempts at revenge. Early in Kaiser William II's administration, however, the alliance system began to work

against Germany. Its formal alliance with Austria in 1879, with Italy joining in 1882, was soon faced with a Franco-Russian formal treaty in 1893. The kaiser looked to England, the kingdom of his grandmother, Queen Victoria, with feelings of admiration and jealousy. Much has been written about the details of Anglo-German relations prior to the war, but suffice it to say that Germany generally tried to bully Britain into an alliance, or at least a guarantee of neutrality in case of a general war on the European continent. One of the primary weapons that Germany wielded in this bullying was the threat of her growing fleet.

The famous state secretary of the Imperial Naval Office, Admiral Alfred von Tirpitz, was the mastermind of the construction of a modern battle fleet for the German navy. A close adviser to the kaiser, Tirpitz argued for a fleet of battleships to assure a "place in the sun" for Germany as a world-class power. More important, his *Risikogedanke* (Risk Theory) explained the less-obvious nature of his building program. This policy called for the gradual construction of a modern fleet of battleships that would challenge British control of the North Sea and English Channel—a direct threat to British home waters. Such a threat—a fleet approximately two-thirds the size of the British navy—would surely scare Britain into neutrality. Even if the German fleet were to lose a naval engagement with the Royal Navy, her flotilla would supposedly be so weakened as to be unable to deal with threats from other enemy fleets. The new fleet would be built slowly, usually with three new battleships laid down each year, in order not to alarm Britain.

The major problem with this building plan was that it assumed Britain would not increase its own building rate to counter the German program. After the Russo-Japanese War and the *Ententes* with France and Russia, Britain naturally scanned the globe for the next challenge and found it across the North Sea. Geography and industrial realities favored the Royal Navy, which welcomed the solitary threat as a way of countering complacency in the fleet. Germany was cursed with a hopeless geographic position because Britain controlled the exits from European waters—the English Channel and the North Sea—which would serve to force the numerically inferior German High Seas Fleet to fight. Additionally, Germany had to consider the presence of the Russian naval threat in the Baltic, albeit a lesser one. But more importantly German shipyards could never challenge those of Great Britain. The Tirpitz building plan of three battleships per year put a tremendous strain on the German shipbuilding industry; Britain, on the other hand, could easily keep up. To illustrate this industrial advantage, Britain laid down no fewer than seven dreadnought battleships and one battlecruiser in 1911 alone.

Admiral Sir John Fisher, the mastermind of the dreadnought battleship design and First Sea Lord from 1904 to 1910, deserves mention as a reformer and ruthless enforcer of efficiency in the Royal Navy prior to the war. His *Dreadnought*, completed in December 1906, was the first battleship to make use of turbine propulsion and all-big-gun armament (ten twelve-inch guns in five turrets). It immediately made all previous battleships obsolete. At the start of the war the Royal Navy possessed twenty-two dreadnoughts in service with thirteen under construction, while Germany countered with only fifteen in service and a further five being built—again, proof of British shipbuilding superiority. Fisher's administrative reforms included the scrapping of obsolete warships on foreign stations, the establishment of a reserve nucleus-crew force, and the redistribution and amalgamation of Royal Navy fleets worldwide—including, of course, a buildup of the Home Fleet, which would have been difficult without the *Ententes* of 1904 and 1907.

The new German fleet angered Britain; a strong battle fleet was a luxury for a continental power such as Germany, but a necessity for maritime Britain. Hostility from Germany was the price Britain was willing to pay in order to protect her world empire, through the ententes with France and Russia, and to maintain the balance of power on the European continent. Concentrating against one enemy, Germany, was much easier than facing France and Russia, and this threat made strategic planning a simple exercise for the Royal Navy. Thus, the naval race was a minor issue in the context of British security interests.

–JOHN ABBATIELLO,
U.S. AIR FORCE ACADEMY

References

Michael Balfour, *The Kaiser and His Times* (London: Cresset, 1964; New York: Houghton Mifflin, 1964).

V. R. Berghahn, *Germany and the Approach of War in 1914*, second edition (New York: St. Martin's Press, 1993).

Paul G. Halpern, *A Naval History of World War I* (Annapolis, Md.: Naval Institute Press, 1994).

James Joll, *The Origins of the First World War*, second edition (London & New York: Longman, 1984).

Paul M. Kennedy, *The Rise of the Anglo-German Antagonism, 1860–1914* (London & Boston: Allen & Unwin, 1980).

Robert K. Massie, *Dreadnought: Britain, Germany, and the Coming of the Great War* (New York: Random House, 1991).

Paul W. Schroeder, "World War I as Galloping Gertie: A Reply to Joachim Remek," *Journal of Modern History*, 44 (1972): 319–345.

Did the Arab uprising of 1916 contribute significantly to the military and political developments in the Middle East?

Viewpoint: Yes. The Arab revolt gave the Allies political leverage in the region and established Arab nationalism as a postwar force.

Viewpoint: No. The Arab revolt represented a minor military event that was peripheral to the more significant fighting taking place west of the Jordan River.

The Arab revolt of 1916 was part of a militant nationalist movement affecting the entire Arab population of the Ottoman Empire—a movement countered by an increasing level of repression from a government itself more ethnically Turkish in orientation since the Young Turk rebellion (1908). The outbreak of war in 1914 offered an opportunity for Husayn ibn 'Ali (King Hussein), Grand Sherif of Mecca and guardian of the Muslim holy places, to negotiate with both his ostensible overlords and their Anglo-French enemies.

Ottoman rule in the Arabian peninsula was in a sense consensual, with the Turks controlling the few railways and key coastal areas while conceding de facto autonomy to Hussein and other powerful tribe and clan leaders. Hussein's ambitions, and those of his son Faisal, ran wider. In October 1915 Sir Henry MacMahon, British High Commissioner in Egypt, promised British recognition and support for Arab independence. The wording of the document was deliberately vague. It nevertheless convinced Hussein and other Arab leaders that Arab rule had been promised for Arab lands—Palestine and Lebanon included.

France and Britain meanwhile had concluded another agreement guaranteeing France a sphere of influence in the Levant. In November 1917 the Balfour Declaration promised Jews a "national home" in Palestine. The toxic mix of ambiguity and mendacity left a heritage that continues to fester. It was enough, however, to lead Hussein to proclaim independence for Arabia in June 1916.

Mecca quickly fell; Medina and the other urban centers proved tougher nuts to crack. For two and a half years Arab insurgents supplied by the British and advised by several British officers, including Thomas Lawrence, waged a colorful campaign against the railroads and the isolated garrisons they sustained. Lawrence in particular proved a master of irregular war at tactical and operational levels while remaining a loyal servant of the Empire: helping to keep the Arabs in the field with promises. Direct effects of the Arab Rising were minimal until the final offensive of the British in Palestine, when the Arab army effectively covered Sir Edmund Allenby's right flank while committing a series of spectacular atrocities. Arab expectation of huge rewards for their services would, however, prove to be mistaken.

Lieutenant Colonel
Thomas Lawrence,
popularly known as
Lawrence of Arabia,
early 1918

Viewpoint:
Yes. The Arab revolt gave the Allies political leverage in the region and established Arab nationalism as a postwar force.

As the last notes of the call to morning prayer quivered in the air and died, a moment of silence hung over Mecca. A rifle shot rang out and hundreds of Arabs moved out of the shadows to rush into the square and begin firing into the barracks of the Turkish army. Sherif Husayn ibn 'Ali (King Hussein) lowered his weapon and smiled. It was the start of the Arab revolt of 1916.

The Arab revolt was badly timed, starting as it did so soon after the Turkish victory against the Allies in the battle of Gallipoli (1915). The Turks had naturally amassed most of their troops in the Dardanelles and on the Russian front. After Gallipoli they could concentrate more on the alternate war objective of capturing the Suez Canal and reconsolidating their Arabian position. That strategy meant increased use of the railroads, which were ripe for sudden raids and guerrilla warfare. Over the next several months, though the Ottoman army managed to keep the vital Hejaz railway

and other main lines of communication open, the rebels captured major towns around Mecca and made a tentative alliance with the British in Egypt. The first liaison officer, a proper military type, was appalled by the Arabs' lack of discipline and their apparently ineffectual way of making war. The Arabs were beginning to feel the same way about the British when Captain Thomas Lawrence arrived.

Lawrence was an intellectual and a man of action—a classicist and a romantic, an Arabist and a warrior—the kind of complex mixture of qualities Imperial Britain occasionally produced. The Bedu were an ancient and proud people who were organized by clans and tribes. Some were purely nomadic, some were settled, and some were in-between. They were mutually suspicious; blood feuds were common. In their five hundred years of occupying the Arabian Peninsula the Turks never really worried about rebellion by the Bedu, because they spent most of their energy fighting one another.

The aims of the two partners, the Bedu and the English, were never quite the same. Amir Faisal I, Hussein's son and field commander, envisioned a greater Arabia incorporating all the tribes into one nation. The British government, ever seeking to enlarge the Empire, envisioned many little states over which it could exert its influence, when not its sovereignty. The British military command for its part seemed to have envisioned molding the Bedu into a type of irregular auxiliary cavalry along lines familiar in the Indian army. Of course, they were not willing to spend any money on training or give them modern arms. Lawrence's personal vision partook of both sides. He wanted to see the Arab revolt successfully unite the Arabs, but believed they would need British oversight to make the leap from what he considered their medieval past to the twentieth century. Lawrence perceived as well that the Bedu would fight only for the Bedu. Their psychology and war aims alike demanded it.

Lawrence in many ways fits Edward W. Said's stereotype of an "Orientalist." He was a brilliant Arabist who genuinely liked the Arabs (the two by no means always go together), understood them, appreciated their strengths, and was tolerant of what he considered their weaknesses. He could inspire them in combat, but his genius was in his diplomatic ability to unite and sustain the Arabs as a fighting force and in his devising a strategy that maximized their military effectiveness. The blowing up of a train, besides being visually impressive, has military value in the temporary destruction of the line and matériel. It also has great psychological value, conveying a sense of power and competence to those carrying out the assault and a corresponding sense of frustration and victimization by those being attacked.

Lawrence, in contrast to his familiar image, was not a guerrilla fighter. Instead, he used the Arabs in what would later be called a long-range penetration force. He generally cooperated in concert with the British main army in Palestine, protecting its right flank, attacking isolated or overextended elements in the Turkish flank or rear, and disrupting communications and rail traffic—all of which are normal military activities. What set Lawrence and his Arabs apart was their use of the desert as an ocean, thus liberating themselves from conventional communications routes, which their more complex logistics forced both the British and Turks to use. The topography and military geography of Arabia favored relatively small mobile units, unhampered by supply trains and artillery. The Turks were for the most part restricted by their rail lines; the Bedu were able to traverse the desert almost at will, as long as they had base areas to which they could return.

The Arabs have navigated the almost-trackless deserts of the peninsula for centuries. This ability and the related fact that it was nearly impossible to form any large, reliable, united force from among the various tribes were used by Lawrence as strengths instead of weaknesses. Lawrence adapted his methods to the forces he had and sought to make problems into possibilities. The habit of the Arabs to loot, then retire to their homes after successful action, for example, became an opportunity to spread the legend of the ever victorious "Aurens."

Even though the Turkish army readily repaired the damage to its railroads, after three years of faceless massacre on the Western Front, the public was famished for heroes and for some success against the enemy. Lawrence had all the prerequisites—looks, dash, and exoticism, a man of intellect and of action. He also benefited from the fact that under Sir Edmund Allenby's command, the British army in Palestine was beginning to advance more than a few hundred yards at a time in an area known to every Christian in the Western world. Allenby's progress, eagerly followed by the world press, served to focus even more attention on Lawrence and his Arabs.

When Allenby began his 1918 invasion of Palestine, with the objective of destroying the Turkish army and moving on Damascus, Lawrence and his Arabs—by this time including a regular brigade, plus a few guns and armored vehicles supplied by the British and French—played the relatively conventional military role of providing cover for the right flank of the

British army. In a strategic context, however, the Arabs did far more. Allenby was able to attack with a two-to-one local advantage in numbers. This favorable ratio reflected Lawrence's success in pinning down thousands of Turks east of the Jordan, and throughout Arabia, as local security against an Arab revolt that became a general insurrection once the British broke through the main Ottoman defenses. While the Arabs could not have overthrown the Turks by themselves, neither could Allenby defeat the Turks without the Arabs.

–JOHN WHEATLEY, BROOKLYN CENTER, MINNESOTA

Viewpoint:
No. The Arab revolt represented a minor military event that was peripheral to the more significant fighting taking place west of the Jordan River.

The Arab uprisings (1916), primarily those of Amir Faisal I and Sherif Husayn ibn 'Ali (King Hussein) in what is now Jordan and Syria, excited the popular imagination of the Allied populations and appeared to make a dramatic contribution to the war effort. This interest was especially true in Britain, which followed the exploits of the heroic Colonel Thomas Lawrence through the exaggerated lens of the press. There were other persons, including Arabs and Frenchmen, who likewise appeared to be doing great damage to the Turkish cause in 1917 and 1918. While blowing up railways made good cinematography, the Arab uprising was, however, peripheral to the real fighting that took place west of the Jordan.

The Ottoman Empire had dealt with dissident Arab uprisings for hundreds of years. The most draining revolts were the ongoing uprisings in Yemen that absorbed almost a tenth of the prewar Ottoman army. The rebel Yemenis were joined by the Sannusi tribesmen in Libya in the first decade of the twentieth century. The nomadic Sharifian Arabs (in what are now Syria, Jordan, and northwestern Saudi Arabia) were quiet, as were the marsh Arabs in Mesopotamia. Relations between the Ottomans and the Arabs were generally good; the Arabs were law-abiding citizens and even provided soldiers for the Ottoman Army in the Balkan Wars (1912–1913).

The onset of World War I changed this relationship forever. Initially the Arabs were supportive of the war effort of the Ottoman Empire. During the first two years of war, Arab levies

THE ARABS DECLARE INDEPENDENCE FROM THE TURKS

On 27 June 1916 Husayn ibn 'Ali (King Hussein) issued a proclamation, portions of which are included below:

I myself, protecting the honor of the State, caused Arabs to rise against their fellow Arabs in the year 1327 [1909 of the Christian era] in order to raise the siege of Abha, and in the following year a similar movement was carried out under the leadership of one of my sons, as is well known. . . .

We have sufficient proof of how they regard the religion and the Arab people in the fact that they shelled the Ancient House, the Temple of the Divine Unity, of which it is said in the word of God, "Purify my House for those that pass round it," the Kibla of Mohammedans, the Kaaba of believers in the Unity, firing two shells at it from their big guns when the country rose to demand its independence. One fell about a yard and a half above the Black Stone and the other three yards from it. The covering of the Kaaba was set in a blaze. Thousands of Moslems rushed up with shouts of alarm and despair to extinguish the flames. To reach the fire they were compelled to open the door of the building and climb on to the roof. The enemy fired a third shell at the Makam Ibrahim in addition to the projectiles and bullets aimed at the rest of the building. Every day three or four people in the building itself were killed, and at last it became difficult for the Moslems to approach the Kaaba at all. We leave the whole Mohammedan world from East to West to pass judgment on this contempt and profanation of the Sacred House. But we are determined not to leave our religious and national rights as a plaything in the hands of the Union and Progress Party.

God (blessed and exalted be He) has vouchsafed the land an opportunity to rise in revolt, has enabled her by His power and might to seize her independence and crown her efforts with prosperity and victory, even after she was crushed by the maladministration of the Turkish civil and military officials. She stands quite apart and distinct from countries that still groan under the yoke of the Union and Progress Government. She is independent in the fullest sense of the word, freed from the rule of strangers and purged of every foreign influence. Her principles are to defend the faith of Islam, to elevate the Moslem people, to found their conduct on Holy Law, to build up the code of justice on the same foundation in harmony with the principles of religion, to practice its ceremonies in accordance with modern progress, and make a genuine revolution by sparing no pains in spreading education among all classes according to their station and their needs.

This is the policy we have undertaken in order to fulfill our religious duty, trusting that all our brother Moslems in the East and West will pursue the same in fulfillment of their duty to us, and so strengthen the bands of Islamic brotherhood.

Source: Charles F. Horne, ed., Source Records of the Great War, *volume four (Indianapolis: American Legion, 1930), pp. 234–237.*

---

fought well for the empire and participated in the defense of Gallipoli, Caucasia, Palestine, and Mesopotamia. To insure Arab loyalty the Turks treated the Arab populations well and implied that greater autonomy was in store for them after the war. In 1916, however, the British and French recognized that the promise of independence, gold, and arms might turn the Arabs into active co-belligerents against the Turks. In that year the Allies sent men, weapons, and gold to the Arab tribes, including Lawrence, then a major. This activity rapidly destabilized the fragile Ottoman-Arab relationship.

The Allied strategy hinged on the idea of creating powerful and highly mobile Arab "armies" (in battalion and brigade strength) that would cut the Damascus-Medina (or Hedjaz) railway and also interdict the logistics and communications of the Ottoman Fourth Army in Palestine. The Hashemite Arab tribes were ideally positioned to accomplish this plan by interdicting the rail junction of Der'a, which was thought to be the "navel" of the Ottoman strategic position. This strategy was never intended to be decisive; it was merely intended to divert scarce Turkish resources from the main campaigns, and it may be thought of as an extension of the concept of the indirect approach at the operational level of war.

There is considerable evidence that the British Foreign Office was already laying the groundwork for the eventual British occupation of the

Ottoman Middle East in the postwar period. The Arabs were, for all practical purposes, pawns in a game of power politics. This concept matured as the war progressed and as French, Russian, and even Zionist interests in postwar regional spoils increased. The Sykes-Picot Agreement (1916) and the Balfour Declaration (1917) were the diplomatic manifestations of these competing interests. Had Russia not collapsed in 1917 there may have been similar treaties regarding Persia and Armenia. In any event, the Hashemite Arab kingdom came to believe that Britain stood behind it and its eventual independence, and open rebellion against the Ottoman Turks broke out in 1916.

At first, the Arab Revolt was held together by the personalities of its leaders and grew slowly. By late 1916 there were three large groups of Arabs ranged from north to south in Syria and Jordan, in Arabia near Medina, and in central Arabia. These groups were armed with an assortment of small arms and light artillery and could put several thousand mounted men into the field. By 1917 both the Turks and the Allies were referring to the collective whole as the Arab army. In that year the Arab army became quite active in conducting mounted hit-and-run raids against the Ottoman lines of communications and was famously noted for the occasional destruction of the railway from Damascus to Medina.

To the east in Palestine the main forces of the British Empire and the Ottoman Turks battled during 1917 on the Gaza-Beersheba line. Finally, on the third attempt the British, under General Edmund Allenby, broke this line and advanced to Jerusalem in November 1917. The anticipated weakening of the Ottoman Fourth Army through Arab raids never materialized and was not a factor in the victory. Unable to advance farther, and stripped of his experienced troops in the spring of 1918 as reinforcements for France, Allenby was forced to pause until September (although his army conducted some large-scale raids across the Jordan River in midyear). During this time the Arab army became more active in its continuing assault on Ottoman logistics; however, these were pinpricks in their effect on the Turks.

In late September 1918 Allenby hit the Turks hard at Meggido in a knockout blow that all but destroyed their armies in Palestine. In the ensuing battles of encirclement Allenby rapidly advanced toward Damascus. Assisting his forces were the Arab armies (and Lawrence), who repeatedly harried and cut the failing Ottoman lines of communications. This phase of the revolt was extensively covered by the western press and included the media-generated legend of "Lawrence of Arabia." Although Allenby actively planned and incorporated the Arabs into his overall strategy, their contribution was minor. Ultimately, it was Imperial cavalry that occupied the key rail junction at Der'a. In any case, a small portion of the Arab army was among the first Allied troops to occupy Damascus. This achievement was widely reported throughout Europe, and, to the public at large, it appeared that the Arabs were the "right wing" of Allenby's army. Turkish involvement in World War I ended on 30 October 1918 with the Hashemites firmly in place in Jerusalem and Damascus, apparently having played an important role in the final victory in the Middle East.

From the Turkish perspective, however, the Arabs played a minor role in the outcome of the fighting in Palestine and Syria. The modern Turkish official campaign histories treat the Arab attacks as a minor inconvenience and the consequent damage is described as easily repairable in a one-to-three day period. The Ottoman General Staff maintained forces in Arabia mainly for reasons of prestige and, in fact, the railway servicing Arabia as far south as Medina was built primarily to move pilgrims to the holy cities.

The Turks maintained four low-priority infantry divisions (armed with mostly small arms and light artillery) in eastern Arabia and Yemen as garrisons for the large cities (Aden, San, Medina, and Mecca). The ongoing revolt in Yemen was considered to be quite serious for the Ottoman Empire and had been an open sore for the Ottoman army since 1908. These garrisons (which amounted to about twenty thousand men) were largely self-sufficient and were impossible to isolate merely by cutting the railway. During the war the Turks never reinforced the original garrisons mobilized in Yemen in August and September 1914. Throughout the course of the war the Ottoman garrisons in Arabia and Yemen fulfilled their mission by holding successfully these key cities.

By mid 1918 the joint Turco-German Yildirim Army Group formed several provisional infantry divisions (roughly three thousand men) to guard the railroad near Damascus and Derna against the growing Arab army. Like the Turkish forces in Yemen, these provisional divisions were small and lightly equipped low-priority formations. While it may be argued that these provisional infantry divisions were diversions that weakened the defense of Palestine by the Yildirim army, their presence at the front probably would not have been of decisive importance against Allenby's massive superiority. Finally, it must be noted that the Turks never sent any of their best infantry or cavalry divisions against the Arabs, nor did they ever conduct serious offensive operations against them. This reactive and defensive strategic posture indicates the extremely low priority that the Ottoman General

Staff gave to the Arab Revolt during the latter stages of the war.

Thus, from both the Allied and the Ottoman perspective the Arab Revolt was a sideshow within a sideshow. Neither side gained much by its efforts, although arguably the British and French expended fewer resources. When analyzing the success of the corresponding missions, however, the Turks were more successful than the Allies and Arabs. The Turks always intended merely to garrison the major cities south of Palestine and to hold them for reasons of prestige. They accomplished this task and in early 1919 the Turks still held the Arabian and Yemeni cities. Furthermore, the Turks had to commit very few additional resources to maintain their grip on the Damascus-Medina railroad in 1917 and 1918. Moreover, they never had to divert first-class troops to deal with the Arab army. Reciprocally, the Allies failed to achieve their objective of creating a serious strategic problem for the Turks. In fact, the raising of the Arab Revolt created some discord among the British and French and laid the groundwork for further Allied disagreements in 1919.

Overall, the Arab Revolt was insignificant militarily during the war and of small consequence to the victors as they divided the Arab lands after the war. The validity of this statement may be seen in the final disposition of the Arab provinces of the Ottoman Empire at the Paris negotiations in 1919. The Arabs had expected to be treated as deserving allies and instead were treated as inferiors. The embittered Lawrence and the Arabs were, in many ways, prisoners of their own legend and therein reflected a fundamental misunderstanding of their own role in the victory. Instead of winning their independence, the Arabs simply replaced one master with another.

—EDWARD J. ERICKSON, NORWICH HIGH SCHOOL, NEW YORK

References

Haifa Alangari, *The Struggle for Power in Arabia: Ibn Saud, Hussein and Great Britain, 1914–1924* (Reading, U.K.: Ithaca, 1998).

David L. Bullock, *Allenby's War: The Palestine-Arabian Campaigns, 1916–1918* (London & New York: Blandford, 1988).

John Darwin, *Britain, Egypt, and the Middle East: Imperial Policy in the Aftermath of War, 1918–1922* (New York: St. Martin's Press, 1981).

Edward J. Erickson, *Ordered To Die: A History of the Ottoman Empire in the First World War* (Westport, Conn.: Greenwood Press, 2001).

Lawrence James, *The Golden Warrior: The Life and Legend of Lawrence of Arabia* (London: Weidenfeld & Nicolson, 1990).

Elie Kedourie, *England and the Middle East: The Destruction of the Ottoman Empire, 1914–1921* (London: Mansell / Boulder, Colo.: Westview Press, 1987).

T. E. Lawrence, *Revolt in the Desert* (London: Cape, 1927).

Edward W. Said, *Orientalism* (New York: Pantheon, 1978).

AUSTRIA-HUNGARY

Did Austria-Hungary's abandonment of great-power status to concentrate on the Balkans play a major role in generating the Great War?

Viewpoint: Yes. Austria-Hungary in 1914 had become, de facto, another Balkan power, and it was correspondingly indifferent to the consequences of its actions in Europe.

Viewpoint: No. The policy of Austria-Hungary after the assassination of Archduke Franz Ferdinand reflected a determination to maintain the Dual Monarchy's status as a great power, able and willing to act independently in defense of its own vital interests.

Long described in the historiography of the Great War as a German cat's-paw, Austria-Hungary is being restored to the status of an independent actor in the diplomacy that led up to the outbreak of hostilities. Since the Bosnian Crisis (1908), the Dual Monarchy's viability was being increasingly questioned. Austria was under increasing economic pressure in the Near East even from its ostensible ally, Germany. British publicists and French diplomats pictured brave futures for the Slavs of southeastern Europe once the Habsburg Empire should disappear. The increasingly strident claims of Austria that its great-power status was being ignored went overlooked—with few questions as to what might happen should Austria not accept its assigned fate and merely fade away.

The issue sharpened as the Balkan Wars (1912–1913) established the small states of the peninsula as military powers to be reckoned with, able and willing to put more men in uniform and to spend a higher percentage of gross national product (GNP) on their maintenance than Austria had been able to consider since the days of Maria Theresa. Austria was generally understood as correspondingly unable to assert itself in the Balkans without a significant effort. Some calculations predicted that as many as a dozen corps would be required to contain Serbia and Romania in case of a general war.

Such gloomy prognostications were encouraged by a growing conviction in Vienna that Serbia in particular was determined to destroy the Habsburg Empire in pursuit of its own self-proclaimed destiny as a Balkan Piedmont and seemed responsive to nothing but force in pursuit of that policy. Pledges from Belgrade to curb subversive propaganda and similar provocations had been repeatedly shown to be nothing but scraps of paper. Great-power diplomacy proved ineffective because no one was willing to put pressure on Russia to curb its unruly client. In the aftermath of the assassination of Archduke Franz Ferdinand it represented no concession to militarism or imperialism to decide that Austrian hawks were being justified by the course of events.

In the next six weeks, Austria-Hungary insisted repetitively that not merely prestige, not merely "vital interests" as an abstraction, were at stake; the issue was the existence of Austria as a great power. The politics of restraint are effective only when pursued from a position of strength. Given the shaky Austrian position in the international community, what Russia did or did not do was of secondary importance. Should Russia choose to support a provocation of this kind by a lesser power, it was an unmistakable statement of intention to Europe as a whole. Austria-Hungary, however, could no longer afford the luxury of making local sacrifices for the sake of a general order. The Serbian boil had to be lanced. The wider consequences of that action were accepted as beyond the control of Vienna.

Viewpoint:
Yes. Austria-Hungary in 1914 had become, de facto, another Balkan power, and it was correspondingly indifferent to the consequences of its actions in Europe.

In 1914 Austria-Hungary had become a de facto Balkan power. Furthermore, it was correspondingly indifferent to the consequences of its actions after the assassination of Archduke Franz Ferdinand in Sarajevo (28 June) for Europe as a whole. World War I became inevitable when leading Viennese statesmen determined that war be declared on Serbia in July 1914. Their goal was to put an end to the years of Great Serbian agitation that threatened the Dual Monarchy (Austria-Hungary), thus destroying the militant South Slav movement while responding aggressively to the assassination. In July Vienna was first to opt for war, indeed a Balkan War, despite the implications of that decision. Dual Monarchy leaders unanimously favored a localized war with Serbia but differed greatly on how exactly to realize it.

Throughout the prewar period (1871–1914) the Dual Monarchy lagged behind its European counterparts in their accelerated armaments race, though only the populations of Russia and Germany exceeded that of Austria-Hungary. The defense budget of the empire equaled only one-fourth that of Germany or Russia, one-third that of Great Britain or France, and even less than that of Italy.

The military weakness of Austria-Hungary would have a profound effect on Viennese foreign policy and lead to growing dependence on German support. The debilitated military position of Russia following the Russo-Japanese War (1904–1905) greatly influenced the Dual Monarchy's foreign policy. Likewise, the steady military recovery of Russia presented a major dilemma to Habsburg diplomatic and army leaders throughout the Bosnian Crisis (1908–1909), the Balkan Wars (1912–1913) and, specifically, during the July 1914 crisis.

As the main supporter of the dynasty and its power position, the Habsburg army was critical to maintaining unity within the empire and keeping its multinational populace *kaisertreu* (loyal to the emperor). After 1912, however, nationality problems, particularly the South Slav question, increasingly came to disrupt domestic, diplomatic, and military matters. The Habsburg army, deficient both qualitatively and quantitatively compared to those of the other Great Powers, required many more reservists in the event of an armed conflict. Such military shortcomings would prove potentially fatal to a multinational army.

The Balkans also served as a focal point for Viennese diplomatic relations with its German ally. The major difficulty facing Habsburg diplomats in the prewar period was inconsistent support of Germany for critical Balkan decisions. This policy became particularly manifest during the Balkan Wars. Nevertheless, regular contact among the allied Chiefs of the General Staffs, primarily in the form of written communiqués beginning during the Bosnian Crisis, continued uninterrupted. The combination of the German drive for *Weltpolitik* (world politics) and the Austro-Hungarian Balkan policy created the tinderbox for a European war.

The role of Germany, as perceived by Vienna, was to prevent Russian intervention in a localized Balkan military campaign. This mission was particularly important at a time when Viennese Balkan policy had been disrupted by the growth in prestige, territory, and population of Serbia as a result of the Balkan Wars. Bulgaria and Turkey, earlier buffers against Serbia, had suffered disastrous military setbacks. Equally disturbing was the apparent loss of Romania to the Triple Alliance. The position of Bucharest was paramount to the Austro-Hungarian military agenda against Russia. Its strategic function was to anchor the Habsburg right flank in a "War Case Russia." Major attention of Vienna, however, was focused on the Balkans.

An energetic Viennese foreign policy in the Balkans dating from the Bosnian Crisis depended upon the support of Berlin. In 1913 the German backing of Balkan policies led both civilian and military leaders in Austria-Hungary to assume a more aggressive stance. This policy had disastrous consequences during the July 1914 crisis.

In 1903 the Serbian royal family was assassinated, and Serbia reversed its diplomatic dependence upon Vienna. The provinces of Bosnia and Herzegovina, home to the majority of Serbs in the Habsburg monarchy, became magnets for the exploding Great Serb propaganda and agita-

tion and the foci of Viennese policy. The provinces served as outposts for an active Habsburg Balkan policy and attracted expanding Great Serb propaganda and agitation.

The brutal murder of Serbian king Alexander and his wife in 1903 and the accession of the rival family to the throne by a military coup transformed Austrian-Hungarian-Serbian relations. The new Belgrade government immediately sought to emancipate itself from the shadow of Habsburg economic dominance. Suppressing this "Greater Serbia" agitation became a primary objective of Viennese policy toward Belgrade.

In Great Power relations, German policy strongly influenced the formulation of the Triple Entente, with the Dual Monarchy increasingly regarded as merely a German ally. This alliance heralded the slow demise of the Great Power status of Austria-Hungary, as it was first buffeted by unfolding Balkan events and then the realization that it could not control them.

Austro-Hungarian foreign minister Alois Aehrenthal's dynamic Balkan policy, initiated in 1906, became a core component of Viennese foreign policy, thus Balkan matters took precedent over other foreign-affairs concerns. The Bosnian Crisis, the Balkan Wars, and the July 1914 crisis can all be attributed to his forceful Balkan strategy and Vienna attempting to maintain the policy even after Aehrenthal's death in 1911.

Shortly after assuming office, Aehrenthal's energetic diplomatic efforts produced an Austro-Hungarian confrontation with Russia and Serbia, stemming from Habsburg reaction to the perceived threat of the Young Turk revolution (1908) in Turkey and its potential effect on the Balkan provinces of Bosnia-Herzegovina. Aehrenthal sought to maintain Habsburg control of the provinces. His vigorous stance was fueled by his firm conviction that the Dual Monarchy's survival hinged upon its ability to demonstrate a new dynamism. As a result, Aehrenthal pursued a foreign policy fraught with risk, as Habsburg power and prestige became fatefully intertwined with the Balkan arena in the decade before the outbreak of World War I.

Convinced annexation would bolster the Great Power status of Vienna and increase its prestige in the Balkan region, Aehrenthal grabbed the two provinces in 1908. In addition, he believed that the annexation would prevent a Serbian unification of the South Slavs in the provinces and dampen the flourishing "Greater Serbia" aspirations.

The decisive outcome of the Bosnian Crisis resulted from the military weakness of Russia following the Russo-Japanese campaign. Foremost, Habsburg-Romanov relations suffered a serious setback, ending an era of cooperation in the Balkans that was replaced by mutual suspicion and personal antipathy. Habsburg relations with Serbia also became inflamed.

Austrian-Hungarian Emperor Charles speaking to soldiers decorated for bravery on the Eastern Front

AUSTRIA-HUNGARY

Support by Berlin of Vienna during the Bosnian Crisis set a dangerous precedent in Habsburg-Hohenzollern relations. The energetic Viennese foreign policy in the Balkans increasingly became dependent on the goodwill of Germany, a further indication of the slipping Great Power situation for Vienna.

The Habsburg military leadership increasingly regarded a war with Serbia as inevitable. The first radical revision to Balkan military planning also introduced the growing possibility of Vienna facing a two-front war against both Russia and Serbia (War Case R + B). This scenario, however, presented an unsolvable military dilemma. Austro-Hungarian armies were incapable of launching successful offensives against both opponents.

Habsburg strategic military planning, ostensibly flexible as a result of the increasing danger of a two-front war, designated Serbia as a secondary foe should the far more dangerous Russia intervene militarily in a Balkan conflict. This strategy, however, did not take into account Franz Conrad von Hötzendorf's (Chief of the Austro-Hungarian General Staff, 1906–1911, 1912–1917) personal obsession with Serbia. Indeed, though Russia posed a far greater military threat, Serbia endangered the all-important Habsburg prestige and standing in the Balkan Peninsula. Conrad gradually increased the allocation of military units to be deployed in the Balkans, at the cost of those to be utilized against Russia, to 40 percent of all troop units in the event of war.

The Balkan Wars revealed the Dual Monarchy's growing diplomatic isolation as Berlin at first displayed indifference to the perceived Balkan problems of Vienna. Thus, Count Leopold Berchtold, Foreign Minister following Aehrenthal's death, had no choice but to adopt a "wait and see" attitude at the commencement of the First Balkan War.

Vienna aggressively sought to preserve its Great Power, as well as its Balkan, position. This stance slowly came to mean utilizing a show of force, if necessary, in its diplomatic dealings in an effort to maintain waning prestige and to counter increasingly failed Balkan diplomatic efforts. As a result of the Balkan Wars, Turkey and Bulgaria, previously military counterweights to Serbia, were militarily neutralized. Romania, allied to the Triple Alliance since 1883 and projected to be a major military factor against Russia, increasingly inclined away from Viennese diplomatic leadership. The once-favorable Balkan military balance now tipped against Vienna and Berlin. Thus, during the winter of 1913 and early on into 1914 an atmosphere of apprehension hovered over Vienna and increased the belief that the very existence of the Dual Monar-

chy was now at stake. Its power in its "sphere of influence," the Balkans, became increasingly challenged.

Intensifying pressure to utilize the military option encouraged Viennese leaders to contemplate a military response to the escalating chronic and demoralizing South Slav situation. The use of force was deemed acceptable if it was needed to halt Serbian machinations. A new militant Habsburg attitude was rapidly forming. Both civilian and military leaders assumed a more aggressive stance. This trend produced disastrous results during the July 1914 crisis.

The role of Germany as a military ally to prevent Russian intervention in a localized Balkan military campaign became particularly important when Viennese policy was disrupted by the growth in Serbian prestige, territory, and population as a result of the Balkan Wars. The long-term results of the 1912–1913 period of cataclysmic upheaval did not bode well for Vienna. Serbia had become a potentially more powerful military power. Its ethnic brethren in the South Slavic territories made the anti-Habsburg policy of Serbia appear to be a life-or-death threat to Vienna.

The consequences of the Habsburg diplomatic moves began to materialize. For example, Romania began casting a more-covetous eye toward Transylvania. The question of maintaining loyalty to the Dual Monarchy in an age of growing nationalistic aspirations became critical to Habsburg diplomacy during 1914—a direct result of the Balkan Wars.

The three Balkan crises solidified the Viennese conviction that only forceful diplomacy, coupled with partial mobilization, threats of invasion, or the issuance of ultimatums, would be effective against a recalcitrant Serbia. Balkan policy making increasingly assumed a more-militant attitude. In just a few months the loss of prestige and self-esteem caused a shift in Habsburg diplomacy from one of caution and prudence to one of desperation, illusion, and exhaustion. Increasingly, armed force appeared to offer the only solution to the predicament of Vienna in the Balkans. This outlook set a dangerous precedent for the July 1914 crisis, as the South Slav provinces became viewed as a source of grave danger to the long-term viability of the Dual Monarchy.

In June 1914 Austria-Hungary became fixated on the more-assertive foreign policy of Russia. The following month, after the assassination of Archduke Franz Ferdinand, the militarized diplomacy of Vienna, ostensibly so successful on three occasions during the Balkan Wars, opted for war on the assumption that the situation would only worsen in time. Austria-Hungary concluded that the Russian and Serbian threats would better be dealt with sooner rather than later. A key factor in understanding the Viennese position in July 1914 is that they would not and could not launch a war against Serbia without German support vis-à-vis Russia, and that, once support had been obtained, Vienna could focus its full attention on preparing to launch a Balkan war that hopefully remained localized regardless of the circumstances.

Once all the leading figures had literally determined that there would be war against Serbia during the first days of July, the die was cast. On 5 July the Hoyos mission to Berlin to receive German backing proved to be successful. With their support secured, Berchtold took control over the next measures and deflected any interference. The Hoyos mission provided the key event that unleashed war.

The point to be emphasized is that, early in the July crisis, the decision to resolve the Serbian problem by a declaration of war emanated from Vienna. Once Germany issued its infamous "blank check" assuring the protection of Austria-Hungary against Russia, Vienna determined the timing and manner of future measures by cutting off any unwanted options.

In fact, by 7 July a major Common Ministerial Council had determined that Austria-Hungary would begin hostilities. Unanswered were the significant questions of "when" and "how." A final decision could not be reached because the powerful Hungarian prime minister István Tisza balked at the decision for war without careful diplomatic preparation. The next week was utilized to convince Tisza to join the other members in their determination to settle militarily accounts with Serbia.

A 19 July Ministerial Council meeting, now with Tisza's approval, agreed to issue purposely an unacceptable ultimatum to Serbia. The mandate, with a forty-eight-hour deadline to respond, was delivered on 23 July. Delivery of the ultimatum was delayed because of a meeting held between the French president and foreign minister with Russian leaders in St. Petersburg to prevent collusion.

The delivery of the ultimatum to Belgrade was accompanied by troubling reports reaching Vienna regarding Russian military measures. Habsburg leaders, nonetheless, continued to pursue their Balkan military campaign plans, hoping that a rapid invasion of Serbia would preclude Russian armed intervention. In addition, Viennese leaders anticipated that allied German support would keep St. Petersburg in line.

However, the partial mobilization was proclaimed on 25 July and the first mobilization day on 28 July, but the actual invasion of Serbia could not occur until August because of the terrible railroad situation (only one rail line led to the Serbian frontier). The diplomatic situation could not last that long. The result was disastrous military defeats on both fronts during the first campaigns.

By 1914 Austria-Hungary was fighting for its preservation. Its sphere of influence was reduced to the Balkans: the Dual Monarchy's days as a Great Power were over. The prolonged conflict of World War I sounded its death knell—and the conflict was initiated by the Austro-Hungarians all for it to remain a Balkan power!

–GRAYDON A. TUNSTALL,
UNIVERSITY OF SOUTH FLORIDA

Viewpoint:
No. The policy of Austria-Hungary after the assassination of Archduke Franz Ferdinand reflected a determination to maintain the Dual Monarchy's status as a great power, able and willing to act independently in defense of its own vital interests.

The policy of Austria after the Archduke's assassination reflected a determination to maintain the Dual Monarchy status as a great power able and willing to act independently in defense, however ineffectively, of its own vital interests. Austria-Hungary fell to the second rank among European powers in 1866 when it was thoroughly defeated by Prussia. The Dual Monarchy nevertheless persisted in sustaining a place at the head diplomatic table through the first six months of the Great War. Emperor Francis Joseph I, ruling longer than any other monarch in the nineteenth century, tottered about his great palaces learning little but forgetting less. He was increasingly suspicious even of any new innovation such as electric lights and was correspondingly hostile to any new ideas he feared might subvert the Empire. His chief of staff in 1914, Franz Conrad von Hötzendorf, saw himself as a worthy successor to Napoleon Bonaparte as a military strategist and filled his days drafting new contingency plans for war against Serbia and Italy—his main phobias even though Italy was an ally of Austria-Hungary, at least nominally.

Serbia in particular seemed to Conrad the major immediate threat to the integrity of the empire, and he regularly sought audience with the emperor to present new reasons necessitating war against the Balkan country he saw as the focal point for south Slav nationalist aspirations. Two conflicting nationalist ideologies were increasingly pitted against each other during the nineteenth century: Germanic *Kultur*

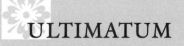

ULTIMATUM

On 22 July 1914 Austria-Hungary sent the Serbians an ultimatum that included assurances that Serbia would refrain from actions promoting the separation of provinces under Austro-Hungarian control. In addition, Serbia would be required:

1. to suppress every publication which shall incite to hatred and contempt of the Monarchy, and the general tendency of which shall be directed against the territorial integrity of the latter;

2. to proceed at once to the dissolution of the Narodna Odbrana to confiscate all of its means of propaganda, and in the same manner to proceed against the other unions and associations in Serbia which occupy themselves with propaganda against Austria-Hungary; the Royal Government will take such measures as are necessary to make sure that the dissolved associations may not continue their activities under other names or in other forms;

3. to eliminate without delay from public instruction in Serbia, everything, whether connected with the teaching corps or with the methods of teaching, that serves or may serve to nourish the propaganda against Austria-Hungary;

4. to remove from the military and administrative service in general all officers and officials who have been guilty of carrying on the propaganda against Austria-Hungary, whose names the Imperial and Royal Government reserves the right to make known to the Royal Government when communicating the material evidence now in its possession;

5. to agree to the cooperation in Serbia of the organs of the Imperial and Royal Government in the suppression of the subversive movement directed against the integrity of the Monarchy;

6. to institute a judicial inquiry against every participant in the conspiracy of the twenty-eighth of June who may be found in Serbian territory; the organs of the Imperial and Royal Government delegated for this purpose will take part in the proceedings held for this purpose;

7. to undertake with all haste the arrest of Major Voislav Tankosic and of one Milan Ciganovitch, a Serbian official, who have been compromised by the results of the inquiry;

8. by efficient measures to prevent the participation of Serbian authorities in the smuggling of weapons and explosives across the frontier; to dismiss from the service and to punish severely those members of the Frontier Service at Schabats and Losnitza who assisted the authors of the crime of Sarajevo to cross the frontier;

9. to make explanations to the Imperial and Royal Government concerning the unjustifiable utterances of high Serbian functionaries in Serbia and abroad, who, without regard for their official position, have not hesitated to express themselves in a manner hostile toward Austria-Hungary since the assassination of the twenty-eighth of June;

10. to inform the Imperial and Royal Government without delay of the execution of the measures comprised in the foregoing points.

Source: "23 July, 1914: The Austro-Hungarian Ultimatum to Serbia, English Translation," World War I Document Archive, Internet website, <http://www.lib.byu.edu/~rdh/wwi/1914/austro-hungarian-ultimatum.html>.

and Slavism. Germany, a unified country for only the past half century, was eager to prove its place as a first-ranked power not only in arms but also in every aspect of a civilized society—the arts, music, sciences, and philosophy. Accompanying this goal was a distaste for, and an atavistic fear of, the developing Slavic cultures to the east—attitudes reciprocated in Russia and the Balkans.

Austria-Hungary was caught in the middle, neither able nor willing to accept the nationalist paradigm. The Empire retained significant great-power credentials: the largest state in Europe in terms of land, not counting Russia, with a developing industrial economy and (on paper) a formidable army. Vienna was an intellectual and cultural capital of the world. Its critics described the Austro-Hungarian Empire as an anachronism among developing nation-states, founded largely on ethnic lines and depending on their inner ethnic culture to bind their social fabrics. The Habsburgs had painstakingly built their empire over 450 years, stitching together a patchwork crazy quilt of a dozen different nationalities, and even more languages, dialects, and cultural traditions. The only common denominators were the army and the emperor. The officer corps, however, identified with the empire. The rank and file proved loyal to the oaths of allegiance they swore—and to the force of habit. That loyalty was enough, in a European system that still measured the status of a state by its men under arms.

With the assassination of Crown Prince Franz Ferdinand and the identification of the killers with a terrorist organization having connections to Serbian intelligence, Conrad had the argument he needed for war against Serbia. Austria had a just cause. As much to the point, failure to act in the face of such a provocation would send an unmistakable message that the empire was as its denigrators described it: hopelessly decadent. An attack on Serbia, he argued, would not trigger a war with Russia. If it did, then Russian hostility was so great that it would only look for another excuse.

Francis Joseph I was less sanguine. At the end, however, he signed the declaration of war—some accounts say, with the phrase "also doch!" a rough Viennese–argot equivalent of "let's roll!" The phrase was apt. Even before Russia declared war, Austria-Hungary was resting the continuation of its great-power status on the ability of its army to win.

Conrad's operational plan relied on the clumsiness and slowness of Russian mobilization. He intended to take Belgrade in two weeks, then shift reserves to attack the Russian southern flank in the Polish salient. Two things went wrong, however. The Serbian army put up a more-determined and more-sophisticated fight than expected, using the broken terrain to flank Austrian attacks and eventually forcing them to retreat with losses of one hundred thousand men. Then Conrad stumbled again. Enraged by the defeat, he began to commit his reserves against Serbia— only to learn that Russian mobilization and concentration was progressing at unexpected speed. The Eastern Front was the exact opposite of the West. Instead of a cramped, crowded theater with no room for maneuver that locked armies in entrenched positions, the East allowed ample scope for moving large units. Therefore, if Conrad gave the Russians the initiative, allowing them to complete their concentrations and to choose their routes of advance, chances were excellent that his armies would be overrun in the field or trapped in the fortress systems of Lvov and Przemysl, which were unlimited vistas for maneuver. The distances, however, were also so large that the primitive air services and inefficient cavalries deployed by both armies were unable to establish enemy locations—until a division, corps, or whole field army crashed into one's own flank to great mutual surprise. Distance also meant marching up to a hundred miles into the battle zone, sending fatigued soldiers into frontal assaults, and creating problems of supply and reenforcement that became insoluble as administrative systems gridlocked. Conrad, true to his nature, abandoned his elaborately constructed prewar plans; divided his armies in the vain hope of trapping the Russians, even though he had no idea where they were or in what strength; and regarded gaps of up to seventy-five miles and little, if any, lateral communication between his subordinate armies as acceptable risks.

So they might have been—to Napoleon's *Grande Armee*, or the Army of Northern Virginia. Both armies blundered about in an intelligence fog, as mismatched forces lunging into each other with varied success. At first the Austrians were lucky, fighting Russian units while possessing a superiority of numbers. Then Conrad's Third Army ran headlong into the Russian main force, which outnumbered them up to three to one. Retreat turned into a general rout. In seventeen days of combat Conrad managed to lose one-third of his effectives. A typical loss rate was that of the Third Infantry Division of the XIV Corps—6,000 casualties out of a force of 10,000, almost all in the infantry, the cutting-edge arm. By the time the Austrian armies reached safety across the border, 100,000 of their men were dead, 220,000 were wounded, and more than 100,000 were taken prisoner. The material booty gained by the Russians included 216 cannons, 15,000 railway cars, and 100 locomotives.

From the first days Conrad stubbornly refused to coordinate with the Germans. The German senior officers, above all Erich Ludendorff and Conrad, held each other in mutual contempt. After regrouping, Conrad launched other offensive strikes in 1915 against both the Russians and the Serbs, but the guns of August were what broke the Austro-Hungarian army as an effective fighting force. The loss of its professional cadres was impossible to replace. Lives were sacrificed to makeup for the lack of tactical and operational skill. Loyalty diminished as casualties mounted. The army was the last claim of Austria to great-power status. Conrad expended it in three weeks and increasingly was forced to cede control of the war in the east to the Germans.

–JOHN WHEATLEY,
BROOKLYN CENTER, MINNESOTA

References

Ludwig Bittner and Hans Uebersberger, eds., *Österreich-Ungarns Aussenpolitik von der bosnischen Krise 1908 bis zum Kriegausbruch 1914: Diplomatische Aktenstücke des österreichisch-ungarischen Ministeriums des Aussern,* nine volumes (Vienna: Österreichischer Bundesverlag, 1930).

Fritz Fellner, "Die 'Mission Hoyos,'" in *Deutschlands Sonderung von Europa, 1862–1945,* edited by Wilhelm Alff (Frankfurt & New York: Peter Lang, 1984).

Imanuel Geiss, ed., *July 1914: The Outbreak of the First World War; Selected Documents,* translated by Henry Meyric Hughes and Geiss (London: Batsford, 1967).

Hugo Hantsch, *Leopold Graf Berchtold: Grandseigneur und Staatsman,* two volumes (Graz: Verlag Styria, 1963).

Conrad von Hötzendorf, *Aus Meiner Dienstzeit, 1908–1918,* five volumes (Vienna: Rikola Verlag, 1921–1925).

John Leslie, "The Antecedents of Austria-Hungary's War Aims," in *Wiener Beiträge zur Geschichte der Neuzeit,* 20 (1993).

Leslie, "Österreich-Ungarn vor dem Kriegsausbruch. Der Ballhausplatz in Wien im Juli 1914 aus der Sicht eines österreichisch-ungarischen Diplomaten," in *Deutschland und Europa in der Neuzeit: Festschrift für Karl Otmar Freiherr von Aretin zum 65. Geburtstag,* edited by Ralph Melville and others (Wiesbaden: F. Steiner Verlag, 1988).

Manfred Rauchensteiner, *Der Tod des Doppeladlers. Österreich-Ungarn und der Erste Wel,tkrieg* (Graz: Verlag Styria, 1993).

Gunther E. Rothenberg, *The Army of Francis Joseph* (West Lafayette, Ind.: Purdue University Press, 1976).

Graydon A. Tunstall Jr., *Planning for War Against Russia and Serbia: Austro-Hungarian and German Military Strategies, 1871–1914* (Boulder, Colo.: Social Science Monographs; New York: Columbia University Press, 1993).

Samuel R. Williamson Jr., *Austria-Hungary and the First World War* (Houndmills, Basingstoke, Hampshire: Macmillan, 1991).

AUSTRIA-HUNGARY

Did the integration of tanks in the British Expeditionary Force (BEF) contribute to the Allied victory?

Viewpoint: Yes. Armor was the central element of British Expeditionary Force (BEF) tactics in the final offensives of 1918.

Viewpoint: No. In the final Allied offensives of 1918 mechanical warfare and tanks were less significant to victory than traditional technologies, especially artillery.

The distinguishing characteristic of World War I in general, and the Western Front in particular, was that firepower so dominated the battlefield that it prevented the attacker from gaining a favorable decision. In all armies the corresponding question was how to reestablish the potential of the offensive. In achieving that goal, the British Expeditionary Force (BEF) reigned supreme. The British army fought its war according to what it considered universal principles, which were never formalized as a doctrine. Instead they emerged from an ethos, a unifying philosophy that structured the military decision-making process at all levels and provided a system for interpreting the problems of combat.

The absence of a war-fighting doctrine as such was not prima facie evidence of anti-intellectualism or lack of imagination. An army such as that of Britain, with widely different theaters of operation and based on a familial regimental system, was likely to tear itself apart before it agreed on a generally applicable doctrine. In any army, however, doctrine conforms to ethos. The British ethos of war was established by the relationship of the army to the British cultural, social, and political order. It was sustained and transmitted by an officer corps, whose professional identity was shaped by its place in society; it was an officer corps that never became self-referencing to the degree of its continental counterparts. It began by insisting on decisive battles won by offensive action in a series of phases, each building on its predecessors. It regarded decision as a function of superior firepower, able to counter the advantages modern weapons gave to the defense, and it understood morale was of primary importance.

Those basic concepts persisted throughout the Great War. Flexibility is overrated as a military virtue by academicians and armchair generals alike. There is no guarantee that radical modification of the ethos by which a nation and an army wage war will result in success. The BEF was able to integrate new techniques, new organizations, and new tactics into a consistent, coherent general concept. The notion of a "learning curve," a period in which the BEF traded lives for know-how, is misleading. There was no easy way to break the deadlock of the trenches. Every army went through a process of trial and error; the British were simply more conscious of their failures in the context of their ethos.

From 1915 to 1918 the history of the BEF is one of constant, incremental adaptation. Its artillery command and fire control, initially decentralized to divisions, came to be concentrated at corps level. Machine guns became not merely a direct support but a barrage weapon, with their own separate corps identity. Gas shells made up as high as 50 percent of some artillery concentrations; smoke was no less important. Tanks were as useful for crushing barbed wire and boosting morale as for their intrinsic firepower and mobility—both limited. Armor was most effective integrated with artillery and aircraft into a support framework for infantry that was itself by 1918 a combined-arms force of rifles, light machine guns, hand and rifle grenades, and mortars organized in mutually supporting combat teams able to advance independently under many circumstances. The eventual results were the semi-mobile managed battles, conducted at corps level, that broke the spine and the spirit of the German army in the final months of 1918.

Viewpoint:
Yes. Armor was the central element of British Expeditionary Force (BEF) tactics in the final offensives of 1918.

In July 1917 the British Expeditionary Force (BEF) under General Douglas Haig launched yet another "big push" against the German lines opposite Ypres. This so-called Third Battle of Ypres was an unmitigated disaster. Apparently believing that his huge artillery preparations for the offensive on the Somme in July 1916 had been inadequate, Haig opened Third Ypres with an even longer and heavier bombardment, the greatest in all of World War I for the British. It extended thirteen days, involved 3,168 guns, and devoured 4,300,000 shells: more than 100,000 tons of high explosives in all. Its principal effect was to bring up so much groundwater in low-lying Flanders that the entire area turned into a morass of thick, glutinous mud. In the last stage of the fighting, a Canadian attack on the village of Passchendaele, the assault troops had to advance in hip-deep mud, dodging German machine-gun fire as they went. Falling off the primitive duckboard paths laid down across the mud meant an unlikely end for a soldier involved in a land battle: drowning. It was, perhaps, the most disgusting fighting of the war—although the connoisseur of World War I battles has many from which to choose. From July to November the British suffered nearly 400,000 casualties to secure another pockmarked piece of nowhere. Haig regarded Third Ypres as a victory for one simple reason, however: as in any artillery-dominated battle of attrition, losses among the German defenders were also heavy, only slightly less than his own.

Was this strategy any way to win a war? Whether a British staff officer visiting the battlefield really did break into tears and cry out, "My God, did we send men to advance in that?" no one who reads accounts of the fighting can fail to be moved. One might wish to evaluate Haig's career in toto; however, it is likely that the word "Passchendaele" will forevermore find a place in his encyclopedia entry, along with "unimaginative" and perhaps even "incompetent."

The problem went beyond any one commander, however. During the trench years the greatest military minds in the western world failed to solve the deadlock of trench, wire, and machine gun. Lengthening the bombardment was just one attempted solution. Others included poison gas, the *Flammenwerfer* (flamethrower), and what was still called the "aeroplane." Taken together, all these new technologies literally revolutionized the face of warfare. What they did not do was solve the problem that they were supposed to solve. Despite all the innovations, the front remained frozen in the deadly embrace of the machine gun and the artillery.

Yet, even before Passchendaele stumbled to its disastrous conclusion, trench warfare had already become obsolete, a form of battle belonging to a different and bygone era. That horrible year of 1917 was also a year of rebirth, ending with two dramatic developments that finally returned mobility to the battlefield. In September a German offensive in the east easily crashed through the Russian lines in front of Riga and seized that major city. Then in October an Austro-German offensive at Caporetto shredded the Italian line along the Isonzo river, inflicting eight hundred thousand casualties on an army of two million and almost knocking Italy out of the war with a single blow. These two battles marked the debut of a new tactical approach worked out by the German army. The term most often used in the West to describe it, "infiltration tactics," is a misnomer. The Germans used the term *Stosstrupp* (shocktroop or stormtroop) tactics.

The second great event of 1917 was the British attack at Cambrai. Here the British used a newly developed weapon, variously called the "landship" or "armored machine gun destroyer." Produced in great secrecy, it eventually came to be known as the "tank" for security reasons. The tank was an armored vehicle mounted on caterpillar tracks, able to cross over the roughest terrain or trench. It was designed to cross no-man's-land, destroy the enemy's wire and machine guns, and open a path for the infantry. It was not intended for long-range, independent operations and, indeed, with a top speed of four miles per hour, that was not likely to happen. By 1917 the British had a "Tank Corps" of three brigades, each of which consisted of three battalions. The

vehicles were a mixture of two types: the "Male," equipped with a six-pound gun, and the "Female," armed with machine guns, intended to protect the male from enemy infantry.

The commander of the corps was Brigadier Hugh Elles, a smart, daring, and extremely charismatic soldier. It was his brilliant but abrasive chief of staff, however, who would become the man most closely associated with the rise and employment of British armor: Lieutenant Colonel John Frederick Charles Fuller. A classic example of a "true believer," Fuller drew up a plan in September 1917 for a surprise offensive in the Cambrai sector by a massed formation of tanks. While tanks had already been in action, they had appeared only in small numbers and had failed to make much of an impact. Fuller wanted something bigger, more dramatic: an operation that would establish the tank as the dominant force on the battlefield.

The battle of Cambrai opened at 6:20 A.M. on 20 November 1917. Without any preparatory bombardment, a force of nearly four hundred tanks came up out of the mist, lumbering toward the German lines. Leading the first great armored assault in history was the dashing Elles himself, in his personal tank *Hilda*, operating "unbuttoned," with his head sticking up out of the hatch for better visibility. Surprise was almost total. The German defenders were stunned. There seemed to be hundreds, perhaps thousands, of tanks, in lines kilometers long! Face to face with this almost inconceivable

armored onslaught, they did what any troops of the day would have done: they threw down their weapons and surrendered or tried to flee or hid themselves in gullies or shell craters. The tanks crossed the wire that had proven so invulnerable to shell fire in the past. As the lead tanks approached the first trench, raking it with fire, the main body of tanks dropped fascines (bundles of wood, sticks, and straw) into it, making an impromptu bridge over which they could cross. They did the same over the second and third trench lines. The entire force passed the enemy's outpost line within nine minutes of the onset of the attack; within the first hour the tanks had torn a hole six miles wide and three miles deep in the Hindenburg Line. To Fuller, messages from the observation post were "more like a railway timetable than a series of battle reports."

Yet, by the next day, the tanks had shot their bolt. The British had no armored reserve. With the German line shattered and a second blow all that was needed to break clear through into open country, the British could launch only limited strikes involving forty tanks here, fifty there. The mechanical unreliability of the tank accounted for far more losses than German fire. As was typical of the day, battlefield command and control was terrible, a situation exacerbated by the much faster pace of the operation. There were at times great gaps in the German line that could have been penetrated, such as that between Bourlon Wood and the village of Fontaine on the night

A British tank in action on the Western Front, circa 1917

(postcard in scrapbook, Joseph M. Bruccoli Great War Collection, Thomas Cooper Library, University of South Carolina)

BEF TECHNOLOGY

of 21 November. Recognizing those opportunities, however, and exploiting them in time proved to be impossible. Finally German reinforcements began pouring into the sector. By 27 November the front had solidified. The British withdrew their tanks and put up barbed wire in front of their new positions.

The spring and early summer of 1918 found the Allies back on the defensive, barely weathering the furious German onslaught known as the Ludendorff offensives. But the inability of the German army to land the knockout blow, coupled with long advances that had stretched its supply chain and manpower to the limit, made it ripe for a counterblow. It began at Soissons, where the French Tenth Army under General Charles Mangin struck the Germans hard, an attack once again spearheaded by some four hundred tanks. The French overran the large German salient seized in General Erich Ludendorff's third offensive (Operation Blücher) and took thousands of prisoners. It was the turning point of the war, the beginning of a nonstop Allied offensive that eventually ground the German army into powder.

On 8 August the British Fourth Army under General Henry Rawlinson launched a massive counteroffensive of its own near Amiens. In the lead were the two most effective shock forces in the Allied camp, the Canadian and Australian corps. Rawlinson had the entire Tank Corps at his disposal, 420 machines in all. Most of them, more than 300, were tanks of the new Mark V design. It was the first heavy tank that could be driven by one man, with a more powerful engine and greater obstacle-crossing ability than older models. There were also 96 Medium A models, or "Whippets," three-man tanks with a top speed of eight miles per hour and an impressive radius of eighty miles. Its mission was to exploit the breach created by its heavier counterparts. Counting supply tanks and gun carriers, the total number of armored vehicles at Amiens was close to 600. More than 500 aircraft also took part. Opposing this formidable array of men and machines were seven under-strength German divisions exhausted by the previous months of fighting.

At 4:20 A.M. the tanks moved out behind a creeping barrage, covered by dark and mist, and headed for the German lines. Again surprise was almost total, and this time thousands of terrified German infantry threw up their hands and surrendered en masse. That first day the tanks tore a great gash some eleven miles wide in the German lines. The German 225th Division reported that, "The entire divisional artillery was lost; of the front line and support battalions practically nothing had come back; and the resting battalions thrown in piecemeal had either been

thrown back or had not got into action at all." Command and control on the German side broke down quickly, a combination of the speed of the Whippets and the low visibility. According to General Paul von Hindenburg, "the thick mist made supervision and control very difficult." German gunners fired into the fog whenever they heard the sound of motors and the rattle of gears, and then came under attack from a completely different direction. The result was a total loss of nerve on the part of the German defenders. "The wildest rumors began to spread in our lines," Hindenburg later wrote.

> It was said that masses of English cavalry were already far in rear of the foremost German infantry positions. Some of the men lost their nerve, left position from which they had only just beaten off strong enemy attacks, and tried to get in touch with the rear again. Imagination conjured up all kinds of phantoms and translated them into real dangers.

No place seemed safe, a lesson hammered home by the aerial bombardment on various rail junctions far behind the lines, such as Péronne.

While panic spread among the defenders, the units that had penetrated the line were having a field day. The exploits of the 17th Tank-Armoured Car Battalion, under Colonel E. J. Carter, were a sign of the new times. Moving out of Villers-Bretonneux and driving deep into the German position, Carter overran a corps headquarters, throwing the staff troops, into a panic. After shooting up a transport column, he overran another corps headquarters. He then proceeded to Proyart and Chuignolles, where his unit surprised German troops at dinner, scattering them. Ordering his cars westward, back towards the start line, he arrived just in time to round up thousands of fleeing men who had been driven from their trenches by the Australians.

That first day the Allies advanced eight miles, taking twelve thousand prisoners and capturing four hundred guns. Over the next three days the Fourth Army took forty thousand German prisoners. Although the Germans managed to reform their lines, their morale had been shattered, and their ability to undertake offensive operations was gone for good. Ludendorff himself called 8 August a "black day" for the German army. "Troops allowed themselves to be surprised . . . and lost all cohesion when the tanks suddenly appeared behind them," he wrote. Fuller called Amiens "the strategical end of the war, a second Waterloo; the rest was minor tactics."

The rest of the war in the West featured three months of slow, but steady, mobile warfare. The Allies grabbed the faltering Germans by the throat, holding them in place with a series of powerful frontal blows, and forced them to shuffle their reserves around until they had no reserves left to shuffle. While the Germans righted themselves after Amiens, turning their rout into an ordinary retreat, they could no longer hope to turn the tide of battle. The Supreme Allied Commander, Marshal Ferdinand Foch, skillfully kept up the pressure, and by 9 September the Allies had rolled the Germans out of all the territorial gains of their spring offensives. All the attacks were essentially the same, unsubtle hammer-like blows, frontal attacks spearheaded by tanks and aircraft. Although they continued to resist Allied infantry attacks, German soldiers often surrendered to tanks without a shot. One office wrote that "their sense of duty is sufficient to make them fight against infantry, but when tanks appear many feel they are justified in surrendering." In his novel *All Quiet on the Western Front* (1929), Erich Maria Remarque painted an unforgettable picture of the tanks at war:

> Armored they come rolling on in long lines, more than anything else embody for us the horror of war. We do not see the guns that bombard us; the attacking lines of the enemy infantry are men like ourselves; but these tanks are machines, their caterpillars run on as endless as the war, they are annihilation, they roll without falling into the craters, and climb up again without stopping, a fleet of roaring, smoke-belching armor-clads, invulnerable steel beasts squashing the dead and the wounded.

The often-repeated claim of German General A. W. H. von Zwehl, "It was not the genius of Marshal Foch that defeated us, but General Tank," is an exaggeration, but tanks played a central role in the crucial Allied victories of 1918. They were the spearhead at Soissons, Amiens, and the drive across northern France in the fall. Though the naval blockade had worn down German resistance and weakened the enemy's will to fight to the point where an Amiens was possible, the tank proved essential in breaking the tactical deadlock of trench and barbed wire that had seemed so hopeless as recently as 1917.

Tanks were not yet the wonder weapons they would become in 1939. Mechanical breakdowns bedeviled them throughout the fighting. Slow and cumbrous, they were not capable of long-range penetrations of enemy territory. Rather, they were tactical weapons, useful in helping friendly infantry cross the "last two hundred meters," that stretch of fire-swept ground that had frustrated so many assaults from 1915 to 1917. And even in that limited sense, they were only one BEF weapon among many. The string of successful British attacks from Amiens to the end of the war was the achievement of combined arms, not the tanks alone. In fact a greatly improved British army beat the Germans

that fall. Its tactical refinements included a greatly superior artillery, employing extremely heavy creeping barrages and effective counterbattery techniques; an aggressive Royal Air Force (RAF), applying both the ground support and interdiction roles; and better planning, which focused on attacks with limited objectives rather than grandiose plans of breakthrough and exploitation to Berlin.

Leading the way, however, were the tanks. Historians have tended recently to stress their weaknesses, their high loss rates, and their mechanical unreliability by the second or third day of an attack. They usually paid for themselves on the first day, however, by punching a hole through the German line in the initial stages of the assault and clearing a path for limited maneuver. Without the tanks, these attacks would not even have made it to the second or third day. German testimony upon this point, usually ignored in the host of modern books on the BEF in 1918, is virtually unanimous. The first day at Amiens cracked open the German defensive position in the West and also broke the morale of the German high command. The Germans never did manage to repair either one.

In evaluating the performance of the tank during World War I, one last point should be called to mind. Unlike other innovations of the war, the tank was completely new technology. It is one thing to build a farm tractor; no one shoots at those. Tanks had not existed anywhere in 1914 outside of a few fertile imaginations and science-fiction stories. Less than four years later, war without them had become virtually inconceivable. Mere months separate Passchendaele from Amiens, but in fact a new era had begun. To many, the tank was not only a key weapon of the present, but *the* weapon of the future. The history of warfare knows no comparable development in such a short period of time.

–ROBERT M. CITINO,
EASTERN MICHIGAN UNIVERSITY

Viewpoint:
No. In the final Allied offensives of 1918 mechanical warfare and tanks were less significant to victory than traditional technologies, especially artillery.

After Erich Friedrich Wilhelm Ludendorff's offensive had run its course late in the spring of 1918, Allied leaders debated the best approach to counterattack the German army. Mechanized warfare appeared to hold considerable promise.

A LATE ARRIVAL

A British soldier, Charles Cole, describes the use of a tank at the Battle of the Somme (1 July–19 November 1916):

Something was brought near to the reserve trench, camouflaged with a big sheet. We didn't know what it was and were very curious and the Captain got us all out on parade. He said, "You're wondering what this is. Well, it's a tank," and he took the covers off and that was the very first tank. He explained what the capabilities were. We was due to make an attack on the Germans in forty-eight hours from the time he showed us, and what we had to do when we made the attack at Zero Hour was just to wait for the tank to go by us and all we had to do was mop up, consolidate our trench.

Well, we were at the parapets, waiting to go over and waiting for the tank. We heard the *chunk, chunk, chunk,* then silence! The tank never came. It was split-second timing, we couldn't wait for it, we had to go over the top. Well, we went over the top and we got cut to pieces because the plan had failed. Eventually, the tank got going and went past us. The Germans ran for their lives—couldn't make out what was firing at them. We didn't know anything at all about tanks, *they* didn't know anything at all about tanks, so the tank went on, knocked brick walls, houses down, did what it was supposed to have done—but too late! We lost thousands and thousands and what was left of us Coldstreams, we didn't know what to do, so we got into shell holes and bits of wall where there was cover.

Source: *Lyn MacDonald, ed.,* 1914–1918: Voices and Images of the Great War *(London: Michael Joseph, 1988), p. 168.*

Tanks had shown their usefulness at Cambrai in November 1917, and by the early summer of 1918 the Allies had developed improved models. At Amiens on 8 August 1918, the so-called Black Day of the German army, 430 Allied tanks tore a twenty-mile hole in German lines. The speed and violence of this assault persuaded Ludendorff that Germany had lost the war. Impressed and intimidated by Mark V medium tanks and fast (eight miles per hour) Whippet light tanks, Ludendorff envisioned nightmare scenarios of hordes of faster and more powerful Allied tanks piercing German lines in the months ahead.

Yet, impressions, although powerful, did not in fact constitute reality. More and faster tanks and increasing mechanization did not bedevil Germany in the last months of the war. Rather, Allied employment of traditional technologies, particularly artillery and machine guns, was more effective in reducing German units to unbearable limits. In the summer and fall of 1918 outnumbered, outgunned, and demoralized German infantry units collapsed under the weight of fresher Allied soldiers who had learned painful lessons in getting the most out of traditional weaponry.

Allied production figures bear out this conclusion. From 1917 to 1918 the United Kingdom produced 2,469 tanks—a considerable achievement, given that only 150 were produced in the first three years of the war. In the same two-year period, however, the United Kingdom produced more than 200,000 machine guns and 13,000 artillery pieces. After three years experience of dealing death, the warring nations built technologies that they knew worked—that they knew to be efficient and effective force multipliers.

Traditional technologies such as machine guns and artillery were in part more effective because doctrine for these technologies had been honed in a Darwinian process. In the struggle for survival on the Western Front, the fittest ideas and weapons survived; faulty ones were winnowed out. Tanks held promise, but the Allies confined them to doctrinal niches that constrained their adaptive skills. Restricted primarily to infantry support roles, tanks also lacked an institutional support structure and high-ranking proponents. Largely ignoring the ambitious proposals of tank enthusiasts such as Giffard le Quesne Martel and J. F. C. Fuller, senior Allied leaders (Douglas Haig most notoriously) continued in 1918 to envision horse cavalry, not tanks, as the combat arm of exploitation par excellence.

Weapons were only as effective as the set of ideas and techniques that propelled them. Excepting visionaries such as Martel and Fuller, Allied ideas and techniques for the employment of tanks remained immature. Indeed, tanks actually exacerbated one of the chief tactical problems of World War I: maintaining effective command and control. With their interiors hot, cramped, dark, noisy, and lacking radios, tank units could not coordinate their battlefield movements and usually proceeded at the pace of infantry in an attempt to maintain cohesion between combat arms. Artillerymen complained that wayward tanks ran over telephone lines, cutting communication between infantry and supporting artillery. Tanks often had to resort to carrier pigeons to communicate with headquarters, hardly an ideal way to promote tactical flexibility or decisive decision making.

Ultimately, it was their mechanical unreliability, limited cross-country capability, lack of speed, and severe logistical demands that restricted tanks to peripheral roles. Although 430 tanks launched effective attacks at Amiens on 8 August 1918, only 155 were available to renew the attack the next day. In exceptional circumstances—favorable terrain, adequate time and rolling stock to concentrate them and their supplies, and sufficient artillery support—tank attacks could be effective, as at Hamel in July and at Amiens. Even at Amiens, however, tanks were less decisive than the 2,000 guns and howitzers that neutralized their German counterparts and provided an umbrella of steel to protect both infantry and tanks. Furthermore, as David J. Childs has noted in *A Peripheral Weapon?: The Production and Employment of British Tanks in the First World War* (1999), mass tank attacks were "confined to operations in the immediate locality of standard gauge railheads," and shortages of spare parts, as well as the difficulty of salvage and of maintaining petrol supply, made repeat attacks impractical. Tanks, Childs concludes, remained "a relatively modest performer on the battlefield, even in late 1918."

What won the war for the Allies was not tank superiority but artillery superiority, both in numbers of guns and improved techniques in employing them. Because of improved calibration techniques, field survey, flash spotting, sound ranging, and aerial photography, Allied artillery by 1918 engaged in effective counterbattery and suppression fire against their German counterparts without having to surrender the element of surprise through preregistration of the guns. Short, intense, and accurate fire replaced the long and often inaccurate barrages of the past. In the closing months of the war Allied attackers could count on local artillery superiority and well-timed creeping barrages that kept German forces off balance and demoralized. It was no idle boast when British prime minister David Lloyd George declared: "We will put the guns wheel to wheel and pound home the lessons of democracy."

Massive and decisive Allied artillery superiority was prominently on display in the attack of the British Fourth Army on the Hindenburg Line on 28–29 September 1918. In twenty-four hours 1,637 guns fired 945,052 rounds, including 30,000 mustard gas shells, against German positions. Even the staunchest German defenders blanched under the weight, accuracy, and intensity of the Allied barrage. To a large extent, Allied artillery conquered the German positions, and heavily armed infantry advanced and occupied. Quite rightly did H. G. Wells conclude in 1916 that "Artillery is now the most essential instrument of war," an observation that remained true until Armistice Day.

Also telling were superior numbers of infantry and greater emphasis on infantry firepower support using machine guns, including the heavy Vickers and the American-designed Lewis light machine gun. Artillery and Vickers machine gun fire were often combined in "hurricane" barrages of great intensity and effectiveness. In his classic account of infantry warfare on the Western Front, *The War the Infantry Knew 1914–1919* (1938), James Churchill Dunn described one of these barrages in July 1918:

> At 11 o'clock, with a sudden terrific uproar, a hurricane bombardment and an intense overhead machine-gun fire, perfectly timed, fell on Hamel. The Battalion rose to its feet and started. "Hamel was a mass of red flames and flashes, and one began to feel a tremendous exultation." After C Company got off the tapes the C.O. and his runner were met in Nomansland. His remark, "You'll have to go into the village for your prisoners; I've been down to have a look, and there aren't any outside the wire," acted as a magnificent tonic, and sent the men forward lightheartedly.

Precisely because artillery and machine guns, and not tanks, were decisive in the final months of the war, the tactical lessons of 1918 proved ambiguous. What had won the war for the Allies in 1918 was a massive advantage in artillery, a growing numerical edge in infantry, the constant shifting of assault fronts by Supreme Allied Commander Marshal Ferdinand Foch, and the resulting deterioration of the German army. In the interwar period the Allies drew perfectly reasonable conclusions that artillery remained the king of battle and infantry the queen. In French and British interwar doctrine, tanks became pawns that attended to the queen—stiffening her resolve and magnifying her power but not operating independently of her. This doctrine drove the technology of French tanks in the 1930s. Lacking radios and with one-man turrets, French tanks were best suited for infantry support and were parceled out in dribs and drabs. Similarly, British "infantry" tanks, such as the Matilda, were heavily armored but slow and undergunned.

By way of contrast, German interwar armored doctrine showed that the vanquished are often more open to innovation than victors. Psychologically scarred by Allied tanks in 1918 and constrained by a Versailles Treaty that ironically reinforced a traditional emphasis on front-loaded, quick, and decisive victories through envelopment, the Germans built panzer divisions that brought Fuller's ideas to fruition. The emphasis on dynamism, technology, and offensive spirit conformed well to Nazi ideology. After Adolf Hitler's rise to power in 1933, moreover, the German army expanded so rapidly that there was little institutional opposition to the panzers since traditional combat arms were getting healthy slices of the fiscal pie. Once again, doctrine drove technology, as the Germans developed tanks with radios and roomy turrets that enhanced crew coordination and intertank communication. What tanks could not do in 1918 in Allied hands they did in German hands in 1940: prove decisive as battle-winning weapons in Western Europe.

–WILLIAM J. ASTORE,
U.S. AIR FORCE ACADEMY

References

Shelford Bidwell and Dominick Graham, *Fire-Power: British Army Weapons and Theories of War, 1904–1945* (London & Boston: Allen & Unwin, 1982).

Brian Bond and Nigel Cave, eds., *Haig, A Reappraisal 70 Years On* (London: Leo Cooper, 1999).

David J. Childs, *A Peripheral Weapon?: The Production and Employment of British Tanks in the First World War* (Westport, Conn.: Greenwood Press, 1999).

Robert M. Citino, *Armored Forces: History and Sourcebook* (Westport, Conn.: Greenwood Press, 1994).

James Churchill Dunn, *The War the Infantry Knew, 1914–1919: A Chronicle of Service in France and Belgium with the Second Battalion, His Majesty's Twenty-third Foot, the Royal Welch Fusiliers: Founded on Personal Records, Recollections and Reflections* (London: P.S. King, 1938).

Paddy Griffith, *Battle Tactics of the Western Front: The British Army's Art of Attack, 1916–1918* (New Haven: Yale University Press, 1994).

J. P. Harris and Niall Barr, *Amiens to the Armistice: The BEF in the Hundred Days' Campaign, 8 August–11 November 1918* (London & Washington: Brassey's, 1998).

Hubert C. Johnson, *Breakthrough! Tactics, Technology, and the Search for Victory on the Western Front in World War I* (Novato, Cal.: Presidio Press, 1994).

Paul Kennedy, *The Rise and Fall of the Great Powers: Economic Change and Military Conflict from 1500 to 2000* (New York: Random House, 1987).

Rod Paschall, *The Defeat of Imperial Germany, 1917–1918* (Chapel Hill, N.C.: Algonquin, 1989).

Robin Prior and Trevor Wilson, *Passchendaele: The Untold Story* (New Haven: Yale University Press, 1996).

A. J. Smithers, *A New Excalibur: The Development of the Tank, 1909–1939* (London: Leo Cooper in association with Secker & Warburg, 1986).

Tim Travers, "Could the Tanks of 1918 have Been War-Winners for the British Expeditionary Force?" *Journal of Contemporary History,* 27 (July 1992): 389–405.

Travers, "The Evolution of British Strategy and Tactics on the Western Front in 1918: GHQ, Manpower, and Technology," *Journal of Military History,* 54 (April 1990): 173–200.

Travers, *How the War Was Won: Command and Technology in the British Army on the Western Front, 1917–1918* (London & New York: Routledge, 1992).

Travers, *The Killing Ground: The British Army, the Western Front, and the Emergence of Modern Warfare, 1900–1918* (London & Boston: Allen & Unwin, 1987).

H. G. Wells, *Italy, France and Britain at War* (New York: Macmillan, 1917).

Wilson, *The Myriad Faces of War: Britain and the Great War, 1914–1918* (Cambridge: Polity Press, 1986; Oxford & New York: Blackwell, 1986).

COMBAT EXPERIENCE

Did blood lust prolong the war?

Viewpoint: Yes. The blood lust exhibited by frontline soldiers throughout the conflict stopped only with the collapse of the German war effort.

Viewpoint: No. The ordinary frontline soldier was no more inclined to act aggressively against the enemy than to adopt a "live and let live" approach toward him.

In literature and history the Great War is generally presented as a tragic calamity for the men who fought it. The victimization of the frontline soldier, expressed in works such as Henri Barbusse's *Under Fire: The Story of a Squad* (1917) and Erich Maria Remarque's *All Quiet on the Western Front* (1929) became a trope for European societies as a whole: from war to the Great Depression, totalitarianism, genocide, and another world war. The image of young men marching away, flowers in their buttonholes and songs on their lips, only to die in the mud and on the barbed wire of the Western Front, is used to mythologize polar images: the old against the young, capitalism against the proletariat, and the West against the rest of humanity.

An alternate perspective, developed by recent research in social history, depicts the World War I soldier as a rational actor. He fought for definable reasons: to expel invaders from France or to safeguard Germany from aggressors. He sought to mitigate and control the conditions of his daily life. Far from being isolated from the civilian world, soldiers transplanted cultures of home whenever possible: sports, entertainments, and newspapers. Their compliance with the military systems depended heavily on the "cultures of competence" established by those systems: the ability to deliver mail and food, as well as to provide medical care and furloughs. At the front, long stretches of time and space were characterized by "live and let live" systems—ad hoc mutual agreements not to do certain things and to regard breaches of the informal local covenants as exceptions to the rule. Even in combat, soldiers "negotiated" their "working conditions" by ceasing to obey orders when those orders no longer seemed to be useful. While official reports might speak of "fighting to the last man," units that were isolated surrendered once their ammunition and water was exhausted—or even earlier, if prospects for relief seemed nonexistent. Attacks stalled when enough men balanced probable risk against probable outcome.

Some soldiers in all armies, moreover, enjoyed the experience of combat, even of killing whether in a heroic vitalist, proto-existentialist sense such as German soldier Ernst Jünger, author of *The Storm of Steel: From the Diary of a German Storm-Troop Officer on the Western Front* (1929); from pleasure in breaking civilian taboos against violence and destruction; or to settle scores for dead friends. Since World War I units as a rule spent much time out of the line, or in quiet sectors, these and similar motivations could be sustained and renewed more readily than under the conditions of constant engagement familiar in World War II. Soldiers' identities and motivations, in short, are by no means as limited as conventional wisdom suggests.

Viewpoint:
Yes. The blood lust exhibited by frontline soldiers throughout the conflict stopped only with the collapse of the German war effort.

For battle to take place over a sustained period there must be, at least to some extent, a will for combat, both individually and societally. At times that will can be filled with a fanaticism hard for those outside one's societal experiences to understand, as with the kamikaze pilots attacking the American fleet off Okinawa (1945) being a classic example. It can be an act of despair, such as the futile last stands of German SS (*Schutzstaffeln*) units on the Eastern Front in 1945, or an act of religious fervor, such as that of Iranian troops charging Iraqi fortified lines in 1981. It can even be motivated by fervent belief in "The Cause," and a shared acceptance that battle is the ultimate test of manhood, concepts that drove Confederate troops forward during the American Civil War at Pickett's Charge (1863) and Franklin (1864).

If a society does not offer significant support for a war effort, eventually the will to do battle disintegrates. Two modern examples of failure of societal belief are the French debacle of 1940 and the final two years of the American ground effort in the Vietnam War (ending in 1975). Troops heading to the front were exhorted to keep their heads down and not get killed in a futile cause. Thus the sons of Verdun (1916) and the sons of Iwo Jima (1945) stayed low, avoided contact, and, in the former case, surrendered in droves.

Usually the key motivators for a society to encourage fanatical combat are religion, ideology, race, or the belief that the very survival of the nation is at stake. World War I was not motivated by any of these key issues, and yet, it became the deadliest war in history for frontline troops. That is the curious aspect of this struggle, for it lacked the traditional motivators usually required to create mass slaughter. Religion played little part in it other than as a tool to boost morale; racial issues were not significant, except perhaps on the Middle Eastern Front; and no society was literally fighting to save itself from annihilation or to preserve an ideology, such as would be seen on the Russian front from 1941 to 1945.

World War I was a new type of war, one created by modern, literate, industrial societies that only months before believed that the age of science would create global harmony and did not perceive how these same tools could be perverted to the creation of mass slaughter. Few truly grasped just how deadly a technologically based war could be, especially when the combatants were equally matched in terms of industrial output and basic resources such as coal, iron, and human blood.

Students by the tens of thousands from all sides who mingled freely in that summer of 1914, at cafés in Paris, Venice, Prague, and Geneva, only weeks later would be primed to kill each other without remorse. The profound shock created by more than a million casualties in the first two months of battle triggered a blood frenzy on both sides. What was truly remarkable to the generations that came after the Great War is the almost instant dehumanization and demonization of the foe, using the new mass media of print, photography, posters, and film that became the tools of state-engineered propaganda.

Even today it is frightful to see how quickly the cultural values changed across Europe, both internally and in relationship to belligerent powers. Boys who had been urged to play the game fairly were now cheered on to learn the fine art of sneaking up on an opponent in the dark in order to cut his throat. The cultured German was now the despised barbarian, an image that lingers even to this day, from a famous poster that depicted an ape-like beast in German uniform dragging a ten-year-old child off to be raped. An allegedly intelligent citizenry was eager to embrace the latest atrocities describing the rape of nuns, the burning alive of children, and the murder of nurses—stories that were cynically turned out by the propaganda organs of the state.

No punishment was deemed too cruel for the barbarians. The use of poison gas was applauded, and serious suggestions were entertained that when victory was won, the male population of the losing side should be castrated to end the vicious breed forever. Theories of Social Darwinism were even brought into play: some argued that the war was Nature's way of proving the superiority of one nation over another, as well as demonstrating individual prowess. Through a perverse logic it was therefore reasoned that war was in fact a healthy process, a purging of weaker blood so that a superior race would emerge. Those who won would thus earn the honor and pleasure of repopulating Europe. It was a moral descent back into the Dark Ages, created by modern techniques of propaganda, cheered on wildly by the mobs on both sides. It revealed a disturbing darkness within the human soul, made even more perverted by the eager willingness of all to call upon a Christian God for victory and the crushing of their opponents.

Society thus primed its young men to the slaughter, raising to heroic martyrdom those who died at the perfidious hands of swine, while in the next breath calling upon the wholesale and pitiless slaughter of the murderers on the other side. The few saner voices who tried to moderate this mad passion were howled down as traitors. Social historians might well find clear connections between the mentality of 1914, the madness of the witch frenzy of the seventeenth century, and the anti-Semitic hysteria that gripped Europe during the Black Death (1347–1351). Thus was the key societal step taken for the mutual slaughter in the trenches of France, Belgium, Italy, and the Eastern Front.

The vast gulf between basic training and the reality of the front was never so clear-cut as it was in World War I. Men were trained in close-order drill as if preparing for Napoleonic assaults. They were taught to go forward in human waves, indoctrinated that it was cold steel and the élan of the man behind the bayonet that would create victory. Always it was the bayonet, the shrill cry of drill sergeants urging their adolescent wards on, encouraging them to rip out the guts of their foes. Recruits were urged to sawtooth their bayonets and, in near sexual terms, told of the joy they would feel when plunging the blade into another man's stomach.

The appalling slaughter of the "Pals" regiments, units made up of British soldiers who enlisted from specific neighborhoods or localities and were allowed to fight together, in their first day of combat on the Somme stands as clear witness to the willingness to close in on the enemy and "have at him" with the bayonet. Their deaths would have been equally useful if they had simply stepped off their ships fully laden with gear while in the middle of the Channel; and perhaps far more merciful. Yet, the butchering of the Pals simply redoubled the shrill cry for more men to go forward to avenge the death of their heroic brothers.

The twin murder matches of the Somme and Verdun, the butcher bill running into the millions, is clear enough evidence that on an individual level both sides were more than willing to face close combat. Though German strategy in the open days of Verdun was supposedly designed to minimize German casualties and lure the French into a grinding machine, this plan was eventually abandoned and raw recruits were shoveled in with reckless determination to win at any cost.

A contemporary best-seller, rarely heard of today, is Arthur Guy Empey's propaganda piece *Over the Top* (1917), which speaks of nighttime trench raiding as a sport, sort of like rugby with the thrill of killing added in. Everything was "cheerio," the boys always singing and joking during the bombardments, and ever eager to get at the Hun and teach him the lesson he truly deserved.

It should also be remembered that the voices of British antiwar poets Wilfred Owen and Siegfried Lorraine Sassoon, though heralded today, were in general ignored or denounced as defeatist in 1917. Even the great moralist of the twentieth century, C. S. Lewis, describes a certain grim resignation to the task rather than a wish to stop the madness or to retreat back from mass slaughter.

Perhaps it is that concept of grim resignation that best describes the lost generation. Deceived in 1914 and slaughtered like sheep in 1916, they were still fighting in 1918. Granted, a large portion of the French army had mutinied and some Commonwealth troops were on the edge of mutiny throughout 1917 and into 1918, yet still they would fight when attacked and do so with determination.

The last-gasp offensive of the Germans in the spring of 1918 shows that the combative spirit was still alive on the Western Front, with Germany sustaining hundreds of thousands of casualties in its final push to the suburbs of Paris. And then there arrived the last of the idealists, the Americans who eagerly went over the top, dashing forward with fey enthusiasm at least for the first attack.

It ended not because the spirit of combat died on one side, but simply because there were no more bullets and shells coming out of German factories. If the industrial output had been able to sustain itself, chances are there would have been no breathing space at all between the killing of 1918 and that of 1939. The world had gone mad and no one understood how to make it sane again.

–WILLIAM R. FORSTCHEN,
MONTREAT COLLEGE

Viewpoint:
No. The ordinary frontline soldier was no more inclined to act aggressively against the enemy than to adopt a "live and let live" approach toward him.

A common image of the Great War is that of a killing machine, with heavy artillery, machine guns, quick-firing rifles, grenades, and mortars mowing down soldiers as they advanced slowly over "no man's land." More than nine million men lost their lives during World War I, and tens of millions more were

CHRISTMAS TRUCE

On Christmas Day 1914 troops from both sides exchanged gifts, fraternized, and played games all along the front. This account, by German soldier Johannes Nieman, concerns a friendly football match played in France.

We came up to take over the trenches on the front between Frelinghien and Houplines, where our Regiment and the Scottish Seaforth Highlanders were face to face. It was a cold, starry night and the Scots were a hundred or so metres in front of us in their trenches where, as we discovered, like us they were up to their knees in mud. My Company Commander and I, savouring the unaccustomed calm, sat with our orderlies round a Christmas tree we had put up in our dugout.

Suddenly, for no apparent reason, our enemies began to fire on our lines. Our soldiers had hung little Christmas trees covered with candles above the trenches and our enemies, seeing the lights, thought we were about to launch a surprise attack. But, by midnight it was calm once more.

Next morning the mist was slow to clear and suddenly my orderly threw himself into my dugout to say that both the German and Scottish soldiers had come out of their trenches and were fraternising along the front. I grabbed my binoculars and looking cautiously over the parapet saw the incredible sight of our soldiers exchanging cigarettes, schnapps and chocolate with the enemy. Later a Scottish soldier appeared with a football which seemed to come from nowhere and a few minutes later a real football match got underway. The Scots marked their goal mouth with their strange caps and we did the same with ours. It was far from easy to play on the frozen ground, but we continued, keeping rigorously to the rules, despite the fact that it only lasted an hour and that we had no referee. A great many of the passes went wide, but all the amateur footballers, although they must have been very tired, played with huge enthusiasm.

Us Germans really roared when a gust of wind revealed that the Scots wore no drawers under their kilts—and hooted and whistled every time they caught an impudent glimpse of one posterior belonging to one of "yesterday's enemies." But after an hour's play, when our Commanding Officer heard about it, he sent an order that we must put a stop to it. A little later we drifted back to our trenches and the fraternisation ended.

Source: Tom Morgan, "The Christmas Truce, 1914," Hellfire Corner, December 1997, Internet Web Site, http://www.fylde.demon.co.uk/xmas.htm

---

crippled or scarred for life. Yet, it would be wrong to assume therefore that soldiers on the front lines were eager, or even willing, to kill their fellow men. Artillery, remote from the battlefield and fired by gunners who rarely saw their targets, accounted for 70 percent of the casualties in the conflict. Most other casualties were incurred during the major offensives that punctuated the war and were not caused by individual soldiers shooting at the enemy's lines.

The memoirs, diaries, and letters of those who served on the Western Front in fact reveal a quite different image of the war, one in which soldiers spent much of their time trying to survive, rather than trying to kill the enemy. One of their most successful survival tactics was the "live and let live" concept, an idea predicated on trust in the common humanity of the enemy. Essentially, soldiers agreed, either explicitly or implicitly, that they would not assault the other side if their enemy would do the same. At times this arrangement even led to the informal negotiation of temporary truces between the opponents. While this idea often failed, especially when officers interfered, the high command decided to change the rules of the game, or men decided to break the tenuous covenants, "live and let live" interactions made the trenches a little more bearable for everyone.

This unique way of dealing with the enemy developed out of the physical, military, and cultural environment of the Western Front. First, an exceptional situation had evolved on the battlefields of France and Flanders. Unlike all other wars, which had consisted of battles that were won or lost and culminated in decisive campaigns that forced the surrender of the hostile government, the Great War on the Western Front became frozen in a devastating stalemate. By the end of 1914 thousands of miles of strongly fortified trenches divided Allied forces from German troops, preventing any decisive battle or indeed any settlement to the war at all. Unable to advance despite the best efforts of their general staffs, and unwilling to retreat, soldiers were in effect trapped, confined to their narrow lines until they were wounded or killed. In these claustrophobic surroundings the belligerent armies endured a strange troglodytic existence, with all the horrors of shelling, mortars, rain, mud, and ever-present death. Frontline soldiers on both sides of the line experienced the same surreal life, and this similar suffering gave the men in the trenches a common language that predisposed them to find a shared solution to the problem all soldiers saw as paramount—how to stay alive. Moreover, the two armies were often in close proximity—in some places the trenches were only a few yards apart—and men were often able to see or even speak to each other. Discussions about politics and sports and even shouted insults across the lines made the enemy more human, and thus, more difficult to kill.

The way that both sides conducted warfare on the Western Front encouraged this predisposition. Not all parts of the front were active at all times. Except during the assault phases of offensives, life in many trenches—the so-called cushy or quiet sectors—consisted of routines that were strictly maintained by officers and high commands alike. Each day British, French, and German soldiers "stood to" at dawn and dusk, fired off a requisite number of mortar shells, dined at precisely the same times, trained a certain amount of time, and suffered through the return fire of their enemies. Only a few other activities punctuated these ordinary routines. The result, at least in the "cushy" trenches, was that both sides could generally, although not always, predict what their daily lives should be like. Over time this predictability meant that combat became a series of rituals that were designed not to inflict injury on the enemy but rather to fulfill obligations to the high command. The way that soldiers embraced routines shows that they were aggressive only when forced to be so, and not because they wanted to destroy the enemy.

Aiding both of these tendencies was the particular social and cultural milieu of early twentieth-century Europe. Both sides of the trench line held unspoken assumptions about what constituted fairness, which helped them to come to understandings, whether openly stated or simply taken for granted, to live and let live. These shared notions about fair play, a "good show," or sportsmanlike behavior (even when they might be understood in a slightly different way by German, French, and British soldiers), meant that men could call upon common "rules of the game" to adjudicate disputes

if someone broke an impromptu truce. Thus, when the other side did not follow the set routine that soldiers had become used to—for instance, lobbing mortars during one's breakfast—this poor sportsmanship was seen as much worse than the random shelling by the enemy's rear. To make the other side pay for their "bad" behavior, as well as to deter them from breaking the routines again, the aggrieved party would retaliate with an equal number of mortars. Retaliation became, in fact, the way to punish opponents who would not respect the "live and let live" system. Nationality also played a role in determining whether soldiers would assault the men across from them or try to work out some sort of modus vivendi. Given the way that the war began, it makes sense that German and French soldiers were less likely to respect unspoken agreements—although this tendency did not prevent them from having quiet sectors. Meanwhile British and German troops seem to have gotten along better. More specifically, British memoirs and diaries repeatedly stress that Saxon soldiers were far less likely to assault them, and, in fact, shouted over greetings and news whenever they were able.

These foundations for undermining aggression were set by the end of 1914, but there was no guarantee that soldiers would embrace such a radical reinterpretation of their role in the war. Two additional factors allowed "live and let live" behavior to actually take place. First, there was the famous Christmas truce of December 1914. Many eyewitnesses have described how Germans, French, and British alike put down their weapons and shared a peaceful holiday, exchanging gifts, singing carols, and even eating Christmas dinners together. The example of this impromptu truce, news of which spread throughout the front, showed soldiers that it was possible to make agreements with their enemies. The second factor was the length of the war. If the war had lasted only a few months it is highly unlikely that soldiers would have had time to develop this unusual response to the dangers of the trenches. Once it became clear that the war would not end quickly or easily, and it also became clear that there would be no dashing charges, successful assaults, or any other way to get at the enemy, frontline soldiers were willing to adapt the example of the Christmas truce to the physical, military, and cultural realities of the Western Front.

Neither high command sat by while parts of their armies made what was, in effect, peace with the enemy. Horrified by the Christmas truce, the militaries of each country tried to prevent fraternization and encouraged their

German dead in a trench after a French artillery barrage, circa 1915

(postcard in scrapbook, Joseph M. Bruccoli Great War Collection, Thomas Cooper Library, University of South Carolina)

COMBAT EXPERIENCE

men to hate the enemy. After December 1914 there were no other large-scale truces, primarily because of the stringent punishments prescribed by these new rules of engagement. Yet, minor truces and other informal agreements with the enemy continued. Realizing that more had to be done, both sides adopted innovative military tactics to ensure that their men would continue to engage actively in the war. Raids, more-frequent minor assaults, and snipers were supposed to make certain that aggression continued even on those parts of the front that were not "active." They were also designed to keep the men aware of the reason for their involvement in the war in the first place—for example, to defeat the enemy through physical force.

Enforcement of these orders, however, depended on the officer corps. If the commander felt strongly about the war and his duty in it, he tried to make certain that his men vigorously fought the enemy. In general, this position only made life much worse for his own troops, as hostile actions provoked retaliation from the soldiers across the way. Conversely, officers who were sympathetic toward the plight of their men and who saw the utility of letting well enough alone, might turn a blind eye to instances of "live and let live" behavior or even engage in it themselves. On these sections of the trenches men were expected to do only

the minimum fighting necessary to placate the high command, and no more.

Thus, despite the best efforts of the high commands, the "live and let live" idea survived and even flourished on certain sectors of the Western Front. Soldiers sang to each other, discussed soccer scores, and made pacts that they would not strafe their enemy if he in turn would not shoot at them. There were limits of these interactions, however, perhaps best shown by a small incident in December 1915. During a heavy downpour, Ernst Jünger, a young lieutenant in the German army and a keen observer of the war, was forced with his men out of their flooded trenches. On the battlefield they met with the British troops whose trenches had likewise filled with water. There in "no man's land" the two enemies traded food, schnapps, cigarettes, and uniform buttons as souvenirs. After the rain stopped, the two commanding officers made a solemn declaration of war to begin three minutes after the parley ended. To the protests of his men, Jünger insisted on shooting at the British as soon as the three minutes were up. The immediate return shot almost knocked the rifle from his hands. "Live and let live" made the trenches a little more humane, but the war was still on and most soldiers were still willing to kill and be killed.

—MARY HABECK,
YALE UNIVERSITY

References

Bernard Adams, *Nothing of Importance: A Record of Eight Months at the Front with a Welsh Battalion, October, 1915, to June, 1916* (London: Methuen, 1917).

Tony Ashworth, *Trench Warfare, 1914–1918: The Live and Let Live System* (New York: Holmes & Meier, 1980).

Henri Barbusse, *Under Fire: The Story of a Squad* (London & Toronto: Dent, 1917; New York: Dutton, 1917).

Rudolf Binding, *A Fatalist at War,* translated by Ian F. D. Morrow (Boston & New York: Houghton Mifflin, 1929).

Carroll Carstairs, *A Generation Missing* (London: Heinemann, 1930; Garden City, N.Y.: Doubleday, Doran, 1930).

Guy Chapman, *A Passionate Prodigality: Fragments of Autobiography* (London: Nicolson & Watson, 1933).

Percy Croney, *Soldier's Luck: Memoirs of a Soldier of the Great War* (Ifracombe, U.K.: Stockwell, 1965).

Giles E. M. Eyre, *Somme Harvest: Memories of a P.B.I. in the Summer of 1916* (London: Jarrolds, 1938).

Niall Ferguson, *The Pity of War* (New York: BasicBooks, 1999).

Huntly Gordon, *The Unreturning Army: A Field-Gunner in Flanders, 1917–18* (London: Dent, 1967).

Robert Graves, *Good-bye to All That: An Autobiography* (London: Cape, 1929).

F. C. Hitchcock, *Stand To: A Diary of the Trenches, 1915–18* (London: Hurst & Blackett, 1937).

Ernst Jünger, *Copse 125: A Chronicle from the Trench Warfare of 1918,* translated by Basil Creighton (London: Chatto & Windus, 1930).

Jünger, *The Storm of Steel: From the Diary of a German Storm-Troop Officer on the Western Front* (London: Chatto & Windus, 1929; Garden City, N.Y.: Doubleday, Doran, 1929).

John Keegan, *The First World War* (London: Hutchinson, 1998).

R. Hugh Knyvett, *"Over There" with the Australians* (London: Hodder & Stoughton, 1918; New York: Scribners, 1918).

Georges Lafond, *Covered with Mud and Glory* (Boston: Small, Maynard, 1918).

Eric J. Leed, *No Man's Land: Combat & Identity in World War I* (Cambridge & New York: Cambridge University Press, 1979).

Thomas Penrose Marks, *The Laughter Goes from Life: In the Trenches of the First World War* (London: Kimber, 1977).

Bernard Martin, *Poor Bloody Infantry: A Subaltern on the Western Front, 1916–1917* (London: Murray, 1987).

Reginald Pound, *The Lost Generation of 1914* (New York: Coward-McCann, 1964).

Erich Maria Remarque, *All Quiet on the Western Front,* translated by A. W. Wheen (Boston: Little, Brown / London: Putnam, 1929).

Reginald H. Roy, ed., *The Journal of Private Fraser, 1914–1918: Canadian Expeditionary Force* (Victoria, B.C.: Sono Nis Press, 1985).

Siegfried Sassoon, *Memoirs of an Infantry Officer* (London: Faber & Faber, 1930).

Edwin Campion Vaughn, *Some Desperate Glory: The Diary of a Young Officer, 1917* (London: Warne, 1981).

Arthur Graeme West, *The Diary of a Dead Officer, Being the Posthumous Papers of Arthur Graeme West* (London: Allen & Unwin, n.d.).

COMBAT EXPERIENCE

CULTURE OF THE OFFENSIVE

Were the war plans of 1914 manifestations of a "culture of the offensive" at any cost?

Viewpoint: Yes. Between 1871 and 1914 European armies moved toward an intellectualized concept of the offensive as a sovereign recipe for victory, without regard for the objective analyses of developments in technology and administration that predicted a prolonged war.

Viewpoint: No. Many military planners before 1914 envisioned a limited offensive war of short duration in which the European balance of power would be maintained.

Viewpoint: No. The general commitment to offensive warfare reflected a careful calculation of prewar armies' perceived strengths, weaknesses, and potential as well as the similarities characterizing those armies.

The war plans of the great powers in 1914 had in common a commitment to the offensive at all levels: tactical, operational, and strategic. The bloody collapse within weeks of the start of World War I of years of professionally directed planning into improvised trench warfare has invited a century of criticism and ridicule. Conventional wisdom describes successive generations of military thinkers as hostile to social change, political democratization, and technical innovation. They substituted for thought a belief that war had changed little since the days of Napoleon Bonaparte. They developed a "cult of the offensive" in which moral force would overcome firepower and systematic planning would compensate for friction. French and German planners, at the least, have been accused of being even more cynical, using morale as a manipulative device to bring their men voluntarily into killing zones.

Closer examination of prewar planning and doctrine suggests that there was a high degree of responsiveness to a crisis generated on one hand by improved weapons and on the other by mass mobilization. Exponential increases in the effect of firepower made it increasingly difficult, when not impossible, to attack with any prospect of general success. The exponential growth of armies, furthermore, restricted opportunities for operational and strategic maneuver. European armies as well were becoming increasingly symmetrical: copying each other's tools and techniques to the point where there were few prospects of spectacular surprises.

Complicating the issue was the unprecedented complexity of European society—a development that in the minds of military planners as well as civilian politicians left it vulnerable to gridlock, disruption, and collapse if subjected to the level of stress certain in a prolonged war. At the human level, young males of Europe, weakened by luxury and Socialism, were not as willing to sacrifice their lives in war as their ancestors had been.

Students of the sharp edge of war, however, clearly recognized that even the most patriotic or the least sensitive privates could hardly be expected to survive the intensified killing zones of the modern battlefield. The challenge remained winning the next war before society collapsed. How to square that particular circle was the question.

Viewpoint:
Yes. Between 1871 and 1914 European armies moved toward an intellectualized concept of the offensive as a sovereign recipe for victory, without regard for the objective analyses of developments in technology and administration that predicted a prolonged war.

The historical record is painfully familiar to even the most-casual students of the Great War: the suicidal French charges in the opening weeks of battle on the German border, the doomed assaults by the flower of German youth against the "old contemptibles" of England in the open pastures of Belgium, and the bloody attacks by the Austro-Hungarians against the Russians. Everywhere it was the same—it was a butcher's bill that would even have made Napoleon Bonaparte flinch. One could almost accept the tactical madness of the first few weeks of World War I, if out of that experience there had emerged a fundamental realization on all sides that until such time as the technology of offensive firepower and unit mobility offset defensive killing power, the bayonet charge was a thing of the past.

Of course, the horrifying record shows different results: Ypres (1914–1915), the Russian offensives of 1915–1916, Verdun (1916), and the Somme (1916). Even as late as 1918, after Commonwealth and French forces refused orders to charge, American troops were still going over the top of the trenches in human waves, driven forward by the doctrine of the offensive spirit and élan; in fact, the Russians never abandoned this mentality even into World War II (1939–1945). This persisting belief in the offensive at the point of the bayonet can be traced back to Napoleon and the Swiss soldier and scholar Henri de Jomini who, in analyzing the campaigns of the greatest soldier in French history, attempted to translate into scientific principles the great master's formula for victory.

The methodology of 1805 was fairly simple, and though bloody, it worked. Pin the opponent through maneuver, hammer with artillery to smash down the ability to effectively mount a response, and then go in with the bayonet, driving forward in massed columns without stopping. It was all predicated on the military technology of the moment: smoothbore weapons, infantry arms that at best could hit a target at seventy-five yards, and artillery that could only be employed as a direct-fire weapon with a maximum effectiveness of little more than half a mile.

A charging column therefore faced a truly lethal killing ground that could be traversed in little more than a couple of minutes. Here was the key factor—to convince troops through ruthless drill, propaganda, social pressure, and idealistic zeal that the charge was everything. Rush boldly forward, cross the killing ground, close with the bayonet, and victory was assured. Always it was the spirit of the bayonet, though careful statistical analysis shows that wounds from bayonets were actually rather rare; one side or the other usually broke ranks before physical contact was achieved. Even this result was understood and became part of doctrine: that the climax of battle was a testing of strength and masculine courage, that at that ultimate moment one's morale and mental powers must transcend that of an opponent, who would melt away at the sight of cold steel and the pitiless gaze of the superior man behind the weapon. Thus were Marengo (1800), Austerlitz (1805), and Wagram (1809) won. Thus was Waterloo (1815) lost, when the thin red lines of the British forces refused to budge and the moral strength of the French Imperial Guard wavered and collapsed.

In the United States this doctrine was taught at West Point by a devotee of Jomini, Alfred Mahan "the Elder," (his son Alfred Thayer Mahan being the great definer of naval doctrine). Mahan shaped the tactical thinking of the generation that charged with such reckless abandon in the Civil War battles at Malvern Hill (1862), Antietam (1862), Gettysburg (1863), and Cold Harbor (1864). Yet, here one sees the clear foreshadowing of the future, for with the introduction of rifled weapons the killing zone was extended out fivefold. At Cold Harbor, fought in the first week of June 1864, General Ulysses S. Grant lost more than eight thousand men in less than thirty minutes, a relative casualty rate that exceeded even that experienced at the Somme, fought just fifty-two years later.

The last great European testing ground for military doctrine prior to World War I was the Franco-Prussian War (1870–1871), and tragically, for the sons and grandsons of the men who fought at Sedan (1870), the offensive against rifled weapons still worked . . . just barely. It was Prussian artillery that did most of the work, but in spite of the severe pounding sustained throughout the battle, the French still inflicted tens of thousands of casualties against the charging Prussian lines. The lesson learned, or at least that which was accepted as truth, was that élan had carried the day on the battlefields of 1870, and that ultimately it was Prussian willpower and moral strength that overcame the French ability to resist. It was a false truth, for German victory came in significant part from poor leader-

CULTURE OF THE OFFENSIVE

ship, outdated equipment, and outmoded doctrines on the part of the French.

The matrix, however, was established and accepted by all Western powers as a basic truth, that the spirit of the bayonet would always be the key to victory. It thus became a point of religious doctrine, as powerful in its influence as the Nicene Creed is to the faithful. Echoes of it are still resonant in the rituals of basic training to this day.

It is well-known that the technological innovations between 1870–1914 were, in general, all but ignored by those who formulated training policy and set the general principles of war-fighting doctrine. Failure to understand the impact of the machine gun on battlefield tactics is pointed out as the classic example, but there were other profound innovations as well: the rapid indirect-fire artillery piece, such as the famed French seventy-five-millimeter gun; bolt-action rifles, with a killing range of one thousand yards; aerial reconnaissance that could direct artillery fire, help to position troops for defense, and divine where the next attack was coming; and even something as simple as barbed wire—a few dozen strands concealed in a wheat field was capable of stopping a charge cold.

There were other factors though, the key ones, of course, being modern logistics and the power of industrialization. At Waterloo and Gettysburg both armies had, at best, enough ammunition on hand for several days of sustained killing and then the fighting simply had to end, with days, even weeks, transpiring before horse-drawn wagons could bring up more supplies. By the end of the Civil War, however, the Union army was employing narrow-gauge railroads to move supplies along the Petersburg siege front (1864) and the key to General William Tecumseh Sherman's battering of Atlanta (1864) rested on the vast array of trains and steamships that stretched clear back to the factories of the North.

The foreshadowing of 1861–1865 was a clear reality by 1914. A single platoon of machine guns could, in a matter of minutes, expend more ammunition than a Napoleonic or American Civil War regiment would fire off in a hard day of battle, while presenting a target silhouette of just a couple dozen square feet compared to six hundred men standing in a line. Within minutes more ammunition would be at hand—moving from factory, to railroad, to narrow gauge line, to motor truck, and finally to the front by bearing parties. All of these advances spelled disaster for anyone ordered to stand up, go forward, and "give them the bayonet."

The clear indicator of how powerfully ingrained this doctrine had become in the mindset of the high command is how long it took for it to be abandoned; in fact, it was not truly discarded throughout the four years of murder during World War I. Though much is made of the German transition to "storm" tactics in late 1917 and into 1918, ultimately the German offensive ended because the unrelenting attacks bled their army dry. A lasting question, which is all but impossible to understand and explain, is why this failure of doctrine was not grasped. One would like to think that in a sane world a combined casualty list on both sides of more than one million men in the first eight weeks of battle would have given everyone reason for pause . . . but it did not.

There are perhaps three answers to this conundrum, the first being the religious-like cult attached to doctrinal training. So intense was this belief that any who dared to question it were apostate. Their masculinity, moral fiber, and courage were called into doubt. A real man can face cold steel and deliver it, victory could be achieved no other way, and to cast the belief into doubt was to question victory itself and the entire cult built up around the means of achieving that victory. Therefore, to raise any serious questions about the doctrine was in fact a setup for defeat, for the mere question being raised automatically began a process of moral breakdown.

Second was the near-total isolation between civilians and military imposed by modern censorship. Word of the true extent of the bloodbaths was concealed on both sides, and perversely an ethic developed to "shield" those at home from the truth of the horror and futility. Without pressure on governments from those called upon to shoulder the burden, there was no reason for the military to change its cherished beliefs.

The third factor is more subtle, a group mind-set that had evolved across the generations since the age of Napoleon. All the major powers had, to varying degrees, adopted a model with an officers' caste that was inbred, elitist, and isolated. Trained in small colonial wars, taught to view civilian authorities with suspicion, and drilled to broker no dissent either from below or from within their own ranks, this officer class was all but impossible to change. "The regiment, after all, has traditions my good man."

The Dreyfus Affair (1898) stands as a classic example of this mentality. A judgment was formed against an innocent man, Captain Alfred Dreyfus. When clear evidence was presented to the contrary the French high command refused to acknowledge it, maintaining that truth was subjective—that protection of the status quo must be maintained at all cost—and then it systematically set out to destroy anyone who dared to question this dogmatic belief. Is it any wonder that military systems that could take part in such a travesty lacked the ability and resilience to clearly see a profound tactical flaw, publicly admit to its failings, and then set it right? It is a phenomenon that is not unique to the military; almost any government bureaucracy can fall into the same model, as can any bloated corporation that is beginning the slide into eventual collapse. It was a mind-set that would put nearly ten million men into their graves.

–WILLIAM R. FORSTCHEN,
MONTREAT COLLEGE

Viewpoint:
No. Many military planners before 1914 envisioned a limited offensive war of short duration in which the European balance of power would be maintained.

It is clear to those looking back that the technology of war changed greatly from 1871 to 1914. War was becoming bigger and more ferocious. However, in the face of these changes, militaries continued to believe that the next general war would be short, offensive, and an acceptable risk for rearranging the European order on their own terms. Therefore, in the years before 1914, European general staffs planned for this short engagement, which never occurred.

By the 1880s the typical European infantryman carried a bolt-action, repeating rifle that held three to nine rounds and was accurate for up to one thousand yards. In addition, team-serviced machine guns, such as the Maxim Gun, designed by English inventor Hiram Maxim around 1884 and manufactured by Vickers, became more common. The three-man-operated Maxim Gun had a water-cooled barrel and could fire four hundred rounds a minute. Black powder was replaced by nitrocellulose, cutting down the amount of smoke on the battlefield. Artillery rounds reached new distant ranges and gained the ability to continually fire on recoilless carriages. On a battlefield lacking smoke, targets were visible to forward observers, who used field telephones to call back locations to firing teams. Firepower became increasingly accurate with these new developments.

Not only was the technology of war changing, but also was its scale. In 1914 Russia had an army of 3,000,000 men in 114 divisions. The entire force could be mobilized against another European power in around forty days. The Austro-Hungarian army could field one and 1,250,000 men and could mobilize its force in around two weeks. In addition, Italy, France, and Germany could all field similar forces within that time span. These national armies were truly massive, and by coupling numbers with technological advancements, Europe was on the verge of a potential tragedy.

One man was convinced of the impracticality of war in the modern age by these facts, but his voice was ignored. Polish banker Jan Bloch, who wrote *The Future of War in Its Technical and Political Relations* (1899), predicted the end of war forever because of practical reasons. He deduced that armies would not survive the destruction and that people would not withstand the famines resulting from the technical improvements of warfare in action. Bloch pointed out to his readers that the modern bullet had more killing power, with greater accuracy, force, and range. The rifle had an increased range of fourteen times, while artillery had increased fortyfold. In the age of smokeless powder, soldiers would no longer be able to anticipate their own demise. Improved weapons would give a greater advantage to the defense on larger battlefields than had ever been seen before. Most importantly, in the industrial age there would never be a shortage of ammunition. Bullets would be cheap and plentiful.

However, the increased ability to supply the battlefield would raise the economic cost of warfare. This factor, linked with conscription, would lead the entire nation to be involved in the next war. The working class would be the hardest hit by conscription and increased taxes. No one would be able to hide from the tragedy of war. Nations would be forced to import grain and foodstuffs, yet shortages would still prevail. Famine would run throughout Europe. In the end the war would not be won on the battlefield but on the home front. Bloch recognized that the sentiments of the people were more important than ever. The side that lost would be the one whose people could no longer withstand the strain and famine of war, and the working class, paying for the war on the battlefield and the home front, represented the potential for revolt.

Though Bloch was wrong in predicting the end of war, the picture he painted of the next war was amazingly true. Bloch saw that it was the officer corps that would be the first to be devastated on the front lines. He believed that Great Britain would be forced to protect its shipping lanes or be forced out of the war. He also predicted that if Russia went to war, the strain on its society would lead to revolution. Bloch argued that the next war would be fought on credit, that no one confrontation would determine the outcome of the war, and that there would be no early decisive battle. In order to pay off their war debt, the winners would force the losers to pay a war indemnity. Unlike those who predicted a short war, Bloch knew that war would drag on for years. In the long conflict, entire nations

CULTURE OF THE OFFENSIVE

VON BERNHARDI ON WAR

In 1912 German general Friedrich von Bernhardi, commander of the Seventh Army Corps, commented on offensive actions in relation to the expected conflict.

Since the tactical efficiency and the *morale* of the troops are chiefly shown in the offensive, and are then most needful, the necessary conclusion is that safety only lies in offensive warfare.

In an attack, the advantage, apart from the elements of moral strength which it brings into play, depends chiefly on rapidity of action. Inasmuch as the attacking party determines the direction of the attack to suit his own plans, he is able at the selected spot to collect a superior force against his surprised opponent. The initiative, which is the privilege of the attacking party, gives a start in time and place which is very profitable in operations and tactics. The attacked party can only equalize this advantage if he has early intimation of the intentions of the assailant, and has time to take measures which hold out promise of success. The more rapidly, therefore, the attacking general strikes his blow and gains his success, and the more capable his troops, the greater is the superiority which the attack in its nature guarantees.

This superiority increases with the size of the masses. If the advancing armies are large and unwieldy, and the distances to be covered great, it will be a difficult and tedious task for the defending commander to take proper measures against a surprise attack. On the other hand, the prospects of success of the attacking general will be very favorable, especially if he is in the fortunate position of having better troops at his disposal.

Finally, the initiative secures to the numerically weaker a possibility of gaining the victory, even when other conditions are equal, and all the more so the greater the masses engaged. In most cases it is impossible to bring the entire mass of a modern army simultaneously and completely into action. A victory, therefore, in the decisive direction—the direction, that is, which directly cuts the arteries of the opponents—is usually conclusive for the whole course of the war, and its effect is felt in the most distant parts of the field of operations. If the assailant, therefore, can advance in this direction with superior numbers, and can win the day, because the enemy cannot utilize his numerical superiority, there is a possibility of an ultimate victory over the arithmetically stronger army. In conformity to this law, Frederick the Great, through superior tactical capability and striking strength, had always the upper hand of an enemy far more powerful in mere numbers.

We arrive, then, at the conclusion that, in order to secure the superiority in a war of the future under otherwise equal conditions, it is incumbent upon us: First, during the period of preparation to raise the tactical value and capabilities of the troops as much as possible, and especially to develop the means of concealing the attacking movements and damaging the enemy's tactical powers; secondly, in the war itself to act on the offensive and strike the first blow, and to exploit the maneuvering capacity of the troops as much as possible, in order to be superior in the decisive directions. Above all, a state which has objects to attain that cannot be relinquished, and is exposed to attacks by enemies more powerful than itself, is bound to act in this sense. It must, before all things, develop the attacking powers of its army, since a strategic defensive must often adopt offensive methods.

. . . From the commander-in-chief, who puts into execution the conceptions of his own brain under the pressure of responsibility and shifting fortune, and the brigadier, who must act independently according to a given general scheme; to the dispatch rider, surrounded with dangers, and left to his own resources in the enemy's country, and the youngest private in the field fighting for his own land, and striving for victory in the face of death; everywhere in the wars of today, more than in any other ages, personality dominates all else. The effect of mass tactics has abolished all close formations of infantry, and the individual is left to himself. The direct influence of the superior has lessened. In the strategic duties of the cavalry, which represent the chief activity of that arm, the patrol riders and orderlies are separated more than before from their troop and are left to their own responsibility. Even in the artillery the importance of independent action will be more clearly emphasized than previously. The battle-fields and area of operations have increased with the masses employed. The commander-in-chief is far less able than ever before to superintend operations in various parts of the field; he is forced to allow a greater latitude to his subordinates. These conditions are very prominent in attacking operations. . . .

Source: Friedrich von Bernhardi, Germany and the Next War, *translated by Allen H. Powles (London: Arnold, 1912).*

CULTURE OF THE OFFENSIVE

would be destroyed. All of these predictions proved true in World War I, but his foresight was ignored by those hoping for a short, generalized conflict.

The European general staffs, instead of being pushed to the defensive by these facts, looked toward the offensive. One of the most important voices in the institutionalization of offensive warfare after 1871 was French Colonel Charles du Picq, who died in 1870 at Metz in the Franco-Prussian War. He based his landmark work, *Etudes sur le combat* (Battle Studies, 1876), on interviews with French veterans. He discovered that moral cohesion was lacking among the soldiers of industrial armies. Du Picq believed that in order for future armies to be successful, they must rediscover this quality. He pointed out that modern weapons were useless in the hands of weakhearted soldiers, while antique weapons would be highly effective with spiritually charged infantrymen. In order to be victorious, an army needed to break the spirit of its opponent. Spirit, not weapons, produced results on the battlefield. Therefore, the army with the most spirit, not the best weapons, would win any conflict. In an ineffective army, rifles are wasted on inaccurate shots, but in a spirited army every shot strikes home. The best form of warfare to instill spirit into men is the offensive. Those men moving toward a positive goal would always be victorious. Meanwhile, the defensive would steal the men's morale.

In addition to du Picq, Continental soldiers feverishly studied German Carl von Clausewitz's interpretation of Napoleon Bonaparte, *Vom Kriege* (On War, 1833), easily one of the most important works of military theory. Like the later du Picq, Clausewitz focused much of his work on the psychological and moral factors of war. In addition, he recognized that the offensive was the most positive form of war. The best method of keeping men motivated was to move forward, not backward. In fact, he stated that all victory, even defensive, was determined by the offense. He also helped to propagate the idea of victory through decisive engagements that he believed a good general could manufacture through talent. He argued that the easiest way to win a decisive engagement was to present the strongest army on the field. Though many of these views could be debated, they were perceptions of Clausewitz that were accepted by European militaries. After World War I, British military historian B. H. Liddell Hart criticized Clausewitz as the "Mahdi of Mass," because of his comments on superior numerical forces at decisive moments. This criticism, though it may not accurately express Clausewitz's true belief, does identify the prewar interpretation of Clausewitz by military men: one can create a

decisive moment. A decisive battle would produce a short war.

A doctrine that relied on spirit and morale, instead of numbers and finances, was extremely popular with the French. They faced a potential German opponent that could field almost twice the number of men. In addition, the Germans were also spending a higher amount of money on the army. If war depended on men and money, the French would lose. However, they relied on spirit; France could fill its men with morale and claim victory. Logically, the only way to keep the men psychologically motivated was to stay on the offensive—the cult of the offensive had won over the French.

The spirit of the offensive became institutionalized in the French army with the adoption of Plan XVII, created by General Joseph Joffre. In the event of a German attack, the French would launch their own offensive into Alsace-Lorraine, one that would be unlinked to German advances. If the Germans attacked through northern Belgium, there would only be a small force to check their advance. The front lines would include both regulars and twenty-five reserve divisions. The French planned to win the war through their positive offensive efforts, not by stopping a German invasion. Many French politicians and soldiers worried that, in the event of a war with Germany, the British would not intervene and assist them. In order to avoid weakening its planned offensive, the French placed the small British Expeditionary Force (BEF) on the left flank as part of the force countering German maneuvers through Belgium. The French offensive had to be insured in order that victory could be won quickly.

The Schlieffen Plan stands as one of the most famous battle plans of all time. The brainchild of the prewar Chief of the German General Staff, Count Alfred von Schlieffen, it called for the German army to knock France out of the war quickly with a flanking maneuver through Belgium and Holland. The Germans would be able to decimate the French army by attacking it through its rear. Schlieffen was so confident that his plan would be able to decimate the French that he placed many of his reserves in the offensive right wing. This placement weakened the left wing of his army, positioned to stop French offensives through Alsace-Lorraine. Meanwhile, in Prussia the Germans prepared to hold off Russia, an ally of France, whom they had anticipated would be slow to mobilize. After the French were defeated, the Germans would then be able to refocus their resources and exhaust the Russian war machine in order to obtain a truce.

The plan was a reflection of the man. Schlieffen planned for the perfect offensive, a double envelopment that would consume the French army. He was obsessed with copying Hannibal's encirclement of the Romans at Cannae in 216 B.C. It was a plan for a short, offensive German triumph. His victory over the French would be so spectacular that the Russians would not wish to fight a lengthy engagement. Much has been made of the changes to the plan by Schlieffen's successor, Helmuth von Moltke (the Younger), who weakened the flanking right wing by restationing troops in the left wing to check the French. He removed twelve divisions from the flanking wing and doubled those assigned to protect Alsace-Lorraine. In addition, he canceled the planned incursion of Holland during the flanking action. Still, the strategy depended on the ability of the German army to obtain victory quickly over the French.

Even on the naval front, offensive thinking dominated. In the United Kingdom and Germany the American Alfred Thayer Mahan's *The Influence of Sea Power Upon History, 1660–1783* (1890) was actively studied in the years before World War I. In his work Mahan extolled the necessary conditions and advantages of sea power. Though he recognized the advantage of a strong navy in economic strangulation, he stressed that the opposing navy was the target of a naval force. Therefore, in order to gain complete command of the seas, one must actively seek out the enemy and their capital ships. Once discovered, they must be defeated in one decisive battle. Admirals, like generals, expected victory in one swift effort. Mahan was so popular in Europe that German kaiser William II read his work and ordered translated copies placed on German naval vessels. After the war began, the admirals were just as frustrated as the soldiers as the largest surface battle of the war, Jutland (1916), was inconclusive rather than decisive.

Throughout Europe every nation assumed that the war would be swift and hoped to use this quick conflict to reform the balance of power to an advantage. The architect of the Franco-Prussian War, Moltke, had predicted that the next war would last for at least seven, to perhaps thirty, years. Yet, his predecessor, Schlieffen, had always assumed that a long war was impossible for logistical reasons. The Austro-Hungarians saw World War I as a short preventive war waged to preserve control over the Balkans. The British assumed the next great war would be short; therefore, Anglo-French staff discussions focused on delivering the BEF to France as quickly as possible. Some Frenchmen saw the possibility of a long war but hoped that speed and optimism during the opening stages would bring a quick French victory. Even the Japanese assumed it would be a short war and grabbed German Pacific holdings as quickly as possible in order to

insure their possession. Everyone assumed or hoped that the next war would be won swiftly.

The illusion of a short war and the cult of the offensive had tragic results for Europe. In 1914 France experienced 995,000 casualties and 1,430,000 more in 1915. These losses were out of proportion with the 2,541,000 lost in the remaining three years. The first fifteen months of the war were horrible. In reality, no nation thought that it could obtain victory without bloodshed. Moltke, Schlieffen, Joffre, and other military leaders all had expected high losses when planning. They received them. However, they saw this slaughter as the necessary cost of victory that, if implemented correctly, would be short, but that did not happen.

Before 1914 European generals had banked on a short offensive war based on morale instead of technology. High-spirited soldiers insured victory over improved military technology. The interpretations of works by du Picq, Clausewitz, and Mahan all helped to institutionalize this vision. Leaders ignored voices of dissent, such as that of Bloch. When World War I began, their plans for offensive short engagements were launched and failed. The conflict would not be short. Instead, it would be tragic, endure for years, and destroy the youth and wealth of Europe. The politicians and generals failed their citizens by not realizing until too late the stresses that war would put upon societies. No one was prepared for what happened.

—DANIEL LEE BUTCHER,
KANSAS STATE UNIVERSITY

Viewpoint:
No. The general commitment to offensive warfare reflected a careful calculation of prewar armies' perceived strengths, weaknesses, and potential as well as the similarities characterizing those armies.

On the outbreak of war in the summer of 1914, all major belligerents immediately undertook major offensives against their enemies. In the west, France attacked Germany in Alsace-Lorraine. In turn, Germany invaded Belgium and Luxemburg to gain access to northern France. In the east, Austria-Hungary began its war with a southern invasion into Serbia and then expanded it by invading Russian Poland to the north. Russia, with its massive army, launched a dual-pronged attack aimed at eastern Germany and Austrian Galicia. Despite these near simultaneous offensives, neither side managed to achieve a success that would allow it to claim victory. In fact, on all fronts, the war quickly degenerated into position warfare, with each side facing the other in long, almost unbroken, trench lines. By November 1914 the war had become stalemated and would remain so until nations began collapsing from within in 1917 and 1918.

The phenomenon of each belligerent beginning the war by attacking its enemies has often been put down to a "cult of the offensive" that reigned in Europe before World War I. The proponents of this interpretation maintain that European armies developed this cult in the face of compelling evidence that modern weapons and the size of conscript armies had rendered offensive action too costly on the modern battlefield. The experiences of the Anglo-Boer War (1899–1902) and Russo-Japanese War (1904–1905) are held up as illustrations of the lessons that European soldiers should have learned about the deadly effectiveness of modern weapons and the indecisiveness of battles in the era of nations in arms. Instead, so the argument goes, conservative European soldiers remained wedded to an outdated idea of warfare, one that held onto the belief that even the massive conscript armies of early twentieth-century Europe could still bring about decisive, war-winning battles by the means of offensive action.

This argument, however, does not bear up under the scrutiny of an examination of why European soldiers undertook their offensives in August 1914. Analysis of the military literature published in Europe before 1914 demonstrates that military leaders were acutely aware of the deadliness of modern weapons and of the difficulties that modern mass armies introduced to the battlefield. Yet, despite this awareness, they believed that they had devised ways of avoiding the inconclusive fighting that had characterized the South African and the East Asian wars at the start of the century. Additionally, a close examination of the strategic goals of each belligerent shows why each army had to adopt the offensive at the outbreak of war for political reasons, despite the battlefield difficulties.

Contrary to popular opinion, European soldiers on the eve of the Great War were not all hide-bound conservatives unwilling to face up to the realities of modern, mass warfare. Far from this rigidity, for the most part, the officer corps of fin-de-siècle Europe were becoming progressively professional, with each army instituting continuing education and specialist journals that fostered the systematic study of war amongst its officers. In Germany, after the Franco-German War (1870–1871), the *Kriegsakademie* (War Academy) was given a larger role in officer education under the watchful eye of Helmuth von Moltke

(the Elder). France followed suit with the establishment of the *École de Guerre* (School of War) in 1876; even in backward Russia the Nicholas Academy of the General Staff was reinvigorated by Mikhail Dragomirov and G. A. Leer in the 1870s and 1880s. In Germany the General Staff edited the *Militär-Wochenblatt* (*Military Weekly*) and the *Vierteljahrsheft für Truppenführung und Heereskunde* (*Quarterly Journal of Troop Leadership and the Knowledge of Armies*), while the French Army published the *Revue Militaire* and the *Journal des Sciences Militaires*. Such structures helped create career paths for the able officer, so that European armies increasingly promoted their officers based upon merit, rather than purely social reasons.

With the study war being required for promotion and a successful career, European officers made use of their professional schools and journals to analyze and discuss contemporary warfare. In the period between the German Wars of Unification (1864–1871) and the outbreak of World War, the classrooms and journals of the European armies teemed with debate about the shape of wars to come and the way in which each army should fight them. In Germany debate was so serious that occasional "courts of honor" were convened to adjudicate between parties with severe differences of opinion. Moreover, this debate was carried out in public, allowing each army to assess the potential of the other and to establish means by which advances in one could be countered in another. In the light of this often acrimonious public debate, each army honed its doctrine repeatedly to take into account the results of the latest wars and debates in each nation.

Events of the German Wars of Unification and the Russo-Turkish War (1877–1878) convinced most European soldiers of what they had suspected for some time: modern, rapid-fire rifles and artillery exacted a heavy, if yet not prohibitive, price for any force advancing in the open on a battlefield. Subsequent wars merely confirmed this conclusion. European military theorists developed two basic tactical responses to this new killing zone. The first was based upon the growing field of psychology. Guided by Dragomirov and Loyzeau de Grandmaison, the armies of Russia and France, after 1894 the Dual Alliance emphasized the need for offensive spirit within their troops. These theorists and their followers recognized the need for some means of getting troops across the fire-swept modern battlefield in order to close with the enemy and complete any attack. Cover could only go so far in providing protection for attacking troops; eventually, they would need to break into the open to cross the last few yards to the enemy. This advance was a daunting prospect for

CULTURE OF THE OFFENSIVE

CULTURE OF THE OFFENSIVE

any infantryman. Wartime experience suggested that troops would often go to ground to avoid being hit, leading to the momentum of the attack breaking down. French and Russian officers believed that if their soldiers could be inculcated with sufficient offensive spirit, they would continue to attack through this deadly, but not devastating, zone of fire. Moreover, they believed that their armies had traditionally displayed such élan and, thus, that such an approach would fit nicely into their long-standing military culture.

In the German army, a different tactical approach to the effectiveness of modern weapons emerged. Although they believed offensive spirit to be important, German theorists emphasized alternative means of avoiding prohibitively high casualties. The first of these was a system of decentralized command, which developed under the tutelage of Moltke the Elder. Such a system was designed to allow small-unit leaders to use their own initiative when attacking the enemy. Commanders would be told what needed to be accomplished rather than how they were to execute their mission. Knowing what needed to be achieved meant that they would not need to wait for orders from above if the situation changed, and being allowed to determine how tasks were to be carried out ensured that units of the German army could take advantage of terrain and of fleeting opportunities on the battlefield in a way that would minimize casualties.

In addition to a decentralized command-and-control system, the German army also placed great emphasis on flank attacks as a means of avoiding the worst of the enemy's fire. This strategy was to be employed on the tactical as well as the operational level in order to avoid the need for attacking into the teeth of an enemy's position. By exploiting poorly defended flanks, German theorists believed that they would strike at the enemy's weakest point and cause resistance to collapse without necessarily having to carry out close combat on a large scale. With such attacks, the German army aimed less at the enemy's physical destruction and more at his tactical position. A successful flanking attack would bring German soldiers into the rear of an enemy position, making it untenable and causing the enemy's soldiers, concentrating on a possible attack from the front, to fear for their safety.

Regardless of which approach to avoiding the worst effects of the fire of modern weapons, either the emphasis on offensive spirit or the decentralized command-and-flank attacks, every European army took steps to improve cooperation between the arms. Throughout Europe, it was recognized that all-arms cooperation, particularly between the infantry and artillery, was key to success on the battlefield. Firepower, both that provided by the infantry's rifles and, increasingly, machine guns and that offered by rapid-fire artillery, was seen as essential in breaking down the enemy's will to resist and as a means of providing suppressing fire with which to cover the advance of friendly infantry. Consequently, in the years before World War I, each nation revised their doctrine to include greater cooperation between the various arms.

Indeed, the evidence provided by the wars fought between 1871 and 1914 seemed to suggest that, despite the increased lethality of modern weapons, the offensive was still effective if proper tactics were employed. Indeed, the conflict seen retrospectively by many to be the precursor to World War I, the Russo-Japanese War, was used by most contemporaries as evidence that their offensive tactics could succeed. The truth of the matter is that frontal attacks were successful in the war, even if the attacker took heavy casualties. Rather than a re-evaluation of the efficacy of the offensive, the war merely occasioned a tweaking of the tactics already in place. Indeed, far from signifying the beginning of a more deadly era in warfare, many observers saw the conflict in East Asia as just the opposite. Alfred von Schlieffen, the Chief of the German General Staff from 1891 to 1905, noted in 1909 that the average daily casualty rate during the Russo-Japanese War was far lower that that of the wars of Frederick the Great and that the fourteen-day battle of Mukden (1905) cost the Russians and Japanese less than an hour's fighting cost the French and Germans in the battle of Mars-la-Tour (August 1870).

The problem of mass armies was one that European soldiers never really resolved before, and one could even argue during, World War I. In August 1914 the nations of Europe fielded armies the size of which the world had never seen. Drawing upon reserves built up after years of conscription, the French army at the start of the war amounted to some 4.4 million men, the German army some 3.9 million, the Austro-Hungarian around 2.5 million, and the Russian a massive 5 million. Such armies not only covered a vast area, but could fill the holes in their ranks caused by fighting. Thus, European armies had the manpower in 1914 to establish a nearly unbroken trench line running from the English Channel to the Swiss border and another that ran from the Baltic Sea to the Carpathian Mountains. Moreover, with large pools of reservists, they could absorb massive casualties and still maintain their positions. No one had experienced warfare on this scale before, and prewar ideas of swirling, highly mobile campaigns with disparate but loosely supporting battles quickly broke down. However, as no one had experience of war such as this, prewar theorists could not conceive of a war that did not possess battles that were in some way decisive, and again the experiences of recent wars seemed to suggest that battles could still decide conflicts.

Regardless of the beliefs of European soldiers as to the continued efficacy of the offensive, the strategic goals of each nation demanded offensive action at the outbreak of war. Since their loss to Germany in 1871, the French had clamored for the return of the provinces of Alsace and Lorraine. From the French perspective, any war would need to reconquer the "lost provinces," and this goal would require an offensive into Germany. Germany, on its part, was sandwiched between two enemies. With an army too small to take on both opponents at once and with the belief that German society could not withstand the pressures of a long war, the German army needed to defeat one enemy quickly and then turn on the other. Knowing that France would field an army before its ally Russia, German strategists were determined to defeat the French army first. This strategy led them to pressure the Austro-Hungarians to attack Russia to tie down Russian forces while the German army attempted to defeat the French. As Austria-Hungary needed her German ally, political reasons forced the army of the Dual Monarchy to contemplate an offensive against Russia that it would not have undertaken under different circumstances. Needing to punish Serbia to maintain her Great Power status, Austria-Hungary tried to launch two simultaneous offensives, despite a relatively small army. Russia was tied to offensive action by her 1894 treaty with France, which required a Russian offensive with substantial forces against Germany within the first several weeks of war. The vast size of their army allowed the Russians to contemplate a simultaneous offensive against their true rival in Eastern Europe and the Balkans, Austria-Hungary.

Thus it was that each major belligerent in August 1914 had strategic goals that demanded offensive action, so regardless of the military beliefs, each nation began World War I with an offensive. The armed forces of each country, however, believed that they could succeed in an offensive against their opponents. The increasing professionalization of the armies of Europe before 1914 led to serious analysis of the problems posed by and potential solutions to the effectiveness of modern weapons. The public nature of the debates about tactics in each nation allowed the belligerent to take stock of the military abilities of the others and to develop tactics

to counter those of their opponents and avoid the worst effects of modern weapons. Far from having a blind adherence to the offensive before 1914, European military leaders had weighed carefully the different options available to a modern army and had decided that the evidence of recent wars and knowledge of the opponent's tactics would allow them to support the strategic need for offensive action upon the outbreak of any future war.

–ROBERT T. FOLEY,
KING'S COLLEGE, LONDON

References

Antulio J. Echevarria II, *After Clausewitz: German Military Thinkers Before the Great War* (Lawrence: University Press of Kansas, 2000).

L. L. Farrar Jr., *The Short-War Illusion: German Policy, Strategy and Domestic Affairs, August-December 1914* (Santa Barbara, Cal.: ABC-Clio, 1973).

Michael Howard, "Men Against Fire: Expectations of War in 1914," *International Security*, 9 (Summer 1984): pp. 41–57.

John Keegan, *The First World War* (London: Hutchinson, 1998).

Jay Luvaas, "European Military Thought and Doctrine, 1870–1914," in *The Theory and Practice of War: Essays Presented to Captain B. H. Liddell Hart*, edited by Michael Howard (London: Cassell, 1965).

Bruce W. Menning, *Bayonets Before Bullets: The Imperial Russian Army, 1861–1914* (Bloomington: Indiana University Press, 1992).

Jack Snyder, *The Ideology of the Offensive: Military Decision Making and the Disasters of 1914* (Ithaca, N.Y.: Cornell University Press, 1984).

Peter Paret, ed., *Makers of Modern Strategy: From Machiavelli to the Nuclear Age* (Princeton: Princeton University Press, 1986).

Douglas Porch, *The March to the Marne: The French Army, 1871–1914* (Cambridge & New York: Cambridge University Press, 1981).

Barbara W. Tuchman, *The Guns of August* (New York: Macmillan, 1962).

CULTURE OF THE OFFENSIVE

DAVID LLOYD GEORGE

Was David Lloyd George an effective wartime prime minister?

Viewpoint: Yes. Lloyd George provided strong leadership when Britain was under intense pressure on many fronts. His personal charm and political skills were major assets, and it is unlikely any of his contemporaries could have done better.

Viewpoint: No. Lloyd George's pursuit of victory at all costs committed Britain to policies that could not be sustained, and the nation's survival depended upon strokes of good fortune.

David Lloyd George was an ambitious man. Of that fact there can be no doubt. His status as a political maverick before World War I reflected as much his refusal to submit to the restraints of party discipline as it did the originality of his ideas and the force of his advocacy. He began as a solicitor, part of the pattern of lawyers moving into politics that has dominated parliamentary/congressional systems in the twentieth century. A Liberal, at least nominally, he made his mark as a radical social reformer, critic of the House of Lords, and advocate of old-age pensions and taxes on the prosperous. Lloyd George opposed the Boer War (1899–1902). His "People's Budget" of 1909, with its relative emphasis on welfare spending, was a direct challenge to the naval programs in particular that dominated British public spending.

In the summer of 1914 Lloyd George was initially hostile to the concept of war with Germany. He soon became an enthusiastic convert, seeing in the conflict opportunities to further both his ideas and his career. A sharp critic of what he considered lack of energy and grip in the prosecution of the war, Lloyd George was able in December 1916 to replace Sir Herbert Henry Asquith as prime minister of a coalition government.

His ideas on how to wage and shorten the war were handicapped by his methods of implementing them. Lloyd George was a schemer and an intriguer, even when those behaviors were counterproductive. His working behind the backs of his senior generals in early 1917 arguably did more to alienate them than the proposals for pursuing decisive victories in non-Western theaters and giving the French supreme command in the West. His insistence on instituting a convoy system over Admiralty opposition in the autumn of 1917 served as a passive check on the German U-boat campaign. His inconsistent approach to the Flanders offensive of 1917, however, contributed heavily to the extension of that operation long after it was doing any good. His refusal to send replacements to the Western Front in the spring of 1918 contributed in part to the initial successes of the German offensives.

Part of Lloyd George's problem was his inability to find suitable replacements for the men—the generals in particular—that he disliked or distrusted. No one in the British Expeditionary Force (BEF) was willing to consider Douglas Haig's job. When Lloyd George finally succeeded in maneuvering the resignation of Chief of Staff Sir William Robertson, the replacement, Sir Henry Wilson, proved just as intransigent while lacking Robertson's personal and professional integrity. As a war premier, Lloyd George might be described as

"Clemenceau lite." He had all of the charisma of his French counterpart, and a good set of the same skills. In the final analysis, however, he lacked the moral force of Georges Clemenceau, and succeeded primarily in confirming his image as a man too clever for anyone else's good.

Viewpoint:
Yes. Lloyd George provided strong leadership when Britain was under intense pressure on many fronts. His personal charm and political skills were major assets, and it is unlikely any of his contemporaries could have done better.

Since the end of World War I a debate has raged among historians about whether David Lloyd George was the best prime minister Britain could have expected during the conflict. His predecessor, Herbert Asquith, premier at the outbreak of the war, was most certainly not the right kind of leader. A patrician and a member of Edwardian society who would not forego his bridge parties and social engagements even under the emergency of the war effort, Asquith could only give the impression that the war was still business as usual for Britain. The problem was that World War I was anything but business as usual. The times required a man of action and energy, a man who could motivate the broader society and provide the British with the means and will to go on fighting until the Germans were defeated. When he was named prime minister, Lloyd George was described by the American ambassador as "not a spent force, but one of the most energetic projectiles I've ever watched or come in contact with. He said more in half an hour yesterday than Asquith ever told me in his life." Lloyd George, a man of energy and one of the first populist-style politicians in Britain, was in fact the best solution for the problem of British wartime leadership in a war that required the mobilization of the whole population of Britain.

War must be won on the material, military, and political levels. However, in 1914, that material and political mobilization were primary responsibilities of the government was not immediately obvious. Classical liberalism, which had given Britain a level of achievement envied around the world, had held that the proper role of government was not to direct the economy, but to stand aside and allow industry and commerce to do its magic: the invisible hand would solve the problems of war mobilization. Lloyd George, a firebrand reformer in the Liberal Party, might well have been expected to follow that line of reasoning, but he did not. As the Chancellor of the Exchequer, Lloyd George dur-

ing a visit to the Western Front in October 1914 was deeply impressed that any victory over the Germans would be largely a material one, and he turned his considerable energies to how to solve this problem, which could damage his role as Chancellor.

In February 1915, Lloyd George presented the Cabinet with a plan for the rational distribution and expansion of industrial output. Calling for a full utilization of the industrial capacity of the nation for the war effort, he projected an expansion of the army by 1.5 million men. This increase would be achieved by a more-direct government intervention in economic planning and management and the complete mobilization of industrial output for the war effort.

Lloyd George got the opportunity to make this vision a reality when Asquith named him the Minister of Munitions in May 1915. As Minister, Lloyd George made the creation of a war economy a reality. Government direction of the economy became one of the distinguishing characteristics of Britain during the war. In part, he was able to achieve this goal because the ministry was a new entity and could be built from the ground up. Minimizing the frictions of bureaucratic turf wars, Lloyd George staffed the ministry with outsiders on the basis of competence. Control over supply and production was centralized and rationalized, and the state opened its own munitions factories. The results were quite readily apparent: shell production, for example, increased by 240 percent in just seven months. Upon the death of Lord Horatio Kitchener in 1916, such success made Lloyd George his obvious successor as Minister of War.

Yet, this post proved to be, as one historian put it, "a gilded cage," for the British military establishment had little respect for its civilian minister, especially a Liberal with a reputation as a populist reformer. The generals could and would circumvent their civilian minister and appeal directly to Tory friends in the Cabinet or even to the King. They could also protect their prestige with political savvy. When Lloyd George, after the catastrophe of the Somme (1916), approached some French generals for advice on a better approach to fighting the war, British military leaders leaked the story to the press, which immediately vilified the minister for a lack of patriotism. Politics, after all, is not the sole province of the politicians.

It is also true, however, that the military need not be the sole province of the generals. World War I, of course, was an arena where nei-

British poster delineating recruitment districts

(Joseph M. Bruccoli Great War Collection, Thomas Cooper Library, University of South Carolina)

ther generals nor statesmen could claim any tremendous success. Cabinet Secretary Maurice Hankey noted in 1917 that British Expeditionary Force (BEF) general Sir Douglas Haig "is the best man we have, but that is not saying much." With such weak faith in the general, it should seem possible that the statesmen could exercise some influence over strategy. Yet, this political

avenue was a dead end. While Lloyd George and others such as Winston Churchill advocated an "Eastern Strategy" to outflank the senseless stalemate of the Western Front, in the end it is uncertain whether this plan would have proven a war-winning strategy. The bloody fighting on the Eastern Front might have been more fluid, but in large part this condition was the result of

DAVID LLOYD GEORGE

"A REAL PEACE"

On 12 April 1917, while giving a speech to the American Club in London, Prime Minister David Lloyd George commented on the United States and the conflict in Europe:

I attach great importance—and I am the last man in the world, knowing for three years what our difficulties have been, what our anxieties have been, and what our fears have been—I am the last man to say that the succor which is given to us from America is not something in itself to rejoice in, and to rejoice in greatly. But I don't mind saying that I rejoice even more in the knowledge that America is going to win the right to be at the conference table when the terms of peace are being discussed. That conference will settle the destiny of nations—the course of human life—for God knows how many ages. It would have been tragic for mankind if America had not been there, and there with all the influence, all the power, and the right which she has now won by flinging herself into this great struggle.

I can see peace coming now—not a peace which will be the beginning of war; not a peace which will be an endless preparation for strife and bloodshed; but a real peace. The world is an old world. It has never had peace. It has been rocking and swaying like an ocean, and Europe—poor Europe!—has always lived under the menace of the sword. When this war began two-thirds of Europe were under aristocratic rule. It is the other way now, and democracy means peace. The democracy of France did not want war; the democracy of Italy hesitated long before they entered the war; the democracy of this country shrank from it—shrank and shuddered—and never would have entered the caldron had it not been for the invasion of Belgium. The democracies sought peace; strove for peace. If Prussia had been a democracy there would have been no war. There are stranger things to come, and they are coming rapidly.

There are times in history when this world spins so leisurely along its destined course that it seems for centuries to be at a standstill; but there are also times when it rushes along at a giddy pace, covering the track of centuries in a year. Those are the times we are living in now. To-day we wage the most devastating war earth has ever seen; to-morrow—perhaps not a distant to-morrow—war may be abolished forever from the category of human crimes. This may be something like the fierce outburst of winter which we are now witnessing before the complete triumph of the sun. It is written of those gallant men who won that victory on Monday—men from Canada, from Australia, and from this old country, which has proven that in spite of its age it is not decrepit—it is written of those gallant men that they attacked with the dawn—fit work for the dawn!—to drive out of forty miles of French soil those miscreants who had defiled it for three years. "They attacked with the dawn." Significant phrase!

The breaking up of the dark rule of the Turk, which for centuries has clouded the sunniest land in the world, the freeing of Russia from an oppression which has covered it like a shroud for so long, the great declaration of President Wilson coming with the might of the great nation which he represents into the struggle for liberty are heralds of the dawn. "They attacked with the dawn," and these men are marching forward in the full radiance of that dawn, and soon Frenchmen and Americans, British, Italians, Russians, yea, and Serbians, Belgians, Montenegrins, will march into the full light of a perfect day.

Source: Charles F. Horne, ed., Source Records of the Great War, *volume 5 (Indianapolis: American Legion), pp. 144–145.*

disparities of the Russian and German armies more than the fact that the battles were fought far from the German homeland. Where the Allied armies had to work at the end of a long logistical train, such as in the Dardenelles, the outcome hardly looked as if it would lead to an Allied victory. Nor would a campaign in the mountainous Balkans, as advocated by "Easterners" such as Lloyd George, be likely to lead to a quick victory. In the end, Lloyd George was not able to restrain his generals and wound up accepting their judgments. Both the Somme and Passchaendaele (1917) were approved by him as war minister and prime minister.

He was fully aware that he had failed to rein in his generals in any substantial manner, and he reflected bitterly on the matter in his postwar memoirs, which portrayed stupid and stubborn generals who were unwilling to see the reality of their method of fighting. To Lloyd George, the

DAVID LLOYD GEORGE

populist who had fought before the war to defend the "little man" against the privileges of the British elite, his generals represented a holdover of the old squirearchy, a dangerous and unjust vestige of the past.

Though success in the strategic and military realm proved elusive, politics was an area where Lloyd George served his country best. Though the material side of the war effort was under control, Britain might not have been able to survive until the collapse of Germany, unless he had been able to master the political storms of the war. Crucial to the war effort was his ability to mobilize the nation for the sacrifices in the war. Already in September 1914, Lloyd George painted the conflict in the most dramatic terms. After describing a brutish, grasping Imperial Germany, he argued

> That is what we are fighting—that claim to predominancy of a material, hard civilization, a civilization which if it once rules and sways the world, liberty goes, democracy vanishes. And unless Britain and her sons come to the rescue it will be a dark day for humanity.

Lloyd George was able to motivate the people to bear the burdens of a total war because he was first and foremost a street-level politician. Before the war he had established his reputation as a great champion of the common man, and that reputation, and the skills it was based upon, proved indispensable as he led the country through the grinder of the war effort. The unprecedented levels of production and sacrifice on the home front and from the empire were constantly tested. Lloyd George was probably the best hope of Britain to keep the country focused and willing to put up with the sacrifices, promising that they were all fighting to build "a land fit for heroes."

–PHILIP GILTMER,
U.S. MILITARY ACADEMY

Viewpoint:
No. Lloyd George's pursuit of victory at all costs committed Britain to policies that could not be sustained, and the nation's survival depended upon strokes of good fortune.

In 1918 the coalition government that had managed the British war effort mounted an election campaign featuring its leader, David Lloyd George, as "The Man Who Won the War." Indeed, after he replaced Prime Minister Herbert Asquith in December of 1916, Lloyd George had been the guiding force providing the men, material, and political will in support of both the war aims of the nation and the tactics of its generals. In this role Lloyd George showed himself to be a flexible improviser, a person capable of adjusting plans and programs to meet the needs of the moment. Such a role had been characteristic of his prewar activities as the creator of social-insurance schemes and as the provider of a "People's Budget" designed to lure the Conservative opponents of Asquith's Liberal Party government into a political confrontation they were sure to lose. In 1915 he applied these skills to the provision of badly needed munitions and ultimately to an agreement with the trade unions whereby unskilled labor, including women, could be fed into war industries while men were recruited into the armed forces. As prime minister he created, at the back of his residence at 10 Downing Street, a "Garden Suburb" in which committees toiled to produce quick results on the enduring demands for guns, men, machines, transportation, and raw materials. These adjustments were clearly important to the demands of war. Set against the laissez-faire policies of prewar governments, they may appear to be radical novelties. Such appearances, however, need to be evaluated according to criteria that both provide historical perspective and assess the consequences of government war policy. An historical perspective shows that Lloyd George's leadership promoted innovations that were common to a nation engaged in a war of attrition. An examination of war policy shows that the goals of Lloyd George's leadership committed Britain to pursue ends it could not reasonably hope to achieve. By these measures it becomes clear that Lloyd George presided over a conflict in which victory meant, at best, survival.

It is well-known that the Western theater settled into an all-consuming stalemate of attrition. The conduct of war in Flanders fields also featured a military leadership determined to break the stalemate with overwhelming frontal assaults. On these terms the war placed prodigious demands upon financial, human, and material resources. Such demands, in turn, inspired governments to undertake extraordinary institutional innovations. This consequence could only be expected and indeed was a common occurrence in British history. One can look back to the wars of William III against Louis XIV (1689–1702) and find a similar pattern of stalemate in Flanders, matched at home by the founding of the Bank of England, the establishment of a Board of Trade, the recoinage of money, and the establishment of a small "war council" to direct policy. By 1916 the need for such innovation was itself generally accepted. Even Asquith was ready to endorse the creation of a small War Committee with extraordinary authority to manage resources. This move, along with plans to introduce conscription of manpower, were also demands of the leadership of Conservative Party politicians who had joined the Liberals in a National Government in 1915. These measures were, therefore, less a novel break with the principles of a peacetime government than the necessary adaptions to the demands war places upon a state.

More novel for the time was the break Lloyd George and the coalition were willing to make with the terms under which the government originally intended to prosecute the war. In the beginning the Asquith government had planned to prosecute the war according to a "blue-water" strategy. The government would build up financial reserves while maintaining a defensive posture on the Western Front. By 1917, so the calculations ran, German strength would be worn down, allowing Britain to intervene in full strength to defeat Germany and dictate the peace terms. By 1915 this plan was in ruins. Early German successes against French and Russian forces caused fears that the allies of Britain would collapse. Sooner than expected Britain would have to provide a greater commitment to the Western Front. The change in government thinking was radical. From a strategy of limited engagement the government shifted its war policy to the all-out commitment demanded by the General Staff. To this decision Lloyd George brought some cautious opinions, but no real dissent. On the one hand, he wanted to minimize British casualties; he also expressed some doubts about the availability of the munitions needed to win on the Western Front. On the other hand, he realized that British opinion needed a military victory to maintain its support for the war. Furthermore, he wanted an outcome that would leave Germany clearly defeated. These considerations led Lloyd George to throw in with his generals and call for the delivery of a "knock-out blow" in the West.

In addition to supporting the goal of a decisive victory, Lloyd George also embraced a wide-ranging menu of strategic goals. The first, proclaimed in public, was to maintain the status of Britain as an independent Great Power. The second, privately held among the policymakers, was to have a peace gaining security for Britain against both its former enemies and its allies. In other words, politi-

cians and generals sought a victory based on British continental, commercial, and imperial interests. Not only would Germany and Austria be defeated, but France, Russia, and later the United States would be treated as competitors for preeminence in the postwar world. Britain would emerge from the war having a "free hand" to determine its own destiny. Pursuit of this outcome drove the policy decisions of Lloyd George's government in 1916 and 1917 to press the offensive in the West, particularly in 1917, with the hope that victory could be had before the American military presence became a significant factor in the final outcome. They also promoted a widening of British military commitments to include a determined effort to dismember the Ottoman Empire and establish British influence in Palestine and Iran. In short, Lloyd George carried out a war policy under which total war would serve broad and ambitious ends.

By 1917 the prospect of achieving these goals faced an uncertain and dubious future. The British nation was bankrupt; its American creditors would no longer grant the loans that fueled its war machine. On the high seas the German U-boat campaign was wreaking havoc on merchant shipping. Food prices were outstripping wages. In eastern Europe the Bolshevik Revolution had taken Russia out of the war. Within the Cabinet, Lloyd George worried that morale at home and in the trenches would not support an offensive in 1918. By any rational standard British leaders should have considered alternatives to knock-out blows and massive offensive maneuvers—but they did not. When in November the London newspaper *The Daily Telegraph* published a letter from the former Conservative Party Foreign Secretary Lord Landsdowne advocating a negotiated peace, Lloyd George and his coalition allies rallied parliamentary and press opposition to its terms. They continued to place their trust in their generals to deliver the victory that would vindicate their strategic goals.

Instead of its own resources, the British government now counted upon the good fortune external events provided. In particular, the decision by Germany in 1917 to prosecute unrestricted U-boat warfare had brought the United States into the conflict. The American government now funded past and future loans to Britain. Also, the prospect of a supply of U.S. manpower inspired the hope that by 1919 fresh and overwhelming fighting forces could finally defeat Germany in the field. Having tried during the summer to win without American assistance, the government now had to accept dependence upon it. Even then, plans for 1919 never materialized. In 1918 the German High Command launched a spring offensive that, when finally stopped and rolled back, brought that country to its knees. In the final analysis, Britain survived the war more through the folly of its adversary than through the skills of its own leadership.

Victory has many meanings. By 1920 it appeared that the status of Britain as a major world power had been maintained. The commercial, financial, and imperial interests of the nation appeared to be intact. In these ways victory meant survival and the chance to rebuild. What victory did not mean was the kind of security the wartime leadership sought for its interests. The imperial system illustrated this point. The Irish fought their way to a measure of independence by 1922. The nationalist movement in India was well established. The dominions, led by Canada, demanded and asserted their independence from British foreign policy. More and more the imperial system showed dependence upon administrative rigidity and military force. Victory over Germany proved to be a dangerous illusion. Lloyd George's achievement had been to insure that Britain paid the highest price possible for its claims to be a Great Power.

–ROBERT MCJIMSEY, COLORADO COLLEGE

References

David French, *The Strategy of the Lloyd George Coalition, 1916–1918* (Oxford: Clarendon Press, 1995; New York: Oxford University Press, 1995).

Bentley Brinkerhoff Gilbert, *David Lloyd George, A Political Life,* volume two, *The Organizer of Victory, 1912–16* (London: Batsford, 1992).

John Turner, *British Politics and the Great War: Coalition and Conflict, 1915–1918* (New Haven, Conn.: Yale University Press, 1992).

David R. Woodward, *Lloyd George and the Generals* (Newark: University of Delaware Press, 1983; London: Associated University Presses, 1983).

DAVID LLOYD GEORGE

EAST AFRICA

Was the 1914–1918 campaign of German general Paul von Lettow-Vorbeck in East Africa a success?

Viewpoint: Yes. As both a military operation and an example of creating a multiethnic army, Lettow-Vorbeck's campaign was brilliant.

Viewpoint: No. The demographic and ecological havoc wrought by Lettow-Vorbeck's operations had little impact on the German war effort.

On the outbreak of war in 1914 both British and German civilian authorities in their respective East African colonies entertained hopes of maintaining neutrality or at least keeping the fighting to a minimum. This desire was partly a manifestation of the paternalism that was a major surface justification for African imperialism. It also reflected widespread fear among the respective settler populations that war between white men would spark black revolution.

Such concerns had little effect on the military commander of German East Africa, Paul von Lettow-Vorbeck. As a German soldier, he considered it his duty to wage war against the enemies of his country. He did so with such success that he became an iconographic figure among both his countrymen and his enemies, much as German general Erwin Rommel was to do in World War II. Leading and sustaining inferior forces by professional skill and will-power, Lettow-Vorbeck was and is frequently described as demonstrating the truth of the old axiom that in war, men are nothing; the man is everything.

Lettow-Vorbeck did not wage a guerrilla campaign in the normal sense of that term. His men were trained as bush fighters—a skill in which they consistently outmatched their opponents, and that depended heavily at the sharp end on ambush and surprise, followed by a swift breaking of contact and a melting back into the "bundu." Lettow-Vorbeck sought battle, however, not attrition. He sought to keep his enemies concentrated, not to disperse them. His operations had meaning not in themselves but in the context of the overall German war effort.

On one level his campaign was a classic illustration of economy of force. With never more than a few thousand men under command, Lettow tied up more than 150,000 British and Belgian troops in the course of the campaign. Relatively few of these soldiers, however, were realistically available for service in Europe. Most were East and West Africans, who proved exponentially superior to Europeans and white South Africans in the terrain and climate of the East African theater, but would have required extensive training and preparation to be deployed effectively under the conditions of the Western Front.

Nor, contrary to a major German myth, did Lettow-Vorbeck emerge as a charismatic leader of Africans. His soldiers fought well and loyally, but they were essentially professionals who fought for pay and for the immediate spoils of victory. Their women and children accompanied them on campaign. Many German *askaris* were recruited outside German East Africa; as the conflict progressed, the army in which they served became a self-sustaining entity in the manner of the Thirty Years' War (1618–1648), living off whatever land it occupied and obtaining military needs such as arms and ammunition by capture. When Lettow-Vorbeck finally surrendered on receiving news of the armistice in Europe, most of his men carried rifles made in Britain. It is ironic that Lettow-Vorbeck, who regarded himself as a modern soldier, achieved his successes by emulating such captains as Flemish general Johann Tserclaes (Graf von Tilly) and Austrian general Albrecht von Wallenstein.

Viewpoint:
Yes. As both a military operation and an example of creating a multiethnic army, Lettow-Vorbeck's campaign was brilliant.

The East Africa campaign of World War I, while considered a sideshow to the war in Europe, nevertheless has captured the imaginations of many. Its subject matter has generated many popular historical treatments, memoirs, and novels. The mystique surrounding this campaign, which lasted from 1914 to 1918, has much to do with its most famous military figure, General Paul von Lettow-Vorbeck. Appointed commander of the German forces in East Africa (the *Schutztruppe,* or "protectorate forces") in 1913, he found himself in the unenviable position of leading the numerically inferior colonial force (260 German officers and 4,600 African troops, or *askaris*) when rumors of war became reality on the European continent in August 1914. He had no illusions that military action in the colonies would have any major impact on the outcome of the war in Europe. Quite the contrary, as he noted in his memoir, "I knew that the fate of the colonies, as of all other German possessions, would only be decided on the battlefields of Europe."

Despite the inherent difficulties involved in mounting a campaign against the Allies in East Africa, he envisioned an important role for the *Schutztruppe* in contributing to the overall prosecution of the war by Imperial Germany. Starting from the premise that a scrappy and well-executed operation could tie up valuable Allied resources and thus weaken their ability to fight in Europe, he assembled a highly effective multiethnic and interracial force, leading this force on an arduous, yet successful campaign (if success is measured, as it should be, against Lettow-Vorbeck's original objective of tying up Allied manpower). Most analysts have considered Lettow-Vorbeck's feat a rare example of highly mobile guerrilla warfare in a wider war stereotypically characterized as stagnant and lacking in mobility. Indeed, the uniqueness of his accomplishments, both in forging an effective fighting instrument out of a polyglot and interracial force and in executing a sustained hit-and-run, but mainly defensive campaign, merits him considerable credit as a military genius.

Lettow-Vorbeck's reputation as a formidable opponent began with the November 1914 defense of the coastal town of Tanga against a disastrous amphibious assault by two British-led Indian colonial brigades. Despite a twenty-to-one disadvantage in troop strength, his troops capitalized on their familiarity with the terrain around Tanga, as well as the ungainliness of British movements on the ground, which Lettow-Vorbeck had accurately assessed before the attack. The assault, equally hampered by British incompetence and poorly trained and travel-weary Indian troops, failed miserably and cost the British some 1,300 casualties. Lettow-Vorbeck's losses were considerably less—only about 60 total deaths—and the British retreat made possible the German seizure of many vital supplies, including machine guns, rifles, ammunition, and clothing. This battle forced the British commanders to reassess their strategy against the Germans and to grapple with Lettow-Vorbeck's skillful employment of his simple advantages—a small, loyal, rugged, and mobile force and a solid knowledge of the operating environment.

Following the Tanga defense, the German forces, which were broken into small tactical units mixing Europeans and eight *askaris,* roved throughout the Kilimanjaro region carrying out small but strategic attacks on bridges, railways, and British baggage convoys. The supplies taken in these ambushes helped Lettow-Vorbeck's supply-starved force to replenish its stocks. Meanwhile, Lettow-Vorbeck recruited a guerrilla army, which grew to include 3,000 whites as officers and noncommissioned officers (NCOs) and 11,000 African *askaris*. By 1916 Britain had been forced to concede that they would have to mount a concerted effort to stop Lettow-Vorbeck and to conquer the last German colony. General Jan Smuts, a South African, became the commander of British forces in 1916. He brought with him the goal of forcing the Germans off balance through a maneuver campaign in which he would "surround and annihilate" Lettow-Vorbeck in short order. Although British efforts forced the Germans from the northern part of the colony in 1916, they were unable to trap the main body of his force. Moreover, the British force, undermined by rampant sickness and sheer exhaustion, could not sustain the southward push and could not immediately pursue the Germans. Lettow-Vorbeck led a masterful tactical retreat into the southeastern corner

EAST AFRICA

A LONG CRAWL IN THE HEAT

In his memoirs, Deneys Reitz, who served under Jan Christian Smuts in East Africa against the Germans in World War I, remembers an encounter with the troops of General Paul von Lettow-Vorbeck:

Von Lettow himself was said to be here, and a few nights before he had launched an attack on our lines that had only been beaten off by fierce hand-to-hand fighting in the dark. The enemy lay in an entrenched position across our front, and with so many of our men out of action from malaria, and with the rest on half rations, van Deventer was unable to continue his attempt to reach the Central Railway, his objective since leaving Mount Kilimanjaro. All this was disappointing, and I for one look back with no pleasure upon the long period of enforced inactivity that followed. Our men were strung out for miles to right and left, facing the German positions, and for the next two months there was stalemate. I was posted to the First Mounted Brigade, holding the left flank of our line in very rugged hills. Food was scarce and sometimes lacking altogether, and cold biting rains, varied by oppressive heat, prevailed much of the time. The Germans were before us in the ravines and gorges, but in such rough country it was difficult to know exactly where their front line ran. Often bullets whipped about our ears from some unexpected quarter, and it was but rarely that we caught more than a fleeting glimpse of the enemy. It was well for us that the Askaris, like all natives, were remarkably poor shots, while the German soldiers were not particularly good either, so that our losses were not heavy, and we probably caused more damage than we received during our frequent brushes.

There was a little six-pounder German gun in our vicinity, daringly handled by an officer whom we learned to know by sight, so often did he appear from behind boulder or thicket, with his field-piece carried on a wooden frame by its Askari crew. In a moment, half a dozen rounds would come screeching at us, after which the gun was taken off to reappear at some other spot. Beyond wounding a few horses once, she did no harm that I know of, and the men laughed at "Big Bertha" as they called her. One morning three of us tried to stalk the gun, but when we closed in on the patch of scrub where we had last seen her, all we found for our pains was a piece of paper bearing a derisive message: "15 Rupees for the bluddy Englisch", a joke at which we were not amused, after our long crawl in the heat.

On another occasion we were ordered to reconnoitre down a rocky gorge giving access to the open country beyond. The Germans, with great speed, rushed up two companies of Askari, who came at us eagerly as hounds on the scent. Young Lieut. Bowden stood on a rock to get a better view, and almost immediately fell back dead, and we had four other men killed and a number wounded, before the attack was staved off. Desultory fighting of this kind went on most of the time, while we were waiting for the fever season to pass, and for the roads to dry. I do not know how many men died of fever, but I think we left over three hundred of our countrymen in the graveyard at Kondoa Irangi.

During all this time the enemy forces confronting us must have been having their own troubles. In some Morogoro newspapers, that were brought in, were many obituary notices of officers and men "gefallen auf der Höhe von Kondoa Irangi" (fallen on the heights of Kondoa Irangi), and the names of many others who had died of fever. Moreover, like ourselves, they had their supply difficulties, for this region is inhabited by a poverty-stricken native tribe. . . .

Source: Deneys Reitz, Trekking On *(London: Faber & Faber, 1933), pp. 84–85.*

of the Tanganyika territory, eventually crossing over into Portuguese East Africa in late 1917, dragging the ragged British troops along behind him as they resumed the chase of the nimble German force.

By the time Lettow-Vorbeck's forces moved deep into Portuguese territory, however, it was apparent that he would soon be surrounded on all sides: the Portuguese were coming from the south, the British from the north (now under General Jacob van Deventer) and from the southwest through Rhodesia (under General Edward Northey), and the Belgians were pressing from the west. Rather than abandoning the cause and surrendering, Lettow-Vorbeck instead crossed back into German East Africa in October 1918 and then into British Rhodesia. Along the way, his forces continued their guerrilla-style attacks on their enemies, seizing supplies and prisoners, both European and African, in the process. Finally, on 13 November 1918, Lettow-Vorbeck received notification that the armistice ending the war had been signed two days earlier. His force then marched to Abercorn (Mbala) at the southern tip of Lake Tanganyika in British Rhodesia, where he surrendered to General W. F. S. Edwards on 25 November.

General Lettow-Vorbeck's performance in this campaign garnered him the respect of his enemies as well as many accolades at home in defeated Germany. How was he able to meet his goals and sustain his campaign for more than four years, despite the lack of outside resupply or allies? Several reasons explain his success. First, he trusted and respected the fighting abilities of his troops, and most important, his African *askaris*. While his force was much smaller than the combined forces of the Allies, it was perhaps the best prepared to fight the war that he envisioned. The core of the force had considerable previous experience in bush warfare because of its primary role in suppressing internal rebellion in the colony. Their harassing attacks on Allied supply lines and strategic nodes were orchestrated to counter enemy numerical superiority while disabling key assets. Rather than forcing the *askaris* to conform to continental ideas of warfare, he recognized the inherent value of allowing them to continue to fight using a means more suitable to the environment in which they fought. He expected his white German officers to do the same. Second, Lettow-Vorbeck knew that his force would be able to provision itself on the march by "living off the land"—they were familiar with the terrain, flora, and fauna of Tanganyika and had a long history of extracting goods from villages in the colony as required. They moved quickly and with little regard to obstacles—natural or human—that crossed their path.

The real reason behind Lettow-Vorbeck's success was his singular military acumen, developed out of a mixture of keen intellect and years of experience in colonial warfare. For example, he had learned firsthand the value of bush warfare while deployed to Southwest Africa for the suppression of the Herero/Nama rebellion (1904). He had observed British clumsiness during the suppression of the Boxer Rebellion in China (1900). Upon his arrival in East Africa in 1913, he assessed his forces and imagined a plan that would both maximize its strengths and minimize its weaknesses. He also benefited greatly from Allied weaknesses—the arrogance and tactical inflexibility of British officers, the poor training and diverse ethnic backgrounds of their troops, and the lack of strategic foresight from

London. Supremely loyal to the Kaiser in Germany, Lettow-Vorbeck believed that the sacrifices he would personally make, along with those to which he would subject the colony, were worthwhile. He thus executed a campaign that by all accounts was disastrous for East African civilians, contributing directly to massive famine and the spread of disease, as well as immense hardship for the *askaris,* their families, and the porters forced to carry German equipment and supplies. He recognized the havoc that his campaign wreaked, but he knew equally well how it exasperated the Allies, and this result was most important to him. He sacrificed his own health and well-being to the cause of the Fatherland as well: as historian Robert Asprey remarked, "By early 1917, he was enduring his fourth bout of malaria; sand flies and jiggers lived in his skin, at times he could scarcely walk on a scabbed and festered left foot, his teeth were infected, and he had scratched his one good eye on long elephant grass." He might easily have surrendered and spent the remainder of the war in the relative comfort of a prisoner-of-war camp. To Lettow-Vorbeck, however, premature surrender was not an option, no matter what the cost. His reputation as a uniquely brilliant general, battlefield commander, and leader of troops unequivocally stands the test of historical examination.

—MICHELLE MOYD, CORNELL UNIVERSITY

Viewpoint:
No. The demographic and ecological havoc wrought by Lettow-Vorbeck's operations had little impact on the German war effort.

The exploits of General Paul von Lettow-Vorbeck in German East Africa (Tanganyika) are the stuff of legend. Vastly outnumbered and outgunned, Lettow-Vorbeck kept a harassing force in the field for four years, relying on maneuverability, superior knowledge of local conditions, and bush tactics to outwit his opponents. For his resoluteness, tactical cleverness, and ability to command the loyalty of the *askaris* (native troops), he won acclaim as the German equivalent to Lawrence of Arabia. Like Lawrence, he was brave, resourceful, dashing—and overhyped, for Lettow-Vorbeck's efforts were confined to a tertiary theater whose strategic importance was marginal to the main war effort in Europe. His dogged resistance in an ultimately hopeless contest served only to lengthen the fighting in East Africa, leading to

EAST AFRICA

wholesale and ruthless exploitation of indigenous labor and widespread ecological devastation. The resulting demographic and ecological damage to Africa echoed the worst of imperialist depredations of previous decades.

Forced enlistment of porters or carriers constituted the most serious demographic impact to Africa. As a result of a lack of water, severe heat, and the tsetse fly (which carried trypanosomiasis), traditional draft animals such as mules died in droves in East Africa. Porters—men, women, and children—replaced draft animals and became both the unsung heroes and unlamented victims of the East African campaign. From 1914 to 1918 both sides together employed approximately one million porters; a conservative estimate for total deaths of these workers is one hundred thousand, with most succumbing to disease, malnutrition, exhaustion, and battle wounds. Africans quickly came to refer to carrier work (porterage) as *thangata* (work without benefit).

Carrier work brought only hardship. Porters routinely carried up to seventy-pound loads in an intensely hot and pestilential environment while subsisting on a daily ration of two and a half pounds of meal. Forced impressment of porters was common, as European recruiters revived the harshest practices of the African slave trade of previous decades: intimidating village chiefs to force them to pick "volunteers," raiding villages in the dead of night to abduct adult males, and offering false promises of high wages and other rewards in aggressive attempts to entice recruits. Impressment, or coerced enlistment, disrupted traditional community work patterns, leading to the breakdown of African families and kinship groups and the loss of vital occupational skills in African villages.

Since German forces had no access to railway lines or shipping, they relied exclusively on porters for logistics. Usually three porters were required for each soldier, with officers requiring more. At peak strength in March 1916 Lettow-Vorbeck's forces consisted of fourteen thousand soldiers (three thousand German and eleven thousand *askaris*) and forty-five porters. In a pinch, both sides used porters as frontline soldiers. Lettow-Vorbeck attempted to set an example by reducing his personal porters to three plus a cook, but European officers usually insisted on as many as fifteen personal porters. Many porters refused to work unless their families or dependents accompanied them, which swelled the ranks even further.

Known in his day as a "good" German for his comparatively compassionate treatment of native peoples, Lettow-Vorbeck nevertheless worked his porters twelve hours a day, seven days a week. For their work, porters received a few handfuls of rice or stale maize. Porters considered lazy or disobedient received *hamsa ishirini* (twenty-five lashes with a hippopotamus-hide whip called a *kiboko*). According to Melvin E. Page, in *Africa and the First World War* (1987), among British African soldiers Lettow-Vorbeck was known as *Lete Viboko,* a corruption of his name that, in Swahili, meant "bring the whips made of hippopotamus hide." Yet, in administering harsh discipline Lettow-Vorbeck was unexceptional. British general Edward Northey reported that porters apprehended while attempting to escape "were shot indiscriminately." Even after the war ended, burdens did not lighten for porters. In the closing weeks of the war many contracted influenza—the infamous and virulent Spanish flu—which they spread to their villages during the homeward trek. Among East Africans the death rate from influenza approached 6 percent of the population.

East Africans proved particularly vulnerable to influenza because of Lettow-Vorbeck's *Hungerstrategie* (hunger strategy). This strategy was based on the German handling of the Maji Maji rebellion (1905). The Germans suppressed this revolt by denying food and agricultural land to the rebels. In the man-made famine that followed, 250,000 Africans died. As German forces retreated through southern Tanganyika in 1917, Lettow-Vorbeck resurrected the scorched-earth policy of 1905 to deny food, cattle, and other agricultural resources to the pursuing Allied forces. This deliberate strategy of agricultural devastation, together with the failure of rains in East Africa in November 1917 and shortages of farm laborers because of the ruthless impressments of porters, led to widespread famine and death in East Africa in 1918. Those East Africans who managed to survive the famine were often left much weakened; falling upon this population, the influenza of 1918–1919 administered the coup de grâce. Perhaps as many as 2,000,000 Africans died before the influenza epidemic ran its course.

This demographic disaster had related ecological effects. As African farm laborers lay dead or dying, crops went unweeded, seeds went unplanted, and fields went untended. Wild animals extended their grazing to these untended fields, and tsetse-fly infestations came with them. These infestations reduced the land available for cattle herding, severely damaging the fragile economy and trade of African communities.

Such widespread demographic and ecological devastation and debilitation might perhaps have been defensible if Lettow-Vorbeck's efforts in the field had garnered proportionate advantages for the German war effort. Tragically for the *askaris* and porters who fought or marched to their deaths in long, scorched-earth retreats, Lettow-Vorbeck wasted their superhuman efforts in a sideshow campaign of marginal strategic significance. Admittedly, Lettow-Vorbeck's force often took the initiative at the tactical level, and his 15,000 *Schutztruppe* (protectorate forces) tied down ten times as many Allied troops. Yet, Lettow-Vorbeck lacked the resources to take the strategic initiative; he could only counterpunch, without ever being able to administer a knockout blow against an often-times clumsy, though ultimately superior opponent.

For the British the campaign in East Africa was always a luxury. When it went poorly, as it did in November 1914 in the botched attack at Tanga Bay, the British responded by placing East Africa on the back burner until December 1915. In prosecuting the campaign in 1916–1917, the British relied primarily on colonial troops, most notably Jan Smuts's Boers, the King's African Rifles, and other native units from the Belgian Congo, Portuguese East Africa, Nigeria, and other regions. Ruthless recruitment techniques meant that native manpower was usually plentiful for the Allies. By February 1918 more than 90 percent of the manpower on both sides was African, with only 4 percent of British infantry forces actually hailing from Britain. Lettow-Vorbeck's resistance may have irritated the British, but it did not force them to divert significant quantities of men or matériel from more important theaters in Europe or elsewhere. Even if the Allied forces had succeeded in defeating Lettow-Vorbeck sooner, the vast majority of the troops fighting against him would not have been shipped to other theaters.

In resources allocated to Lettow-Vorbeck, the Germans themselves recognized the backwater nature of the East African theater. *Askaris* initially fought with obsolete weaponry such as the Mauser M1871 pattern rifle: a single-shot .450 breech-loader that used black-powder cartridges. The black smoke spewed by this rifle often gave away the position of the soldier firing it, a liability of fatal consequences in bush warfare where concealment was everything. Lettow-Vorbeck may have worked wonders in capturing Allied supplies or in improvising artillery from the wreckage of the *Königsberg*, but he could never obtain the supplies he needed to attain decisive victories. With Britain controlling the African lakes and blockading the coastline, Lettow-Vorbeck was essentially constrained to maneuver (at times brilliantly) in a geographically vast, yet strategically vapid, arena of combat.

Everyone loves an underdog, especially a respectable underdog such as Lettow-Vorbeck, who was known for his correct and courteous behavior and his fluency in English. The campaign in East Africa, moreover, was certainly more exciting and colorful than the trench warfare and stalemates that characterized fighting on the Western Front from late 1914 to 1918. Yet, the romance of Lettow-Vorbeck's exploits should not obscure the fact that he was engaged in a futile campaign in a theater of marginal importance. His limited victories, such as they were, had little discernible effect on the Allied war effort, but they did have a devastating impact on African demographics and ecology. By prolonging a futile conflict in East Africa, Lettow-Vorbeck may have been doing his duty as a Prussian officer, but it came at the expense of hundreds of thousands of Africans who died grievously and tragically for European colonial interests and military vainglory.

–WILLIAM J. ASTORE,
U.S. AIR FORCE ACADEMY

References

Michael Crowder, "The First World War and its Consequences," in *General History of Africa,* volume 7, *Africa under Colonial Domination 1880–1935,* edited by A. Adu Boahen (London: Heinemann; Berkeley: University of California Press, 1985), pp. 283–311.

Byron Farwell, *The Great War in Africa, 1914–1918* (New York: Norton, 1986).

Brian Gardner, *German East: The Story of the First World War in East Africa* (London: Cassell, 1963).

Geoffrey Hodges, *The Carrier Corps: Military Labor in the East African Campaign, 1914–1918* (New York: Greenwood Press, 1986).

Edwin P. Hoyt, *Guerilla: Colonel von Lettow-Vorbeck and Germany's East African Empire* (New York: Macmillan, 1981).

David Killingray, "The War in Africa," in *World War I: A History,* edited by Hew Strachan (Oxford & New York: Oxford University Press, 1998), pp. 92–103.

Paul Emil von Lettow-Vorbeck, *My Reminiscences of East Africa* (London: Hurst & Blackett, 1920).

Charles Miller, *Battle for the Bundu: The First World War in East Africa* (New York: Macmillan, 1974).

Leonard Oswald Mosley, *Duel for Kilimanjaro: An Account of the East African Campaign, 1914–1918* (London: Weidenfeld & Nicolson, 1963).

Melvin E. Page, "The War of *Thangata:* Nyasaland and the East African Campaign, 1914–1918," *Journal of African History,* 19 (1978): 87–100.

Page, ed., *Africa and the First World War* (London: Macmillan, 1987; New York: St. Martin's Press, 1987).

Hew Strachan, *The First World War,* volume 1, *To Arms* (Oxford & New York: Oxford University Press, 2001).

EAST AFRICA

90

Did German occupation policies in Eastern Europe prefigure those of the Third Reich?

Viewpoint: Yes. The Nazis, who added genocidal racism to the mix, perpetuated German views of the East and its peoples as fields of conquest and development.

Viewpoint: No. The German occupation of Eastern Europe was concerned initially with providing administration and security and subsequently with reorganizing the conquered territory along traditional imperialist lines.

As the Eastern Front stabilized after the great battles of 1915, grandiose projects of exploitation increasingly appeared in memoranda at the highest levels of the government and the army. A Central European customs union, new thrones in the Baltic states and Poland, German colonization of lands vacated by wartime migrations—all seemed possible. German general Erich Ludendorff suggested annexations of land ranging as far east as the Caspian Sea. The discourse reflected a developed consciousness of the East as a source of both current German power and endless possibilities for the future.

On an everyday level, the German army had instituted what it considered a civilizing campaign behind its lines, regulating the movement of refugees, cleaning streets, disinfecting schools and bathhouses, and establishing public toilets. The soldiers and civil administrators paid little attention to the populations they proposed to benefit. Their normal reaction to the Jews, Poles, and Russians were a mixture of amusement and contempt on one hand, fear and hostility on the other. They reflected a developing prewar sense of racially based superiority to the *Ostvölker* (Eastern peoples), as well as other experiences that reinforced a sense of cultural alienation. One officer put the matter bluntly: "Only when the population has learned to wash themselves can we think of political measures."

An increasingly racialized imperialism was balanced, if not checked, by the fact that the German occupation of the east overwhelmingly involved involuntary participants. Whether running delousing stations or killing Russian soldiers, the "new Teutonic Knights of the East" were conscripted conquerors and homesick racists. They saw nothing that was not exponentially better in Germany—certainly nothing worth the effort of ruling over the local peoples on a long-term basis. The concept of a German imperium may have attracted generals and politicians. Almost everyone else was marking time until he could return back home. Their feelings about the East were negative: keep these aliens, their folkways, and their diseases as far from Germany as possible. It was a moral compound unpalatable but not as yet toxic. It would require development by racist scholars and Nazi ideologues in order to become the stuff of genocide.

Viewpoint:
Yes. The Nazis, who added genocidal racism to the mix, perpetuated German views of the East and its peoples as fields of conquest and development.

Imperial German policies on the Eastern Front during World War I were geared to achieve two basic aims: to make it easier for the *Wehrmacht* (German army) to rule newly conquered peoples while fighting the war and to ensure a continued German presence in the region after the conflict. Their policies and methods did not differ much from those of the National Socialist German Workers' Party (Nazis) a generation later; any contrast is essentially a study of the differences between the nineteenth-century world of the Kaiser and the twentieth-century one of the Führer. Many of the excesses and horrors of Nazi occupation could be seen in a slightly more primitive form earlier, during Imperial German occupation and government of the same lands, and both groups of Germans based their policies and methods on similar ways of viewing the world.

It is a problem of recent historians to perceive the Nazis as existing somehow in a vacuum. There seems to be a desire to see the Nazis and their policies as somehow separate from Western European tradition, as an anomaly, an aberration unlike anything that had come before. This conclusion is a mistake. It leads to many faulty interpretations of their policies and of the motivations of the men who conceived and implemented them. It is more accurate, and probably more helpful, to view fascism in general and the Nazi Party in particular as a logical (if despicable) outcome of the Enlightenment. A fundamental belief of post-Enlightenment thinkers is that society can be "shaped," if necessary by force, into a more pleasing, efficient, or "better" form. This belief, that some men know better how to reshape society, led nineteenth-century German philosopher Friedrich Nietzsche and others to conclude that a superior breed of man would then emerge, free of traditional moral constraints. Eventually these "super-men" would triumph over the weak and inferior, if necessary by exterminating them. These Enlightenment ideas of forging a perfect society have had a great impact in Germany and elsewhere and have led many people to try and restructure society the way they would like it.

It is therefore reasonable to expect that Nazi German policies evolved from Imperial German ones: if it was believed to be acceptable to attempt to enslave millions of people to build a better society in World War I, how would it be less so only twenty years later? To the extent the Imperial German General Staff were products of Prussian monarchical, militaristic traditions, they did not embrace the notion of inherent inferiority of other peoples. They saw instead only the glory of the German state—not necessarily of the German race. Adolf Hitler's *Wehrmacht* officers were another generation removed from the "kinder, gentler" world of the past, another generation down the path of the superman. Like the Communists (who also sought Utopia), the Fascists predicted not the triumph of a German state but of a "race" (equivalent to the Communist "class") of Aryans.

The basic difference between the two periods is the relative importance of the military versus the political elements of the German government. In World War I the military took precedence, as it had for generations. However, once the precise battlefield operations were set in motion, the German army had little planned as far as governing the newly conquered peoples of Eastern Europe. Much of their policy was improvised, largely by professional military officers unaccustomed to making political decisions. By the time World War II began in 1939, the military men had been pushed into the background and policy decisions were made according to long-held plans, conceived by politicians who were members of the Nazi Party. These men saw themselves as learning from the "mistakes" of World War I, and they sought to ensure German domination by planning ahead.

If German rule in Eastern Europe was less harsh during World War I than World War II, it was perhaps because of the type of men making the decisions on how the subject peoples would be treated. They were largely Prussian aristocrats, who were stirred by a sense of honor and duty, and they felt an obligation toward defeated enemies. Furthermore, they were professional soldiers, who are by and large a practical group: nothing so stiffens the enemy's resolve as knowing they will be massacred or enslaved if they lose the war. Under the Third Reich, however, the decisions were made by political figures, who tended to be harsher on subject peoples than military men. Both groups of German decision-makers sought to alleviate immediate problems and accomplish their long-term aims at the same time. The Imperial German General Staff did not have concrete plans going into the war for what to do with the Poles, for example, because that was something they were going to leave to the politicians to solve after the war. Their immediate problem was fighting the Russians, Romanians, and Serbs. Hitler's government already had plans for the Poles and everyone else in Eastern Europe, and they incorporated their "solu-

tions" into the war itself, going so far as to redraw borders and begin population transfers while the fighting was still going on.

In both wars there was massive pressure from the German civilian public to make a "Greater Germany"; that is, to enhance not only the size of Germany but to ensure her protection and economic well-being in whatever world emerged after the war. A "Petition of the Intellectuals" was signed by 1,300 artists, professors, students, and industry leaders in June 1915, which stated that Germany was "entitled" to territorial gain. Only "a few, a very few German subjects," according to Max Hoffmann in *War Diaries And Other Papers* (1929), thought the demands for expansion would come back to haunt them. Twenty years later the Nazis argued that Germany suffered starvation and postwar revolution because it failed to secure a just peace after World War I—millions of Germans were convinced the only way to prevent this tragedy from happening again was to set Germany above all its neighbors, both militarily and economically. The Germans learned from what they perceived as their mistakes in World War I: it is difficult and expensive to control an unwilling subject population with ad hoc and improvised solutions. In addition, twenty years of independence from German overlordship left many of Germany's neighbors capable of acting on long-standing anti-German sentiment and offering significant resistance. German methods of implementing policy in World War II therefore went beyond brute, physical intimidation by occupation troops and reached into the realm of terror and wide-scale extermination of potential enemies.

Seeds of later Nazi policies and methods can be seen in an examination of five specific cases of World War I German occupation policy: Poland, the Baltic countries, Serbia, Romania, and the Russian Empire as a whole. Poland received perhaps the most prewar attention by German thinkers and writers. Heinrich von Treitschke was a popular German philosopher of the nineteenth century. He and other "Pan-German" authors argued that it was "natural" and "just" that Germans rule over Poland. By and large the prevailing opinion in Germany was that sooner or later a major, victorious war against the Russian Empire would result in the absorption of millions of non-Germans—mostly Poles—into the German Empire. Many thought the lands of the Medieval Teutonic Order, populated by Lithuanians, Poles, Latvians, Estonians, Germans, and other peoples, could over time be "Germanicized"—made more German. The notion ran that some nations were stronger than others, and eventually only a few strong nations would survive, absorbing all the "weaker" nations. This perversion of English naturalist Charles Darwin's theory of evolution into political reality was particularly popular in America, Britain, and Germany at the turn of the twentieth century.

The two men most responsible for Imperial German strategy and policy on the Eastern Front were General Erich Ludendorff and Field Marshall Paul von Hindenburg—both important figures in twentieth-century German history. Ludendorff went on to be a founding member of

Russian soldier attempting to stop two deserters on the Eastern Front

(from The Illustrated War News, *12 September 1917, page 13, Joseph M. Bruccoli Great War Collection, Thomas Cooper Library, University of South Carolina)*

EASTERN EUROPE

the Nazi Party in the 1920s; Hindenburg was President of Weimar Germany from 1925 until his death delivered near-absolute power into Hitler's hands in 1933.

Ludendorff, in particular, wrote and spoke a great deal during the war on what to do with newly conquered territory. World War I began well for Germany—they conquered vast amounts of territory from the Russian Empire and were by 1916 responsible for governing more than 100,000,000 non-Germans. The generals commanding on the Eastern Front had to devise local governments, largely by themselves or with imported administrators and technicians, since much of the local population had fled east as the Russian army retreated. Strict martial law, school closures (except those taught in German), and cessation of all political activity were the immediate "benefits" the German army brought with them. The Nazis issued similar orders, but went further in "securing" the country by closing all Polish churches and limiting the amount of food individual Poles were allowed to eat.

Ludendorff espoused total political annihilation of the Polish state, at best characterizing this policy as a "severe reduction" of Poland. According to Werner Conze, Ludendorff argued "it is all a matter of power"; that while Poland had great potential for recruiting armies and workers for German factories, Germany would not be safe with an independent Poland on its borders. The land itself would be used for "German colonization": German landlords would run vast estates worked by Polish peasants, who would be bound to serve their German masters. Naturally, this scenario would create some problems, especially since there were so many Poles and would be so few German "settlers," at least at first. Ludendorff solved that problem by suggesting forcibly resettling "undesirables" to a location "further east." The final details would be decided after the war, but in the meantime Hindenburg and Ludendorff set about creating as much hostility between local populations as possible. There are many examples of Lithuanians being imported to run Polish shops, Jewish merchants getting all the local contracts, and Polish workers being brought into Ukrainian towns—all with the purpose of preventing the formation of a united front against the German conquerors.

There was a larger German concern for security in the East. The principal German ally in World War I was the Austro-Hungarian Empire: a collection of German, Hungarian, and Slavic nations ruled over by an Austrian emperor from the Hapsburg family. The two allies' interests collided in Poland; both wanted to annex large swaths of territory. To reduce friction with Austria during the war, the Imperial German government showed some flexibility by proposing several divisions of spoils that greatly reduced the amount of territory, and therefore people, that Germany would take at the end of the war. According to Robert B. Asprey in *The German High Command at War: Hindenburg and Ludendorff Conduct World War I* (1991), "Many influential Germans had turned to the idea of *Mitteleuropa* or 'Middle Europe,'—a Central European union under the aegis of Germany." The idea came from a novel of the same name, a best-seller in 1915 Germany, by Friedrich Naumann. This concept shows there was a diversity of opinion in Germany about what to do with Poland—but the range of debate was only over specifics. Poland would still be dismembered and its people ruled by foreign kings.

The Nazis also reached an accommodation during the World War II with their then-ally, the Soviet Union, and divided Poland between them. After its attack on the Soviet Union in 1941, Germany annexed much of Poland outright and established military rule over the rest. "Undesirable" Poles were again shipped eastward, mirroring Ludendorff's policies; but what the prudent military thinker Ludendorff would never have thought feasible was the next step of the Nazis: wholesale liquidation of the Slavic population. German plans for clearing their "elbow room" in Eastern Europe required that thirty million Slavs die to make room for German settlers. The death camps at Auschwitz and elsewhere in Axis Europe, where millions of Poles, Serbs, Russians, Jews, and Gypsies were murdered, were technologically unfeasible for Ludendorff to implement. Ludendorff could be credited, however, with laying the foundation for the mentality and psychology of the death camp. A forty-year-old concentration camp guard in World War II was, after all, a product of Imperial Germany. He was probably a World War I veteran with a good chance of having fought on the Eastern Front; he certainly had his opinions formed long before Hitler left art school in Vienna to pursue a career in politics. And at least some people were already thinking this way if the Nazis could staff a "Race and Settlement Office" in 1935.

A similar picture emerged in the Baltic territories of Kurland (now part of Latvia), Lithuania, Latvia, and Estonia. Independent in Medieval times, these lands had been incorporated over the centuries into the German, Polish, or Russian empires. Arguments in Germany during the war ranged from calls for independence to outright annexation. For his part, Ludendorff saw a strategic necessity for cutting off Russian access to the Baltic Sea by making these regions part of Germany. He also seemed to see Germany as the liberator of these people from "Russian oppression." The "historically Germanic" lands north of Poland and west of Russia along the Baltic Sea were treated differently than the Slavic lands. "Virtually every cultured and politically engaged German [was] dreaming of the 'liberation of the land of the Teutonic Order'," argued Gerhard Ritter in *The Sword and the Sceptre: The Problem of Militarism in Germany* (1969–1973), for the Medieval Germanic knights, whose hereditary foes were the Slavs. Though Ludendorff did not have much of a chance to implement his policies here, the Nazis again took the next logical step: during their offensive against the Soviet Union they recruited tens of thousands of Lithuanian, Latvian, and Estonian troops into special *SS* (*Schutzstaffeln*) units to fight against the Russians. They were granted "Honorary German" status and were generally exempted from the harsh treatment meted out to others conquered by the Nazis. In return, the newly independent states really did regard the Nazis as liberators and signed the Tripartite (Axis) Pact with Hitler's Germany, Benito Mussolini's Italy, and Hirohito's Imperial Japan.

Further south, the Austro-Hungarian and Bulgarian allies of Germany became bogged down by 1915 in a war of conquest against Serbia. The German General Staff reluctantly committed troops to help. German policy in World War I regarding the Balkans was less concerned with details of occupation than with overall outcome. As early as the Conference of Berlin in 1878, Germany had encouraged Austria-Hungary to move further into the Balkans, which the latter did, eventually annexing Bosnia-Herzegovina in 1908. When the Austrians and Serbs might have peacefully resolved territorial and other disputes following Archduke Francis Ferdinand's rash visit to Sarajevo, the Germans put immense pressure on the Austrians to go to war. Again, the Austrians did what their much stronger ally wanted—at the cost of their empire, as it turned out.

Within weeks of entering the Balkans, there was much agitation in Berlin for an increased German presence, but what the German government was most interested in was a strong Austro-Hungarian neighbor to the south. German XI Army Chief of Staff General Hans von Seeckt lamented "we shall conquer this beautiful land for someone else," meaning the Austrians, when they could have taken it for themselves. To attain the goal of a strong Austria, there could be no strong states on the Balkan Peninsula. Postwar plans called for dividing existing countries up among German allies such as Bulgaria, Turkey, Italy (until 1915), and, of course, Austria-Hungary.

This policy was similar to those employed by the Third Reich in the next war. Though Austria-Hungary was dissolved at Versailles (1919), its successor states became Nazi allies: Croatia and Hungary were used to fight against the Serbs. German war aims did not involve annexation of Serbia, but rather its dissolution into an impotent agricultural region dominated by German business, and with large sections of Serb territory annexed by German allies. The Croatian Nazis ran into the same problem in Serbia as the German Nazis did in Poland: there were too many people to rule them effectively. Their "solution" to the problem was also similar: they established death camps, such as Jasenovac in Croatia, where hundreds of thousands of Serbs, Jews, and Gypsies were tortured and killed.

Another Balkan country that met a tragic fate at the hands of German policymakers in World War I was Romania. A nominal German ally before the war, Romania stayed neutral until 1916, when the Entente Powers (Britain, France, Russia, and, by then, Italy) convinced it to join the war against Germany and Austria-Hungary. It was a terrible miscalculation: within six months the Romanian Army was shattered, with no hope of assistance from its new allies. According to John W. Wheeler-Bennett, in *Wooden Titan: Hindenburg in Twenty Years of German History, 1914–1934* (1936), the Treaty of Bucharest (1918) drafted by Germany was, in the words of a contemporary observer, "without precedent or equal in modern history." In fact, its terms made Romania no more than a degraded colony of the German Empire. This punishment served as a warning not only for smaller nations, but also for France and Italy; "is this what will happen if we surrender to Germany?" It was much worse than nineteenth-century peace treaties, which generally amounted to an exchange of fees for damages and the redrawing of borders in favor of the victor. It was an innovation the Germans would regret, as the Treaty of Bucharest (1918) and the Treaty of Brest-Litovsk (1918) were used as examples by the Entente Powers when they drew up the Versailles Treaty. The policy of total annihilation of a subject people, while not new for the world, was new for Europe in modern times. Hitler's government would impose similar treaties on its defeated enemies two decades later, which would also encourage resistance as the only alternative to slavery or death.

The best examples of Imperial German policies serving as a precursor to Nazi German conduct were within the lands of the Russian Empire proper. After several years of bitter and uncertain struggle, the Russian Empire virtually disintegrated. Hindenburg and Ludendorff, against perhaps the better judgment of others in the German government, had brought Lenin and his Bolshevik intimates to Russia in the famous "sealed train" like a dangerous virus in a germ-warfare experiment. The virus worked: as the Russian Empire collapsed into revolution and its armies melted from the field, the German Empire soon controlled an area ten times its size before the war. Since the collapse was so sudden and largely unexpected, the task of structuring the conquered territory fell to Hindenburg and Ludendorff. In addition, the United States had recently entered the war following President Woodrow Wilson's reelection, and Germany faced new dangers on the Western Front in France. Things had to be settled quickly and efficiently.

Along with a German-dominated Kingdom of Poland (created on 5 November 1916 and ruled by a German prince), several vaguely defined "buffer" states were created along the Baltic Sea out of Lithuania, Latvia, and Estonia—the details were to be worked out following the conclusion of the war. The rest of the Russian Empire was tentatively carved into "independent" states, though in reality they were garrisoned by German troops and forced to devote almost 100 percent of their monetary, agricultural, and industrial output to the German war effort. The conquered territory was stripped bare. A puppet state was created under a local anti-Russian government in the Ukraine, which furnished 140,000 horses to the German Army as well as cattle and much-needed grain. The Germans generally let them make their own internal decisions (especially those aimed at combating the new Soviet Russian government or the remnants of Russian Imperial forces). Nonetheless, there were almost one million German troops in the Ukraine and surrounding territories, even at the end of the war. General Wilhelm Groener's army of occupation was constantly harassed by Ukrainian peasants and Bolshevik partisan units; by October 1918 German troops were completely unable to transport the vital grain harvest back to Germany because local militias had destroyed railways, bridges, and what few roads existed. Contemporaries viewed the situation in the Ukraine and the other German-occupied sections of Russia as chaotic, and the viability of the new "states" as extremely tenuous and fraught with practical difficulties. None of the local satraps the Germans set up, even in the Ukraine, survived long after the withdrawal of German troops, suggesting that they really were nothing but temporary German puppets.

The sons of General Groener's troops fared no better in World War II: they also came under consistent attack in the Ukraine. To try to deal with this situation, the Nazis also set up client states, carved from the Soviet Union; so, too, did they make distinctions between Germanic and non-Germanic peoples in the way they were treated. They even mirrored their Imperial pre-

decessors in perceiving themselves (and to a great extent in turn being perceived) as liberators of peoples suffering under Communist rule. To their credit, Hindenburg and Ludendorff did not immediately go back on promises of autonomy and freedom the way the Nazis did, but one gets the impression that any clemency shown to conquered peoples was based as much on the practical concerns of winning the war as on humanitarian grounds. Hitler, on the contrary, saw his position as secure enough to dismiss as "futile" German Nazi leader Alfred Rosenberg's ideas of establishing permanent allies among the Slavs.

Elsewhere in Russia Ludendorff indulged in empire-building that was a virtual blueprint for Hitler twenty-five years later. Going beyond initial war aims of establishing a buffer zone to protect Germany, a Berlin newspaper announced that the Crimea would be turned into a "German Riviera," compliments of Field Marshal Hindenburg. Ludendorff "gave" the German navy villages along the Crimea and on the Ukrainian coast from which to cull a labor pool to support the newly acquired shipyards at Sevastopol. This last decision proved to be a violation of an agreement with the Turks, but either way it shows that German policy in the region was harsh, and those subject to German rule were little more than tools. When it was not convenient to pose as a liberator, the German General Staff used brute force to acquire what it needed: in the Caucasus Mountains region of Georgia and Azerbaijan, local nationalist (indeed, pro-German) uprisings were violently suppressed because they threatened to interrupt oil drilling and exploration deemed vital to the German war effort. These policies would be repeated by the armies of the Third Reich, albeit with more mechanical efficiency, but hardly with less brutality or concern for the welfare of the conquered peoples.

In general, Imperial German policy toward conquered Russia was a microcosm of German policy toward their enemies in general; certainly it was viewed this way by many at the time. The Treaty of Brest-Litovsk, which the Provisional Government of Soviet Russia was forced to sign literally at gunpoint, was branded the "Peace of Violence" and used as an excuse to crush Germany after the war. It is rightly considered the harshest peace treaty in modern times. Compared to its draconian and impoverishing conditions and demands, the Treaty of Versailles was a slap on the wrist: nearly everything that could be eaten, ridden, or melted down was to be rounded up and hauled to Germany, by rail, oxcart, or where necessary, on Russian backs. Nothing important to the economy, whether industry or large-scale agriculture, was to remain in non-German hands. Hundreds of thousands of people were forcibly resettled into areas where they could be better controlled or more efficiently put to work for new German landlords. It was a massive undertaking, poorly conceived and requiring vast numbers of soldiers to implement. However, it is easy to imagine the Treaty of Brest-Litovsk as a blueprint for Nazi strategists twenty years later as they planned how to manage the invasion of the Soviet Union. Again the Nazis proved more ready to kill large numbers of people, where Ludendorff was content to make them serfs.

What is perhaps most strikingly similar about the Eastern European plans of both Kaiser and Führer is that they achieved (or failed to achieve) similar results. Throughout the war both had to contend with uneasy and fragile situations in the wake of their temporarily victorious armies. In Poland, Romania, Serbia, and Ukraine it was the same: nowhere was the dream of a free, dominant German master ruling fields toiled in by Slavic peasants to become a reality; it was a "peace" based on bayonets or, later, Panzers. Ludendorff and others wrote that the only unifying force in Eastern Europe was mutual hatred of Germany. If the way in which the many nations of the Soviet Union (even languishing under Joseph Stalin's Communist Party) banded together to defeat the Germans is any indication, they were right. Perhaps what united these peoples, however, was not hatred of Germans but hatred of *domination* by Germany. They could see clearly, in both wars, that they would be second-class citizens, and possibly much worse. The Germans did not simply seek to enforce their laws on another people, they sought complete hegemony. In carving out an empire larger than Rome, they sought to enforce their *kultur* (culture) even to the extent of destroying that of their victims.

This theme is largely the same in all times and places, and was certainly not unique to Imperial Germany or the Nazi Party. Conquest is conquest; any differences between conquerors and their policies is quite probably irrelevant to those on the receiving end. To be conquered by a foreign army, and to have them set up a government sympathetic to them, whose first goal is to perpetuate at the very least economic slavery, can never be an occasion for celebration. Ludendorff and his kind, bad as they were, paled beside the Nazis—but not for lack of trying. It is small comfort to think that the children of your oppressors, who themselves gassed your villages and forced you to work on their farms, would reserve the more efficient evils of the gas chamber and the concentration camp for your children.

-LAWRENCE A. HELM,
NASA HEADQUARTERS

Viewpoint:
No. The German occupation of Eastern Europe was concerned initially with providing administration and security and subsequently with reorganizing the conquered territory along traditional imperialist lines.

The impressive military success of Imperial Germany on the Eastern Front during World War I gave it the power to determine the future political structure of much of the Russian Empire. In many ways the power that Kaiser William II held over the region after the signing of the Treaty of Brest-Litovsk in March 1918 was equaled by the power to which Adolf Hitler aspired a generation later. The occupation policies carried out by the governments of these two different leaders, however, had practically nothing in common and were oriented toward radically dissimilar goals.

The most critical difference between the German approach to Eastern Europe in 1918 and 1941 (when Hitler launched his invasion of the Soviet Union) derived from the enormous contrasts in the political philosophies of the regimes. The German Empire was firmly rooted in the traditional conservatism of Central Europe. The Kaiser's strategic planners aimed at establishing German hegemony over the continent through economic and diplomatic preponderance. German territory might be expanded territorially in minor ways, for instance in Belgium, but the principal vehicles of hegemonic domination were to be the weakening of the opponents of Germany, the acquisition of overseas colonial possessions, and a more-pronounced domination of European markets.

It was the first of these means that dominated Imperial German policy toward Russia. The aims devised during the war, and their elaboration during the peace negotiations, were not as much about German expansion as they were about decoupling a significant amount of territory from the Russian state, now led by Lenin's Soviet government. Broadly defined, the lands in question were inhabited by non-Russian peoples who had been conquered by the Russian Empire in its long history of expansion. German strategy for a postwar East Central Europe involved establishing new states based roughly on ethnic lines. With that goal in mind, German military and diplomatic efforts supported the emergence (or reemergence) of such historical entities as Finland, Poland, Lithuania, and Georgia as independent states. In places where the historical record was more ambiguous, in Ukraine, Belarus, Livonia, and Estonia, the Germans backed nascent

AN AMERICAN OBSERVES THE GERMAN OCCUPATION OF POLAND

Frederick C. Walcott, an American member of the Belgian Relief Commission, visited Poland in 1916 and reported some of his findings:

Wicker baskets were scattered along the way—the basket in which the baby swings from the rafter in every peasant home. Every mile there were scores of them, each one telling a death. I started to count, but after a little I had to give it up, there were so many.

That is the desolation one saw along the great road from Warsaw to Pinsk, mile after mile, more than two hundred miles. They told me a million people were made homeless in six weeks of the German drive in August and September, 1915. They told me four hundred thousand died on the way. The rest, scarcely half alive, got through with the Russian army. Many of these have been sent to Siberia; it is these people whom the Paderewski committee is trying to relieve.

In the refugee camps, 300,000 survivors of the flight were gathered by the Germans, members of broken families. They were lodged in jerry-built barracks, scarcely waterproof, unlighted, unwarmed in the dead of winter. Their clothes, where the buttons were lost, were sewed on. There were no conveniences, they had not even been able to wash for weeks. Filth and infection from vermin were spreading. They were famished, their daily ration a cup of soup and a piece of bread as big as my fist. . . .

In that situation, the German commander issued a proclamation. Every able-bodied Pole was bidden to Germany to work. If any refused, let no other Pole give him to eat, not so much as a mouthful, under penalty of German military law.

This is the choice the German Government gives to the conquered Pole, to the husband and father of a starving family: Leave your family to die or survive as the case may be. Leave your country which is destroyed, to work in Germany for its further destruction. If you are obstinate, we shall see that you surely starve.

Staying with his folk, he is doomed and they are not saved; the father and husband can do nothing for them, he only adds to their risk and suffering. Leaving them, he will be cut off from his family, they may never hear from him again nor he from them. Germany will set him to work that a German workman may be released to fight against his own land and people. He shall be lodged in barracks, behind barbed wire entanglements, under armed guard. He shall sleep on the bare ground with a single thin blanket. He shall be scantily fed and his earnings shall be taken from him to pay for his food.

This is the choice which the German Government offers to a proud, sensitive, high strung people. Death or slavery.

Source: Charles F. Horne, ed., The Great Events of the Great War, *volume three (New York: National Alumni, 1923), pp. 426–427.*

---

nationalist movements that appeared to have the most chance of success. Territory that was historically Russian by ethnicity was left untouched, and the Muscovite core of the old Russian Empire was to remain under the control of the revolutionary Soviet state. Revealingly, the German government took proactive steps to exclude its Austro-Hungarian ally from a role in the East in order to prevent Vienna from attaching Polish and Ukrainian territory directly to its existing domains. In a caveat developed after the Bolshevik Revolution (1917), German strategic thinkers also identified independence movements in the lands that Lenin's government gave up at Brest-Litovsk as buffers to hold back the spread of communism into continental Europe.

Scholars who compare Imperial occupation policies in the East to those of Nazi Germany often argue that these political formations were just puppets for German domination, and therefore not all that different from what Hitler pursued, but the differences are astonishing. Although princes of lesser states of the German Empire were advanced to become the monarchs of Finland, Lithuania, and Poland, their presence did not imply anything close to what the Nazis were planning. In each case there were few existing political institutions prepared to govern. More than anything else, everyone involved desired the stability of these new nations as trading partners and benevolent small states on the border of Germany. Monarchies led by experienced rulers were a reasonable way to create such stability. The Finnish Diet actually approved a German king in a democratic vote. Some German strategists spoke of incorporating these states into a pan-European federative structure centered around a German core, but no long-term plans for such a development were ever laid out in detail or endorsed officially. Favorable diplomatic, economic, and strategic relations, even if they could be fairly described as biased in its favor or existing for the benefit of the long-term position of Germany in Europe, were the limit of the ambitions of the Imperial government. In other parts of the former Russian Empire, Imperial Germany had no problem leaving government firmly in local hands. In Ukraine the Germans supported a predominantly leftist regime that had specifically invited their intervention to fight the Bolsheviks. After their weak policies failed to bring order, the Germans supported a monarchic state based loosely on the historic political structure of the Ukrainian Cossacks and led by a tsarist general of Ukrainian backgrounds, Pavlo Skoropadsky. Rather than treat Skoropadsky as a colonial agent or puppet ruler, the Germans gave him much military and economic aid and at the same time encouraged him to develop a stable and independent Ukrainian nation-state. In the far-off Caucasus, Imperial Germany secured the independence of the historic Georgian state under a moderate socialist government as part of the Brest-Litovsk agreement. When a German military expedition arrived there in the summer of 1918, it came not to impose German colonial control but to support the independent Georgian government against its regional antagonists.

Nazi Germany pursued policies that were unimaginably more ambitious than, and represented a definitive break with, the policies of Imperial Germany. Advocated by Adolf Hitler in *Mein Kampf* (1925–1927), the Nazi program desired nothing less than total German domination of the entire landmass between the Vistula and the Urals. Its "subhuman" population was to be reduced to abject slavery for German masters, and ultimately exterminated and replaced by German settlers who would develop the new *Lebensraum* (living space) for the health and benefit of the Aryan race. The populations of peripheral regions, such as the Baltic littoral and the Crimea, were to be "Germanized." Nazi plans included no place for national states and, in sharp distinction from the policy of the Imperial government, the Russian state was to be destroyed and was targeted as the main object of the genocide and resettlement.

Even though Hitler never had the opportunity to realize the full extent of his vision, Nazi policies in the East clearly established his seriousness. As Nazi Germany extended its control over Eastern Europe, it took calculated and effective steps to insure that the region would be in the permanent thrall of the Thousand Year Reich. Beginning with the occupation of Bohemia, Moravia, and Poland in 1939, the direct annexation of territory that had never previously belonged to Germany—and which the Imperial government had never considered annexing—became a leading indicator of Hitler's designs. This geographic transformation was followed in short order by the forced resettlement, or "ethnic cleansing," of several million ethnic Poles and Jews from the new lands of the "Greater German Reich" to the truncated "General Government of Poland." After Germany invaded the Soviet Union in 1941, special execution squads began the methodical extermination of the Jewish population, another preparatory step for German resettlement. The Nazi government also initiated the process of replacing the expelled Poles and Jews with German settlers, people who had been more or less forced to relocate there from ethnic German enclaves in the Soviet Union and elsewhere in Eastern Europe. Although the eventual defeat of Nazi Germany in World War II precluded the further development of these policies in Poland and prevented their application in Soviet territory, there was no doubt that Hitler's government was planning to pursue them to greater lengths in the future.

While the Imperial government had actively supported capable nationalist leaders on the territory of the former Russian Empire, the Nazis targeted them for destruction. Directives issued by the Nazi government and security services ordered the wholesale elimination of the traditional social and political elites (if they still existed), as well as the new communist elite that had sprouted up in Soviet territory. Nationalist agitators of any political stripe who attempted to get the German government to support their ambitions were either arrested right away or used for short-term military and political purposes and then eliminated. The ultimate goal of these policies was to destroy the forces of organization among the Slavic peoples of Eastern Europe and thus facilitate the enslavement of the leaderless peasantry. For administrative purposes the Nazis carved up the East into "Reich Commissariats," ruled by Nazi government officials for no other purpose than to insure the full implementation of Hitler's goals for the region.

If the tangible differences between approaches of Imperial and Nazi Germany to Eastern Europe were clear, their theoretical and intellectual inspirations were also widely divergent. The German Empire had developed an official ideology of pursuing its "special path" or "place in the sun," but both its means and ends conformed to the traditional European pattern of imperialism and diplomacy. As far as this approach touched on Eastern Europe, Imperial German leaders advocated the reorganization of the region in a way that would give Germany strategic and economic advantages.

No longer having to deal with a large and powerful Russian Empire, Imperial Germany could gain highly favorable diplomatic and trade relations with its successor states. This development in turn would enable it to maintain a broad hegemony over the entire European continent, assuming it could also win the war on the Western Front.

The Nazi approach was truly revolutionary. Hitler's policy was to pursue the complete subordination of the whole continent to direct German control. The intellectual roots of this ambition came from a relatively small number of extremist academics and publicists who had been marginal cranks in the intellectual life of the Empire but who became cultural icons in Nazi Germany. While the inherently intense racism and genocidal proclivities of such authors had sprouted before World War I, their ideas were never adopted by the conservative officers of the Imperial German Army or by the conservative and tradition-minded administrative bureaucracy. Indeed, experienced colonial administrators of the Imperial government knew that encouraging German out-migration to underdeveloped regions was an impossible task. Only a few thousand settlers ever went to German-controlled parts of Africa, while the overwhelming majority of emigrants went to the prosperous Americas. Indeed, why should anyone leave the comfort, security, and high living standards of modern Germany to farm an undeveloped wasteland in Tanzania or, for that matter, a depopulated battle zone in Russia? It was the Nazis alone who embraced the obscure and fantastic ideas of conquest and resettlement, which plain demographic facts had long contradicted, and made them the basis of their expansionist policies. Much like the Nazis' general approach to traditional German conservatism after 1933, the Imperial elite's vision of Eastern Europe was discarded in favor of a radical new vision that bewildered and disgusted the traditionalists.

Another argument advanced by those who try to compare the two approaches to the East is that regardless of their different ideological backgrounds and professed long-term goals, the occupation policies employed by Imperial and Nazi Germany were uncomfortably similar. In both cases, they argue, the German High Command established military administrations that treated the indigenous populations harshly, and ruthlessly exploited people and resources for the benefit of the German war effort. General Erich Ludendorff, the de facto head of German military planning in World War I, in other words, was merely the predecessor of the Nazi satraps responsible for the region during World War II.

This comparison is misleading for several reasons. First, the exploitation of occupied territories for expedient military reasons was not a policy shared merely by two separate German regimes, but one that has been employed by many armies of many nations throughout modern history. If Imperial German occupation policies in Eastern Europe prefigured Nazi occupation policies on this basis, so did those of every other country that occupied enemy territory while engaged in a desperate war.

Second, although the Imperial German Army was by any objective standard excessive in its application of martial law, summary justice, and extemporaneous violence, it approached neither the method nor the magnitude of what the Nazis perpetrated. While the Imperial government dealt with the region through trade relationships that were concluded under German diplomatic pressure and possibly biased in the favor of Germany, the Nazis carried out the unabashed exploitation of the entire region. To cite one example, that of Ukraine, Imperial Germany bought grain from Skoropadsky's regime at negotiated rates and traded with it in other commodities under the same tariff agreements that had governed trade between Germany and the Russian Empire before 1914. After the Nazi armies occupied Ukraine in 1941, however, German administrators confiscated virtually all of the agricultural produce, livestock, and industrial machinery directly and without compensation. When the Nazi war machine needed laborers, the occupying authority abducted millions of Ukrainian civilians (as well as millions of Poles and Russians) and reduced them to slavery in German mines and factories. Eventually, Nazi plans called for the removal of the entire Slavic population and its replacement with German settlers. There were plainly no antecedents to such policies in even the most determined quarters of the Imperial government, nor is there even the slightest amount of evidence to suggest that it was planning such activities in the future. Certainly the mass murder of millions of East European Jews by the Nazis bore no comparison to the worst atrocities of Imperial German forces a generation earlier.

Third, Ludendorff's directives for occupation and economic exploitation in the territories of the Russian Empire were indistinguishable from those he employed elsewhere. The industrial capacity and agricultural produce of occupied Belgium and northern and eastern France were also adapted to fill the needs of the Imperial German war machine, and the German military administration of those areas shared the reputation of the Eastern Command for ruthlessness and cruelty to civilians. Yet again, neither zone of occupation included genocide or ethnic cleansing among its policies. Nazi German rule over the East was completely different from its control over the rest of occupied Europe. Mainly for "racial" reasons, West European populations were to be given a place in a new European order centered around Germany. Even if their political independence and aspects of their sovereignty were to be limited sharply, the states were to continue to exist and there was no question that their peoples would survive. This policy contrasted essentially with the Nazis' planned genocide of the Slavic peoples and the projected use of their lands for German settlement. If Ludendorff's policies in the East truly foreshadowed the barbarism of the Nazis there, why did his identical treatment of occupied Western Europe not preconfigure an identically radical and genocidal set of Nazi policies?

Despite superficial points of comparison, Imperial German policies in Eastern Europe had nothing in common with Nazi behavior in the region. Although both regimes exploited the East for immediate military purposes, the approach of the Imperial government was entirely determined by existing military and diplomatic conventions, and was infinitely more humane in its practice and goals than that of Hitler's Germany. While the kaiser and his strategists planned the formation of a buffer zone of independent nation-states with close ties to Germany, the Nazis desired the total subordination of a much larger region (including Russia and extending all the way to the Urals) to German domination, the wholesale obliteration of its indigenous population, its resettlement by ethnic Germans, and its physical inclusion in a previously unthought of Germanic Empire. The difference in these approaches was amply indicated by developments in the region before each German regime lost control of it. The Imperial government facilitated the creation of nation-states from Finland to Georgia over the course of 1918. It began setting up stable diplomatic and commercial relationships that respected their independence, as well as the independence of the Soviet Russian state that had taken over from the tsars. The Nazis, on the other hand, stamped out as much potential for Slavic nationhood as they possibly could, thoroughly ravished the economy of the region, began eliminating the Slavic and Jewish populations through mass murder and deportation, and even started to move in German settlers to repopulate the vacant lands. Military defeat ultimately prevented both regimes from realizing their strategies, but the enormous differences in their conception and execution are undeniable.

–PAUL DU QUENOY,
GEORGETOWN UNIVERSITY

References

Robert B. Asprey, *The German High Command at War: Hindenburg and Ludendorff Conduct World War I* (New York: Morrow, 1991).

Roger Chickering, *Imperial Germany and the Great War, 1914–1918* (Cambridge & New York: Cambridge University Press, 1998).

Alan Clark, B*arbarossa: The Russian-German Conflict, 1941–45* (New York: Morrow, 1965).

Werner Conze, *The Shaping of the German Nation: A Historical Analysis,* translated by Neville Mellon (New York: St. Martin's Press, 1979).

Alexander Dallin, *German Rule in Russia, 1941–1945: A Study of Occupation Policies* (London: MacMillan; New York: St. Martin's Press, 1957).

Oleh S. Fedyshyn, *Germany's Drive to the East and the Ukrainian Revolution, 1917–1918* (New Brunswick, N.J.: Rutgers University Press, 1971).

Wilhelm Groener, *Lebenserinnerungen: Jugend, Generalstab, Weltkrieg* (Göttingen: Vandenhoeck & Ruprecht, 1957).

Max Hoffmann, W*ar Diaries and Other Papers,* translated by Eric Sutton (London: Secker, 1929).

Eric Ludendorff, *My War Memories, 1914–1918,* 2 volumes (London: Hutchinson, 1919).

Robert Proctor, R*acial Hygiene: Medicine Under the Nazis* (Cambridge, Mass.: Harvard University Press, 1988).

Paul du Quenoy, "The Skoropads'ky Hetmanate and the Ukrainian National Idea," *Ukrainian Quarterly,* 56 (Fall 2000): 245–271.

John S. Reshetar Jr., *The Ukrainian Revolution, 1917–1920: A Study in Nationalism* (Princeton: Princeton University Press, 1952).

Gerhard Ritter, *The Sword and the Sceptre: The Problem of Militarism in Germany,* 3 volumes, translated by Heinz Norden (Coral Gables, Fla.: University of Miami Press, 1969–1973).

Joseph B. Schechtman, E*uropean Population Transfers, 1939–1945* (New York: Oxford University Press, 1946).

Woodruff D. Smith, *The Ideological Origins of Nazi Imperialism* (New York: Oxford University Press, 1986).

Heinrich Gotthard von Treitschke, P*olitik,* 2 volumes (Leipzig: Hirzel, 1897–1899).

John W. Wheeler-Bennett, B*rest-Litovsk: The Forgotten Peace, March 1918* (London: Macmillan, 1938).

Wheeler-Bennett, W*ooden Titan: Hindenburg in Twenty Years of German History, 1914–1934* (New York: Morrow, 1936).

Gordon Wright, *The Ordeal of Total War, 1939–1945* (New York: Harper & Row, 1968).

EASTERNERS AND WESTERNERS

Was the conflict between Prime Minister David Lloyd George and Chief of Staff Sir William Robertson the result of a basic disagreement on war strategy?

Viewpoint: Yes. David Lloyd George emphasized military operations in the East while Sir William Robertson advocated continuing the offensive in the West.

Viewpoint: No. David Lloyd George and Sir William Robertson had flexibility in their respective positions, but they were unable to find a way of working together systematically.

In principle, David Lloyd George and Sir William Robert Robertson should have been able to achieve a harmonious relationship. Both were outsiders in a system brutally depending on contacts and patronage. Lloyd George was a Welshman, of humble social origins, a radical reformer, and a habitual intriguer. "Wully" Robertson, of equally common origins, enlisted in the British Army in 1877. At a time when few enlisted men achieved line commissions, he became an officer—with the enthusiastic endorsement of the officer corps of his regiment, the Sixteenth Lancers, one of the most exclusive units in the army. A hard worker with a reputation for talent and self-discipline rather than genius, he not only was the first former enlisted man to pass the staff college, he later became its commandant. His competence as a planner and administrator brought him appointment as Chief of Staff to the British Expeditionary Force (BEF) in 1916 and then promotion to Chief of the Imperial General Staff (CIGS). In the same time frame Lloyd George was rising from gadfly backbencher to prime minister of a coalition government that promised more vigorous prosecution of the war than its discredited predecessor.

These outsiders-become-insiders promptly locked horns. On one level the clash involved priorities. Robertson had been since 1914 a confirmed "Westerner," believing the only path to victory involved committing all available resources to France and Flanders. Lloyd George was less certain. While his memoirs present him as a principled opponent of the gridlocked slaughter on the Western Front, he was on record as demanding a decisive attack. He supported the abortive French offensive of 1917, to the point of formally subordinating the BEF to the French high command for the duration of the operation.

That position was a good deal more than the "Westerners" were willing to accept. Robertson in particular saw the entire episode as proof of Lloyd George's mendacity and opportunism—a contrast to Robertson's loyalty to the side he chose to back. Lloyd George saw Robertson as typifying the worst features of the regular officer: not merely stubborn, but a yard dog who substituted loyalty for judgment.

The British Passchendaele offensive (1917) further deepened the antagonism between the men. As the offensive bogged down, Lloyd George could neither decide to give it his complete support, or terminate it, even at the price of relieving Douglas Haig. Robertson became even more of a symbol of what the premier considered the obstructionism of the army, opposing Lloyd George's support for sending troops to Italy and frustrating his proposal for a full-scale Palestine offensive. By 1918 the antagonism had deepened to a point where the war effort itself was at risk. Resolution came only when Haig accepted proposals, backed by Lloyd George, to take over a larger sector of the front and contribute forces to an Allied general reserve. Robertson, deprived of his commander's support, was exiled to Versailles and a figurehead assignment.

Viewpoint:
Yes. David Lloyd George emphasized military operations in the East while Sir William Robertson advocated continuing the offensive in the West.

Conflict between David Lloyd George and William Robert Robertson was inevitable. The two men came from radically different backgrounds, had forceful and dynamic personalities, and inherited a flawed system at the British War Office that placed the two in direct opposition from the start of their professional relationship. Lloyd George was the consummate politician, becoming the youngest member of the House of Commons upon his election to that body in 1890. He remained in politics until the outbreak of World War I, making a name for himself in radical circles and making few friends within the armed forces along the way. Robertson's career was no less remarkable. After serving as an enlisted man for eleven years, he received his commission in 1888 and served in India, attended the prestigious British staff college at Camberley, and fought in the Boer War (which Lloyd George had vocally opposed from the House of Commons). At the start of World War I, Robertson was serving as Quartermaster General of the British Expeditionary Force (BEF), then became chief of staff to BEF commander Sir John Denton Pinkstone French.

In prewar Britain, where soldiers and politicians were equally contemptuous of one another, conflict between the career politician and the career soldier was unavoidable. By the end of 1915 Robertson had been named Chief of the Imperial General Staff (CIGS, the first former enlisted man ever to hold that position), theoretically placing him under the supervision of Lord Horatio Herbert Kitchener, the Secretary of State for War. Kitchener's own appointment was constitutionally questionable as he was the first serving soldier to hold the post. Kitchener and Robertson further muddied the legal waters by concluding what became known as "The Bargain." Under this agreement the Secretary of State for War retained only those powers that

pertained to his office in peacetime. All wartime powers remained the preserve of the Chief of the Imperial General Staff. Such an arrangement effectively made the Secretary of State for War a figurehead and gave the Chief of the Imperial General Staff unprecedented power. The Bargain was on shaky legal grounds, placing Robertson in charge of many matters that were constitutionally the responsibility of the Secretary of State for War.

Shortly after Kitchener's death in 1916, Lloyd George assumed the office of Secretary of State for War. He soon informed Robertson that he was unwilling to continue to operate under the terms of The Bargain. In a long letter to Robertson, Lloyd George reminded the Chief of the Imperial General Staff that the Secretary of State for War "retains the ultimate responsibility for the War Office. The Prime Minister, Parliament, and the Country must hold him accountable." Robertson was unwilling to cede any authority to Lloyd George, telling him at one point that the only responsibility of the Secretary of State for War was to feed and clothe the army. Robertson believed that he alone had the authority to advise the government on strategy and issue orders to commanders. He even denied that he had to inform Lloyd George of any decisions that he made.

Robertson had envisioned that Lloyd George should act as his own voice at the cabinet. He was enraged when Lloyd George openly criticized the performance of the army at the Somme in July 1916 and grew even more irate when Lloyd George interviewed French general Ferdinand Foch as to the causes of British failure. Lloyd George then proposed to send Robertson to Russia to complete the mission that Kitchener had been on when his ship sank. Robertson (rightly) saw the mission as a way to get him out of London for an extended period of time and refused to go, fearing that in his absence Lloyd George would convince the prime minister to nullify The Bargain and reverse the power relationship between the two offices.

Lloyd George grew so frustrated at the situation that he told Prime Minister Herbert Henry Asquith that he would resign if satisfactory changes were not imposed from above. Under the system Lloyd George envisioned, strategy would still be the preserve of the soldiers, but would thereafter be "checked by the common sense of the civilians." As recorded in an article in *Lloyd George: Twelve Essays* (1971), edited by A. J. P. Taylor, Lloyd George went on to challenge the competence of Robertson and BEF commander Douglas Haig: "The soldiers in this war have not been a conspicuous success. Up to the present there has not been a plan conceived and carried out by them which has not ended in bloody failure." Asquith understood the crisis brewing at the War Office but refused to step in. In the end, Lloyd George did not offer his resignation but vowed to undermine Robertson's authority from within. He immediately began to ignore The Bargain and assume responsibilities that he believed were constitutionally the responsibility of his office.

Their personal clashes reflected a growing professional estrangement as well. Lloyd George had grown increasingly discouraged by the inability of Robertson and Haig to come up with alternatives on the Western Front. Strategically, he had become a staunch "Easterner," favoring operations in Turkey, Syria, and Salonika instead of renewed offensives in France. Despite the disaster at Gallipoli (1915–1916), Lloyd George argued that victory would only come after the Allies had first eliminated the Ottoman Empire and Austria-Hungary from participation in the conflict. Robertson and Haig disagreed with what they saw as an amateurish approach last heard in force from another politician, Winston Leonard Spencer Churchill. Robertson consistently argued that victory was only possible by concentrating in France against Germany and that Britain lacked the resources for an Eastern offensive of the magnitude envisioned by Lloyd George.

This fundamental strategic disagreement, on top of the deteriorating personal relationship, prevented any system from emerging that might have allowed the two men to work together. Lloyd George grew angrier when he learned that Robertson had written a letter to British press baron Alfred Charles William Harmsworth, Viscount Northcliffe that read: "The Boche gives me no trouble compared with what I meet in London. So any help you can give me will be of Imperial value." When Northcliffe's personal threat to Lloyd George failed to have its desired effect, Northcliffe began a "Hands Off the Army" campaign in his newspapers. Lloyd George quickly discerned that Robertson was behind the campaign and wrote to him to warn: "You must not ask me to play the part of a mere dummy. I am not in the least suited for the part."

Lloyd George not only survived the media attacks, soon afterward, in December 1916, he became prime minister in a new coalition government. He would have liked nothing more than to remove both Robertson and Haig, but his Conservative coalition partners would not allow it. Instead, Lloyd George looked for ways to reduce the influence of both men. In 1917 he fell under the influence of the new French commander-in-chief, General Robert-Georges Nivelle, who spoke fluent English thanks to his English mother and convinced Lloyd George that he had found the solution to breaking the stalemate on the Western Front—a proposed joint English-French offensive along the Chemin des Dames.

Lloyd George was so persuaded that he asked Haig to accept a unified command under Nivelle. This proposal, which effectively would have put British troops under the command of a French general, violated a fundamental principle of the British army. Eventually, the anger of the British generals, who were suspicious of Nivelle's plan, caused Lloyd George to rescind the suggestion. Events soon proved Haig and Robertson right on at least this score. The Chemin des Dames offensive failed miserably. Soon, nearly half of the French army was refusing to attack. As a result, Lloyd George became further convinced of the futility of trying to win the war in France. Robertson, for his part, was further convinced that the prime minister was out of his league on questions of strategy.

The disaster on the Chemin des Dames did not lead Robertson to give up his Western approach. He and Haig wanted to resume the offensive in France and Flanders as quickly as the French could recover from the disasters of the spring. Lloyd George, on the other hand, agreed with the French that any future offensive should await the arrival of the Americans, but his support of the disgraced Nivelle had put him in a weakened position. He could not support the recently humbled French generals over his own. Robertson took advantage of Lloyd George's temporary weakness to convince the French to support a British operation in Flanders later in the year.

In strategic eclipse as a result of his support for Nivelle's disaster, Lloyd George could not stop the Westerners from launching the offensive that became known as the Third Ypres or Passchendaele. Lloyd George feared that he might lose the prime ministry if he overruled the generals. Guessing the weakness of his position, a united front of military officers, led by Robertson, received the final approval from the War Policy Committee on 18 July 1917. Lloyd George was able to get the committee to agree that if the offensive turned into another Somme, it would be stopped and Britain would concentrate on defeating Austria-Hungary by sending troops to Italy. Robertson and Haig feared that Lloyd George might call a premature halt to the

Deserted German trench, circa 1915

(postcard in scrapbook, Joseph M. Bruccoli Great War Collection, Thomas Cooper Library, University of South Carolina)

offensive in order to switch British efforts to Italy. As a result, Robertson kept his own doubts about Haig's plan from Lloyd George and the cabinet, causing him to look even more inflexible than he was. Although Robertson doubted Haig's plans, he feared a switch to Italy or Salonika even more.

Such a switch was exactly what Lloyd George had in mind. With the Passchendaele offensive literally drowning in a sea of mud, Lloyd George argued at an interallied conference to end the offensive. An offensive in Italy, he argued, was the only alternative to an endless stalemate in France. The French generals disagreed with any diminution of British (to say nothing of French) effort in the West, ending Lloyd George's hopes for a major operation on the periphery. Robertson was incensed at the Prime Minister for suggesting in front of French generals that a British offensive be halted.

Lloyd George was now convinced that Robertson's adherence to a Western approach was irretrievably at odds with his own strategic understanding. When, in February 1918, Lloyd George asked Robertson to represent Britain at the Supreme War Council at Versailles, Robertson saw the move as a politically motivated way to get him out of London and refused. Lloyd George took the occasion to report to the king and tell him that differences

between the two men had made it impossible to continue the status quo: either the king would accept the resignation of his Prime Minister or he would accept the resignation of his Chief of the Imperial General Staff. Lloyd George won. Robertson heard of his own resignation through a government announcement later that day, ending the battle between the fiercest British "Westerner" and "Easterner."

—MICHAEL S. NEIBERG, U.S. AIR FORCE ACADEMY

Viewpoint:
No. David Lloyd George and Sir William Robertson had flexibility in their respective positions, but they were unable to find a way of working together systematically.

William Robert "Wully" Robertson, Chief of the Imperial General Staff (CIGS) from December 1915 until his dismissal in February 1918, is often portrayed as an inveterate "Westerner" who fought David Lloyd George and other "Easterners" tooth and nail. "Westerners," or those who preferred making the main

British push on the Western Front in France and Belgium, and "Easterners," or those who preferred British operations in peripheral theaters such as the Balkans and the eastern Mediterranean, occupied opposite poles of a seemingly inflexible strategic compass. Yet, Lloyd George and Robertson displayed flexibility in their strategic views that belied rigid "west versus east" compass headings. Demonstrating a grudging respect for each other, even as they fought intense bureaucratic battles to define the best direction for British strategy, Lloyd George and Robertson never quite found a way of working together systematically.

Older than Lloyd George by three years, Robertson rose from humble origins as a lowly trooper to attain the rank of field marshal. Gruff, laconic, and headstrong, Robertson made the British army and the study of warfare his life. His formidable military record made him a natural choice for CIGS in 1915. The equally headstrong and determined Lloyd George also rose from humble origins in Wales to become Minister of Munitions from May 1915 to June 1916, Secretary of State for War in July 1916, and later Prime Minister after the fall of the Asquith government in December 1916.

Possessing a Welsh flair for language (it was said he "could charm a bird off a bough"), Lloyd George distrusted the taciturn CIGS and the equally reserved and much more imperious Douglas Haig, commander of the British Expeditionary Force (BEF) on the Western Front. Often it was the near-total inability of Lloyd George to talk to these men—rather than disagreements in strategy per se—that led to misunderstandings and estrangement.

Communication difficulties and personality conflicts tended to obscure commonalities in outlook. Both Lloyd George and Robertson agreed that universal conscription for all men, single or married, between the ages of eighteen and forty-one was necessary for victory. They further believed that, without decisive victory on the battlefield, a negotiated settlement would prove inconclusive. They thus sought a decisive theater and campaign to end the war quickly while avoiding costly battles of attrition.

Whereas Robertson argued consistently for the Western Front, Lloyd George advocated an indirect approach. By supporting Serbia against Austria or attacking Turkish interests in the eastern Mediterranean, Lloyd George hoped to "knock away the props" to the German war effort. The rhetorical appeal of the indirect approach, however, faded with the disastrous Gallipoli campaign (1915–1916). Shortly thereafter, the German onslaught at Verdun (February 1916) redirected attention to the Western Front. Lloyd George put aside his "Eastern"

schemes and reluctantly supported an attack on the Western Front to relieve German pressure on the French.

As Minister of Munitions, Lloyd George had rationalized production of artillery shells and ammunition, thereby establishing a reputation for dynamism and providing Haig and Robertson the matériel they needed to launch a massive assault at the Somme (July 1916). Nevertheless, what was planned by Haig as a breakthrough attack to defeat the German army on the Western Front became a bloody stalemate. The slaughter sickened Lloyd George and Robertson alike. The CIGS was put in the unenviable position of begging Haig for reports of progress (or lack thereof) while airing serious concerns about high casualties and Haig's lack of progress to the Cabinet. Confronted by Haig's rosy projections of eventual British success, Lloyd George and Robertson saw little choice but to stand by Haig and the Somme campaign.

By the end of 1916 Robertson, frustrated by Prime Minister Horatio Herbert Asquith's indecisiveness, found Lloyd George a viable alternative. According to Frank Owen, in *Tempestuous Journey: Lloyd George, His Life and Times* (1954), the CIGS declared on 24 November 1916 that, "The only man who can decide quickly, say 'Yes! Or No!' without hesitation, is Lloyd George. He might say the wrong Yes! or sometimes say the wrong No! But I prefer that to no decision at all. I am for more power for Lloyd George, not to interfere with military operations, but to direct War policy."

The catch here, of course, was that Lloyd George was "not to interfere" with military strategy. In Haig and Robertson's view, Lloyd George was a meddlesome frock (politician) who displayed rank amateurism in trying to define operational strategy. There was a measure of truth in this view. In 1917 the newly minted prime minister called for British support of an attack in Italy against the Austrians, or perhaps renewed assaults against Turkey. Both operations were impractical. In Italy the geography was decidedly unfavorable and the Italians themselves skeptical and unenthusiastic. Meanwhile, shortages of shipping as a result of German U-boat attacks torpedoed large-scale offensives in the eastern Mediterranean.

Revealingly, Lloyd George did not fight tenaciously for his strategic flights of fancy. He essentially agreed with Robertson that the Western Front should take priority in the spring of 1917. But Lloyd George wanted General Robert-Georges Nivelle, the French commander and a hero of Verdun (1916)—not the lordly and devious Haig—to lead a general offensive on the Western Front. Lloyd George and Nivelle got along famously; both shared a gift for gab, which Nivelle employed to persuade the prime minister to support whole-

NO PEACE TILL WE HAVE A ROW

On 8 November 1916 General William Robert Robertson sent a secret note to General Douglas Haig. This communication concerned the attempt by David Lloyd George to send Robertson to Russia.

I am going to tell you some of my worries. But treat them as an entertainment. They do not generally trouble me.

Did I tell you before that about six weeks ago L. G. tried to shove me over to Russia, saying I was such a splendid fellow to go & see Alexeieff & buck up Russia in general—about which we hear, still, rumours of a separate peace with Germany—which I *do* not believe.

I told him I could not go. Also told the Prime Minister. The King took up matter strongly, & it was dropped. The idea was to let L. G. become top dog here & have his wicked way. Like he used to get rid of poor old K. I could not do the trip under a month, & he would keep me there for weeks more once he got me there. He has been a good deal with Winston & F E Smith, & French is also not far distant at times. Last Friday, in McKenna's absence (a friend of ours) he got up a War Committee at which there were no naval or military experts. He got together another yesterday. Result was a telegram to Briand saying L. G. & Prime Minister would come over on Tuesday next to discuss general matters & to arrange an Allied conference at Russian Headquarters, as the only useful way of securing real cooperation etc etc. Also that Chantilly Conference should be postponed for at least a week as it could not usefully meet until it had before it the decisions of the Tuesday (political) Conference. To represent us in Russia L.G. told me last night it was thought that Grey & I should go; France, Joffre (or Castelnau) &

a minister; Italy, Cadorno (or Poroo). Of course, Italy will send no one. France may refuse the whole thing. On the other hand Briand may be in the plot, (he would welcome my absence from the helm) & agree to send representatives to Russia—including old Joffre, if he wants to be rid of him. No answer has yet come. Its reply depends upon whether Briand in the plot or not. If he is not, I imagine he will refuse the Russian idea & the Chantilly Conference may not be postponed for more than 1 or 2 days. If he agrees to Russia, I imagine there will be no Chantilly Conference at all, as it will be superceded by the Russian one.

But I am not concerned except as regards myself. I have no intention of going. The idea is absurd. The Prime Minister ought to have said so. But he is very weak. It is a devilish clever plot & L. G. has misled the War Committee. I have seen McKenna & he says he will stick by me. I have *no* intention of going. But it is a nice mess. And takes so much of my time. Of course I have told the King, & he is lying low, on my advice, for the time being—like myself. Salonika is at the bottom of it all. L. G. is always saying the West is a failure & will be so. He is egged on by Winston & F. E. Smith. There will be no peace till we have a row.

Good luck to you. What awful mud you are in. Such very bad fortune. Never mind. No answer. Will tell you *if* Chantilly is postponed. I have wired Joffre & am wondering what his reply will be.

Source: *David R. Woodward,* The Military Correspondence of Field-Marshal Sir William Robertson, Chief of the Imperial General Staff, December 1915–February 1918 *(London: Bodley Head, 1989), pp. 104–105.*

sale assaults against German positions. The dismal failure of the Nivelle Offensives (April and May 1917) shook Lloyd George's confidence and diminished his authority. Taken together with his underhanded tactics in attempting to shackle and subjugate Haig and the BEF to Nivelle's direction, Lloyd George had succeeded in straining relations with his CIGS nearly to the breaking point.

Lloyd George and Robertson, nevertheless, agreed that Haig should avoid further costly assaults on the Western Front in 1917. How, then, did Third Ypres (Passchendaele) come to pass later that year? Both Robertson

and Lloyd George shared misgivings about Haig's ambitious plans for major attacks near Ypres in August. Despite their misgivings, they were both seduced by the grandiose nature of Haig's designs. Lloyd George was a less-than-willing accomplice, but he and his war cabinet could not articulate a viable strategic alternative (Italy remained a nonstarter). Robertson was a more willing accomplice to Haig's plan. The CIGS believed that limited attacks, closely coordinated with massive artillery support, would help exhaust German reserves, thereby setting the stage for Allied victory in 1918. Both men, however, were betrayed by Haig's purblind optimism and boundless ambition.

In some ways, Third Ypres initially vindicated Robertson's strategy of exhaustion. After disappointing results in the first two weeks, Haig scaled down his objectives, employing a "bite and hold" strategy that wore down the Germans. Haig's decision to press ahead in October, however, despite horrendous battlefield conditions, turned qualified success into utter failure. It was not German but British morale that was slackening, as Robertson recognized. As early as mid-September 1917 the CIGS was hinting to Lloyd George (through Andrew Bonar Law, Chancellor of the Exchequer) that Haig's offensive held little promise. The situation only worsened as heavy rain fell throughout October.

The CIGS dared not communicate his concerns to Lloyd George. Fearing that criticism of Haig's plans would embolden Lloyd George to divert precious resources to Italy or some other secondary front, Robertson held his tongue. His own belief that ultimate decision in the war would come on the Western Front—and Haig's cajoling of him "to play the man" to limit civilian meddling in military operations—hamstrung Robertson. Tortured by yet another bloodletting on the Western Front, Lloyd George decided he had had enough of Robertson's opposition and prevarication (for which Haig bore the lion's share of the responsibility). Unable or unwilling to run the risk of replacing Haig, Lloyd George did what he believed was the next best thing. He sacked Robertson in February 1918, replacing him with the more pliable Henry Hughes Wilson. (Ironically, Wilson proved less able than Robertson to limit Haig's machinations.) The prime minister also renewed calls for an Allied generalissimo, in part to coordinate strategy and the allocation of reserves on the Western Front, but also to weaken Haig's authority. Fortunately for the Allies, French general Ferdinand Foch filled the post admirably.

Thus, the "Easterner" Lloyd George recognized in 1918 that the endgame of the war would come on the Western Front, a view that the now-demoted Robertson could only applaud from the sidelines. The events of 1918 would vindicate Robertson's "Western Front first" philosophy and his strategy of exhaustion.

Conflicts between Lloyd George and Robertson may have captured headlines, but they also tended to obscure commonalities in purpose and flexibility in strategic objectives. Yet, even commonalities of purpose could be derailed by disdain and distrust. The unbridgeable sociological gap between soldiers ("brass hats") and politicians ("frocks") accounted for mutual misunderstandings and mistrust. Another source of dissension was

professional pride and sense of duty. For Robertson, operational strategy was a soldier's job and defining it his sacred duty. Civilian oversight of the military did not warrant interference in this sacred duty. Robertson may have respected Lloyd George for his dynamism and energy, but not for his inconstant and nonconformist strategic insights. Likewise, Lloyd George recognized Robertson's military skills and grudgingly accepted the need to strike on the Western Front, but he grew increasingly incensed with Robertson's obdurate resistance to any peripheral campaign. By 1918, an unnegotiable chasm had opened between these two men that prevented them from finding common ground upon which their considerable egos and talents could coexist. They nevertheless contributed mightily, each in his own way, to eventual British victory.

—WILLIAM J. ASTORE,
U.S. AIR FORCE ACADEMY

References

Victor Bonham-Carter, *The Strategy of Victory, 1914–1918: The Life and Times of the Master Strategist of World War I: Field-Marshal Sir William Robertson* (New York: Holt, Rinehart & Winston, 1963).

David French, *The Strategy of the Lloyd George Coalition, 1916–1918* (Oxford: Clarendon Press; New York: Oxford University Press, 1995).

David Lloyd George, *War Memoirs of David Lloyd George,* six volumes (London: Nicolson & Watson, 1933–1936; Boston: Little, Brown, 1933–1936).

Peter Lowe, "The Rise to the Premiership, 1914–1916," in *Lloyd George: Twelve Essays,* edited by A. J. P. Taylor (London: Hamilton, 1971), pp. 95–133.

Frank Owen, *Tempestuous Journey: Lloyd George, His Life and Times* (London: Hutchinson, 1954).

William Robertson, *Soldiers and Statesmen, 1914–1918,* two volumes (London: Cassell, 1926; New York: Scribners, 1926).

Peter Rowland, *David Lloyd George: A Biography* (New York: Macmillan, 1975).

Frances Stevenson, *Lloyd George: A Diary,* edited by A. J. P. Taylor (London: Hutchinson, 1971; New York: Harper & Row, 1971).

David R. Woodward, *Lloyd George and the Generals* (Newark: University of Delaware Press: London: Associated University Presses, 1983).

EASTERNERS AND WESTERNERS

FIREPOWER AND MOBILITY

Was the crucial military problem of World War I an imbalance between firepower and mobility on the battlefield?

Viewpoint: Yes. By successfully addressing the tactical problem of the "last 300 yards of no man's land," the Allies won the Great War.

Viewpoint: No. The crucial military problem of World War I was that Allied leaders formulated offensive strategies that never accommodated the realities of trench warfare.

The familiar excoriation of World War I generals as "donkeys" who sacrificed millions of men to barbed wire and machine guns is matched in academic circles by critiques of the statesmen for their inability to make a way out of a conflict that within eighteen months had clearly escalated both beyond its causes and beyond any gains any of the belligerents were likely to achieve. In recent years that position has been balanced by a renewed focus on the objective circumstances of the war: in particular, a fundamental imbalance between firepower on one hand, mobility on the other. This interpretation stresses the rapid incremental development after 1871 of a technology that at all levels—tactical, operational, and strategic—facilitated stagnation.

By 1914 rifles were effective against targets at more than a mile away and were able to fire a dozen rounds per minute. Machine guns had evolved from unreliable crank-operated devices into recoil-operated weapons whose precision-manufactured cartridges reduced jamming to a minimum. Artillery now was a precision weapon able both to smother particular targets with rapid fire and destroy them with heavy shells. Weapons systems, however, were only one element of the gridlocked battlefield. A second was the exponential growth in army size, facilitated by the capacity of even partially industrialized states to remove large numbers of young men from the economy and support them in the field for long periods of time. Flanking operations became impossible when flanks did not exist; maneuver warfare became a chimera when an opponent's forces physically occupied the relevant battle space. That physical occupation, moreover, did not necessarily depend on mass, at least in the initial stages. Relatively small numbers of men, if equipped with machine guns and supported by artillery, were able to hold their ground long enough for reinforcements to arrive and replicate the previous status quo.

Tactical and operational mobility at the outbreak of war remained essentially unchanged from the Napoleonic era, depending primarily on the physical strength and endurance of men and animals. Both were severely limited on a modern battlefield—animals by their size, men not least by the loads they had to carry if they were to sustain themselves in situations when resupply ranged from difficult to impossible. The internal-combustion engine remained too fragile and too low powered to be useful except for logistical purposes. While trucks and tractors played increasing roles in Africa and the Middle East as well as on the Western Front, armored fighting vehicles made no more than marginal contributions in particular circumstances. What trucks and railroads could do was shift reserves behind the lines, choking off breakthroughs at operational levels before they could become strategic breakouts. The end result was an increasingly desperate search for ways of overcoming tactical gridlock—a search extending, albeit vainly, to the operational, strategic, and policy levels of the Great War.

Viewpoint:
Yes. By successfully addressing the tactical problem of the "last 300 yards of no man's land," the Allies won the Great War.

World War I began as a war of movement; German armies swept into Belgium and France in August 1914 in an audacious, if overly ambitious, flanking maneuver known as the Schlieffen Plan. On the Eastern Front the war remained one of movement, but ominous signs of the coming stalemate on the Western Front could already be discerned in disastrous attacks launched by the French in Lorraine. Placing their faith in *l'attaque à outrance*—unbridled frontal assaults carried forward with considerable élan and heroic vitalism—the French suffered 300,000 casualties, or nearly 25 percent of the attacking force, in the span of two weeks. Yet, German units also suffered high casualties. After the German army failed to envelop French and British units before Paris, each side raced to outflank the other. Known somewhat misleadingly as the "race to the sea," by November 1914 the end result of these unsuccessful flanking movements was a continuous line of fortified trenches, 475 miles long, from Switzerland to the Belgian coast.

Commanders on the Western Front were thus confronted with the unexpected challenge of constant siege warfare and of coming to grips with a well-fortified, dug-in, and highly motivated opponent. How was one to come to grips with the enemy without suffering debilitating and ultimately unsustainable losses? The problem of crossing "the last 300 yards" plagued commanders for four years and resulted in the deaths of millions of soldiers. More so than strategic decisions, eventual Allied successes in crossing the "last 300 yards of no man's land"— though such victories nevertheless came at high, yet sustainable, cost—proved decisive in 1918 in sapping the will of the Germans to fight.

What had happened on the Western Front to shift the balance so dramatically in favor of the defensive? The combination of well-designed defensive fortifications, incorporating rapid-firing machine guns with interlocking fields of fire and barbed wire (in some places exceeding ten feet in height and arrayed in dense fields of coils hundreds of feet deep) posed nearly insuperable obstacles to would-be attackers. To attack, soldiers had to leave the comparative safety of their trenches, exposing themselves to the withering firepower of defenders who remained largely concealed behind cover. As attackers dispersed in an attempt to reduce casualties, command and control became increasingly difficult, whereas stay-at-home defenders had the advantage of familiar surroundings and the moral support of men and officers in close proximity.

Attackers, in essence, had no enemy asymmetries to exploit. Battles became costly slugging bouts between two unevenly matched opponents, one of whom (the defender) exposed only his jaw, the other (the attacker) who exposed all his vitals. The outcome of such mismatches was rarely in doubt. Thus, soldiers on each side preferred to jab at a distance, using artillery, rather than to risk knockout attacks that usually proved far more costly to the aggressor.

With the exception of a major offensive at Verdun from February to July 1916, Germany stayed on the defensive until 1918, preferring to counterpunch on the Western Front. Taking the fight to the enemy was the task of French and British forces from 1915 through 1917—an approach that proved costly and largely futile. While the British were still building their first-ever million-man conscript army, the British Expeditionary Force (BEF) nevertheless took the offensive at Neuve-Chapelle in the spring of 1915. Unprepared to exploit their initial successes, the British attack sputtered as the Germans quickly deployed reinforcements. A dozen German machine guns were sufficient to thwart British counterattacks on the second day of the battle. Also in the spring of 1915 the French took the fight to the Germans at Champagne and Artois. Limited and local "break-ins," however, proved fruitless. French and British offensives were like so many "Pickett's Charges": gallant in sentiment, glorious in bravery, yet ghastly in their wanton expenditure of men and matériel for limited ends.

From 1915 to 1917 the toll exacted in crossing the last three hundred yards prevented decisive victories for either side. Lack of timely reinforcements, breakdowns in communications, and murderous firepower employed by steadfast defenders defeated the gallantry and bravery so remarkably displayed by attackers. Thus, to Allied troops the Western Front became known as the "Sausage Grinder" because it was fed with live soldiers, churned out corpses, and yet remained firmly in place.

British artillery crew preparing to fire a 60-pounder "Long Tom" gun in 1914

(from The Illustrated War News, 2 September 1914, page 33, Joseph M. Bruccoli Great War Collection, Thomas Cooper Library, University of South Carolina)

Indeed, the persistence of frontal assaults requires explanation. Most commanders with colonial experience had never encountered extensive fortifications or dealt with million-man armies in which the force-to-space ratio inhibited maneuvers or the exploitation of breakthroughs. Commanders, in essence, had to learn the hard way. They first tried what they were familiar with and continued to stress traditional martial virtues such as bravery and unflinching devotion to duty. When this approach failed to work, they improvised. Yet, it was difficult to improvise when one was constantly being probed, tested, and attrited by a skillful opponent. In preferring direct approaches, commanders could preserve a measure of control over their troops, thereby reducing the uncertainty of war, although ironically increasing the certainty of crippling casualties.

By the summer of 1916 the British believed they had a solution: weight of shell combined with meticulous planning. Prior to their attack at the Somme on 1 July 1916, the British fired 1.5 million artillery shells for six days against German positions. This massive and meticulous barrage, the British hoped, would cut German wire, smash trenches, and obliterate machine-gun emplacements. British soldiers would merely have to walk across "no man's land" to defeat the few dazed German defenders fortunate enough to have survived the preliminary bombardment.

The reality was somewhat different: 60,000 British casualties on the first day, including nearly 20,000 killed. By the end of the Somme campaign, the British had suffered 420,000 casualties, the French 205,000 and the Germans nearly 500,000. Just as at Verdun, the Somme campaign became a horrific attritional nightmare. Each side proved unable to weather the storm of steel, shrapnel, and lead of the last 300 yards to make an appreciable impact on the enemy.

Yet, wars are not won by staying on the defensive. Near the end of the Verdun campaign, limited French attacks led by General Robert Nivelle succeeded in driving the Germans back. Encouraged by these limited and highly contingent successes (German troops in the theater were quite literally exhausted), Nivelle launched a new series of offensives in April 1917. Once again, French troops were bled white by German firepower as they attempted to traverse the last 300 yards. After suffering 120,000 casualties, the French army would go over the top no more. Instead, it mutinied. Fifty-four divisions—nearly half the French army—literally went on strike and refused to participate in further, patently suicidal, frontal assaults. Until the summer of 1918 the French army, its offensive will shattered, remained on the defensive.

The perils of crossing the last 300 yards took its toll on every army, as the British rediscovered in 1917 in the Third Battle of Ypres near the village of Passchendaele. Heavy rains and artillery barrages turned the battlefield into lakes and rivers of mud. Staggering through nearly impassable terrain, the British lost 70,000 men killed and another 170,000 wounded for inconsequential territorial gains (although the attacks succeeded in distracting German attention from French sectors that had been weakened by mutinies).

These troops were not lions led by an officer corps composed of unimaginative donkeys. Innovative officers on both sides—perhaps the most famous being Erwin Rommel—were developing

FIREPOWER AND MOBILITY

tactics to address the question of how best to advance while under heavy fire. Bravery and willpower were necessary but hardly sufficient, as many battles had shown. Massive artillery barrages hurt the enemy, but in the process tore up the ground; were often inaccurate because of wear and tear on gun barrels; tied infantry assaults to rigid and predictable timetables; and forfeited any pretense to surprise. Yet, what other options were available?

The fundamental issue was how to restore maneuver warfare and effective, sustainable offensives to the Western Front. Both the Germans and the Allies developed solutions that helped to restore the balance between offense and defense. The German solution was to combine speed, firepower, and shock in highly trained infantry units composed of *stosstruppen* (storm troops). These storm troops adopted so-called *Hutier* tactics (named after General Oskar von Hutier) in which attacks were preceded by short, intense artillery barrages using high explosives, smoke, and gas to confuse and disrupt defenders, followed by rapid infiltration by heavily armed storm troops trained to bypass enemy strongpoints to attack instead artillery positions, road junctions, and headquarters. Heavy columns of infantry, supported by artillery, followed the storm troops to deal with obstinate Allied units in the bypassed forward defenses.

The new German tactics proved successful at Riga and Caporetto in 1917, contributing to an Italian military collapse in November. In the early stages of the Ludendorff Offensive (Operation Michael) in March 1918, the storm troops advanced up to forty miles, destroying the British Fifth Army in the process. Yet, although the Germans had made great strides in operational art—reducing casualties incurred in crossing "no man's land" to tolerable levels—they had simply run out of troops by April 1918 with which to reinforce their initial successes. They forced the Allies to bend, but could not break them. At the end of Michael each side had suffered approximately nine hundred thousand casualties, but the Allies could afford these losses, as more than one million American doughboys were crossing the Atlantic to augment Allied forces. For the German army, it was a case of too little, too late.

Learning the hard way at the hands of the Germans, the Allies applied similar infantry tactics reinforced by the new technology of tanks. Employed en masse first at Cambrai on 20 November 1917, tanks provided firepower and protection for soldiers, helping them to bridge the last three hundred yards with reduced losses. The shock transferred by more than three hundred tanks disrupted German cohesion, allowing the British to advance five miles along a front six miles long. Yet, tanks were still an immature technology. More importantly, British units at Cambrai got bogged

down in attacking German strongpoints instead of bypassing them. Despite the visionary ideas of tank proponents such as J. F. C. Fuller, the British still lacked a tactical doctrine that allowed commanders flexibility to improvise.

In 1918 the Allies finally developed a mix of technology, tactics, and training that reduced losses incurred in crossing the last three hundred yards to acceptable limits. The Germans helped them in this achievement. The Ludendorff Offensive had extended German lines to little purpose, complicating the defensive assignments of German units and decreasing the force-to-space ratio. Tearing through the extended lines of the Germans came Allied infantry armies reinvigorated by fresh divisions from the United States and supported by artillery, tanks, and airplanes. By appointing Ferdinand Foch as supreme commander, the Allies ensured that their attacks were coordinated, which negated the German advantage of interior lines in moving reinforcements to stem breaches. Unable to transfer troops quickly enough to meet powerful and coordinated Allied attacks, the German army met its Götterdämmerung on 8 August 1918, although the sun would not fully set on Germany until that November.

In their use of tanks and airplanes for firepower, shock, and psychological dislocation; close coordination of infantry with supporting artillery; and renewed emphasis on surprise, unit initiative, and tactical flexibility, the Allies hit on a synergistic formula in 1918 to sap the German will to continue. In prosecuting the war, the political leaders on both sides had largely abnegated their authority to the generals, who, as was their wont, sought tactical solutions to the stalemate on the Western Front. The Allied success in solving the most challenging tactical problem of the war—crossing the last three hundred yards—ultimately proved decisive.

—WILLIAM J. ASTORE,
U.S. AIR FORCE ACADEMY

Viewpoint:
No. The crucial military problem of World War I was that Allied leaders formulated offensive strategies that never accommodated the realities of trench warfare.

It may seem obvious that the crucial problems in World War I occurred at the tactical level. In his book *On War* (1833), the nineteenth-century military theorist Carl von Clausewitz defined tactics as the use of armed forces in battles. In simpler terms, tactics can be understood as a limited perspective from the ground level.

FIREPOWER AND MOBILITY

During World War I, the machine gun, as well as other technological advances in weapons, gave significant advantages to those soldiers in defensive trench emplacements. When other factors, such as artillery barrages and railway transportation, are added to this tactical mix it becomes clear that the defender possessed overwhelming firepower and logistical superiority against enemy forces making an offensive assault across "no man's land." Likewise, it may also seem obvious that these problems should have been solved on the front lines. Indeed, the German army eventually developed "storm trooper" tactics with some tactical effectiveness. In another instance the British army employed tanks in significant numbers at the Battle of Cambrai (November 1917) with limited tactical success.

These examples of tactical innovations were, however, exceptions to the rule. In most battles during World War I the attacking force laid down a prolonged artillery barrage and then sent foot soldiers over the top into the meat grinder to be chewed up by enemy artillery fire, mowed down by machine-gun fire, sniped by rifle fire, cut by barbed wire, bludgeoned by entrenching tools, and skewered by bayonets. Those who survived this gauntlet enjoyed a brief respite until the enemy counterattacked from their trenches behind the lines. This futile scenario repeated itself ad nauseam in battles such as the Somme (1916), Verdun (1916), and Isonzo (1915–1917). Casualties rose into the millions. No decisive victory, however, was possible because no army could turn a tactical victory into a strategic one by using maneuver warfare and mobile forces. Armies lacked the mobility to mount a sustained attack, break through enemy lines, and exploit that penetration. Thus, according to historian Eric J. Leed, in *No Man's Land: Combat and Identity in World War I* (1979), an inverse relationship existed between the intensity of the defender's firepower and the mobility of the attacking forces.

Tactical mistakes were made and tactical solutions were invented throughout World War I. The crucial military problems, however, did not lie in tactics. On the contrary, they were found in strategy and policy. Clausewitz defined strategy as the use of armed forces to achieve objectives such as self-defense, territorial expansion, or retribution. Military analyst Edward N. Luttwak, in *Strategy: The Logic of War and Peace* (1987), argues that a hierarchy extends from strategy down to tactics. Decisions or policies made at the strategic level filter down to the tactical level and effect the outcome of a given battle. Any good strategist must also understand tactics because it is the means to achieve strategic ends; tactics, although subordinate, still affects

A FRENCHMAN AT VERDUN

A French Army officer describes the slaughter at Fort Douaumont on 20–23 May during the Battle of Verdun (1916):

Verdun has become a battle of madmen in the midst of a volcano. Whole regiments melt in a few minutes, and others take their places only to perish in the same way. Between Saturday morning [May 20th] and noon Tuesday [May 23rd] we estimate that the Germans used up 100,000 men on the west Meuse front alone. That is the price they paid for the recapture of our recent gains and the seizure of our outlying positions. The valley separating Le Mort Homme from Hill 287 is choked with bodies. A full brigade was mowed down in a quarter hour's holocaust by our machine guns. Le Mort Homme itself passed from our possession, but the crescent Bourrus position to the south prevents the enemy from utilizing it.

The scene there is appalling, but is dwarfed in comparison with fighting around Douaumont. West of the Meuse, at least, one dies in the open air, but at Douaumont is the horror of darkness, where the men fight in tunnels, screaming with the lust of butchery, deafened by shells and grenades, stifled by smoke.

Even the wounded refuse to abandon the struggle. As though possessed by devils, they fight on until they fall senseless from loss of blood. A surgeon in a front-line post told me that, in a redoubt at the south part of the fort, of 200 French dead, fully half had more than two wounds. Those he was able to treat seemed utterly insane. They kept shouting war cries and their eyes blazed and, strangest of all, they appeared indifferent to pain. At one moment anesthetics ran out owing to the impossibility of bringing forward fresh supplies through the bombardment. Arms, even legs, were amputated without a groan, and even afterward the men seem not to have felt the shock. They asked for a cigarette or inquired how the battle was going.

Our losses in retaking the fort were less heavy than was expected, as the enemy was demoralized by the cannonade—by far the most furious I have ever seen from French guns—and also was taken by surprise. But the subsequent action took a terrible toll. Cover was all blown to pieces. Every German rush was preceded by two or three hours of hell-storm, and then wave after wave of attack in numbers that seemed unceasing. Again and again the defenders' ranks were renewed.

. . . .Some shell holes were thirty feet across, the explosion killing fifty men simultaneously.

Before our lines the German dead lie heaped in long rows. I am told one observer calculated there were 7,000 in a distance of 700 yards. Besides they cannot succor their wounded, whereas of ours one at least in three is removed safely to the rear.

Source: *Charles F. Horne, ed.,* Source Records of the Great War, *volume four (Indianapolis: American Legion, 1930), pp. 223–224.*

strategy. Thus, a dynamic sliding scale exists between tactics and strategy. Policy comes into play because, as historian Russell F. Weigley asserts in *The American Way of War: A History of United States Military Strategy and Policy* (1973), it includes both the structure of armed forces and determination of a strategy in which these forces can be employed. This explanation of policy could also be said to extend to the determination of tactics in which units can be utilized.

During World War I, many of the military leaders failed to overcome the tactical advantages enjoyed by defensive forces. The commanders did not take tactical or logistical matters into account when determining strategic goals, nor did they account for either of these things in establishing policies to achieve those goals. Moreover, their collective ignorance or negligence stemmed from rigid strategies and inflexible policies.

Before 1914 strategic planners assumed that mobile warfare would be possible in a future conflict. All nations entered World War I with offensive-minded strategies—what political scientist Jack L. Snyder, in *The Ideology of the Offensive: Military Decision Making and the Disasters of 1914* (1984), has called "offensive biases." For example, the Schlieffen Plan started with the basic premise that the German army was better than the French army. This plan laid out the whole campaign to defeat France in a few weeks; it anticipated a swift, decisive victory similar to the Franco-Prussian War (1870–1871). However, the German Plan did not make sufficient allowances for unforeseen contingencies such as the stiff Belgian resistance or the gallant French stand at the Marne. The Schlieffen Plan ignored the constraints of time, space, and technology. Ultimately, the scheme was foiled when the lines on the Western Front solidified.

Once the war started, most of the commanders remained loyal to this offensive mind-set. French Marshal Ferdinand Foch advocated the *offensive à l'outrance* (all-out offensive). He firmly believed that a massive charge of courageous men could overcome the concentrated firepower of machine guns, artillery, and bolt-action rifles. By 1915 Foch came to the conclusion that a strategy of coordinated attacks would wear down the enemy. Yet, his own French forces were also worn down.

British Field Marshal Douglas Haig also followed an offensive mind-set. He outlined three stages of battle: artillery barrage, rapid attack, and exploitation beyond enemy front lines. The Battle of the Somme (1916) stood as a prime example of how naive his faith in the offense really was. Haig had hoped for quick and decisive strategic victory. However, his troops, as well as the German army, experienced high casu-

alty rates with no substantive gains. The real strategic effects were exhaustion and attrition on both sides. Haig did not comprehend these realities in part because he remained aloof from the conditions on the battlefield. He would decide on a strategic goal and then pursue this objective with no understanding of tactical realities or the capabilities of his own forces. His strategic goal-setting did not coincide with tactical realities. Haig wanted a war of mobility, movement, and maneuver; but he actually fought a war of attrition.

Even with the experiences of 1914 to 1916 in recent memory, military leaders still did not reject the offensive biases. French general Robert Nivelle, French marshal Joseph Joffre, and American general John Pershing all believed that the stalemate on the Western Front could be ended by just one more assault against the German trenches. The Somme, the Second Battle of the Aisne (or Nivelle's Offensive, 1917), and the Battle of Meuse-Argonne (1918), respectively, showed that these commanders failed to learn lessons from their predecessors.

Unlike so many of their Allied counterparts, German commanders gained a swifter and more thorough understanding of strategy and policy in relation to tactics. At the beginning of World War I General Helmuth von Moltke attempted to put the Schlieffen Plan into action. His attempt slowed and stopped at the Battle of the Marne (1914), partially as a result of hesitation of a junior officer at the battle. Moltke resigned his command. The lines stabilized as trenches were dug and supply lines were established.

General Erich von Falkenhayn, who succeeded von Moltke, realized that massive offensives would be futile at both strategic and tactical levels. No breakthrough or exploitation would be possible. He therefore set about creating a new approach: attack the French and British, establish a foothold in their trenches, and force them to mount costly counterattacks. At the Battle of Verdun (1916), the German forces exacted a heavy price in 362,000 French casualties; the Germans, however, also paid dearly with 337,000 casualties. By 1916, Falkenhayn was relieved of his command.

Field Marshal Paul von Hindenburg and General Erich Ludendorff took over command of the German army in 1916. Earlier in 1914 they had effectively established and executed a successful strategy against Russia on the Eastern Front, winning the Battles of Tannenberg (1914) and the Masurian Lakes (1914). At both battles, the German army benefitted from good tactics and logistics, as well as from some appreciation for how they affected strategy; the Germans also profited from good policies outlined by their staff planning officers. The Russians, at one point or another, suffered from poor commanders, inadequate logistics, unfavorable terrain, or bad intelligence.

On the Western Front facing the British and French, Hindenberg and Ludendorff solidified the strategies and policies of the German army. Ludendorff adjusted German strategy, policies, and tactics to the realities of the machine gun and trench warfare. For example, the German army went on the strategic defensive on the Western Front, breaking with the offensive mentality. This strategy included an elaborate defense-in-depth with three lines of supporting trenches. Meanwhile, the Germans worked to eliminate the Russian threat in the East. Having accomplished that task by 1917, Ludendorff set the German army in the West back on offensive in order to achieve decisive strategic victory before too many American soldiers arrived to support the French and British. In terms of policy, the German field commanders increasingly exercised local control over their tactical decisions. The decentralized system allowed commanders more flexibility. Moreover, the storm-trooper tactics became accepted as offensive tactics. Heavily armed soldiers in two groups would leapfrog one another, with the rearmost group providing fire support for the forward unit as they advanced against the enemy. Such tactics differed from the mass-assault waves employed by so many Allied commanders. Though none of these strategies, tactics, or policies changed the outcome of the war, they did indicate German adaptability and pragmatism under Hindenberg and Ludendorff. The mutual interaction among tactics, policy, and strategy can also be seen.

At the tactical level in World War I, technology and logistics frustrated success on the battlefield. These two areas illustrate some of the challenges and problems facing the armies. The mistakes in, and misunderstandings of, the two areas held serious ramifications at higher levels. The strategists and policymakers never recognized realities on the battlefield as they attempted to win the war with the wrong strategies and policies.

Technological developments ushered in many changes in warfare. New rifles increased the killing efficiency of regular infantry. The British Lee Enfield No. 1 Mark III or the German Mauser Gewehr 98 were shoulder-fired, bolt-action firearms that held five shots; they could be quickly reloaded. These rifles delivered accurate fire out to several hundred yards. In addition to rifles, artillery also saw advances in range and accuracy. The airplane, tank, and poisonous gas appeared on or over battlefields in World War I. Although some tactical innovations were made, all these weapons largely remained at the experimental stage. None could offset the advantages of those soldiers defending trenches.

The machine gun proved to be the most important weapon in World War I. It could fire automatically while a soldier pressed the trigger; a machine gun would fire bullets at a rate of ten rounds per second, until the barrel melted, or until no more rounds were left. When used from the safety of a trench emplacement, the machine gun created a lethal killing zone out to several hundred yards. In the calculus of trench warfare, attacking positions defended by these automatic weapons was foolhardy. No amount of courage, patriotism, or élan on the parts of attackers could overcome such firepower.

As the months dragged on into years, World War I gradually became a war of attrition. Logistics, both supply and transportation of military forces, emerged as important a military factor as strategy, tactics, or technology. Consequently, the British, French, Germans, Italians, Austro-Hungarians, and eventually the Americans found themselves fighting a static war of attrition. They had not expected this type of war on the tactical or strategic level—a type of war in which policies were not adapted to achieve victory.

Armies required thousands of tons of food, water, ammunition, and other supplies every month to maintain their war efforts. French pre-war plans, for example, anticipated using one hundred thousand artillery rounds per month during a conflict. This estimate was much too low, because by 1916 the French army was using more than four million rounds per month. To their credit, most of the nations fighting in World War I achieved and maintained high levels of production and transportation. Still, although production levels and transportation schedules were maintained, logistics favored the defenders of trenches much more than the attackers, because attacking forces quickly moved beyond the immediate supply lines and railheads. At the same time, the defenders could bring food, water, supplies, ammunition, and other items close to their sedentary trench system. Then, in the event of an attack, the defenders could use the same transportation system to remove their wounded soldiers.

Collective military mentalities and individual military leaders remained rigid in their strategies and policies. According to historian Leed, a dysfunctional relationship existed in the trench warfare of World War I. At the strategic level, military leaders hoped to overrun the enemy trenches and move deep into enemy territory. The necessary tactics, however, did not exist. The relationship between strategic ends and tactical means was thus dysfunctional. The more manpower and matériel resources committed by an attacking force, the slower the assault—the slower the assault, the more manpower and matériel resources were committed by the defending force. The desired result of decisive victory did not occur. Instead, casualty rates rose on both sides, with no correspondingly significant strategic success to show for the battle. For the most part, individual officers and the officer corps did not understand this strategic aspect of World War I, nor did they establish satisfactory policies to solve the tactical and strategic problems of this conflict.

–DAVID J. ULBRICH, TEMPLE UNIVERSITY

References

John Ellis, *A Social History of the Machine Gun* (New York: Pantheon, 1975).

Paddy Griffith, *Battle Tactics of the Western Front: The British Army's Art of Attack, 1916–18* (New Haven: Yale University Press, 1994).

Bruce I. Gudmundsson, *Stormtroop Tactics: Innovation in the German Army, 1914–1918* (New York: Praeger, 1989).

Michael Howard, "Men Against Fire: The Doctrine of the Offensive in 1914," in *Makers of Modern Strategy: From Machiavelli to the Nuclear Age,* edited by Peter Paret, and others (Princeton: Princeton University Press, 1986), pp. 510–526.

John Keegan, *The Face of Battle* (London: Cape, 1976; New York: Viking, 1976).

Keegan, *The First World War* (London: Hutchinson, 1998).

Eric J. Leed, *No Man's Land: Combat and Identity in World War I* (Cambridge & New York: Cambridge University Press, 1979).

B. H. Liddell Hart, *The Real War, 1914–1918* (Boston: Little, Brown, 1930).

Edward N. Luttwak, *Strategy: The Logic of War and Peace* (Cambridge, Mass.: Belknap Press of Harvard University Press, 1987).

John Mosier, *The Myth of the Great War: A New Military History of World War I* (New York: HarperCollins, 2001).

Erwin Rommel, *Infanterie Greift An* (Potsdam: Voggenreiter, 1941), translated as *Attacks* (Vienna, Va.: Athena Press, 1979).

Jack L. Snyder, *The Ideology of the Offensive: Military Decision Making and the Disasters of 1914* (Ithaca, N.Y.: Cornell University Press, 1984).

Tim Travers, *How the War Was Won: Command and Technology in the British Army on the Western Front, 1917–1918* (London & New York: Routledge, 1992).

Travers, *The Killing Ground: The British Army, the Western Front, and the Emergence of Modern Warfare, 1900–1918* (London & Boston: Allen & Unwin, 1987).

Russell F. Weigley, *The American Way of War: A History of United States Military Strategy and Policy* (New York: Macmillan, 1973).

Robert H. Zieger, *America's Great War: World War I and the American Experience* (Lanham, Md.: Rowman & Littlefield, 2000).

GALLIPOLI

Was the Allied effort on the Gallipoli Peninsula doomed from the start?

Viewpoint: Yes. Allied planners seriously underestimated Turkish fighting capabilities and defensive preparations.

Viewpoint: No. Poor decisions made on the strategic, operational, and tactical levels determined the failure of the Gallipoli campaign.

The Gallipoli campaign (March 1915–January 1916) remains one of the most provocative and controversial operations of World War I. It has been interpreted as anything from a tantalizing "might-have-been" to an effort objectively doomed from its inception. Gallipoli had its strategic sources in the desire of the Western allies to open a reliable warm-water route to Russia and drive the Ottoman Empire, seemingly the most vulnerable of the Central Powers, out of the war. Arguably, the roots of the operation lay even deeper: to find a way around the developing gridlock of the Western Front—specifically, to bring British sea power to bear directly on a war that was being fought from trenches. Nor was Winston Churchill, the prime advocate of the plan, alone in his mixture of the romantic with the pragmatic. To a generation of British public-school boys raised on classics they imperfectly understood, the chance to fight on ground made hallowed by Homer seemed at times to obscure the common-sense factors mitigating against the operation.

Gallipoli required, first of all, a belief that the second team of the Royal Navy, the pre-dreadnought battleships no longer fit for the line of battle, could force their way through the well-defended straits of the Dardanelles (connecting the Sea of Marmara with the Aegean Sea)—especially given a climate of opinion that recoiled from the idea that even elderly capital ships were expendable assets. When the naval option failed, it required a second act of faith to assume that leftovers from the Western Front—a cobbled-together British regular division, Australian and New Zealand citizen soldiers in improvised armies, and French formations scraped from what was left in the depots—could sweep aside a Turkish army that for all its shortcomings had proved in the Balkan Wars (1912–1913) that its tough, thrawn rank and file were formidable opponents on ground they occupied.

When the initial landings went awry, as much from failures of command as from any extraordinary Turkish performances, it evoked still more faith-based behavior to pour division after division of raw British territorials and New Army volunteers, commanded by superannuated generals, into the broken ground of the Gallipoli Peninsula and expect them somehow to break through increasingly sophisticated Turkish defenses, without even the rudimentary tools coming into use on the Western Front. Yet, despite all the negatives, the culmination of Gallipoli, the August 1915 assault on the high ground of Chunuk Bair that dominated the Straits of Marmara and the way to Constantinople, came within a handspan of success. Fog and friction, including one successful force being shelled off its objective by its supporting warships, were compounded by Turkish heroism, embodied in the sector commander Mustafa Kemal (Atatürk), who led one decisive counterattack himself.

After the failure at Chunuk Bair and the accompanying Suvla landings, a new commanding general recommended evacuation. This withdrawal was accomplished with a competence and flair sadly missing from the actual fighting. Not a man was lost; they were spared instead to die in other places from Mesopotamia to the Somme. Churchill's political career would take a quarter century and an even greater crisis before it recovered from Gallipoli. More than forty-five thousand Allied soldiers from the four corners of the world, and as many as two hundred thousand Turks, did not get a second chance.

Viewpoint:
Yes. Allied planners seriously underestimated Turkish fighting capabilities and defensive preparations.

The historiography of the Gallipoli campaign (March 1915–January 1916) contains a certain "what if" mystique that endures today. Evolving primarily from the pen of Winston Churchill, there are three principal themes that reinforced the idea that with a little extra effort the Allies might have successfully taken the Gallipoli Peninsula or at least broken through the narrows, thus placing Constantinople under the guns of the Royal Navy. The principal myths are that the peninsula was almost undefended until March 1915; the Turks were almost out of ammunition for their heavy coastal guns; and the Allied commander, General Sir Ian Hamilton, should have gone ashore to push his subordinates into action. These themes have endowed the campaign with mythic characteristics and "might-have-beens" when, in fact, the Allied effort at the Dardanelles was doomed from the start.

The Turks began seriously to fortify the peninsula in the fall of 1912 when the Greek fleet threatened invasion during the First Balkan War. By December 1912 the Turks had one regular and three reserve infantry divisions on the Gallipoli Peninsula and a divisional equivalent on the Asian shore. These formations began to fortify the landing beaches and to establish the basic defensive plans. These plans relied on small-unit defenses overlooking all beaches and heavy concentrations of reserves in protected positions on the adjacent high ground from which counterattacks would be launched. After the conclusion of the Balkan Wars, the Turkish staffs retained and refined these defensive plans.

The Ottoman army was ordered to mobilize on 2 August 1914. The most combat-capable corps in the army was assigned the mission to defend the peninsula. This group was the III Corps under the command of Lieutenant General Esat Paşa, a highly regarded general staff officer who had commanded an infantry division in Gal-

lipoli itself in 1911. Moreover, Esat Paşa was one of the most successful Ottoman commanders in the recently ended Balkan Wars and was experienced in actual corps-sized defensive operations. The III Corps mobilized in twenty-two days (the only Ottoman corps out of thirteen to meet its timetable) and began to move into the peninsula in mid September. By the end of October 1914 both the Seventh and Ninth Infantry Divisions were on the peninsula and were occupying battle positions that had evolved in 1912.

The coastal defenses of the straits themselves were organized as a fortress commanded by Cevat Paşa, who had led an infantry division in the Balkan Wars. The fortress had its ninety-one heavy coastal guns manned by 17 August 1914 and the Turks had laid three naval minefields as well. Batteries of 120 millimeter howitzers were deployed on 23 August, a full regiment of 150 millimeter howitzers was ordered there in late September, and by October three more minefields were laid in the narrows. Thus, by the outbreak of war between Britain and the Ottoman Empire on 2 November 1914, the Turks had substantial forces commanded by experienced generals in position to defend the straits.

By February 1915 the Turks had more than fifty thousand trained soldiers on the peninsula, who were armed with more than three hundred cannons. Furthermore, a new infantry division, under the command of the aggressive Mustafa Kemal (Atatürk), was training near Gallipoli itself. By March the straits were the most heavily defended position in the empire. Clearly there was no point after the declaration of war at which the Turks were unready for an Allied landing.

An Allied naval attack on the straits failed in February; a more determined assault was carried out on 18 March 1915, which was a disaster for the Allies, costing them three battleships sunk and three more badly damaged. The heavy firing convinced some Allied officers (and later the memoirs of several German staff officers convinced Churchill as well) that the Turks were running dangerously short of ammunition for their coastal artillery. However, modern official Turkish General Staff histories contain ammunition expenditure reports that contradict this idea

An Anzac sniper with a periscope rifle preparing to fire on a Turkish position on the Gallipoli Peninsula

(from The Anzac Book; Written and Illustrated in Gallipoli by the Men of Anzac [1916], Joseph M. Bruccoli Great War Collection, Thomas Cooper Library, University of South Carolina)

(total Ottoman ammunition expenditures for 18 March 1915 show 2,200 rounds fired in total, of which only 201 were from heavy coastal guns). On 19 March the Turks still had more than a thousand shells remaining for their modern heavy coast artillery, more than four thousand shells remaining for their semimodern heavy coast artillery, and more than six thousand shells remaining for their howitzers. Furthermore, they had laid a total of eleven minefields, consisting of more than four hundred underwater mines, in the narrows. There was more than adequate ammunition with which to continue the fight and, although the Allied navies might have eventually broken through the straits, the cost would have been unacceptably high.

General Otto Liman von Sanders, the commander of the German Military Mission, arrived in Gallipoli in late March 1915 to command the new Ottoman Fifth Army in defense of Gallipoli and the straits. With him came additional combat formations. In his memoirs Liman von Sanders took credit for orchestrating the defense by the Fifth Army; however, in reality, all he did was confirm the existing defensive plans that dated back to 1912. His role in planning the battle is greatly exaggerated, although he must be given credit for affirming the Ottoman plans. Significantly, he did not alter the plans of the III Corps for peninsula defense nor did he choose to relieve Esat Paşa in favor of a German officer.

The actual amphibious invasion on 25 April 1915 set 212 full-strength Allied infantry companies against 120 smaller Ottoman infantry companies in less than five days. Moreover, the Allies enjoyed surprise at the operational level and also lavish logistical and naval superiority. Nevertheless, the Turks held them to tiny beachheads. The superb performance of the Ottoman Army was a tribute to the soundness of the defensive planning and to the overall high quality of Turkish leadership.

The commander of the Allied Mediterranean Expeditionary Force was General Hamilton, who has come under criticism by official and popular historians for his alleged failure to actively push his subordinates into decisive action. Hamilton has been particularly criticized for his failure to go ashore to determine the tactical situation, and then to urge his commanders onward. His failure to do so in late April 1915 is perhaps forgivable; however, in August 1915 he

GALLIPOLI

ANZAC LIONS!

A German officer serving under General Otto Liman von Sanders, commander of the German Military Mission and Ottoman Fifth Army, describes the defense of Gallipoli:

Any one who observed the ensuing conflicts will unhesitatingly give the highest praise for to the death-defying courage of the troops who landed on Suvla Bay. The "Anzacs," as the English newspapers called the Australian-New Zealand Army Corps, fought like lions. If the brilliantly planned operation failed, it was because Sir Ian Hamilton met in the commander of the Fifth Turkish Army a master who in a few moves answered "check" with "checkmate."

The night of the 6th of August settled down pitch black. All day the rain had fallen unceasingly. Not a ray from the moon, not a sparkle from the starts, could penetrate the thick canopy of clouds. It was so dark that a man could scarcely see his hands before his face. . . . Without a word, without a sound, the troops entered the lighters brought for the purpose. On the northern and southern promontories and opposite Tuslagöl Australians and New Zealanders landed with noiseless steps.

The Turkish outposts before the main positions on the rim of the heights which on the west overlook the lowland of Tuslagöl drew back in the face of overwhelming numbers, and immediately a field telephone informed the army high command of the landing of strong forces. Liman Pasha without delay sent an alarm to the two divisions stationed in the northeastern part of the peninsula for the protection of the Gulf of Saros, and started them for Anatolia by forced marches. At the same time a division of Djemil Bey, part of the right wing of the southern troops, was started toward Kodja Djemendagh. The enemy on Suvla Bay at once made bridgeheads of Softa and Laletepe to assure the safety of further landings. . . .

On the same morning a regiment of the enemy moved from the landing place at Softatepe, the northern promontory of Suvla Bay, toward Kiretschtepe and attacked a battalion of Gallipoli gendarmerie. These were oldish men—the beards of some were white—recruited entirely from the peninsula. But they were defending their homes, and the greater strength of the enemy was unable to drive the gallant fellows from their carefully prepared positions. Another body of the enemy had proceeded through Tuslagöl, now almost completely dried up, and from Laletepe against Mestamtepe. At this point the attackers succeeded in holding their positions.

During the night of the 7th–8th still other troops in considerable numbers disembarked on Suvla Bay. The lack of heavy artillery and the shortage of ammunition were seriously felt by the Turks. Had conditions in this respect been different, the enemy's transport and battle fleet, which was now calmly anchored between the two tongues of land formed by the bay, protected against U-boat attack by a steel net stretched between the two headlands, could not have stayed there, and the landing of troops would have been very much more difficult. . . .

. . . Up on Kodja Djemendagh two divisions were stationed under the command of Djemil Bey. He had placed his men so skillfully in the numerous fissures, ravines, and declivities of the mountain that they were enduring fairly well the terrific fire from the ships' guns. Signals flashed among the fleet, and suddenly, at one stroke, every cannon stopped firing. This was the moment Djemil Bey was waiting for. Quickly he hurried to the observer's stand of the mountain artillery, which high above on Jonkbahir was stationed in the front line. His surmise was right. There they came, the Anzacs, ascending the heights in broad storming columns. In good order so far as the difficulty of the ground permitted. Even the new Kitchener troops had learned much during their short period of training.

The artillery commander, trembling with excitement and eagerness for the fray, looked questioningly but vainly at Djemil Bey, whose orders had so far condemned him to inactivity. Further waiting was exacted by that man of iron nerves. Now the attackers, climbing laboriously, were crowded closely together in the ravines and gullies, two thousand meters away; they drew nearer—to fifteen hundred meters, to a thousand. White stones visible only to the defenders, the other side being painted dark, marked for the Turks the exact distances from their lines. Att his moment the mountain artillery started its salvos; the machine guns began to crackle and snap; from the lines of riflemen a hail of bullets sped forth against the Anzacs. It was a scene of Death, of raging, frightful Death, mowing down all. Not a man of those that peopled the slope survived.

Source: *Charles F. Horne, ed.,* The Great Events of the Great War, *volume 3 (New York: National Alumni, 1923), pp. 268–272.*

repeated this error by failing to insist that the lethargic General Sir Frederick Stopford rapidly seize his objectives at Suvla Bay. In each case the school of the "missed opportunity" has created a counterfactual assessment of reality.

It has appeared in retrospect that a more energetic Australian and New Zealand Army Corps (ANZAC) might have pushed inland rapidly to seize their assigned objectives on 25 April. In fact, had they done so it would only have created a meeting with Lieutenant Colonel Kemal's oncoming Nineteenth Infantry Division. Although this engagement might have eliminated the Turkish counterattack that afternoon, it would have placed the ANZACs in an offensive posture on ground thoroughly understood by their enemy. Moreover, three additional infantry regiments, released by Liman von Sanders, were marching to reinforce the Nineteenth Infantry Division. Given the confusion on the ANZAC beachhead, it remains problematic that Hamilton might have inspired a decisive push that would have achieved a breakthrough.

Later in the campaign, Hamilton sought to outflank the Turks by landing a corps at Suvla Bay on 6 August. Although opposed by weak Turkish forces, the British commander, Stopford, was very slow to move aggressively inland. Within three days the Turks moved in three regular infantry divisions to cordon off the Allied beachhead. Assuming that Stopford had moved more rapidly, he simply would have met these same Turkish divisions a bit later and would have had a slightly larger beachhead perimeter. Throughout the campaign the Turks maintained substantial reserves in the Bulair and Saros area of the peninsula and near Kum Kale in Asia.

Some writers have assumed that the immediate and active presence of Hamilton himself would have changed the tactical balance in favor of the Allies. However, this idea flies in the face of the tactical dynamic operative in 1915; offensive operations had failed almost everywhere, and this failure had little to do with the commanders at the corps and army levels. Presuming that Hamilton could have instilled action in a moribund and stagnant command climate, it would have only led to the same result but in different locations. Marginally larger beachheads would not have improved the Allied position nor would this situation have improved their opportunities for success. Furthermore, it must be remembered that an essentially amateur army, commanded by inexperienced leaders, confronted a combat-tested continental army commanded by experienced leaders trained in German methods.

In April 1915 the Turks had twenty regular infantry divisions stationed around the periphery of the Sea of Marmara. By August they had moved three more infantry divisions into the area

from Palestine and formed four new infantry divisions there as well. The Gallipoli campaign acted as a magnet that attracted most of the Ottoman regular army. Significantly, most of the army formations sent to Gallipoli were Anatolian Turkish units that were highly regarded by the British. While the Allies maintained significant forces on the peninsula, which actually outnumbered the Turkish defenders throughout the campaign, they were not able to achieve a decisive numerical superiority sufficient for victory.

It is important to consider that the British were generally unsuccessful against the Turks, at the operational and tactical levels of war, until the battle of Third Gaza (October 1917), where General Edmund Allenby's British offensive operations were based on a huge superiority in tactical methods, numbers, and logistics they did not have on the Gallipoli Peninsula in 1915. Even then Allenby had to wait an entire year (while retraining his depleted army) to deliver a second, and deadlier, blow to the greatly debilitated Ottoman armies. In Mesopotamia the British and Indians were likewise not particularly successful against the Turks until later in the war in spite of huge advantages in resources. This point has somehow become lost in contemporary assessments of Allied potentialities in operations against the Turks at earlier periods in the war.

In fact, there never was a favorable opportunity for the Allies to deliver a decisive naval or military blow that might have achieved victory at Gallipoli. The Allied efforts to seize the straits were doomed from the start, as were almost all offensive operations (by any nation) at that point in the war. The strategic grandeur and unrealized potential of the campaign tends to obscure the operational and tactical realities facing the Allies. This reality, that the Allies had to conduct successful offensive operations against a determined, well-prepared Turkish opponent, was simply not achievable in 1915.

—EDWARD J. ERICKSON, NORWICH HIGH SCHOOL, NEW YORK

Viewpoint:
No. Poor decisions made on the strategic, operational, and tactical levels determined the failure of the Gallipoli campaign.

While the Gallipoli campaign is easily stigmatized as a tragedy of compounded illusions, a case can be made that the operation suffered more from execution than conceptualization. The basic notion of a grand-strategic envelopment, driving Turkey from the war and simultaneously opening a warm-water supply route to Russia, merits credit in a war where creative energy was primarily focused on solving narrow tactical problems. Winston Churchill's initial notion of forcing the Straits by a naval attack foundered less on its demerits than on First Sea Lord Sir John Fisher's reluctance to shift priorities away from the North Sea; on the slowness with which the naval task force was assembled; and finally on the reluctance of French and British naval officers brought up regarding battleships as "sacred vessels" to accept the expendability of the obsolete pre-dreadnoughts composing most of the squadron.

Turkish defenses at the Dardanelles had been improved since the start of the war. They were, however, by no means impassable—especially given the prizes lying beyond them. In the event, however, a combination of gunfire and mines that sank three ships and damaged another half dozen broke the morale of the senior naval officers on the spot. The first Royal Navy admiral commanding the Dardanelles operation had a nervous breakdown and asked to be relieved. His successor, and most of the captains and staff officers, believed a land operation was necessary to clear away the guns, so that minesweepers could clear the Straits for the men-of-war to steam triumphantly into Constantinople. The minesweepers in turn needed high levels of support because they were fishing trawlers manned by civilians. Risking instant death by a mine explosion was bad enough; the heavy shells of the Turkish shore batteries were one thing too many. Eventually the trawlers were remanned, and old destroyers with sweeping gear assumed the main responsibility for mine-clearing. However, that transition too took time, and handed time to the Turks.

The land forces under discussion were leftovers from the Western Front: a hastily assembled British division of regulars, and another of naval and marine reservists; a French division cobbled together from the depots; and two completely inexperienced divisions from Australia and New Zealand. The plan was even more improvised than the force, with projected landing beaches scattered up and down the Gallipoli Peninsula, administrative measures trusting to fortune, and a command system that offered too much initiative to subordinates unable to use it to advantage.

Even then, the rank and file in General Sir Ian Hamilton's attacking formations almost pulled it off. Australian and New Zealand battalions, which landed at the wrong beach, nearly made it to the right one, driving forward to high ground on their own initiative before bogging

down from lack of support. On several other beaches, the landings met no consequent opposition, but instead of pushing forward the attackers waited for orders. Only in the far south, at W and V Beaches, did the landing become a disaster, and there too, the commanders on the spot were left to cope with their own devices.

This lack of grip was a direct product of the character of the British commander in chief Hamilton, who had a distinguished record in the kind of long-range shoestring operations that the Gallipoli landings became. Nothing in his previous career in command indicated a lack of grip. If Gallipoli had a chance in its early days, however, that chance depended on a combination of imagination and energy at all levels of command. Hamilton, however, followed a policy of outlining a general course of action and leaving the implementation to subordinates. He suggested instead of ordering. He exercised command from a distance, on a warship that constantly shifted locations to perform fire missions, then later stationed himself on the island of Mudros.

There were good men in plenty of subordinate assignments, men who would eventually rise to command corps and divisions. They were still learning the higher levels of their craft. None of Hamilton's chief subordinates were anything but mediocre. One, General Sir Aylmer Hunter-Weston, of the Twenty-Ninth Division and later of VIII Corps, was a positive danger commanding anything larger than a battalion. The result was a pattern of operational drift. When Hamilton finally exercised command as opposed to supervising, he allowed Hunter-Weston to talk him into reinforcing the southern sector at Cape Helles and allowing the Australian and New Zealand Army Corps (ANZAC) front to sink into a bloody stalemate.

At its best, attacking north from the Cape Helles beachhead involved a long, hard slugging match up the entire length of the Gallipoli peninsula. The lack of even the limited scales of supporting weapons normal at that time for the Western Front doomed the attacks to repeated failure. Hamilton requested and received reinforcements. Eventually the equivalent of a dozen more divisions, poorly trained territorial soldiers and untrained New Army recruits, dismounted cavalry, French Senegalese and North Africans, Gurkhas, Sikhs, and more ANZACS, were sent to the peninsula, where they found a high command still committed to blasting its way through despite its continuing lack of supporting firepower.

Infantry casualties mounted correspondingly. Hamilton finally attempted a second end run. An amphibious landing at Suvla Bay, well to the north of the other landing sites, was meant to complement a strike across the center of the peninsula for Chunuk Bair and the Sairi Bair ridge line, the high ground commanding the Straits of Marmora. The Suvla operation failed when ineffective commanders at every level from army corps to battalion failed to move their units forward against limited opposition. Hamilton, instead of ruthlessly relieving these ineffective veterans, again allowed them an independence they were incapable of using. The thrust for Chunuk Bair is for its part a classic example of the risks of using tired troops and the dangers of disrupting organizations. The overall effect was of throwing boiled peas at a wall. Yet, again, it almost worked. New Zealand and Gurkha troops reached the objective then were shelled by their own warships and driven back by a ferocious Turkish counterattack.

After the Suvla/Chunuk Bair fiasco, the Dardanelles theater remained stagnant. By that time the Turks had almost as many troops on the peninsula as the allies—in a war where a three-to-one superiority was the minimum ratio for even local tactical successes. Hamilton was relieved, and his successor Sir Charles Monro arrived in the theater convinced withdrawal was the only feasible remaining option. The successful evacuation at the turn of the year ended a campaign as inglorious as it had been promising.

The Turkish opposition receives and deserves much credit for the Allied failure at Gallipoli. Turkish tactical and operational effectiveness steadily improved during the campaign, as officers and men learned from experience and passed their knowledge on to the replacements. The Turkish learning curve, however, was facilitated because of the slow pace of operations. The Turkish army, moreover, was not the German one. Its reaction times were slower; it was subject to disruption by the kind of hard-driving attack that a first-rate Western army might reasonably be expected to deliver. The Allies at Gallipoli faced all the well-known Great War obstacles to offensive operations, plus several others specific to the theater: no rear area to speak of; no bases close to hand; and no economically developed civilian infrastructure. Nevertheless, avoidable lapses in command and control determined the outcome of the campaign even apart from the objective factors.

–DENNIS SHOWALTER,
COLORADO COLLEGE

References

Eric Wheler Bush, *Gallipoli* (London: Allen & Unwin, 1975; New York: St. Martin's Press, 1975).

Edward J. Erickson, *Ordered to Die: A History of the Ottoman Army in the First World War* (Westport, Conn.: Greenwood Press, 2001).

Michael Hickey, *Gallipoli* (London: Murray, 1995).

John Keegan, *The First World War* (London: Hutchinson, 1998).

John Laffin, *Damn the Dardanelles!: The Story of Gallipoli* (London: Osprey, 1980).

Geoffrey Miller, *Straits: British Policy Towards the Ottoman Empire and the Origins of the Dardanelles Campaign* (Hull, U.K.: University of Hull Press, 1997).

Alan Moorehead, *Gallipoli* (New York: Harper, 1956).

Geoffrey Penn, *Fisher, Churchill, and the Dardanelles* (Barnsley, South Yorkshire, U.K: Cooper, 1999).

John Robertson, *Anzac and Empire: The Tragedy and Glory of Gallipoli* (London: Cooper, 1990).

Nigel Steel and Peter Hart, *Defeat at Gallipoli* (London: Macmillan, 1994).

Jeffrey D. Wallin, *By Ships Alone: Churchill and the Dardanelles* (Durham, N.C.: Carolina Academic Press, 1981).

GALLIPOLI

GENDER ROLES

Were women excluded from the Great War?

Viewpoint: Yes. World War I essentially was a masculine activity.

Viewpoint: No. The Great War was an experience that both transcended and denied sex-role stereotyping.

Before 1914 war was universally regarded as a male activity. The few women who had disguised themselves or otherwise managed to serve directly in various armed forces were anomalies. Women were considered nurturers and supporters, objectified as something to be protected and as prizes to be won by the brave. Feminists who addressed the subject of war tended to accept the paradigm, describing it as a male manifestation and expressing not merely the hope but also the certainty that the empowerment of women would at least diminish the frequency and ferocity of armed conflict.

The outbreak of war seemed to confirm women's roles as facilitators. The well-worn cliché of women handing white feathers to men not in uniform is even more ironic because that symbol of cowardice was borrowed from cockfighting, among the most brutal and macho of sports, where a rooster with a white feather was considered a crossbreed and therefore lacking the killer instinct. In a deeper sense, women acted as enablers. Instead of refusing to participate, they stepped in at both family and public levels to assume a broad spectrum of social and emotional roles previously filled by men: street-car conductors, factory workers, and disciplinarians.

This process has been described as enhancing both women's self-esteem and their position in society. By filling the gaps caused by mobilization and casualties, women laid the foundations for political gains such as suffrage and psychological ones such as gender equity. An alternate position is less sanguine. It describes women's participation in the war effort as instrumental. They were cheap labor, whose wages seldom rose above two-thirds those paid to males. They seldom had the chance to acquire the skills that might have improved their marketability. They were substitute men: women who took jobs made available by the war were left with no doubt that they were only holding them either until the males returned or peace made the jobs redundant.

Women during the Great War were arguably most important in traditional feminine roles. As lovers and nurturers, as givers of life to the next generation, they came to symbolize both a future that at times seemed far away and a past whose rough edges eroded under the pressures of war. Nor was the notion of being valued as women—or at least as females—entirely unattractive to many women whose lives had been dislocated by the war, who found themselves doing hard work for low pay, with the full responsibilities of de facto single parenthood or the anxiety of whether they would even have a chance for a husband, a home, and a family—all of which grew more attractive the more they seemed out of reach.

Viewpoint:
Yes. World War I essentially was a masculine activity.

Before the outbreak of World War I, the so-called war myth portrayed combat as a means for boys to achieve manhood. The war myth furnished a cultural process to fulfill this transition. Unlike females, who had menstruation and childbirth as physiological proofs of their womanhood, males needed to find some other means to prove their manhood. This transition necessarily excluded women. Indeed, it was from the feminine virtues of softness and passivity that boys were trying to break away. Men had to remain war-like to avoid slipping back into a boyish condition or falling into a more feminine condition. Men, not boys, exhibited the masculine virtues of courage, decisiveness, and vigor. War was both rite of passage to manhood and guarantor of that passage.

In the late nineteenth century and early twentieth century, European cultural norms demanded that women remain in separate spheres from men. Men occupied public, political, and economic spheres. Their masculine duties included that of provider and protector, both for their families and their nations. They exercised authority over those family members under their protection. Conversely, women occupied private, moral, and domestic spheres, tending to domestic functions such as housework and childbirth. Frequently, working-class women did double duty by laboring outside the home to supplement family income. Those women who crossed over into the public, political, or economic spheres dominated by men did so without absolute security. Middle- and upper-class women enjoyed more flexibility in their daily schedules, while their husbands worked outside the home as lawyers, doctors, engineers, accountants, or bureaucrats.

In every European nation the overwhelming majority of people—regardless of class, gender, or ideology—rallied to the colors in 1914. Men blindly followed the war myth and entered military service. Parades and rallies occurred in all the capital cities as the standing armies mobilized. Nationalistic and militaristic fervor gripped Europeans. The fervor emphasized masculinity as well as misogyny. Propaganda played up the masculine symbols of a given nation. Posters portrayed the enemy as effeminate or barbaric. The enemy, the propaganda stated, possessed inferior masculine qualities or even feminine qualities and would have to be defeated by soldiers with proper masculine qualities.

The actual experience of combat in World War I excluded women, both literally and figuratively. With the exception of some Russian women fighting on the Eastern Front, only men experienced combat. Soldiering established and reinforced their masculinity. A typical battle might look like the following: a lengthy artillery bombardment of the enemy, sometimes lasting for days; waves of thousands of soldiers climbing over the top of their own trenches and racing across "no man's land" toward the enemy trenches; enemy artillery, machine guns, rifles, and hand grenades inflicting many casualties on soldiers as they struggled to get through barbed wire; fierce hand-to-hand combat in the enemy trenches, causing still more casualties on both sides; and then the eventual enemy counterattack frequently pushing the soldiers back to their original starting point. This futile scenario recurred ad nauseam in battles such as the Somme (1916), Verdun (1916), and Isonzo (1915–1917). Casualties for men in uniform of all nations rose into the millions. Unless they served as nurses or support personnel and were caught in enemy fire, few women perished on battlefields.

During World War I the warring nations assembled massive armed forces. These nations also suffered enormous casualties who were killed, wounded, missing, or taken prisoner. The British Empire mobilized a military nearly 9 million strong, drawing most from the 46 million people in Great Britain proper. Casualties numbered more than 3 million, or 36 percent, of that total British military force. France and its empire marshaled almost 8.5 million military personnel, drawing most of its manpower from the 40 million people in France proper. Casualties numbered more than 6 million, or 73 percent, of French military strength. Germany amassed some 11 million men from a nation of 65 million people. Casualties numbered more than 7 million, or 66 percent, of the total military strength of Germany. Russia mobilized some 12 million men and women from among its population of 167 million. Casualties numbered 9 million, or 75 percent, of the total Russian military strength. The Austro-Hungarian Empire cobbled together almost 8 million men from 50 million people. Casualties numbered 6.7 million, or 86 percent, of the total military manpower. And, although it did not enter the conflict until spring 1917, the United States called up more than 4 million men from its population of approximately 100 million. American casualties numbered 260,000, or 6 percent, of its total military strength. Of the 4 million Americans in service, however, only 1 million actually saw combat.

FOUR YEARS IN THE FIGHT
The Women of France
We Owe Them Houses of Cheer

UNITED WAR WORK CAMPAIGN

Most nations also lost civilians to the war as a result of malnutrition, starvation, or mismanagement of food resources. Some 6 million civilians perished in World War I, with Russian losses accounting for 2 million of those. Included in these civilian casualties were women and children.

In these cases, the conflict affected people other than soldiers on the front.

According to historian George L. Mosse in *Fallen Soldiers: Reshaping the Memory of the World Wars* (1990), the war myth also offered camaraderie to the soldiers. Known by many

THE MAKING OF A MAN

In a chapter titled "The Making of a Man," in Donald William Hankey's memoirs, A Student in Arms (1917), the author describes the changes that occur to the recruit that age and season him for war:

On the barrack square of a Special Reserve battalion you may see both the raw material and the finished product—the recruit but newly arrived from the depot, and the war-worn veteran, with anything over one year's service, just discharged from hospital. The change wrought in one year is remarkable. It "sticks out all over." It is seen in their physique, their bearing, the poise of their head, their expression, and most of all in their eyes. The recruit is not set. He stands loosely. He is never still. His expression is always changing. His eyes are restless. Now he is interested, and his pose is alert, his eyes fixed on the instructor. Now his attention is distracted elsewhere, his attitude becomes less tense, his eyes wander. Now he is frankly bored, his head and shoulders droop forward, he stands on one leg, his eyes are fixed on the ground. His movements reflect every passing mood. His will is untrained, his character unformed, his muscles undeveloped. He has no control over his mind or his limbs. He is just a boy. The fascination about him lies in his potentialities, in the uncertainty as to how he will turn out. There are so many pitfalls ahead of him. . . . The trained soldier, who has fought, seen death, suffered wounds, endured hardness, offers a complete contrast. He is thicker. His limbs are quiet and under control. He stands solidly motionless and upright. His mouth is firmly shut. His eyes are steady, and their expression unvarying. His whole attitude and his expression suggest quiet expectancy. He is still; but he is ready to move at a seconds notice. He is intensely self-controlled. Of course all generalizations are untrue. But probably this is how the contrast between the recruit and the trained soldier would present itself to anyone who watched a number of them as they paraded on the barrack square. . . .

Then came the time when his mates began to disappear. Posters stared at him from the hoardings telling him that his King and country needed him. Recruiting sergeants eyed him doubtfully. He did not look much more than sixteen. Here was a chance of variety. His restless temperament responded to the suggestion with enthusiasm. He loved change, and feared monotony above all things. Besides, he would be on his own. Even the shadow of parental control would be removed. He would be a man, and his own master. So he reckoned! "Mother" noticed his excitement, and with a sure instinct guessed what was the matter. "Our George is going for a soldier," she remarked to her husband. "I can see it in 'is eyes." "Father" taxed him with it, and waxed indignant. "Ain't yer satisfied with yer 'ome?" he demanded. "Ain't yer got no gratitood to yer mother? Don't know when yer well off, yer young fool." This clinched matters. The boy said nothing. He could afford not to. His answer was to enlist next day. When it was done "Mother" shed a surreptitious tear, and "Father" grunted; but both were secretly proud of him, though it meant seven shillings a week less in the family exchequer. He went away feeling a little lost and young, and with a lump in his throat for the sake of the home that he had valued so cheaply. . . .

The recruit is developing rapidly. His perspective is altering hourly. Old prejudices are vanishing, and new ones forming. His old selfishness is giving way to good comradeship, his individuality is being merged in a bigger corporate personality. As he becomes less of an individualist, he becomes quieter, and more contented. In a few months he will be drafted out to the front, there to learn harder lessons still, and lessons even better worth learning. He will learn to endure without complaint, to be unselfish without "making a song about it," to risk life itself for the good of the world, the honor of the regiment, and the safety of his comrades. A man does not rise much above that. Perhaps he will make the supreme sacrifice, and so be taken hence at his best. Perhaps he will return to "Blighty." If he does the latter he will be no longer a boy but a man.

Source: *Donald William Hankey, A Student in Arms (New York: Dutton, 1917).*

GENDER ROLES

terms—such as small-unit cohesion, group identification, or male bonding—the camaraderie felt among soldiers leveled class distinctions, ethnic backgrounds, and national allegiances. Soldiers "loved" one another, not in a physical but in an emotional sense. They gradually lost their individual "me" and replaced it with the collective identity "us." The experience of combat further strengthened this bond among veterans. Time and time again, veterans made references in novels and memoirs to their great loyalty to their squad of several fellow soldiers. Every bombardment, every charge, every meal brought these men closer together. The small groups of soldiers became surrogate families. A darker side to all-male combat also existed. World War I required men to prove their manhood by brutally killing other men, who were not unlike themselves. Women did not find any place in combat or the camaraderie that grew out of it.

Soldiering and combat in World War I also excluded women in the figurative sense. Male veterans of combat felt estranged from the civilian home front. The construction of gender gave femininity a cultural meaning diametrically opposed to masculinity. This polarity can be broken down into the following examples: women were feminine, and men were masculine; women acted emotionally, and men acted rationally; women resided in the domestic sphere, and men resided in the public sphere; women acted as nurturers, and men acted as warriors; women gave life, and men took life.

Demonstrating the exclusion of women is not to say that women performed no significant functions in World War I, nor is it to say that men ignored women altogether. Women helped their national war efforts in a variety of ways. Laboring long hours in factories under wretched conditions for low wages, millions of women built the machines and weapons with which men killed one another in the Somme or Verdun. Although these female factory workers invaded a traditionally male work environment, they were limited to lower, feminine status. For example, as a total and modern war, World War I required complete support from combatants and civilians alike. A majority of women offered patriotic and essential support for the war efforts of their nations.

Women played several acceptably feminine roles in World War I. All were unmasculine and unwar-like. Women were caregivers. They served as medical personnel. Either as trained nurses in a medical unit or volunteers in the Red Cross, women worked long hours under sometimes wretched conditions to provide assistance to sick and wounded soldiers. Some women doctors even served as military surgeons when the need exceeded the availability of male doctors.

Women were the objects of war, often as sexual conquests or rewards of war. Whether older or younger, married or single, soldiers frequently visited brothels and employed prostitutes during World War I. Their sexual activities often had a medical penalty. In the British army alone, 27 percent of all diseases were classified as "social diseases" or, in modern terms, as venereal diseases. More than four hundred thousand British men required treatment for their conditions. Moreover, in Paris in 1914 and 1915 almost four thousand girls were arrested for prostitution; of these women about half had contracted venereal diseases. If these numbers of hospitalized and diagnosed cases were any indication, then there must have been millions of additional male soldiers exploiting women as objects of war.

Women were the stewardesses of home fronts for the duration of the conflict. They kept up the households in the absences or deaths of their husbands and fathers. They also took up masculine job occupations such as in munitions factories. When World War I ended and men returned to their prewar status as heads of households, however, women were expected to return to their prewar gender status.

Whether in hospitals, in brothels, or at home, women provided some level of refuge, release, or escape for male soldiers. Whatever the roles women played, they were separate from the male soldiers. Men who fought in World War I performed essentially masculine and belligerent activities, neither feminine nor civilian.

—DAVID J. ULBRICH, TEMPLE UNIVERSITY

Viewpoint:
No. The Great War was an experience that both transcended and denied sex-role stereotyping.

The Great War was not a watershed for permanent changes in women's rights or opportunities. During the war, women gained the right to vote in the United States and Great Britain, but this victory reflected the culmination of decades of activism by suffragettes; it was not a reward for women's contributions to World War I. Nevertheless, during the conflict women moved in large numbers into traditionally male occupations and roles, often despite considerable opposition from organized, male-dominated unions. Usually paid less than men, women nonetheless proved themselves highly capable and courageous as munitions workers, ambulance drivers, police officers, and even as soldiers in the case of some Russian women. Viewed collectively, women's experiences in the Great War both transcended and denied sex-role stereotyping.

Obviously, "women" as a category of analysis must be qualified. As Gerda Lerner has noted in *Why History Matters: Life and Thought* (1997), women's experiences differed by social class, race, ethnicity, religion, country, region, education, and several other categories. These categories themselves were gender specific, notes Lerner. For example, men and women of the same class experienced notions of class identity differently, with women's identity being mediated and shaped by husbands, fathers, or other male figures of authority. Notions of "correct," or "proper," behavior for women, moreover, were socially constructed within contested spaces where gender—the identities, roles, and expectations ascribed to each sex within specific cultural settings—was constantly being challenged, negotiated, and contingently reconstructed.

Recognizing that "women" as a Platonic explanatory category is always simplistic and misleading, one can nevertheless make generalizations about prewar attitudes about gender roles. Prior to the Great War, bourgeois women were restricted primarily to traditional roles as mothers, wives, and daughters within a "cult of domesticity." If married, they were expected to be childbearers and loyal companions, not breadwinners. Men put women on pedestals as the upholders of moral virtue within a nation but also shackled them to this role. Divorce was rare and brought scandal from which few women recovered. Peasant women wore tighter fetters than their social superiors; they usually had to toil, sometimes side-by-side with men, in fields, coal mines, factories, and in the home, among other patriarchal settings. Within patriarchal societies in Europe and the United States, women were actively discouraged from becoming entrepreneurs or politicians or obtaining any position that exposed them to the male gaze in the rough-and-tumble competition of a male-dominated Darwinian world. President Theodore Roosevelt's "champion in the ring" was always to be male, never female.

Shackles and fetters loosened for women during the Great War, but they never disappeared. Female warriors served with distinction on the Russian front (as in the famous Women's Battalion of Death), but they were exceptions. European and American women proved their mettle initially in more-traditional roles such as nursing. As the war entered its second year, however, nations realized that attritional warfare required national mobilization. With millions of men marching to the front, women patriotically sought ways to fill in for the men by "doing their bit" for their respective national war effort.

Facing the enormous demands and horrendous losses of attritional warfare at Verdun (1916), the French employed nearly 370,000 women in defense-related industries. They constituted nearly a quarter of the French factory force. Rightly did General Joseph Joffre conclude that, "If the women in war factories stopped for twenty minutes, we should lose the war." Employment of women also drove increased mechanization to compensate for women's comparative lack of physical strength that ultimately improved the efficiency of French war production. There was nothing new about women working in factories, of course, but the scale of their involvement was much larger. More importantly, women excelled at traditionally male jobs that required skills and physical strength that supposedly (yet not in reality) placed these jobs outside of the women's sphere.

Britain too witnessed the mass recruitment of women to fill traditionally male jobs. Before 1914 the Royal Ordnance Factories employed only a handful of women; by 1918 they employed more than 24,000. National Shell Filling Factories employed an additional 50,000 women. Known affectionately as "canaries" because of the yellow streaking of their faces from TNT, these "munitionettes" worked twelve-hour days under dangerous, sometimes fatal, conditions. Wages lagged in comparison to male workers, but the salary of 40 shillings a week women earned by 1918 was nearly five times what they earned in factory work before the war. With Tommies in the trenches earning just a shilling a day, women's pay actually exceeded that of the poor blighters at the front by a comfortable margin.

After the bloodletting of the Somme campaign (1916), Britain also founded auxiliary military formations for women to free up men for battle at the front. Thus, the Women's Army Auxiliary Corps (WAAC) came into being in March 1917, the Women's Royal Naval Service (WRNS, knows as Wrens) in November 1917, and the Women's Royal Air Force (WRAF) in April 1918. Nearly 100,000 women served in these auxiliary forces. Although they served in noncombat roles such as telephonists, stenographers, messengers, secretaries, kitchen help, and similar positions, women's administrative contributions were vital in a war in which telephones and typewriters were critical to the mass mobilization and control of multimillion-man armies.

Demands for men at the front led to renegotiation of gender roles at the home front. "Unlady-like" jobs were redefined as the patriotic duty of qualified women. Thus, women drove trams and ran the Métro in Paris or drove buses in London. Police work—a traditional male bastion of blue-collar respectability—was opened to women. Six women helped to found the Women's Police Volunteers in Britain in November 1914. By 1917, 650 women served on the force. That same year, a quarter of a million British women donned trousers and served in the Women's Land Army in Britain. When off-duty, they often continued to wear their "male" trousers unselfconsciously. The transgressive practices of flappers of the 1920s—with their bobbed hair, audaciously short skirts, and gender-blurring behavior—owed much to their older sisters' and mothers' work and attitudes during the Great War.

Other countries witnessed similar redefinitions of gender roles. In the German machine industry, women workers increased from 75,000 in 1913 to nearly 500,000 in 1918. The United States was only in the war for a little more than a year, yet American women's representation in the workforce increased 250 percent between April 1917 and the end of 1918. As white working-class women moved from domestic service into higher-paying jobs in industry, blacks moved into positions in households that whites had vacated. Eleven thousand American women also served as nurses in support of the American Expeditionary Force (AEF).

Largely unheralded and unsung after the war, women's contributions were nonetheless vital and indispensable to the respective war efforts of their nations. Yet, despite these contributions, women were pressured after 1918 to return to the domestic sphere. Most women could do little but comply with societal pressures, especially in Europe, where recession and unemployment followed the Armistice. Thus, in 1929 English novelist Virginia Woolf was still penning polemics that called for women to gain "rooms of their own" in which they could excel. Clearly, the Great War did not revolutionize women's position in society or lead to equality of opportunity.

Yet, the glass was more than half full. In filling more-interesting jobs with greater responsibility and higher pay, women found themselves transformed by the experience. Societal pressures and conformity may have forced most women to give up their jobs after the war, but women experienced what is referred to as "empowerment." They won respect, not just as moral weather vanes but also as bellwethers of change, by contributing to the war effort in ways that transcended traditional gender roles. Women assumed even more-prominent roles in World War II (1939–1945); the dynamism, courage, hardiness, and patriotism exhibited by women in the Great War made it possible. As women activists recognized, deeds spoke louder than words—and women's deeds in the Great War spoke loudly and unequivocally of women's equality.

–WILLIAM J. ASTORE,
U.S. AIR FORCE ACADEMY

References

Bonnie S. Anderson and Judith P. Zinsser, *A History of Their Own: Women in Europe From Prehistory to the Present*, revised edition, volume 2 (New York: Oxford University Press, 2000).

Gail Braybon, "Women, War, and Work," *The Oxford Illustrated History of the First World War*, edited by Hew Strachan (Oxford & New York: Oxford University Press, 1998), pp. 149–162.

Braybon, *Women Workers in the First World War: The British Experience* (London: Croom Helm, 1981; Totowa, N.J.: Barnes & Noble, 1981).

Malcolm Brown, ed., *The Imperial War Museum Book of the First World War: A Great Conflict Recalled in Previously Unpublished Letters, Diaries, Documents, and Memoirs* (London: Sidgwick & Jackson, 1991).

Diana Condell and Jean Liddiard, *Working for Victory?: Images of Women in the First World War, 1914–18* (London: Routledge & Kegan Paul, 1987).

Ute Daniel, *The War from Within: German Working-Class Women in the First World War*, translated by Margaret Ries (Oxford & New York: Berg, 1997).

Margaret H. Darrow, *French Women and the First World War: War Stories from the Home Front* (Oxford & New York: Berg, 2000).

Modris Eksteins, *The Rites of Spring: The Great War and the Birth of the Modern Age* (New York: Houghton Mifflin, 1989).

John Ellis, *Eye-Deep in Hell* (London: Croom Helm, 1976).

Jean Bethke Elshtain, *Women and War* (New York: Basic Books, 1987).

Lettie Gavin, *American Women in World War I: They Also Served* (Niwot: University Press of Colorado, 1997).

Joshua S. Goldstein, *War and Gender: How Gender Shapes the War System and Vice Versa* (Cambridge: Cambridge University Press, 2001).

Maurine Weiner Greenwald, *Women, War, and Work: The Impact of World War I on Women Workers in the United States* (Westport, Conn.: Greenwood Press, 1980).

Margaret Randolph Higonnet, and others, eds., *Behind the Lines: Gender and the Two World Wars* (New Haven, Conn.: Yale University Press, 1987).

John Keegan, *The Face of Battle* (London: Cape, 1976; New York: Viking, 1976).

Keegan, *The First World War* (London: Hutchinson, 1998).

Eric J. Leed, *No Man's Land: Combat & Identity in World War I* (Cambridge & New York: Cambridge University Press, 1979).

Gerda Lerner, *Why History Matters: Life and Thought* (New York: Oxford University Press, 1997).

George L. Mosse, *Fallen Soldiers: Reshaping the Memory of the World Wars* (New York: Oxford University Press, 1990).

Mosse, *The Image of Man: The Creation of Modern Masculinity* (New York: Oxford University Press, 1996).

Sharon Ouditt, *Fighting Forces, Writing Women: Identity and Ideology in the First World War* (London & New York: Routledge, 1994).

David J. Ulbrich, "A Male-Conscious Critique of *All Quiet on the Western Front*," *Journal of Men's Studies*, 3 (February 1995): 229–240.

Angela Woollacott, *On Her Their Lives Depend: Munitions Workers in the Great War* (Berkeley: University of California Press, 1994).

Robert H. Zieger, *America's Great War: World War I and the American Experience* (Lanham, Md.: Rowman & Littlefield, 2000).

GENDER ROLES

GERMAN COMMERCE RAIDERS

Were German surface-commerce raiders effective?

Viewpoint: Yes. Surface raiders exercised continuous pressure on commercial shipping in open waters.

Viewpoint: No. Surface-commerce raiding was obsolescent as early as 1914, having no more than a nuisance value against the British maritime empire.

In the years prior to 1914 German naval strategy increasingly emphasized seeking an immediate decisive battle with the British Royal Navy. This notion of *der Tag* (the day) to which toasts were regularly drunk in officers' messes, took little account of the real anxiety of British strategic planners: maintaining the commerce on which the heavily industrialized British Isles were considered to depend. The British approach to future war might have accepted a continental commitment as its focus. However, it was expected to be minimal in terms of men and guns. Instead Britain would act as the bank and the arsenal for its French and Russian allies. That in turn required not merely maintaining but enhancing overseas trade. In contrast to the days of Napoleon Bonaparte, by 1914 the British Isles were no longer able to feed their population. The nightmare of politicians and admirals alike was an interruption of commerce on the outbreak of war that would first create financial anxiety in the West End of London accompanied by hunger in the slums, followed rapidly by respective slides into panic and rioting.

In that context the limited preparation of the German navy for a blow at British lifelines is further proof of the failure of Germany to think strategically about the prospects of war with Britain. Like the Royal Navy, the German navy had concentrated its principal assets in home waters. Their only significant overseas force was the East Asian Squadron stationed at Tsingtao: two armored and three light cruisers, all of them older ships. Three more light cruisers were deployed singly on routine show-the-flag missions. The commerce-raiding potential of these ships was limited by the lack of defensible bases and by neutrality laws restricting the amount of time they could spend in non-belligerent ports. In that sense they were an expendable asset. The decision of Admiral Maximilian Graf von Spee, however, to keep his squadron together as a miniature "fleet in being" only facilitated its eventual destruction by a superior British force. The one cruiser he detached, the *Emden,* was disproportionately successful as a raider, not only for the ships it sank but also for its moral impact. Of the three others, one joined Spee, another blew up by accident, and the third eventually was blockaded in an East African river. A half-dozen, or even a dozen, warships operating along the *Emden*'s lines, commanded by officers believing in the concept of war against maritime commerce, would not have changed the outcome of the war, but might have rewritten its story.

The Germans initially put faith in the prospect of arming fast ocean liners and using them as commerce raiders. These ships turned out to consume too much coal at high speed, to be too easily recognizable, and to be too vulnerable to gunfire. Far more useful relative to their tonnage were the few armed merchantmen the Germans were able to slip past the British blockade in the later years of the war. Disguised as neutral freighters, armed with concealed four- or six-inch guns, they wreaked havoc with relative invulnerability. Finding a single tramp steamer before the days of aircraft and radio was a matter of serendipity. The *Mowe,* a converted banana boat, accounted for thirty-four ships sunk in two cruises between 1915 and 1917. The *Wolf,* with a seaplane for scouting and its guns supplemented by a minelaying capacity, cost the Allies more than a hundred thousand tons of shipping in 1916–1918 and made port to tell her story. The Germans even deployed a sailing ship: the *Seeadler* bagged ten of her own kind before being wrecked in 1917.

Like the warships, the merchant raiders were too few, too late. They nevertheless left a memory, and a suggestion that even in a developing undersea age, surface action against commerce was a profitable investment. In a later war German methods would be more sophisticated and more successful.

Viewpoint:
Yes. Surface raiders exercised continuous pressure on commercial shipping in open waters.

Commerce warfare (attacking the enemy's trade rather than their warships) received little attention before World War I. Navies focused on a decisive battle rather than on slowly choking their enemy's supplies. Britain planned a blockade of Germany, however, and had examined how to achieve this objective safely and effectively. Although it would have made sense for the Germans to do more, they paid little attention to commerce raiding.

As a result, when war came the vast majority of the German fleet was in home waters where the British blockade trapped it, preventing much commerce raiding. The largest ship that was not near a German port was the battle cruiser *Goeben,* and it quickly steamed to Turkey, where it played an important role in getting the Ottoman Empire to join the Central Powers, but soon was bottled up by powerful British forces. With that exception, the German Asiatic Squadron and a few light cruisers scattered around the world were all that were not blockaded.

Admiral Maximilian Graf von Spee, commander of the Asiatic Squadron, detached the light cruiser *Emden* to raid the Bay of Bengal while taking the rest of his squadron (two more light cruisers and two heavy cruisers) across the Pacific in an effort to return to Germany. *Emden* captured seventeen ships (74,305 tons) and made headlines all over the world. Part of its fame came from its boldness: nobody had embarrassed the Royal Navy this badly for more than a century. By mid November, however, the *Emden* had been wrecked, caught at the obscure Cocos Island by the more powerful Australian cruiser *Sydney.*

Von Spee, meanwhile, had disappeared into the vast spaces of the Pacific, forcing the Allies to devote substantial resources in hunting him. (The hunting forces were in addition to the warships needed to escort large troop convoys from Australia, New Zealand, and India.) Crisscrossing the Pacific and Indian Oceans and looking for the proverbial needles in a haystack were, along with large numbers of British ships, the bulk of the French Pacific forces, the cream of the Japanese navy, and even a few Russian ships. Von Spee eventually reached the Chilean coast, refilled his coal bunkers, and continued toward home. En route he encountered an inferior British squadron at Coronel where he sank two cruisers—handing the Royal Navy their first substantial defeat in decades. The British soon more than evened the score: on 8 December 1914 at the Falkland Islands a vastly superior force sank four of von Spee's five ships. *Dresden* was the only German ship to escape, remaining a potential threat until it was forced to be scuttled in March 1915, but it spent its time hiding rather than raiding.

Elsewhere the light cruiser *Königsberg* left German East Africa just long enough to sink two ships (one an antiquated cruiser) before returning to hide in the twisting Rufiji River delta. It hid there for six months; for a long time the British did not know where it was and had to patrol the areas where it might be. Eventually it was found and then neutralized on 11 July 1915 by long-range fire. The *Leipzig* had been showing-the-flag on the west coast of the Americas, and it captured a few ships as far north as British Columbia before joining von Spee. The *Karlsruhe* had been stationed in the Caribbean in peacetime; it sank sixteen ships (17,805 tons) but had to spend much of its time dodging British patrols.

To augment their commerce-raiding strength, the Germans also armed some of their merchant ships, mainly the fast Atlantic liners, as auxiliary cruisers. (Every nation had plans for auxiliary cruisers, either to protect trade or to attack it.) The results were mixed: while a few raiders were successful, others achieved nothing. Since all the liners consumed large quanti-

A lifeboat of Australian sailors approaching the beached German commerce raider *Emden* in the Indian Ocean in 1914

ties of coal, they rapidly ran out of fuel and had to intern themselves in neutral ports.

Now the Allies had unchallenged control of the seas beyond Europe. Before the war, the British had analyzed the question of trade protection. The conclusion was simple: facing a weak enemy, there was no need to worry about convoying or escorting thousands of merchantmen around the world. It was better to hunt the warships, which had few bases and could not stay at sea for long, and accept the small number of ships sunk. They believed this strategy would quickly solve the problem, freeing most of the warships from distant stations for use in European waters. By and large they had stuck to this plan when war actually came—even though at times the *Emden* had frightened shipping companies into holding ships in port. They only escorted the troop convoys; as a result, in exchange for losing seventy-one ships of about 225,000 tons, the high seas were then clear of German raiders.

The Germans, on the other hand, were in a strategic bind. They had little chance of winning a decisive victory in the North Sea for two reasons. First, the British fleet had a larger and roughly equally good fleet, so if the two met, the odds favored the British. Second, the British would not risk their fleet under unfavorable circumstances.

The Germans were forced to turn to commerce warfare, and under the circumstances it could only be conducted by submarines. Although submarines could sink ships around Britain and in the Mediterranean, they had severe limits. Bases in Belgium could only handle medium and small subs that could only reach the North Sea or the west coast of Ireland. The large subs based in German ports faced a longer voyage to their hunting grounds if they went around Scotland, or a riskier voyage if they tried to get past British patrols in the English Channel.

Regardless, the subs could only operate in the North Atlantic. In 1916 the Germans built two large (for the day) subs that were supposed to carry high-value cargoes bought in America under the Allied blockade. One of these boats, *Deutschland,* made several trips, and in 1916 one of the larger ordinary subs operated for about three days off the American coast. By 1918 some of the new subs could operate as far away as Gibraltar, but these were exceptions. The long cruises were typically inefficient, sinking few ships but taking a long time to deploy and return, and also a long time to refit. The bulk of German subs was only a threat in European waters.

Since no German warship managed to sneak through the British blockade during World War I (unlike World War II when several managed it in the early years), they had to use something else. The Germans therefore took some ordinary-looking merchantmen, fitted them with concealed guns, torpedoes, and mines (and some with floatplanes), and gradually slipped them out through the blockade. The first of these ships was the *Mowe,* which operated in the Atlantic in 1915 and 1916; in that time it sank fourteen ships of 49,739 tons. Of four raiders dispatched later in 1916, two failed to slip through the blockade, but two others (the *Wolf* and the sailing ship *Seeadler*) did. The *Mowe* went back to sea and sank another twenty-five ships of 124,707 tons in the North and South Atlantic. The *Wolf* spent fifteen months at sea, going around South Africa and through the Indian Ocean to the Pacific, and it sank twenty-seven ships of 114,279 tons. *Seeadler* meanwhile sank twenty-seven small ships (many were other sailing vessels, since she had trouble chasing steamers) for a combined 30,099 tons. The last raider to try and run the blockade was intercepted and sunk in early 1917. Combined, the surface raiders sank around 200,000 tons of shipping. This tonnage was a useful amount, but only about two ordinary months of what the U-boats sent to the bottom.

Were the merchant raiders worth the effort? Yes, they were. They were inexpensive to convert and operate; the Germans knew how risky these operations were and did not gold-plate the ships they sent. They only involved a total of some 1,500 crewmen, not enough to man a single battleship. While the men could have crewed about fifty subs, the Germans did not have fifty spare subs. The shipyards were building subs as fast as they could, but the work involved to convert the handful of merchantmen/raiders would not have produced an equal number of subs, much less fifty.

In addition, the raiders accomplished more than the subs could have, since the surface vessels operated around the world. Raiders worked, literally, on the far side of the globe, in places no submarine could reach. They also tied down dozens of Allied cruisers, keeping thousands of sailors steaming back and forth, chasing the latest report of where the raider was. *Wolf* was chased by up to fifty Allied warships at one point; *Mowe* was pursued by two dozen British, and some French, ships. To be fair, the Allies would never have removed all their ships from everywhere except European waters—but the raiders forced the Allies to use more ships and men in remote areas unproductively pursuing raiders. If the German raiders had not been at sea, many of the Allied cruisers in distant parts of the world would have been decommissioned and the men transferred to antisubmarine ships in the North Atlantic and Mediterranean. So the results of the surface-raiding strategy for the Germans were good. They sank a bit more tonnage for a small investment in men and matériel. They stretched the Allies resources in men and ships, which reduced the effort the Allies could put into antisubmarine patrols.

In fact, while it would not have done decisive damage, the Germans might have been better off if von Spee's squadron had been used as raiders. Although their return to Germany would have boosted German morale, the ships would hardly have affected the naval balance. His bigger cruisers were out of date, so the net effect would have been a few more light cruisers to patrol the North Sea. Had he instead scattered his squadron, with orders to sink as many merchantmen as possible while dodging pursuers, they would have done more long-term damage than the two old cruisers they sank at Coronel. Going further, the Germans were ill advised to station the armored cruisers in the Pacific since they had little wartime use. They were too slow and too powerful for efficient commerce raiding; the Germans only needed a handful of light cruisers in the Pacific if the main role of their Asiatic Squadron was to fight Britain or France. The Asiatic Squadron was there for prestige purposes and proved of little use in wartime.

–SANDERS MARBLE, WWW.EHISTORY.COM

viewpoint:
No. Surface commerce raiding was obsolescent as early as 1914, having no more than a nuisance value against the British maritime empire.

In Vice-Admiral Maximilian Graf von Spee's plaintive 1914 letter to his wife, he summed up both his specific predicament and the general situation that affected any attempts by the Imperial German Navy to conduct cruiser warfare. "We possess no secure harbours in the world, I have to strike through the oceans and cause as much disruption as I can, until our ammunition is depleted or a far superior enemy does me in." Although the exploits of the German commerce raiders, and in particular the story of the light cruiser SMS *Emden,* are among the most colorful and dramatic events of World War I, they remain more curiosities than successful attempts to conduct a worldwide *guerre de course* (war on trade), a war on Allied maritime commerce. The technology and laws of war no longer permitted the effective adoption of such a strategy. The German Navy achieved greater success than it could have hoped for during its brief foray into cruiser warfare, but the entire campaign could never amount to more than a nuisance.

Part of the success of the British during the previous three centuries of naval warfare had been the result of reliance on attacking enemy commerce, performed both by the Royal Navy and by a

THE *EMDEN* AT SEA

Lieutenant Hellmuth von Müecke from the German cruiser Emden, *which raided Allied commerce in the Indian Ocean, reports on the sinking of an enemy vessel:*

. . . very early in the morning of September 11, a few hours after our squadron hat received its first addition, with the rising of the sun, a large steamer appeared dead ahead who, thinking we were an English man-of-war, was so overjoyed at our presence that she hoisted a huge British flag while still at a great distance. I do not know what kind of expression came over her captain's face when we hoisted our flag and invited him most graciously to tarry with us awhile. The steamer had left Calcutta and, having been detailed for transport duty between Colombo and France, was fitted out in fine style. Especially were we touched by the fact that she did not disown the English desire for cleanliness and therefore had taken such a big cargo of soap that our small crew, itself in the greatest need of this most necessary assistant to Kultur, would have enough to last a whole year. We also found a beautiful racehorse aboard. A bullet behind the ear saved the animal the agonies of a death by drowning. We had less compassion for the numerous built-in, beautifully numbered, horse stalls and gun mounts aboard the ship. A half hour later the sharks could, at closer quarters, occupy their attention with these.

The crew of the ship was transported to our "lucky bag." The "lucky bag" was always one of the captured ships which was either empty or in ballast and therefore of little value, or which contained neutral cargo and could therefore not be sunk without a loss. At the end of the war, all neutral cargo destroyers must be paid for. The "lucky bag" always followed along behind the *Emden* until she was finally filled up with people taken from the captured vessels. Then she was detached and sent into the nearest harbor. Under these circumstances, the *Pontoporros* was detailed to the rule of "lucky bag."

A seaman always has a peculiar feeling when he sees a ship sinking. Even we, accustomed to helping vessels in distress, were affected not a little by the sight of sinking vessels, even those that we had to destroy. The destruction was usually done in the following way: We went into the engine-room and removed the bonnet of a main overboard discharge valve. The water immediately came into the engine room in a stream twice a man's height and more than a man's thickness. The watertight doors to the adjoining fire-room were opened and secured against closing, so that at least two large compartments of the ship would certainly fill up with water. In addition, two smaller compartments were also filled, either by exploding bombs—this at night or by firing shells into them. . . . Then the *Emden* would go ahead to meet the next oncoming mast head.

Source: *"2 August–9 November, 1914: Cruise and Destruction of the Emden," World War I Document Archive, Internet website, http://www.lib.byu.edu/ ~rdh/wwi/1914/emden.html.*

---

host of private investors using war as a method of speculation. This strategy was as much economic warfare as military, relying on the capture of enemy goods and ships to make even more profit.

The circumstances that made commerce warfare such an appealing prospect changed over the course of the nineteenth century. First, the Declaration of Paris (1856) abolished privateering, the use of private enterprise for war on maritime trade, placing the burden of carrying out such a strategy on naval forces. Second, the events of the American Civil War (1861–1865), and in particular the exploits of the Confederate commerce-raider CSS *Alabama,* convinced nations of the importance of observing the laws of neutrality in war. Third, the effects of the Industrial Revolution on naval technology produced a type of warship that was in

many ways superior to its predecessors, but it possessed a fatal flaw that hampered its ability to conduct a long-range war on enemy commerce. The second and third points are the most relevant to any discussion of German commerce raiding in World War I and are closely linked.

Warships in the Age of Sail were not self-sufficient by any means. They required regular stocks of fresh water and food, and repairs were a fact of life. The introduction of steam propulsion, however, created a new problem for the long-range raider. While the steam engine provided a reliable and faster means of propulsion, it required a steady supply of coal to keep the boiler fires going. Long-range cruisers built for overseas service in the second half of the nineteenth century were equipped with both engines and sails to permit greater mobility, but by 1890 such warships were obsolete.

The use of steam propulsion was necessary by this time in order to deal with the merchant fleets of the world, which also were under steam power. The *Alabama* and her sister raiders were able to use sails for cruising, conserving precious coal reserves for chasing down prey. No such luxury was available to the German cruisers of 1914. The armored cruisers *Scharnhorst* and *Gneisenau* were both heavy consumers of coal. Attempts to turn large passenger liners such as the *Kaiser Wilhelm der Große* into auxiliary cruisers by mounting a few medium-caliber deck guns were hampered even further by the appetite for fuel of these vessels; they were built for speed and comfort, not economic long-range cruising.

From where was the German Navy to get its coal? This requirement was where the laws of neutrality came into play. After the favored treatment received by the *Alabama* from several nations and subsequent protests by the American government, restrictions on the use of neutral ports by belligerent warships were enforced more uniformly by foreign governments. Most importantly, a warship was allowed to coal only once within a three-month span in a port of a neutral nation. This restriction meant it was nearly impossible for a warship to conduct operations far from its own bases.

As well as coal, other supplies played a crucial role in limiting the effectiveness of overseas cruisers. In particular, the ammunition for the guns was impossible to replenish; whereas coal could be seized from passing vessels, munitions were much harder to come by, and they would not have fit any other of the guns used by another country. In a single action, the encounter at Coronel on 1 November 1914 forced von Spee's ships to use up 42 percent of the irreplaceable 8.2 inch ammunition for the main guns of his two large armored cruisers, *Scharnhorst* and *Gneisenau*.

The German Empire had not been created with the needs of the navy in mind. Naval leadership had been lobbying for secure coaling stations, German-controlled ports, and even colonial possessions as far back as 1848. Those cries had been ignored, however, especially by Otto von Bismarck during his tenure as Imperial Chancellor (1815–1898). Consequently, the empire possessed only one base of any significance in the Pacific Ocean, Tsingtao, on the northern China coast, which it obtained in 1897. With the entry of Japan into the war, however, Tsingtao became vulnerable to blockade and invasion. As a result, von Spee was ordered not to use it as a base of operations. With the rapid loss of all German possessions in the Pacific after the beginning of the war, von Spee had to hope for the benevolent neutrality of either the United States or the Netherlands. Neither proved cooperative, and the possibilities for action in the crucial regions around Indonesia, the west coast of Australia, and the eastern waters of the Indian Ocean were severely curbed by the rigorously enforced neutrality of the Dutch East Indies.

The East Asian Cruiser Squadron was left on its own to devise means of obtaining coal, and on finding places secure enough to engage in the dirty, time-consuming, and laborious task of transferring coal from supply ships to its warships. Coaling at sea led to ships banging together in the swells, with eventual damage to hulls, boilers, and engines. The performance of warships thus decreased without regular and proper maintenance.

The brief history of the East Asian Cruiser Squadron illustrated its difficult situation. The entry of Japan into the war made operations in East Asia impossible; as well, von Spee had to avoid Australian waters for fear of the battle cruiser HMAS *Australia*, which outgunned his most powerful ships. He was able to detach *Emden* for operations in the Indian Ocean solely because *Emden* would be operating on its own. This resourceful light cruiser was able to wreak havoc in the Bay of Bengal but was still trapped by its own needs. Of the ten coaling refills it carried out during its cruise, five were from captured prizes.

The rest of the squadron—the armored cruisers *Scharnhorst* and *Gneisenau*, and the light cruisers *Nürnberg*, *Leipzig*, and *Dresden*—made their way south and east, keeping away from superior forces and always looking for their next coal supply. Their destruction at the Battle of the Falklands (8 December 1914) by the British battle cruisers HMS *Inflexible* and *Invincible* was the ideal illustration of why this class of warship had been developed by the Admiralty under Sir John Arbuthnot Fisher, to hunt down and destroy enemy commerce raiders.

The few other German commerce raiders fared little better. The light cruiser SMS *Königsberg* was a nuisance off the coast of German East Africa, but it was unable to attack British shipping. Within a year the *Königsberg* was bottled up and sunk in the Rufiji River delta. Its only further contribution to the war was its guns, put to better use in the defense of the colony by the army. The light cruiser SMS *Karlsruhe* accidentally blew up off the coast of Brazil in November 1914, after moderate success; its main contribution to the war effort was that news of its loss was kept secret until the following spring. There was even a proposal put forward by Vice-Admiral Franz von Hipper in November 1914 to sail his battle cruisers from Wilhelmshaven to the West Indies or South Atlantic as commerce raiders; to solve the coaling problem, Hipper wanted to enlarge the coal bunkers of his ships, and he also believed he could coal, by force of arms, at least once at a British overseas harbor. The idea was rejected.

Ultimately, German surface raiders were little more than an inconvenience, especially in comparison to the later unrestricted U-boat campaigns. Between the outbreak of the war and January 1915, German commerce raiders sank seventy-five cargo ships of 273,000 tons; from February 1915 until the Armistice (1918) they sank a further 227,000 tons, making a grand total of 442,000 tons. In comparison to the 6.5 million tons sunk by U-boats, the surface raiders made barely a dent in the total number of British merchant vessels sunk. Their exploits made for great stories but had little impact, physically or psychologically, on the progress and outcome of the war.

–DAVID H. OLIVIER, SASKATOON, SASKATCHEWAN, CANADA

References

Roy Alexander, *The Cruise of the Raider "Wolf"* (New York: Yale University Press, 1939).

John F. Beeler, *British Naval Policy in the Gladstone-Disraeli Era, 1866-1880* (Stanford, Cal.: Stanford University Press, 1997).

British Admiralty Staff Study, *Review of German Cruiser Warfare, 1914-1918* (Unpublished, London, 1940).

Bernard Brodie, *Sea Power in the Machine Age* (Princeton: Princeton University Press; London: Oxford University Press, 1941).

A. Harding Ganz, "Colonial Policy and the Imperial German Navy," *Militärgeschichtliche Mitteilungen,* 41 (1977): 35–52.

Paul G. Halpern, *A Naval History of World War I* (Annapolis: Naval Institute Press, 1994).

Holger H. Herwig, *"Luxury" Fleet: The Imperial German Navy, 1888-1918* (London & Boston: Allen & Unwin, 1980).

Nicholas A. Lambert, "Admiral Sir John Fisher and the Concept of Flotilla Defence, 1904–1909," *Journal of Military History,* 59 (October 1995): 639–660.

R. K. Lochner, *The Last Gentleman-of-War: The Raider Exploits of the Cruiser Emden,* translated by Thea and Harry Lindauer (Annapolis: U.S. Naval Institute Press, 1988).

Arthur J. Marder, *From the Dreadnought to Scapa Flow: The Royal Navy in the Fisher Era, 1904–1919,* volume two, *The War Years: To the Eve of Jutland, 1914–1916* (London & New York: Oxford University Press, 1966).

D. P. O'Connell, *The International Law of the Sea,* volume two, edited by I. A. Shearer (Oxford & New York: Clarendon Press, 1984).

Peter Overlack, "The Force of Circumstance: Graf Spee's Options for the East Asian Cruiser Squadron in 1914," *Journal of Military History,* 60 (October 1996): 657–682.

Paul Schmalenbach, *German Raiders: A History of Auxiliary Cruisers of the German Navy, 1895-1945,* translated by Keith Lewis (Cambridge: Patrick Stephens, 1979).

Hans-Ulrich Wehler, "Bismarck's Imperialism, 1862-1890," *Imperial Germany,* edited by James J. Sheehan (New York: New Viewpoints, 1976), pp. 180–220.

GERMAN ECONOMIC MOBILIZATION

Was the 1916–1917 Hindenburg-Ludendorff program for German economic mobilization a failure?

Viewpoint: Yes. The mobilization of national resources intended by the program took little account of German economic realities.

Viewpoint: No. The program eventually did succeed in integrating the army, industry, and labor behind the war effort to a significant degree.

German economic mobilization during World War I is usually described in negative terms. Before the war, the argument runs, neither the armed forces nor the government were willing to face squarely the demands of the relatively long war the military planners increasingly believed Germany would have to fight. In consequence the Reich entered the conflict with few reserves of raw materials, no plan to acquire them externally under the conditions of Allied blockade, and no preparations for converting the economy to a war footing. For a year and a half businesses sought to maximize profits, labor tried to improve working conditions, and bureaucracies worked at cross purposes. "Deputy Corps Commands," given extraordinary powers in the expectation they would not be exercising them for long, instead found themselves deciding questions of production and allocation far beyond the experience of the retired generals holding the posts.

Things became even worse, according to conventional wisdom, when the Hindenburg-Ludendorff team took over command of the army in 1916. Determined to institute a program of total national mobilization, the generals succeeded for a while in getting business, labor, and administration to work together. Within months, however, over-regulation cost the government much of its public legitimacy. Micromanagement could not prevent profiteering. Command authority failed to avert labor-management strife that culminated in paralyzing strikes.

For most of the century, conventional wisdom described the German failure in terms of inexperience and halfway measures. Managed, controlled economies were seen as desirable norms until the collapse of the Soviet Union (1991) introduced an alternate interpretative structure arguing that there are some things government does not know how to do and never will know how to do: control is as likely to gridlock a developed economy as to enhance its effectiveness. Certainly Germany, like other European countries, sought to dismantle its regulatory apparatus after World War I, and during World War II did not come close to replicating it until after its defeat at Stalingrad (1943).

Viewpoint:
Yes. The mobilization of national resources intended by the program took little account of German economic realities.

Prior to 1914 German soldiers and politicians alike were reluctant to address the question of long-term economic mobilization in a general war. The domestic order of the country was generally perceived as too fragile to survive serious hardship. Germans were used to living well by any standards, enjoying the highest level of calorie consumption in Europe, with ample room for "luxury calories" such as beer and red meat. Apart from the brutal political infighting characteristic of the semiparliamentary empire, the state in Germany—more accurately, the states of the federal system—were perceived as service institutions, expected ultimately to deliver more than they demanded. The massive armed forces of the Second Reich were expected not to wage warfare but to deter it—a major reason why military service was not merely acceptable but popular among young men of all social classes.

As a consequence, no relevant specific preparations existed for the situation that developed during the first year of World War I. The Reich called millions of men to arms—but found there were no arms, at least no modern ones. Nor were there boots, underclothes, or toothbrushes. The high levels of autonomy allowed the army, on the assumption that the war would soon be over, to duplicate effort and patterns of bureaucratization that defied even the German skill at paperwork. Walther Rathenau's War Raw Materials Department, the ad hoc umbrella agency created to facilitate converting private enterprises to war production, established systems that by October 1914 had increased the output of ammunition to 1,300 percent of August 1914 levels, and other war-related items were produced in similar proportion.

This level of production was not enough. From the outbreak of war Germany faced a financial crisis: it could not borrow money from any nation. At the same time both the central and state governments were extremely reluctant to tax their citizens. That situation left one alternative: to finance the war by winning it, and somehow making the Allies pay. Germany faced a raw materials crisis as well. The Allied blockade inspired remarkable feats of innovation and improvisation among a German scientific community second to none in the world. Ultimately, however, regulation was the only way of controlling the allocation and use of scarce material resources. Food was a third problem. The pattern of the army purchasing what it needed without concern for civilian requirements increased prices as supplies shrank. Military demand for nitrates reduced the supply of fertilizer as the demand for soldiers diminished the physical labor that might have produced the needed chemicals. Farmers, soldiers, and administrators pursued mutually antagonistic, mutually contradictory policies culminating with the great hog-killing of 1915. Ordered by the military authorities to save scarce fodder, the slaughter generated almost immediate shortages, causing meat rationing. Bread was already on the restricted list. Finally, Germany confronted a labor crisis. Mobilization emptied factories and farms alike, without regard for maintaining production in either area. Returning skilled men to the factories, a logical response, did nothing to improve morale among their comrades expected to remain at the front.

As stresses mounted, the Prussian War Ministry, responsible for the mobilization effort, did its best to balance concerns among interest groups, using negotiation and compromise to counter discontent and modify the social dangers of the kind of war their own army consistently calculated that Germany could not win. That approach changed in 1916, with the appointment of Paul von Hindenburg as Chief of Staff and his right-hand man Erich Ludendorff as quartermaster general. They and their technocratic staff officers, with support from both industrialists and intellectuals, reorganized the administration of the economy by creating the War Office, implemented an Auxiliary Service Law intended to stabilize labor resources and prevent profiteering, and authorized a Hindenburg Program for the increased production of munitions.

The end result was gridlock. The Auxiliary Service Law, which for a while resulted in an unprecedented cooperation among labor, business, and the increasingly militarized government apparatus, eventually foundered because of its failure to control profiteering and provide compensation for the sacrifices it demanded from both labor and capital. The Hindenburg Program exhausted already limited reserves of coal and metals, and produced transportation bottlenecks that finally overstrained the railway network of the country. The War Ministry passed increasing numbers of regulations, which impinged more and more on everyday life and correspondingly were unenforceable in a system that at bottom still depended on the willing consent of ordinary people to sustain the war. Germany was not a totalitarian society; its capacity to repress protest remained limited.

By 1917 Germans were eating less than one-third of the meat they had consumed in 1914

and only a fifth of the butter. Milk was so scarce that by 1918 only babies and children were authorized a ration. At the same time, farmers refused to deliver foodstuffs at government-established prices, instead trading what they raised for durable goods or eating it themselves. The cost of food staples doubled. Inflation flourished, reaching 250 percent by the end of 1918. Industrial workers' wages increased by as much as 150 percent—but real wages fell 25 percent across the board. The real income of junior officials fell to 70 percent of 1914 levels; senior officials suffered a 50 percent loss. The social consequences of these changes were exacerbated by a burgeoning black market in scarce or regulated goods that moved increasingly into the open as the war progressed. "Respectable" burghers were reluctant to patronize it; industrial workers often lacked the time. Smuggling nevertheless became a common weekend activity—more or less controlled by a growing police force, whose presence and behavior served less to

reinforce the authority of the state than to foster resentment against it.

Hunger reinforced war weariness. An initial wave of strikes in the major ports in March 1917 was checked by the delivery of extra food. Tensions and resentments smoothed over in the early years of the war resurfaced: city against country, farmers against townsmen, workers against bourgeoisie. By the end of 1917 German society was approaching a negative consensus: rejection of a regulatory apparatus that was unable to deal with either the physical realities of scarcity or the psychological consequences of deprivation.

On January 1918 Germany was rocked by another wave of strikes, whose leaders this time combined economic and political demands: more food and freedom of employment along with suffrage reform and, above all, peace. Proclamations of martial law were met with serious violence. The March Offensive and the Treaty of Brest-Litovsk only temporarily checked an ero-

German civilians receiving rations of potato peels in 1917

(Hulton Picture Library, London)

NECESSARY MEASURES

In his memoirs of service in Germany during the early years of World War I, U.S. ambassador to the Imperial German court James W. Gerard recalls the economic impact of the war:

On the fourth of August, 1914, a number of laws were passed, which had been evidently prepared long in advance, making various changes made necessary by war, such as alteration of the Coinage Law, the Bank Law, and the Law of Maximum Prices. Laws as to the high prices were made from time to time. For instance, the law of the twenty-eighth of October, 1914, provided in detail the maximum prices for rye in different parts of Germany. The maximum price at wholesale per German ton of native rye must not exceed 220 marks in Berlin, 236 marks in Cologne, 209 marks in Koenigsberg, 228 marks in Hamburg, 235 marks in Frankfort a/M.

The maximum price for the German ton of native wheat was set at forty marks per ton higher than the above rates for rye. This maximum price was made with reference to deliveries without sacks and for cash payments.

The law as to the maximum prices applied to all objects of daily necessity, not only to food and fodder but to oil, coal and wood. Of course, these maximum prices were changed from time to time, but I think I can safely state that at no time in the war, while I was in Berlin, were the simple foods more expensive than in New York.

The so-called "war bread," the staple food of the population, which was made soon after the commencement of the war, was composed partially of rye and potato flour. It was not at all unpalatable, especially when toasted; and when it was seen that the war would not be as short as the Germans had expected, the bread cards were issued. That is, every Monday morning each person was given a card which had annexed to it a number of little perforated sections about the size of a quarter of a postage stamp, each marked with twenty-five, fifty or one hundred. The total of these figures constituted the allowance of each person in grammes per week. The person desiring to buy bread either at a baker's or in a restaurant must turn in these little stamped sections for an amount equivalent to the weight of bread purchased. Each baker was given a certain amount of meal at the commencement of each week, and he had to account for this meal at the end of the week by turning in its equivalent in bread cards.

As food became scarce, the card system was applied to meat, potatoes, milk, sugar, butter and soap. Green vegetables and fruits were exempt from the card system, as were for a long time chickens, ducks, geese, turkeys and game. Because of these exemptions the rich usually managed to live well, although the price of a goose rose to ridiculous heights. There was, of course, much underground traffic in cards and sales of illicit or smuggled butter, etc. The police were very stern in their enforcement of the law and the manager of one of the largest hotels in Berlin was taken to prison because he had made the servants give him their allowance of butter, which he in turn sold to the rich guests of the hotel.

No one over six years of age at the time I left could get milk without a doctor's certificate. One result of this was that the children of the poor were surer of obtaining milk than before the war, as the women of the Frauendienst and social workers saw to it that each child had its share.

The third winter of the war, owing to a breakdown of means of transportation and want of laborers, coal became very scarce. All public places, such as theatres, picture galleries, museums, and cinematograph shows, were closed in Munich for want of coal. In Berlin the suffering was not as great but even the elephants from Hagenbeck's Show were pressed into service to draw the coal carts from the railway stations.

Light was economized. All the apartment houses (and all Berlin lives in apartment houses) were closed at nine o'clock. Stores were forbidden to illuminate their show windows and all theatres were closed at ten. Only every other street electric light was lit; of the three lights in each lamp, only one.

Source: *James W. Gerard,* My Four Years in Germany *(New York: Doran, 1917), pp. 406–408.*

GERMAN ECONOMIC MOBILIZATION

sion of support for what increasingly seemed a meaningless war.

By November 1918, as Allied troops approached the Rhine, the Imperial system had lost the legitimacy it needed to survive the approaching defeat in the field. A solid case can be made that the loss of legitimacy was a consequence of overcontrolling the economy. Attempting to micromanage a complex industrial economy created not a "war socialism" that was the beginning of a new era, but a distortion of the "peace capitalism" that had created the prosperity of 1914.

—DENNIS SHOWALTER,
COLORADO COLLEGE

Viewpoint:
No. The program eventually did succeed in integrating the army, industry, and labor behind the war effort to a significant degree.

Critics of the programs of the German Army for total economic and social mobilization in 1916–1917 argue that the Hindenburg-Ludendorff plans not only failed to meet stated objectives and proved ineffective in mobilizing the full potential of domestic resources, they also made an already difficult situation even worse. The critics are much too harsh. From the start of World War I the government confronted two enormous challenges. One was the fundamental problem of a manpower shortage that affected every area of national mobilization. There simply proved to be too few men available to meet the requirements of both the army and industry. No program, no matter how efficiently conducted, could overcome this basic dilemma. The other challenge involved maintaining a balance between compulsion and volunteerism. In August 1914 the so-called *Burgfrieden* (civil truce) brought together all German parties in an unprecedented display of unity and patriotism. German leaders remained convinced that cooperation rather than compulsion would best maintain this unity and the support required of industry and labor. In light of competing institutional interests, divided authority, and structural flaws in the German political system, a policy of cooperation was the only sensible course of action. Yet, genuine collaboration among business, labor, and the army proved elusive.

These dilemmas notwithstanding, Germany realized significant successes in mobilizing industry and labor for prosecution of the war. In short, business and labor were allowed to pursue their own "enlightened self-interest," with the army mediating conflicting priorities and mobilizing both sides to support the troops in the field and help maintain a unified home front. With its self-image as the school of the nation, the army intended to use "field grey socialism" to lead a united Germany to victory. If the army proved not quite up to this ambitious task, it nonetheless achieved remarkable results in its mobilization efforts.

Prior to 1916 the army, represented by the Prussian War Ministry, and heavy industry engaged in a two-year struggle over manpower because of the short-war illusion. The indiscriminate call-up of skilled workers in 1914 caused serious shortages in the most vital industries once it became clear the war would not be over by the first Christmas. Although the War Ministry assumed responsibility for manpower, the production and distribution of munitions and food supplies, as well as labor relations, it provided no cohesive plan and found its authority on the home front challenged by the Deputy Commanding Generals of military districts and political leaders in the individual states. Under these circumstances, its efforts to mediate between labor and industry served to alienate the latter without winning the allegiance of the former. By 1916 inefficient management and mounting casualties from the Verdun and Somme battles created overwhelming pressure to reorganize management of the war under a military dictatorship. Like other belligerents, Germany traveled the path toward total war.

The Hindenburg-Ludendorff plan for total mobilization consisted of two elements. First was the Hindenburg Program, announced by the government of Chancellor Theobald von Bethmann Hollweg in August 1916 when the two military leaders, Paul von Hindenburg and Erich Ludendorff, assumed the reigns of power. Favoring heavy industry, the Hindenburg Program set Spring 1917 targets of a 50 percent increase in munitions and a 75 percent increase in weapons and called for a massive industrial plant construction program. To coordinate this huge effort, the army created a War Office and placed in charge General Wilhelm Groener, a respected General Staff officer with wide economic experience and a strong technical background.

The Auxiliary Service Law was the second aspect of the total war effort of Germany in 1916. Passed by the *Reichstag* that December, the legislation represented the triumph of labor and sought to alleviate the manpower shortage by mobilizing all Germans between the ages of seventeen and sixty for military or civilian service. To enlarge the labor market, it would reduce military exemptions, call up the temporarily unfit, close the universities, eliminate nonessential industries, reallocate labor to vital industries, mobilize women for the workforce, and control food distribution. The Auxiliary Service Law also formally recognized an array of labor-union prerogatives and the right of labor to equality in arbitration with employers.

Both parts of the Hindenburg-Ludendorff program failed to meet established objectives. Although arms-production goals were achieved, munitions output actually fell, the construction program was canceled, and the domestic labor shortfall continued unresolved. The high command actually released 125,000 men at the front for industrial work, but to no avail. Moreover, the ambitious output quotas for war production led to crises in the coal and railroad sectors, while bad weather and the resulting poor harvest produced widespread food shortages and the so-called Turnip Winter (1916–1917). At the same time, industry and labor seemed determined to further their own interests.

Industry refused to rely on extensive employment of women or juveniles, or to fill available skilled-worker jobs with unskilled labor. Universities remained open and an experiment to import Belgian and Polish labor ended in failure. Labor, for its part, seized the opportunity to press its demands for better working conditions, equitable grievance procedures, mixed arbitration boards to settle wage disputes, and the right of workers to switch jobs for higher wages. The War Office was charged to alleviate these difficulties, but Groener saw his authority increasingly undermined by the War Ministry as well as by Hindenburg and Ludendorff. He also proved unable to reconcile the special and competing interests of industry and labor. Industrial leaders complained of excessive privileges of labor and called for restrictions on the movement of workers, while labor officials demanded limitations on industrial war profits. Groener found himself caught in the middle, with no common manpower plan, and unable and unwilling to coerce the parties involved. His was not the central military agency that possessed the dictatorial powers required to incorporate the existing, competing bureaucracies. By the summer of 1917 he clearly had failed to achieve the cooperation of industry and labor in realizing the target objectives. That August, Ludendorff dismissed Groener and established a full-blown dictatorship to achieve his dream of the total militarization of German life.

During the final two years of the war, however, Ludendorff found himself as dependent as his predecessors on the good offices of labor, industry, and the civilian and military bureaucracies. Moreover, because he had little understanding of social and economic issues, he had to rely on his advisers to formulate and carry out policy. The erstwhile dictator might rule with an iron fist in foreign affairs but not on the home front. He, too, attempted to strike a balance among the competing groups through conciliation, especially in light of the growing food, fuel, housing, and clothing shortages during the last year of the war. "Dictatorial" Germany, unlike "democratic England," proved far less successful in creating a centralized, integrated administration to prosecute the war. Given the German domestic milieu, however, the political and military authorities realized that compulsion would fail to raise significant additional manpower while causing more unrest and threatening *Burgfrieden* unity. Their policy of cooperation and conciliation best reflected German realities.

Critics who have accused labor and industry, as well as the army, of economic and political opportunism and a general lack of community spirit might be correct. Yet, in pursuing their own selfish interests, they also supported the war by keeping the army in the field and the public united behind the war effort. The 1914 *Burgfrieden* was no illusion. Despite the labor strikes of April 1917, the German population continued to support the war until the late summer of 1918, when victory was no longer possible. If German manpower inferiority required the most rational use of the labor market, moreover, the best of total war plans could not alter the fact that available manpower resources were insufficient to meet the needs of both the armed forces and war industry in a long war of attrition. By 1918 clearly Germany was running short of laborers to work and soldiers to fight, while the Allies reveled in the prospect of unlimited American reinforcements.

Both business and labor exited the war strengthened from their experiences. Industry grew and profited from wartime contracts and influence, while labor achieved significant wage and living-standard improvements for workers in war industries. The army, for its part, emerged with a legacy of national stewardship it would long remember. During the death throes of the Weimar Republic, army veterans of the Great War sought to apply the lessons of "field grey socialism" to a Germany beset by economic disaster and political upheaval. It was a noble, if futile, effort that mirrored their earlier role in Germany's hour of need. One must continue to marvel that during World War I, Germany, beleaguered and surrounded by enemies, remained unified at home and undefeated on the battlefield through four long years of attritional conflict. In this context, the army program of 1916–1917 was far more than a paper exercise that resulted in spectacular failure. It accounted for German realities and achieved the best results possible under incredible challenges.

–DAVID N. SPIRES, UNIVERSITY
OF COLORADO

References

Robert B. Armeson, *Total Warfare and Compulsory Labor: A Study of the Military-Industrial Complex in Germany during World War I* (The Hague: Nijhoff, 1964).

Robert B. Asprey, *The German High Command at War: Hindenburg and Ludendorff Conduct World War I* (New York: Morrow, 1991).

Roger Chickering, *Imperial Germany and the Great War, 1914–1918* (Cambridge & New York: Cambridge University Press, 1998).

Gerald D. Feldman, *Army, Industry, and Labor in Imperial Germany, 1914–1918* (Princeton: Princeton University Press, 1966).

Holger H. Herwig, *The First World War: Germany and Austria-Hungary, 1914–1918* (London & New York: Arnold, 1997).

Andreas Hillgruber, *Germany and the Two World Wars,* translated by William C. Kirby (Cambridge, Mass.: Harvard University Press, 1981).

Martin Kitchen, *The Silent Dictatorship: The Politics of the German High Command Under Hindenburg and Ludendorff, 1916–1918* (New York: Holmes & Meier, 1976; London: Croom Helm, 1976).

Jürgen Kocka, *Facing Total War: German Society, 1914–1918,* translated by Barbara Weinberger (Cambridge, Mass.: Harvard University Press, 1984).

GERMAN ECONOMIC MOBILIZATION

INTERNAL FRENCH POLITICS

Did internal French politics prior to World War I significantly weaken relations between the civil government and the military?

Viewpoint: Yes. The mutual suspicion and hostility of the years before 1914 endured throughout the conflict and negatively shaped French conduct in the war.

Viewpoint: No. Prewar political animosity dissipated with the need to confront a common challenge and enemy.

The relationship between the government and the army of the Third French Republic was characterized by high levels of discord after the 1870s. The army that emerged from the Franco-Prussian War (1870–1871) depended on conscripts but sought to professionalize them as far as possible by relatively long terms of active service. The Republic sought its military inspiration in the *levees en masse* of the French Revolution and the second half of the recent war. The Republic was increasingly secular; the army grew increasingly Catholic. The Republic sought to control an army that correspondingly insisted on autonomy.

The Dreyfus Affair, in which the army demanded that its honor be served at the price of an innocent staff officer's wrongful conviction for espionage, split France down the middle. In 1901 the government set out to republicanize the army and strengthen political control of the military by selectively promoting "politically correct" officers to senior ranks. The term of service was cut to two years, an overt effort to reduce the exposure of young Frenchmen to Right-wing influences. Many soldiers responded by rejecting the Republic as unrepresentative of the "real France." Institutionally, the army increasingly emphasized mass attacks as the only form of war their half-trained men could be expected to execute.

A new War Ministry pulled back from the brink in the years before World War I by modifying the detested promotion policies, increasing the high command's authority, and restoring three-year service. The rifts, however, remained. The army participated only grudgingly in this final wave of reform, objecting in principle to what the soldiers regarded as micromanagement and unwarranted interference by unqualified amateurs. The ill feeling did not dissipate when on the outbreak of war in 1914 the civilian authorities turned virtually the entire conduct of operations over to the generals in order that they could win the quick victory they had promised for years. When Plan XVII, the aggressive French mobilization plan, faded into the gridlock of the trenches, tensions resurfaced—with increasingly spectacular consequences.

Viewpoint:
Yes. The mutual suspicion and hostility of the years before 1914 endured throughout the conflict and negatively shaped French conduct in the war.

Perhaps no nation in Europe had such tumultuous relations between its army and the society it served as did France. The most-direct roots of these conflicts lie in the memories of the Franco-Prussian War (1870–1871) and the Paris Commune (1871). Both the French Right, which largely controlled the officer corps, and the French Left could (at least after the passage of time) point with pride at their efforts to resist the Prussian invaders. Legacies of the Commune, however, were considerably more ambiguous. To most members of the French officer corps, the Commune had been an illegitimate experiment in Left-wing politics led by a dangerous mob. The destruction of the Commune in the "bloody week" of 21–28 May 1871, along with twenty thousand dead Communards and innocent bystanders, had been grim, but was considered necessary to stop a new reign of terror. To the Left, however, the violence with which the army put down the Commune conflicted sharply with the poor performance it displayed in the defense of France the previous fall and winter. Even as the regular army was engaged in crushing the Commune, the occupying Prussian army that it had failed to defeat stood at the gates of the city watching as the French engaged in internecine civil war.

Out of the bloody and divisive events of the Paris Commune was born the star-crossed Third Republic, which had tumultuous relations with the French army from the very beginning. As Douglas Porch noted in *The March to the Marne: The French Army, 1871–1914* (1981), the army was "an unwelcome guest at a republican feast." Many French republicans accused the army of being dominated by royalists and Jesuits. At its least subversive, the army existed in the minds of many Frenchmen as a potential antidemocratic tool in the hands of a future dictator. At most, many republicans feared that the army might plot a coup d'état in order to install a more orderly, but antidemocratic, political system. Indeed, such a coup seemed probable in 1889 when the French government had to issue an arrest warrant on grounds of treason for the popular retired general Georges Boulanger.

The army, for its part, constantly feared political purges and a French political system that did not understand or promote the interests of national security. Fears of a government controlled by a Commune-like mob haunted the minds of many senior army officers. Continual conflict over military training and education systems further soured army-government relations.

The general instability of the Third Republic contributed to these problems. France had forty-two war ministers between 1871 and 1914. In 1898 alone France had five war ministers. In the same year Emile Zola's famous "J'accuse" appeared in the newspaper *L'Aurore,* accusing the French army of a high-level cover-up in the Dreyfus Affair. Space forbids a complete recap of the events of the infamous scandal. For present purposes, the Dreyfus Affair should be seen as heightening all of the tensions, fears, and stereotypes of the Third Republic. The Left accused the army of being jingoistic, anti-Semitic, and antirepublican. The French Right, for its part, rallied to the side of the army, accusing the Dreyfussards of pursuing their case to the point of being antipatriotic or even treasonous. The Dreyfus Affair, which confirmed each side's worst images of the other, continued to poison relations between the state and the army long after the central figure of the scandal, Captain Alfred Dreyfus, was finally cleared of all charges in 1906.

Also in 1906 one of the chief nemeses of the army (and one of Dreyfus's most vocal defenders), journalist and politician Georges Clemenceau, became prime minister. He quickly cut military salaries and pensions and placed Zola in the Pantheon. He also ordered that political files be created on all generals in the French army. The *fiches* scandal that resulted led to the resignation of a war minister who had the rare combination of being both a general and a republican. After the *fiches* incident, Clemenceau, ever suspicious of what he saw as repressive tendencies in the royalist officer corps, oversaw a plan to promote noncommissioned officers over graduates of the French military academy at St. Cyr. He also tried to force all St. Cyr graduates to perform one year of service as privates. The French officer corps recoiled to such an extent at this perceived insult to their honor that Clemenceau eventually withdrew his plan.

Political divisions inside France played a considerable role in the ascendancy of General Joseph Joffre to the position of Army chief of staff. Several of Joffre's main competitors for the job proved unsuitable because of their antirepublican politics. One of them even insisted upon the right of the chief of staff to have a seat in the cabinet. Many of his peers believed that Joffre, though a man of tremendous char-

ZOLA CRITIQUES THE MILITARY

On 13 January 1898 the novelist Emile Zola wrote a letter, which was published in L'Aurore. It was critical of the French army and its handling of the infamous Alfred Dreyfus case, in which a Jewish officer was court-martialed for treason.

I am not even talking about the judges, who could have been chosen differently. Since these soldiers have a lofty idea of discipline in their blood, isn't that enough to disqualify them from arriving at an equitable judgement? Discipline means obedience. Once the Minister of War, the supreme commander, has publicly established the authority of the original verdict, and has done so to the acclamation of the nation's representatives, how can you expect a court martial to override his judgement officially? In hierarchical terms, that is impossible. General Billot, in his statement, planted certain ideas in the judges' minds, and they proceeded to judge the case in the same way as they would proceed to go into battle, that is, without stopping to think. The preconceived idea that they brought with them to the judges' bench was of course as follows: "Dreyfus was sentenced for treason by a court martial, therefore he is guilty; and we, as a court martial, cannot find him innocent. Now, we know that if we recognize Esterhazy's guilt we will be proclaiming Dreyfus's innocence." And nothing could make them budge from that line. . . .

As I have already shown, the Dreyfus Affair was the affair of the War Office: an officer from the General Staff denounced by his fellow officers on the General Staff, sentenced under pressure from the Chiefs of the General Staff. And I repeat, he cannot emerge from his trial innocent without all of the General Staff being guilty. Which is why they War Office employed every means imaginable—campaigns in the press, statements and innuendos, every type of influence—to cover Esterhazy, in order to convict Dreyfus a second time. The republican government should take a broom to that nest of Jesuits (General Billot calls them that himself) and make a clean sweep! Where, oh where is a strong and wisely patriotic ministry that will be bold enough to overhaul the whole system and make a fresh start? I know many people who tremble with alarm at the thought of a possible war, knowing what hands our national defence is in! and what a den of sneaking intrigue, rumour-mongering and back-biting that sacred chapel has become—yet that is where the fate of our country is decided! People take fright at the appalling light that has just been shed on it all by the Dreyfus Affair, that tale of human sacrifice! Yes, an unfortunate, a "dirty Jew" has been sacrificed. Yes, what an accumulation of madness, stupidity, unbridled imagination, low police tactics, inquisitorial and tyrannical methods this handful of officers have got away with! They have crushed the nation under their boots, stuffing its calls for truth and justice down its throat on the fallacious and sacrilegious pretext that they are acting for the good of the country!

Source: Emile Zola, The Dreyfus Affair: "J'accuse" and Other Writings, edited by Alain Pagès, translated by Eleanor Levieux (New Haven & London: Yale University Press, 1996), pp. 43–44.

acter and courage, did not possess the intellectual background and command experience necessary to become an effective chief of staff. He was named to the post primarily because he had no outspoken political beliefs and was thus an inoffensive compromise choice.

The overly aggressive French war plan, Plan XVII, was largely Joffre's creation. It inadvertently placed French troops into a trap that the German Schlieffen Plan had set for them. The price was nearly the loss of Paris. Joffre's army lacked any doctrine or operational standards that could have met the challenges of 1914. Instead, Joffre continually fell back on moral force and the supposed superior élan of the French soldier as the bases for grand strategy. It is, of course, impossible to know if another general would have handled the crisis of 1914 any better. The main point here is that Joffre's appointment did not depend primarily on military qualifications. Rather, it depended on his lack of political disqualifications. Prewar French civilian leaders were thus sufficiently afraid of the Army playing an antirepublican role in domestic politics that they were willing to select a commander on the basis of his lack of strong political convictions.

To Joffre's credit, he did not take politics into account during his large-scale removal of ineffective generals in the early months of the war. Poor civil-military relations, however, continued to hamper French war efforts throughout the conflict. It is important to keep in mind that the French army of 1914–1918 was largely made up of peasants and proletarians in the enlisted ranks and professionals and bourgeoisie in the officer corps. At the most-senior ranks, French officers were either long-term professionals or descendants of royalists who had populated the officer corps of the Second Empire, or both. Preexisting social tensions thus constantly underscored relations between enlisted men and their officers. Moreover, military training and the processes of converting civilians into soldiers, which might have relieved these tensions in the quest for national unity, more often exacerbated them instead.

Furthermore, the September 1914 removal of the French government to Bordeaux as German armies approached Paris left the army as the sole agent capable of exercising control. The inglorious return of the government (at Joffre's invitation) in December left it in a weak political position. As Parliament reconvened in Paris, it accepted the principle of "Sacred Union" of the political parties, muting partisan criticism in the interest of national unity. As a result, parliamentarians (two hundred of whom were in the army) generally refrained from public criticism of Joffre and his staff.

Joffre took advantage of the power vacuum to create what Jere Clemens King, in *Generals & Politicians: Conflict between France's High Command, Parliament, and Government, 1914–1918* (1951), has accurately called a "military dictatorship." Even parliamentarians and cabinet members were forbidden from visiting military zones without Joffre's approval. In 1915 Joffre threatened to arrest Minister of War General Jean Pédoya if he came into the Zone of the Armies in eastern and northern France. His obstinacy and recurrent refusal to permit parliamentarians to visit the front caused tremendous acrimony.

The worst indignity, however, was still to come. In July 1915 Joffre replaced General Maurice Sarrail as commander of the Third Army. Sarrail was known as the "republican general" and the darling of most republican and socialist parliamentarians. They saw his removal as an overtly political act and a reminder of the nefarious use to which the Right wing and the army were using the silence of the Sacred Union. After arranging for Sarrail to save face by commanding the new army based near Salonika, Greece, French politicians resolved to involve themselves more in politics. The Sarrail Affair was the first step along the road to Joffre's removal as chief of staff.

Joffre's replacement, General Robert Nivelle, was aware of the political landmines that he had to negotiate. In a quest for symbolism that would please the Right and the Left, he divided his headquarters into two buildings, one a former abbey, the other a school founded by anticlericals. With Joffre gone, Parliament reasserted its powers, visiting Nivelle's headquarters and insisting on ill-conceived changes to Nivelle's already flawed plan. The enormous failures of the Chemin des Dames offensive (1917) laid bare the lingering poisons and mutual suspicions in the French military system. The mutinies that soon followed were in large part a protest against the prewar French military system, in which aristocratic officers disdained their men as a democratic, and dangerous, rabble. Officers therefore wasted little time worrying about the morale or physical conditions of their troops. Discipline was harsh because of an abiding fear of the power of an aroused mob.

The mutinies were, if nothing else, a demand by the men for more say in how their own lives were to be run. As citizens of a republic, they insisted upon the rights that they believed they were owed as their birth-

right from the French Revolution (1789–1799). French army leaders, however, were largely unsympathetic to republicanism and saw the Revolution as a less stirringly positive model. They saw the men not as republican citizens but as military resources to be used as the general staff saw fit. It is therefore hardly surprising that one common demand of the mutineers was for more enlisted men to be made officers. In effect, they were demanding a republicanization of the military. Here again, memories and myths of the Commune of 1871 shaped French civil-military relations.

The return of the old nemesis of the army, Clemenceau, to the position of prime minister in 1917 promised to make the situation even worse. At first, many army officers, accustomed to manipulating French politicians, hoped to outwait the man known as The Tiger. France had already had five prime ministers, eight war ministers, and eleven foreign ministers since 1914. Waiting out another round of politicians seemed like a reasonable and profitable policy. Clemenceau, however, had no intention of going away. Instead, he strengthened his hold on the French war-making apparatus by integrating the jobs of war minister and prime minister and holding both offices for the duration of the war.

Moreover, Clemenceau knew much about war and was as determined as any Frenchman to see this conflict to a victorious conclusion, with or without the assistance of professional military minds. Clemenceau had lived in the United States during its Civil War (1861–1865) and was mayor of the twentieth arrondissement of Paris, which included the heavily fought-over Montmartre area, during the Franco-Prussian War and the Commune. He also once served as president of the Senate Army Committee and was one of Dreyfus's most ardent supporters. Clemenceau was, therefore, a man fully suited by experience and temperament to transform the nature of civil-military relations in France. One of Clemenceau's most often-quoted statements, "War is too important a business to be left to the generals," reveals his open distrust of French army leadership.

Although the senior army leadership disliked and distrusted him, Clemenceau could not be ignored. He was immensely popular with the troops and the French populace in general, in part because of his commitment to win the war at all costs and in part because of his proven willingness to challenge the entrenched army leadership structure. Whatever his faults, he had that rare combination France so desperately needed in 1917 and

French propaganda poster with the quotes of government ministers declaring the treason of a Jewish army officer, 1898

(Archive Nationales, Paris)

1918: the heart of a soldier and the head of a republican.

Clemenceau's answer to the abiding tensions between the army and French society was near-total centralization under him. When General Philippe Pétain attempted to influence policy through a time-honored tactic of threatening to resign, Clemenceau dismissed him, pointing out that "There can be no question [of resignation]. I alone am responsible here." In a heated argument with General Ferdinand Foch the following year, Clemenceau shouted, "Shut up! It is I who represents France here!" Clemenceau's tight-fisted control of the French army, combined with changing battlefield fortunes by the summer of 1918, smoothed issues long enough to ensure victory. But the civil-military crisis was not yet over. Clemenceau and Foch, his senior military adviser at the Paris Peace Conference, publicly disagreed over how to deal with Germany. Clemenceau, in his fashion, won the day, but tensions and problems remained the norm after World War I, contributing to the great disaster that befell France in 1940.

—MICHAEL S. NEIBERG,
U.S. AIR FORCE ACADEMY

Viewpoint:
No. Prewar political animosity dissipated with the need to confront a common challenge and enemy.

Until recently, there was little historical dispute about the attitude of the French people in July 1914. Even historians with little sympathy for workers and peasants, or for the parties of the Left, accepted the image of a nation united, at the outbreak of World War I, in manifestations of "sacrificial joy." Accounts of French mobilization emphasized the unexpectedly tiny number of deserters and the decision by the government not to authorize the preemptive arrest of potential subversives listed in the notorious file known as *Carnet B*. The best recent studies of French behavior in 1914 have demolished the fiction that Frenchmen marched to war with zeal and optimism. Instead, they remind us that, as Paul-Marie de la Gorce points out in *The French Army: A Military Political History* (1963), "songs and warlike slogans helped to make the moment of leave-taking bearable" and that "in the villages . . . there was no crowd, no band, no popular enthusiasm to hide the simple truth that the men were going." Correcting the myth that French citizens eagerly raced "*à Berlin!*" should not be an excuse, however, to create an equally fictional vision of a country in which animosity between soldiers and civilians undermined the national effort. Frenchmen marched dourly off to war, but they directed their bitterness at the German foe, not the army in which they would serve.

It would be otiose to deny the tensions between substantial parts of the French Third Republic and its army before 1914 or that French political leaders took antimilitarist sentiments into account in their handling of the July Crisis. Whatever their feelings about the army or about obligatory military service, however, the French people loved their country and resented, to say the least, German aggression. The carefully advertised restraint of French policy during the crisis contrasted starkly with German bellicosity, cementing people and army into a united front.

It is, moreover, a mistake to exaggerate the antimilitarism of the French Left during the early twentieth century. When the Third Republic emerged in the aftermath of the military debacle of 1870–1871, its founders embraced general (though not quite universal) military conscription. The Right emphasized the military advantages of the new system, while the Left saw conscription as a national unifier and a teacher of republican virtue. Both sides acknowledged the citizen's obligation to serve the nation and rallied behind the notion of armed recovery of the lost provinces of Alsace and Lorraine. This period was the "golden age" of the French army.

The ardor of the Left for military service cooled during the 1890s for several reasons. The Dreyfus Affair raised suspicions about the loyalty of the army. The officer corps became increasingly a haven for men whose aristocratic birth and Catholic, monarchist sentiments set them apart from the egalitarian and fiercely anticlerical Republic. Contemporary novels emphasizing the nastier aspects of military life indicate that, while the theory of universal military service appealed to the intellectual Left, the reality of squalid living conditions, subordination to authority, and propinquity to peasants and proletarians appalled many who experienced it.

Antimilitarist writings usually combined the language of socialism, pacifism, and internationalism with that of patriotism and republicanism. People who saw war as unlikely and unnecessary dismissed the army as an anachronistic and antirepublican institution. That antimilitarism in France rarely implied lack of patriotism can be seen in the work of Socialist Party leader Jean Jaurès. Rejecting contemporary military institutions as instruments of class oppression, Jaurès was, however, no pacifist. He believed that France had to remain strong so that "foreign tyranny" did not replace capitalist oppression. Instead of disarming France, Jaurès proposed in *L'Armée nouvelle* (1910) to replace the standing army of professionals and conscripts backed by reservists with a wholly reserve militia organization reflecting the French tradition of the "nation-in-arms."

Though not sharing the Socialist rejection of the standing army, Left-wing governments took steps to recast the political views of the officer corps. Most notably, War Minister General Louis André moved control over military promotion from the army to the ministry in order to favor men certified as republicans. From informants within the army, the prefectures, and, notably, Masonic Lodges, the ministry collected information about the political and religious affiliations of individual officers and recorded it on file cards. Thus, the resulting controversy became known as the *affaire des fiches*. This effort to republicanize the officer corps naturally aroused resentment in that intensely conservative body. The most antirepublican officers dreamed of using a victorious war against Germany not only to restore the international stature of France and recover Alsace and Lorraine, but also to put an end to parliamentary government.

These were, however, extreme views. Partisan rhetoric aside, the Left could no more abolish the army than the Right could abolish the republic, and the estrangement between army and republic was a short duration. In 1905 Kaiser William II's inept and aggressive diplomatic démarche in Morocco reminded France of the unsated desire of Germany for international status. A second Moroccan incident in 1911 (and other similar provocations) hinted at this insatiability and reinforced the impression that Germany would continue to push France until met with force. In this atmosphere both the government and citizens of France once again treated their army as a bulwark against aggression rather than a political threat. In 1912, under War Minister Alexandre Millerand, the army resumed a public face that was hidden during the rule of his Left-wing predecessors. Military ceremonies once again enlivened life in garrison towns, and soldiers were encouraged proudly to wear their uniforms when off duty.

Fostering the reconciliation of army and population was the general understanding of the peaceful intentions of France. Calls for a war to regain Alsace-Lorraine had virtually disappeared. One important recent study of French policy by Jean Doise and Maurice Vaïsse, *Diplomatie et outil militaire, 1871–1991* (1992), bluntly asserts that by 1911, "France had not only renounced revenge but even begun to believe that there would never be another war." It was easier to support an army that was not tied to aggressive intentions. Moreover, the war plan in force from March 1909 to May 1914, Plan XVI, called for the French army to meet a German attack by deploying in a defensive orientation and awaiting events, a strategy inoffensive to the French Left.

Strong evidence for the improving relations between army and populace as war approached comes from studying the military service law of 1913, the most controversial piece of military legislation of the period. The measure extending the period of compulsory military service from two years to three was presented to the voters as a necessary response to military expansion by Germany in 1912. Passed in parliament with a substantial majority, it aroused great anger among the population. There were mutinies among soldiers subject to the additional year of service and cries of outrage from families and from those who saw the measure as unnecessary concession to the requirements of the Franco-Russian alliance. The Radical Party included the return to two-year service in its platform for the 1914 elections. These events worried President Raymond Poincaré and his Right-wing supporters, who feared that the parliamentary elections of May and June 1914 would become a referendum on the three-year law. In fact, although the successes of Left and Center-Left parties in those elections have been attributed to the voters' hostility to military service, careful study of the results suggests that candidates opposed to the three-year law did not do particularly well. The election results actually serve to demonstrate how far the French population had come in accepting the need for increased national military effort.

The same concern about popular antimilitarism that made President Poincaré fear the outcome of the parliamentary elections led him to direct French policy carefully during the July Crisis. If war came, it was essential that the French people believe themselves to have been the victims of German aggression. Poincaré played his cards well. Even today, few people are aware of the extent to which French support for Russian policy made war more likely in 1914. While the French president's astute policy was partially driven by fear of stimulating antiwar feelings, it suggests that he did not doubt that his people would support their army in a just, defensive war. In that assumption he was absolutely correct.

Frenchmen did not like military service in 1914. Nor did they venerate their army as they had in the 1870s. Four decades had stripped away the illusion that any single institution could apolitically represent the much-divided Third Republic. In the Dreyfus Affair, moreover, the army had served as the focus for the bitterest factional struggle of the Third Republic. What was left for the French people after the "affairs" of Boulanger, Dreyfus, and the *fiches* was not love for military service but an unromantic appreciation of the army as their only protection against the increasing threat from Germany. Since French citizens knew where they stood vis-à-vis Germany, they went to war in August 1914 firmly committed to the army of their republic.

–EUGENIA C. KIESLING,
U.S. MILITARY ACADEMY

References

Jean-Jacques Becker, *1914, comment les Français sont entrés dans la guerre: contribution à l'étude de l'opinion publique printemps-été 1914* (Paris: Presses de la Fondation nationale des sciences politiques, 1977).

Roger Chickering and Stig Förster, eds., *Great War, Total War: Combat and Mobilization on the Western Front, 1914–1918* (Washington, D.C.: German Historical Institute, 2000; Cambridge & New York: Cambridge University Press, 2000).

INTERNAL FRENCH POLITICS

Jean Doise and Maurice Vaïsse, *Diplomatie et outil militaire, 1871–1991* (Paris: Editions du Seuil, 1992).

Paul-Marie de la Gorce, *The French Army: A Military Political History,* translated by Kenneth Douglas (London: Weidenfeld & Nicolson, 1963; New York: Braziller, 1963).

John V. F. Keiger, *France and the Origins of the First World War* (London: Macmillan, 1983; New York: St. Martin's Press, 1983).

Jere Clemens King, *Foch Versus Clemenceau: France and German Dismemberment, 1918–1919* (Cambridge, Mass.: Harvard University Press, 1960).

King, *Generals & Politicians: Conflict between France's High Command, Parliament, and Government, 1914–1918* (Berkeley: University of California Press, 1951).

Douglas Porch, *The March to the Marne: The French Army, 1871–1914* (Cambridge & New York: Cambridge University Press, 1981).

David B. Ralston, *The Army of the Republic: The Place of the Military in the Political Evolution of France, 1871–1914* (Cambridge: M.I.T. Press, 1967).

William L. Shirer, *The Collapse of the Third Republic: An Inquiry into the Fall of France in 1940* (New York: Simon & Schuster, 1969).

Eugen Weber, *France, Fin de Siècle* (Cambridge, Mass.: Belknap Press of Harvard University Press, 1986).

H. L. Wesseling, *Warrior and Soldier: French Attitudes Toward the Army and War on the Eve of the First World War,* translated by Arnold J. Pomerans (Westport, Conn.: Greenwood Press, 2000).

INTERNAL FRENCH POLITICS

IRISH INDEPENDENCE

How did the Great War affect the Irish independence movement?

Viewpoint: The Great War renewed the historical divisions of British intransigence and Irish nationalist factionalism, resulting in the drift of the independence movement into militancy.

Viewpoint: The Great War afforded the Irish independence movement with an opportunity to strike against Britain while its attention was concentrated on the Continent.

Viewpoint: By declaring the defense of the rights of small nations among its war aims, Britain lost its moral authority in Ireland and inadvertently strengthened the independence movement there.

The securing of Irish independence—or partial independence—between 1916 and 1922 reflected both long-term and short-term factors. The British government had been moving steadily toward some form of "Home Rule" since the days of Prime Minister William Gladstone (1868–1874, 1880–1886, 1892–1894). The impossibility of governing a recalcitrant Ireland directly from Westminster was highlighted as Irish parliamentarians grew increasingly adept at obstructing debate and legislation at a time when both foreign and domestic affairs put increasing demands on successive governments to discuss matters other than the Irish Question. The South African War (1899–1902) had also provided a wake-up call as radical Irish nationalists volunteered for service on the Boer side, and ordinary Irish nationalists supported them. With Anglo-German rivalry developing, Britain also did not need to risk a repetition of the uprisings of the 1790s.

The prospects for a peaceful solution seemed to improve as "mainstream" Irish nationalist leaders grew more "responsible." Men such as John Redmond insisted the days of Fenians (Irish nationalists of the later nineteenth century) were long past—if Britain should prove reasonable. The major problem seemed to lie in the northern provinces, where an increasingly militant Protestant/Loyalist movement in the province of Ulster insisted it would fight against the Crown to remain part of Great Britain rather than trust itself to the good will of Papist Home Rulers. The Ulstermen made their point by a massive arms-smuggling campaign, by drilling in public, and by soliciting support from a British officer corps generally sympathetic to the cause of Ulster.

The possibilities of civil war over Home Rule in 1914 should not be exaggerated. The subject was still under political control when the outbreak of World War I put it on the back burner. The Ulstermen went off to die on the Somme. A surprising number of nationalists joined them. And a small group of radicals seized their chance by staging an uprising in Dublin during Easter Week, 1916. The expected general rebellion did not materialize, but the execution of the leaders of the uprising provided a fresh set of martyrs for the cause. The breakdown in local control caused by the demands of war enabled the radicals to establish a virtual shadow government even before the Armistice. In addition, the return of the "hard boys" from the trenches led to an environment of terror and repression that led the postwar government of a war-weary Britain to decide the game was no longer worth playing. Home Rule and partition, each in slightly different form than originally intended, became realities in 1921—and have remained points of contention ever since.

Viewpoint:
The Great War renewed the historical divisions of British intransigence and Irish nationalist factionalism, resulting in the drift of the independence movement into militancy.

It is possible for warfare to carry forward an agenda of domestic policy. During World War I, for example, the patriotic support women gave to the British war effort made an important contribution to their winning the right to vote. In 1914 it was also possible to believe that patriotic support for the Liberal Party government of Herbert Asquith would allow for passage and implementation of a Home Rule Bill granting self-government to the whole of Ireland. Indeed, at the outbreak of war the leader of the nationalist Irish parliamentary party, John Redmond, supported the effort of Britain to mobilize its troops to defend Belgium from German invasion. Redmond offered to join his National Volunteers to the Protestant Ulster Volunteers to form a home-defense force, allowing British troops stationed in Ireland to go into Europe. By this move the Irish nationalist leader hoped to win public and political support for the Home Rule Bill. The Protestant leadership of northern Ireland also accepted the political inevitability of Home Rule but vowed to keep Ulster out of its provisions. The prospect of a peaceful settlement seemed to be close at hand. Subsequent events, however, would prove this promise to be illusory. By the end of the war the nationalist struggle for self-government had been transformed into a militant campaign to gain full independence from British rule, while the Protestant North successfully remained within the union with Great Britain. The war thus frustrated political and diplomatic efforts to resolve the destiny of Ireland by constitutional means and fostered a period of conflict extending well beyond its conclusion.

Two events were central to this transformation. The first was the formation in 1916 of a coalition government, joining Asquith's Liberal Party with the Conservative and Unionist Party (Unionist standing for the commitment of that party to keeping Ireland within the British fold). Although seen as a necessary step to provide unified support for the war effort, this move brought a Conservative Party leadership that had continually opposed Home Rule and particularly had been willing to support the determination of Protestant Ulster to resist Home Rule by violent means. By the end of 1916 the Liberal Party had split over the replacement of Asquith with David Lloyd George, believed by the majority to be better qualified to lead the war effort. This split left Lloyd George and his remaining Liberal allies dependent for their survival in Parliament upon Conservative support. It was also important that Redmond's Irish Party did not join the coalition. Not only did Redmond have to keep a respectable political distance from any British government, now he had to deal with Conservatives who steadfastly opposed Home Rule. This circumstance created a deadlock over any plans to carry Home Rule forward and led to a period of political drift in which the government took little or no notice of developments in Ireland. When the second event occurred, the Easter Rising of 24 April 1916, the government was thus unprepared and unable to react to its consequences.

The Rising itself was the work of a faction within the militant Irish Republican Brotherhood. Lacking expected German support and accepting that the Irish people would not join the rebellion, the leader of the Rising, Patrick Pearse, went ahead in the hope that the rebels would become martyrs to the cause of Irish freedom. Other rebels hoped that a wartime insurrection would make Irish freedom an international issue. As it turned out, Pearse's expectation proved to be more accurate. Although the rebels' efforts, centered in and around Dublin, were quickly suppressed, the treatment of the leaders inflamed Irish nationalist opinion. Instead of treating the leaders as political insurrectionists and imprisoning them, the London government allowed the army commander in Ireland to try, condemn, and execute them under articles of martial law. The fact that one man, badly wounded in the fighting, was tied to a chair so the firing squad could carry out its orders only underlined the ferocity and unfairness of the British reaction. Local Irish newspapers featured the courage of the insurgents, and leaders of the Catholic clergy rebuked the British officers for their treatment of prisoners who had surrendered to them.

The Irish reaction to the aftermath of the Rising undermined the influence of Redmond's parliamentary party. Initially, Redmond accepted the renewal by the British government of an offer to grant immediate Home Rule, while temporarily leaving out six counties of the Protestant North. An upsurge of Conservative Party opposition, coupled with the unwillingness of the government to declare the Protestant exclusion only temporary, wrecked the plan. This failure left Redmond with nothing to show for his protest against British reaction to the Rising. Back home, nationalist opinion was outraged that the partition of the nation could even be considered. The breakdown of the constitutional process became only too apparent during a convention held in Dublin between July of 1917 and April of 1918. Although the convention was meant to be a meeting of all parties to negotiate a settlement over Home Rule, the radical nationalist Sinn Féin (Ourselves Alone) Party refused to attend, the northern Irish representatives resisted all initiatives at compromise, and southern Irish Protestants insisted that Britain retain control over external trade and national defense. These latter terms were unacceptable to the bulk of nationalist opinion. When in April 1918 the government in London introduced a bill to conscript Irishmen into the armed forces, the leadership of the Irish parliamentary party walked out, returned to Ireland, and joined Sinn Féin, trade unionists, and Catholic bishops to resist the bill. On their side the Irish Protestant leaders of the Conservative Party insisted that conscription be imposed throughout Ireland. The divisions over conscription signaled the end of negotiation. When parliamentary elections were held, after the war ended, southern Ireland returned a delegation dominated by Sinn Féin. The transformation of the nationalist movement into a militant struggle for independence was complete.

One possibility for a political settlement of Anglo-Irish relations remained. Throughout the war American political opinion had followed Irish developments closely. After the Easter Rising, Irish Americans offered both arms and money to the nationalist cause. Within the Congress, discussions of Irish affairs continued to spring up. Because the British government deeply desired American support for its war effort, its leaders were aware that President Woodrow Wilson might apply pressure to settle Irish Home Rule. In particular there was a chance President Wilson's stance in favor of self-determination for national groups might be applied to Ireland. Certainly the Irish nationalists hoped that Wilson would bring their cause before international opinion and possibly would support it at a peace conference.

Although Wilson continued informally to encourage the British leadership to settle on an Irish government, his efforts were hampered by the slipping of nationalist politics toward the radicalism of Sinn Féin. Not only had Wilson no sympathy for Pearse and the Irish Republican Brotherhood, he also equally detested the militancy of Sinn Féin. In addition, the complexity of working out a peace settlement at Versailles in 1919 submerged Irish concerns. Thus, Wilson alternately avoided any specific commitment to Irish independence while hoping that such a goal might be reached within the context of the League of Nations. To gain support for the League, Wilson had, in turn, to work with the British leader Lloyd George. This necessity meant that Wilson could not antagonize the British government, now even more under the control of the Conservatives. Over the course of 1919 the American president could do nothing to arrest the shooting war that had broken out between British forces and Sinn Féin's militant force, the Irish Republican Army (IRA). When the U.S. Senate rejected the Versailles Treaty and refused to join the League of Nations, the American role in an Irish settlement became even more problematic.

The story of the Irish nationalist movement during World War I is thus one of lost opportunities and the failure of a constitutional settlement. When in 1922 the British government negotiated a treaty granting southern Ireland the status of a Free State, it did so with representatives of Sinn Féin and the IRA. This outcome resulted not from the pressures of the European war but from the familiar and enduring elements of British intransigence and the factionalism that characterized the nationalist movement in Ireland. As the statesmen stood by, that nationalist movement transformed itself into an organization dedicated to another kind of warfare, a war of liberation.

—ROBERT MCJIMSEY,
COLORADO COLLEGE

Viewpoint:
The Great War afforded the Irish independence movement with a opportunity to strike against Britain while its attention was concentrated on the Continent.

To write off the importance of World War I to Irish independence is to ignore eight hundred years of Irish history. It was no mistake, twist of fate, or quirk of history that the Irish nationalist

IRISH DECLARATION OF INDEPENDENCE

On 21 January 1919 the Dáil Eireann (House of Representatives) proclaimed an independent Ireland:

Whereas the Irish people is by right a free people;

And whereas for seven hundred years the Irish people has never ceased to repudiate and had repeatedly protested in arms against foreign usurpation;

And whereas English rule in this country is, and always has been, based upon force and fraud and maintained by military occupation against the declared will of the people;

And whereas the Irish Republic was proclaimed in Dublin on Easter Monday, 1916, by the Irish Republican Army, acting on behalf of the Irish people;

And whereas the Irish people is resolved to secure and maintain its complete independence in order to promote the common weal, to reestablish justice, to provide for future defense, to insure peace at home, and good will with all nations and to constitute a national policy based upon the people's will, with equal right and equal opportunity for every citizen;

And whereas at the threshold of a new era in history the Irish electorate has in the general election of December, 1918, seized the first occasion to declare by an overwhelming majority its firm allegiance to the Irish Republic;

Now, therefore, we, the elected representatives of the ancient Irish people, in national parliament assembled, do, in the name of the Irish nation, ratify the establishment of the Irish Republic and pledge ourselves and our people to make this declaration effective by every means at our command.

To ordain that the elected representatives of the Irish people alone have the power to make laws binding on the people of Ireland, and that the Irish Parliament is the only parliament to which that people will give its allegiance.

We solemnly declare foreign government in Ireland to be an invasion of our national right, which we will never tolerate, and we demand the evacuation of our country by the English garrison;

We claim for our national independence the recognition and support of every free nation of the world, and we proclaim that independence to be a condition precedent to international peace hereafter;

In the name of the Irish people we humbly commit our destiny to Almighty God, who gave our fathers the courage and determination to persevere through centuries of a ruthless tyranny, and strong in the justice of the cause which they have handed down to us, we ask His divine blessing on this, the last stage of the struggle which we have pledged ourselves to carry through to freedom.

Source: Ireland's Declaration of Independence and Other Official Documents: Including Letters to the President of the Peace Conference and the General Memorandum Submitted in Support of Ireland's Claim for Recognition as a Sovereign Independent State *(New York, 1919), p. 3.*

rebels struck when they did. They discussed and debated the merits of striking while "perfidious Albion" was otherwise occupied. That is not to say that these actions were universally popular—some thought it was the coward's way—attacking Britain at her time of greatest peril and need. Home Rule, the right to have their own government, had already been agreed upon, but was suspended for the duration of the war. Where was the need to fight the British? The Home Rule Party under John Dillon and John Redmond already had assurances for the future. Yet, Home Rule was a poor second to the concept of an independent Irish Republic envisioned by the republicans. Home Rule was greater independence from Britain than they had, but nowhere near what the radical republicans wanted: total and complete separation. The radical nationalists saw nothing wrong with attacking Britain; in fact, they argued they could only be successful while the full attention of the empire was elsewhere. They were simply taking advantage of the world situation that Britain had helped to create.

The cause of Britain in World War I was not as strong a pull on Irishmen as it was on other groups in the United Kingdom. The Irish did not flock to the colors in the same proportions as did recruits in the other parts of the country. To be sure, there were about one hundred thousand Irishmen already serving in the British Army, but there were smaller enlistments from Ireland. There was also a definite political divide among the Irish. Unionists, or Irishmen who wanted to remain united with Britain, living mostly in the north, joined in much higher numbers than did their nationalist brethren in the south. The Ulster Volunteer Force (UVF), a pro-Union armed group, joined the British Army en masse; they were virtually annihilated at the Somme in 1916. There was also a difference between Home Rulers and radical nationalists, with the former being more likely to serve than the latter. Even then, there were a surprising number of radical nationalists serving during the war. In fact, the Germans tried to form an "Irish Brigade" from Irish prisoners of war held in Germany, although this scheme failed because of a lack of interest on the part of the detainees.

This disparity was all too apparent to the British public and government. Ordinary people and members of Parliament began to ask why Ireland was not pulling its "fair share." As a direct result of this criticism, and the mounting losses, the government moved to begin conscription in Ireland in 1917. This move brought the question of nationalism to a head, for why should Irish lads go to Flanders to fight for others' rights? The Conscription Crisis, as the situation came to be called, exploded when Irish public opinion, which had been largely supportive of the British to that point, quickly turned against them. The ensuing demonstrations and strife not only doomed the implementation of conscription but also brought a hitherto little-known organization called Sinn Féin (Ourselves Alone; founded in 1905), to popularity. This upheaval also brought about the demise of the Home Rule Party (which had been the dominant nationalist group to that point).

World War I changed the nature and character of the Irish struggle for independence, modifying the manner in which Ireland would separate from the United Kingdom. This transformation would, in turn, lead to the eventual creation of an Irish Republic. Rather than being a peaceful, legislative process, it became violent and usually brutal. Yet, it was precisely these changes that ensured that the Anglo-Irish Treaty (1921) was fundamentally different from the Home Rule Bill of 1914, thereby bringing the radical nationalists closer to their goal of total independence. This turmoil also allowed them to negotiate with Britain from a position of relative strength rather than the weakness that existed before the fighting.

The entire struggle took on the militancy born of 1916, from both the Easter Rising on the nationalist side and the Somme on the Unionist side, changing the face of Irish politics. Unionists hardened their opposition to the separation from the United Kingdom, in part, because of their extreme sacrifice for king and country during the war, especially at the Battle of the Somme. However, the Rebels experienced a similar sense of sacrifice as a result of the way they were treated after the Rising, especially the "martyrdom" of their leadership in front of British firing squads.

On 24 April 1916 a force of the radical nationalist Irish Volunteers and the Irish Citizen Army marched into Dublin, seized key buildings and strategic points, and proclaimed an independent Irish republic. Within two days the British government diverted troop ships bound for the Western Front and began a counterattack to retake the city. Using gun ships steaming up the Liffey River, the British bombarded the city while their troops advanced in the open under heavy fire from the rebel positions. By Saturday the 29th, it was over; the rebel commander, Patrick Pearse, surrendered his force. The British then tried the rebel leadership by secret courts, sentenced dozens to death, and executed fifteen of them without allowing them an opportunity to appeal their judgments. In all, about three thousand people were killed or wounded in the Rising, which also caused millions of pounds in damage, many people to be homeless, the city to be on the verge of starvation, and three thousand others arrested and/or exiled.

The Rising of 1916 can be seen as a World War I battle. There is an obvious connection between the Germans and the rebels. The Germans attempted to land arms to the rebels the previous week but were intercepted by the Royal Navy. But one cannot press the German connection too closely. The action of the British must be understood within the framework of an empire fighting against a serious threat to its survival. Their actions against the rebels were only legal under the Defense of the Realm Act (DORA, 1914), which required conspiracy with the enemy—which the rebels provided, albeit minutely. The harsh treatment of Dublin by the British more closely resembled the occupation of an enemy city than the restoration of order in a coequal member of the United Kingdom.

Similarly, the later British actions—early releases of prisoners in late 1916 and early 1917 (including those sentenced to life imprisonment), the reoffering of Home Rule, and the convening of a convention to discuss independence—can only be understood when one considers what the British were trying to do, which was to enforce conscription. These measures were

CONSCRIPTION AND DESIRE FOR INDEPENDENCE CAUSES OF REVOLT IN IRELAND

[The chief cause of present discontent in Ireland, beside the century old grievances of the irreconcilables who favor complete separation from England, is conscription. Although neither the draft measure now in force nor that being considered in England will apply in Ireland, opposition to conscription has nevertheless been used as an argument by the agitators who seized points in Dublin. The leaders of the opposition have been spreading the report that it is only a question of time when the conscription measures will be applied to the Irish as well as to the English. In the accompanying pictures No. 1 is Lord Wimborne, lord lieutenant of Ireland, whose capture by the rebels was reported; No. 2, John E. Redmond, leader in parliament of the Irish who adhere to the connection with England while favoring home rule; No. 3, Augustine Birrell, chief secretary for Ireland in the British government; No. 4, Sackville street, Dublin, one of the principal thoroughfares of the Irish capital and the scene of rioting.]

Newspaper account of the Easter Rebellion

(scrapbook, Joseph M. Bruccoli Great War Collection, Thomas Cooper Library, University of South Carolina)

IRISH INDEPENDENCE

designed to gain public support. This issue furthered the cause of Irish nationalism by exposing the supposed hypocrisy of the British. The strong, sometimes violent, reactions of the Irish public to conscription doomed any attempts to enforce the law. It also brought attention to what would become the leading nationalist party—Sinn Féin. The Conscription Crisis passed without Irish submission to the law and the war ended, but the nationalists were still working toward their goals and had been strengthened by the conflict.

The postwar independence movement reaped many benefits from, and was shaped by, World War I. There were a surprising number of nationalists in the British army. At one point in the debate on conscription, the British government worried about the effect of the return of three hundred thousand trained, battle-hardened Irishmen to Ireland. While they did not return in those numbers, the British did have cause for fear. Although there were many more-moderate Home Rulers who served, both the moderates and radicals returned with more-extreme views on independence and desensitized views toward violence. In the case of the former, they returned with a sense of entitlement that went unfulfilled with the failure of the British to implement Home Rule in Ireland following the war as promised. This betrayal tended to anger both the moderate and radical nationalists, as they had "fought for the rights of small nations to be free." What was Ireland if not a "small nation"?

However, the nationalists were not the only Irishmen to return home from the army. The Ulster Unionists who fought returned with a greater militancy than when they left. The UVF became even more militant as a result of the war, partly because of the aforementioned sacrifice, but also because of the training and battle-hardening they endured as well. They felt entitled to remain within their empire and to use force to achieve this goal. Their presence in the north helped steel the opposition to Home Rule.

Adding to this turmoil was the great influx of weapons left over from the war. Returning British soldiers in need of easy cash were particularly lucrative targets, as were the depots where their weapons were turned in (if the arms were not already stolen or sold). Further, the tens of thousands of German weapons were also available to the warring parties. With Germans strapped for cash, they were willing participants in the weapons trade. Another odd example is that during the war civilian explosives used in construction and mining were diluted to allow for greater military production. The potency was increased to prewar levels in 1920, thereby increasing the destructive potential, not to mention their greater abundance.

If it were not for the war, the Black and Tans, members of the Auxiliary Division of the Royal Irish Constabulary that was formed from former soldiers, would likely have been much different altogether. These former soldiers needed work, had been trained for mass killing, and were surprisingly ill disciplined. Their legend of brutality was fairly well deserved but had polarizing effects: sometimes cowing the rebels and sometimes making them fight harder—usually by responding in kind.

There were many who declared that the Anglo-Irish Treaty was no different than what was offered in earlier Home Rule settlements. This argument usually goes on to say that the war was a waste because the republicans gained only what they had already been offered. While there is some truth to this argument, there is no doubt that what the republicans gained in this treaty was the almost complete removal of Brit-

ain from their country, whereas they would not have had the same results with Home Rule. Further, they gained powers never offered before, especially the rights to maintaining an army and navy. This "dominion" status—the same as Canada, Australia, New Zealand and South Africa—granted greater sovereignty than they otherwise would have had and allowed for the "leaving alone" of Ireland for decades to come, which harmed it economically. The fighting changed this situation; without it, the split, which was probably inevitable, would have been more amicable.

–WILLIAM KAUTT, UNIVERSITY OF ULSTER AT JORDANSTOWN

Viewpoint:
By declaring the defense of the rights of small nations among its war aims, Britain lost its moral authority in Ireland and inadvertently strengthened the independence movement there.

The century from the Battle of Waterloo (1815) to the outbreak of World War I (1914) was the British century. As the European power broker, Britain helped keep the peace. It built the largest world empire, covering more than a quarter of the globe, and its colonies were relatively well managed, peaceful, and prosperous. The Royal Navy kept order in the far reaches of the world, and the British free-trade policy and financial acumen made it the leading industrial nation. In short, Britain won the admiration and envy of the world for the judicious conduct of its foreign affairs and financial policies. Britain of the nineteenth and early twentieth centuries was often a model of competent and effective government.

Given its success in ruling so many far-off lands, it is, perhaps, surprising that Britain did so badly in its dealings with the nation closest to home—Ireland. Of course, the whole history of the British involvement in Ireland since the Middle Ages had been fraught with friction and conflict. In the nineteenth and twentieth centuries, however, successive British governments had many opportunities to eliminate the causes of conflict and to establish a friendly partnership that would have kept Ireland as a loyal nation within the empire. Yet, every opportunity for a peaceful resolution to "the Irish question" was rejected by the British government until most Irishmen felt there was no alternative but to go to war with England.

Irish nationalism had been ruthlessly suppressed by Britain for centuries to the point that most Irishmen by the nineteenth century were reconciled to the concept of British rule. The Fenian rebellions of 1848 and 1867 failed to attract strong support. What most Irish wanted was "home rule": the right to elect their own parliament and regulate Irish affairs themselves, while foreign and military affairs would remain the purview of the British parliament. It was a reasonable desire and did not threaten either British interests or fundamental authority. Indeed, Ireland watched as Canada, Australia, New Zealand, and South Africa became self-governing dominions within the empire—a policy carried out with the support and approval of the British government. Britain found that allowing the creation of strong, self-governing dominion nations did not weaken the empire but actually strengthened it. Granting such a status to nearby Ireland, on the other hand, was somehow unthinkable.

In 1886 the first real attempt to solve "the Irish question" was made when a "home rule" bill was introduced to the House of Commons. Home Rule would not have granted full dominion status for Ireland, as in Canada, but would have at least established an Irish parliament with the authority to tax and administer their own nation. Home Rule was violently opposed by the small Protestant minority in Ireland, which was concentrated in the six northern counties of Ulster. The Ulster Protestant politicians tended to be a viciously anti-Catholic group in a country that was overwhelmingly Catholic. Yet, as obnoxious as the Ulster politicians were, they commanded a small but tightly knit voting block needed by a government to stay in power. Under the Ulster Protestant slogan "Home Rule is Rome Rule," consideration of home rule was repeatedly blocked.

From the 1880s to the outbreak of World War I the Irish nationalists followed a peaceful and moderate course of trying to change the status of Ireland through the parliamentary process and social action. In the 1890s the Gaelic League, dedicated to reviving the Irish language and culture, was started and gained a large membership. Sinn Féin (Ourselves Alone), was founded in 1905 with a more radically nationalist agenda but did not gain wide acceptance before World War I. By 1912 the moderate Irish Nationalist Party was the dominant political force in Ireland and British prime minister Herbert Asquith supported introduction of another home-rule bill because he needed the eighty-two Irish Nationalist votes in Parliament.

Seeing the probability of Irish home rule, the northern Irish Protestants, under the leadership of Sir Edward Carson, began to organize paramilitary forces and openly threaten civil war if Ireland were granted Home Rule. Twenty thousand Northern Irishmen signed a covenant to refuse to recognize Home Rule and, by June 1913, fifty thousand Northern Irish Unionists were organized into military units, called "The Ulster Volunteers," under command of a retired British general.

The threat to fight was no mere bluster. In April 1914, as the Home-Rule bill was ready to pass, the Ulster Volunteers smuggled 24,600 German Mauser rifles and 3,000,000 rounds of ammunition into Northern Ireland with no interference from the police or military. Ulster Volunteers, armed with modern rifles and machine guns, paraded openly in the northern counties. Alarmed, the government ordered the British army garrison in Ireland to guard arms depots to ensure that the Unionists would not loot them. In what became known as the "Curragh Mutiny" the commander of a cavalry brigade and the majority of his officers declared that they would resign their commissions rather than undertake any action against the northern Unionists. The mutiny had support from some of the top generals in the army, and the action radicalized an already incendiary atmosphere. When the home-rule bill was passed on 6 May 1914, Ireland was on the verge of a civil war.

In the south of Ireland, nationalists had organized their own paramilitary forces, known as the "Irish Volunteers," who had 180,000 men organized by the Spring of 1914. The Irish Volunteers also tried to smuggle arms in from Germany, but their attempts to arm their forces met with a different response from a British army that was overwhelmingly sympathetic to the Northern Protestant cause. In July 1914 Irish nationalist Robert Childers landed 15,000 old Mauser rifles near Dublin. This bit of arms smuggling resulted in a bloody confrontation with British troops in Dublin, where British soldiers fired on an Irish crowd, killing 4 and wounding 38.

The only thing that prevented an all-out civil war in 1914 was the start of World War I in August. The Home Rule Bill, which was due to take effect with the royal assent scheduled for 1 September, was postponed until the end of the war. The Irish nationalist parliamentary leader, John Redmond, who saw the war as an opportunity to gain British government support for home rule, committed the Irish Volunteers to the British cause and encouraged Irishmen to join the army and fight for Britain. Many followed Redmond's lead and enlisted. In fact, 300,000 Catholic Irishmen fought in the British Army in the war and 40,000 were killed in service of the empire. Britain ought to have been grateful, but in typical fashion, it was not.

From the beginning of the war, the British government reneged on promises made to the Irish. The Ulstermen were allowed to form an army division of their own while the government promised that Irish units would be organized into an Irish corps—but these units never materialized. Indeed, the southern Irish were not allowed a division or even a specific brigade. Almost no Irish Catholics were given commissions; Southern Irish regiments were commanded by officers who were Protestants and Ulstermen. As a further insult to Irish loyalties, the British Army press releases refrained from mentioning the superb performance of Irish regiments in the bloody fighting in Flanders and Gallipoli. The final act that pushed the Irish over to fight for independence was the formation of a new coalition government in May 1915. Prime Minister Asquith brought eight Unionists into the cabinet and gave a cabinet seat to Carson, the virulently anti-Catholic Ulster leader who had arrogantly threatened civil war the year before. Redmond, whose moderate pro-British stance was causing his following in Ireland to rapidly evaporate, called putting Carson in the cabinet an act of "infinite harm."

By mid 1915 many of the Irish nationalist leaders decided that Ireland had no recourse but open rebellion. Decades of trying to win a small degree of autonomy by democratic means had been betrayed time and again by the British government. When the war began, the British government damaged its own case against Irish self-government by declaring that the conflict was being fought for the rights of small nations, such as Serbia and Belgium. What was Ireland, then, if not a small nation with a claim to national autonomy and self-government every bit as strong as that of Belgium? In short, Britain no longer had a moral case for its policy and gave no cause for moderate Irishmen to trust the British government. Well before the Easter Rising of April 1916, Irish leaders no longer doubted that a full-scale rebellion was necessary; the only question was the timing.

The more militant Irish nationalists who led the Easter Rebellion, such as James Connolly, Patrick Pearse, and Thomas J. Clarke, rightly saw the war as their best chance to commit Ireland to independence from Britain. Nationalists of every stripe were angry and disillusioned by British conduct toward Ireland during the war. Most of the Irish nationalists did not hope for a German victory but rather expected that Britain would be so weakened by the war that it would be possible to win independence. As it turned out, this thinking was pretty sound. After winning World War I, Britain had little stomach to fight yet another war on its doorstep.

A coalition of 1,600 men from several Irish nationalist groups seized Dublin and declared the Irish Republic on Easter Monday (24 April 1916). The rebellion was planned with the expectation that German arms and aid were on the way. Yet, even though the aid failed to arrive, the nationalists could not call off the rebellion. The Irish groups,

now styled the Irish Republican Army, conducted a brilliant fight against the British Army, inflicted heavy casualties on British forces, and held the center of Dublin for a week before being compelled to surrender to overwhelming force and firepower. After the rebellion the British, given their last chance to repair their relationship with Ireland, characteristically came down with a heavy hand, quickly executed 14 rebel leaders after secret trials, and arrested more than 3,000 Irish nationalists. The British, infuriated by what they considered to be treason in wartime, failed to look beyond the rebellion and into the broad sympathy that the rebels enjoyed among the Irish population. The executions provoked an explosion of nationalist sympathy in Ireland, so much so that in the December 1918 elections the independence-minded Sinn Féin Party won seventy-three of one hundred Irish parliamentary seats, with the Unionists winning twenty-six seats and the moderate nationalists of Redmond's party winning only six seats. After the 1918 election there was simply no turning back for the cause of Irish independence.

World War I—with the postponement of Home Rule, a string of broken promises, and the brutal repression of the Easter Rebellion—radicalized the Irish Catholic population as nothing else could have. Moreover, with a declared aim of fighting the war for the rights of small nations, Britain gave up its moral authority in its relationship with Ireland. The Easter Rebellion and its aftermath could not have taken place outside the conduct of the World War. In the end, the nationalist's idea that the war that would weaken the empire so much that Ireland could win independence proved to be correct.

−JAMES S. CORUM, USAF SCHOOL OF ADVANCED AIRPOWER STUDIES

References

Thomas Hennessey, *Dividing Ireland: World War I and Partition* (London & New York: Routledge, 1998).

Lawrence J. McCaffrey, *Ireland: From Colony to Nation-State* (Englewood Cliffs, N.J.: Prentice-Hall, 1979).

John Turner, *British Politics and the Great War: Coalition and Conflict, 1915–1918* (New Haven: Yale University Press, 1992).

Alan J. Ward, *Ireland and Anglo-American Relations, 1899–1921* (London: Weidenfeld & Nicolson, 1969).

JEWISH COMMUNITY

What impact did the war have on the European Jewish community?

Viewpoint: Physical devastation and a surge in anti-Semitism combined to make the lot of European Jews far worse in 1919 than in 1914.

Viewpoint: By the end of the war Europe was more tolerant of Jews as evidenced by their greater role in political, cultural, and intellectual life.

From one perspective the Great War was a significant instrument of Jewish emancipation. For the first time in modern history Jews were fully integrated into the armed forces of at least the Western powers, providing infantrymen and fighter pilots as well as doctors and clerks. The German Jewish community, less than a half million in number, put eighty-eight thousand of its men in uniform. More than twelve thousand never came back. If blood was the price of citizenship, Jews had paid in full measure. For those disaffected from the bourgeois nation-states that had waged the war, the Russian Revolution (1917) promised a new order in which religious and ethnic identities would be irrelevant—and seemed on its way to delivering on the promise, at least in principle. For Jews seeking to withdraw from the Gentile world, the Balfour Declaration (1917) had opened the door to international recognition of a Jewish homeland in Palestine.

On the other side of the ledger, Jewish communities in Western Europe had suffered from the same kinds of loss and dislocation as their Gentile counterparts. In the East, Jewish communities had been devastated by contending armies—a pattern that endured after 1918 as civil wars bade fair to become endemic in that region. The postwar peace settlement created several new states and enlarged others—such as Romania—whose emphasis on cultural nationalism as a focus of identity boded ill for their Jewish minorities. The negotiators at Versailles were unwilling to go beyond legal and contractual formulas in securing Jewish rights. Furthermore, the national homeland proved heavily dependent for both development and basic security on the goodwill of a British Empire far more concerned with placating its large Arab and Muslim components.

No less a problem than these specifics was the solvent effect of the Great War on patterns of civility. Verbal and physical violence became normative after 1918 to degrees considered impossible in 1914. Ideas previously considered fit at best for circulation among like-minded cohorts in dingy beer halls became part of the public discourse. Jews were unlikely to benefit from that aspect of the new European order—unless they bought guns themselves.

Viewpoint:
Physical devastation and a surge in anti-Semitism combined to make the lot of European Jews far worse in 1919 than in 1914.

World War I did not produce the traditional Jewish strategy of keeping heads down while the Gentiles shot it out. European Jews went to war with as much enthusiasm as did any ethnic minority. Ten percent of Russian Jews served during the war, despite the notorious anti-Semitism of that country and its ruling elite. Eleven percent of Austro-Hungarian Jews served, as did 14 percent of British Jews, 18 percent of German Jews, and 20 percent of Jews in France. Across Europe, Jews were anxious to show that their national loyalty made them reliable citizens. Jews were, however, in the unfortunate position of being too well assimilated to avoid the calling of nationalism, yet too marginalized by their respective societies to win the benefits of participation.

Despite active and loyal service, the image of Jews as the alien "other" continued to dominate across Europe. Consequently, Jewish participation in European armed forces did not bring any long-lasting positive changes to the Jewish communities of Europe. Despite the willing service and sacrifice of Jews, Europeans remained suspicious of Jewish minorities and went to great lengths to marginalize and persecute Jews wherever they could. In a war in which Jews found themselves in the unusual position of fighting on opposing sides, they also found that their adopted homelands were unwilling to accept them as full and participating members of the nation at arms.

Most European states forbade Jews from occupying senior leadership positions. In Russia the officer corps was officially closed to Jews, although a select few served as surgeons. In Germany, all senior military ranks were closed to Jews, and the reserves used a variety of formal and informal mechanisms to discourage Jews from serving. In France, aftershocks of the Dreyfus Affair continued to complicate the movement of Jews into senior ranks. Only in Austria-Hungary did Jews serve at senior ranks; eight Austro-Hungarian generals were Jewish. As a result of this marginalization, Jews disproportionately served as frontline soldiers and, as a consequence, they died at disproportionately high rates.

Despite the ten thousand Jews who died serving Germany, including the only Reichstag member to die in service, Jews became an easy target for Germans as the war began to turn against them. German definitions of the *Volk* (people) excluded Jews and identified them as internal aliens and a threat to Germany. Theobald von Bethmann Hollweg, the German foreign minister, made this point abundantly clear when he declared that the war was a "battle between the objectives of German Jewry and Germanic Germans." The kaiser declared in February 1918 that German problems were a result of an international conspiracy led by American president Woodrow Wilson and "international Jewry." At the end of the war, the kaiser refused demands that he resign, saying: "I wouldn't dream of abandoning the throne because of a few hundred Jews and a thousand workers." Clearly the "stab in the back" can be traced directly back to the war years and the immediate consequences of German defeat.

Civilians suffered terribly during World War I. Jewish civilians were singled out for especially brutal treatment, especially in Russia, the most violently anti-Semitic country in Europe. Despite the heroic service of Russian Jews (one even won the Cross of St. George, the Russian equivalent of the Victoria Cross), they were still denied full citizenship. In western Russia and Poland, according to David Vital in A *People Apart: The Jews in Europe, 1789–1939* (1999), the Russians began a "continuous series of massive, arbitrary, and wholly unnecessary expulsions of the civilian Jewish population." Because the majority of young Jewish men were, in fact, serving in the tsar's army, these expulsions disproportionately impacted women, children, and the elderly. Germans, Poles, and Russians alike looted Jewish shops, confiscated Jewish property, and destroyed synagogues.

The Russian army claimed that the expulsions were required for national security, but in reality Jews became a scapegoat for the incompetent performance of the army. Blaming Jews for treasonous cooperation with the Germans was easier for Russia than admitting its battlefield failures. In three districts (Courland, Kovno, and Grodno) the Russians expelled two hundred thousand Jews in a forty-eight-hour period. Seven thousand Jewish refugees were denied permission to leave freight trains at Kursk for more than a month, forcing them to live in the freight cars in inhuman conditions. Thousands of Jews were hanged without trial.

Moreover, the particular conditions of World War I worked against the Jews finding a champion among the great powers. Russia was so pathologically anti-Semitic that many Jews, even in Britain and France, hoped for a German victory, at least in the east. German occupation, however, turned out to be no better than the Russian occupation had been. Polish Jews openly expressed the feeling that they had only

THE COUNTRY'S CALL FOR MEN
HAS BEEN NOBLY RESPONDED
TO BY JEWS OF ALL CLASSES

ARE YOU HOLDING BACK?

On the VICTORY OF THE ALLIES depends
THE CAUSE OF FREEDOM AND TOLERATION
which is the cause of England

Apply at the Recruiting Office at
Messrs. ROTHSCHILD'S
New Court, St. Swithin's Lane, E.C.
and Major Lionel de Rothschild, M.P., will enlist you

THERE MUST BE NO JEWISH SLACKERS
JEWISH YOUNG MEN!
Do your duty to your faith and your Country
All British Born Jews ENLIST NOW

DON'T FORGET—Ask advice of
Major LIONEL DE ROTHSCHILD, M.P.

exchanged one form of slavery for another. The report of one international charitable organization noted that the Germans in Poland treated Jews "with a severity that is at least equal to that which was once displayed by the tsar's administration. A strong anti-Semitic current prevails everywhere in the occupation authority and every measure of harassment . . . is permissible."

There was, of course, little that the Western Allies could do to stop German anti-Semitism, short of winning the war. They could, at least theoretically, reduce the worst aspects of Russian anti-Semitism by pressuring their Entente partner. The complexities of alliance warfare, combined with the already fragile nature of the Russian state, worked against British and French politicians putting pressure on the tsar to stop new waves of pogroms. The Russian Revolution (1917) led to the immigration of thousands of Russian Whites to France where they united

with the French Right to slander Jews as pro-German in Right-wing journals such as *Libre Parole* and *Action Française*.

Of course, the notion of Jews as pro-German was complicated at best. In October 1916 the German Catholic Centre and Liberal parties joined Right-leaning parties in voting for a *Judenzählung* (Jew count). Acting on accusations that Jews were not doing their part, the *Judenzählung* took a census of Jews serving in the trenches. This hostile and unwarranted act hurt a Jewish community that was in fact serving and dying in proportions equal to those of the city of Munich. The *Judenzählung* also violated the spirit of the *Burgfrieden* (civic truce), a national agreement to end domestic discord similar to the French *union sacrée*. Germany was at the same time forbidding Jews from serving in high ranks and erroneously accusing them of not fully participating in the war effort. Anti-Semitic accusa-

**British Jews reading a
recruitment poster
during the war**

(Ulstein Bilderdienst, Berlin)

tions from other Right-wing groups led to the resignations of German finance minister Walther Rathenau and Warburg bank director Carl Melchior, the only two German Jews who served in senior posts during the war.

The Ottoman Empire looked upon the ninety thousand Jews in Palestine as a potential fifth column. The Ottoman governor of Palestine, Jemal Pasha, disbanded a proposed Jewish militia group that had volunteered to defend Jerusalem from the British. The Ottomans also sent thousands of civilians to hard-labor camps in Syria (where many died) and deported twelve thousand Jews to Alexandria, Egypt. Many of these deportees joined a Jewish brigade of the British army that fought at Gallipoli. Other Jews formed the Nili spy ring inside Palestine that provided crucial intelligence for the British until the Turks uncovered it in October 1917.

Partly as a reward for Jewish efforts, Britain supported the creation of a Jewish homeland, though that support was lukewarm. The Balfour Declaration (1917), normally cited as a great step forward for Jews, was bereft of immediate benefit. Its passage did not produce a Jewish homeland nor did it set a timetable for such a homeland to be established. Nor could one have been established, since Britain had promised the same strip of land to the Arabs. Thus the Jews believed that Palestine was theirs, while the Sherif of Mecca believed that the British had promised Palestine as an eventual Arab homeland. Britain squared the circle by making Palestine a "mandate," effectively adding it to the British Empire, and by banning Jews from the part of the mandate known as Trans-Jordan. It would take another world war to make the theoretical British support for a Jewish homeland worth more than the paper that the Balfour Declaration was printed on. Any connection between the Balfour Declaration and the creation of the state of Israel must be understood as indirect at best.

World War I did not improve the lives of Jews in any meaningful way. Instead, the war presaged the violent anti-Semitism and genocide of the 1930s and 1940s. The new nation of Poland, where terrible pogroms became commonplace, refused to grant citizenship to Jews. Long before Adolf Hitler came to power, Jews had become convenient scapegoats for German military defeat. In 1922 Rathenau, then serving as the German foreign minister, was assassinated by nationalist anti-Semites in Berlin. World War I also broke apart Jewish villages in Eastern Europe, scattered individuals, and left traditional Jewish communities less well prepared to deal with the Nazi onslaught of World War II. The history of Nazism and genocide did not begin in 1933. Its roots in the World War I period cannot be ignored.

–MICHAEL S. NEIBERG,
U.S. AIR FORCE ACADEMY

Viewpoint:
By the end of the war Europe was more tolerant of Jews as evidenced by their greater role in political, cultural, and intellectual life.

If one accepts the British historian A. J. P. Taylor's argument that World War I and World War II were actually a single conflict separated by a twenty-one-year truce, it would follow that the Jewish population of Europe emerged from the first portion of the conflict in a much worsened state. Did not Adolf Hitler and other anti-Semites of the interwar period blame Jews for precipitating the war and ending it on terms that were disastrous for Germany? If the flaws of the Versailles peace settlement (1919) laid the foundations for the belligerence and genocide of Nazi Germany, how could one possibly regard the conclusion of World War I as a positive development for European Jews? These observations, however, are influenced by a hindsight that simply cannot ignore the unimaginable tragedy of the Holocaust. From the perspective of 1918, however, European Jewish communities had many reasons to believe that a new day had dawned.

At the most basic level, the end of World War I ushered in sweeping political changes that thoroughly democratized virtually every major country in Europe. The authoritarian empires of Central Europe were transformed into pluralistic democratic republics, where traditional modes of social hierarchy were swept away. Jews may have been legally emancipated in the Habsburg realms as far back as 1781 and throughout the German Empire at its inception in 1871, but the post–World War I political climate increased their social acceptance and integration to unprecedented levels. The abolition of the favored–and virtually exclusive–position of the traditional aristocracy in state service in those countries meant that careers in public life would now be open to talent and subject to meritocractic competition. Applications from Jews, almost totally excluded from the traditional elite for religious reasons, were for the first time just as valid as those of any other citizen. The great wartime and postwar legitimization of Socialist and other left-wing political parties–with which Jews tended to identify more strongly than traditional conservative parties—as parties of government opened political life to them as well.

European cultural and intellectual life in the interwar period was also thoroughly enriched by the contributions of Jews, particularly in Germany and Austria. Composers such as Alban Berg and Arnold Schoenberg, director Max Reinhardt, physicist Albert Einstein, and psychologist Sigmund Freud all achieved fame and popularity in the 1920s. The leading international performer of the era of the quintessentially German (and personally anti-Semitic) composer Richard Wagner's forceful baritone roles was the Hungarian-Jewish singer Friedrich Schorr. Anti-Semitic extremists targeted these leading figures as examples of "degeneracy" in the public sphere, but they could hardly have done so if these Jewish figures were not in fact as prominent and popular as they had become. Indeed, one recent explanation for the eventual rise of Nazi anti-Semitism was that the Jews' newfound prosperity made it appear that they had benefited from a war that Germany had lost and through which the other nations of Europe had suffered. Naturally, all the shame belonged to the bitter and resentful, but many historians believe that their bitterness and resentment stemmed from their inability to accept a world where Jews could succeed too.

Extremist anti-Semitism in interwar Germany has received much scholarly attention, but it is nevertheless important to remember that there was at the time little reason to believe that its adherents would seize the levers of power and embark on genocide. When Hitler joined the National Socialist German Workers' (abbreviated "Nazi") Party in 1919, it had only a few dozen members. Even at the time of his failed putsch in Munich in November 1923, the Nazis were still only a provincial party with no serious mass following. In the relative stability of the mid 1920s the Nazi Party was briefly banned and received only an insignificant number of votes for years afterward. Only shrewd alliance-building with gullible moderate conservatives, shamelessly deceptive politicking, a skewed electoral system of proportional representation, the general incompetence of the political mainstream, and—most of all—the catastrophic economic conditions of the Great Depression enabled the Nazis to become a serious contender for political leadership. Even at the height of their popularity, in the parliamentary elections of July 1932, they still only received 37 percent of the national vote. Germans who supported Nazi candidates, moreover, were much more likely to have voted for their statist economic policies and aggressive foreign policies. Anti-Semitism was far from the average German's radar screen during the Great Depression.

BALFOUR DECLARATION

On 2 November 1917 British foreign secretary Arthur James Balfour wrote a letter to Lionel Walter Mayer, Second Baron Rothschild, detailing the British policy on Zionism, the Jewish movement that desired to establish a homeland in Palestine:

I have much pleasure in conveying to you, on behalf of His Majesty's Government, the following declaration of sympathy with Jewish Zionist aspirations which has been submitted to, and approved by, the Cabinet.

"His Majesty's Government view with favour the establishment in Palestine of a national home for the Jewish people, and will use their best endeavours to facilitate the achievement of this object, it being clearly understood that nothing shall be done which may prejudice the civil and religious rights of existing non-Jewish communities in Palestine, or the rights and political status enjoyed by Jews in any other country."

I should be grateful if you would bring this declaration to the knowledge of the Zionist Federation.

Source: *"Balfour Declaration 1917," Israel Information Service, Internet website, http://www.accessv.com/~yehuda/ Balfourdec1.html.*

In the world of 1918 there was extremely little evidence to suggest that the position of German Jews would be so horribly different fifteen years in the future.

In other major European states Jews had equally strong reasons to be optimistic. The Polish and Baltic successor states to the Russian Empire also instituted broad civil equality for their Jewish populations, even if society continued to harbor anti-Semitism. Even revolutionary Russia itself presented opportunities to the traditionally most persecuted Jewish community in Europe. The Provisional Government established in February 1917 abolished all of the distinctions of birth, class, religion, and nationality in the Empire. The Soviet government established after the Bolshevik coup d'état in October 1917 reaffirmed that commitment, at least in principle, and subsequently adopted policies aimed at the physical destruction of the old elites. Although most Communists were not Jews and most Jews were certainly not Communists, the harsh oppression by the Russian Empire of its Jewish community had left it impoverished and in many cases politically well-disposed toward the revolutionary movement. Prominent Bolshevik leaders such as Leon Trotsky, Grigory Zinovyev, and Lev Kamenev rejected their Judaism as doctrinaire Marxists but reached levels of power and responsibility to which no one of their background could have aspired under the Empire.

Certainly there was much violence against Jews living in the former territories of the Russian Empire during the revolutionary period. The pogroms in Ukraine in 1919, for example, were the bloodiest since the seventeenth century. Yet, these atrocities were committed by rogue elements of the anti-Bolshevik White Russian armies, by rabid nationalists, or by hateful individuals and mobs operating in the absence of order and authority. Nor were Jews the only victims in a brutal and multifaceted civil war in which indiscriminate violence was directed against a large number of ethnic groups, religious faiths, social classes, and political organizations. All of the violent anti-Semitic groups, however, were crushed by the Bolsheviks in the course of the war. Lenin's government even instituted a policy of recruiting party, government, and police officials heavily from minorities who had been oppressed by tsarist Russia, including Jews, in the belief that their terrible treatment before the Revolution would increase their enthusiasm and vigilance for the new regime.

In the early years of Soviet rule, Jews, like other officially recognized national minorities, also received heretofore unknown rights of national self-expression. Permitted to use Yiddish as its official language, the Soviet Russian Jewish community was free to publish its own newspapers, to develop its own literature, to operate its own schools, and to enjoy its own artistic and theatrical life. Of course, Soviet Jews had no license to use their new linguistic and cultural freedoms to engage in political dissent, and their religious life was subject to persecution under the official atheism of the regime. Nevertheless, in the immediate aftermath of the war and revolution, Soviet citizens of Jewish background could aspire to high positions in the government and Communist Party (although those avenues became more closed off to them over time), and could use (at least for a while) their native language in public situations.

In keeping with its liberal tradition, Western Europe offered even better prospects for European Jewish communities. The most important development was the public support of the British government for a Jewish state in Palestine, a policy elaborated by Foreign Secretary Arthur Balfour in a letter to a leading Zionist in November 1917. Although the Balfour Declaration was consistent with the postwar goal of the Allies of dividing the possessions of the Ottoman Empire along ethnic lines, it was notable for two reasons. First, Balfour himself was neither a great liberal nor a maverick politician. As a wealthy landowner, a former Conservative prime

minister and opposition leader, the nephew of his predecessor as prime minister, the Marquess of Salisbury, and a direct descendant of Queen Elizabeth I's chief minister, he was at the very center of the British political establishment. For such a man to make a public statement favoring the controversial issue of Jewish statehood showed that even the greatest British traditionalists were sympathetic to the leading ideal of Jewish cultural and intellectual life. Second, the territory that Balfour tentatively promised had only a small minority population of Jews. By promising them statehood in Palestine, he showed his willingness to offend the Muslim majority of the region as well as Arab peoples in general. The audacity of the declaration actually limited the ability of Britain to follow a pro-Zionist policy immediately after the war, when it risked alienating the populations of its League of Nations mandates in Jordan and Mesopotamia, its Red Sea and Persian Gulf colonies, and its Egyptian protectorate—to say nothing of its Muslim subjects in India. Despite its immediate postwar strategic concerns, Britain eventually kept Balfour's word when it withdrew from Palestine in 1948 and consented to the creation of the state of Israel.

Despite individual examples of racism and anti-Semitism, Jews in both Britain and France were free to enter public life and to live in an atmosphere of tolerance. Britain, having granted equal civil rights to its Jewish population (along with Catholics and dissenting Protestants) in most spheres nearly a century before World War I, continued its tradition of tolerance. British Jews were unencumbered in their daily lives, no serious politician advocated their exclusion from the public sphere, and prominent members of the Jewish community could expect inclusion at the highest level of power. Well before World War I, Benjamin Disraeli, a Jewish-born convert to the Anglican Church, had served two terms as prime minister. Rufus Isaacs, a politician who kept his Jewish faith, served before the war as a cabinet minister and Lord Chief Justice, and after the conflict as Viceroy of India and Foreign Secretary. His illustrious career earned him national respect and advancement through the ranks of the aristocracy, culminating in Conservative prime minister Stanley Baldwin's decision to give him the high title of marquess after Isaacs returned from India in 1926.

France also continued its broad toleration of Jews. Emancipated in 1790, the native Jewish population was already well assimilated into French society. When Captain Alfred Dreyfus, a Jewish officer serving on the French general staff, was framed on espionage charges and fraudulently convicted of treason in 1894, an impassioned national movement came to his defense and achieved his full exoneration. After the war, when large numbers of East European and Russian Jews began to arrive in France, resentment against them had much more to do with their status as poor immigrants who took jobs and relied on social services than it did with ethnic or religious identities. Significantly, the anti-immigrant attitudes directed toward them were often shared by assimilated French Jews. Nevertheless, the French Republic maintained a relatively easy system of naturalization for citizenship, and the common public attitude was tolerant. When a Jewish immigrant assassinated the exiled Ukrainian nationalist leader Symon Petlyura, who had been responsible for some of the pogroms of 1919, in Paris in 1926, a sympathetic French jury acquitted him although there was no doubt of his guilt. Twelve years later the French people elected a left-wing coalition government presided over by Léon Blum, the Jewish leader of the French Socialist Party. French Jews, even the recent immigrants among them, felt so comfortable in their homeland that many preferred living in France to the prospect of immigrating to the United States. Ironically and tragically, one of the reasons why French Jews—and West European Jews generally—were so easily identified by the Nazis in the 1940s was that they had been so well integrated into national life that they, as good law-abiding citizens who trusted their governments, obeyed instructions to identify themselves as Jews on mandatory census forms.

The end of World War I generally represented progress for European Jews. Despite significant violence in war-torn and revolutionary Russia, the massive political transformations that swept the Continent made life easier for Jews. In the major European countries, Jews occupied senior offices of state in the interwar period and played an unprecedentedly distinguished role in cultural and intellectual life. Although the roots of the anti-Semitic movements that culminated in Nazi Germany and regimes sympathetic to it were present in the 1920s, they long remained marginal and attracted little mass support. Even their later successes had less to do with anti-Semitism than they did with aggressive nationalist ideologies and promises of economic recovery. Although the new day would end in a horrible nightmare, Europe in the years after World War I was more tolerant and inclusive of the Jewish people than it had ever been before.

–PAUL DU QUENOY,
GEORGETOWN UNIVERSITY

References

Esther Benbassa, *The Jews of France: A History from Antiquity to the Present,* translated by M. B. DeBevoise (Princeton: Princeton University Press, 1999).

Peter Gay, *Weimar Culture: The Outsider as Insider* (New York: Harper & Row, 1968).

Martin Gilbert, *The First World War: A Complete History* (New York: Holt, 1994).

Gilbert, *The Jews in the Twentieth Century: An Illustrated History* (New York: Schocken Books, 2001).

Paula Hyman, *From Dreyfus to Vichy: The Remaking of French Jewry, 1906–1939* (New York: Columbia University Press, 1979).

Paul Johnson, *A History of the Jews* (New York: Harper & Row, 1987).

Charles S. Maier, *Recasting Bourgeois Europe: Stabilization in France, Germany, and Italy in the Decade After World War I* (Princeton: Princeton University Press, 1975).

Peter Pulzer, *Jews and the German State: The Political History of a Minority, 1848–1933* (Oxford, U.K. & Cambridge, Mass.: Blackwell, 1992).

Howard Morley Sachar, *The Course of Modern Jewish History* (Cleveland: World, 1958).

David Vital, *A People Apart: The Jews in Europe, 1789–1939* (Oxford & New York: Oxford University Press, 1999).

Susan Zuccotti, *The Holocaust, the French, and the Jews* (New York: BasicBooks, 1993).

KERENSKY

Did the Kerensky government make a mistake when it tried to keep Russia in the war?

Viewpoint: Yes. The decision of the new government antagonized the proponents of the slogan "Peace, Land, Bread!"

Viewpoint: No. The new government needed all the help it could get, and the promise of generous French and British support made staying in the war a reasonable calculated risk.

The first Russian Revolution (March 1917) grew out of a complex synergy of factors, all traceable to a common source: comprehensive war-weariness. The Provisional Government that replaced the Tsarist Empire had no general mandate. It consisted of an uneasy coalition of politicians and bureaucrats from the more-conservative parties and the more-liberal element of the former administration. It began by breaking sharply with its predecessor on many fronts. The new government proclaimed freedom of speech, press, and assembly. It abolished restrictions based on class, nationality, and religion. It declared its intention to call for a freely elected national assembly. It shared de facto power with the radical Petrograd Soviet, and the two bodies worked together in the early days of the revolution despite mutual suspicion.

The prospect of the new order must not be overstated. The swift and easy collapse of tsarism had not solved any of the deeply rooted social or political problems the Empire had been accumulating for decades. At best it had created an environment in which solutions could be developed. Within weeks, as self-demobilizing soldiers returned to their villages and as peasants began to realize that the traditional authority was indeed gone, disorder began and escalated.

A major focal point of popular discontent was the decision by the Provisional Government to keep Russia in the war. Its first head, Prince Georgy Lvov, and his successor, Aleksandr Kerensky (Alexander Kerensky), were committed to keeping the new Russia in the camp of the Western democracies, a position enhanced by the April entry of the United States into the war. Fulfilling previously assumed international obligations seemed a necessary first step—especially since France and Britain were willing to promise financial and military aid in amounts far greater than those furnished to the vanished Empire. Prowar socialists were dispatched to make the case that continuing the struggle against German tyranny did not violate Marxist canons. Convincing as well was the argument that continuing the war would stabilize the internal situation in Russia. All the factions would rally to the support of the government, setting aside their differences at least temporarily.

The Russian army had been eroding for months before the revolution. Radical-Left political groups, the Bolsheviks in particular, called for "peace, land, and bread." Soldiers listened. Frontline units, as well as the rear echelons, were hemorrhaging men. Discipline was unraveling as junior officers with wartime commissions abandoned even a pretense of enforcing command authority. Officers who expressed pessimism were considered counter-revolutionaries; Kerensky in his original capacity as Minister of War had dismissed many of them.

In April an All-Russian Council of Soviets called for a negotiated peace without annexations or indemnities. The Provisional Government responded by reaffirming support for "guarantees and sanctions" to prevent future conflicts. This stance precipitated a conflict leading to mass demonstrations in Petrograd and to the formation of a new coalition government supported by the major radical parties. That government took the step of solidifying its position by a major military offensive, similar in conception to that of the previous year. This time, however, the attacks petered out as division after division refused to advance. By mid July the extent of the fiasco was such that the Provisional Government reintroduced courts-martial and capital punishment. Conservative generals planned a coup. Radicals, Bolshevik and otherwise, rejoiced in the fulfillment of the classical proverb that whom the gods seek to destroy, they first drive mad.

Viewpoint:
Yes. The decision of the new government antagonized the proponents of the slogan "Peace, Land, Bread!"

Ending a war is harder than starting one. There are both political and psychological reasons for this phenomenon. Politicians who start wars put everything on the line when they do so: they risk their careers, their honor, and their place in history. Thus, they tend to avoid a negotiated peace when it is still possible to win the war. Given the general reluctance of political communities to change leaders in the midst of a conflict, the men who start wars are normally the ones who are leading the country when it is necessary to end them. This structural factor prolongs warfare. Psychologically, wars are difficult to end because each side sacrifices human lives and material goods in order to obtain victory. The more that these losses pile up, the more important it becomes to gain something from victory. World War I was particularly difficult to end because the losses were so great and the contest so close. As the human and economic costs rose, so too did the expectations of large rewards from victory, despite the fact that the enormous costs were in large part the result of the balance of power that existed between the warring parties. As a result, though it was becoming increasingly clear that the war was a tie, military and political leaders pushed in vain for lopsided victories.

Something revolutionary had to change in order for the war to end with a stable European order. That event actually occurred in February 1917, when the Romanov dynasty was toppled by urban protestors and dissatisfied soldiers in the Russian capital city of Petrograd. Unfortunately, political mismanagement by the Provisional Government that assumed power after the abdication of Tsar Nicholas II led instead to a prolongation of the war, an intensification of domestic conflict within the Russian Empire,

and the rise of radical Communists to power eight months later. Though many factors accounted for the dramatic events that occurred in Russia in 1917, war or peace was the largest political question of the day and the one that ultimately decided the fate not only of the Provisional Government but of twentieth-century Europe. The hostilities, of course, ended in 1918, but the failure of Russian politicians to seize the opportunity to conclude it in 1917 resulted in a postwar world marked by radicalism, bitter grievances, and endemic violence. Ultimately, unresolved issues found expression in an even more-devastating war that came a generation later.

What could the new generation of Russian politicians have done to stop this madness? They should have ended the war as soon as they came to power. Russia was in a unique and temporary position in the early months of 1917, when both the political and psychological impediments to ending the war were, in effect, suspended. In political terms the February Revolution had opened the door for new policies. Those responsible for starting the war and many of its disasters were now ousted from power and replaced by members of the Duma (a quasi-parliamentary legislature), who had spent much of the past year and a half actively denouncing the government's actions. They took "provisional" power until a Constituent Assembly (roughly the equivalent of a Constitutional Convention) could be convened, but they all proclaimed themselves to be democrats responsible to the will of the people. That will was solidly in favor of bringing about a rapid peace settlement. In terms of domestic politics, Russian politicians had not only the capability to end the war but a mandate to do so. Nearly all of the many riots and outbursts of the war years had included a call to put a stop to hostilities. "Down with the War!" and "Down with the Autocracy!" were favorite slogans well before the February Revolution, and they almost always appeared together. Some Russians still wanted to fight the war to a "victorious conclusion," but they were a distinct minority. Among the most crucial segment of the population—the soldiers of the Russian army—the consensus throughout

THE *1917* OFFENSIVE

In his memoirs, Aleksandr Kerensky (Alexander Kerensky) considers the need for ordering the final Russian offensive against the Germans:

The fact is that the resumption of active operations by the Russian army after two months of paralysis was dictated absolutely by the inner development of events in Russia. To be sure, the representatives of the Allies insisted on the execution by Russia, at least in part, of the strategic plan adopted at the Inter-Allied conference in Petrograd, in February 1917. But the insistence of the Allies would have been of no avail if the necessity for the offensive had not been dictated by our own political considerations. The insistence of the Allies (France and England) played no part, if only because they no longer considered themselves bound by any obligations to Russia after the Revolution. As I have already said, the German General Staff having stopped according to plan, all active operations on the Russian Front, there ensued a condition of virtual armistice. It was the plan of the German High Command that this armistice be followed by a separate peace and the exit of Russia from the War. Berlin's efforts to come to a direct agreement with Russia were begun as early as April. Of course, these efforts failed to make any impression on the Provisional Government and the whole Russian democracy, which were determined on peace as quickly as possible, but a general, not a separate peace. . . .

. . . It was necessary to make a choice—to accept the consequences of the virtual demobilization of the Russian army and capitulate to Germany, or to assume the initiative in military operations. Having rejected the idea of a separate peace, which is always a misfortune for the country concluding it, the return to new action became unavoidable. For no army can remain in indefinite idleness. An army may not always be in a position to fight, but the expectancy, at all times, of impending action constitutes the fundamental condition of its existence. To say to an army in the midst of war that under no circumstances would it be compelled to fight is tantamount to transforming the troops into a meaningless mob, useless, restless, irritable and, therefore, capable of all sorts of excesses. For this reason and to preserve the interior of the country from the grave wave of anarchy threatening from the front it was incumbent upon us, before embarking upon the main problem of army reorganization and systematic reduction and readjustment of its regular formations, to make of it once more an army, i.e., to bring it back to the psychology of action, or of impending action.

Source: *Alexander F. Kerensky,* The Catastrophe: Kerensky's Own Story of the Russian Revolution *(New York & London: Appleton, 1927), pp. 207–209.*

most of 1917 was that Russia should end the war as soon as possible without ceding territory or treasure.

The question of peace was a bit messier in the international arena. The political leadership of the main allies of Russia, Great Britain, and France still sought victory at any cost. The continued presence of Russia in the war was crucial for their plans, as the Russian army forced the Central Powers to fight the war on two fronts. The British and French were opposed to any negotiated peace and were highly agitated about the possibility of a separate peace between Russia and the Central Powers. The major stumbling block to ending the war in 1917 was the refusal of the Allies to contemplate a negotiated political settlement. This stance, however, did not mean that peace was impossible. To the contrary, the potential for Russia to sign a separate peace was quite real. The Russian army had been pummeled by German forces in 1915, but it had rebounded in 1916 to win significant victories over both the Ottoman and Austro-Hungarian Empires. Neither of these crumbling empires had either the desire or the capability to refuse an armistice with Russia if Germany could be brought on board, and the Germans were ready to deal. The Germans had gambled desperately on a campaign of unrestricted submarine warfare in the winter of 1916–1917 and were losing that gamble. The United States was in the process of declaring war on Germany when the February Revolution occurred, and massive numbers of American troops were expected to arrive in Europe in 1918, which gave Germany about a year to salvage their war effort. A separate peace was a golden opportunity. Throughout April, May, and June 1917 the German High Command repeatedly tried to get the Provisional Government to come to the table to work out terms of an armistice.

Politically and psychologically, the potential for ending the war was also there. Most Russian soldiers had not been enamored of the war from its beginning and were right to believe that it held little promise of gain for common Russians, not to mention the enormous threat of personal and social destruction. Most Russians were therefore justifiably antiwar, but few were defeatist. The general feeling both in the ranks and at home was that the war should be ended without any expectation of annexation or indemnity by any of the warring parties. Continuing the conflict was throwing good money (and lives) after bad. In addition, the Revolution itself had opened the possibility for psychological reward. If no far-off ports or trading concessions were to be gained, something far greater could be achieved: liberty, equality, fraternity. Ending the war to consolidate freedom and to recognize the

KERENSKY

sacrifices and efforts of Russian citizens had a pleasant ring to it, and calls to cease hostilities in the name of the revolution sprang forth from all corners of the country.

Even more significantly, Russia now had the chance to be the true moral leader of the Continent through her Revolution. With little prospect that traditional political gains could be won on the battlefield by any side, some hoped that this untraditional war might result with the end to traditional diplomacy and perhaps with an end to war itself. This psychological reward was of the highest order, and enthusiastic Russians sought to claim it immediately. The most famous formulation of this type came from social democrats in the Petrograd Soviet on 15 March 1917 in their "Appeal to the Peoples of All the World." "Toilers of all countries," the appeal read, "extending our hands as brothers across the mountains of our brothers' corpses, across the rivers of innocent blood and tears, across the smoking ruins of cities and villages, across the ruined treasures of civilization, we appeal to you to restore and strengthen international unity. In this is the pledge of our future victories and of the complete liberation of humanity." Socialists, such as the ones who wrote this appeal, counted on the Russian peace offensive to trigger a social revolution across the continent that would unseat kings and topple governments, but even those with a less panoramic vision of the probable results of a separate peace could see that the withdrawal of Russia from the war, coupled with the entrance of the United States, would put new pressures on all warring parties to end the conflict before a decisive outcome was reached. A politically negotiated peace, without annexations or indemnity, would have been difficult to achieve, but the potential for it had increased dramatically.

Thus, the Provisional Government had the motive, means, and opportunity to get out of the war. They failed to do so, not just once but twice. The first chance was on the heels of the Revolution itself, when crowds of people thronged the streets, the powerful Petrograd Soviet prepared its appeal to the world for peace, and German diplomats drooled at the chance to close one of their fronts. Instead, the liberal historian and parliamentarian Pavel Milyukov, who had been named Foreign Minister, announced without delay on 4 March 1917 that Russia would remain "faithful to the treaty that binds her by indissoluble ties to her glorious allies" and would "shoulder to shoulder with them fight our common foe to the end, unswervingly and indefatigably." So long as this war was, as Milyukov also declared, being fought to prevent the "shame of being dominated by Prussian militarism," there was a chance of maintaining the effort. When it

leaked out later that Milyukov was also insisting to the Allies that Russia be granted Constantinople and the Straits as the reward for their sacrifice, however, Milyukov was discredited, removed from the government, and destroyed as a politician. Thus ended the first opportunity.

The moderate socialist Aleksandr Kerensky (Alexander Kerensky) had played an active role in the furor over the Straits and Milyukov's continuation of old-style diplomacy. His stand against annexations, combined with his long history in the Duma of being the voice of the common soldier and his position as a go-between between the Provisional Government and the Soviet, propelled him to the top of the revolutionary scene in the wake of Milyukov's departure. He became minister of war and prime minister, and he had that most unusual of political opportunities: a second chance to seize a golden moment. Instead of ending the war, however, he did the opposite. He rebuffed new German peace plans, ordered his generals to prepare an offensive against the Central Powers, and personally went on a morale-raising tour of the front lines to lecture soldiers on their duty to fight and die for the glorious Russian revolution. The offensive, which began at the end of June, had initial success but was crushed by a counteroffensive days later. The army was shattered by the experience. Units that had been held together by a thread after the February Revolution now broke apart. Desertion and indiscipline ran rampant. Brutalized, war-weary soldiers terrorized the civilian population on their way home, and chaos became the common daily condition.

Several viable political groupings stepped forward to try to reinstill order, including Kerensky's government and the military high command. By the end of the summer, however, the group that was growing most rapidly was the one that had been most strident in its call to end the "imperialist war." This group was the previously small but rapidly growing Bolshevik Party led by radical communist Lenin. The Bolsheviks grew from less than 24,000 members at the time of the February Revolution to 350,000 by October 1917, at which point they swept to power and delivered on their promise, signing an armistice with Germany less than a month after their seizure of power and a peace treaty three months later. The Treaty of Brest-Litovsk, however, was far more punitive than what the Germans had offered less than a year earlier. During the spring of 1917 a large if wavering army still faced German troops. By the winter of 1918 those men had gone home. The German High Command therefore was able to dictate terms in a way that would have been impossible a year earlier. They would get a taste of their own medicine a year later in Versailles, when a vengeful peace embittered a generation of Germans and gave birth to violent schemes of revenge. In the meantime, the armed political factions that emerged from the Russian rubble in 1918 launched a civil war against one another that lasted another three years, completely devastated the economic and social life of the country, and resulted in a brutal communist dictatorship.

Why, then, did Milyukov, Kerensky, and other decision makers in the Provisional Government fail to save their careers, country, and continent by concluding peace? The answer was as simple as it was unsatisfactory. They rejected German calls for a separate peace as "shameful and incompatible with the honor and dignity of Russia." Thus, the options they saw before them were dismal. The most obvious choice, to conclude a general peace along with the British and French, foundered immediately on Western recalcitrance. With peace out of the question, only war remained, and if all policymakers were well aware that a Russian military victory was out of the question, all also placed great hopes in the American intervention. The question was therefore not winning, but just surviving. Indeed, as Kerensky noted in his memoirs, the great summer offensive of 1917 was undertaken not for territory or any other strategic gain, but simply to maintain morale in the army, since "no army can remain in indefinite idleness." This situation was the absurd position that the Russian government put itself in by insisting on maintaining treaty obligations. Kerensky was asking soldiers to fight for nothing, while Lenin was promising them everything if they refused to fight. The fact that soldiers overwhelmingly preferred the Bolsheviks to Kerensky by October was thus not a reflection of their being duped by propaganda (as Kerensky would later claim), but because the Bolsheviks better represented their own personal and political interests.

Still, it is hard not to have at least a little sympathy for the men in the Provisional Government. Refusing to sign the separate peace and remaining engaged with and committed to their allies was their way of being honorable and trustworthy public figures of international importance. They were fulfilling promises and acting according to their consciences and their own understanding of Russian interests. Unfortunately, they failed to see what many other Russians saw with remarkable clarity. The commitments the Provisional Government kept were ones they had not made—ones agreed to by a government they despised on the basis of an imperial policy they rejected. The commitments they broke were to the people they claimed to represent and to the democratic idea that in times of crisis politicians should submit to the clearly expressed will of the vast majority of their constituency. They would pay for these egregious political mistakes with their careers. Many more, both in Russia and across Europe, would pay with their lives in the century to come.

–JOSH SANBORN, LAFAYETTE COLLEGE

Viewpoint:
No. The new government needed all the help it could get, and the promise of generous French and British support made staying in the war a reasonable calculated risk.

For many historians of the Russian Revolution, one the most fateful decisions of the Provisional Government that assumed power after Tsar Nicholas II's abdication was its determination to keep Russia in World War I. It has been argued that this decision was the most obvious catalyst for the collapse of the fragile Russian democracy and that it greatly exacerbated the existing social and political tensions that beset the country. In many ways, however, this argument relies upon hindsight and does not take into account other critical factors of the time. The fact of the matter is that there were many other reasons behind the collapse of the Provisional Government. Continuation of the war was neither the main cause of its fall, nor was it an imperative course of action at the time.

When the Provisional Government assumed authority in March 1917, its greatest problem was the inexperience of its leading personnel. Although it was no fault of their own, the men who took up executive power after the collapse of tsarism had never been entrusted with any serious responsibilities in government administration. All of the new ministers came from parties of either the liberal center or socialist Left. After the legalization of political parties and the creation of a quasi-parliamentary legislature (Duma) in 1905, and until literally the last days of the empire, the tsarist regime had viewed even the moderate Duma politicians with great suspicion and indignantly refused to allow them into government. In addition to their ideological differences with the regime, most of the new ministers came from the professional or commercial middle classes, which the tsarist government mistrusted and generally discriminated against when it came to making appointments to positions of power. The first prime minister of the Prince Provisional Government, the liberal aristocrat Georgy Lvov, had substantial experience in the limited *zemstvo* (local government) institutions established in the 1860s, but their activities were sharply circumscribed by the powers of the Imperial government. Although many of the new Russian leaders in 1917 were accomplished in law, business, academia, or other sectors of civil society, none of them had ever held any responsible government position at the national level, and most had no government experience at all. This inexperience immediately became evident. Approaching government more from their own philosophical abstractions rather than from administrative pragmatism, they displayed little talent, efficiency, or political savvy.

Their first major difficulty was their problematic legitimacy. The new executive authority was never elected to national leadership and had quite simply assumed its powers as tsarist authority evaporated in the crisis that shook Petrograd in February-March 1917. In a technical legal sense, the new ministers did not even have formal standing as Duma members, since Nicholas II prorogued the sitting session of the body shortly before his abdication. Even if they had a legal basis for assuming power, the ministers still had to face the fact that the Duma elections that had brought them to national prominence in the first place were indirect, undemocratic processes designed to favor the wealthiest elements in society and rural areas over cities. The new government's claim to democratic legitimacy was thin.

When the Provisional Government came to power, all it had was the broad sanction of the politically active population in the capital and the tepid acquiescence of its main rival for executive power, the Petrograd Soviet (council), an erratically elected assembly of representatives chosen by a large segment of the soldiers and factory workers in the city. Despite the Soviet's tacit acceptance of the Provisional Government, however, it began to issue decrees and legislation in its own right. Even as the Provisional Government tried to consolidate its authority, it had to contend with a more-radical and often antagonistic body that, to complicate matters, actually met in the same building. As if this "dual power" were not enough of a challenge, many of the radical delegates in the Soviet called with increasing vehemence for it to depose the Provisional Government and assume all power.

The Provisional Government was keenly aware of its flawed democratic credentials, yet its leaders were unforgivably lax in their attempts to remedy the situation. After coming to power, its ministers made clear that their role was temporary. Even the name they used for themselves, "Provisional Government," is inaccurately translated from the Russian *vremennoe pravitel'stvo*, which has the more literal (and politically significant) meaning of "temporary government." With no pretensions about its fleeting role, the Provisional Government promised that the future

political structure of the country would be decided by a democratically elected Constituent Assembly. Nevertheless, it took the assiduously professional officials several months just to draft the necessary laws to govern the elections, which were finally scheduled for late November 1917, fully ten months after the Provisional Government had assumed power and, incidentally, one month after the Bolsheviks had made the whole issue irrelevant by overthrowing it. In the intervening time, the Russian people were held in a suspense that bred the disillusionment and apathy that made the October coup all too easy.

Worse still, the Provisional Government further declared that the resolution of pressing issues such as land reform, long-range economic policy, and national minority rights, among many others, would also be decided by the Constituent Assembly. In addition to the more abstract question of the future form of government, important decisions impacting the daily lives of the Russian people were also to be deferred for what many came to believe would be an indefinite period of time. Faced with a government that had essentially absented itself from leadership on most crucial issues, many Russians simply took the law into their own hands. As the revolutionary year went on, there were more and more illegal seizures of privately owned agricultural land by peasants. Factory workers increasingly used physical intimidation to dictate working conditions to their employers, and minority nationalists gravitated more resolutely toward independence from Russia. Having abolished the tsarist police, the politicians were offering apparently empty promises that could do little to curtail the growing civil unrest.

Most ominous of all was the status of civil-military relations. In a crucial test of any democratic government, the new democratic government of Russia generally failed to subordinate the military to its control. Within a few days of its assumption of power, the famous Soviet Order No. 1 authorized soldiers and sailors to elect administrative councils (also called soviets) within their units. This development fundamentally altered the power structure of the Russian army. It effectively deprived officers of their authority, seriously impaired military discipline, dramatically undermined the centralized command structure, and eventually threatened the effectiveness of the military as a fighting force. By the autumn of 1917, desertion, mutiny, and a general unwillingness to fight were common phenomena in the Russian army.

The collapse of military order, together with the general weakness of the Provisional Government, also alienated Russian officers. Although many of them embraced fundamental political reform and rejected tsarism, few supported the ineffectual Provisional Government and the chaotic situation over which it presided. In August 1917 its new commander in chief, General Lavr Kornilov, independently ordered a corps of the most reliable units on the front to march on Petrograd. While Kornilov's motives remain unclear and appear to have had the initial support of the government, his move was denounced as a plot against the Revolution and he and his officers were arrested. Whether the new democracy chose to stay in the war or not, its control over the military was dangerously limited.

What did the Provisional Government accomplish? Despite its fatal timidity with regard to important affairs of state, it managed to reform some of the worst abuses of the tsarist system. As convinced democrats who wanted Russia to become "the freest country in the world," the new ministers almost instantly embraced far-reaching changes in the Russian legal system. To the plaudits of Western liberals (and sympathetic historians), the Provisional Government introduced a truly progressive program of civil liberties, which included the amnesty of all political prisoners, full freedom of speech and assembly, and the abolition of capital punishment. In an unstable situation, however, these reforms only weakened the new democracy further. The amnesty, first of all, extended to all political offenders imprisoned or exiled by the tsarist regime, even those who had committed violent crimes for (ostensibly) political reasons, and not only to people whom the contemporary world would consider prisoners of conscience. With strong traditions in Russia of underground revolutionary movements, political terrorism, and Marxist extremism, many of the "political" offenders amnestied in 1917 had in fact been imprisoned or exiled for their violent crimes rather than their ideas. As a result, political extremists who were fundamentally opposed to the new democracy and advocated further violent revolutionary change, including the Bolshevik leader Lenin, were allowed to return to the center of the action. The lifting of censorship and the advent of completely free speech enabled Lenin and other radicals to advocate with impunity the revolutionary overthrow of the weak new government and the existing social and economic order. The abolition of capital punishment, regardless of whatever humanitarian value it may have had, both emboldened extremists who no longer faced death if they attempted to make a revolution and removed the strongest sanction of military discipline from the ranks of collapsing army.

Clearly, the Provisional Government had plenty of internal problems unrelated to the war. Although some historians point to the contin-

ued participation of Russia in the conflict as yet another serious problem that the government could not handle, the alternative of withdrawing from it was for several reasons an even less attractive option. First, it was clear that after three years of consistent military reversal, any peace settlement with the belligerent and imperialist German government would have been little more than a negotiated surrender. Political turmoil in Russia in the spring of 1917 actually emboldened German ambitions in Eastern Europe and, as the Bolshevik government realized a year later when it made a peace settlement, the price of Russian departure would have been the loss of an enormous amount of territory to direct or indirect German influence. This option was especially unattractive, as the territory in question included many of the richest industrial and agricultural regions in Russia, and much of its natural resources. Second, it was widely believed that Imperial Germany would use military victory over Russia to install a more palatable government of its own choosing, probably a restoration of the monarchy in modified form. Leaving the war, therefore, was regarded as a major threat to Russian democracy. Third, peace would also have meant the immediate demobilization of several million soldiers who were becoming increasingly radicalized and whose reintegration into the chaotic and fractured civilian world would have exacerbated an unstable domestic situation.

The most far-reaching consequence, as Russian strategic planners had long feared and as Western diplomatic missions constantly pointed out to the Provisional Government, was that a separate peace in the East would enable Germany to concentrate all of its armed forces in France and quite possibly win the war decisively in the West. In other words, informed opinion at the time believed, not unreasonably, that withdrawing from the war in 1917 would both doom Russia to long-term subordination to Germany and quite possibly contribute to permanent German hegemony over continental Europe.

Obviously, no responsible politician who wanted to assure the future of an independent, democratic Russia could have embarked on such a path. Even when the Bolsheviks, facing great domestic instability and a desperate civil war after they seized power, came to terms with the Germans, they did so only reluctantly and after pronounced internal debate. Although Lenin argued that peace with Germany, however costly, would enable the Bolsheviks to consolidate power at home, he still faced challenges to the decision and even to his leadership over the issue. Only the twisted Marxist argument that a successful revolution in Russia would touch off a worldwide revolution that would negate German

Alexander Kerensky (left) at the Russian Front in the summer of 1917

(from The Illustrated War News, 11 July 1917, page 29, Joseph M. Bruccoli Great War Collection, Thomas Cooper Library, University of South Carolina)

gains convinced the party hierarchy to support the separate peace.

Long before Lenin had to accept the punitive peace settlement, however, the Provisional Government had even less inclination to withdraw from the war than either the short-term political damage or the dire long-term strategic implications suggested. In many ways the Provisional Government believed that despite internal problems and military reversals, it could nevertheless see the war through to a successful conclusion. In the abstract political calculus of the new leadership, it was widely believed that the new democratic government could galvanize the demoralized Russian troops to fight for their freedom. Aleksandr Kerensky (Alexander Kerensky), Lvov's successor as prime minister, affected a military bearing (he wore a uniform although he had never been a soldier and faked an ostensibly combat-related arm injury) and made dramatic speeches urging the rank and file to fight for a free Russia. Although this attempt to instill a kind of civic patriotism into the ranks was a failure, it failed not so much because the war was a lost cause but because the politicians were unable to deliver on issues that could have made a real difference in the soldiers' attitudes toward the war.

Further, the new Russian government received a great deal of attention and encouragement from its democratic allies in the West. The entry of the United States into the war in April 1917 offered the prospect of both a stronger effort against the Germans on the Western Front

KERENSKY

and a huge increase in badly needed shipments of Allied military hardware to Russia. This development convinced the Provisional Government not only to stay in the war, but even to maintain the tsarist plans to annex territory from the Ottoman and Austro-Hungarian Empires. Although the disclosure of these ambitions angered the public and led to the resignations of the responsible ministers, the imperialist plans nevertheless indicated what the government believed to have been possible at the time. With the Western Allies' urging and encouragement, the Provisional Government also had enough confidence to mount a major offensive in July 1917. Despite domestic political strife and the growing problems in the military, the attack enjoyed substantial initial success.

Staying in the war was not crucial to the collapse of the Provisional Government. In domestic politics it proved itself almost totally ineffectual on the leading issues of the day, and it was increasingly unable to maintain law and order. It was also incapable of asserting its authority over the competing Soviet institution in Petrograd and over the restive and rebellious army. Nor could it deal effectively with the radical revolutionaries fighting against the existing social and political order. As a result, the Provisional Government inspired little domestic confidence. When it was finally overthrown by the Bolsheviks in October 1917, its lack of decisive leadership had left it with almost no supporters. Even without the war, the Provisional Government was doomed.

From a diplomatic perspective, the leaders of the Provisional Government correctly believed that a peace settlement with Germany would be so punitive that it would destroy the status of Russia as a great power and would likely mean the end of its democracy. They also had sufficient reasons at the time to believe that if Russia stayed the course, the Allies, bolstered by the entry of the United States into the war, would end the stalemate on the Western Front and defeat Germany before it could do further harm to Russia. The conclusion of a separate peace before that happened would have given the Germans the opportunity to transfer their massive Eastern armies to the Western Front long before decisive American forces arrived in France. The consequences of a potential German victory in the West in 1917 were incalculable, for the world and for Russia.

–PAUL DU QUENOY,
GEORGETOWN UNIVERSITY

References

Richard Abraham, *Alexander Kerensky: The First Love of the Revolution* (New York: Columbia University Press, 1987).

Edward Acton, and others, eds., *Critical Companion to the Russian Revolution, 1914–1921* (Bloomington: Indiana University Press, 1997).

Robert Paul Browder and Alexander F. Kerensky, eds., *The Russian Provisional Government, 1917: Documents,* volume 2 (Stanford, Cal.: Stanford University Press, 1961).

Orlando Figes, *A People's Tragedy: The Russian Revolution, 1891–1924* (London: Cape, 1996).

Figes and Boris Kolonitskii, *Interpreting the Russian Revolution: The Language and Symbols of 1917* (New Haven: Yale University Press, 1999).

George Kennan, *Soviet-American Relations, 1917–1920,* volume 1, *Russia Leaves the War, 1917–1920* (Princeton: Princeton University Press, 1956).

Alexander F. Kerensky, *The Catastrophe: Kerensky's Own Story of the Russian Revolution* (New York & London: Appleton, 1927).

Paul Miliukov, *Political Memoirs, 1905–1917,* edited by Arthur P. Mendel, translated by Carl Goldberg (Ann Arbor: University of Michigan Press, 1967).

Richard Pipes, *The Russian Revolution* (New York: Knopf, 1990).

Robert Service, "The Bolsheviks on Political Campaign in 1917: A Case Study of the War Question," in *Revolution in Russia: Reassessments of 1917,* edited by Edith Rogovin Frankel, and others (Cambridge & New York: Cambridge University Press, 1992), pp. 304–325.

Melissa Kirschke Stockdale, *Paul Miliukov and the Quest for a Liberal Russia, 1880–1918* (Ithaca, N.Y.: Cornell University Press, 1996).

Rex A. Wade, *The Russian Revolution, 1917* (Cambridge & New York: Cambridge University Press, 2000).

Alan K. Wildman, *The End of the Russian Imperial Army,* two volumes (Princeton: Princeton University Press, 1980, 1987).

KERENSKY

LORRAINE

Was the 1914 German offensive in Lorraine an appropriate response to altered circumstances on the Western Front?

Viewpoint: Yes. Having defeated the initial French offensive in Lorraine, the Germans were justified in committing reserves to reinforce their position.

Viewpoint: No. Diverting forces to a secondary theater in the south seriously hampered German efforts in Belgium.

Few of the decisions made by Helmuth Johannes Ludwig von Moltke (the Younger) in his brief term as field commander of the German armies have been so excoriated by military specialists as his authorization of a sector offensive in Lorraine on 27 August 1914. Not only did it violate the principle of concentration of force on the grand sweep through Belgium, it assigned a half-dozen as yet uncommitted divisions to what, in hindsight, seemed an extrinsic operation instead of using them to reinforce the right flank, as so often urged by Alfred von Schlieffen.

To a degree the Lorraine offensive was a consequence of an earlier French attack into the provinces lost in 1871. Undertaken with drums beating and colors flying, it achieved some local successes, then was sent reeling back by superior German forces entrenched around Morhange and Sarrebourg. The German commander on the ground, Crown Prince Rupprecht of Bavaria, confident that he could counterattack successfully even with the forces at his disposal, mounted a series of limited operations and asked permission to expand them into a general offensive. Moltke agreed with no significant demur. The German command system stressed initiative on the part of subordinates, and it was part of the German approach to war to reinforce success, expanding local opportunities and tactical victories into operational success. Breakthrough in Lorraine might set the stage for a real Cannae (a Roman defeat engineered by the Carthaginian general Hannibal in 216 B.C.E.): a double envelopment of the French army on a scale beyond even Schlieffen's vision. Pressing the French in the south, moreover, was the best way to prevent them from detaching troops to reinforce their left wing, which was already enjoying a greater degree of relative success against the German right than Moltke found comfortable. The French in the north were losing, but they were also disengaging and falling back successfully. Even without a breakthrough, an offensive in Lorraine might help fix them in place. As for the divisions Moltke sent south, they were Ersatz formations, composed of men with little or no peacetime training, intended primarily for rear security until they found their feet. Giving them to Rupprecht would help clear a badly strained rail network. War is the province of uncertainty, and in the contexts of late August, the Lorraine option seemed a worthwhile gamble.

Viewpoint:
Yes. Having defeated the initial French offensive in Lorraine, the Germans were justified in committing reserves to reinforce their position.

The essential feature of the Prussian/German way of war was to take advantage of an enemy's mistakes. Even the Schlieffen Plan, with its aura of a doomsday machine, allowed scope for revision as the operational situation changed. In August 1914 the major unexpected development came in an unanticipated theater: Alsace-Lorraine. German concentration plans provided for the deployment of two armies in that region, a total of eight corps. The Sixth Army was composed primarily of Bavarian troops, with the XXI Corps from the Lorraine frontier; the Seventh Army had two corps from Baden; and the XV Corps, another frontier formation.

When on 14 August 1914 the French First and Second Armies crossed the frontier, the Germans initially conducted a fighting retreat, but under protest. The commander of the Sixth Army was the crown prince of Bavaria, Rupprecht; former Prussian war minister Josias von Heeringen led the Seventh. Both men ranked high in the pecking order of the army; both were capable field soldiers; and both, supported by their staffs, argued with Supreme Headquarters that they should make a stand. Alfred von Schlieffen himself had never intended German forces in Lorraine to be entirely passive, assuming instead that the French would stand on the defensive in that sector and must correspondingly be held in place by German initiatives. Rupprecht's chief of staff, Konrad Krafft von Dellmensingen, similarly had before the war regarded the Sixth and Seventh Armies as being responsible for protecting the German sweep through northern France—first by screening it, then by advancing to cover its movements.

Perhaps—just perhaps—if the French in Lorraine were sufficiently weakened, there might be an opportunity to launch a general offensive: one strong enough to crush the enemy right while the grand envelopment finished them off in the north. That possibility appealed strongly to Rupprecht as well, and to his Bavarian corps and division commanders, unwilling to be tied to a secondary role while the Prussians hogged the glory in front of Paris. As modified by Schlieffen's successor, Helmuth von Moltke (the Younger), the German left was initially expected to remain inactive to encourage a French attack. That aim, argued the commanders on the spot, had been achieved. Now it was crucial at least to fix the French in place, preventing them from transferring forces to meet the massive sweep of the German right wing through northern France and Belgium.

By 18 August the generals had made their case. "Strike, and God be with you!" the Quartermaster General finally said to Krafft. On 20 August a full-strength counterattack took the French by surprise around Sarrebourg and Morhange. Amid some ugly scenes of panic, the overextended French fell back toward their start lines while Rupprecht, by now de facto commander of the sector, demanded that Moltke reinforce success. The German chief of staff temporized—until reports began arriving of an even more vigorous French offensive in the center of the front, through the Ardennes and along the Sambre and Meuse Rivers.

If his enemy was so obliging as to thrust his head into the noose, Moltke saw advantages to developing the initial success in Lorraine by advancing on Nancy and finishing off the French right wing as their left was being crushed in the north. In any case the railroad network was not yet able to shift forces from Lorraine to the German right. Lines and rolling stock were available, however, to move a half-dozen improvised second-line divisions into Lorraine, where they would give what weight they could to Rupprecht's offensive.

On 25 August German advance guards came up against French positions on the Meurthe River. Krafft had a reputation as a theorist of battle and before the war had argued cogently that the flanking movements so popular in peacetime maneuvers would be impossible to execute on a modern battlefield. Armies had become too large, he contended. Firepower had become too strong. The only way to victory was not around an enemy position, but through it! He sent the men from southern Germany against French trenches, supported by some of the heaviest artillery bombardments seen in more than a century. They made little headway. The advance entered a region, the "Charmes Gap," long designated as a potential killing ground for a German offensive, and the French at all levels were determined to fight for it. Reconnaissance aircraft revealed German movements. French counterattacks slowed, then stopped, the advance. On 26 September it began to rain, and exhausted German infantry stumbled to a halt under fire from the French guns.

For almost two weeks the Lorraine sector remained stable. The Germans had exhausted their immediate resources. Replacements and supplies had to come forward as wounded were evacuated to the rear. Companies and battalions needed to be sorted out and their chains of

LORRAINE

DECISIVE ACTION?

British scholar George H. Perris, who was in France during the attack in Alsace, provided this analysis of the French actions:

When the new start was made in the plain, the chief crests and passes of the Vosges had been captured after hard fighting, and were firmly held. The retirement five miles from the frontier on the eve of the war here involved a peculiarly hard penalty upon the mountain troops. . . . More to the north, the central Vosges offered much greater difficulties, the French sides being the steeper, so that it was difficult to bring up artillery; while the Germans had been able to strengthen their positions on the narrow, thickly wooded summits by cutting down trees, putting up wire entanglements, and digging trenches. The Col du Bonhomme (3,120 feet) and the lower Col Ste. Marie, captured after a five-day's struggle before the middle of August, gave protection to the French right in its progress toward Saales, at the head of the valley leading to Schestadt; but the direct way to Colmar was blocked by German field-works and by heavy artillery on the lower slopes. A further northward advance was, therefore, made along the mountain crests, and artillery was brought down from the head of the Bruche Valley upon the German flank. This operation, in which material losses were sustained, opened the way for the occupation of Mount Donon (3,300 feet), the most northerly of the Vosges summits, on August 14th. This quasi-Alpine campaign had been skillfully directed, and met with a deserved success. The numbers of men engaged were not large, varying at first from a battalion of Chasseurs to a regiment of infantry, and being gradually increased. The most considerable French loss officially named was 600 killed and wounded in the Bonhomme and Ste. Marie passes. Apart from cannon and material, the German losses were larger.

The little manufacturing town of Thann had now been reoccupied; and at St. Blaise, a village near Ste. Marie-aux-Mines, in a sharp combat, General von Deimling, commanding the 15th German Army Corps, was wounded, and the French took their first standard, to the great joy of Paris sightseers a few days later. On August 18th, General Joffre issued from eastern headquarters the first dispatch bearing his own signature. It reported steady advance along the Alsatian valleys, and declared that "the enemy retreated in disorder, everywhere abandoning his wounded and material." General Pau had received strong reënforcements with a view to a "decisive" action. Advancing simultaneously from Belfort and the Vosges, but on a narrower front than previously, with their right supported on the Rhone-Rhine Canal, they had stormed Thann and Dannemarie, and, bringing the left round toward Colmar, while the center attacked Mulhouse, threatened the German forces with a serious breach of their communications. After severe street fighting, in which twenty-four guns were taken, Mulhouse was again in French possession on August 20th.

The whole of the ground thus gained was abandoned a few days later. This was a grave blow to French pride, and brought a severe punishment upon the Francophile Alsatians. Naturally, the whole southern campaign aroused severe criticism. Several high officers were retired for mistakes in the first advance, which was afterwards officially described as "a mere reconnaissance." If any less eminent soldiers than General Joffre and General Pau had been responsible, there might have been more trouble. But Joffre "the taciturn," the cool-headed engineer whose powers had been tested in many a colonial field, and confirmed in long labors of fortification and organization, and the veteran Pau, who had been second in consideration for the post of Generalissimo, could not be regarded as reckless adventurers, aiming at a political advantage they could not hold.

Source: *Charles F. Horne,* Source Records of the Great War, *volume 2 (New York: National Alumni, 1923), pp. 111–113.*

LORRAINE

command reorganized. Before the war the railway network in eastern France had been significantly improved; between 27 August and 10 September, French general headquarters took advantage of the pause to move twenty divisions from the French left wing to shore up its right. The fighting around Nancy, however, was far from over. On 4 September, following Moltke's order to continue attacking toward the Moselle in support of the redirected movements of the right wing, the Germans drove forward again—this time hard enough to convince the commanding general of the French Second Army that his depleted force could not hold on much longer. French supreme commander Joseph Joffre, depending on his southern flank to hold during the developing Battle of the Marne (1914), complained in his memoirs that the situation in that sector was a "grave source of apprehension." Nevertheless, the Second Army held its ground. As would happen time and again later in the war, German attacks broke down. They could not break through and they could not break out.

In the aftermath of the Marne, both German and French troops were drawn away to reinforce the "race to the sea" that culminated in the Battle of Ypres (1914). Lorraine became a quiet sector, a zone where exhausted divisions came to renew their energy and where new formations, eventually including several divisions of the American Expeditionary Force (AEF), were sent for initiation into trench warfare. "Live and let live" became the rule. The effort to take advantage of the initial French defeat in Lorraine had, however, generated enough anxiety on the French side of the line to support the argument that it was a line of operations worth pursuing—as much worth pursuing, at least, as were any operational possibilities in the summer of 1914.

—DENNIS SHOWALTER,
COLORADO COLLEGE

Viewpoint:
No. Diverting forces to a secondary theater in the south seriously hampered German efforts in Belgium.

In the eight years leading up to 1914, German military strategy was dominated by the thinking of the chief of the general staff from 1891 to 1906, Count Alfred von Schlieffen. Schlieffen's operational plan for a two-front war with France and Russia called for a quick envel-

opment campaign against French forces in the west and then the concentration of German forces on the eastern front for a protracted struggle with the Russians. The success of the operation depended on the ability of Germany to deliver a lightning strike against France. After Schlieffen's retirement in 1906, however, his successor, Helmuth von Moltke (the Younger), became more and more squeamish about extending a German advance too far forward. While Schlieffen had originally planned an advance through neutral Belgium to be followed by a dramatic pivoting maneuver between Paris and the English Channel, Moltke's final drafts of the plan focused instead on a less risky envelopment that would confine the German advance to the territory east of Paris. The consequent shortening of the front and the weakening of the more-ambitious movement through Belgium was a crucial factor in the failure of the German offensive in 1914. It also set the stage for another crucial mistake, the German offensive in Lorraine in August and September.

When Schlieffen presented the first draft of his plan in 1906, he correctly assumed that French war plans were defensive. With a smaller population and lesser military potential than the German Empire, and still haunted by their defeat in the Franco-Prussian War (1870–1871), French strategic planners long believed that France could only fight a defensive war against Germany. Their side of the Franco-German frontier was hilly and forested country defended by modern fortresses such as those at Verdun, Maubeuge, and Belfort. If the French army could hold back the Germans at the border, it could bide its time until its Russian ally attacked Germany in the East. The two-front situation would divide the superior forces of Germany and allow for a successful French counterattack.

Neither Schlieffen nor his successor knew, however, that French strategic thinking changed in the years immediately before the war. Under the direction of the new commander in chief, General Joseph Joffre, the French general staff had reconsidered the defensive approach and decided instead that the best defense would be a moderately aggressive offense. At the same time, French tactical thinking embraced the idea of *offensive à outrance,* that is, the basing of military operations on forward attack rather than cautious, defensive movements. Plan XVII, the French strategic plan in effect from 1913, was influenced by these ideas and called for an immediate attack in the event of war. Since French military planners presciently expected the bulk of a German offensive to come through Belgium, they could see that an immediate French attack at the

Sheet music for a song about the French province ceded to Germany by the Treaty of Frankfurt in 1871

(Joseph M. Bruccoli Great War Collection, Thomas Cooper Library, University of South Carolina)

northernmost part of the common frontier, in Lorraine, would threaten German communications. The French would be countering the German advance by attacking its rear areas, as if it were striking a swinging gate at its hinges.

As German troops rolled into Belgium, Joffre ordered the French First and Second Armies to begin offensive operations in Lorraine. After the attack began on 14 August, it enjoyed a few days of successful forward movement into German territory, mainly because the Germans acted according to Schlieffen's original plan and conducted a tactical withdrawal. It was not long, however, before the German

forces that Moltke's version of the operational plan had positioned in the area checked the advance. By 20 August the French were in headlong retreat back to their starting point along the Meurthe River.

In some respects the immediate containment of the French advance into German Lorraine could not have been possible without Moltke's prewar rearrangement of the Schlieffen Plan. Because more forces were concentrated in a defensive position along the common border than would otherwise have been the case, the Germans had an easier time stopping the French in their tracks. The main

LORRAINE

German units in the region, the Sixth Army under Crown Prince Rupprecht of Bavaria and the Seventh Army under General Josias von Heeringen, disposed substantially larger forces than the French had anticipated in their plans. While the French general staff had correctly guessed the details of Schlieffen's original plan, there was no accounting for Moltke's hesitation. Their successful riposte to the French incursion emboldened the Germans to contemplate a counterattack in Lorraine. Schlieffen had specifically warned his successor and other readers of his plan that a diversion of resources from Belgium to an alternate front along the Franco-German border would imperil the larger envelopment maneuver. If the envelopment failed, in Schlieffen's calculations, France would survive his projected six-week campaign against it, and Germany would be left with a protracted, two-front war it might not be able to win. Moltke's inclination to launch offensive operations in Lorraine endangered not only the campaign in the West, but also the position of Germany in the entire conflict.

Moltke could not resist pursuing the weakened and retreating French forces in Lorraine, however. The massive statue of his uncle and predecessor as chief of staff—Helmuth von Moltke, who had devised the great victories of Prussia in 1866 and 1870–1871—that he could see from his office window every day cast a shadow under which the uninspired younger Moltke pined for victories in his own right. In August 1914 he had added pressure from Crown Prince Rupprecht, who urged him to take the offensive in Lorraine. Since the prince was heir to the throne of the second largest state after Prussia in the German Empire, Moltke's decision was doubtlessly colored by the delicate prestige politics of the Second Reich. Even if Prussia dominated the political and military landscape of the Empire, it nevertheless had to concede some laurels to the lesser states, particularly the Catholic monarchies of southern Germany, which had joined the united nation last and with circumspection. A victory won by Bavarian troops under their crown prince would have given them a measure of regional pride and deepened their bonds with the Empire.

These factors did not change the fact that Schlieffen had been right about the folly of an offensive in Lorraine. Indeed, Moltke's counterattack had no far-reaching benefits for the German campaign and actually worsened the strategic situation on the Western Front, though it did enjoy some modest success after it began on 24 August. The French troops on the Meurthe, especially the XX Corps under the future hero of the Marne, General Ferdinand Foch, offered heavy resistance, but in the next two weeks the superior German forces pushed them back into French territory. The Germans captured about ten thousand prisoners and a substantial amount of French supplies over the course of the offensive, yet a major breakthrough remained elusive. At its deepest, the German advance drove only twenty-five miles into France before it encountered strong defensive positions in the wooded high ground along the Meuse and Moselle Rivers. The front there barely moved for the rest of the war.

Ironically, German strategic planners had long dismissed the effectiveness of an attack through Lorraine precisely because of its difficult topography. A large modern army that had to move fast in order to ensure victory in the West, and ultimately the success of Schlieffen's two-front strategy, needed a highly developed infrastructure, which that part of France lacked.

Although the German high command was certainly aware of the problems of moving armies through Lorraine, it persisted nevertheless. After a month of active warfare, the surprisingly stiff resistance of the Belgian army and the resilience of the British and French forces opposing the larger German attack in the West had frustrated any swift conclusion of the campaign. The transfer—needless as it turned out—of two entire corps to meet an unexpected Russian offensive in East Prussia had further weakened German capabilities in Belgium and northern France. With their initial repulse of the French incursion into German Lorraine and subsequent successes on French soil, the armies under Rupprecht and Heeringen seemed to command their sector and offered a solid prospect of success, perhaps even a breakthrough that would effect a "double envelopment" of the French forces. Even though the German armies moving through Belgium proved to be in need of reinforcements, there was little likelihood that high-quality, experienced troops would be transferred from the Lorraine front. When Moltke proposed that course of action on 3 September to save the larger campaign, Prince Rupprecht strenuously contested his orders. The coincidental presence of Kaiser William II at Rupprecht's headquarters and his personal support for a continued attack in Lorraine persuaded Moltke to retract the command. A more confident chief of staff, such as his uncle before him, might have stood his ground and made a strong case for transferring troops to Belgium, but Moltke was too weak and indecisive to stand up to the kaiser. Instead he backed down and accepted the stalemate that dominated the Western Front for most of the war.

LORRAINE

Most significantly of all, the Lorraine offensive actually eased the task of the French army forestalling the main German attack in the north. By moving forward into French territory, the German attack blunted the contours of the "sack" in which Schlieffen had planned to encircle the bulk of the French forces and shortened the main front that the French had to defend. As the German forces moving through Belgium turned south, the French were more concentrated and better able to offer effective resistance. Had Moltke ordered the Sixth and Seventh Armies to fall back before the French or merely hold back their initial advance into German territory, the French First and Second Armies would have been arrayed in exposed forward positions that would have been several days' march from the developing front along the Franco-Belgian frontier. Since the German offensive had pushed the French invaders back to the defensible line of the Moselle, however, the rested and resupplied French troops could quickly and easily be shifted to meet the Germans advancing over the northern plain. No less a figure than Foch, the victor of the Marne, was transferred from his corps in Lorraine to take command of the Ninth Army in early September. Several corps from the French First and Second Armies were transferred in their entirety to the Marne, where they played an instrumental role in the battle that stopped the larger German offensive.

If these forces had been engaged in offensive operations inside German territory at that critical time, the ease and speed of their transfer would have been much less assured. By driving the French troops in Lorraine back into interior lines of defense, the Germans helped cripple their own campaign.

–PAUL DU QUENOY,
GEORGETOWN UNIVERSITY

References

Otto Friedrich, *Blood and Iron: From Bismarck to Hitler, the von Moltke Family's Impact on German History* (New York: HarperCollins, 1995).

Hermann Gackenholz, *Entscheidung in Lothvingen 1914* (Berlin: Junker & Dünnhaupt, 1933).

John Keegan, *The First World War* (London: Hutchinson, 1998).

Konrad Krofft von Dellmensingen, *Die Führundes Krunprinzen Rupprecht von Bayevn . . . bin zur Schlacht im Lothringen in August 1914* (Berlin: Mittler, 1925).

Barbara W. Tuchman, *The Guns of August* (New York: Macmillan, 1962).

LORRAINE

LOST GENERATION

Did the Great War create a "lost generation"?

Viewpoint: Yes. The war did in fact exact a disproportionate physical and psychic toll on Europe's "best and brightest" young men.

Viewpoint: No. The "lost generation" was an invention of the interwar years, a convenient excuse for those who failed to meet the challenges that arose after 1918.

World War I democratized service: about one-half of the men between eighteen and fifty years of age in the major combatant countries were put into uniform. World War I democratized sacrifice: nearly half of the men who served died or became casualties. It is correspondingly unsurprising that after 1918 one of the most-frequent images was of a "lost generation," a term used by Gertrude Stein to describe a group of American writers who experienced World War I and wrote in the 1920s, and also used by Ernest Hemingway in the epigraph for *The Sun Also Rises* (1926). Initially this concept was built around those returned veterans who seemed to have lost their way and themselves at the front. For many of its participants, the war experience could not be processed into their postwar lives. The literary examples offered by such writers as Robert Graves, Hemingway, and Erich Maria Remarque were replicated in every village and every urban neighborhood. Veterans of previous wars had also returned traumatized, but their numbers had been small enough to enable their marginalization. After 1918 the veterans who could find no peace reached critical mass.

Increasingly the concept of a "lost generation" acquired another context. There arose in all the major combatant nations an image of youthful talent destroyed in the trenches before it had time to flourish. The concept involved not only artists, musicians, and writers. In universities, parliaments, and foreign offices as well, those who eventually replaced the wartime generations expressed a consistent sense of taking the places of better, more-qualified men killed at the Somme (1916), Verdun (1916), or Passchendaele (1917).

This belief was a logical, almost a natural, consequence of what might be called a generalized case of survivor's syndrome. Processes of memory and mourning were insufficient to overcome traumatic grief on the scale that Europe was experiencing. These processes were insufficient as well to provide perspective to men who frequently processed their survival as an accident: being on a course when the rest of their companies were wiped out in an attack; or even as a form of cowardice: letting someone else go forward with the wire cutters, or taking a staff job behind the lines while the real men went back to the front. It was not a good attitude to bring to the overlapping crises of the 1930s—especially when confronting men such as Adolf Hitler, who believed the war had spared them for a higher purpose.

Viewpoint:
Yes. The war did in fact exact a disproportionate physical and psychic toll on Europe's "best and brightest" young men.

When the Great War at last ended, Europeans hoped to pick up their lives where they had been interrupted four years before. It would not be easy. The war had killed greater numbers of soldiers than all other conflicts in European history put together, and maimed even more. Horrifying as the losses were, German, British, and French survivors had to deal with other factors that further complicated a return to normal life. The majority of those who served in the war, and thus the majority of those killed, were young men in the prime of their lives. To lose a loved one or friend was difficult; to lose so many innocents was almost unbearable. The way that the war was fought also ensured that a disproportionate number of its young victims came from the educated elite of Europe. When the war ended, entire classes at the prestigious universities of Britain, France, and Germany did not return, and there were many budding poets, writers, and other artists who would never realize their full potential. It was no wonder that Europeans felt that a generation had been lost in the mud of the Western Front. There was another "lost generation" as well. The experience of trench warfare scarred the survivors just as deeply as enemy shelling. Millions of men became the walking wounded, truly lost souls who would never be able to adjust to the postwar world.

In terms of sheer numbers, the Great War exacted a terrible toll from Europe: almost 9.5 million men died during the conflict, while another 15 million were seriously wounded. Men who fought at the front at times saw the loss of entire units, mostly the result of the grinding attrition that both sides eventually adopted as their strategy. What did this loss mean in real-life terms? Guy Chapman, a thoughtful soldier who participated in some of the worst fighting in Flanders, wrote in *A Passionate Prodigality: Fragments of Autobiography* (1933) that of the 350 men in his battalion who entered the Somme at the end of September 1916, only 8 were left a week later. Giles E. M. Eyre, who saw himself as but one of the "poor bloody infantrymen," noted in *Somme Harvest: Memories of a P.B.I. in the Summer of 1916* (1938) that after just twenty days at the front he was the sole survivor of his section. The 29th Division, one of the best British units, lost the equivalent of seven times its official strength during the war. During the battles of Verdun (1916), the Somme (1916), Ypres (1917), and other major offensives, entire divisions melted away before the intense shelling and machine-gun fire "like snow before the sun," one soldier, R. Hugh Knyvett, wrote in *"Over There" with the Australians* (1918).

Added to the horror of these losses was the fact that so many of those who died were very young. Some had not even finished secondary school—they lied to be able to join up—and many more were just beginning their adult lives as fathers, husbands, and scholars. Memoirs, diaries, and even paintings from the war emphasize the extreme youth of so many who fought and died on the Western Front. This toll was not, of course, unusual. Most armies are made up of the young, and military service in Europe since the nineteenth century had focused on early adulthood to provide the most promising soldier material. The Great War was, however, the first conflict in which entire age groups were drafted en masse in all of the belligerent countries, and therefore the first to see such extensive losses of one age group. Scholars have estimated that Germany, for instance, sacrificed about 36 percent of its young men aged nineteen to twenty-two, and the losses for France and Britain (which experienced proportionately higher casualties than Germany overall) were just as terrible. The deaths of such a significant proportion of European youth left a gap that was felt by every family.

The other cohort of men lost in the trenches of the Western Front was from the young university- and public-school-educated elite of Europe. There were two reasons that a disproportionate percentage of these men became casualties of the Great War. In the first place, higher education was for the privileged few, and university-educated men were groomed to lead from the moment they began their studies. When the war broke out, the most conscientious of the elite volunteered to serve, prompted by their sense of duty to their nation. The development of the stalemate would later force Germany, France, and Britain to mobilize even larger armies, whose demand for junior officers far exceeded the supply of regular and reserve officers available. To fill the gap, it was only natural to recruit these future leaders from the universities. Once on the battlefield, a second factor came into play. Because there was no way to communicate with one's soldiers other than by being physically present (radios, telegraphs, and telephones were not yet suitable for this purpose), junior officers had to lead from the front. This requirement meant that they were generally among the first "over

LOST GENERATION

the top" during an offensive, and on "quiet" sectors they were expected to lead dangerous raids into the enemy's lines. The result, naturally, was carnage. As recorded in *Memoirs of an Infantry Officer* (1930), when Siegfried Sassoon's battalion assaulted the German lines in a minor offensive that is barely mentioned in the history books, every officer except for one became a casualty. This slaughter was not unusual. As more than one memoirist noted, the average life span of a British subaltern on the Western Front was three weeks.

Among these educated young men were a large number of intellectuals, artists, and sons of statesmen, many of whom were being groomed for leadership positions throughout Europe. While it would not be fair to say that Europe lost all of its "best and brightest" in the Great War, each of the men who died took with him a talent and potential that could never be replaced. One study of Britons who perished in the war—Reginald Pound's *The Lost Generation of 1914* (1964)—lists hundreds of young scholars, poets, writers, musicians, children of noble birth, and even Olympic athletes who died in battle or from disease on the Western Front. This attention to one group is not to denigrate the sacrifices made by others, but Europeans believed that there was something especially tragic about a life like that of the poet Rupert Brooke, which was cut short in 1915 before all of his genius could be realized.

Then there was the "lost" generation that returned from the battlefields. Men who survived the Great War knew that they were not the same people who had marched off to battle so willingly a few years before. Again, this circumstance is not unusual. Every soldier who fights in the front lines has experiences that alter his perceptions and life and make it difficult to fit into peacetime existence. The soldiers who struggled on the Western Front, however, had special problems reintegrating into ordinary life, and many of them felt like strangers in their own countries for the rest of their lives. The harsh and unearthly conditions of trench warfare created a world for its dwellers that was like nothing any humans had ever undergone. Yet, somehow, men learned to adjust to trench existence in order to survive and they became familiar, if not comfortable, with this strange new world. Having learned to fit into an alien landscape and the deadly routines of war, soldiers nonetheless found even before the conflict ended that old friends in their home countries understood neither them nor the trenches that had become the central focus of their lives. The feeling was mutual. Men who returned from the front saw their homelands with new eyes and became critical of the hypocrisy that they believed they saw all

around. Each time Sassoon returned to Britain, he was more and more alienated from his family, friends, and nation. Civilians, he felt, could never understand the war, and there was "no earthly use trying to explain things to them." After the armistice this alienation was expressed in antiwar books such as Remarque's *All Quiet on the Western Front* (1929), Robert Graves's *Good-bye to All That: An Autobiography* (1929), and Henri Barbusse's *Le Feu* (1917); in the paintings of Otto Dix, Max Beckmann, and Paul Nash; and in such cases as the fiction of dozens of writers who fought in the war or, in works by John Dos Passos and Hemingway, who at least were at the front. Not only were men "lost" because of the war, but some of European art had been as well.

Lost in an even more profound sense were soldiers who suffered shell shock or who went insane because of their experiences at the front. About 65,000 former British soldiers drew disability pensions because of various nervous disorders after the war ended; German and French soldiers experienced similar rates. This sum does not include the far larger number of men who suffered shell shock at any point during the war—most never fully recovered—nor those who endured decades of what we would now call "post-traumatic stress disorder." For the Great War taught Europe, as the war in Vietnam (ended 1975) would teach America: that a generation may be lost in more ways than one.

—MARY HABECK,
YALE UNIVERSITY

Viewpoint:
No. The "lost generation" was an invention of the interwar years, a convenient excuse for those who failed to meet the challenges that arose after 1918.

The concept of a lost generation rests on dubious demographic premises and is in essence a myth in the strictest sense of the term. That is to say, it was an explanatory narrative used to make sense of the world rather than a simple reflection of reality. There were distinct national variations, but they were bound together by concerns that antedated the war: long-term demographic anxiety, cultural disorientation, and a crisis of confidence within the social elite. These factors had relatively little to do with actual death tolls.

The proposition that demographic loss automatically undermines the cultural, politi-

The remains of soldiers on Deadman's Hill, Verdun, 1916

(postcard in scrapbook, Joseph M. Bruccoli Great War Collection, Thomas Cooper Library, University of South Carolina)

cal, and economic vitality of a society is readily and easily proved false. The most obvious example is the impact of the Black Death on late-medieval Europe. Catastrophic demographic loss on the order of 25 to 35 percent of the whole European population had genuinely traumatic effects on a population living under the shadow of "King Death." In the Europe of 1400 it was perfectly plausible on empirical grounds to believe the world was coming to an end. The objective result of the plague, however, was not cultural, economic, and political decline but the transformation generally referred to as the "Renaissance." To take another example nearer chronologically to World War I, between 1840 and 1900, contrary to global demographic trends, only one European nation suffered catastrophic population loss. Ireland experienced first the mass death of the famine, followed by a slow but major drain from emigration. Yet, again, there is no question that Ireland was economically, politically, and above all culturally a more dynamic society in 1900 than it had been in 1840.

It is worth noting that both of these examples represent high absolute levels of demographic loss. The European experience of 1910 to 1920 did not even come close to reaching a similar statistic. Significant population decline in Europe during the decade that spanned World War I is almost unknown. Only in Serbia is it clear that the population was actually reduced during this period. Out-side of Europe the only radical population decline was in Anatolia, scene of brutal ethnic cleansing. This population reduction was in the context not only of the war but also the global Spanish influenza pandemic (1919) which, measured globally, killed more people than the war.

For all the murderous horror of World War I, it did not stop, or even appreciably slow, the overall growth of the European population. In fact, the population of Europe (outside the U.S.S.R.) grew from 295 million in 1900 to 393 million in 1950 despite the impact of two world wars. While this figure is a slower rate of growth than in the previous half century, the difference is almost entirely attributable to radical fertility decline rather than increased war-related mortality, which was comfortably compensated in most cases by radical improvements in ordinary life expectancy.

The European nations went into World War I on the back of a demographic explosion. Taken overall, the birth cohort 1890–1900, the "war generation," was one of the largest in European history. Did the war destroy them? Nowhere is the mythology of a lost generation stronger than in the United Kingdom. If one compares the censuses of 1911 and 1931 one finds that the absolute number of young, middle-aged males (for example, between thirty and thirty-nine years of age) was almost precisely the same in the two censuses (2.7 million). Furthermore, when

LOST GENERATION

EARLY SACRIFICE

Some Americans did not wait for the United States to join the war but volunteered to serve in a variety of capacities, such as infantrymen, pilots, doctors, and ambulance drivers. A generation of young men served early in World War I, some of whom are remembered here by E. A. McKenzie:

What have the Americans done? Many of them, the very pick of the nation, gave themselves as volunteers. The great Universities, headed by Harvard, have sent doctors and hospital staffs to nurse the sick and wounded. Groups of rich young men crossed the Atlantic when war broke out, bringing their own automobiles with them, and formed the nucleus of the splendid ambulance services that have been of incalculable service of France. . . .

Americans were so eager to join the ranks of the French Army that military laws were relaxed for their benefit. The record of the American Flying Squadron in the French service is one of great brilliancy, even in that corps d'elite of France. The British roll of honor gives frequently the names of American born soldiers who have laid down their lives for the Allies.

Look at the record of Americans who have died for Britain and France. It is a very remarkable list, more especially for the quality of the men enrolled. There are Harold Chapin, born in Brooklyn, at the beginning of a brilliant career as a dramatist, and Alan Seeger, of old New England stock, whom three nations to-day hail as poet and hero. Kenneth Weeks, who died at Givenchy, twenty-four years old, had already done notable work in letters. Dilwym Starr, of Philadelphia, a Harvard man, took his place in the ranks of the British Expeditionary Force, won

his commission, and died on the Somme. Officers in the United States Army like Major Stewart and Captain Wood, on the staff of General Leonard Wood, resigned their commissions to join us, and fell for us. American students from the Latin Quarter, University men galore, sturdy plainsmen and men from the West, have died side by side with the sons of Britain fighting for justice and liberty. Many others, happily, are still alive, wearing on their breasts the ribbons of medals they have won for gallant conduct in the field.

What drew them to us? Some came because of the instinct of race and blood. "The army of my race and tongue," said Frederick Palmer, the distinguished war correspondent, when he found himself with the British Forces. Some came because of historic memories. "I am paying for Lafayette and Rochambeau," said Kiffin Rockwell, the steel-nerved airman, shortly before his death. . . .

Alan Seeger, shortly before he died, gave another reason:

"Can sneerers triumph in the charge they made,
That from a war where Freedom was at stake,
    America withheld and, daunted, stood aside.
Now heaven be thanked, we gave a few brave drops;
Now heaven be thanked, a few brave drops were ours."

Source: *Charles F. Horne, Source Records of the Great War, volume 4 (Indianapolis: American Legion, 1930), pp. 262–264.*

---

one looks at the next younger generation in the 1931 census, the postwar generation aged twenty to twenty-nine, one sees a significant increase from 2.9 million to 3.3 million. If by a lost generation one is implying a shortage of young adult males "in the prime of life" in the postwar period, then it is clear demographic nonsense. Both in absolute numbers and as a proportion of society as a whole, 1931 represents a historic peak in the United Kingdom.

This demographic spike should not be too surprising. British deaths in World War I represented just more than 12 percent of the men mobilized for the armed forces. The mobilized

population in turn represented about 50 percent of the men of military age. So 6 percent of British males of military age died during the war. Even though these casualties were heavily concentrated in the 1891–1900 cohort, it was, it should be remembered, a huge cohort (numbering almost 3 million in 1911), the overwhelming majority of whom were not killed during the war.

As a result to a large extent among prominent, opinionated individuals, not least the recurrent conservative Prime Minister Stanley Baldwin, for whom it was a favorite lachrymose theme, the British seemed to have

LOST GENERATION

accepted the idea of a lost generation peculiarly strongly, despite the day-to-day evidence otherwise. In fact, Britain got off lightly in demographic terms compared with some European nations. The cut was much deeper in France, which overall lost substantially more men from a significantly smaller population of military age. The demographic consequences of the war were far more severe in France. Even though a majority of young Frenchmen survived, it was a more narrow majority than in the British (or indeed German) case based on a smaller initial population. The lost generation had a greater degree of empirical reality in France, but it cannot and should not be considered in isolation. Postwar concern in France was more concentrated on the demographic "hollow years," less concerned with the dead themselves than with the children they had failed to have. This central concern of strategic demography did not begin in 1919; it had raged for two generations before World War I. The conflict intensified but did not create an existing trend.

So if the lost generation was not about actual deaths, what was it about? It is interesting that the term has a particular and specific resonance in the United States. The Americans took to the term in a sense that did not relate to the war dead at all—unsurprisingly because, however personally painful, American deaths in the war bordered on the demographically trivial. Instead the "lost generation" explicitly referred to the survivors, or rather a small subset of survivors: the American émigré writers in Paris. The application of the term to Ernest Hemingway and F. Scott Fitzgerald, alive and prolific, shows the degree to which the word *lost* was being used in a different sense, indicating drift, confusion, and disorientation.

The war had killed people, but to a much greater extent it had killed certainty. That this result was far more about the living than the dead should be self-evident. The world was not suffering from any obvious loss of creative energy in the post–World War I period—quite the contrary. In just about any sphere of creative human endeavor, the interwar years were almost feverishly dynamic—a continuation rather than a break with the prewar era. Arguably only one of the prewar artistic giants, French poet Guillaume Appolinaire, fell victim to the war and his loss is an arguable case. German painter Franz Marc (killed at Verdun in 1916) was probably a serious loss. A roll call of other major artistic figures—Pablo Picasso, Fernand Léger, Henri Matisse, Marc Chagall, Max Beckmann, Gustav Klimt, Emilio Marinetti, T. S. Eliot, Ezra Pound, Marcel Proust, James Joyce, Alfred Döblin, André Gide, Igor

Stravinsky, and on ad infinitum—produces a loud cry of "present" in 1919. Judged as collective biography, the history of European art could more or less ignore World War I. Much the same could be said of philosophy and the social sciences—the war interrupted but did not derail the careers of Ludwig Josef Johan Wittgenstein and John Maynard Keynes.

The loss of talent in wartime is in the end speculative. One cannot judge lost potential. To take two of the most famous and poignant cases, what was the real loss to British poetry through the death in action of Wilfred Owen and Isaac Rosenberg? Poignant as Owen's poetry is, it is difficult to imagine him becoming a literary giant to equal Eliot or W. H. Auden; Rosenberg might have achieved literary fame, but it is unproven. The postwar career of Siegfried Lorraine Sassoon does not suggest a major literary loss if he had been killed rather than seriously wounded in summer 1918. Likewise, if Robert Graves had been killed rather than wounded in 1916, the world would have lost a great deal of interesting prose, but no major work.

This conclusion sounds callous and to a degree it is, but the lost-generation mythology has its own dubious assumptions. The mythology was inherently elitist and even eugenic. At the heart of the myth was the disproportionate casualty list of the social elites. The casualty rate of Oxford University was approximately double that of the national average; similar comments can be made about the German *Gymnasien* or French *Grand Ecoles*. When interwar politicians were mourning the lost generation, they were not particularly mourning a lost generation of clerks and shop workers (although these groups, too, suffered heavily). The assumption behind this mythology was implicitly and often explicitly aristocratic—the war was interpreted as a dysgenic disaster because those of the best birth had been killed. The fact that the prewar elite was far from meritocratic was never allowed to enter into the argument and the possibility that the death toll among the elite might in fact have led to improved opportunities for some of lower social status (including a small number of women) was not seriously entertained.

Regarding politics, given that under normal circumstances political careers reach their peak when individuals are in their fifties and sixties, it is unsurprising that the "generation of 1914" did not dominate interwar politics. They were not missing so much as in junior positions. In fact, by the 1940s and 1950s this generation emerged in dominant roles, as one would expect. From 1940 to 1964 five successive British prime ministers were veterans of the trenches. This political genesis was not atypical. Future American president Harry S Truman was a veteran of the campaign in France, while Dwight David Eisenhower, another future American president, had held a staff position in World War I. French premier Charles de Gaulle was a veteran both of the front lines and of German prisoner-of-war camps; Yugoslav president Tito had served in the Hapsburg army and had been captured by the Russians. In two peculiar cases the war generation had come to prominence much earlier. In Fascist Italy and Nazi Germany, self-consciously "youthful" political regimes, the war generation was prominent. That, however, is scarcely good advertising for the legend of the lost.

–ADRIAN GREGORY,
OXFORD UNIVERSITY

References

Guy Chapman, *A Passionate Prodigality: Fragments of Autobiography* (London: Nicholson & Watson, 1933).

Giles E. M. Eyre, *Somme Harvest: Memories of a P.B.I. in the Summer of 1916* (London: London Stamp Exchange, 1938).

Niall Ferguson, *The Pity of War* (New York: BasicBooks, 1999).

Ernst Jünger, *The Storm of Steel: From the Diary of a German Storm-troop Officer on the Western Front* (London: Chatto & Windus, 1929).

John Keegan, *The First World War* (New York: Knopf, 1999).

R. Hugh Knyvett, *"Over There" with the Australians* (New York: Scribners, 1918; London: Hodder & Stoughton, 1918).

Bernard Martin, *Poor Bloody Infantry: A Subaltern on the Western Front, 1916–1917* (London: Murray, 1987).

Reginald Pound, *The Lost Generation of 1914* (New York: Coward-McCann, 1964).

Erich Maria Remarque, *All Quiet on the Western Front,* translated by A. W. Wheen (London: Putnam, 1929).

Siegfried Sassoon, *Memoirs of an Infantry Officer* (London: Faber & Faber, 1930; New York: Coward-McCann, 1930).

NEW WEAPONS

Did World War I accelerate the technological development of weaponry?

Viewpoint: Yes. The synergies of technical development of weaponry during World War I represented a marked change in the conduct of war as well as the attitudes about it.

Viewpoint: No. The technological innovations introduced in 1914–1918 were part of a continuum of increasingly improved firepower capabilities.

From the first days of the Great War the armies showed unusual degrees of flexibility and adaptability. When the shock approach employed in August and September failed, the generals turned to mass, emphasizing numbers of men and weight of shell to the point where within a year officers were complaining that their men had forgotten how to use their rifles and were neglecting the bayonet in favor of the hand grenade. Even the cavalries were largely reorganized as semi-mobile infantry or dismounted and converted to foot soldiers.

All that flexibility resulted in the loss of millions of men and the expenditure of tons of material for nothing resembling proportionate gains. Armies coped not by becoming technology centered but by becoming machine, as well as manpower, intensive. Increasing amounts of material, organic and manufactured, were transported by internal combustion engines, not only in Europe but also in such unlikely theaters as Mesopotamia and East Africa. The aviation industry developed under forced draft from machine-shop improvisation to assembly-line mass production, while the pace of aircraft technology rendered cutting-edge designs obsolete in a matter of months.

Closer to the front lines, artillery incorporated electronics, topography, and ballistics to the point where gunnery became a science. Light machine guns, hand and rifle grenades, trench mortars, and light guns combined in "platoon technologies" that made subalterns de facto commanders of combined-arms formations. The Germans broke ground with assault battalions that included flamethrowers and light artillery, with squadrons of specialized ground-attack aircraft, and by employing artillery by function instead of organization. The allies, especially the British, carried the combined-arms battle to the army corps level, integrating direct air support, armored-fighting vehicles, and infantry able to help itself by improvisation, and holding the whole together by a communications system increasingly depending on radios.

Machine war produced technowarriors. The French taught hundreds of Vietnamese peasants to drive trucks. High-performance aircraft weeded out the incompetent in ways as unmistakable as they were unpleasant. Tank crews spent as much time learning to understand their machines as how to use them to fight. The infantryman in all armies evolved toward the German archetype of the storm trooper—no longer victim, but master, of the modern battlefield. The armed forces of World War I may have seen new technologies less as a paradigm shift than as a way of doing the same things more effectively. Nevertheless, World War I witnessed a faster tempo of change than any subsequent conflict.

Viewpoint:
Yes. The synergies of technical development of weaponry during World War I represented a marked change in the conduct of war as well as the attitudes about it.

Before Europeans discovered in 1939 that they would have to number their "world wars," World War I was known as the "Great War." The implications of "great" were manifold: the geographical extent of the war, its intensity, the nearly nine million soldiers who died, the demise of four empires, and many other factors. An undeniable aspect of the "greatness" of World War I was the dramatic change in the technologies and associated ideas of waging war. The campaigns of 1914 were fought with the weapons and attitudes of fin de siècle Imperialist Europe, if not of the age of Napoleon Bonaparte. Yet, the campaigns of 1918 powerfully foreshadowed and largely determined the technologies, tactics, and techniques of mid-twentieth-century mechanized warfare. Indeed, the campaigns of 1939 resembled those of 1918 much more than 1918 resembled those of 1914. Developments in weaponry during the Great War, in short, constituted a military-technical revolution in warfare.

Weapons that emerged as practical and effective (if not decisive) technologies during World War I included aircraft (reconnaissance, pursuit or fighters, and both tactical and strategic bombers), tanks, poison gas, and submarines armed with long-range, self-propelled torpedoes. Viewed collectively, these weapons constituted much more than an incremental or evolutionary change in waging war. Rather, they were radically new ways of fighting and of thinking about war.

Aircraft constituted the most radical change in waging war. Fulfilling the dreams of visionaries such as the Italian Renaissance inventor Leonardo da Vinci, aircraft opened the skies not only to human travel but also to combat in three dimensions. By 1911 the element of air had joined earth and water as realms of human strife. After it became clear that World War I was not coming to a speedy conclusion, combatants actively sought technical advantages over their respective opponents. Aircraft held considerable promise, and the sheer quantity of resources devoted to their production was in itself astonishing. From humble beginnings in 1914 of 200 aircraft produced, British factories produced 14,700 aircraft in 1917 and another 32,000 in 1918.

Equally astonishing was the pace of aircraft qualitative development. In 1914, single-seat biplanes such as the British Bristol Scout went unarmed into battle in largely empty skies, relying on a then unprecedented speed of 90 miles per hour for protection. By 1918 thousands of scouts and fighters armed with synchronized machine guns fought for control of the skies, reaching speeds of 150 miles per hour and ceilings of nearly twenty thousand feet. More remarkable still was the rapid development of bombers. In 1914 bombers simply did not exist. By 1917 German multiengine *Gotha* bombers were carrying six 110-pound bombs in cross-Channel raids, with Britain responding in 1918 with the larger Handley Page, which carried sixteen 112-pound bombs (later models were designed to carry 3 tons of bombs). Recognizing contemporary contributions and the enormous promise of airpower, Britain created in 1918 a new, independent combat service—the Royal Air Force (RAF)—that by the end of the war counted 165,000 men on its roster. The RAF provided institutional confirmation that airpower had revolutionized warfare.

This revolution was not just restricted to the institutions or machinery of warfare but also included the very nature of war itself. Since civilians were essential to the war effort, especially in the production of munitions in factories, they became legitimate targets of aerial bombardment. Thus, the killing zone of World War I extended from the Western Front to the home front, as nations targeted their opponent's population in an attempt to weaken fatally its will to continue. Together with more traditional naval blockades and the torpedoing of ships without prior warning, aerial attacks on cities represented an unprecedented expansion of war to noncombatants.

On land, tanks served as catalysts for change in land warfare nearly equal to results achieved by aircraft. Rushed prematurely into combat during the Somme campaign in 1916, tanks initially proved cumbersome, prone to mechanical breakdown, and slow (two miles per hour cross-country). Scarcely two years later, however, the Allies possessed hundreds of tanks, instead of a few dozen, and improved models that included "fast" Whippet tanks that achieved eight miles per hour in favorable terrain. Used primarily to support infantry attacks, tanks served as force multipliers to previous, incremental, advances in infantry combat power achieved with light machine guns, trench mortars, improved grenades, and flamethrowers.

The synergistic combination of Allied tanks and aircraft with well-armed and supported infantry helped to restore a balance among shock, firepower, protection, and maneuver on the Western Front. This combination proved devastating to the German army at Amiens in August 1918. Subsequent Allied infantry

German zeppelin L-49, circa 1915

(postcard in scrapbook, Joseph M. Bruccoli Great War Collection, Thomas Cooper Library, University of South Carolina)

assaults, supported by tanks and aircraft and coordinated by improved command technologies (telegraphs, field telephones, and wireless radios), proved an effective if still costly operational approach that led ultimately to the collapse of Germany. Impressed by this Allied technological coup de main, the Germans developed their own interwar operational and tactical doctrine—known after the fact as blitzkrieg—based on shock, maneuver, and rapid exploitation by tanks supported closely by ground-attack aircraft. Such tightly coordinated, combined-arms assaults were impossible without well-integrated command and control networks.

Such networks encouraged new codes of behavior. Commanders began to reward subordinates, not for dronish displays of discipline or reverent adherence to "standard operating procedures," but for demonstrating initiative and a cultivated irreverence for SOPs. New technologies of war stimulated fresh habits of mind that rewarded militaries that encouraged imagination, decentralization, and interservice cooperation.

Poison gas provided more cautionary lessons but also lent its considerable reputation to World War I, which became known as "the chemist's war." (World War II, by contrast, became known as "the physicist's war" because of the development of radar and the atomic bomb, among other inventions.) For complicated reasons, poison gas in its various forms (ammonia, mustard, and phosgene) proved little more than a (sometimes) deadly nuisance on the Western Front. Techniques for delivery of gas against the enemy remained immature, with gas sometimes drifting unpredictably to incapacitate its users. Yet, used in combination with conventional artillery barrages, poison gas forced soldiers to don masks and other chemical gear that restricted their vision and sapped their endurance. The horrors of gas—made evident by more than half a million gas-related casualties on the Western Front and its frightening potential for reducing wars of the future to unheroic and inglorious exercises in human extermination—led thirty-eight countries to sign the Geneva Protocol in June 1925 that outlawed chemical attacks.

In World War I revolutionary, yet still immature, weapons such as tanks and aircraft proved most effective as supplements to established weapons such as artillery and machine guns (although tanks and aircraft largely replaced cavalry in its roles of exploitation and reconnaissance). That they served more as supplements than as war-winning weapons highlighted the critical importance of doctrine and the dynamic nature of technology and warfare on land. If tanks had been employed in the thousands in independent tank brigades, as proposed in J. F. C. Fuller's "Plan 1919," they may well have been

NEW WEAPONS

war-winning weapons. Correct doctrine was essential, as Fuller envisioned the enemy's headquarters, whose destruction would result in strategic paralysis, not its troops, as the main objective. As in science-fiction writer Robert A. Heinlein's *Starship Troopers* (1959), Fuller's tanks would risk all to capture or destroy the enemy's "brain bug," while avoiding costly attritional exchanges with infantry drones. Similarly, poison gas, dropped by the Italian general Giulio Douhet's proposed "battleplanes" on unprepared civilian populations, promised decisive if gruesome results. That tanks and poison gas demonstrated promise, not decisiveness, on the battlefield highlighted the primitive nature and complexity of land warfare, qualities that served to limit the effectiveness of any single weapon system.

In comparatively simpler environments such as air or sea, technological advances often proved to be of singular import and effectiveness. Such was the case for submarines and torpedoes. Confined initially to coastal defense in 1914, German submarines (known as U-boats) quickly proved their mettle against the superior British Royal Navy. The threat of surprise U-boat attacks restricted the movements of the Dreadnoughts, creating a virtual "No Man's Sea" in large swaths of ocean off the eastern coast of Britain. Instead of enforcing a close blockade, the Royal Navy redeployed the Grand Fleet to Scapa Flow in the Orkneys to enforce a "distant blockade." When the Dreadnoughts sallied forth from their sanctuaries, they employed nearly one hundred destroyers to screen them from torpedo attacks.

Of course, U-boats were most effective as commerce raiders, sinking nearly 750,000 tons of shipping in 1915 and millions more when the Germans resumed unrestricted submarine warfare in February 1917. German efforts to strangle the economy of Great Britain, however, ultimately failed because U-boats were simply too few in number. The Allies also developed effective tactics and weapons as countermeasures, the most important being the convoy system and extensive networks of magnetic mines and nets. Although not used until 1918, primitive ASDIC (named after the Anti-Submarine Detection Investigation Committee, and known in the United States as SONAR) also helped the Allies to locate submerged U-boats.

The asymmetrical threat posed by torpedo-firing U-boats fundamentally altered naval warfare. Caution and cunning—often informed by painstaking signals intelligence and code breaking—supplanted boldness and impetuous Nelsonian attempts to close with the enemy's fleet. The delivery of destruction at long distances, attained through technical proficiency in long-range gunnery, became de rigueur. Aircraft car-

riers loomed just beyond the naval horizon, which in the 1930s would extend the strike range of navies to hundreds of miles, instead of thousands of yards.

Unprecedented leaps in performance meant that the first-line ships of 1900 often became the funeral barges of 1916, with the pursuit aircraft of 1917 reduced to flying coffins if forced to dogfight with the new class of 1918. Rapid technological obsolescence was a new phenomenon associated with industrialized warfare accelerated by extensive research and development. Brown Bess muskets had outfitted the British infantry for more than one hundred years; Horatio Nelson's flagship, HMS *Victory,* had served its commander well at Trafalgar at the ripe age of forty. Yet, the ships and aircraft of World War I became death traps in a matter of years, even months.

Rapidity of change confounded commanders who were initially haunted more by memories of Napoleon or Nelson than by echoes of the ancient Greek god of fire Hephaestus's forge. Many officers, however, came to follow the echoes of the forge instead of Napoleon's ghost. B. H. Liddell Hart was among them. He concluded in 1933 that "The increasing influence of science on war, and the consequent acceleration of change . . . clearly indicate the need for intellectual ability in the higher posts of the Army equal to that of the leaders in other spheres." Americans responded with intelligence quotient (IQ) tests to distinguish innovators from cannon fodder.

To present-day readers accustomed to rapid and often decisive changes in technology, Liddell Hart's words appear unremarkable. Yet, they were remarkable for leaders of the World War I generation, who were more likely (at least initially) to dismiss science and technology as frivolous subjects for boffins. Especially notable in retrospect, however, was not the stodginess but the openness to innovation demonstrated by militaries, in spite of their rigid structures and emotional investment in tradition.

World War I witnessed the "invention of invention" within a military milieu. This new *mentalité* included a strong commitment to operational research and the creation of institutions to develop improved weaponry and associated doctrine. Mobilizing scientists and engineers for sustained and deliberate military research and development became a common trope. In Britain the Admiralty established the Board of Invention and Research in the summer of 1915. Not to be outdone, that same summer the army created the Munitions Inventions Department for land warfare, followed by an Air Inventions Committee in May 1917. France quickly mobilized its scientists in 1915 with the *Direction des*

Inventions Intéressant la Défense Nationale, among other boards and commissions. Similarly, the United States created the National Advisory Committee for Aeronautics (NACA) and the Naval Consulting Board (chaired by Thomas Alva Edison) in 1915 and the National Research Council in 1916 to respond directly to military needs. These institutions created a culture of scientific and technical competence within militaries that set the pattern for future relations among scientists, engineers, industrialists, and military men. They also set the stage for the emergence of massive military-industrial complexes during World War II.

Arguably the most significant change in this military-technical revolution was attitudinal. In 1914 many senior officers were much like C. S. Forester's fictional character Herbert Curzon in *The General* (1936): a cavalryman in no need of mental diversion, who boasted of his ignorance of artillery and machine guns. Yet, under conditions of seemingly ceaseless siege warfare on the Western Front, officers as technical experts reemerged as respectable figures. In some ways World War I represented a return to warfare of the early modern period, when military engineers such as Sébastien de Vauban wielded considerable power. Indeed, after the war the French built the Maginot Line, thereby placing their faith not in élan but in the power of defensive fortifications engineered with consummate skill. Thus, the specter of Vauban supplanted the ghost of Napoleon Bonaparte in French minds in the interwar period.

The rise of a military technocracy reflected the radical mechanization and bureaucratization of warfare that emerged by the end of the war. Taylorism and efficiency experts promoted warfare by timetable and production by automated assembly lines. Increasing specialization in combat roles led to the creation of Signal Corps—experts in the complexities of new command technologies. Carbon paper and typewriters proved as indispensable as shells and bullets to supporting combat formations and to extracting the maximum combat power from the limited economic and logistical resources of a nation.

As Dennis Showalter has rightly concluded in an article in *Great War, Total War: Combat and Mobilization on the Western Front, 1914–1918* (2000), edited by Roger Chickering and Stig Förster, "Men did more than adapt to Great War technology. They mastered it." Yet, in mastering it, they also became victims of its dynamic—of firepower, massive casualties, and warfare affected by even more uncertainty than in the past—for technology often produced uncertainty rather than determinism. While some postwar commentators railed against the "merchants of death," others recognized that "merchants of vic-

tory" might be a more accurate description of the synergistic potential of military-industrial-scientific collaboration. How best to maximize the potential of revolutionary technologies such as aircraft and tanks in synergistic combinations became the postwar question to answer. The Germans answered it best initially. They missed the subtlety, however, of the physics that ultimately led to the Manhattan Project and atomic weapons—a military-technical revolution that continues to haunt humanity to this day.

–WILLIAM J. ASTORE,
U.S. AIR FORCE ACADEMY

Viewpoint:
No. The technological innovations introduced in 1914–1918 were part of a continuum of increasingly improved firepower capabilities.

During World War I, commanders failed to adapt and adjust strategy and tactics to coincide with existing technological reality because they had rarely faced such technology. While there were a few exceptions to this rule, they simply neglected to learn obvious lessons from recent history.

When one considers the advancement of weapons technology since 1850, it is clear that the greatest change had taken place in military rifles. The U.S. Civil War (1861–1865) was fought almost entirely with muzzle-loading, "cap-and-ball," single-shot rifles, despite the fact that repeating rifles had already been developed by several gun manufacturers. The designs of the repeaters were rejected by the Army Ordnance Department because of the strain these weapons would cause in the already strapped supply system—there were too many varying types of ammunition. There was an increase in the casualty rates as a result of the change to rifles, primarily a result of the increased accuracy and range of the weapons. Although the war began with Napoleonic tactics, trench warfare evolved over time to increase survivability. By the Battle of Fredericksburg (1862) the typical scene more resembled the trenches of World War I than a Napoleonic battlefield.

The first use of military breech-loading rifles on both sides of a conflict occurred in the Franco-Prussian War (1870–1871). The Prussians used the "needle gun," named for its abnormally long firing pin, which used paper cartridges; the French used the Chassepot rifle, which had a tighter breech and was in

NEW WEAPONS

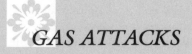

GAS ATTACKS

Captain A. F. P. Christison of the 6th (S) Battalion, Queen's Own Cameron Highlanders, recalls a gas attack in the trenches on 13 July 1917.

. . . . I was going round my forward trench when the Germans started shelling steadily, but with small stuff, and we could not understand why the shells all seemed to be duds. One shell landed in my trench almost beside me and did not burst—just a sort of plop. I felt a burning sensation just above my right knee and heard the man next to me cough and retch. I realised this was something very odd and shouted 'Gas' and quickly put on my respirator. The gas alarm immediately sounded and, as we were good at our gas drill, only five or six of my Company were gassed. Captain Rowan heard the gas alarm and his men put on respirators. After wearing them for some time in the heat of the morning and no attack developing they thought the original alarm was false as no gas had been smelt. What they did not know was that this was mustard gas, had no smell, and had delayed action. The C Company trenches were saturated with stuff and the whole Company were struck down. By nightfall every officer and man was either dead or in hospital.

Corporal H. Bale of the 242nd Brigade, Royal Field Artillery, recalls a gas attack on his position:

We had about eight hours of mustard gas shells, churning into the ground at the side of the battery. I was on duty on the signalling pit, working by a candle and with a mask on. After about six hours, the masks were no good. They'd been neutralized, and we were starting to choke. No. 6 Gun was quite close to the battery pit which was like a shed with a few sandbags on the top of it and a tarpaulin over the doorway, and every time No. 6 Gun went off, it blew out my candle. What with a mask on and doing everything by buzzer, it was rather difficult! By morning, everyone was round the shell holes vomiting and they had to send quite a lot of people out to bring us in. We need one on each side of us, we were in such a bad way, and they took us back into a trench by the side of the road to wait for transport. The fellows were getting a bit panicky, couldn't get their breath, and I remember saying to myself, "Hold tight and take no notice," but breathing was very difficult. Eventually, they brought down a GS wagon, a great big thing, and we got into that. I had a terrible cramp in the stomach through vomiting, and as we were going slow, the road gradually seemed to fade away. By the time we got to Vlamertinghe we were blind, we couldn't see anything. They led us down into the dressing-station, sat us on a plank and told us, "Open your mouths." We waited with out mouths open and suddenly someone shot something like 200 per cent ammonia into your mouth. It nearly knocked the top of your head off. We got bathed and put into bed and I don't remember anything more till I woke up in the hospital at the base. It was the 4th Canadian General, and I was there for a long time. Stone blind!"

Source: *Lyn MacDonald, ed., 1914–1918: Voices and Images of the Great War (London: Michael Joseph, 1988), pp. 222–223.*

general a superior weapon. The next time such mass armies would gather on the continent, it would be with magazine-fed, bolt-action, repeating rifles. The sheer volume of fire increased in addition to its accuracy. Furthermore, the Europeans and the Americans began to focus some attention on marksmanship during training—something almost unheard of until the late nineteenth century.

Many commanders claimed they did not know what would happen with this increase in firepower, but they should have, especially the British and Americans. British forces suffered significant casualties in the Second Anglo-Boer War (1899–1902) against the Boers armed with Mauser rifles—almost the same weapon the Germans used twenty years later; while the Americans faced Mausers in the hands of the Spanish during the Spanish-American War (1898). Both countries were victorious despite the superiority of the Mauser, and were determined not to repeat the same mistake of having inferior weapons.

In the United States, Colonel John Thompson of Springfield Armory was directed to copy and improve the Mauser. He copied it, but said he could not improve it, so he changed the caliber to .30–06 (from 7.92mm) and created the M1903A1 "Springfield," which became the mainstay of the U.S. military until the 1930s (in fact the U.S. Marines continued to use it until late 1942).

NEW WEAPONS

The British produced their own bolt-action rifle, the .303 Lee-Enfield, which remained in service until the 1950s.

As these weapons were in the inventory for almost fifteen years before World War I, and since both the British and the Americans had seen what they were capable of under battlefield conditions, there was no excuse for what happened. Part of the answer was a cultural myopia. The French, long considered as having the best military in the world, along with the best military theorists, had an almost cultural affinity for offensive action. The lesson they took from Napoleon Bonaparte was that the offensive is always superior to the defensive. That idea fit perfectly with the French soldier's psyche and affinity for the attack. Around this concept grew what has come to be known as the "Cult of the Bayonet" or of the "Offensive." Their defeat by the Prussians in 1870–1871 did not change this outlook. For when they read the Prussian theorist Carl von Clausewitz, they read into his works what they wanted, thereby "validating" their preconceived notions despite the unmistakable reality of their defeat. Strangely, although Clausewitz was Prussian and his theories were used successfully by the Prussians against the French, most countries accepted the French interpretation of his writings. This reading produced French, British, and, to a lesser extent, American armies with an imbued sense of the Cult of the Bayonet, which doomed millions unnecessarily during the war.

Rapid-fire weaponry had been in use since the U.S. Civil War and should have been no surprise to World War I commanders, as its effect on the battlefield was well known to those who cared to look. Regardless of the ignorance of World War I commanders of this situation, the effects of these weapons were well known to the troops in the trenches. However, the machine gun was seen as a "defensive" weapon and both the French and British eschewed practices "contrary" to offensive doctrine (for example, building adequate trenches and fortifications). They believed such actions would diminish the "offensive spirit," or elán, of their fighting forces.

Despite all the emphasis thus far on light weapons, the truth is that the majority of the casualties during the war came as a result of artillery fire. Yet, in this realm too, there was little that was "revolutionary." Artillery had been getting bigger and heavier, as well as more deadly, with greater range and mobility, for three hundred years. A perfect example of this advance is the Gribeauval System of artillery boring from France, which led to modern artillery. Instead of casting the cannon around the bore or hole, the eighteenth-century French general Jean-Baptiste de Gribeauval cast the cannon in one solid piece and used a precision drill to bore the hole. This method ensured uniformity of barrel thickness and, when combined with better metallurgical practices, enabled greater charges to be used with more devastating effect. Further, the Gribeauval system called for the use of horse-drawn limbers to take the guns directly onto the battlefield, thereby increasing their mobility and agility. During the U.S. Civil War, the Union developed rifled guns and exploding projectiles, while later, the Prussians developed steel, breech-loading guns to add to those advances. These changes made the guns more accurate, sturdier, and lighter. They used these new guns during their three wars of unification (1864–1871), and the British faced these developments in the Anglo-Boer War after the Germans supplied the Boers with Krupp guns. Again, these weapons were a known entity.

Air warfare would, seemingly, be the most "revolutionary" technology of the entire war, yet, air power did not change the outcome of the war by a single day, according to the official postwar air-power survey. Although this conclusion seems overly harsh, it is true nonetheless. The greatest problem was that later developments demonstrating just how devastating air power really could be were still several decades away. The airplane of 1914 was primarily useful for only limited missions. At first, airplanes were used for many of the same roles as mounted cavalry; scouting and reconnaissance in particular. In fact, the French discovered the Germans turned too soon when executing the Schlieffen Plan in 1914 through an aerial observer. Once they confirmed this maneuver, they stopped the evacuation of Paris and sent every available soldier to meet the Germans. The ensuing battle was soon called the "Miracle at the Marne."

Initially, the airplanes of both sides were insufficient to do much more than take a single man aloft to conduct reconnaissance. It quickly became clear, however, that the war would continue into the air when aviators started assuming additional cavalry roles, such as pursuit. The engines were initially not powerful enough to lift the plane, aviator, and a machine gun into the air. This problem was the engines—the airframe was not sturdy enough to withstand the vibrations of powerful motors. At the same time, even if the engine could get the pilot and gun aloft, the recoil of the machine gun would have been too much for the plane. The development of sturdier airframes, stronger engines, and lighter machine guns all helped to create a new breed of aviator—the pursuit, or fighter, pilot. Units of these aviators patrolled sectors of the front and hunted for enemy airplanes.

A similar development of better airframes helped to create more powerful bombers. Aerial bombardment using lighter-than-air ships was a natural extension of the concept of air power; and the Germans, with their zeppelins, were at a distinct advantage over the Allies. Still, the use of heavier-than-air ships was desirable because they could fly faster than the pursuit fighters, albeit at lower altitudes than the zeppelins.

Along with this change came the slow development of aerial tactics that made the air war worthwhile. Foremost among the World War I aerial tacticians was the German Oswald Boelcke, whose "Dicta Boelcke" are still taught to fledgling fighter pilots around the world. That the air war did not shorten the conflict notwithstanding, air power was not without potential. The main reason the use of planes in combat did not achieve a greater outcome was the result, in part, to the nullification of advantage by one side over the other.

Chemical weapons also had the potential to be revolutionary, as these weapons were truly new. Although the Germans achieved decisive results on the Eastern Front using CS gas (a class of tear gas that was outlawed in 1993 for use in war), the same did not hold true with their use of more deadly chemical agents such as "mustard" gas. First used at the Second Battle of Ypres in 1915, mustard gas devastated the unprotected Algerian (French) line of defense. Although the potential for a critical breakthrough lay before them, the Germans could not advance far into the breach because they had not anticipated such success and therefore had no gas masks of their own. Their gas was as dangerous to them as to the enemy. Gas never achieved the status of a breakthrough weapon critical to winning the war because by the time the Germans had enough gas masks, the Allies did too, which nullified the German advantage and ended any decisive exploitation.

The real problem of World War I was not that technology outpaced doctrine. Rather, it outpaced many generals on both sides, their prejudices, and their refusal to change their thinking to match reality. They were faced with stalemate and were intellectually ill prepared to deal with it because their concept of doctrine, which was decidedly Napoleonic, albeit with a Clausewitzian flair, did not allow for stalemate. Under their concept of reality, which was imbued with the Cult of the Bayonet/Offensive, the moral (motivated men with bayonets) would always overcome the physical (fortified trenches, machine guns, and artillery). The consequences of their false paradigm never seemed to come home to them, for their answer always lay with creating better motivation in the men and then throwing them forward.

A large part of the problem lay in the fact that none of these armies had faced a "first class," or a European, army in almost three generations. Further, colonial experiences led World War I commanders to a false sense of superiority—in spite of the battle of Isandhlwana (1879) as well as the Anglo-Boer War. They should not have been so smug.

The greatest irony of the war was that the solution to the stalemate was with them all along—combined arms. They had tried combining infantry with artillery in the rolling barrage, where the shells would land close enough to the advancing infantry to protect them but not too close as to harm them. In practice, this strategy failed because of a lack of adequate maps and the need to maintain precise schedules. Armor made its first appearance at the Somme in 1916 but was really just a failure of expecting too much, too soon. The tanks broke down and were unable to keep up or be of any real use. Then, in late 1917, the Allies developed better tanks (with stronger engines and more reliable treads) and accurate maps and combined these improvements with their infantry, artillery, and flying squadrons into a coordinated offensive. The artillery weakened the enemy as the tanks led the infantry advance with the airplanes in support. This redefinition of the doctrinal concept of combined arms, which had existed for centuries, combined with technological evolution of existing technologies resulted in the first significant Allied gains in the three years of the war to that point.

The Germans were paying attention, however, and launched their own combined-arms offensive in the spring of 1918. To the same choreography, with the same branches of forces, the Germans added two new innovations. They put armor plating on the fuselages of some aircraft dedicated to ground attack, thus protecting both the plane and pilot trained for ground attack. The other German innovation was in creating shock troops. These specially trained soldiers operated in a completely new manner. Rather than charging headlong like lemmings, they moved with purpose, using any cover available. They penetrated the enemy defenses and opened paths for the main combined arms advance. When the Germans launched their offensive, it succeeded even more than they could have hoped. They advanced thirty-five miles in a war that had, hitherto, measured success in yards. They finally stopped only because of fatigue and supply problems. Strangely, just when both sides had discovered a formula for success in this war, it ended. The Germans were not really defeated on the battlefield but at home when their government fell apart from the civil unrest caused by the war and the ensuing blockades that devastated their homeland.

There were technologies in World War I that were unseen before: gas and tanks. However, it was mostly an improvement of already existing technologies and the inability of the generals on both sides to change the thinking that caused the stalemate. The answer did not lie with creation of new technologies but rather with an evolution of existing doctrine, strategy, and tactics to meld with the evolution of technologies. The German Spring offensive of 1918 was a success without adequate armor support. The answer was there all along. It just needed the right minds to develop it.

—WILLIAM KAUTT, UNIVERSITY OF
ULSTER AT JORDANSTOWN

References

Giulio Douhet, *Il dominio dell'aria* (1921), translated as *The Command of the Air,* by Dino Ferrari (New York: Coward-McCann, 1942).

C. S. Forester, *The General* (London: Joseph, 1936).

Ludwig F. Haber, *The Poisonous Cloud: Chemical Warfare in the First World War* (Oxford & New York: Oxford University Press, 1986).

Guy Hartcup, *The War of Invention: Scientific Developments, 1914–18* (London & Washington: Brassey's, 1988).

Basil H. Liddell Hart, *The Ghost of Napoleon* (London: Faber & Faber, 1933).

Williamson Murray and Allan R. Millett, eds., *Military Innovation in the Interwar Period* (Cambridge & New York: Cambridge University Press, 1996).

Dennis Showalter, "Mass Warfare and the Impact of Technology," in *Great War, Total War: Combat and Mobilization on the Western Front, 1914–1918,* edited by Roger Chickering and Stig Förster (Cambridge & New York: Cambridge University Press, 2000), pp. 73–93.

Tim Travers, *How the War Was Won: Command and Technology in the British Army on the Western Front, 1917–1918* (London & New York: Routledge, 1992).

NEW WEAPONS

ORGANIZED RELIGION

Did organized religion support the war efforts of the various nations involved in the Great War?

Viewpoint: Yes. Many Christian denominations, motivated by patriotism, viewed the struggle as a spiritual test of their respective nations' moral virtue.

Viewpoint: No. The churches provided one of the first influential sources of challenge to specific aspects of the war's conduct.

Perhaps no single Western institution emerged from the Great War more damaged than did organized Christianity. From the beginning of the conflict, clergymen of all faiths blessed the war and its artifacts, urged enthusiastic participation by their communicants, and proclaimed God's support for activities that direct participants saw as having more to do with Satan. The interconnect of war and religion was a logical consequence of the synergy of church and state that took place in the course of the nineteenth century. In return for noninterference in ecclesiastical affairs, the various state churches abandoned prophetic and minatory functions relative to the public sphere, concentrating instead on cultivating private piety and excoriating private vices.

It was a comfortable system. European society before and during the war was identifiably and affirmatively Christian, though actual churchgoing was increasingly optional. Nor was it remarkable that from the beginning of the war churches provided what comfort they could to civilians mourning lost sons. Clergymen were largely drawn from the middling reaches of their respective societies and from those men who aspired to rise in the secular world by serving the spiritual. It was not promising ground for dissenters, and even the most bitter opponent of the war in principle was hardly likely to denounce the conflict at a memorial service for its dead. Predictable too was the integration of Christian imagery and metaphor into wartime propaganda by politicians raised and educated in Christian contexts. As for the enthusiastic support of clerics at all levels for the war effort, it was the first time many of them had actually been listened to by their congregations since ordination, and they responded with alacrity.

Individual soldiers of all armies found or strengthened religious convictions during their military service. In few cases, however, did that process have anything to do with an institutional church. Combatants instead frequently noted the absence of military chaplains from the combat zones. This condition was no reflection on the personal courage of clergymen in uniform. The German army was strict about keeping its chaplains in rear areas. The French army, serving an avowedly secularist republic, went to war with only four chaplains at each corps headquarters and an additional one for each division—a "parish" that would be considered excessively large in a big city. British ratios were closer to one chaplain to a battalion—but there too regulations and, to some degree, custom restricted where and when he could be present. An often-remarked exception were the Roman Catholics, mostly Irish, who saw their duty in the front lines, ministering directly to the stricken. The contrast with their Anglican counterparts was so often remarked upon that a British Expeditionary Force (BEF) legend had a colonel requesting a Catholic chaplain for his battalion, on grounds of the mass conversion of his men.

Study of the records shows that Church of England padres in no way stood behind Roman Catholics, "RCs," in taking risks. The point seems to have been that the spiritual consolations they conveyed paled before the everyday facts of large-scale death and mutilation. A Catholic chaplain who anointed a dying man conveyed a sense of certainty about the afterlife that few Anglicans—and few Continental chaplains of any faith—were able to do. Again, an exception must be made for the thousands of French priests conscripted as ordinary soldiers. Many served in the ranks; others were assigned, for obvious reasons, as stretcher-bearers. They too seemed better able than their official counterparts to convey a sense of salvation and immortality—perhaps because, like the Roman Catholic chaplains of the BEF, they were perceived as "outsiders" relative to the state system that demanded and took lives on such an unprecedented scale.

Viewpoint:
Yes. Many Christian denominations, motivated by patriotism, viewed the struggle as a spiritual test of their respective nations' moral virtue.

If the nineteenth century witnessed the "death of God" in some quarters, in the years leading up to World War I there was increased evangelization by individuals from Christian countries cooperating in international agencies. Evangelicals were particularly optimistic in the United States. Yet, Christian optimism and international cooperation were early casualties when the guns of August sounded in 1914. Churches in Britain, France, Germany, and (later) the United States were quick to ally themselves fully with the war efforts of their respective nations. In the major Christian denominations, virulent declarations of nationalism and jingoism commonly supplanted traditional and ecumenical professions of faith.

Moral righteousness and outrage characterized the rhetoric of the Allies from the start. The heavy-handed German violation of neutral Belgium, the burning of the library at the University of Louvain, and extensive damage to Rheims Cathedral became immediate Allied *causes célèbres*. The novelist Henry James spoke for many when he wrote to Edith Wharton on 21 September 1914 that

> Reims *is* the most unspeakable & immeasurable terror & infamy—& what is appalling & heartbreaking is that it's *forever & ever*! But no words fill the abyss of it—nor touch it, nor relieve one's heart nor light by a spark the blackness; the ache of one's howl & the anguish of one's execration aren't mitigated by a shade even as one brands it as the most hideous crime ever perpetrated against the mind of man.

Accounts of German atrocities of unprecedented hideousness captured headlines in Allied nations throughout the autumn of 1914. German war crimes were exaggerated, then roundly condemned, as rhetoric replaced reality. The demonization of the "Hun" made compromise nearly impossible.

In this vituperative climate of "crusading-apocalyptic war hysteria," concludes Albert Marrin's *The Last Crusade: The Church of England in the First World War* (1974), clergymen of all persuasions in the Church of England "took up the call for a holy war." Prominent Anglican clergy such as the Bishop of Chelmsford implored "all men of military age, as a religious duty, to take their stand with their brothers at the Front." Union Jacks replaced Christian pulpit cloths as Anglican clergy attempted to persuade eligible males in their flocks to enlist and to fight overseas in defense of all that was good, noble, and just. Not to be outdone, Scottish Presbyterians also embraced the war with evangelical fervor. Belgium, declared the Reverend Walter Mursell of Paisley, "is Christ for us today." More than half a million Scotsmen answered the call of the British Empire for a holy crusade against the barbarous and treacherous Huns.

Forbidden by canon law to enlist for combat, Anglican clergy nevertheless contributed their own sons to the war effort. They filled a disproportionate 30 percent of the officer billets in Lord Horatio Kitchener's army. The clergy themselves volunteered for National Service projects that included work as engineers, auto mechanics, and constables. Some served at the front as chaplains, although Anglican chaplains were forbidden to go forward of brigade headquarters, a stipulation that did not apply to Catholic chaplains. "Sacrifice" became the operative word in the struggle for the soul of Europe—a struggle steeped in blood at the Somme (1916), Ypres (1917), and other battlefields.

Ministers who suggested bloodless sacrifices found themselves ostracized. After suggesting in 1915 that Britain should provide an example of political compromise and high-minded magnanimity by internationalizing Gibraltar, the Reverend Edward Lyttelton, headmaster of Eton, was hounded from his position for supposedly scheming to hand "the Rock" to Germany. Writing in November 1914, British journalist Rebecca West succinctly captured the reactionary conformity of British public opinion, which extended to secular intellectuals as well as clergy:

> Disgust at the daily deathbed which is Europe has made us hunger and thirst for kindly ways of righteousness, and we want to save our souls. And the immediate result of this desire will probably be a devastating reaction towards conservatism of thought and intellectual stagnation. Not unnaturally we shall scuttle for safety towards militarism and orthodoxy. Life will be lived as it might be in some white village among English elms; while the boys are drilling on the green we shall look up at the church spire and take it as proven that it is pointing to God with final accuracy.

Many nations, not just Great Britain, believed that God guarded and guaranteed the rectitude of their war efforts. In France, vicious anticlericalism and patent distrust of Catholics gave way to the *Union Sacrée*. Distrusted before the war as antirepublican agents, French curés (priests) gained newfound respect as they shared in the sacrifices of the *poilu* (the common soldier). Unlike Anglican clergy, curés were subject to conscription. They served in the trenches as soldiers and medics, lending their moral weight to the French war effort. Their frontline feats, combined with the triumphs of Ferdinand Foch—a devout Catholic whose brother served in the Jesuit order—showed that Catholics could fight for France with the same ferocity, tenacity, and commitment as socialists and Dreyfusards. In their unhesitating embrace and support of the war effort, echoed in their calls for righteous revanche, French Catholics found redemption in the eyes of their countrymen.

Equally as convinced of the moral rectitude of their war efforts were German Protestants. Seeing themselves as the rightful inheritors of Martin Luther's legacy, German Protestants celebrated their own sacred union between church and state, altar and throne, crucifix and sword. German soldiers had only to glance down at their belt buckles, engraved with *Gott mit uns* (God is with us), to be reminded of their national belief that God marched with them. In their eagerness to embrace the German military, a few Protestant ministers raised their own boys' battalions, an effort that made even the Prussian War Ministry blanch. Disseminating radical, nationalistic propaganda became the modus operandi, even the raison d'être, of the German Protestant League, a mainly petit bourgeois organization that recruited half a million members in three thousand local chapters. Germany witnessed the complete formalizing of religion in the service of the state, one that at its fringes advanced an Aryan myth of racial superiority that became a progenitor of the racist state religion of Nazi Germany.

All of these nations, including the United States, viewed the war as a spiritual test of moral fitness. Initially, President Woodrow Wilson, joined by most Americans, found moral virtue in remaining studiously neutral. Dissenting voices were muted. As the United States drifted toward war, however, critics became more numerous and vocal. One of the more vocal was William Jennings Bryan, who resigned as secretary of state in 1915 to protest warmongering criticism of Germany in wake of the sinking of the *Lusitania*.

The decision of Germany to resume unrestricted submarine warfare as of 1 February 1917, however, persuaded most Americans that President Wilson's description of the Great War as a moral crusade that would make the world safe for democracy was fitting and morally proper. Stern Presbyterian that he was, Wilson found plenty of like-minded supporters. Statements by three prominent Protestant clergymen might be taken as typical. According to Lyman Abbott, the German army was the "most efficient band of brigands" yet known to world history. The evangelist Billy Sunday went further and declared: "If you turn hell upside down, you will find 'Made in Germany' stamped on the bottom." The sober and more established Shailer Mathews of the University of Chicago Divinity School concluded that "for an American to refuse to share in the present war . . . is not Christian."

The popular anti-German testimony of ministers such as Newell Hillis was simply too lurid and compelling for Americans to ignore. A prominent Congregational clergyman, Hillis tore across the country in 1917, selling Liberty Bonds for the war effort (his campaign raised an impressive $100 million in forty-six days). Author of such books as *German Atrocities, Their Nature and Philosophy, Studies in Belgium and France during July and August of 1917* and *The Blot on the Kaiser's 'Scutcheon* (both published in 1918), Hillis portrayed every German *boche* as benighted fiends—denizens of Hieronymus Bosch's spectacularly twisted canvases

Interior view of the
Cathedral of Notre Dame
in Amiens, France, 1918;
the sandbags are for
protection against
bombardment.

(Roger Viollet)

of hell. The German, Hillis wrote, will never "realize the wickedness of his own atrocities and the crimes of militarism until he sees the horrors of war with his own eyes, hears the groans of his own family, and sees his own land laid desolate." Ultimately responsible were German officers, "men who have given up all faith in God, who practise the Ten Commandments with the 'not' left out, who have stamped out of the souls of their soldiers every instinct of pity and sympathy." In Hillis's inflamed account, only total victory could extirpate the total depravity of the Hun butchers of Belgium. Here Hillis cited the words of an anonymous physician: "I have seen Belgium; I have seen a lamb torn by the wolf; I am on the side of the lamb."

The religiosity of language in the Great War was intense and widespread, as Paul Fussell noted in his groundbreaking study *The Great War and Modern Memory* (1975). Words and concepts such as "sacrifice," "atonement," "higher calling," "mission," and many others were redolent with Christian imagery and spiritual meaning. But, whereas Fussell saw irony as the key concept of Oxbridge-educated war poets, "sacrifice" was more suitable, and unironic, to middlebrow shopkeepers and minor bureaucrats, who saw nobility in the

sacrifice of their nation despite the meanness, dirtiness, pettiness, and seemingly random brutality and futility of trench warfare.

Unwavering commitment to the state and national military service was evident even in supranational churches. Prior to 1917, American Catholics tended to uphold neutrality. Naturally, German-American Catholics tended to sympathize with the Central Powers, as did English-hating Irish Americans. Yet, in April 1917 American Catholics quickly fell into line with the declaration of war by Congress against Germany. On 5 April 1917, the day before Congress declared war, Cardinal James Gibbons proclaimed that "The primary duty of a citizen is loyalty to country. This loyalty is . . . exhibited by an absolute and unreserved obedience to his country's call." Once Congress issued the call to arms, Gibbons declared that "the members of both Houses of Congress are the instruments of God in guiding us in our civic duties." Not surprisingly, Gibbons won high praise for his manly patriotism from former president Theodore Roosevelt.

Catholic laity showed by their deeds that they agreed with Wilson's crusade. More than a million Catholics joined the American Expeditionary Force (AEF), with Catholic chaplains expanding from 28 to 1,525 in number

A BELGIAN CARDINAL ADDRESSES THE GERMANS

On 24 November 1915 Cardinal Désiré J. Mercier, the Archbishop of Malines, wrote a letter to the German bishops about the atrocities carried out by German troops during the occupation of Belgium. After denying reports that the citizenry had savagely attacked German soldiers, he wrote:

. . . the Bishop of Namur asked for an interview with the Military Governor of Namur, and protested against the accusation which the Emperor sought to make against the Belgian clergy. He maintained the innocence of all the members of the clergy who had been shot or ill-treated, and declared that he was himself ready to publish any guilty deeds which were in reality established.

The offer of the Bishop of Namur was not accepted, and his protest had no result.

Calumny was thus given a free course. The German Press fomented it. The organ of the Catholic Centre, the *Cologne Peoples' Gazette* rivaled the Lutheran Press in its chauvinism, and on the day when thousands of our fellow citizens (ecclesiastics and laity from Visé, Aerschot, Wesemel, Hérent, Louvain, and twenty other localities, as innocent of deeds of war or of cruelties as you and we), were taken prisoners, led through the stations of Aix-la-Chapelle and Cologne, and for hours were exhibited as a spectacle for the morbid curiosity of the Rhenish metropolis, they had the pain of finding that their Catholic brethren poured out as many insults on them as the Lutherans of Celle, Soltau and Magdebourg.

Not a voice in Germany was raised in defense of the victims.

For we, through direct experience, know and declare that the German army gave itself up in Belgium, in a hundred different places, to plundering, incendiarism, imprisonments, massacres and sacrileges, contrary to all justice and to every sentiment of humanity.

We declare this, notably in the cases of the communes, the names of which appeared in our Pastoral Letters and in the two notes addressed by the Bishops of Namur and of Liége, on October 31st and November 1st, 1915, respectively, to His Holiness, Pope Benedict XV, to His Excellency, the Nuncio at Brussels, and to the ministers or representatives of neutral countries in residence at Brussels.

Fifty innocent priests and thousands of innocent Catholics were put to death; hundreds of others, whose lives have been saved by circumstances independent of the will of their persecutors, were in danger of death; thousands of innocent persons, with no previous trial, were imprisoned; many of them underwent months of detention, and, when they were released, the most minute questioning, to which they were submitted, revealed no guilt in any of them.

These crimes cry to heaven for vengeance.

If, in formulating these denunciations, we are calumniating the German army, or, if the military authority had just reasons for commanding or permitting these acts which we call criminal, it is to the honour and the national interest of Germany to confute us. So long as German justice is denied we claim the right and the duty of denouncing what, in all sincerity, we consider as a grave attack on justice and on our honour.

Source: *Désiré Mercier,* The Voice of Belgium: Being the War Utterances of Cardinal Mercier, *with a Preface by Cardinal Bourne (London: Burns & Oates, 1917), pp. 159–160, 167–168.*

to serve the AEF. The most famous chaplain was Father Francis Duffy of the "Fighting Sixty-Ninth" New York Regiment, whose statue in battle dress occupies a commanding position in Times Square in Manhattan. American Catholics also banded together to create the National Catholic War Council to support war-loan drives and chaplains serving overseas with the troops.

Like Catholics in France, although for different reasons, American Catholics wanted to demonstrate their patriotism to their fellow, non-Catholic countrymen. Still strongly distrusted by Nativists—supposedly because of their supranational loyalty and commitment to the Pope—American Catholics charted a via media (middle way) between the prejudice of their countrymen and the opposition to the war expressed by Pope Benedict XV.

For German Catholics, justifying a fratricidal war against fellow Catholics in France posed more troublesome questions. Heinrich Schrörs, professor of theology at the University of Bonn in West Germany, answered them by shifting the focus of the debate. Russian militarism was the immediate cause of the war, Schrörs suggested, and German Catholics were fighting to contain the spread of Pan-Slavism and Eastern Orthodox Christianity, which, if left unchecked, would end in the "Greek-Russian Church" dominating the world. Like their counterparts in France and the United States, German Catholics had their loyalty and patriotism questioned by their fellow countrymen (Otto von Bismarck's *Kulturkampf* had provided the sternest test). Catholics in all three countries attempted to show their true colors by marching to the colors and by supporting unreservedly the wartime policies of their respective governments.

One might suggest other reasons why major Christian denominations expressed few reservations concerning the war. Guilt experienced by some ministers may have been a factor. Secure in comfortable surroundings in the village parish, forbidden by canon law to serve in combat, Anglican clergymen perhaps felt an overriding need to assert their patriotism and manliness by supporting the government and its policies to prosecute the war. The need to provide consolation to parishioners who had lost loved ones in the war may also have silenced doubt and suppressed dissent. Condemning the activities of the enemy—both internal slackers and external foes—also made for stimulating sermons that parishioners found more relevant and compelling than standard theological fare. Opposition to the war, moreover, was associated more with "fringe," or nonconformist, religious sects such as Quakers, not with the muscular Christianity of committed believers of the main Protestant sects. Conscientious objectors, it was believed, were more likely to emerge from the ranks of godless radicals, not God-fearing Christians.

In the years leading up to World War I the main Christian denominations also faced increased competition from secularism, mysticism, and spiritualism. If ministers objected too strenuously to war, against the prevailing sentiment of their flock, they risked becoming irrelevant as shepherds. That their charges might wander away from Christianity to search for comfort, solace, and a sense of purpose in the greener pastures of non-Christian belief systems was a legitimate concern shared by many ministers. After the war, many of the bereaved turned to spiritualism and other non-Christian practices in an attempt to find consolation and closure.

To the chagrin of Christian clergymen in many countries, rabid displays of nationalism and unqualified support of government policies and war directives did not win the permanent allegiance of Christians, many of whom became alienated by the war and its less-than-satisfying resolution at Versailles (1919). Having abandoned the moral high ground during the war, Christian denominations found it difficult to reoccupy it in the interwar period. Many efforts to outlaw war went forward, such as the Pact of Paris (1928); many international condemnations of war were made. Tragically, none proved compelling, as nations began to beat plowshares into swords again in the 1930s with little opposition from mainstream Christian denominations.

—WILLIAM J. ASTORE, U.S. AIR
FORCE ACADEMY

Viewpoint:
No. The churches provided one of the first influential sources of challenge to specific aspects of the war's conduct.

The answer to this question is problematic as it presupposes that "organized religion" is, or was, unified in its response to World War I. This question is not one of "it," but rather "they," for even inside specific religions or belief systems, there were deep divides between denominations and sects. Truly, what must be discussed is "how did Christianity respond to the war?" For although there were non-Christians involved (citizens in the Ottoman Empire, Arabs, Jews, Indians, and other Asians, not to mention Africans) in large numbers, most discussions of the war assume a Eurocentric view, which means that Christianity was in the fore. Christianity claims the allegiance of two-fifths of the world population—about two billion people—and has three main branches: Catholicism, Protestantism, and Orthodoxy. Yet, while there is one Catholic Church (with its Roman and other rites united under the Pope) and about a dozen Orthodox national churches (which are loosely confederated), there are approximately 36,000 denominations of Protestantism. To suggest that this great multitude of believers agree with one another is ludicrous. So then, to speak in terms of what "religion" in some generic sense did or did not do during the war is simply impossible. However, what is possible is to examine the roles of specific groups within Christianity and their reactions during the war.

The Catholic Church is the natural choice of subject, as it is the largest single denomination of Christianity, with slightly more than one billion members. It is also the most global of all religious groups. Still, many people have an interestingly dichotomous attitude toward the Catholic Church. These people frequently are in vehement opposition to it for doctrinal or other reasons, yet have a peculiar tendency to look to Rome for vicarious leadership, some kind of moral compass, in spite of their religious attitude against it. Finally, the Catholic Church holds an unusual place among the religions of the world in that it is the only religious group to have its own sovereign nation—Vatican City. It is important to note that the status of the Vatican during World War I was not quite what it is today, as it was technically still under siege by the Italian state. The Lateran Treaty, which ended the state of hostilities between the Vatican and Italy, was not signed until 1928. This treaty also guaranteed the sovereign status of the Vatican. Yet, many countries retained diplomatic relations with the Holy See throughout this era.

This status, neutrality, and broad representation throughout the world, however, gave the Church a special position. It was beholden unto no political master as other churches were. While this condition was also true of many denominations in the United States, none of them had the reach of the Catholic Church. Most Christian denominations in Europe were either disunited or the official religion of their country and therefore were under the influence of the government. In the British Empire the Anglican Church supported the war effort, but this stance was only to be expected, as the head of the Church could not be neutral. This wholehearted support from the Anglican Church extended from the United Kingdom to Canada and Australia, to India and South Africa, and to the colonies. This situation was also true of the Orthodox Greeks, Russians, Serbs, and Armenians. A similar point can be made about Islam in the Ottoman Empire, but the similarity cannot be taken too far as Islam does not have the same hierarchical structure. Jewish Zionists also supported the war after they were promised a homeland in Palestine in the Balfour Declaration (1917). The other Protestant groups in Europe, such as the Lutherans, were also fairly nationalistic. The Catholic Church was the only religious group with any significant num-

bers in all the belligerent countries (although there were few in the Ottoman Empire). It truly was the only neutral group capable of even attempting to stop the war or to change it.

While the Catholic Church was unified and doctrinally identical throughout the world, the structure of national churches offers some interesting national distinctions. Ireland is a good case in point; the Church in Ireland originally supported the war effort against Germany but then turned against it over time. When Germany executed the Schlieffen Plan in 1914, they had to march through predominantly Catholic Belgium in order to reach the proper position to begin their swing to the southeast. This violation of the neutrality of Belgium brought Great Britain into the war—or gave it the excuse to get involved, depending on one's point of view. During the march through Belgium, reports began to surface about the most horrific crimes being committed by the invaders, prompting the Allies to label the Germans "Huns." While there were some incidents of civilians being killed by "collateral damage," and some who were shot for resisting, there was no organized campaign of terror. Worse still, reports also came back claiming the Huns were committing atrocities against Catholic priests, monks, and nuns. These reports, likewise, were propaganda, created to stir up public sentiment against the Germans; it was the beginning of the dehumanization campaign against them.

As the reports of mass casualties returned from the front, the Church responded with the same horror as everyone else. People steeled themselves with the grim determination it would take to see the war through. The Church cooperated with the national efforts to provide relief to the victims of war—widows of soldiers, their children, the wounded and maimed, and the families of these people. The extent of devastation is difficult to comprehend on a human scale. Fully an entire generation of young men died on the Western Front. So devastating was the carnage that society was hard-pressed to deal with it. The Church helped where it could.

The Catholic Church in the United Kingdom reacted with horror at these reports and decided that the war against Germany was "just" according to doctrine. Under this determination, since the cause of the war was not against the laws of God, the Church in the United Kingdom was free to assist the state in this war. They lent their support, moral and otherwise, to the recruiting campaign. There was also an initial outpouring of popular support that lasted for some considerable time.

The same was true, to a lesser extent, in Ireland, but to many Irishmen it made no sense to go to the Continent to "fight for the rights of small nations" when they could do the same at home.

By 1916 the situation began to change in Ireland. In April of that year, Irish rebels began what would come to be known as the Easter Rising. They seized key points in Dublin and proclaimed an Irish Republic. The rebellion lasted six days and was put down by British troops, who were cheered by the Dubliners as they marched in. During the Rising, the Catholic Bishops of Ireland condemned the revolt, for rebellion against lawful authority is considered a sin under Canon Law. Yet, when the Rising ended and the British continued a reign of terror in which loyal subjects were murdered, the Church also took notice. It protested the secret trials of the rebel leaders, in which they were not permitted any defense, as well as their immediate execution without the right of appeal. Indeed, the mood throughout Ireland shifted. The Church continued its support for the British war effort, albeit without as much vehemence as before, while keeping one eye on the situation in Ireland.

By 1917 the war in Europe showed no signs of abating; in fact, the loss of Russia to Bolshevism meant that hundreds of thousands of German and Austrian troops were freed for another assault in the west. This news made Britain all the more desperate to replace their losses and add more men to their defensive line. As conscription was not in effect in Ireland up to that point, the logical choice was to use this as yet untapped manpower source. The only problem with this plan was that it would prove to be horrendously unpopular with the Irish people.

When the government moved to extend conscription to Ireland in 1918, it was met with mass demonstrations and rallies by the "ordinary" Irish people (with republicans fomenting this rebellion). Mindful of their treatment at the hands of British troops after the Rising, the idea of fighting for king and country or for "small nations" rang particularly hollow to the average Irishman. As the situation intensified, with both sides increasing their rhetoric, the Irish Council of Bishops came down squarely on the anti-Conscription side when they said: "We consider that conscription forced in this way upon Ireland is an oppressive and inhuman law which the Irish people have a right to resist by every means that are consonant with the law of God." The situation ended with the British government backing down.

All of this vacillation suggests that there was no organized response from Rome itself during the war. This situation is not the case. Cardinal Secretary of State Pietro Gasparri and Secretary of the Congregation of Ecclesiastical Affairs Eugenio Pacelli were directed by Pope Benedict XV to maintain diplomatic relations with the warring powers. They also set about ceaselessly working on behalf of the victims of war. They organized relief, provided aid to all in need, and spearheaded assistance to civilians on all sides of the conflict. They also advocated on behalf of prisoners of war to ensure their safe return and humane treatment.

In 1917 Monsignor Pacelli was ordained a bishop and consecrated an archbishop for his assignment as Papal Nuncio to the German kingdom of Bavaria—the only German state with which the Vatican had diplomatic relations. The assignment of Archbishop Pacelli to Munich was critical to the efforts of the Vatican to end the war. That they ultimately were unsuccessful notwithstanding, the Pope and his representatives did all they could while maintaining their neutrality. Yet, this posting to Munich was extremely important to the future history of the world, for Pacelli remained there until 1928, when he became Cardinal Secretary of State under Pope Pius XI. During his time in Munich, Pacelli saw the rise of socialism and communism and their replacement by National Socialism. Pacelli would learn, firsthand, what the Nazis were about and begin his opposition to them. As Pope Pius XII during World War II he maintained the Church's official neutrality, but he also helped save almost one million Jews.

During the World War I, however, Archbishop Pacelli tried to do what he could to ease suffering. He handed out food to the poor in the streets of Munich, even though he himself did not have enough to eat. He helped create a peace plan, which was similar to the one that President Woodrow Wilson put forward about a year later, to end the fighting. It was rejected by Kaiser William II. He assisted in the repatriation of 65,000 prisoners of war and helped the Vatican spend money to ease suffering wherever it could. Upon his death in 1922, Pope Benedict XV had spent so much money on relief to those in need from the war that the Vatican had to borrow to pay for his funeral.

The question of whether religion did enough during World War I depends largely upon whom one asks and which religion one asks about. It is also a question of what could religion really do? The "official" religions may have been guilty of not being neutral, while the others may have been too neutral. Clearly, the Catholic Church and other denominations exerted what influence they had based on their moral determinations. Their actions, especially in the Catholic Church, were always undertaken to lessen the real suffering of people where they could.

–WILLIAM KAUTT, UNIVERSITY
OF ULSTER AT JORDANSTOWN

References

Ray H. Abrams, *Preachers Present Arms* (New York: Round Table Press, 1933).

Charles E. Bailey, "Gott Mit Uns: Germany's Protestant Theologians in the First World War," dissertation, University of Virginia, 1978.

Paul Fussell, *The Great War and Modern Memory* (New York: Oxford University Press, 1975).

Newell Dwight Hillis, "The Atrocities of Germany," in Frank H. Simonds, *History of the World War,* volume two (New York: Review of Reviews, 1919), pp. 328–345.

Gerlof D. Homan, *American Mennonites and the Great War, 1914–1918* (Waterloo, Ontario & Scottsdale, Pa.: Herald Press, 1994).

Arlie J. Hoover, *God, Germany, and Britain in the Great War: A Study in Clerical Nationalism* (New York: Praeger, 1989).

Gangolf Hübinger, "Religion and War in Imperial Germany," in *Anticipating Total War: The German and American Experiences, 1871–1914,* edited by Manfred F. Boemeke, Roger Chickering, and Stig Förster (Cambridge & New York: Cambridge University Press, 1999), pp. 125–135.

Albert Marrin, *The Last Crusade: The Church of England in the First World War* (Durham, N.C.: Duke University Press, 1974).

John F. Piper Jr., *The American Churches in World War I* (Athens: Ohio University Press, 1985).

Lyall H. Powers, ed., *Henry James and Edith Wharton: Letters, 1900–1915* (New York: Scribners, 1990).

Ronald J. Rychlak, *Hitler, the War, and the Pope* (Huntington, Ind.: Our Sunday Visitor, 2000).

OTTOMAN EMPIRE

Did the collapse of the Ottoman Empire during the war establish the conditions for the rise of the Turkish state afterward?

Viewpoint: Yes. Conflict with various European nations and internal Arab rebellion reduced the Ottoman Empire to a core Turkish state.

Viewpoint: No. The achievements of the Ottoman Empire during the war were remarkable, and its weaknesses and handicaps in no way prefigured a Turkish nationalist successor state.

The Ottoman Empire, like other multiethnic polities, underwent an identity crisis during the nineteenth century as two competing forms of nationalism influenced it. "State nationalism," like its counterpart in the Habsburg lands, emphasized patriotic identification with the Ottoman experience, reestablishing a common imperial identity, and modernizing at least two key institutions: armed forces and administration. This form of nationalism was at best accepting of the patchwork of ethnic identities that formed the Ottoman Empire; at best willing to tolerate a certain cultural autonomy if exercised with discretion. Its opposite pole was an ethnic nationalism that defined "homeland" not in the context of a multiethnic empire but as a particular community bound together by a specific ethnic and cultural heritage.

Initially, religion played a major role in the development of this latter form of nationalism. The Christian peoples of the Balkans and Anatolia had long been restive under an Islamic rule whose tolerance was often more apparent than real. Culture was significant as well. As early as the 1820s intellectuals in the Arabic-speaking provinces of the Empire began a process of rediscovering their particular histories—a process that often involved depicting Turks as "others": aliens, outsiders, and barbarians. The Turkish response, slow in developing, was nevertheless predictable. Like the Serbs, the Turks described themselves as deserving special recognition as bearers of an idea that transcended particular ethnic groups: in this case the idea of an Islamic empire dominating the Middle East.

The link between Turkish identity and Islamic unity persisted as the primarily Christian provinces of the Empire broke away in the second half of the nineteenth century. It endured after the Young Turk revolution (1908) brought a modernizing government to Constantinople and transformed the Sultan to a figurehead. The Balkan Wars (1911–1912), however, and the accompanying spread of open, armed revolt in the Arab provinces generated an alternative perspective: a vision, as yet unformed, of a Turkish or Turanian state, ethnically and culturally homogeneous. During World War I that vision took concrete form as conquest and rebellion sheared away more and more of the historic Ottoman Empire. The Russian Revolution (1917) provided fuel by offering the ephemeral hope of absorbing Turanian peoples of the fallen empire. In the end, however, Turkish nationalism took on a local form as a response to the Allied occupation of Anatolia and to the accompanying plans for parceling it out into spheres of influence. Kemal Atatürk, hero of the Great War, led a revolt that was initially both Islamic and nationalist, driving out Allied forces unwilling to embark on a fresh war of imperialist conquest, arranging population transfers with Greece, continuing persecution of other minority ethnic and religious communities in Anatolia, especially Kurds and Armenians. Kemal's victory was heralded throughout the Islamic world. It was doubly ironic that he used it as a springboard for the modernization and secularization of the new state of Turkey.

Viewpoint:
Yes. Conflict with various European nations and internal Arab rebellion reduced the Ottoman Empire to a core Turkish state.

The Great War for Turkey really lasted from September 1911 to July 1923. Except for a pause between September 1913 and November 1914, Turkey was at war during that entire twelve-year period. During the course of this series of wars, Turkey fought (in rough chronological order) Italy, Montenegro, Bulgaria, Serbia, Greece, Russia, Britain, France, Italy (again), and Greece (again). The Ottoman Empire also faced internal rebellions across the Arab world, most notably in Palestine, Arabia, and Mesopotamia. Given the preindustrial and fragmented nature of the Ottoman state, decline and contraction around a Turkish core were inevitable.

The inability of the Ottoman Empire to offer more than negligible resistance to an Italian invasion of Libya (1911–1912) did not bode well for the future. The Turkish army, far from supply lines, quickly abandoned Tripoli. The Turkish navy was unable to support the army, nor could it prevent the Italian navy from demonstrating in the Dardanelles and seizing the Dodecanese Islands. A little more than a year after the war began, the Treaty of Ouchy (18 October 1912) recognized conditions on the ground, with the Ottomans ceding Rhodes, the Dodecanese Islands, and all of Libya to Italy.

The Ottomans were forced to sign the Treaty of Ouchy because of more-pressing concerns closer to home. Seeing Ottoman defeat in the war with Italy as an opportunity, Montenegro, Bulgaria, Serbia, and Greece had formed a loose coalition known as the Balkan League dedicated to separating the empire from its European territories. The control of the Aegean Sea by the Greek navy limited Ottoman ability to reinforce their European fronts and left them unable to prevent the Balkan League from launching several simultaneous attacks. The alliance soon overran Albania. Bulgaria then moved into Thrace at the same time that Serbia invaded Macedonia. Shortly thereafter the Greeks took Salonika. Adrianople fell to a joint Bulgarian-Serbian army the following spring.

The First Balkan War might have ended even more catastrophically for the Ottomans had

not Great Britain organized a cease-fire and then hosted a peace conference. The Treaty of London, signed in May 1913, was humiliating enough. The Ottoman Empire ceded Crete to Greece and surrendered all European territory west of a line running from the Black Sea port of Midye to the Aegean Sea town of Enez. The empire had lost Thrace, Macedonia, Albania, and almost all of its Aegean Islands. The Ottomans recovered some of the land lost to Bulgaria when it took advantage of hostilities between the erstwhile allies of the Balkan League (the so-called Second Balkan War), but the overall trend was a loss of non-Turkish lands to the European rivals of the Empire.

To some Turkish leaders, this trend was not all unforeseen. Some members of the Young Turk movement, including Kemal Atatürk, looked forward to a national state built around Turkish identities. A centralized, multiethnic Ottoman Empire, they argued, was becoming an anachronism. Although replacing it with a Turkish Republic was a goal, the Young Turks despised the sight of the empire and its army being humiliated on the battlefield. Kemal himself was from Salonika and his family was forced to flee their home in the face of invading Greek armies.

The alliance of the Ottoman Empire with Germany was largely a function of Ottoman desires to recover territory it had lost during the recent wars. The Entente Powers had remained neutral during the war with Italy, and England had negotiated the painful Treaty of London (1913). Moreover, England and France were allied with Russia, the traditional enemy of the Ottoman Empire. Germany seemed to be the better option for recovering lost lands and preventing further fragmentation.

Nevertheless, even an alliance with Germany could not compensate for the overwhelming weaknesses of the Empire far from home. The highly touted Baghdad Railway had three significant gaps, requiring that all people and equipment be unloaded, carried by hand to the next railhead, and loaded again. Ottoman troops in the Caucasus Mountains had no rail communications with Constantinople, and forces in Yemen were isolated from all land communications. Furthermore, Allied naval superiority ensured that the Ottomans would not be able to use sea communications either. The movement of divisions from Thrace to eastern Anatolia in 1914 took nearly six months to complete.

The main concerns of the Empire were close to home, necessitating a weakening of forces stationed in non-Turkish parts of the empire. The first major campaign in the Caucasus Mountains cost Turkey more than sixty thousand casualties before the end of 1914. The following year, the Allied landing on the Gallipoli Peninsula occupied the main military efforts of the Ottoman Empire. Over the course of the campaign the Ottomans engaged more than five hundred thousand men and suffered almost 50 percent casualties. With the capital threatened and Gallipoli consuming so much manpower, outlying areas received few supplies and little reinforcement.

Even after the British evacuation, Ottoman strategy focused on areas close to the Turkish homeland. By the end of 1916 half of all Ottoman troops were concentrated against the Russians in Anatolia, Armenia (the scene of a terrible war against the Armenian civilian populace), and the Caucasus Mountains. Indeed, here Ottoman forces enjoyed their greatest successes, seizing the cities of Batum and Kars, which had been lost to Russia in 1878. The collapse of Czarist Russia opened the door for Ottoman troops to seize Baku as well.

All of this effort in the Turkish core left precious few resources to guard the outer reaches of the Ottoman Empire. An offensive against the Suez Canal in January 1915 failed, as did another

attempt the following July. In Mesopotamia, minimal British forces took Basra in the opening months of the war, then proceeded (despite a stunning Ottoman victory at Kut) to seize Baghdad, Samara, and Tikrit by the end of 1917.

The situation could have been even worse for the Ottomans. Germany was able to restrain the pro-German king Constantine, whose wife was the Kaiser William II's sister, from renewing Greek designs on Constantinople. Another Turkish enemy from the Balkan Wars, Bulgaria, had joined the Central Powers. Thus the Turkish Balkan front was, ironically enough, its calmest. Still, even that advantageous situation could not stop the inevitable fragmentation of the non-Turkish regions of the Ottoman Empire.

Renewed British offensives out of Egypt finally broke Ottoman lines in Palestine, capturing Jerusalem in late 1917. Within a year, British forces under General Edmund Allenby had seized all of Palestine, Lebanon, and Syria. Along the way, Allenby defeated an impressive array of Ottoman and German senior officers that included Erich von Falkenhayn, Liman von Sanders, and Kemal. Allenby's advance was so quick that the War Office in London, unaccustomed to reports of such rapid advances, warned him to slow his offensive down lest he outrun his supply lines.

The Ottoman Empire also had to face uprising from within. In 1915 Sir Henry McMahon

Allied beachhead on the Gallipoli Peninsula

(from The Anzac Book; Written and Illustrated in Gallipoli by the Men of Anzac *[1916], Joseph M. Bruccoli Great War Collection, Thomas Cooper Library, University of South Carolina)*

OTTOMAN EMPIRE

of Great Britain concluded a series of agreements with the Grand Sherif of Mecca in which Britain agreed to recognize Arab independence in Mesopotamia and much of Syria. These agreements fulfilled long-standing desires by Arab members of the Ottoman Empire to remove themselves from Turkish rule. According to Martin Gilbert, in *The First World War: A Complete History* (1994), McMahon made it clear that in order for Arab independence to be meaningful in the postwar world, Arab forces must "afford no assistance to our enemies. It is on the success of these efforts, and on the more active measures which the Arabs may hereafter take in support of our cause, when the time for action comes, that the permanence and strength of our agreement must depend."

The following year, building on British promises and Ottoman weakness, the Grand Sherif declared Hejaz independent of the Ottoman Empire. On 5 June 1916 the Arab Revolt began in earnest with support from British gunboats and seaplanes. On 13 June, Arab forces seized Mecca, and on 16 June, Jiddah fell as well. Outnumbered and outgunned, Ottoman forces began a steady withdrawal out of the Arabian peninsula. Arab forces, led by the Emir Faisal I and British captain Thomas Lawrence (Lawrence of Arabia), began a guerrilla war, disrupting Ottoman communications and destroying rail lines. Jewish units in Palestine also conducted guerrilla raids, destroying communications and working behind Ottoman lines.

By the time of the armistice, signed off the island of Mudros in October 1918, the Ottoman Empire had vanished. Turkey agreed to evacuate its last remaining Arab territories, open the Bosporus and Dardanelles, and demobilize its army. The Treaty of Sèvres (1920) formally separated Arab territories from the empire, although, much to the disappointment of Arabs and Jews, they became British and French mandates rather than independent states. The Ottomans were forced to cede all European territory except Constantinople and also were forced to recognize an independent Armenia.

The weakness of the new, as yet undefined, Turkey led to renewed invasions by Italy in April 1919 at Antalya and in May by the Greeks at Smyrna. In 1920 the British landed a force under General George Milne to keep the Bosporus and Dardanelles open, support the Sultan's tottering government, and protect the Armenians. The Greco-Turkish War (1920–1922) would have led to the further dismemberment of Turkey had it not been for the rise of a powerful nationalist force led by Kemal. In due course, Kemal convinced the Italians, Soviets, French, and British to leave Turkish territory. The Greeks, however, kept fighting, with

150,000 troops in Turkey. In September 1922, Kemal's forces recaptured Smyrna and turned toward Constantinople. Turkey was thus able to end this humiliating period with the triumphant Treaty of Lausanne (1923), which superceded the Treaty of Sèvres. It gave Thrace back to Turkey and witnessed the birth of the Turkish Republic.

Still, the overall pattern of the period 1911 to 1923 was clear and represented the decline of the Ottoman Empire to a Turkish core. All Arab parts of the empire were in British and French hands, though in some places, such as Trans-Jordan, Arab leaders had significant autonomy. European Turkey had been reduced to the immediate area around Adrianople and a Soviet Armenian Republic had been created as well. The Sultan was gone and in his place emerged Kemal, who committed himself to recognizing reality. His future state would be Turkish, not Ottoman. Conquest and rebellion had destroyed the empire, but Kemal would ensure that the Turkish Republic endured.

–MICHAEL S. NEIBERG,
U.S. AIR FORCE ACADEMY

Viewpoint:
No. The achievements of the Ottoman Empire during the war were remarkable, and its weaknesses and handicaps in no way prefigured a Turkish nationalist successor state.

The final surrender of the Ottoman Empire did not inevitably prefigure a Turkish nationalist successor state. Given the weaknesses and handicaps of the Ottoman Empire, its achievements during World War I were remarkable. Indeed, although suffering enormously, it may be argued that the Ottoman Empire experienced surprisingly little internal political, economic, social, or military collapse during the course of the war. In actuality, the origins of the modern Turkish state lie in the ill-advised attempts to partition Anatolia after the war.

The Ottoman Empire began mobilization on 2 August 1914, although it would not be at war for three more months. In the wake of the disastrous Balkan Wars (1912–1913), the Ottoman General Staff had no offensive war plans, nor did the government have any coherent war aims or objectives. The empire entered the war unprepared and still recovering from huge losses of men and equipment. The mobilization and concentration plan itself provided neither levers for the dip-

THE FINAL ACT

H. Collinson Owen, a British observer in Constantinople, describes the defeat of the Ottoman Empire in November 1918:

The final act to one of the greatest dramas of the war was enacted yesterday when, in accordance with the terms of the armistice with Turkey, British troops landed unopposed to occupy the Gallipoli Peninsula. . . .

Later in the day, up toward the Narrows, we saw the remains of submarine *E-15,* which ran ashore when trying to ascend the strait and was torpedoed from a launch by our own men under heavy fire, and a little further up, the rusty bottom of the Turkish battleship *Messudiyeh,* looking like an immense turtle, marked one of our submarine successes. We passed over deep waters that concealed the remains of sunken British and French battleships, the *Ocean, Irresistible, Majestic, Goliath, Triumph,* and *Bouvet.* We anchored just off V beach, where the *River Clyde* was run ashore.

The Turkish troops occupying the peninsula had been removed some days before, and for the time being not a single Turk was to be seen. V Beach along to Cape Helles and so to W Beach is as unlovely and barren a strip of coastline as can be imagined. Above us to our right were the remains of the old fort of Sedd el Bahr, which the fleet knocked to pieces in the first bombardment. We walked up the steep ground, passed over old trenches, both our own and the enemy's, and saw new ones constructed in case of the further attack which for months past the Turks had been expecting. Everywhere, too, were elaborate telephone connections. Here, on the ground which we had won and given up again, the Turks were expecting to fight us once more. The two heavy guns which we captured and blew up were still lying there, not far from a modern heavy battery with deep ammunition dugouts cut in rocky soil and a plentiful supply of six-inch shells neatly arranged in galleries.

We embarked again near the *River Clyde* in a patrol launch, and proceeded up the strait. Intelligence officers on board, maps in hand, were marking down various points of information and verifying the positions of batteries. Altogether, on both sides of the strait, there are about fifty batteries containing guns ranging from 6-inch to 14-inch, a considerable portion of which are modern. We passed within five yards of an ugly Turkish mine floating on the surface. We went ashore at Chanak and walked to Hamidieh battery, a mile and a half away, which is the strongest on the strait. At Chanak were Turks in plenty, both soldiers and otherwise, and everybody appeared quite well fed. The population appeared pleased to see a group of British officers walking about, glad that the war for them was over.

Hamidieh fort was quite deserted. It has played a big part in the operations against the Dardanelles. It has three 14-inch guns, dating back to the eighties, and six 9.2-inch guns. Looking from one of the emplacements one could see right down to the mouth of the strait and beyond. A small party of Turkish soldiers will be temporarily left to put the guns clean and in order, and we shall hold the forts until such time as the Allies shall have decided what is exactly to happen to the Dardanelles in the future.

Source: *Charles F. Horne, ed.,* Source Records of the Great War, *volume 6 (Indianapolis: American Legion, 1930), pp. 341–343.*

---

lomats nor swords for the generals and only served to alienate the empire from the Entente. In the absence of clear war aims, the Ottoman prime minister issued limited foreign policy directives that sought the ending of the capitulations, monetary compensation, and the return of the Aegean coastal islands. In retrospect, it is difficult to rationalize the entry of the Ottoman Empire into the war based on these objectives alone.

The Ottoman Empire entered the war with a primitive, agrarian, peasant economy. Its incomplete railroad net was built by foreigners with profit in mind (as opposed to the European railroads, which were subsidized by military staffs for the purposes of mobilization) and serviced only limited areas of the empire. The road network was in a similar condition and an easily interdicted coastal trade provided most commercial commerce. The Ottoman economy produced inconsequential amounts of steel, chemicals, fuels, and weapons, and produced only hides and fruit in abundance. Technical and professional skills of every kind were lacking in the largely illiterate population. Of a total population of around twenty-two million people only ten million were ethnic Turks; moreover, millions of citizens were

OTTOMAN EMPIRE

potentially dangerous Greeks, Armenians, Yemenis, or Arabs. Additionally, war losses aside, the Ottoman Empire had lost its most valuable European provinces in the Balkan Wars and millions of Muslim refugees had flooded the empire. By any measure the Ottoman Empire was ill-equipped to engage in a multifront modern total war.

Entering the war with poorly conceived offensives against Russian Caucasia (1914) and against the Suez Canal (1915), the Ottoman army failed. Losses at Sarikamish (1914) in Caucasia were particularly severe. Shortly thereafter, the British, Anzacs, and French invaded the Gallipoli Peninsula (April 1915), the Russians launched offensives in Caucasia, the Armenian population in eastern Anatolia revolted, and the British and Indians mounted offensive operations in Mesopotamia. Combat was intensive and the number of Ottoman soldiers killed and wounded in combat in the first year of the war exceeded the total combat losses for the remaining three years of war. For the Ottoman Empire 1915 proved to be a trial by fire during which disaster was narrowly avoided.

In 1916 the Turks met with some success as the Allies withdrew from the Gallipoli Peninsula and the Russian offensives were met by Ottoman counteroffensives. At Kut-al-Amara in Mesopotamia (April 1916), the Turks forced the surrender of thirteen thousand British and Indian troops. Victorious Ottoman infantry divisions also helped crush Romania and helped to contain the Allied beachhead at Salonika in Greece. The entry of Bulgaria in late 1915 reconnected communications with Germany, which by 1916 was providing increasing amounts of war matériel. Battle casualties fell off by 60 percent in 1916, but the mortality rate of diseases doubled. Despite the loss of Erzurum, Trabzon, and Erzincan in Caucasia, 1916 was a year of triumph during which the Ottoman Empire again had military heroes.

Because of the Russian revolutions and British preoccupation with the Western Front, 1917 proved to be a much-needed year of respite for the Ottoman army. Battle deaths reached an all-time low, although deaths from diseases remained high. The Turks lost Gaza, Beersheba, and Jerusalem in Palestine. They also lost Baghdad in Mesopotamia. While these cities were important for political, as well as religious, reasons, their retention was not critical in the strategic sense. In fact, 1917 provided the Turks with a final opportunity to consolidate their scant reserves into the Yildirim Army (a combined force that included Turkish, Syrian, Iraqi, German, and Austrian elements that fought in Palestine) and to again plan offensive operations.

The Ottoman Empire entered the final year of the war with a general sense of optimism. Serbia and Romania had been crushed. The ancient Russian enemy had collapsed and had taken itself out of the war. The active fronts, formerly three to five in number, had been reduced to two, and the long-delayed completion of the Amanus and Pozanti railroad-tunnel complexes was imminent. The principal ally of the Empire, Germany, was transferring troops westward for a knockout blow against the British and French. Even the Austrians appeared to be doing well against the Italians. The strategic outlook was so hopeful that the General Staff launched a full-scale invasion of Armenia, Georgia, and Azerbaijan in the late spring of 1918 that advanced all the way to the Caspian Sea by fall. It was not until September 1918 that the Ottoman strategic posture collapsed, first in Palestine at Meggido and simultaneously in Greece with the collapse of the Bulgarian perimeter surrounding Salonika. Austria-Hungary began to collapse internally in the fall of 1918, as did Bulgaria, and Germany appeared to be heading in the same direction. By October 1918 Allied troops had conquered all of Palestine and Syria and stood at the threshold of the Turkish Anatolian heartland. Allied armies from Salonika were advancing toward Adrianople and the Ottoman capital. While the General Staff was preparing for the defense of Anatolia against General Edmund Allenby, there were almost no troops left with which to defend the capital, the Bosporus, and the Dardanelles from General George Milne's advancing army. Facing such dismal strategic prospects, the Turks decided to request an armistice, and on 30 October 1918 the Ottoman forces laid down their arms.

The cost of the war had been terrible. In combat the Ottoman military lost 305,000 men dead or missing and suffered a further 467,000 men dead from disease. An equal number of men had been wounded in action. The overall mortality rate for men mobilized was almost 27 percent. Additionally, the Turks had lost their provinces in Palestine, Syria, and Mesopotamia, which had been Ottoman territory since the tenth century. The economy was decimated, the productive Armenian minority was either killed or deported, and the Greek minority had been savaged as well. By any measure World War I was a disaster for the Ottoman Empire.

Remarkably, neither the Ottoman state nor its army collapsed under the pressures of the war. The empire still maintained a million men under arms on 31 October 1918, which were organized into twenty-five combat infantry divisions under competent command and control. Moreover, after the armistice the Ottoman state continued in being, unlike the governments of its German and Austrian partners, until after 1920.

The Mudros Armistice (30 October 1918) provided the Ottoman Empire with a reasonable peace considering the position that the empire was then in. Although it demobilized, the Ottoman army did not cease to exist and returned proudly home to its garrison locations in Turkish Thrace and in the Anatolian heartland. The victorious troops in Azerbaijan and Armenia reluctantly returned also. The postwar Ottoman army contained twenty infantry divisions manned and equipped at the same level as their prewar counterparts. Thousands of surplus machine guns and artillery pieces were stored in the depots of the Anatolian heartland as well. Many experienced officers, including most of the general staff, remained in the army. Importantly, in the postwar Turkish consciousness the myth that the Germans had lost the war began to take hold.

Over the course of the war many other states had collapsed or had been rendered ineffective by the exigencies of war. The Serbian and Romanian armies were reduced to exiled bands. Russia collapsed entirely in 1917, and in the same year perhaps sixty infantry divisions of the French army mutinied. Much of the Austro-Hungarian army either deserted or proved a liability in combat, and the Austro-Hungarian empire itself collapsed in October 1918. Likewise, Bulgaria collapsed in September 1918. In Germany itself, the fleet mutinied and the government was facing a condition of anarchy. None of these states (save Serbia) suffered casualty rates as severe as the Ottoman Empire and all had been in a better financial, military, and economic posture than the Turks in 1914. Yet, at the end of the conflict the Turks held their government and army together. It could be said that the Turks began with less, suffered more, and nevertheless held on longer in the war than many other European states.

The actual genesis of the modern nationalist Turkish successor state began as a result of the Allied effort to partition and to retain Ottoman territory that had not been physically lost during the war. This process began at the Paris Peace Conference (1919) and continued until the Treaty of Sèvres (1920). While the Turks were willing to give up their Arabian and Mesopotamian provinces, they were unwilling to accept the partition or the loss of either the Turkish Thrace or the Anatolian heartland. In 1919 the Italians and French were busily occupying parts of southern Anatolia, and the British had occupied the straits region. Urged on by the Allies, both the Greeks and Armenians were carving huge enclaves in the Smyrna area and in Caucasia, respectively. These heavy-handed attempts to partition the Ottoman Empire into nothingness finally galvanized Turkish nationalists to mobilize the now all-Turkish army and to reclaim their lands. Although shattered by war the Turks rallied behind their myths that they had not been beaten on the battlefield and put their armies back into the field. Led to victory by the experienced commanders of World War I, the Turkish people found deliverance as the much-despised and underestimated Turkish army arose from the ashes of disaster to confound and to defeat their enemies.

–EDWARD J. ERICKSON, NORWICH HIGH
SCHOOL, NEW YORK

References

David L. Bullock, *Allenby's War: The Palestinian-Arabian Campaigns, 1916–1918* (London & New York: Blandford Press, 1988).

Edward J. Erickson, *Ordered to Die: A History of the Ottoman Army in the First World War* (Westport, Conn.: Greenwood Press, 2001).

Martin Gilbert, *The First World War: A Complete History* (New York: Holt, 1994).

Lord Kinross, *The Ottoman Centuries: The Rise and Fall of the Turkish Empire* (New York: Morrow, 1977).

T. E. Lawrence, *Seven Pillars of Wisdom: A Triumph* (New York: Doran, 1926).

A. L. Macfie, *The End of the Ottoman Empire, 1908–1923* (London & New York: Longman, 1998).

Andrew Mango, *Atatürk: The Biography of the Founder of Modern Turkey* (Woodstock, N.Y.: Overlook Press, 2000).

Alan Moorehead, *Gallipoli* (New York: Harper, 1956).

Alan Palmer, *The Decline and Fall of the Ottoman Empire* (New York: Evans, 1992).

Stanford Shaw, *History of the Ottoman Empire and Modern Turkey* (Cambridge & New York: Cambridge University Press, 1976).

Ulrich Trumpeter, "Turkey's War" in *World War I: A History,* edited by Hew Strachan (Oxford & New York: Oxford University Press, 1998), pp. 80–92.

Naim Turfan, *The Rise of the Young Turks: Politics, The Military and Ottoman Collapse* (London: Tauris, 1999).

OTTOMAN EMPIRE

PASSCHENDAELE

Should the Passchendaele offensive of 1917 have been called off once it became clear that a breakthrough was impossible?

Viewpoint: Yes. Because of the early high casualties and failed initial assaults, the British should have stopped the offensive before the heavy rains began.

Viewpoint: No. A steadily increasing British battlefield superiority legitimated Sir Douglas Haig's belief that the attack was worth pursuing, even under the appalling weather conditions.

The Battle of Third Ypres (1917), more commonly known as Passchendaele, was until recently replaced by the Somme (1916) as the "defining event" of the Great War in general, and of war for Britain in particular. Its images are of soldiers from every part of Britain and the Empire sent day after day into attacks in endless rain, across featureless ground so waterlogged that mules and men drowned in shell holes, for no better purpose than the capture of a few more acres of swamp and the hope of killing or maiming more Germans. The cri de coeur attributed—albeit erroneously—to a British staff officer getting his first sight of the battlefield: "My God! Did we really send men to fight in that?" is matched by the equally apocryphal reply of his escort: "it's worse farther up."

While less melodramatic than its mythology, the history of Passchendaele is depressing enough. The original objectives of the campaign were to relieve pressure on a French army tried to the limits of its endurance in the Nivelle Offensive (April 1917) and to capture the Belgian coastal ports that were—mistakenly—considered the major bases for a submarine campaign that was tightening its grip on the British maritime lifeline. The attack began on 31 July and initially achieved reasonable levels of success. The high command, however, was unable to resolve the claims of a breakthrough strategy along lines favored by Field Marshal Douglas Haig with the "bite and hold" approach tested in the later stages of the Somme campaign, which accepted limited gains in any one phase of an offensive, followed by consolidation that led to another set-piece attack. A revised German defense system emphasizing depth, built around networks of front-line pillboxes made of concrete impervious to all but heavy shells or lucky hits, and featuring rapid counterattacks kept even the best British and Dominion troops off balance, forcing them back to their original start lines with not even ground to show for their sacrifices. Autumn brought rain, which saturated what remained of a complex and fragile prewar drainage system. The British nevertheless floundered forward, finally capturing the village of Passchendaele, at a cost of almost three hundred thousand casualties, most of them from the "poor Bloody Infantry." That loss of men meant that up to a dozen divisions were not in the line when the German offensive struck in 1918—for most students of the battle, a classic example of attrition on the wrong side of the ledger.

**Viewpoint:
Yes. Because of the early high
casualties and failed initial assaults,
the British should have stopped the
offensive before the heavy rains
began.**

The Third Battle of Ypres, better known
as Passchendaele from the name of the Belgian village where it reached its tragic denoue-
ment, was the brainchild of Field Marshal
Douglas Haig, commander in chief of the
British Expeditionary Force (BEF). Preceded
by a ten-day artillery barrage by three thousand guns firing nearly 4.3 million shells, the
attack went forward from the Ypres salient on
31 July 1917. After modest gains the attack
quickly bogged down because of torrential
downpours on 1–4 August, exacerbated by the
destruction of the Flemish drainage system
during the preliminary bombardment.
Although the weather improved in September, heavy rains in October and November
1917 stymied any opportunity for the decisive
breakout that Haig had so optimistically predicted in July. An effective system of elastic
defense employed by the Germans, moreover,
made the BEF pay dearly for nearly every
meter captured. The result was 70,000 British
and Dominion soldiers killed, at least another
180,000 wounded, all for the gain of a few
miles of chewed-up, shell-wasted land.

The high casualties and meager results of
Passchendaele have become synonymous with
the idea that British and Dominion soldiers
were lions led by donkeys. Admittedly emo-
tive and simplistic, the idea is valid in this
case, since both Haig and British prime minister David Lloyd George had opportunities to
call off the campaign based upon the high
casualties and strategic indecisiveness of the
initial assaults. Haig's persistence in attacking
despite horrendous weather in October highlighted his stubbornness and strategic solip-
sism. Meanwhile, Lloyd George's reluctance
to rein in Haig constituted a breakdown in
civil-military relations. Certainly, the limited
territorial gains of October and November
provided no recompense to the tens of thousands of men who died or suffered crippling
injuries while launching near impossible
attacks across muddy quagmires.

Many were the reasons for the failure of
Passchendaele. An overly optimistic and ambitious plan was one. After the Allied success at
Messines in early June, Haig put into action
plans for a major offensive at Ypres in the
direction of the Flemish coast in order to

seize German U-boat bases at Ostend and Zeebrugge. A separate amphibious assault was to
aid in the capture of Ostend, after which Haig
planned to clear the Flemish coast of Germans.
The offensive took six weeks to prepare, however, during which time the Germans built an
active and elastic system of defense-in-depth. It
incorporated pillboxes and interconnected
strong points supported by specially trained
troops held in reserve for timely counterattacks. In spite of protracted delays, Haig
insisted on attacking into the teeth of these
defenses.

Expecting that a lengthy artillery barrage
of unprecedented weight would destroy the
bulk of German defenses, Haig disregarded
warnings that it would also destroy the Flemish system of drainage, turning reclaimed
marshland into renascent swamp. Combined
with climatological data that showed that substantial rain was normal for August, the result
should have been predictable: a nearly impassable battlefield composed of glutinous mud.
As French general Ferdinand Foch dismiss-
ively remarked when he heard of Haig's plans,
Third Ypres promised to become "a duck's
march" in which British attackers would wal-
low in fetid swamps of their own making. In
disregarding climatological data and the coun-
sel of Belgian experts, Haig demonstrated
obduracy if not obtuseness.

Haig also erred in his selection of General
Sir Hubert Gough, commander of the Fifth
Army, to lead the initial attacks. A former cavalry officer, Gough lacked experience,
although he did share with Haig a marked
preference for the offensive. One might say of
Gough what some American soldiers said of
General George Patton nearly thirty years
later: "Our blood; his guts." In the summer
and fall of 1917 Tommies came to look upon
an assignment to Gough's Fifth Army as a virtual death sentence. Gough's impetuosity and
indifference to casualties eventually led Haig
to shift in late August the main responsibility
for further attacks to General Sir Herbert
Plumer and the Second Army.

The choice of Plumer constituted a capit-
ulation on Haig's part to the goal of achieving
a decisive breakthrough. Known for methodical preparation and careful husbanding of
troops' lives, Plumer launched a series of set-
piece, "bite and hold" offensives from mid
September to early October. Unlike Gough's
ambitious assaults, Plumer's offensives had
modest objectives. They were also carefully
planned, launched across firmer ground in
drier weather, and supported by tanks and
well-timed and coordinated creeping barrages.
At the Battles of Menin Road and Polygon

Wood (26 September–3 October), Plumer used artillery to take ground and infantry to occupy it. Particularly successful was his attack at Broodseinde on 4 October, during which British artillery caught the German Sixth Guard Division in the open and pulverized it.

If Haig or Lloyd George had ordered Plumer to stop here, Third Ypres would perhaps be remembered today as a costly yet justifiable example of *Materialschlacht* (material battle). Yet, despite incessant and unseasonably heavy rains after 4 October, Haig insisted on launching three more offensives that damaged his own forces far more than those of the enemy. Optimistic as ever and encouraged by Plumer's modest advances as well as rosy intelligence reports from Brigadier General John Charteris, Haig surmised that German forces were reeling from the strain of nine weeks of intense fighting. One or two more shocks, he believed, might make them snap.

Such optimism was, however, unfounded. Atrocious battlefield conditions favored the defense. The ooze and slime that typified the approach to Passchendaele Ridge swallowed up men, swamped equipment, and smothered shells. Thus, when Plumer renewed the attack at Poelcappelle on 9 October, according to Robin Prior and Trevor Wilson in *Passchendaele: The Untold Story* (1996), the result was—given the wretched condition of the battlefield—"a predictable and quite unwarranted calamity." Three days later, in what became known as the First Battle of Passchendaele, the BEF lost 13,000 men for no gain. During the battle Australian and New Zealand soldiers crawled across treacherous mire only to encounter unsuppressed German machine-gun fire and uncut wire. Trying desperately to cut its way through thick belts of wire, the New Zealand division was a sitting duck for German machine gunners. One thousand resolute Kiwis were cut down and another 2,000 wounded before the survivors had no choice but to retreat.

In Leon Wolff's memorable description, *In Flanders Fields: The 1917 Campaign* (1958), Passchendaele in October became a "slough of despond" for the BEF. Yet, Haig remained unperturbed either by grievous losses or by horrendous weather. Never bothering personally to reconnoiter the front, he relied on his staff as his eyes and ears. Passchendaele had to be lived firsthand, however, not heard about secondhand. Lacking firsthand knowledge, Haig authorized two more costly offensives for 26–30 October and 6–10 November. Canadian units bore the brunt of these assaults. As they advanced further into the neck of the salient, they restricted their own ability to employ artillery while increasing their exposure to German flanking fire. Despite heavy losses, they succeeded in capturing what little was left of the village of Passchendaele and the surrounding heights. Even these meager territorial gains soon proved insupportable, however. They would be surrendered to the Germans without a fight during General Erich Ludendorff's offensive in March 1918.

In continuing to press ahead regardless of horrendous battlefield conditions, Haig earned a reputation for wanton disregard of life that eroded the morale and fighting power of the BEF. Leadership is the art of the possible, not the striving for the impossible. Throughout Third Ypres, Haig committed among the worse blunders a leader can make: he continued to reinforce failure. Thus, when unexpected success came two weeks after Third Ypres during the Battle of Cambrai, Haig lacked reserves to exploit it. Lack of reserves stemming from Third Ypres proved even more costly to Haig's army in March 1918. Bearing the brunt of Ludendorff's offensive, Gough's Fifth Army—still recovering from its mauling at Third Ypres—nearly disintegrated.

After the war, Haig argued that painful sacrifices at Passchendaele—although regrettable—had been necessary, both to keep the German army busy while French forces recovered from mutinies earlier in the spring, and to wear down the German forces, thereby weakening the will of Germany to continue. These arguments do not survive careful scrutiny, however. By the end of July 1917 the French army under Philippe Pétain had recovered sufficiently to launch limited attacks. Meanwhile, the Russian Revolution, the Italian collapse at Caporetto, and the withdrawal of Romania all proved a remarkable tonic to the German will to continue. Attrition was also quite disproportionate. Whereas Germany suffered approximately 220,000 casualties (killed, wounded, or missing) during Third Ypres, Haig's army suffered at least 250,000, with some estimates running as high as 350,000. By transferring forty divisions from the Eastern to the Western Front by mid March 1918, the German army made good its losses at Passchendaele with far more alacrity than did Haig's army. Haig, in contrast, had to wait for the arrival of American forces.

The British did have approximately three hundred thousand men in the Home Islands, but after the profligacy of the campaign at Ypres, Lloyd George deliberately starved Haig of men—a policy that proved nearly fatal when Ludendorff attacked in March 1918. Open distrust, sharp recriminations, and outright bitterness between Haig and Lloyd George was yet another outcome of the carnage of Passchendaele. Always suspicious of Haig's motives and abilities—in fact, Lloyd George considered Haig to be a second-rater who was devoid of imagination—the prime minister and his War Cabinet gave only grudging assent to the opening phases of

Third Ypres. Yet, once Lloyd George abnegated his authority (he is quoted as saying he would leave vital military decisions to military commanders), he found it difficult to reclaim it.

In part, Haig—supported by a gullible and misguidedly patriotic press—simply misled the prime minister. Press reports in August and September 1917 attested to the success of the initial attacks and went uncorrected by Haig. As it became increasingly evident by mid October that Passchendaele was more like the Somme than Messines, Lloyd George considered relieving Haig of command. He could not bring himself to do so, however. Relieving Haig of command, concluded Lloyd George, would probably lead General Sir William Robertson, the Chief of the Imperial General Staff (CIGS), to resign in sympathy. The prime minister knew that Robertson had colluded with Haig to discredit proposals to emphasize the Italian Theater or Palestine in 1917 at the expense of the Western Front. Yet, Lloyd George also knew that Haig's dismissal and Robertson's resignation, coming on the heels of the Russian Revolution and Caporetto, would further hurt Allied morale while encouraging the Central Powers. Haig's dismissal would also have violated one of the three conditions Conservatives had insisted upon prior to forming a coalition government. As much as Lloyd George wanted to relieve Haig for his misleading dispatches from headquarters, his imperious mien, and his Pyrrhic victories, the prime minister dared not risk provoking a major political crisis, especially one that might bring aid and comfort to the enemy.

Instead, Lloyd George sought to diminish Haig's power and autonomy. In November 1917 he supported the creation of the Supreme War Council to coordinate Allied war plans, selecting General Sir Henry Maitland Wilson, a critic of Haig, as the British representative. Robertson's outspoken opposition to this council led to his dismissal as CIGS in 1918. Lloyd George also insisted that Haig submit to Marshal Foch's authority as the latter took over as generalissimo of Allied operations on the Western Front in 1918.

In his detachment, brusqueness, and arrogance, Haig gave the appearance of a commander who was callously indifferent to the suffering of his men. Yet, it was not indifference so much as it was optimism so heightened in intensity by a belief in his own rectitude (guided by the Hand of Providence, he believed) that blinded Haig to the futility of Passchendaele. He succeeded in deluding

APPALLING SLAUGHTER

In a letter to his parents, Private Leonard Hart, of the First Otago Infantry, Fifth New Zealand Reinforcements, describes his participation in an assault during the Battle of Passchendaele in October 1917:

For the first time in our brief history as an army the New Zealanders failed in their objective with the most appalling slaughter I have ever seen. My company went into action 180 strong and came out thirty-two strong. Still, we have nothing to be ashamed of, as our commander afterwards told us that no troops in the world could possibly have taken the position, but this is small comfort when one remembers the hundreds of lives that have been lost and nothing gained. . . .

The weather had for some days been wet and cold and the mud was in places up to the knees. The ground had all been deluged with our shells before being taken from the Germans, and for those five miles leading to our front line trench there was nothing but utter desolation, not a blade of grass, or tree, numerous tanks stuck in the mud, and for the rest, just one shell hole touching another. The only structures which had stood the bombardment in any way at all were the German machine-gun emplacements. . . .

At three o'clock on the third morning we received orders to attack the ridge at half-past five. It was pitch dark and raining heavily. When all was ready we were told to lay down and wait the order to charge. Our artillery barrage curtain of fire was to open out at twenty past five and play on the German positions on top of the ridge a hundred and fifty yards ahead of us.

At twenty past five to the second, and with a roar that shook the ground, our guns opened out on the five-mile sector of the advance. Through some blunder our artillery barrage opened up about two hundred yards short of the specified range and thus opened right in the midst of us. It was truly an awful time—our men getting cut to pieces in dozens by our own guns. . . . At length our barrage lifted and we all once more formed up and made a rush for the ridge.

What was our dismay upon reaching almost to the top of the ridge to find a long line of practically undamaged German concrete machine-gun emplacements with barbed wire entanglements in front of them fully fifty yards deep! The wire had been cut in a few places by our Artillery but only sufficient to allow a few men through at a time. Dozens got hung up in the wire and shot down before their comrades' eyes. It was now broad daylight and what was left of us realised that the day was lost. We accordingly lay down in shell holes or any cover we could get and waited. Any man who showed his head was immediately shot. They were marvellous shots those Huns. We had lost nearly eighty per cent of our strength and gained about three hundred yards of ground in the attempt. This three hundred yards was useless to us for the Germans still held and dominated the ridge.

. . . .When daylight came some of us, myself included, crawled out to some adjacent shell holes from where the cries were coming and were astonished to find about half a dozen Tommies, badly wounded, some insane, others almost dead with starvation and exposure, lying stuck in the mud and too weak to move. We asked one man who seemed a little better than the others what was the meaning of it, and he said that if we cared to crawl about among the shell holes all round about him we would find dozens more in similar plight. We were dumbfounded, but the awful truth remained, these chaps, wounded in the defence of their country had been callously left to die the most awful deaths in the half-frozen mud while tens of thousands of able-bodied men were camped within five miles of them behind the lines.

Source: *Lyn MacDonald, 1914–1918: Voices and Images of the Great War (London: Michael Joseph, 1988), pp. 243–247.*

himself that the climactic battle was in sight, that a supreme effort (and concomitantly high casualties) would ultimately be redeemed, because Passchendaele would constitute the last sacrificial push. Many would find the *Memorial Tablet* of English author and World War I veteran Siegfried Lorraine Sassoon, however, not the providential vision of Haig, as providing the most powerful lesson of Passchendaele:

Squire nagged and bullied till I went to fight,
(Under Lord Derby's Scheme). I died in hell—
(They called it Passchendaele). My wound was
   slight,
And I was hobbling back; and then a shell
Burst slick upon the duck-boards: so I fell
Into the bottomless mud, and lost the light.

–WILLIAM J. ASTORE,
U.S. AIR FORCE ACADEMY

Viewpoint:
No. A steadily increasing British battlefield superiority legitimated Sir Douglas Haig's belief that the attack was worth pursuing, even under the appalling weather conditions.

The British Flanders Offensive (1917) has been excoriated so often and on so many grounds that the facts behind it risk disappearing entirely under successive waves of analysis and polemics. In part, Passchendaele was a response to the increasingly desperate condition of a France that since August 1914 had borne the brunt of the war in the West. Its casualties had been almost beyond counting. Its economy had borne the strain of losing some of its central areas to German occupation. Verdun might in retrospect emerge as an epic victory, but in immediate terms it had in fact succeeded in bleeding white the French army. The prospects for success of the Nivelle offensives were objectively never great. France believed because it had to believe, like a desperate gambler staking his remaining resources on the turn of the next card.

Even before then, however, British political and military leaders were well aware that 1917 must be "Britain's year," when the Empire assumed a burden France could no longer carry. In some respects the politicians were ahead of the generals in recognizing that fact. David Lloyd George, on becoming premier in December 1916, saw its costs clearly enough and sought to develop an alternate solution. The British General Staff and the high command of the British Expeditionary Force (BEF) had by this time no illusions. Britain must take stage center in the crucial theater of the war: the Western Front, where the bulk of German forces were deployed and where the threat to the chief ally of Britain was mortal.

BEF commanding general Sir Douglas Haig favored an offensive in Flanders. The geographic limits of the sector made it attractive. In contrast to the Somme, where the Germans had miles and miles of expendable territory behind them, Flanders offered no room for operational or strategic withdrawal. The enemy must stand and fight the kind of head-on slugging match at which the BEF was developing considerable expertise. Flanders, moreover, had been British turf since late 1914. Its rear areas were firmly under British control. Even if the German army was not broken, as Haig expected, a Flanders offensive would wear down both German fighting forces and morale. As a bonus, Haig offered the possibility of conquering the Belgian ports

that were considered central to the U-boat offensive. The Royal Navy was sufficiently enthusiastic to give its support to a projected division-scale amphibious landing on the Flanders coast—a kind of mini-Anzio (1944).

The Passchendaele offensive, in short, was the product of policy rather than strategy, and strategy more than operations. Britain could not avoid mounting a major offensive in a critical sector; Flanders was the best of a list of dubious choices. The small size of the theater made concealment, deception, and surprise virtually impossible: this attack would be mass war in its ultimate form. Nor had the German army shown serious signs of general deterioration, either in the final stages of the Somme (1916) or the early battles of 1917 around Arras. Common sense indicated that its fighting power would have to be countered with firepower. Yet, the ground in the principal combat zones was a low-lying mix of clay, sand, and silt unable to absorb either heavy rain or heavy damage to the centuries-old networks of canals and ditches that provided drainage. Even given a good or normal summer and early fall, tactical conditions could be expected to deteriorate. August and October 1917 would be abnormally, unpredictably wet.

The course of events from the opening bombardment in mid July to the capture of Passchendaele village in mid November are less important for this essay than an analysis of the reasons why the BEF, its commander, and his military and political superiors continued to attack. The justifications for continuing the operation were the same as those mandating its initiation. For practical purposes, nothing had changed for the better on the policy level during the summer and fall of 1917. The U.S. entry into the war was widely regarded in both France and Britain as a political gesture, whose military effects were unlikely to be manifested until the spring of 1919. Aleksandr Kerensky's Russia was staggering toward entropy well before the Bolshevik Revolution (1917) put the Provisional Government out of its misery. The gallic acid that infused much contemporary French comment on Third Ypres has an unmistakable flavor of sour grapes. The French army concealed the worst details of its own slide into disaffection and mutiny, but the most insular British officer with any contacts to his ally knew that all was not well in the ranks of an army "waiting for the Americans and the tanks." Without British sacrifice, in other words, the Germans might well have gained significantly in relative fighting power merely by standing still.

Nor were events at the front the top-to-bottom fiasco of myth and memory. Haig certainly merits criticism for an uncertain grip on the battle, at times revealing his intentions and at times withholding them; at times leaving events in the hands of his subordinates and at times micromanaging. Fifth Army commander Sir Hubert Gough was the wrong man in the wrong spot—but the Tommy's alleged friend, Herbert Plumer of the Second Army, was not much less committed to a policy of pushing on in the face of bad weather and heavy losses. At divisional levels and below, British warfighting capacities steadily and significantly improved. Artillery fire control developed along with systems of ammunition supply. In the infantry, company and platoon tactics, at best in their embryonic stages on the Somme, during Third Ypres enabled the BEF to cope effectively with pillboxes and machine-gun nests and to repel increasing numbers of German counterattacks often already disrupted by artillery. Even the mud could be compensated for to a degree, though never overcome. That tactical effectiveness in turn encouraged division and corps commanders to "give it one more go" rather than to complain to their superiors and to risk being relieved.

It also eroded a German army whose best units by the end of 1917 had often been through three hecatombs: Verdun, the Somme, and Passchendaele. Each had its own distinguishing feature. At Verdun the Germans had held the initiative. The Somme was fought against a BEF whose raw courage was no substitute for its collective inexperience. At Passchendaele, for the first time in the war, the enemy was showing a learning curve—under physical conditions no less miserable for the Germans than the British. German reports and correspondence convey an almost universal sense of being set back on their heels, of losing not merely the military but the moral initiative to an enemy that just kept coming against every tactical and technical artifice, and under the most brutal weather conditions. If the professional German army, its cadres of regular officers and noncommissioned officers (NCOs), died on the Somme, a case can be made that the German citizen army, the reservists and wartime conscripts, was eviscerated at Passchendaele. The innovations preceding the March 1918 offensive were no more than cosmetic modifications to a force whose spine had been snapped during the death grapple in the mud and which was no longer able to stand up to comprehensive adversity.

None of these arguments make a prima facie case for the Passchendaele operation as it was implemented. Put together, however, they suggest that Haig's determination and the perseverance of the BEF were not altogether in vain. Third Ypres was something more than a gruesome one-sided catastrophe.

—DENNIS SHOWALTER,
COLORADO COLLEGE

References

Brian Bond and Nigel Cave, eds, *Haig: A Reappraisal 70 Years On* (London: Cooper, 1999).

Glyn Harper, *Massacre at Passchendaele: The New Zealand Story* (Auckland: HarperCollins, 2000).

B. H. Liddell Hart, *The Real War, 1914–1918* (Boston: Little, Brown, 1930).

Lyn Macdonald, *They Called It Passchendaele: The Story of the Third Battle of Ypres and of the Men Who Fought In It* (London: Joseph, 1978).

Geoffrey Powell, *Plumer: The Soldier's General: A Biography of Field-Marshal Viscount Plumer of Messines* (London: Cooper, 1990).

Robin Prior and Trevor Wilson, *Passchendaele: The Untold Story* (New Haven: Yale University Press, 1996).

Siegfried Sassoon, *The War Poems of Siegfried Sassoon,* arranged and introduced by Rupert Hart-Davis (London: Faber & Faber, 1983).

Nigel Steel and Peter Hart, *Passchendaele: The Sacrificial Ground* (London: Cassell, 2000).

John Terraine, *The Road to Passchendaele: The Flanders Offensive of 1917: A Study in Inevitability* (London: Cooper, 1977).

Edwin Campion Vaughan, *Some Desperate Glory: The Diary of a Young Officer, 1917* (London: Wayne, 1981).

Philip Warner, *Passchendaele: The Story Behind the Tragic Victory of 1917* (London: Sidgwick & Jackson, 1987).

Denis Winter, *Haig's Command: A Reassessment* (London & New York: Viking, 1991).

Leon Wolff, *In Flanders Fields: The 1917 Campaign* (New York: Viking, 1958).

PERMANENT ALLIANCES

Did the system of permanent alliances that arose in Europe after 1871 cause World War I?

Viewpoint: Yes. The alliances encouraged belligerence and risk taking by making all the great powers believe they would be supported by their allies in almost any situation.

Viewpoint: No. If any factor shaped diplomacy, it was the perceived weakness of pre-1914 alliance treaties, all of which featured escape clauses and reservations as opposed to affirming mutual support.

The system of permanent alliances between and among the great powers that emerged in Europe between 1871 and 1914 has generally been described as a major factor in causing the Great War. Contemporaries and historians have described a "poisonous medicine" that locked states into two mutually exclusive, mutually hostile systems with less and less internal or external flexibility. It started with the "dual Alliance" of 1879 between Germany and Austria. The inclusion of Italy in 1882 was a second step down a path that took definitive form with the Franco-Russian alliance of 1894. From that date Europe was partitioned into two antagonistic camps. If the alliances were often characterized by internal dissension—well before 1914 Italy was considered unreliable by its ostensible partners—they nevertheless resisted periodic and strenuous efforts to "split the pairs."

Traditional, more flexible arrangements such as the successive Three Emperors' Leagues linking Germany, Russia, and Austria between 1872 and 1878, and then between 1881 and 1888, proved unviable in this new atmosphere. Limited mutual agreements such as the Russo-German Reinsurance Treaty (1887–1890) proved less attractive than the apparent security offered by the comprehensive arrangements of an alliance. Another attractive factor was the growing uncertainty the respective military systems felt about their probable effectiveness in case of a general war. Alliances offered an opportunity to share burdens and to complement weaknesses. France, for example, had money and factories but was increasingly short of men. The industrial and financial shortcomings of Russia were outweighed by its seemingly endless manpower.

Proof of the strength of the alliance system is the accession of Britain to what became the Entente by treaties with France in 1904 and Russia in 1907. A British Empire long priding itself on its ability to take as much or as little as it willed of Continental affairs was, by the turn of the century, suffering from "overstretch." Tentative overtures from Berlin foundered on a lack of mutual interests. The Franco-Russian connection, on the other hand, offered an opportunity to settle a spectrum of long-standing imperial grievances and provided as well security against a Germany whose economic and maritime ambitions were becoming too great for the comfort of London.

The alliance systems were not doomsday machines. It may indeed be said that their relatively loose structure contributed significantly to the outbreak of war. Every agreement incorporated mutual-escape clauses, usually predicated on one's partners acting "aggressively" and provoking a conflict. However, in 1914 those clauses encouraged a mutual pushing of envelopes, so as to be sure the partners would honor the agreement rather than question it. Loose or rigid, the alliances set the stage for the Great War. The stage was set for the final scene.

Viewpoint:
Yes. The alliances encouraged belligerence and risk taking by making all the great powers believe they would be supported by their allies in almost any situation.

Since the great powers went to war in 1914, they obviously felt justified in risking hostilities at that particular time. One must understand, however, how diplomatic and military developments between 1875 and 1914 combined to create the situation that resulted in the cataclysm of 1914. In 1875 only France had foreign-policy objectives that could be secured by a victorious war against Germany. By 1914 all of the great powers found themselves in situations where war was considered a necessity to achieve desired ends.

In the aftermath of the Franco-Prussian War (1870–1871), French foreign policy was essentially set in stone for the next forty-three years. The goal of every French government, revanchist or not, was the recovery of Alsace-Lorraine. Since that objective could only be accomplished by war, German chancellor Otto von Bismarck sought to keep France in a perpetual state of diplomatic isolation. During his tenure Bismarck was able to accomplish this scheme through means both unworkable (the two ill-fated Leagues of the Three Emperors in 1872 and 1881) and the potentially sustainable combination of the Triple Alliance (1882), the Reinsurance Treaty (1887–1890), and the Mediterranean Agreements (1887).

Bismarck's dismissal by German kaiser William II in 1890 initiated a series of events that fundamentally changed the nature of the alliance system. The lapsing of the Reinsurance Treaty led to the Russian rapprochement with France, thus giving the French the ally they needed. The combination of the Kaiser's ardent desire to build a navy, plus his ham-fisted diplomacy, then succeeded in alienating Britain, driving it into the *Entente Cordiale* with France. The other German ally, Italy, began to back out of the Triple Alliance in wake of the Bosnian Crisis (1908–1909). Indeed the events of 1914 showed how radically the nature of the Austro-German alliance in the first place was to act as a brake against Austrian expansion in the Balkans. By the terms

of the alliance, if Austria was the aggressor in a war with a third party, Germany was under no obligation to come to the aid of the Austrians. By 1914 Germany was in such a position that the kaiser had to follow precisely the course of action that Bismarck sought to prevent in the first place. Thus did William II sign the "blank check."

Military developments also served to make the great powers willing to risk war in 1914. In general, the size of the armies roughly tripled between 1870 and 1914. Given the criticality of railroads to the execution of both mobilization and war plans, by 1914 the mere act of mobilization was essentially the equivalent of an act of war. The fear that the other side would mobilize, complete its deployment, and attack first certainly helped propel countries, once mobilization had been declared, to take the ultimate step.

Matters were made worse by the ossified nature of the planning systems the major powers had in place by 1914, which was amply demonstrated by German general Helmuth von Moltke (the Younger)'s near panic at the kaiser's request for a change in the mobilization plan in an attempt to localize the impending conflict. Likewise, Austrian attempts to shift troops between the Serbian and Russian fronts resulted in complete chaos. Russian tsar Nicholas II's attempt to order a partial mobilization directed only against Austria-Hungary foundered on a combination of suspicion of Germany and remonstrations by the Russian General Staff that a partial mobilization was impossible to carry out.

The impetus toward war was also reinforced by the expectations on the part of the great powers that the conflict would indeed be short. The great powers all believed that the nature of modern economics was of such fragility that no economy could withstand the strain of a prolonged war. Although the experiences of the American Civil War (1861–1865), Franco-Prussian War, Russo-Turkish War (1877–1878), and Russo-Japanese War (1904–1905) might have suggested otherwise, the war plans of the great powers all reflected the expectation of a short war.

Further, all of the major powers were under the influence of many of the destructive tendencies so prevalent in the nationalism of the late nineteenth century. The glorification of violence and the promotion of war as the most noble of human endeavors was present in all of the great powers. Manifestations of these tendencies were

THREE EMPERORS' LEAGUE

On 18 June 1881 the leaders of Austria-Hungary, Germany, and Russia attempted to restore peace in Eastern Europe by signing the following agreement:

The Courts of Austria-Hungary, of Germany, and of Russia, animated by an equal desire to consolidate the general peace by an understanding intended to assure the defensive position of their respective States, have come into agreement on certain questions. . . .

The Courts of Austria-Hungary, of Germany, and of Russia, animated by an equal desire to consolidate the general peace by an understanding intended to assure the defensive position of their respective States, have come into agreement on certain questions. . . . With this purpose the three Courts . . . have agreed on the following Articles:

ARTICLE I. In case one of the High Contracting Parties should find itself at war with a fourth Great Power, the two others shall maintain towards it a benevolent neutrality and shall devote their efforts to the localization of the conflict.

This stipulation shall apply likewise to a war between one of the three Powers and Turkey, but only in the case where a previous agreement shall have been reached between the three Courts as to the results of this war.

In the special case where one of them shall obtain a more positive support from one of its two Allies, the obligatory value of the present Article shall remain in all its force for the third.

ARTICLE 2. Russia, in agreement with Germany, declares her firm resolution to respect the interests arising from the new position assured to Austria-Hungary by the Treaty of Berlin.

The three Courts, desirous of avoiding all discord between them, engage to take account of their respective interests in the Balkan Peninsula. They further promise one another that any new modifications in the territorial status quo of Turkey in Europe can be accomplished only in virtue of a common agreement between them.

In order to facilitate the agreement contemplated by the present Article, an agreement of which it is impossible to foresee all the conditions, the three Courts from the present moment record in the Protocol annexed to this Treaty the points on which an understanding has already been established in principle.

ARTICLE 3. The three Courts recognize the European and mutually obligatory character of the principle of the closing of the Straits of the Bosporus and of the Dardanelles, founded on international law, confirmed by treaties, and summed up in the declaration of the second Plenipotentiary of Russia at the session of July 12 of the Congress of Berlin.

They will take care in common that Turkey shall make no exception to this rule in favor of the interests of any Government whatsoever, by lending to warlike operations of a belligerent Power the portion of its Empire constituted by the Straits.

In case of infringement, or to prevent it if such infringement should be in prospect, the three Courts will inform Turkey that they would regard her, in that event, as putting herself in a state of war towards the injured Party, and as having deprived herself thenceforth of the benefits of the security assured to her territorial status quo by the Treaty of Berlin.

ARTICLE 4. The present Treaty shall be in force during a period of three years, dating from the day of the exchange of ratifications.

ARTICLE 5. The High Contracting Parties mutually promise secrecy as to the contents and the existence of the present Treaty, as well as of the Protocol annexed thereto.

ARTICLE 6. The secret Conventions concluded between Austria-Hungary and Russia and between Germany and Russia in 1873 are replaced by the present Treaty.

Source: *"The Three Emperors League,"* World War I Document Archive, *Internet website <http:// www.lib.byu.edu/~rdh/wwi/1914m/liga3.html>.*

PERMANENT ALLIANCES

present in every level of society. Although recent scholarship has somewhat challenged the notion that the soldiers of the European powers went to war as joyfully as had been traditionally assumed, it is nevertheless clearly the case that in 1914 the armies of the great powers marched off to war with considerably more enthusiasm than they would a generation later. Certainly, at the very least, the prospect of a short and presumably victorious war offered a welcome escape from the boredom and humdrum of everyday life.

Such attitudes were every bit as pronounced in the upper echelons of European society. Colonel Edward Mandell House, personal envoy of U.S. president Woodrow Wilson, described the mood in the higher levels of British and English government and society as "militarism run stark mad." Russia, stung badly by both the loss of the Russo-Japanese War and the humiliation of having to back down to a German ultimatum during the Bosnian Crisis, was struck by a fresh surge of Pan-Slavism. In Germany the social, intellectual, political, and military elite alike were caught up in the morose ideology defined later by Oswald Spengler's *The Decline of the West* (1918–1922) and its application to power politics, best expressed in the notion of "world power or decline." Even Austria-Hungary went to war armed with extreme confidence. Thus did intellectual influences common to both alliances contribute to the onset of war in 1914.

This interpretation of prewar foreign policy conditions does not assert that alliances are bad things in and of themselves. In the case of 1914, however, the alliance system, or rather its degeneration, combined with the dangerous tandem of intellectual trends and military developments that seemed to make war a more palatable alternative, played a critical role in bringing about World War I.

—RICHARD L. DINARDO, USMC COMMAND
AND STAFF COLLEGE, QUANTICO, VIRGINIA

Viewpoint:
No. If any factor shaped diplomacy, it was the perceived weakness of pre-1914 alliance treaties, all of which featured escape clauses and reservations as opposed to affirming mutual support.

Many conventional treatments of World War I argue that the conflict was caused by a rigid system of alliances that unavoidably led the major European powers into a conflict that they did not necessarily want to fight.

Although these alliances were important elements of European diplomacy in the prewar period, their relevance to the outbreak of war has been greatly exaggerated. The powder keg that exploded in 1914 had much more to do with competing national interests, extensive great-power ambitions, and tactical military considerations than it did with the objective existence of alliances.

The rival alliance structures that emerged after 1871 were remarkably weak institutions. The oldest alliance in effect when World War I broke out, the Dual Alliance that Germany formed with Austria-Hungary in 1879 and then extended into the Triple Alliance with Italy in 1882, required each country to come to the aid of an alliance partner only if it were attacked by at least two other countries. In other words, a limited conflict between an alliance partner and one other country, even a conflict in which the ally was the victim of aggression, would not have triggered the alliance obligation and thus would not have assured a general European war. Any offensive conflict initiated by an alliance partner, it goes without saying, was also not covered by the provisions of the alliance.

When Archduke Francis Ferdinand was assassinated in Sarajevo in 1914, therefore, the Triple Alliance was essentially irrelevant. Under its provisions, the Austro-Hungarian declaration of war against Serbia left Vienna on its own. Even when Russia mobilized its armies against Austria following the declaration of war, the alliance was still not a factor since the attack implied by Russian mobilization was coming from only one country, not the required two. At no point did the provisions of the alliance require Germany or Italy to come to the aid of Austria-Hungary. Germany supported Austria against Serbia, but it had agreed to do so in a completely separate private assurance for which the Austrian foreign minister, Count Leopold Berchtold, had specifically asked the German government before pursuing war. Italy was neither asked to do anything, nor did it volunteer to become involved.

The rationale of Germany for supporting its Austrian ally had to do with nothing but its long-term strategic ambitions. By supporting Austrian prestige in the Balkans, the German government hoped to enhance its own strategic and economic positions in southeastern Europe and the Middle East. The construction of the Berlin-to-Baghdad railway, the dispatch of a military mission to Constantinople in 1913, and increasing German commercial investment in the Ottoman Empire were clear indications of the goals of Berlin. If Austria could swat Slavic nationalism with a decisive

blow against Serbia, the most territorially ambitious state in the Balkans, German backing was to be expected.

The categorical support of Germany for Austria was also determined by immediate military considerations. The Austrian war against Serbia threatened Russian intervention on behalf of Belgrade. Although the military mobilization of Russia in late July 1914 was at first partial and only directed against Austria, Russian strategic planners were convinced that anything less than a full mobilization (against both Germany and Austria) was the only effective way to prepare for war. The Russian high command and the responsible ministers believed that since Germany was backing Austria against Serbia, Germany might mobilize its armies preemptively against Russia in the event of an Austro-Russian conflict. In that case a partial mobilization would have left the unprepared Russian forces on the German frontier at a tactical disadvantage. At the insistence of his advisers and despite direct warnings from Kaiser William II, Tsar Nicholas II canceled the partial mobilization orders and instead issued orders for a full mobilization. This action led to a German countermobilization against Russia. Since German military strategy was based on the worst-case scenario of a two-front war and called for the quick defeat of France, the ally of Russia, Germany

had no partial mobilization plans and had no choice but to mobilize against France when it mobilized against Russia. Again, practical considerations about national security rather than alliance obligations drove the mobilization showdown.

German declarations of war on Russia on 1 August 1914, and on France two days later, were neither mandated by its alliance commitments, nor, since Germany was the party declaring war, did the declarations force its alliance partners to follow suit. Austria-Hungary and France remained technically at peace until France declared war on Austria on 12 August. The position of Italy is even more interesting, for although it remained a full partner in the Triple Alliance, nothing that had happened in the crisis of July and August 1914 required it, or the other two members of the Triple Alliance for that matter, to enter the conflict. On 3 August, Rome declared official neutrality.

If the Triple Alliance was unimportant for the development of the general European War, the "rival alliance" that connected Britain, France, and Russia was even less important for the emerging conflict. Strictly speaking, there was no single alliance that connected all three nations. In 1891 Russia and France concluded an agreement to consult with one another in the event of an international crisis, and three years later they agreed that each country

German general Paul von Hindenburg reviewing troops

(postcard in scrapbook, Joseph M. Bruccoli Great War Collection, Thomas Cooper Library, University of South Carolina)

PERMANENT ALLIANCES

would come to the aid of the other if it were attacked by Germany or by one of its Triple Alliance partners with German support. The mobilization of Russia against Austria in 1914 had nothing at all to do with its French ally. Instead, it was following a long tradition of supporting the Slavic and Orthodox Serbian state as a means of enhancing its own influence in southeastern Europe. The internal weaknesses of Russia, however, had prevented it from taking an active role on Serbian behalf during the Bosnia-Herzegovina crisis of 1908 and during the Balkan wars of 1912–1913, occasions when Serbian interests and ambitions had been directly and successfully challenged by Vienna. In 1914 many Russian officials believed that if their country failed to come to the aid of Serbia a third time, it would forfeit its credibility as a great power. For that reason alone it was willing to engage Austria in war. As the situation developed into a general European war, furthermore, the Franco-Russian military alliance did not even have the opportunity to function as it had been envisaged. Since Germany had almost simultaneously declared war on both France and Russia, neither was drawn into an unwanted conflict by their alliance obligations.

The position of Britain was anomalous. Traditionally it had resisted forming alliances with Continental powers and cooperated with them only when it served its interests. This policy was maintained up to and after 1914. At no time did Britain enter into a formal alliance with either France or Russia. Instead, its interests dictated that it settle its differences with each of those countries to counter what appeared to be a German challenge to its global leadership. In 1904 Britain resolved outstanding colonial disputes with France and promised to fight on its side if the vital interests of both countries were at stake. The British government, however, was careful to prevent this "entente," or "understanding," from developing into an explicit military alliance, even one limited by the complicated escape clauses and reservations that characterized the Austro-German-Italian and Franco-Russian axes. The use of the word "entente" to describe the Anglo-French relationship illustrated this fact. When Britain smoothed over colonial conflicts of interests with Russia in a similar entente agreement in 1907, the rapprochement remained vague and the two countries made no separate military agreement at all.

When Germany presented France and Russia with war in 1914, British involvement was by no means assured. Like every other power involved in the early days of World War I, Britain had no explicit alliance obligation to enter the conflict. Since a Franco-German war had no direct bearing on British interests in the objective sense, the provisions of the Entente for joint military action remained inert. To the consternation of the French government, Britain refused to commit to the war for several days after it had begun. When it finally did, at midnight on 4 August 1914, it was only because Germany refused to withdraw troops that were moving through neutral Belgium to invade France. While this maneuver violated an international agreement of 1839, which guaranteed Belgian neutrality, the British view—going back to the sixteenth century—was that control of the strategic Low Countries by any major power posed a threat to their security. Britain eventually may have become involved in the war without the German violation of Belgian neutrality, but it remained significantly outside of the conflict until the strategic threat posed by a German occupation of Belgium became certain. In the decision of Britain to go to war, in other words, the belligerent status of France was not objectively a decisive factor.

As the assassination crisis developed into a wider conflict, the prewar alliance system proved to be even less important. The Ottoman Empire and Bulgaria joined Germany and Austria-Hungary because of their favorable prewar relations with Berlin and because fighting on the German side offered the best prospect for postwar territorial gain. The same factor motivated Italy, Greece, Romania, and Japan to join the Entente powers. Of those six nations, three (Bulgaria, the Ottoman Empire, and Greece) had no previous alliance connection with even one nation in either camp. Italy had been an ally of Germany and Austria but had no obligation to fight with them. Instead it fought with the Entente powers after they promised that it could annex Austrian territory after the war. Romania had been a nominal German ally before 1914. Japan had a mutual defense alliance with Britain that dated from 1902, but since Britain had declared war on Germany and not vice versa, the Japanese government was not obliged to enter the war on the British side. The United States, perhaps the most significant power in the war, had spent much of its history following George Washington's advice from 1796 to avoid entangling alliances with any European power. When it entered the war in April 1917, it was motivated by German submarine attacks on its shipping and, more significantly, the unattractive prospect of a German-dominated Europe.

No country entered World War I because a rigid alliance obligation required it to.

Although the alliances for the most part delineated the two opposing camps years before the war broke out, their provisions were in every case too weak to compel the signatory nations to go to war. The great powers of Europe fought each other because they had ambitions, security requirements, and concerns about national prestige that were plainly incompatible. These factors were the true engines of the conflict. The system of opposing alliances that developed after 1871 was less significant.

-PAUL DU QUENOY,
GEORGETOWN UNIVERSITY

References

V. R. Berghahn, *Germany and the Approach of War in 1914,* second edition (New York: St. Martin's Press, 1993).

Fritz Fischer, *Griff nach der Weltmacht,* translated as *Germany's Aims in the First World War* (New York: Norton, 1967).

James Joll, *The Origins of the First World War* (London & New York: Longman, 1984).

John Keegan, *The First World War* (London: Hutchinson, 1998).

David MacLaren McDonald, *United Government and Foreign Policy in Russia, 1900–1914* (Cambridge, Mass.: Harvard University Press, 1992).

Zara S. Steiner, *Britain and the Origins of the First World War* (London: Macmillan, 1977; New York: St. Martin's Press, 1977).

Barbara W. Tuchman, *The Guns of August* (New York: Macmillan, 1962).

PERMANENT ALLIANCES

PLAN XVII

Was Plan XVII the blueprint for a French offensive?

Viewpoint: Yes. Plan XVII was an aggressive military strategy that dictated the need to seize the initiative from the Germans and not allow them time to coordinate a proper defense.

Viewpoint: No. Plan XVII made provisions only for the mobilization and concentration of French troops and not their offensive use on the battlefield.

French planning for war with Germany after 1871 had the common denominator of emphasizing offense. Apart from a general conviction in military circles that the debacle of 1871 had been caused by resigning initiative to the enemy, the social contract of the Republic with its citizens implied protection against another Boche invasion. Initially an elaborate system of frontier fortresses had been built to check attacks and channel attackers onto killing grounds. Increasingly the French generals proposed to take the war to the Germans. The inadequate training and short service provided for conscripts gave the French army, at least in the minds of its leaders, a brittle quality. Élan, dash, and courage were the French soldier's traditional qualities, best used quickly and likely to erode in sustained operations.

A variant on that collective wisdom briefly emerged in Plan XVI. The strategy was predicated on a German invasion of Belgium and a French counterattack. It was, however, rejected as politically unacceptable because it involved violating Belgian neutrality. Its successor, Plan XVII, was formulated a few years before World War I erupted and also assumed a German invasion of Belgium—one confined, again for purposes of international relations, to the southern portion of the country. General Joseph Joffre proposed to counter by bringing virtually the entire strength of France, organized in five armies, to the eastern frontier. If Germany behaved as expected, and as French intelligence predicted, three armies would swing northeast and meet them in Belgium. Should the Germans instead come straight ahead, the primary French axis of advance would be an offensive on either side of the Metz-Thionville fortifications.

Plan XVII determined concentration not strategy. Its most serious weakness was its deployment of more than three quarters of the army south of Verdun. Given the offensive emphasis of French doctrine, that deployment set the stage for a premature attack into Alsace-Lorraine, undertaken before the Germans showed their hand. When on 4 August 1914, Joffre received definite information that the invasion of Belgium was under way, he ordered a full-scale offensive into the lost provinces. His goal was to pin down German reserves to the south while his northern armies drove into Belgium and Luxembourg, across the presumed axis of a German advance now stripped of support.

In the event, French shortcomings at tactical and operational levels produced not a headlong rush into disaster but a slow, poorly coordinated stumble forward that led to the same results. In less than two weeks the

French army was back on its starting lines—minus one-third of a million of its men dead, wounded, or missing as Plan XVII was overtaken by events.

Viewpoint:
Yes. Plan XVII was an aggressive military strategy that dictated the need to seize the initiative from the Germans and not allow them time to coordinate a proper defense.

During the period 1871–1913 the French army went through a series of operational plans and strategies in preparation for the inevitable rematch with the German Empire that the French high command believed would avenge their defeat in the Franco-Prussian War (1870–1871). Each plan, in many ways, built upon the other and reflected the changing military theories of the French army and the evolving geopolitical situation of the late nineteenth and early twentieth centuries. In addition to developing plans of operation during this period, the French also wrestled with the lessons that they believed should be learned from their defeat and strove to conceptualize and implement as doctrine the fundamental aspects that would bring success in modern warfare. Plan XVII, formally adopted in 1913, was thus the culmination of decades of French military planning and political maneuvering. It embodied their latest military doctrine, which urged that, above all else, an army must be aggressive and that the offensive was the highest expression of the military art.

Without question, Plan XVII was a scheme for the concentration of the French army along the eastern frontier, but to what purpose? If one looks carefully at the development of Plan XVII, and the preceding Plan XVI that it replaced, it is abundantly clear that the reason for this concentration along the eastern frontier was designed to begin an offensive action against Germany at the earliest possible moment after the commencement of hostilities. French military theory, political objectives for the war, and the Franco-Russian alliance all dictated that when war came with Germany, France must immediately attack; thus, Plan XVII, developed in response to these prerogatives, committed the French army to an offensive strategy in 1914.

It is impossible to overstate the shock and feeling of disbelief that swept over the French army in the wake of its defeat in the Franco-Prussian War. Heirs to a tradition of martial excellence, including the legendary *Grande Armée* of Napoleon Bonaparte, the French army had long considered itself, and been considered by others, as the leading army in the world. In the years after the Napoleonic Wars (1792–1815), victories in the Crimea (1854–1856), Italy (1859), and in its wars of empire in North Africa and Indochina in the nineteenth century reinforced this image and lent an aura of invincibility to the French army. Thus, the rapid and disastrous defeat of the French army at the hands of Prussia and its German allies constituted a monumental shock to the army and the nation that provoked a major reassessment of national defense policy and military theory.

Hardly had the guns fallen silent before the French began to prepare for the inevitable rematch. In the initial years after the Franco-Prussian War, the French focused on a defensive strategy. The newly created German Empire was superior to France in population, industrial output, and, of course, in the size and strength of its army. These factors seemed to dictate that merely halting the next German onslaught should be the primary focus of the French army. To this end the French began to develop a series of "fortified regions," studded with fortresses and defensive works, along the new Franco-German border. Under the able direction of General Séré Rivière, the French army constructed modern forts designed for a war fought with artillery and machine guns and that emphasized the defensive advantages that modern firepower brought to the battlefield. French army plans for the next war with Germany revolved around this concept of the primacy of the defensive expressed by these new forts and envisioned the concentration of French forces behind the fortified regions. The fortifications along the eastern frontier would restrict the frontage of the German offensive and channel their attacks into killing zones where the French army, poised behind the forts, would be able to pounce upon the invaders in a series of counteroffensives that would destroy the enemy in detail.

The final expression of this "defensive-offensive" doctrine was Plan XVI, adopted in 1909, which firmly embraced the concept that when war came France must, at least initially, be on the defensive. Under Plan XVI, three French armies would concentrate in defensive positions behind the fortified regions of Toul and Verdun, with two more armies forming a second line to the rear and one army in reserve for local counterattacks. Thus, Plan XVI provided a defense in depth with some flexibility for limited offensive action.

Yet, even while mainstream French military thought accepted a defensive role, there was a strong movement among young officers that decried the passivity of fortifications and defensive tactics. Led by military theorists such as Louis de Grandmaison and Ferdinand Foch, and inspired by the writings of the late Charles du Picq, these officers began to call for an aggressive military strategy based upon their belief in the primacy of the offensive in warfare. The "cult of the offensive" was founded upon an intensive study of the French victories in the Napoleonic Wars and the French defeats during the Franco-Prussian War. The offensive theorists argued that the foundation of Napoleon's success was his aggressiveness. Regardless of the odds or overall situation, the emperor routinely took the offensive at both the strategic level while initiating a conflict and at the tactical level on the battlefield itself. By thus seizing the initiative, Napoleon was able to control the flow and tempo of both the campaign and the battle and dictate his will to his enemy, forcing them to react to his moves, keeping them off balance, and eventually destroying them.

As a counterpoint to Napoleon's legendary successes, the offensive theorists pointed out that during the Franco-Prussian War the French were essentially on the defensive throughout the opening stages of the conflict. With the exception of an initial probe by French forces in the opening days of the war, which led to one of the few French successes, the armies of the Second Empire were constantly on the defensive throughout the engagements that essentially decided the conflict in its opening weeks. The French fortresses became traps for retreating French armies that were quickly shut inside, isolated, and knocked out of the conflict by the aggressive Germans. With these two examples firmly in mind, the conclusion was obvious: glorious victory through an aggressive offensive or ignominious defeat from a passive defense. For the attack-minded theorists, the offensive must be conducted aggressively at both the tactical and strategic level. To them Plan XVI, with its establishment of the French army into defensive lines based on fortifications, would doom France to a repetition of 1870.

The offensive-minded theorists soon developed a powerful political following as French foreign policy became increasingly bent on *revanche* and the recovery of the lost provinces of Alsace and Lorraine. Hence Plan XVI, which dictated a defensive strategy that not only eschewed any early recovery of the lost territories but also advocated sacrificing areas of eastern France to the invader, was a difficult sell for its supporters. In addition, the offensive-minded theorists argued that political circumstances now made an offensive possible. The signing of the Franco-Russian alliance in 1890 assured France that it would not face Germany alone and that the powerful German army would be divided in order to fight enemies to the east and to the west. Thus, the French offensive-school believed they would be facing far

better odds in the coming war than initially forecast and hence there was no reason to remain passive. In addition, France wanted to assure Russia that they would not simply sit back and watch while the Russian army did all of the fighting. A strong commitment by the French army to an offensive at the earliest moment would be matched by a similar Russian commitment, and thus Germany would be faced with a two-pronged invasion that it could not hope to stop.

It was amid this swirl of new military theory and political pressure that the head of the French army and author of Plan XVI, General Victor Michel, was relieved of command in 1911 by the French government and replaced by General Joseph Joffre. The move was instigated by the younger officers of the French army who were increasingly demanding a more aggressive approach to warfare that the conservative Michel had opposed. While Joffre was no Grandmaison or Foch, he was enamored with the possibilities of an early offensive and indeed owed his rise to supremacy within the French army to the support of the offensive-school theorists.

Joffre soon made it clear that he would not countenance any plan for military operations that envisaged the sacrifice of yet more of the sacred soil of France to the Germans. He was also determined that, whatever else may come from the inevitable rematch with Germany, Alsace and Lorraine must be recovered. French military theorists, like most European strategists, believed that the next war would be a brief and violent affair. Thus, Joffre theorized that there would be no time to obtain the ultimate objectives of the lost provinces through a "defensive-offensive" strategy that depended upon a counteroffensive at some ill-defined moment in the future. It was also of vital importance to French foreign policy that the Russians were assured that when war came with Germany, France would strike a blow. Quite plainly, then, vigorous offensive action at the outset of the conflict was of the foremost importance, and therefore a new war plan emphasizing the offensive must be developed. This concern was the genesis and background of the plan for military operations drawn up by Joffre and his staff during the years 1911–1913 that eventually became known as Plan XVII.

While Plan XVII was indeed designed to concentrate the French armies along the Franco-German border, from its inception it was developed as a scheme for offensive action. Whereas Plan XVI had concentrated the French armies in Lorraine by placing them behind the barriers of the Meuse and Moselle Rivers and the fortified regions of Verdun and Toul, the new Plan XVII deployed the French army in front of these defensive positions and massed along the Franco-German border. Although Joffre retained some tactical flexibility

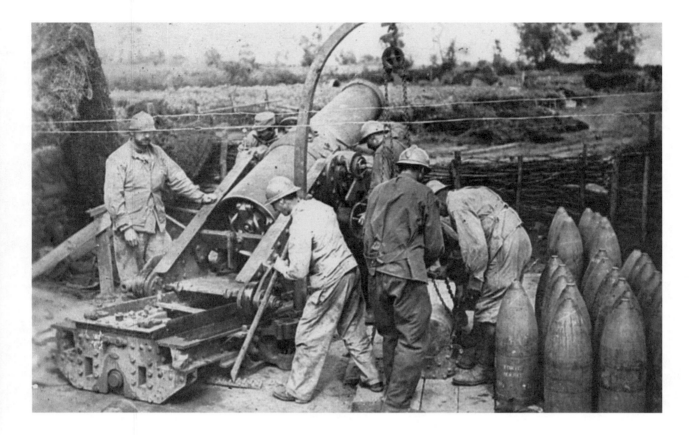

French heavy mortar crew in action, circa 1915

(postcard in scrapbook, Joseph M. Bruccoli Great War Collection, Thomas Cooper Library, University of South Carolina)

with this concentration of forces, it was clear that the obvious targets for the inevitable French offensive were the lost territories of Lorraine and Alsace. The greater preponderance of force, and the more fully developed lines of communication, existed in Lorraine and hence it would, under Plan XVII, be a perfect location for the decisive battle that the French believed would settle the war. From this location, the French could also threaten the German flanks should they advance through neutral Belgium or Switzerland. When considering the possibility that the main German attack would be through Lorraine, Joffre fully intended to meet the Germans head-on rather than rely on static defensive positions. The impact of the 1870 campaign was clearly stamped on the minds of Joffre and the offensive theorists of the French army. There would be no French armies shut up in fortresses in the next war. They would instead hurl themselves upon the invader in an all-out offensive that would take full advantage of the French soldier's natural élan and defeat the Germans in the open field.

Although Joffre later stated that he reserved the final decision regarding his exact plan of operations to the days immediately following the outbreak of hostilities, there is little question that, based upon the deployment provided by Plan XVII, he intended to launch an offensive at the earliest possible moment. There was no pretense to defensive action in Plan XVII. Any thoughts of forming up behind fortified regions with armies deployed for a defense in depth had been tossed aside with the departed Michel. French military

theory, political objectives, and their obligations to Russia all pointed to offensive action when war came. Thus, the French were committed to launching their army into a major offensive at the outset of hostilities and Plan XVII reflected this mind-set by concentrating the French army in forward positions designed as a jumping-off point for a massive assault against the Germans.

–ROBERT B. BRUCE, SAM HOUSTON STATE UNIVERSITY

Viewpoint:
No. Plan XVII made provisions only for the mobilization and concentration of French troops and not their offensive use on the battlefield.

It seems perverse to argue that Plan XVII could have been anything but an offensive plan. *L'offensive à l'outrance* (an attack to the utmost) was the favored doctrine of General Joseph Joffre, who directed French military planning as the Chief of Staff of the French Army and its designated wartime commander-in-chief. When he assumed authority over French planning on 28 July 1911, Joffre explicitly rejected the existing Plan XVI as too defensive. Under his guid-

JOFFRE ON PLAN XVII

There is one observation, however, which I feel bound to make. It is that, in my view, the movements were not necessarily to be carried out exactly as laid down in these instructions. As I have already said, I considered that arrangements for concentration were only fixed, in definite fashion, up to the Regulating Stations. Beyond these, decisions would have to be governed by the development of the situation, and the instructions modified accordingly.

In my opinion, the instructions for the concentration were not comprehensive. They did not provide for all contingencies. It was impossible for them to do so, for the final decisions of the Government were, in large part, dependent on the attitude of Belgium, which remained enigmatic up to the very last moment. This was brought out very well by Lord French when he said, "It is most regrettable that Belgium could never be persuaded to decide in advance on her attitude in the event of a general war." It would have simplified in very large measure our task in the days preceding the war. In a document to be issued to a comparatively large number of persons, I could only, officially, take into account operations outside Belgian territory. I was obliged to contemplate a violation of Belgian neutrality, but I preferred to put nothing in writing in the plan of operations, and had to be satisfied with a concentration lending itself to various ends. I confined myself to asserting my intention of pursuing an offensive in a general north-easterly direction, as soon as the whole of the French forces were assembled.

This reserve on my part appeared to me at the time to be perfectly well justified, and seems to be still more so today.

To take a case in point. Our mobilization might be delayed by circumstances of a domestic nature, or the Germans might so well conceal their preparations as to complete their mobilization before ours. It is quite evident that, in both of these cases, we should be obliged to concentrate in a rearward zone. It will be seen, moreover, that it was exactly this contingency that I had to fear during the period of political tension.

When the Instructions were being fully drawn up, it was suggested that a paragraph should be added to the effect that they did not claim to provide for every contingency. I refused to do this, for I thought it better to issue directions for studies to be made of modifications having in view the concentration of our main forces in the northern portion of the theatre of operations. I considered that the Instructions, as they stood, met the case sufficiently well and formed a good basis for the work of the staffs of the various armies. I felt sure that these staffs were quite capable of carrying out any modifications I might have to order, and judged it dangerous to disclose in advance the various manoeuvres I had in mind.

As a matter of fact, it was found, in August, 1914, that a great part of these Instructions required no alteration.

It is, moreover, to be noted that, for reasons of secrecy, no mention was made in the Instructions of British co-operation, of the rôle the Belgian Army might eventually play, of how the troops form Algeria were ultimately to be employed, and also our Alpine troops, in the event of Italy remaining neutral.

Source: *Joseph Joffre,* The Personal Memoirs of Joffre, *volume 1, translated by T. Bentley Mott (New York & London: Harper, 1932), pp. 105–107.*

---

ance, the new regulations of 1912, as recorded by Ferdinand Foch's memoirs, proclaimed "The French Army, reviving its old traditions, no longer admits for the conduct of operations any other law than that of the offensive." Joffre's preferences aside, a swift eastward drive promised both to protect French soil and to achieve its foremost war aim, the recovery of the "lost provinces" of Alsace and Lorraine. Offensive action was also more likely to produce a short war, the only kind France would choose to fight. Most important, the threat of coordinated French and Russian attacks would upset German plans or possibly even deter war altogether. A French defensive policy would, on the other hand, offer Germany the freedom to defeat Russia before turning her attentions westward. France relied on a Russian offensive to hold German forces in the east; she could hardly expect Russia to fling her army against Germany without her own promise to follow suit. In any case, who could expect defensive thinking from the country whose parliament voted in July 1914 against replacing the celebrated red trousers of the French army with a less aggressively visible green?

For all of these reasons, Plan XVII ought to have been the "virtual incarnation of the *offensive à l'outrance*," as described by historians such as Samuel R. Williamson Jr. in *The Politics of Grand Strategy: Britain and France Prepare for War, 1904–1914* (1969). That was the kind of plan that French soldiers wanted and that the crucial Russo-French alliance demanded. Nonetheless, the evidence that Plan XVII was merely a plan for the mobilization of French armies, albeit one offensively inclined, is incontrovertible. Crucially, Joffre insisted as much in his memoirs. "I," he said, "determined to delay my decision as to the manoeuvre to be undertaken until the first days following the declaration of war." There is every reason to believe Joffre on this point. Any incentive to dissimulate was in the other direction, that of describing a more comprehensive plan than actually existed. Instead, Joffre argued that the army could not make a campaign plan until the enemy's line of approach became clear. Nothing that the French army did in August 1914 contradicts Joffre's unabashed portrayal of the campaign as one of improvisation.

The next question is why the French army accepted an allegedly "offensive" war plan that did not look past the mobilization and concentration of the troops. Logistical imperatives, at the very least, ought to have stimulated more detailed planning. For, although French generals did not foresee the exact shape of the next conflict, they did know that the huge armies involved would require unprecedented quantities of supplies. French soldiers could march over the frontier as they had done under Napoleon Bonaparte, changing direction at their commander's whim, but supplies were a different matter. Since armies were now too large to live off the land, their commanders should have wanted to predict when and where they would have to be fed. Ammunition supply, especially, posed unprecedented challenges, thanks to the voracious appetites of bolt-action rifles, machine guns, and the new quick-firing artillery. This logistical argument in favor of advanced campaign planning did not sway Joffre, who persisted in leaving his options open.

One possible reason for the vagueness of Plan XVII is that there had not been time to complete the campaign details. Joffre began developing a replacement for the defensive Plan XVI as soon as he became Chief of Staff. It took until May 1913 for the general scheme to pass muster at the War Ministry, at which point the general staff began working on the details of mobilization. The plan was distributed to army commanders in February 1914

and came into effect during the following May. Although the process was lengthy, almost none of the two years and ten months was devoted to operational details. During the period 1911 to 1913 the discussion focused on the political issue of whether the attack would drive eastward into Germany or, as Joffre preferred, violate the neutrality of Belgium. The ten remaining months from War Ministry acceptance to implementation may have been enough time only for mobilization planning, not for detailed plans as to what to do next.

The more important reason Joffre refused to produce a specific campaign plan was the desire to retain flexibility in the face of uncertainty about German intentions. The French army leadership had long suspected that the eventual German onslaught would come through Belgium. The best response to such an attack, Joffre advised his government in February 1912, would be for the French army also to enter Belgium. By such a movement "the problem presented to us would be simplified and our chances of victory would be singularly increased." An attack through Alsace-Lorraine, on the other hand, was not likely to achieve the desired decisive results. The government replied to Joffre that, since neither Britain nor Belgium would tolerate a French violation of the neutrality of Belgium, his proposal was diplomatically unacceptable. Later that year, British general Sir Henry Hughes Wilson, himself a firm advocate of Anglo-French military understanding, reminded Joffre that the British commitment to defend neutral Belgium would prove "embarrassing" in the event of a French démarche into that country. In consequence, Joffre reported that he was obliged definitely to renounce all ideas of a "manoeuvre *a priori* through Belgium."

His official "renunciation" of the Belgian plan, however, did not prevent Joffre from contemplating a northward movement if German actions made it necessary. He claimed to have been "obliged to contemplate a violation of Belgian neutrality" while not committing such impolitic ideas to paper. It is easy to see how Joffre's belief that the French army ought to fight in Belgium discouraged him from developing concrete plans for operations in a contrary direction. Apparently he declined to commit to plans that would prevent taking advantage of changes in diplomatic situation and the consequent opening of the Belgian frontier.

Thus, Joffre's own testimony amply demonstrates that Plan XVII was more a mobilization scheme than an offensive-campaign plan. Presenting Plan XVII as a framework for operational flexibility rather than a recipe for a reflexive attack does not mitigate the deficiencies of Joffre's concept. While he claimed to have delayed committing to an eastward line of operations so as to allow a riposte to a German entry into Belgium, Joffre never established the intelligence capabilities necessary to ascertain German intentions early enough to shift troops northward. German troops crossed the Belgian frontier on 4 August 1914, but it was 6 August before Joffre sent an officer to Brussels to learn what was going on. Under such circumstances, the French army could not counterattack against the main German line of advance in Belgium.

Joffre designed Plan XVII as a mobilization plan in order to keep his options open but then moved too slowly to take advantage of the freedom of action gained thereby. In sum, Plan XVII was not a strategy of unlimited offensive, for which Joffre has so often been criticized. Rather, it was less a plan at all than an effort by the French High Command to avoid facing the realities of a strategic conundrum.

–EUGENIA C. KIESLING, U.S. MILITARY ACADEMY

References

Ronald H. Cole, "'Forward With the Bayonet:' The French Army Prepares for Offensive War, 1911–1914," dissertation, University of Maryland, 1975.

Ferdinand Foch, *De la Conduite de la Guerre: La Manoeuvre pour la Bataille avec 13 cartes et croquis* (Paris: Berger-Levrault, 1915).

Foch, *The Memoirs of Marshal Foch,* translated by T. Bentley Mott (Garden City, N.Y.: Doubleday, Doran, 1931).

Adolphe Goutard, *La Marne: Victoire Inexploitée* (Paris: R. Laffont, 1968).

Joseph Joffre, *The Personal Memoirs of Joffre, Field Marshal of the French Army,* volume 1, translated by Mott (New York & London: Harper & Row, 1932).

B. H. Liddell Hart, *Reputations: Ten Years After* (Boston: Little, Brown, 1928).

Charles Mangin, *Comment Finit la Guerre: Avec Onze Cartes* (Paris: Plon-Nourrit, 1920).

Barthélemy Palat, *La Grande Guerre sur le Front Occidental,* fourteen volumes (Paris: Chapelot, 1917–1929).

Douglas Porch, *The March to the Marne: The French Army, 1871–1914* (Cambridge & New York: Cambridge University Press, 1981).

Samuel R. Williamson Jr., *The Politics of Grand Strategy: Britain and France Prepare for War, 1904–1914* (Cambridge, Mass.: Harvard University Press, 1969).

POISON GAS

Was the poison gas used in World War I essentially a nuisance weapon?

Viewpoint: Yes. Gas was used primarily for harassment, increasing the misery of war and lowering morale.

Viewpoint: No. When used properly, in conjunction with small arms fire and artillery barrages, gas was a lethal weapon.

Gas was first used in World War I by the German army made aware of its possibilities by the German chemical industry, the most advanced in the world in 1914. It was introduced on the Russian Front in January 1915, when a few tear gas rounds were fired into Russian positions with no effect. By April, however, the Germans had a more powerful agent available in larger quantities. Chlorine gas was a by-product of the dye industry: a vesicant that killed by overproducing fluid in the lungs, essentially drowning its victims. Instead of shells, as yet unreliable, the Germans released it from cylinders in the Ypres sector on 22 April 1914. French North African troops panicked and fled before it. That the Canadians on their flank held on owed something to their grit and something as well to the presence in the ranks of enough men with enough chemistry training to be able to name the horror they faced. Cloths soaked with water, or better yet urine, provided some elementary protection as British researchers developed protective masks—not only for men, but for dogs and horses as well.

The Ypres front held, and the British launched their own gas clouds at Loos in September—again with limited results. German gas clouds, however, played a significant role in their successes on the Russian Front during 1915, and by the time of Verdun (1916) and the Somme (1916) gas was a part of the arsenal of any modern army. Phosgene joined chlorine to form an increasing number of lethal compounds utilized as weapons. Artillery shells and, for the British, special mortar bombs became the preferred method of delivery. In 1917 mustard gas was first used in the war. Not directly lethal in the way of its predecessors, it inflicted soft-tissue burns, lung damage, and temporary blindness (which became permanent often enough to terrify its victims).

Gas was often described as a weapon of denial, to keep enemy troops from utilizing a particular area, or to diminish their effectiveness by forcing them to wear masks. Its deadliness has often been questioned as well: most gas victims in the second half of the war survived. Gas in sufficient quantity, however, could saturate masks to the point where they no longer offered protection. Putting masks on too late, taking them off too early, or being ignorant of such facts as that gas, being heavier than air, lingered in shell holes and dugouts, or that mustard gas contaminated water enough to inflict serious burns, was no less fatal. The green soldiers of the American Expeditionary Force (AEF) suffered particularly from the sophisticated gas warfare techniques of 1918, when as many as half the rounds fired in an action might be gas or smoke. Few soldiers of any army would agree with the post facto generalization that gas was a "nuisance weapon." It was arguably the most terrifying, as well as among the most effective, weapon introduced in the four years of the war.

Viewpoint:
Yes. Gas was used primarily for harassment, increasing the misery of war and lowering morale.

Despite the 1899 Hague Convention prohibition of poison gas use in warfare, both sides during the Great War employed chemicals as a means of overcoming the immobility of trench warfare on the Western Front. The shock and panic it created in the enemy ranks led the public to view gas as one of the most lethal, diabolical weapons of the war. Such was not the case. From its initial use by the Germans in 1915, gas warfare proved to be an amateurish, unorganized effort whose effect was to terrorize and incapacitate rather than to kill.

Gas appeared in three essential varieties. Tearing agents represented the least harmful category. The popular xylyl bromide, for example, produced temporary blindness and inflamed the nose and throat, but could be effectively neutralized with a gas mask. More injurious than the tearing agents were the asphyxiates, or poisonous gases: chlorine, phosgene, and diphosgene. Chlorine appears as a greenish-yellow gas and creates havoc by creating hydrochloric acid when in contact with moisture found in the lungs and eyes. Colorless phosgene achieves a rapid hydrolysis and has twice the toxicity of chlorine. Diphosgene is deadlier still and could not be effectively filtered by standard issue gas masks. The third variety, blistering agents, were the most dreaded of all gases used in the war. Of these, mustard gas, the infamous yellow cross, proved most effective as an incapacitating weapon. While the other gases affected the respiratory system, mustard gas, which was thirty-six times more poisonous than chlorine, attacked exposed skin, creating burnlike blisters that healed slowly. Often the symptoms only appeared well after exposure, and the gas itself persisted sometimes for days after its dispersal. The gas mask could protect only the eyes and nose from blistering agents.

Although munitions filled with irritants had been used from start of the war, the first major use of gas came on 22 April 1915, when the Germans released 168 tons of chlorine from 520 metal cylinders built into the front trench parapet against the French and Algerians near Langemarck. A five-mile cloud produced panic and an eight to nine-kilometer gap in the French lines. This action proved to be the first of nearly 200 chemical attacks using gas cylinders. Two days later the Germans again used chlorine, this time against the Canadians,

French, and British. Although 25 percent of the 20,000 troops gassed were killed, this initial high figure would decline over the course of the conflict, as the Allies quickly responded with countermeasures and gas attacks of their own. For the Germans, however, this first test of gas was just that: a minor experiment employed without careful planning. Had the focus been on its wide-scale use, in conjunction with reserves to exploit the shock effect, gas might have created the all-important, decisive breakthrough early in the war.

Improvement came with the gas shell, which was unaffected by the wind, required no special training, and could be fired quickly against specific targets by devices such as the Livens projector and Stokes mortar. As such, it represented a more mobile form of warfare. Yet, results with the new British phosgene gas shells fired from Livens projectors at Arras in April 1917 proved once again that gas was not a critical, decisive factor. Although the gas shelling created temporary panic in the German ranks, the stalemate continued. Moreover, with 80 percent of the Germans gassed having been wounded rather than killed, the weapon served mainly to incapacitate. Both sides began extensively using phosgene in 1916, and the Germans first used diphosgene at Verdun on 22 June 1916, causing 1,069 casualties, including 120 killed. Once again, however, gas facilitated only temporary battlefield gains through its nuisance value. The Germans were also the first to use mustard gas, when they assaulted the Ypres Salient on the night of 11–12 July 1917. During the next six weeks mustard gas produced more than 20,000 casualties, with the vast majority being wounded, not killed.

The most skillful use of mustard gas to penetrate the enemy line appeared with the Hutier tactics (named after Oskar von Hutier) first employed by the Germans on the Eastern Front in September 1917. Applying these tactics in the 1918 German offensives, General Erich Ludendorff used phosgene and mustard gas to incapacitate the defenders and destroy enemy morale prior to the main attack. Although his tactics initially proved successful, as seen in the forty-mile penetration of the British lines at Arras in March, insufficient reserves and Allied countermeasures blunted the German advance. Earlier the Germans had waited until they had a sufficient supply of mustard gas before introducing it in their 1917 offensive at Ypres, making it difficult for the Allies to rapidly catch up. Indeed, the French did not respond with mustard gas until June 1918, followed by the British that September. During their counteroffensive of 1918 the Allies gave no indication that they viewed mustard gas as other than a terror weapon that might aid in their advance. By that time the critical manpower situation proved most decisive in the German retreat.

The central question involves the combat effectiveness of gas warfare. As an incapacitating agent, gas proved particularly effective against troops unprepared for the attack. Surprised soldiers often left the trenches in panic, choking and dying, or were temporarily immobilized, thus creating an opportunity for the attacker to exploit. It was better for the attacker to wound than to kill because the wounded soldiers required men to move them to safety and facilities to provide care. Even when expectation of an attack allowed time for donning the gas mask, the device hampered performance and, psychologically, proved demoralizing. Against artillery positions, poison gas often forced gun crews to keep their masks on for hours. At the same time, gas killed the horses, thereby preventing the arrival of new supplies of ammunition. Mustard gas was the most effective because it left the artillery untouchable for hours or sometimes days. Initially during an attack often one had to wear the gas mask until it was clear that only high explosives and not gas shells were being used. Both sides continued to increase their use of gas artillery shells, and by 1918 one in every four artillery shells were gas projectiles. This trend, however, should be viewed against a backdrop of increasingly capable countermeasures.

Preparing for a gas offensive took considerable time and involved hauling thousands of canisters or Livens projectors across a wide front. Often the enemy could see the preparations unfolding and react accordingly. At first the Allies countered the chlorine cloud with makeshift masks of gauze bandages with ties, moistened with water or urine. They followed in 1916 with the box respirator and steadily improved the gas mask throughout the war. The gas cloud also had its drawbacks for the attacker. The cylinders proved cumbersome and demoralizing for troops who had to live in constant contact with them, while the wind direction could and often did shift during the battle. Although even increasingly capable gas masks offered inadequate protection against mustard gas, the persistent qualities of the powerful vesicant made its use dangerous for both sides.

Military planners considered all forms of gas a terror weapon that would create confusion and panic prior to an offensive. Given the problems with its use and the development of countermeasures, gas increasingly wounded troops rather than killed them. In the final analysis, authorities such as Augustin M. Prentiss and George J. B. Fisher, in *Chemicals in War: A Treatise on Chemical Warfare* (1937), and Ludwig F. Haber, in *The Poisonous Cloud: Chemical*

Warfare in the First World War (1986), estimate that gas caused only one-third of 1 percent of all the casualties in the Great War, and the vast majority of these were nonlethal. Among the American forces, for example, 27.4 percent of the total 258,338 casualties are attributed to gas. Yet, of the 46,419 American wartime deaths, gas accounted for only 1,400, or 2 percent. Most of these casualties resulted from mustard gas. Although British casualties from chemical agents are considerably higher, as one would expect, less than 5 percent died from exposure to gas. The other combatants reflect the same pattern of losses.

Clearly, exposure to poisonous gas was a horrible experience, and veterans of the war often suffered physically and emotionally for years to come. Adolf Hitler, for one, ended the war temporarily blinded by gas, and that experience might well have persuaded him to refrain from using chemical agents against foreign troops in World War II. The incapacitating effects of gas warfare led General J. F. C. Fuller, the British Tank Corps chief of staff in World War I, to declare that, "contrary to popular belief, gas was the most humane weapon used in the war." While an effective weapon, gas was not critical to wartime operations. Apart from Ludendorff's temporary successes in 1918, it produced no significant breakthroughs on the Western Front. Throughout the Great War, gas remained relatively nonlethal, and military planners used it primarily for harassment and denial.

–DAVID N. SPIRES,
BOULDER, COLORADO

Viewpoint:
No. When used properly, in conjunction with small arms fire and artillery barrages, gas was a lethal weapon.

When gas warfare was first proposed to the German high command in 1914, it was conceived as a possible "war winning" weapon that could punch a large hole in the enemy defense lines and allow the German forces to break through. When the Allies first used gas, they also viewed chemical weapons as being potentially decisive on the battlefield. Although the use of gas in warfare did not turn out to be as effective as its practitioners hoped, it was still much more than just a "nuisance weapon." Indeed, gas warfare played a central role in the German Spring offensive of 1918, which came close to breaking the Allied armies on the battlefield.

GAS PIONEER

German soldier Otto Hahn recalls his participation in gas warfare:

In the middle of January I received orders to go and see Geheimrat Haber, who was in Brussels on behalf of the Ministry of War. He explained to me that the Western fronts, which were all bogged down, could be got moving again only by means of new weapons. One of the weapons contemplated was poison gas, in particular chlorine, which was to be blown towards the enemy from the most advanced positions. When I objected that this was a mode of warfare violating the Hague Convention, he said that the French had already started it—though not to much effect—by using rifle-ammunition filled with gas. Besides, it was a way of saving countless lives, if it meant that the war could be brought to an end sooner.

Haber informed me that his job was to set up a special unit for gas-warfare, Pioneer Regiment No. 36. We received our first special training in Berlin, being instructed in the use of the poison gases and the relevant apparatus, including what was called the Drägersche Selbstretter, a protective device that had to be worn when discharging the gas. We also had to learn something about wind and weather, of course.

From the training-course I returned to Flanders and was attached to Infantry Regiment No. 126 as their gas pioneer. My first task was to be what was called a front-line observer, i.e., I had to evaluate positions from which gas might be used. Our position was in the vicinity of Gheluvelt, directly opposite the English lines, and so at times we could only talk in whispers. We were not yet very well entrenched and we were constantly under enemy fire, so the installation of the gas cylinders for the proposed attack was very difficult indeed.

The gas warning was given a number of times, but the attack had to be postponed again and again because of weather conditions. Every time the time of the attack had to be fixed—which had to be twenty-four hours earlier—the wind changed and blew towards us, and the units brought up from the rear had to be taken back again. In the middle of April High Command decided to remove the gas cylinders again and take them to a sector of the front north-east of Ypres, where wind conditions were more favourable.

The reason why it was not entirely successful was probably that both the troops and the Command had become nervous as a result of the many abortive attempts, and also that by then there were no longer sufficient reserves available to consolidate the gains.

Source: Lyn MacDonald, *1914–1918*: Voices & Images of the Great War *(London: Michael Joseph, 1988), pp. 81–82.*

When the Western and Eastern fronts settled into a stalemate by late September 1914, both the Allied and Central Powers looked for some technological means of breaking through the lines of powerful entrenchments that had become characteristic of the war. Shoving masses of infantry at dug-in troops armed with machine guns and protected by trenches and barbed wire was simply a recipe for slaughter; some means had to be found to either incapacitate the enemy or to neutralize the power of the machine gun/trench combination. Some of the most technically minded of the Allies proposed the construction of armored, tracked vehicles to overcome the enemy trenches and machine guns. Both Britain and France began to develop tanks in late 1914. Germany, on the other hand, had the most advanced chemical industry in the world in 1914, and it was natural that the Germans might turn to chemistry as a means of breaking the power of the defense.

In the fall of 1914 chemist Fritz Haber proposed filling artillery shells with tear gas and firing it at enemy lines to incapacitate the enemy long enough for German soldiers to cover the deadly ground before the trenches and break into the defenses. The idea appeared sound and was approved. However, the problem was in the delivery technology. Gas warfare first emerged at Neuve Chappelle on the Western Front in October 1914 when the German army fired some 105-mm artillery shells filled with tear gas at the Allied front lines. The shells were badly designed and the gas was not dispersed. In fact, the French and British had no idea that they had even been on the receiving end of a gas attack. Another attempt to use gas, this time on the Eastern Front in January 1915, also failed. At Bolimov the Germans fired a large number of shells filled with tear gas at the Russian lines to support a counterattack. The cold weather simply froze the tear gas and, for the second time, gas warfare failed.

The Germans were still desperate to find some means of using chemicals to break the stalemate on the Eastern and Western Fronts. Until effective artillery shells were developed, they decided to wait for the right wind conditions and to release gas directly from large canisters. This time it would be chlorine gas, lethal in large doses. It worked by affecting the membranes of the lungs and choking soldiers. Even a small dose could incapacitate a soldier for days or weeks. The German gas attack on the Allied lines at Ypres on 22 and 24 April 1915 was so successful that the Germans were unprepared to follow up their success. The gas cloud, rolling slowly across the battlefield, sent two French divisions into headlong retreat and opened a five-mile gap in the Allied lines. Thousands of Allied soldiers

became casualties to the new weapon as there were no effective gas masks or experience in dealing with gas. The Germans, who had only the most primitive gas protection of their own (cotton masks with applied chemicals) were not prepared to follow up the opportunity for a breakthrough that gas had given them.

Now that gas warfare had become known, every combatant country raced to equip its armies with poison gas and with gas countermeasures in the form of effective gas masks. By September 1915 the British were ready to make their first gas attack to support their offensive against the Germans at Loos. Unlike the German attack of April, the British gas attack was a flop. The wind blew much of the gas back on British lines and the British found that gas had no effect upon the thick field of barbed wire in front of the German trenches. In fact, although the British used poison gas extensively during the war, they never seemed to get the hang of using it to the maximum tactical advantage.

By 1916 the Germans and French could deliver gas by means of artillery shells, which meant that gas could be fired on enemy troops and positions miles behind the front. Phosgene gas, much more lethal than chlorine, was introduced. Phosgene could kill a man in aerial doses of only two hundred parts per ten million. A further refinement to chemical warfare was added with the introduction of mustard gas in 1916. Mustard agent was generally not lethal unless one had a massive dose, but it could incapacitate

soldiers by inflicting severe burns on exposed skin. It could temporarily or permanently blind soldiers. From the tactical viewpoint, it was important because it was persistent. Mustard gas remained potent and disabling for days or even weeks after it was fired and one could cross ground covered in mustard gas only with the greatest precautions.

Both the Allies and the Germans used gas extensively in the war. Total German gas production during the war was 68,100 tons, matching the combined British, French, and American production of 68,905 tons. For the Allies, poison gas was primarily a harassment weapon. Gas canisters or shells would be mixed with smoke shells in the hope of catching the Germans by surprise and killing and disabling a few enemy soldiers. Even if German gas discipline was good, forcing soldiers to wear gas masks for long periods exhausted and demoralized them.

For the Germans, however, gas was much more than a harassment and attrition weapon. If used properly, gas could be effective in increasing the firepower of the army. By 1917 the Germans developed effective tactics for chemical warfare. In making a gas attack, the artillery would first fire salvos of shells containing powerful sensory irritants (known as blue cross for the marking on the shells), the slightest whiff of which would cause sneezing and coughing and make it difficult for the defender to put on his mask. Then the defender would be hit by a heavy concentration of lethal phosgene

American troops with gas masks marching through Chateau-Thierry, 1918

(postcard in scrapbook, Joseph M. Bruccoli Great War Collection, Thomas Cooper Library, University of South Carolina)

POISON GAS

gas (known as green cross). The Germans even brought forward professors of chemistry and meteorologists to calculate the best wind and weather conditions for making a lethal gas attack. Another tactic was to fire highly persistent mustard gas to cover the flanks of an attack to create a chemical barrier between the Germans and any Allied counterattack. These tactics were used in all the major defensive and offensive operations of 1917 and 1918.

The largest and most decisive use of gas in the war was during the German Spring offensive of March 1918 that broke open the Allied front. Stormtroops and gas were an effective combination, and German gas operations helped their infantry restore maneuver to the battlefield in 1918. Gas was used to cover the flanks, to block Allied counterattacks, and to disable Allied artillery as a counterbattery weapon. Throughout the war, and especially in 1918, the Germans proved that gas could be one of the most useful weapons on the battlefield. While both sides employed approximately the same amount of gas during the war, better tactics made the German use of gas far more effective. During the war the Germans and Austrians lost 12,000 men killed by gas with another 288,000 wounded. German gas attacks, on the other hand, killed 78,198 Allied soldiers and wounded another 908,645.

Gas was certainly one of the uglier weapons to be used in the Great War. Yet, despite the prohibitions against gas warfare in the Hague Treaties of 1899 and 1907, there was no great outrage or protest against the new weapon. It was quickly accepted as "just another weapon of war" by both sides. Despite the great effect when first used, both sides adjusted to gas warfare, just as they did to trenches and heavy-artillery bom-

bardments. While the Allies tended to use gas as part of a harassment and attrition strategy, the Germans showed some real finesse in gas warfare, and in 1917–1918 it came close to being one of the decisive weapons of the war.

–JAMES CORUM, USAF SCHOOL OF
ADVANCED AIRPOWER STUDIES

References

Tim Cook, *No Place to Run: The Canadian Corps and Gas Warfare in the First World War* (Vancouver: UBC Press, 1999).

Ludwig F. Haber, *The Poisonous Cloud: Chemical Warfare in the First World War* (Oxford & New York: Oxford University Press, 1986).

Charles E. Heller, *Chemical Warfare in World War I: The American Experience, 1917–1918* (Fort Leavenworth, Kans.: Combat Studies Institute, U.S. Army Command and General Staff College, 1985).

William Moore, *Gas Attack!: Chemical Warfare 1915–18 and Afterwards* (London: Cooper; New York: Hippocrene Books, 1987).

Albert Palazzo, *Seeking Victory on the Western Front: The British Army and Chemical Warfare in World War I* (Lincoln: University of Nebraska Press, 2000).

Augustin M. Prentiss and George J. B. Fisher, *Chemicals in War: A Treatise on Chemical Warfare* (New York: McGraw-Hill, 1937).

Donald Richter, *Chemical Soldiers: British Gas Warfare in World War I* (Lawrence: University Press of Kansas, 1992).

SCHLIEFFEN PLAN

Was the Schlieffen Plan of the German General Staff a sound war strategy?

Viewpoint: Yes. The various directives that made up the German war plan indicate a high level of flexibility and a willingness to respond to events.

Viewpoint: No. The Schlieffen Plan was predicated on an inexorable progression to an all-or-nothing victory.

Viewpoint: No. The Schlieffen Plan seriously underestimated the capabilities of enemy forces and did not take into account their tenacity and rapid deployment.

Alfred von Schlieffen, Chief of the German General Staff from 1891 to 1906, invited description, when not caricature, as an archetype of the specialist with tunnel vision, a man who would send staff problems to subordinates on Christmas Eve and expect a solution on his desk the morning of 26 December. The operational plan bearing his name is usually described in corresponding terms, as a comprehensive, detailed scheme for deploying the German army so as to conquer France by destroying the French army in one giant enveloping movement through the Low Countries.

In the years after the Great War supporters of the plan—most of them German officers—presented it as a design for victory, disrupted by the mistakes of Schlieffen's successor. Critics, whose numbers have steadily increased, describe it as a doomsday machine triggering general war by its emphasis on a first strike and as a military myth, requiring its details to go impossibly right in order to have any real chance of succeeding.

The Schlieffen Plan was no straitjacket, but a series of annually revised memoranda, reflecting current military and political developments as well as the results of particular staff inspections and maneuvers. The general outline, however, was shaped by Schlieffen's long-standing convictions that first, Germany could not win or indeed survive a general war of any length; and second, the developing alliance between France and Russia meant Germany must prepare for a two-front war as a military certainty. The French army, developed since the 1870s as a virtual carbon copy of the German original, was the enemy Schlieffen considered the easiest to defeat in a short time; a corresponding focus on Russia ran too great a risk of being sucked into the vast, undeveloped wastelands of the east.

To implement this strategy, Schlieffen concentrated on developing the offensive capacities of the army, including establishing a command system based on electronic technology that he expected would make possible the fine-tuning of large-unit movements from a central headquarters. He emphasized reducing as far as possible the time required to mobilize and concentrate a field army that grew ever larger—though not as large as Schlieffen considered necessary for his grand design. For the tactical advantage of gaining a few hours, he was willing to accept the risks of violating the neutrality of both Belgium and Holland. Above all, Schlieffen's approach denied the possibility of fine-tuning by diplomats and politicians. It was at best a strategic solution to a problem of policy.

Schlieffen's retirement in 1906 led to some modifications of his plan, but on the whole the German army and general staff accepted its principles and pursued its ends with a single-mindedness that came closer to success in 1914 than is generally realized. The problem was that the limitations of the plan were exposed by events while no military alternatives existed—which in turn threw added burdens on a political system ill equipped to cope with them.

Viewpoint:
Yes. The various directives that made up the German war plan indicate a high level of flexibility and a willingness to respond to events.

Perhaps no other war plan has attracted as much attention as Alfred von Schlieffen's memorandum to his successor as Chief of the General Staff—the so-called Schlieffen Plan. In this memorandum, Schlieffen provided the outline for a future German deployment plan that envisioned the rapid and total defeat of the French army within weeks of the outbreak of war. Schlieffen aimed to achieve this decisive victory in the open field by marching the bulk of the German army through the neutral countries of Luxembourg, Belgium, and the Netherlands and thereby bypassing the heavily fortified Franco-German border. While Schlieffen wrote this document around the time of his retirement at the end of 1905, his memorandum served as the basis for the German war plan of 1914 and has excited commentators ever since.

Immediately after the German defeat in World War I, German officers began writing in support of the ideas embodied in Schlieffen's memorandum. The stature of these officers, most of whom had served in high-level staff posts during the war, lent credence to their assertions that had Schlieffen's plan been followed to the letter, then Germany would have won World War I in the first weeks of the conflict. Writers such as Wilhelm Groener, the head of the Railway Section of the General Staff from 1914 to 1916, and Hermann von Kuhl, the Chief of Staff to the First Army and later to Army Group Crown Prince Rupprecht, castigated Schlieffen's successor, Helmuth von Moltke (the Younger), for altering Schlieffen's master plan and thereby causing the German defeat at the battle of the Marne (1914). By the beginning of World War II, this interpretation—that the Schlieffen Plan had been a sure recipe for success, but was tinkered with by an unworthy successor—had become standard. Most Germans, and indeed most other observers, held the Schlieffen Plan to be a brilliant plan worked out meticulously by a great mind years before the outbreak of hostilities.

It was only in the aftermath of the Nazi defeat in World War II that this interpretation began to be reexamined. In the 1950s Gerhard Ritter, a historian from Freiburg University, began publishing a monumental study of German "militarism." In the process of writing this work, he came across drafts of Schlieffen's plan in the documents captured by the Allies at the end of World War II. These he published, along with a biting attack on the standard interpretation of the Schlieffen Plan developed in the interwar years. In contrast to the retired officers writing in the 1920s and 1930s, Ritter maintained that the Schlieffen Plan far from being a sure recipe for success was, in fact, an act of desperation.

One error, however, links these two different interpretations of Schlieffen's eponymous plan. Both sides of the debate saw the Schlieffen Plan as being a scrupulously detailed prescription that was meant to be followed to the letter. The writers of the interwar period and those of the post–World War II era believed that Schlieffen had meant his plan to be used under all political circumstances and to be carried out exactly as he had written it down. However, a careful reading of Schlieffen's prewar writings and an examination of the orders issued by Moltke the Younger in 1914 proves this interpretation to be untrue. In fact, the Schlieffen Plan was meant to be utilized in specific strategic circumstances and was designed to provide overall guidance for a campaign that could unfold in several different ways. Rather than being prescriptive, the German war plan was intended to be applied with judgment based upon the situation.

First, it must be remembered that the Schlieffen Plan was in fact titled "War Against France," and was one of two plans worked up by Schlieffen and his subordinates on the General Staff in late 1905 and early 1906. Since 1900 Schlieffen had been developing two separate war plans, one for a war against France and Russia, for example, a two-front war, and the other for a war against France alone, a one-front war. Schlieffen's famous memorandum of 1905 was written to provide the guidance for the construction of the German plan for 1906–1907 for a one-front war against France unsupported by Russia. This mainte-

SCHLIEFFEN PLAN

German artillery unit riding through Brussels in 1914

(from The Illustrated War News, 2 September 1914, page 18, Joseph M. Bruccoli Great War Collection, Thomas Cooper Library, University of South Carolina)

nance of two plans would allow the German army to react as needed in the case of a war. If Germany found itself at war with France alone, then Aufmarschplan I (Deployment Plan I) would be used. On the other hand, if Germany found herself fighting France and Russia simultaneously, then Aufmarschplan II would be put into effect.

It is clear that by the time of his retirement in 1905, Schlieffen believed that Aufmarschplan II was not of great use. He favored a western offensive as such an attack would offer the best prospects for Germany to defeat the army of one of her foes quickly. However, he maintained the dual-plan system in order to be ready for all contingencies. Such a system was kept in place until 1913, when Schlieffen's successor as Chief of the General Staff, Moltke, decided to scrap Aufmarschplan II. While Schlieffen had felt this plan would not be used because of the poor quality of the Russian army and the time it would take for it to mobilize, Moltke decided it was unlikely to be used for other reasons. In the years between 1906 and 1913 Moltke had watched an increasing bond develop between the French and Russian armies. This cooperation manifested itself in an ever greater amount of aid being given by the French to improve the combat capability of the Russian army and, importantly, its ability to mobilize vast manpower reserves quickly. Thus, while Schlieffen could all but discount the Russian army in a future war, Moltke could only expect a more dangerous and rapid threat from the east. This apprehension led him to scrap his plan for a two-front war, as he

believed it was no longer viable to divide the German army in the face of two capable foes.

Moltke's decision to concentrate on the west was built upon rational calculation of the changed strategic situation. He concentrated on improving the timing of Schlieffen's plan in an effort to ensure the defeat of the French army, and Moltke believed that this strategy could be accomplished rapidly. Despite Russian advances, the French army would still be fielded first. This situation offered the Germans the opportunity to engage the French before the Russians had completed their mobilization. Moreover, the French did not have the geographic space in which to withdraw in the face of a German attack. Thus, Moltke believed that they could be brought to battle and defeated decisively before the Russians could do serious damage in the east.

Despite the necessity for a faster victory in Moltke's time, however, he did not change the essence of Schlieffen's plan. The goal remained the destruction of the French army, wherever it might be found. In war games conducted during the writing of his plan, Schlieffen had experimented with a variety of scenarios for the defeat of the French army. In the wake of the defeat of the Russian army in the Russo-Japanese War (1904–1905), Schlieffen believed that the French would be unlikely to leave the safety of their fortresses and attack the German forces. Nonetheless, he, and Moltke after him, conducted war games with the French attacking Germany through several different routes. The results of all these games were the destruction of the French army by the powerful German right wing advocated by Schlieffen's plan that had advanced in various depths into France through neutral

Belgium and Luxembourg. These projections demonstrate that, for Schlieffen and later for Moltke, it did not matter where the French army was destroyed so long as it was defeated quickly. The games proved that the strong right wing called for by Schlieffen's memorandum offered the best prospect of success for the German army whether the French attacked Germany or whether they remained on the defensive behind their fortress line.

This goal was reflected in the plan itself. Although Schlieffen's plan is often seen as being formulaic and as demanding the German army reach "phase lines" by specified times, this interpretation is not supported by a close reading of Schlieffen's 1905 memorandum. In fact, Schlieffen's plan merely outlined how the German army was to advance behind the fortified Franco-German border. How the decisive battle would be fought once the German army was in northern France was dependent upon French reaction. Although he made plans for a German advance on Paris, Schlieffen clearly hoped that the decisive encounter would take place long before German forces reached the strong French capital. Hence, his memorandum makes provision for a variety of possible scenarios in which the French stand at different points to fight the invading German army.

The fact that no firm guidance could be given by Schlieffen or Moltke as to where the decisive encounter with the French would take place influenced how they expected the German army to fight. German planners had to leave matters largely in the hands of the commanders of the operational units of the German army—the seven armies deployed in the west. In doing so, they were also following the long tradition of decentralized command within their army. This tradition maintained that commanders on the ground would invariably have better information than the commander in chief behind the fighting and should therefore be allowed to conduct operations as they saw fit within the overall intent of the commander in chief. Thus, when war broke out in August 1914, Moltke issued his army commanders "directives" that contained what he hoped to achieve (the destruction of the French army) and only as much detail as was needed to coordinate the advance of the seven separate armies. Where the French were to be engaged depended on what the French did. How they were to be engaged was left largely to the commanders in the field.

The Schlieffen Plan was not designed by its author to be the "secret to victory." Both Schlieffen and his successor Moltke viewed the plan as one that should be employed flexibly. The overall strategic situation was to dictate how and when it should be used. Until 1913 it was one of two plans and was meant to be employed in the case of a war against France alone. As the strategic situation changed, so Moltke changed German war plans and shelved Aufmarschplan II. Additionally, neither Schlieffen nor Moltke could be sure exactly how the French would react to a German invasion of France by way of Belgium; hence the plan itself was written to take into account several different possible scenarios once the German army began conducting operations, which was to be left to the discretion of the commanders of the seven Western armies. The course of the campaign was not to be dictated by a detailed plan drawn up during peacetime. Both Schlieffen and Moltke were well acquainted with Helmuth von Moltke (the Elder)'s dictum: "No plan survives first contact with the enemy."

—ROBERT T. FOLEY, KING'S COLLEGE, LONDON

Viewpoint:
No. The Schlieffen Plan was predicated on an inexorable progression to an all-or-nothing victory.

Once one of the constants in the ever-changing constellation of historical interpretation, historians' understanding of the Schlieffen Plan has recently come under question. Yet, while flawed in many respects, Gerhard Ritter's famous work, Schlieffen Plan: Critique of a Myth (1958), correctly characterizes the Schlieffen-Moltke Plan as a "daring, indeed an over-daring, gamble whose success depended upon many lucky accidents." For Ritter the plan demonstrated the consequences of rampant militarism and of military planning conducted without any reference to economic or political realities and without concern for political aims. He went so far as to call it a "curse" that ultimately brought catastrophe to Germany and Europe. One scholar, Terence Zuber, has exposed the flaws in Ritter's analysis, especially his conclusions about the time-phasing of the operation and the envelopment of Paris. However, Zuber's own contention—that the Schlieffen Plan was not a plan at all, but a ruse to influence the German parliament to increase the budget of the Imperial Army—is less than persuasive. Terence Holmes has successfully refuted Zuber's main argument by showing the many continuities that existed between the initial planning conducted before 1900 and that around 1905–1906, and Helmuth von Moltke's adjustments thereafter. However, in so doing Holmes has raised additional questions about the overall intent of what historian Dennis E. Showalter, in *Tannenberg: Clash of Empires* (1991), maintains should be called the Schlieffen-Moltke Plan after its two primary authors. Nonetheless, despite the contributions of recent scholarship, the evidence remains decisively in favor of the view that the German war plan of 1914 was a doomsday machine designed to gain an all-or-nothing victory for the Reich.

Count Alfred von Schlieffen began working on the plan shortly after he became Chief of Staff of the German Great General Staff in 1891. The age-old military problem of Germany had been how to avoid a war on two fronts. This dilemma—always a possibility—became a probability in 1890, when Friedrich von Holstein and others in the German Foreign Ministry advised against renewing the Russo-German Reinsurance Treaty (1887–1890) that the renowned Chancellor of the Reich, Otto von Bismarck, had established with Russia to protect the eastern flank of Germany. This strategic faux pas eventuated in a Russian-French rapprochement and the subsequent alliance of Russia with France and Great Britain, transforming the German "nightmare" of encirclement into a reality. Chancellor Bernard von Bülow's aggressive foreign policy, *Weltpolitik* (World Policy), and Admiral Alfred von Tirpitz's maritime strategy, *Flottenpolitik* (Fleet Policy), of making allies by intimidation, merely hardened that circle against Germany instead of providing the international prestige and alliance with Britain that the Kaiser desired. With a vengeful France in the west and the "Russian danger" in the east, the threat of a two-front war became greater every year. More important, it posed a near-insoluble problem for the war planners on the General Staff. In 1900, for example, Britain, France, and Russia outnumbered Germany and Austria-Hungary by more than 2.75 to 1 in military personnel (army and navy) and 5.2 to 1 in warship tonnage. By 1914 the gap had closed to 2 to 1 in personnel and 2.6 to 1 in warships. However, the central position of Germany and its inability to carry on a protracted war meant that the situation was still grave.

The key to success of the plan, as revealed in Schlieffen's Cannae essays, published in the General Staff's *Quarterly* between 1909 and 1913 and later as a collected volume, was based on a so-called strategy of annihilation—*Vernichtungsstrategie*—that aimed at destroying the enemy's physical capacity to fight by totally defeating his army in the field, usually by means of a single or double envelopment that would cut their lines of reinforcement and retreat. To achieve this annihilation of the French army, Schlieffen planned to launch his armies on a great wheeling motion through Belgium into northern France to cut off the French armies and crush them against the Swiss border. While in military usage, the German term *Vernichtung* did not equate to "extermination"—as translated in the English edition of the Cannae essays—Schlieffen's plan, nonetheless, called for "decisive" results, which essentially meant destroying enough of the French army (perhaps 75 percent) so as to remove it as an offensive threat, thereby permitting the bulk of the German forces to be shifted toward East Prussia to fight the Russians. Schlieffen himself admitted that, if it could be achieved, the total destruction of the enemy's force in a single blow—as Hannibal had effected against the Roman armies at Cannae (216 B.C.E.)—amounted to a work of the highest military genius. Although he admitted that such a battle was "very rarely possible," he eventually came to see it as the only hope for Germany. The envelopment of Paris was included as a contingency in the plan, but it would occur only if the French did not launch an offensive of their own, or chose not to stand and fight before or along the Oise and Aisne Rivers. The French could not be allowed to fall back in the direction of the Marne and Seine, otherwise, as Schlieffen concluded, the war would "be endless." Thus, in a manner of speaking, under Schlieffen's tutelage, the mentality within the General Staff was that what was desirable—the destruction of the French army—had become necessary; and what was necessary was possible.

Although Schlieffen's successor, Moltke the Younger, nephew of the elder Field Marshal Helmuth von Moltke, made significant modifications to the plan during his eight-year tenure (1906–1914). Moltke reduced the arc of the wheel so that the German advance did not violate Dutch neutrality; and he strengthened the German left wing against a possible French offensive in the south. He, therefore, essentially accepted the underlying premises of the Schlieffen Plan, especially the need to defeat France first. A fatalist who believed war was inevitable, Moltke kept a close eye on developments in Russia. The Russian army had recovered faster than expected from its thrashing at the hands of the Japanese in the war of 1904–1905. By 1910, German intelligence reports indicated that the Russians had received new equipment and undergone significant organizational and doctrinal reforms. A central reserve of seven new divisions had been created in European Russia, with plans to create eight more. By 1911 the Russian mobilization schedule had been shortened to only half what it had been in 1906. In 1912 a great railroad-building program was launched that was to result in ten thousand kilometers of new track by 1922. This new railroad system would better link the Russian interior with its borders, enabling the Russian army to reinforce

A MASTER PLAN

Immediately following World War I, military officers and strategists throughout Europe reviewed the prewar plans of Germany. The following selection comes from a British military journal:

Schlieffen detailed 10 divisions for the Eastern front; Moltke, 8. Moltke, still less Schlieffen, never had the number of corps and divisions which the Schlieffen plan assumed to exist—the latter's plan was only a "project." But, taking the above figures: In Schlieffen's plan the defensive wing is to the offensive as 4 to 37 1/2 (1 to 9 3/8), in Moltke's 8 to 27 (1 to 3 3/8); but Schlieffen's with the forces available in 1914, would have been 4 to 31 (1 to 7 3/8). . . .

The reasons for strengthening the left wing are given by Dr. Bredt as follows: Moltke could not abandon Alsace, as Schlieffen designed to do, for the Italians might take part on the German side; General Pollio, the Italian Chief of Staff until his death in 1914, had assured him they would. As they were to be brought to Alsace, Moltke considered it necessary to hold that province with two corps. If the Italians did not appear, then the question of the transport of the two corps to the right wing would arise. As we know, the French attack towards Mulhausen fatally delayed this. These two corps, plus the two corps sent from France to Russia, would, if added to the right wing, have made it as strong as Schlieffen intended.

It emerges incidentally that the Schlieffen plan was worked out for war on the Western front only; for when drawn up, Russia was still very weak as a result of the Manchurian War. It also contemplated additions to the army that did not take place. There was only a general statement that in the case of Russia intervening, ten divisions should be withdrawn from the Western front and sent to the East, without altering the proportion of the two wings.

More important than the changes in the technical details was the alteration of the plan politically. In the Schlieffen plan "there was no ultimatum to Belgium, but the German army, without any notification, was first to deploy on the Dutch-Belgian frontier." As the German plan would be divulged by this, it was assumed that the French would take countermeasures. These, according to Schlieffen's views, could only be the occupation of the natural defensive position in the Meuse valley south of Namur; and thus the French would themselves violate Belgian neutrality. Such a plan must have been at least considered by the French, and in 1914 the German General Staff took it for granted that they would advance to the Meuse. All this presumed that Belgian neutrality would not be broken by Germany first. Such a step Graf Schlieffen desired, if possible, to avoid. He wished to leave sufficient time so that, in one way or another, the German statesmen would be able to evade the reproach of the violation of Belgian neutrality. "That Liege would always be captured sufficiently soon after the entry of the German army into Belgium, to serve as the railway junction for reinforcements and supply, could be accepted . . ."

"Schlieffen did not consider it out of the question, in view of the then [*1905*] political situation, as he judged it, that German diplomacy might succeed on the outbreak of war against England in obtaining from the Netherlands Government by an amicable arrangement *(auf geftlichen Wege)* permission for the German army to cross the Dutch province of Limburg (Maastrich, Roermond). By this means the fortress of Liege would be avoided by passing north of it, and could quickly be brought to surrender by threatening it in the rear."

Moltke did not believe that Holland would give permission to traverse her territory, and dropped the idea of an advance of the German right wing by this route. On the other hand he feared that Liège could not be taken quickly enough by an accelerated artillery attack to prevent a delay in the general advance of the right wing. It was most important not to give the Belgians time to put the fortress in a state of defence, and in particular to construct defences in the intervals between the forts and destroy the important railways passing through Liege. It also appeared to him that it was impossible to march an army between Liege and the Dutch frontier. He therefore decided to take Liege by a *coup de main* carried out by troops of the peace establishment without mobilization immediately on outbreak of war. "Two days and the following night were allowed for the execution of the *coup de main.*"

Source: The Army Quarterly, 18 (July 1929): 286–290, as found in the World War I Document Archive, Internet web site, http://library.byu.edu/~rdh/wwi/1914m/schlieffen.html.

SCHLIEFFEN PLAN

critical areas more quickly. Hence, in Moltke's view, not only would a war in the east not yield decisive results because the Russians could retreat into their vast interior, it was only a matter of time before slim prospects for success had vanished altogether. The main effort of Germany, then, had to be against France.

Accordingly, Moltke began to push for war sooner than later. To wait only meant that chances for German victory would diminish further. In 1913 Moltke suspended all contingency planning for a conflict with Russia, effectively limiting the Reich to one war plan. Regardless of the actual political aims and the particular circumstances that could occasion the outbreak of the next European war, therefore, Germany would have to attack France and to do that, she would also have to invade Belgium and bring Britain into the war. Moltke appears to have known that his plan was a desperate gamble. He hoped—rather than expected or assumed—that France could be defeated quickly and that the war would be short. Operational estimates for the duration of the war ranged from one and one-half to four years, though economic and logistical preparations seem to have been for a much shorter period.

The Schlieffen-Moltke Plan put tremendous logistical and timing demands on the German armies, though the time-phasing of the plan was not as rigid as historians once believed. Army and corps commanders were to execute their assigned tasks according to the prescribed plan, though German actions were actually somewhat contingent upon the success (or failure) of enemy and friendly operations. To be sure, time was not on Schlieffen's or Moltke's side, and this situation precluded extending complete freedom of action to subordinate commanders. Whereas in the wars against Austria (1866) and France (1870–1871) Moltke the elder, Chief of Staff of the Great General Staff (1857–1888), could afford to wait for his opponent to make a mistake, the younger Moltke had to try to induce his adversary into making one. Moltke had to prevent the Entente armies from going to ground and drawing the German army into a stalemate, as that would ultimately prove disastrous. The political and military leadership of Germany feared that a long war might lead to a Socialist revolution and the overthrow of the political system of the Reich. The Entente did not have to fight an offensive war to defeat the Central Powers, though it intended to do so. It merely had to dig in behind defensive fieldworks in combination with a naval blockade to strangle the Central Powers slowly. Thus, the Schlieffen-Moltke Plan was an all-or-nothing gamble because its designers believed Germany had no other choice

militarily. Anything less would have meant the inevitable eclipse of German military power.

—ANTULIO ECHEVARRIA, STRATEGIC STUDIES INSTITUTE

Viewpoint:
No. The Schlieffen Plan seriously underestimated the capabilities of enemy forces and did not take into account their tenacity and rapid deployment.

The Schlieffen Plan, named after its architect Alfred von Schlieffen, German Chief of Staff from 1891 to 1906, was a product of several elements that grew from the wars of 1866 and 1870. Its direct inspiration was the growing realization by the General Staff that in any realistic scenario for a major continental war Germany must expect to be forced to fight on two widely separated fronts, against France and Russia, which had completed a mutual defense pact in 1894. These two countries were reacting to the status of Germany as the dominant power in Middle Europe after having thoroughly defeated France in 1870 and Austria in 1866. France, determined not to be humiliated militarily as it had been at mid century, had fortified its German frontier heavily with a system of formidable works such as Verdun and Belfort, designed to channel any invasion into preselected killing grounds. The thought of confronting the fortresses bristling along the French border triggered the preference of the German General Staff for envelopment over attack

Schlieffen and his successors knew, moreover, they could not afford a long war on two fronts. Correspondingly, it was imperative to achieve a quick victory against either France or Russia, then turn against the remaining foe. Because of the vast distances involved and the general disorganization of the Russian army, the General Staff calculated that it would take at least forty days for Russia to mobilize fully. That lag time gave Germany a "window of opportunity" to swiftly and safely envelop the left flank of the French army, even though that strategy involved violating the neutrality of Belgium and the Netherlands. At the end of Schlieffen's projected maneuver, the German army would be outside Paris, free to attack the retreating French army from the rear, occupy Paris, and deal with any surviving French forces in the south and west, much as had been done in 1870–1871.

Once Schlieffen's grand strategy had been accepted, all else involved working out schedules and details. Railroads became the dominant element of mobilization because they made it possible to mobilize large numbers of reserve troops quickly and move them to the theater of war with unprecedented precision and rapidity. That mass, however, created its own problem: dealing with armies of unprecedented size. No general, no planning staff, had ever handled an army of three million men. The slightest error could create what modern chaos theory calls a "butterfly effect," with troops and trains piling up on every railroad line in Germany. It was scarcely remarkable that for the German General Staff war planning became a game of railroad timetables and telegraph operators. It was a plan of immense complexity. In the final version that was perfected by Schlieffen's successor Helmuth von Moltke the Younger, nephew of the first great Chief of Staff, Field Marshal Helmuth von Moltke, 200,000 telegraph employees and 100,000 telephone operators using 32,847 telephones were needed just to initiate the mobilization. The plan then called for 30,000 locomotives, 65,000 passenger cars, and 100,000 freight carriers to move 25 German army corps to disembarkation points.

Two-thirds of the available troops would be involved in the envelopment through Belgium, initially funneling into an area twelve miles wide because of Moltke's decision to respect Dutch neutrality for the sake of securing a window to the outside world. The end of the line came at frontier cities such as the ancient Carolingian capital, Aachen. Here the luxury of railroad travel ended and the joys of the march began. Each corps stretched out for almost forty miles, counting road space for guns and supply trains. The march plans were designed to enable the 40,000 men of a corps to enter battle in a single day, coordinating its movements with the three or four other corps that made up a field army. That was wargaming. Maps and sand tables incorporated train schedules, marching orders, and the logistics of providing 2 million tons of hay for the horses and 1 million rations a day for the troops. They did not incorporate broken axles, exhausted men, or horses with harness galls.

Nor did they allow for changing circumstances. In the last hours before the main troop movements began, German kaiser William II received information leading him to believe France might after all remain neutral. When he told Moltke that now Germany could just turn the whole army against Russia, the Chief of Staff went into shock. With great difficulty Moltke convinced the emperor that it was impossible to turn around or even slow the invasion without courting disaster. He took up field command of

the invasion a broken man from the effort. The Schlieffen Plan as it had been constructed could not allow for anything but victory.

Based as it was on abstract theories of force and movement, the Schlieffen Plan ignored its opponents. It did not envision the tenacity of the British Expeditionary Force (BEF) at Mons and Le Cateau. It did not allow for the coolness of French generalissimo Joseph Joffre, who detached troops facing the German infantry in Lorraine and brought them quickly in good order to the Marne. Schlieffen's grand design took no account of the French taxicabs that bought time by moving troops from the south through Paris without their meters running. Forced to consider withdrawing lest an emerging seventy-five-mile gap between his two armies be exploited by the French, Moltke and his successor Erich von Falkenhayn had no contingency plans and were forced to improvise their next moves. The eventual result was four years of stalemate.

On the Eastern Front the Schlieffen Plan ran into another set of difficulties and misjudgments. The plan postulated that Russia would not be able to mobilize its forces before the defeat of France enabled transferring the main German force to the Eastern Front. Russia, however, sufficiently improved its rail network and its mobilization plans that the High Command was able to send two full armies into East Prussia in less than two weeks. A badly shaken German army retreated toward the Vistula, its commander becoming the first field army chief in modern German history to be relieved. The new command team of Paul von Hindenburg, Erich Ludendorff, and Max Hoffmann found their chance to reverse the situation when the First and Second Russian Armies, divided by the Masurian Lakes, lost contact with each other and allowed the Germans to concentrate against first one, then the other, defeating them in detail.

What was supposed to be a holding action became the first major victory for the German army in World War I. Even its immediate fruits were wasted as the German ally, Austria, marched into disaster. The intended role of Austria in the Schlieffen Plan was to hold Russia in check to the south. Instead, Habsburg chief of staff Conrad von Hötzendorff allowed his strategic reserve to dangle in space between the Balkan and Russian fronts, then sent his limited available forces blindly forward until flanked by the Russians and suffering nearly one million killed, wounded, or captured in a forced retreat back across the Austrian border.

The Schlieffen Plan was based on the model of a railroad timetable—or better put in modern terms, an airline schedule—on full bookings, cooperative weather, and standard operability. Even small, unexpected contingencies disrupt flights across a continent. The French and British were not supposed to be in position to do what they did in the Marne campaign. The outcome of that operation in turn forced a stalemate in the west. The Eastern Front, supposed to be a stalemate until victorious troops from the west arrived, instead became a killing field covering hundreds of square miles instead of thousands of square yards. The Schlieffen Plan, indeed, was a doomsday machine—but not the kind its creators intended.

–JOHN WHEATLEY, BROOKLYN
CENTER, MINNESOTA

References

Arden Bucholz, Moltke, Schlieffen and Prussian War Planning (New York: Berg, 1991).

D. N. Collins, "The Franco-Russian Alliance and Russian Railways, 1891–1914," Historical Journal, 16 (1973): 777–788.

Martin van Creveld, Supplying War: Logistics From Wallenstein to Patton (Cambridge & New York: Cambridge University Press, 1977).

L. L. Farrar Jr., "The Short War Illusion: The Syndrome of German Strategy, August–December 1914," Militärgeschichtliche Mitteilungen, 31 (1972): 39–52.

Robert T. Foley, Alfred von Schlieffen's Military Writings (London: Frank Cass, 2002).

Foley, Attrition: Its Theory and Application in German Strategy, 1880–1916. Dissertation, Kings College, 1999.

Stig Förster, "Der deutsche Generalstab und die Illusionen des Kurzen Krieges, 1871–1914, Metakritik Eines Mythos," Militärgeschichtliche Mitteilungen, 54 (1995): 61–95.

Holger H. Herwig, The First World War: Germany and Austria-Hungary, 1914–1918 (London & New York: Arnold, 1997).

Herwig, "From Tirpitz Plan to Schlieffen Plan: Some Observations on German Military Planning," Journal of Strategic Studies, 9 (1986): 53–63.

Terence M. Holmes, "The Reluctant March on Paris: A Reply to Terence Zuber's 'The Schlieffen Plan,'" War in History, 8 (2001): 208–232.

Paul M. Kennedy, ed., The War Plans of the Great Powers, 1880–1914 (London & Boston: Allen & Unwin, 1979).

Annika Mombauer, Helmuth von Moltke and the Origins of the First World War (Cambridge & New York: Cambridge University Press, 2001).

Gerhard Ritter, The Schlieffen Plan: Critique of a Myth, translated by Andrew and Eva Wilson (London: Wolff, 1958).

Ritter, The Sword and the Sceptre: The Problem of Militarism in Germany, volume 2, European Powers and the Wilhelmine Empire, 1890–1914, translated by Heinz Norden (Coral Gables, Fla.: University of Miami Press, 1972).

Gunther Rothenberg, "Moltke, Schlieffen, and the Doctrine of Strategic Envelopment," in Makers of Modern Strategy: From Machiavelli to the Nuclear Age, edited by Peter Paret (Princeton: Princeton University Press, 1986), pp. 296–325.

Dennis E. Showalter, Tannenberg: Clash of Empires (Hamden, Conn.: Archon Books, 1991).

David Stevenson, Armaments and the Coming of War: Europe, 1904–1914 (Oxford & New York: Clarendon Press, 1996).

Jehuda L. Wallach, The Dogma of the Battle of Annihilation: The Theories of Clausewitz and Schlieffen and Their Impact on the German Conduct of Two World Wars (Westport, Conn.: Greenwood Press, 1986).

Terence Zuber, "The Schlieffen Plan Reconsidered," War in History, 6 (1999): 262–303.

SOCIALISTS

Did European Socialists give their ultimate loyalty to national governments rather than the universal proletariat during the war?

Viewpoint: Yes. Socialist parties sustained national war efforts with recruits, votes, and propaganda.

Viewpoint: No. Socialists took advantage of the general war weariness to advance the cause of workers.

The outbreak of war in August 1914 came as a seismic shock to a European Left that was well on its way to making terms in practice with the capitalist society it continued to challenge in principle. Anarchism and Anarcho-Syndicalism, influential for decades in Spain, Italy, and France, was in retreat before states whose intelligence and security services were proving all too capable of coping with "propaganda of the deed." Marxism had been more successful, both in organizing workers and securing representation in the parliamentary systems of the Continent.

Repressive measures such as those undertaken by the German Empire had ultimately proved too costly for states whose legitimacy depended on doing things for their citizens, not to them. Government-sponsored insurance and welfare programs provided a different sort of challenge, one involving defusing Socialist movements by diminishing the sources of envy, grievance, and resentment on which Socialism depended for recruits. One Socialist response had been "Revisionism": abandoning any belief in the inevitability and necessity of revolution in favor of building on specific gains to produce de facto socialization of political and economic systems. That view was too strong for an orthodox majority that continued to insist on revolution—but revolution as an eschatological experience rather than a political one, something that would come at an unspecified future date but for then was best neither dwelt on nor discussed. In consequence Socialism—and many Socialists—became "at ease in Capitalism," developing alternative societies in which it was possible to do everything from birth to burial in Socialist contexts, making no more concessions to "the system" than the minimum imposed by registry offices, tax collectors, and conscription officials.

The internationalism of which Socialism historically boasted was far from dead, but it was also far from being strong enough to provide a workable alternative for the tide of patriotism that moved both the leaders of the movement and its rank and file behind their respective countries in 1914. Socialist belligerence, however, was less principled than circumstantial. In all the belligerent countries, Socialists proclaimed support for a defensive war to defend threatened or violated rights. In all belligerent countries Socialists hoped as well that the conflict would bring the final victory of Socialism closer—albeit by domestically peaceful means. Even as the costs of the conflict escalated, relatively few Socialists seriously considered revolution to be an option.

That pattern began to change by 1916, as radical Russian exiles made their case for violence to Socialist leaders and intellectuals willing to take the risks of meeting in neutral countries. Events in Russia that same year brought the question of revolution to center stage. Even before the Bolsheviks seized power, the notion of a synergy between peace abroad and change at home began affecting Socialist parties in the other major belligerents. Tensions arose between advocates of increasing influence, who eventually assumed power in the dirigiste (state economic control) systems generated by the war, and supporters of drastic action to sweep away the entire system in favor of a new paradigm. The radicals triumphed in Russia; the statists won in Germany. Elsewhere the issue continued to be a source of tension and weakness in leftist ranks throughout the interwar years.

Viewpoint:
Yes. Socialist parties sustained national war efforts with recruits, votes, and propaganda.

The outbreak of World War I in 1914 galvanized European populations behind their governments to an unprecedented—and unexpected—degree. The political figures, ideologues, and ordinary individuals who reflected that enthusiasm included Europeans of all political persuasions, including socialists. Rather than acting as dogmatic fanatics committed to the solidarity of the international working class, the overwhelming majority of European Socialists actively supported their national governments in the war.

The major reason for this unexpected show of socialist patriotism was that by 1914 revolutionary Marxism had been by and large discredited as a political philosophy. A rising generation of "revisionist" socialist intellectuals had come to realize that their ideals of social justice, populist democracy, and economic reform were best served by competition in a free marketplace of ideas and dedicated work through the existing institutions of government and society. Establishing a socialist government through violent revolution was thought to be a counterproductive goal, for abstract political radicalism oriented toward the future both obscured and discredited the more-immediate needs of the working class. Many socialists came to see revolutionary violence as ultimately unnecessary, believing that the main goals of their movement were more compatible with stable liberal democracy and regulated capitalist economics than they were with the turmoil of revolution and dictatorship that Karl Marx had both predicted and demanded. In European countries ruled by constitutional monarchies—even authoritarian ones such as Imperial Germany—a large number of socialists were monarchists.

Although the transformation of European socialism into an essentially democratic force was neither fully understood nor widely trusted in the years leading up to World War I, it became astonishingly clear in August 1914. As the series of war declarations crisscrossed the Continent, armies mobilized in good order in the absence of socialist antiwar agitation and with no palpable resistance from trained soldiers who supported socialism in civilian life. In France more than 98 percent of the reservists called up in August 1914 responded promptly, and this punctuality was only typical among the combatant powers. The 2,500 French socialists and other radicals whom the Ministry of the Interior had identified as potential subversives to be arrested in the event of war made no trouble, and four-fifths of them eventually served in uniform. In Britain, where the Labour Party (founded only in 1900) remained a marginal political force until after the war, many socialist volunteers, such as the fighter ace Edward Mannock, became war heroes. Others were entrusted with significant responsibility.

The attitudes and actions of socialist political leaders across Europe confirmed the truth about the new moderation of socialism. In France the socialist movement had been thrown into initial disarray by the assassination of its de facto leader, Jean Jaurès, by a right-wing fanatic a few days before war was declared. Although Jaurès and most of his supporters had long advocated peaceful solutions to international problems and had worked against efforts to increase military spending and prolong obligatory peacetime military service, French socialists closed ranks behind the government when conflict could no longer be avoided. The socialist leader of the largest French labor union, the General Confederation of Labor (CGT), proclaimed his support for the government in a setting no less dramatic than Jaurès's funeral. The socialist delegations in both the National Assembly and Senate voted in overwhelming numbers for war appropriations. In late August Prime Minister René Viviani, himself an independent socialist and a pragmatic politician, expanded his government to include all shades of political opinion represented in Parliament, and two leading Socialist Party deputies accepted ministerial portfolios. A former socialist, Alexandre Millerand, also became minister of war at that time, and in December 1916 Viviani's successor, Aristide Briand, appointed the

Bolshevik leader Vladimir Lenin addressing a crowd in Petrograd, 1917

(from The Illustrated War News, 19 December 1917, page 33, Joseph M. Bruccoli Great War Collection, Thomas Cooper Library, University of South Carolina)

Dissent from the official line of the French Socialist Party remained quite minor. A small number of party members and CGT officials attended antiwar socialist conferences in the Swiss resorts of Zimmerwald (1915) and Kienthal (1916), but they were marginal figures whose views never had a serious impact on either the trade union or the party. Although intraparty dissent became more pronounced as the war dragged on, and when Prime Minister Georges Clemenceau rocked the boat by breaking strikes and cracking down on the free expression of dissent, the Socialist Party remained cohesive until a small, radical minority broke off to form the French Communist Party in December 1920.

The German socialist movement had more problems preserving its unity, but its mainstream nevertheless remained committed to the war. As conflict became imminent in late July 1914, only fourteen members of the parliamentary delegation of the Social Democratic Party (SPD), which held the largest plurality in the *Reichstag* (German Parliament), declared their opposition to the war in the party caucus. Yet, all of them accepted and publicly supported the party line. When the *Reichstag* voted on the first appropriation of German war credits on 4 August 1914, the measure was approved unanimously. The catch phrase for the Social Democrats became "in the hour of peril we shall not leave the Fatherland in the lurch."

Like the French socialists, a small minority of German Social Democrats soon became disillusioned with the war and the heavy-handed government administration. Even as early as December 1914 the radical SPD *Reichstag* delegate Karl Liebknecht voted against a second appropriation of war credits, and a small faction of other SPD members supported him. Yet, Liebknecht's action was and remained decisively out of step with the sentiments of the overwhelming majority of German socialists. Although the Social Democrats lost their outward unanimity early on, most socialists realized—as their French counterparts had—that their growing respectability in the German political landscape would be endangered if they were thought to be sabotaging the war effort supported by the rest of the country. One strand of socialist thought actually tried to justify the war in Marxist terms, arguing that since backward and autocratic Russia was a major national enemy, a military victory would lead to its political liberation. When Russia unexpectedly invaded Germany in August 1914, rallying to the defense of Marx's homeland and the arguable birthplace of socialism was a compelling battle cry.

Socialist deputy Albert Thomas as minister of armaments. It was quite clear that the French Socialist Party had abandoned its rhetorical emphasis on proletarian internationalism in favor of national solidarity with other social classes and national interests. This stand, truly, was a *union sacrée*, or "sacred union," as the wartime system of political relationships in France came to be called.

In addition to the revisionist influences on their ideology, the French socialists had additional justifications for their actions. Since Germany had declared war and stood poised to invade French territory, socialists argued that their patriotism represented the defense not only of their homeland but also of the "cradle of the liberty" for which the French Republic stood. Rather than sourly weakening France from within and taking on the burden of an unpopular antiwar position, they positioned themselves as conscientious republicans fighting for their homeland against an authoritarian empire.

Thus, the Social Democratic Party entered into a German version of *union sacrée*, the so-called fortress peace, or *Burgfriede*. On the basis of a series of informal understandings with the Imperial government, German Socialists agreed to support the war in exchange for guarantees that the war situation would not be used as a pretext to mistreat labor unions or reverse democratic gains in the Empire. The Imperial government to a large degree kept up its end of the bargain. When a war economy was organized, many government officials included trade-union representatives and socialist politicians in their decision-making processes. Union rights were generally respected. Socialists who supported the war remained free and politically active. Only Liebknecht, his associate Rosa Luxemburg, and a few other socialists were briefly jailed for radical political agitation.

At the same time, the socialists were willing to tolerate many aspects of wartime civil administration that contradicted their ideals. Under laws passed in Prussia in the 1850s and 1860s, the Imperial government was empowered to declare a national state of siege in wartime and place broad powers in the hands of district military commanders. In law as well as in practice, these generals came to exercise virtually unchecked authority over freedom of speech and political assembly. In some cases they applied political labels to unions in order to curtail their activities. At other times they closed socialist newspapers with a zeal that a growing number, yet still a decided minority, of socialists found alarming. In December 1916 General Erich Ludendorff was given, among his other responsibilities, the authority to organize the national economy along military lines, and he implemented a compulsory labor draft. Although his original intention of drafting all adult men and women under the age of sixty was abandoned, and many of the other onerous provisions of his plan were dropped or softened, Ludendorff's policies were a direct provocation to the ideals of German socialists who, out of respect for national defense, largely did nothing.

German political opposition to the war did develop, but it was never officially sanctioned by the SPD. When a grouping of pacifist party members formed a working group to agitate for a "democratic peace," that is, one without territorial acquisitions or financial indemnities, the Social Democratic leadership expelled them from the party. The new political party that these dissidents formed in April 1917, the Independent Social Democrats (USPD), commanded little popular support, had no major electoral impact, and split when a dissident faction formed the German Communist Party (KPD) in late December 1918. The most serious

peace initiatives, moreover, came not from the leadership of any socialist party but from a faction of the moderate Catholic Center Party led by Matthias Erzberger, which energetically criticized the government's handling of the war and called for its end. Socialist politicians supported Erzberger's peace resolution in July 1917, but this stance only betrayed their desire for a reasonable peace, not a philosophical unwillingness to support their country.

Ultimately, the late-hour political reforms and formal request for an armistice by the Imperial government came not from back-stabbing socialists who had seized the reins of power but from an army High Command that could foresee nothing but total defeat, a society that was incapable of enduring more sacrifices for the war, a broad domestic political consensus that could no longer support the kaiser, and an international community that would not enter into negotiations with an authoritarian Germany. Rather than lead the agitation or drive the political reforms, the Social Democrats were thrust into power by default. The liberal constitutional monarchy envisioned by the reforms of October 1918 required democratic, parliamentary rule, and hence a transfer of power to the plurality holding SPD. Its leader, Friedrich Ebert, a monarchist who had lost two sons in the war, became a republican only after William II abdicated and Ebert unexpectedly found himself chancellor of a democratic Germany.

The majority of socialists in Austria-Hungary were also supportive of the war, though their attention was divided by the multiethnic dilemma of the Empire. The most prominent leaders of the Austrian Social Democratic Workers' Party, Karl Renner and Otto Bauer, actually incorporated the nationalities issue into their support for the war effort by calling for the transformation of the Habsburg Empire into a federation of national territories. In their view this policy would, at least early in the war, have satisfied minority grievances and included the further democratization of political life. The projected reform also had Marxist cachet because if such a state were under socialist leadership, Renner and Bauer maintained, it would pay homage to Marx's ideal of an international socialist polity. Leaving that bizarre theoretical construction aside, the Socialists' projected reform was not unlike the liberalized federal structure elaborated by Emperor Karl I in October 1918. Although the reform was too little and too late, both the Socialists and the emperor believed it would create an Austro-Hungarian state for which all of its people would fight. Despite the best of intentions, however, the spirit of nationalism became too strong and was too heavily backed by the Allies for any amount of imperial loyalty to tame.

Even the most radical national grouping of socialists, those of the Russian Empire, were supportive of the war effort in their country. Of the myriad of socialist circles and political parties that had sprouted in late Imperial Russia, only the Bolshevik faction of the Russian Social Democratic Party, led by the ideologue Vladimir Lenin, dismissed the war as an imperialist struggle that the workers of the world should refuse to fight. In 1914, however, Lenin's call was a small, insignificant voice, for the members of his party were scattered abroad, sitting in jail or Siberian exile or living precariously on the edge of the law in Russia. By virtue of the Bolsheviks' own criteria for party membership, which had formed the basis of their split from the Menshevik faction of the Social Democratic Party in 1903, their party was restricted to an elite of professional revolutionaries. Opposition to the war marginalized the Bolsheviks even further because many of their prominent members and activists in Russia were promptly arrested for amateurish antiwar agitation.

The overwhelming majority of Russian Socialists—the Mensheviks, the populist Socialist Revolutionary (SR) Party, and a few other minor parties and independents—immediately ignored Lenin's views and advocated "defensism." Like their peers throughout continental Europe, these socialists believed first and foremost in the patriotic defense of their homeland and in the pursuit of broad political transformation later. Fighting on the side of the French Republic and a democratizing Britain against the authoritarian empires of Central Europe had a definite ideological appeal and raised hopes for the future of Russia. When the proto-parliamentary *Duma* institution voted to support the war, only the tiny Bolshevik delegation and a small number of disaffected Mensheviks and SRs voiced opposition. Even most Russian socialists who were obliged to live in foreign exile for political reasons came out in support of the war. Georgy Valentinovich Plekhanov, the grand old man of Russian Marxism, who lived in Parisian exile, worked to enlist Russian volunteers in the French army in 1914. The antiwar Bolsheviks were treated as virtual outcasts in the socialist movement at large.

As the war continued, socialist support for the Russian war effort remained solid. Assassinations of Tsarist officials by revolutionary terrorists, common before the war, virtually ceased after 1914, and the most spectacular wartime murder, that of the Siberian mystic and Imperial family intimate Grigory Rasputin in December 1916, was carried out by conservative monarchists who objected to his suspicious influence and activities. Labor unions and other workers' associations ignored Bolshevik admonitions and compliantly elected representatives to the "special councils" and War Industries Committee that Tsar Nicholas II had agreed to introduce to organize the Russian war economy in 1915. When many other problems in Russia eventuated the collapse of the monarchy in February 1917, socialist agitation was not a factor. Most socialists believed that the inevitable revolution was still far in the future and were surprised that the popular demonstrations that swept Petrograd toppled Nicholas II so easily. Ultimately, the tsar's downfall came from the growing unreliability of the military and his own de facto abdication of political leadership, not from socialist disloyalty.

After the fall of the tsar, all Russian socialist parties except the Bolsheviks (after some initial confusion) supported both the Provisional Government that took power as a temporary executive and the continuation of the war. Appealing to strict Marxist theory, they argued that the new government represented the "bourgeois-democratic phase" of human development and would have to exist for a long period of time before a socialist revolution could occur. The attitude of most socialists, therefore, was to engage the Provisional Government in cooperation while seeking a supervisory role over its rather undemocratic executive authority. As part of this strategy, socialists were even willing to enter the government. Only one, the nominal Socialist Revolutionary Aleksandr Kerensky (simultaneously a vice chairman of the Petrograd Soviet), entered its first cabinet as minister of justice, but more opportunities for socialists became available as the political situation changed.

When the imperialist ambitions of the Provisional Government were accidentally discovered in April 1917, socialist politicians led the uproar, but their objections were to the long-term strategic ambitions of the government rather than the war in principle. On the contrary, many socialists presciently argued that an immediate peace would put Germany in a commanding position that would both endanger the achievements of the February Revolution and enable Berlin to establish long-term hegemony over all Europe. When Petrograd was rumored to be threatened by German advances or "counterrevolutionary" activity by Russian armies, the socialists were the first to call out reliable military units and workers' militias to meet them. Like the radicals of the French Revolution, Russian social-

ZIMMERWALD DRAFT (1915)

This document was written in August 1915 by Socialists meeting in Zimmerwald, Switzerland, as Europe faced the calamity of World War I:

The present war has been engendered by imperialism. Capitalism has already achieved that highest stage. Society's productive forces and the magnitudes of capital have outgrown the narrow limits of the individual national states. Hence the striving on the part of the Great Powers to enslave other nations and to seize colonies as sources of raw material and spheres of investment of capital. The whole world is merging into a single economic organism; it has been carved up among a handful of Great Powers. The objective conditions for socialism have fully matured, and the present war is a war of the capitalists for privileges and monopolies that might delay the downfall of capitalism.

The socialists, who seek to liberate labour from the yoke of capital and who defend the world-wide solidarity of the workers, are struggling against any kind of oppression and inequality of nations. When the bourgeoisie was a progressive class, and the overthrow of feudalism, absolutism and oppression by other nations stood on the historical order of the day, the socialists, as invariably the most consistent and most resolute of democrats, recognised "defence of the fatherland" in the meaning implied by those aims, and in that meaning alone. Today too, should a war of the oppressed nations against the oppressor Great Powers break out in the east of Europe or in the colonies, the socialists' sympathy would be wholly with the oppressed.

The war of today, however, has been engendered by an entirely different historical period, in which the bourgeoisie, from a progressive class, has turned reactionary. With both groups of belligerents, this war is a war of slaveholders, and is designed to preserve and extend slavery; it is a war for the repartitioning of colonies, for the "right" to oppress other nations, for privileges and monopolies for Great-Power capital, and for the perpetuation of wage slavery by splitting up the workers of the different countries and crushing them through reaction. That is why, on the part of both warring groups, all talk about "defence of the fatherland" is deception of the people by the bourgeoisie. Neither the victory of any one group nor a return to the *status quo* can do anything either to protect the freedom of most countries in the world from imperialist oppression by a handful of Great Powers, or to ensure that the working class keep even its present modest cultural gains. The period of a relatively peaceful capitalism has passed, never to return. Imperialism has brought the working class unparalleled intensification of the class struggle, want, and unemployment, a higher cost of living, and the strengthening of oppression by the trusts, of militarism, and the political reactionaries, who are raising their heads in all countries, even the freest.

In reality, the "defence of the fatherland" slogan in the present war is tantamount to a defence of the "right" of one's "own" national bourgeoisie to oppress other nations; it is in fact a national liberal-labour policy, an alliance between a negligible section of the workers and their "own" national bourgeoisie, against the mass of the proletarians and the exploited. Socialists who pursue such a policy are in fact chauvinists, social-chauvinists. The policy of voting for war credits, of joining governments, of *Burgfrieden*, and the like, is a betrayal of socialism. Nurtured by the conditions of the "peaceful", period which has now come to an end, opportunism has now matured to a degree that calls for a break with socialism; it has become an open enemy to the proletariat's movement for liberation. The working class cannot achieve its historic aims without waging a most resolute struggle against both forthright opportunism and social-chauvinism. . . .

The imperialist war is ushering in the era of the social revolution. All the objective conditions of recent times have put the proletariat's revolutionary mass struggle on the order of the day. It is the duty of socialists, while making use of every means of the working class's legal struggle, to subordinate each and every of those means to this immediate and most important task, develop the workers' revolutionary consciousness, rally them in the international revolutionary struggle, promote and encourage any revolutionary action, and do everything possible to turn the imperialist war between the peoples into a civil war of the oppressed classes against their oppressors, a war for the expropriation of the class of capitalists, for the conquest of political power by the proletariat, and the realisation of socialism.

Source: *"The Draft Resolution Proposed by the Left Wing at Zimmerwald," in V. I. Lenin,* Collected Works, *volume 21, fourth edition, edited by Julius Katzer (Moscow: Progress Publishers, 1964), pp. 345–348.*

SOCIALISTS

ists discovered a militant patriotism when their political gains were threatened.

Socialist resolve also applied to high politics. After the liberal ministers of war and foreign affairs resigned over the war-aims crisis, Kerensky took over the War Ministry, and four additional Socialists were brought into the cabinet. As the authority of the government waned amid military reversal and civil strife in the summer, political discord led to the departure of more-liberal ministers and their replacement by still more socialists who hoped their presence could stabilize the situation. By late July they controlled a majority of the cabinet, with Kerensky as premier.

Ultimately, however, the Provisional Government failed, no matter what the moderate socialists did. Although Kerensky tried his best to rally the army, it became increasingly disaffected by political instability and declining military fortunes, and it melted away. In urban areas radical workers and garrison soldiers began to favor extreme solutions and were disappointed with the moderate Socialists' timidity and willingness to shore up the hated Provisional Government. During one demonstration in July 1917 a worker seized a socialist minister by his collar and screamed, "take power, you son of a bitch, when it's given to you!" When Lenin's Bolsheviks, untainted by cooperation with the discredited regime and posing as defenders of the democratic revolution, managed to seize power and to establish their dictatorship in October 1917, it was largely at the price of the moderate socialists' involvement in the decaying internal stability and war effort of Russia.

The cases of France, Germany, Austria-Hungary, and Russia—the countries with the strongest socialist movements in Europe—indicate how far European Socialists had departed from the founding principles of international solidarity and revolutionary violence. Mainstream socialist parties not only failed to work against the war, they supported it outright by voting war credits, entering cabinets, and accepting government policies that betrayed their most fundamental ideals, and sacrificing the lives of their supporters and, in the case of Ebert and many others, their own sons. The Austrian Socialists actually twisted Marxist internationalism in a vain attempt to create a workable multiethnic state that could remain effective in the war. Renegade Marxists such as the German Independent Social Democrats, the French internationalists, and the Russian Bolsheviks were fringe groups whose members would later break decisively with the majority socialist movement, label it "social fascism," and in many cases fight violently against it.

Although the Bolsheviks eventually supplanted the moderate socialists in their country, they only did so through the incompetence of their opponents, years of desperate armed struggle, and ruthless terror. The overwhelming majority of socialists backed their governments and supported their efforts in World War I.

–PAUL DU QUENOY,
GEORGETOWN UNIVERSITY

Viewpoint:
No. Socialists took advantage of the general war weariness to advance the cause of workers.

In the half century before the outbreak of the Great War, European Socialists had demonstrated consistent hostility to the idea of war. In Germany the Social Democratic Party mounted a drumfire of propaganda against the military system and the state that underwrote it; voted consistently against military budgets; and encouraged Socialist conscripts to do their duty but took no abuse from superiors. French Socialists voted against the introduction of a third year of obligatory service in 1913. In other states the pattern was similar—and now to a point where most armies included arresting Socialist leaders and activists in their mobilization plans. The founding of the Second International in 1889 offered an alternative to both militarism and nationalism, emphasizing the cooperation of the working class of Europe in moving forward the inevitable triumph of socialism by economic and political means.

In that context one of the major surprises of August 1914 was the quietism of European Marxists. Instead of standing for the brotherhood of the workers and the commonwealth of mankind, Socialist parties affirmed declarations of war, and Socialist party members fell into line at regimental depots throughout Europe. Far from the International becoming the human race, it seemed that the workers had fatherlands after all. Generals pigeonholed orders for mass incarcerations, congratulating themselves on the rightness of their assumption that it would take no more than a little whiff of gunpowder to return the deluded followers of Karl Marx to their patriotic duty.

It all seemed simple in August, but as the war endured and evolved into one of production, the worker, specifically the stereotypical proletarian, the industrial worker, became at least as important as the soldier. A conflict evolving into a war of machinery borrowed more and more of its tropes and images from mines and factories. Chronic labor shortages, especially in jobs requiring physical strength and endurance, gave corresponding leverage to laborers and their representatives—leverage that increased as public opinion turned against high profits crossing the line into profiteering. War economies began shifting from free-enterprise models to an emphasis on management and direction that to Socialist intellectuals prefigured at least the initial stages of a Socialist order. The capitalists themselves were putting the machinery of a new world in place; it would only be necessary to change the hands on the crank. Socialists, moreover, were laying down their lives like everyone else, paying in full the blood price of citizenship. While strikers might be unpopular among frontline soldiers, they could also emerge as homefront heroes to those workers lacking the organization, or the nerve, to put their own jobs on the line to protest shortages and declining real wages. In short, from being considered borderline members of their respective societies before 1914, Socialists were rapidly becoming social archetypes.

As more and more people of all classes and conditions began questioning the need to fight the war to a finish at whatever the cost, Socialists benefited from their prewar standing as an organized opposition. That process varied by country. In Britain and France, where legitimacies in the prewar regime were broad and wartime dislocations relatively limited, Socialist opposition was muted, expressed through the system and focused on specific issues rather than general principles. In Germany, wartime hardships merged with prewar disaffection to split the Socialists in April 1917, with a new Independent Social Democratic Party challenging the continuation of the war. In Austria-Hungary, Italy, and Russia—all states whose infrastructure suffered heavily under the strains of war—Socialist parties moved further along the path of opposition toward overt resistance to the war effort. Protest rallies, strikes, and military mutinies testified alike to growing war weariness and possible opportunities for parties or movements willing to seize them.

International interaction by the organized Left began as early as 1915, when neutrals from Holland, the Scandinavian countries, and still-uncommitted Italy organized meetings and acted as clearinghouses for the belligerents. Dissident Socialists from France and Germany joined exiles from tsarist Russia to pass resolutions denouncing the war at Zimmerwald (1915) and Kienthal (1916). These were not major industrial centers throbbing with proletarian ressentiment. They were Swiss villages—but the demand for peace echoed no less powerfully for that.

Radicals such as Lenin argued the only way to end militarism was to end capitalism, and the only way to end capitalism was by revolution. Socialism in the decades prior to 1914, however, had acquired something like a Jeffersonian aspect, presenting the good life as being a quiet one, where a man—or a couple—could go to work, put in a fair day, and enjoy the full fruits of their labor. Socialism was about bicycle riding and pigeon racing, about chess clubs and gymnastic societies—about bringing men home safely to the women and children who waited for them. As the chaos of war threatened to engulf civilization, Socialists all over Europe yearned not for revolution but for stability.

The Russian Revolution of March 1917, if anything, served to strengthen that mind-set. For the first months the forces of popular protest emphasized ending the fighting rather than reconstructing society. It was that demand for a negotiated peace, with no annexations and no reparations, that engaged Socialists throughout Europe—and led to an increased scale of popular protest, outside the existing institutional channels. Even in Britain, socialist opposition groups called for Workers' and Soldiers' Soviets on the Russian model.

Proposals for an international Socialist conference at Stockholm in September foundered on a growing split between "defense Socialists," who more or less accepted the legitimacy of their respective national causes and hoped to construct Socialism on a framework of wartime institutions and experiences, and were advocates of outright revolution. It was these men and women who dominated the rump meeting actually held at Stockholm, which insisted on the inseparability of peace and revolution. When in October 1917 the Bolsheviks unseated the Provisional Government, they legitimated their unilateral seizure of power by translating the principle into action, removing Russia from the war and simultaneously proceeding to establish the foundations of a revolutionary social order.

French and British Socialists denounced the Bolsheviks for leaving them in the lurch before the Germans. German Socialists criticized the Bolshevik belief that a Socialist economy could be created by a political revolution. Socialist "establishments" everywhere were attracted by President Woodrow Wilson's ideas of liberal internationalism as means for securing the kind of peace that would—eventually—make Socialism possible. Increasing numbers of the respective rank and file, however, turned in desperation to the only approach that seemed to offer an end to the years of destruction. This division would continue to burden the European Left in the postwar years. Its existence is final proof that Socialism was anything but passive in face of the challenge of war.

–DENNIS SHOWALTER,
COLORADO COLLEGE

References

Maurice Agulhon, *The French Republic: 1879–1992,* translated by Antonia Nevill (Oxford, U.K. & Cambridge, Mass.: Blackwell, 1993).

Michael Balfour, *The Kaiser and His Times* (London: Cresset, 1964; New York: Houghton Mifflin, 1964).

Roger Chickering, *Imperial Germany and the Great War, 1914–1918* (Cambridge & New York: Cambridge University Press, 1998).

Gerald D. Feldman, *Army, Industry, and Labor in Imperial Germany, 1914–1918* (Princeton: Princeton University Press, 1966).

Orlando Figes, *A People's Tragedy: The Russian Revolution, 1891–1924* (London: Cape, 1996).

Hajo Holborn, *A History of Modern Germany,* volume 3, *1840–1945* (New York: Knopf, 1969).

Lonnie R. Johnson, *Central Europe: Enemies, Neighbors, Friends* (New York: Oxford University Press, 1996).

John Keegan, *The First World War* (London: Hutchinson, 1998).

Richard Pipes, *The Russian Revolution* (New York: Knopf, 1990).

Rex A. Wade, *The Russian Revolution, 1917* (Cambridge & New York: Cambridge University Press, 2000).

Eric D. Weitz, *Creating German Communism, 1890–1990: From Popular Protest to Socialist State* (Princeton, N.J.: Princeton University Press, 1977).

Gordon Wright, *France in Modern Times: From the Enlightenment to the Present,* fifth edition (New York: Norton, 1995).

SOCIALISTS

SOLDIERS' MOTIVATIONS

What motivated soldiers in all armies to fight?

Viewpoint: The essential reason why millions of soldiers continued to fight was consent, derived from love of country, hatred of the enemy, and a crusading spirit.

Viewpoint: Comradeship and coercion ultimately kept soldiers at their posts.

The issue of motivation remains one of the most obscure, and most debated, questions in the historiography of the Great War. After 1918 a myth arose of a "great illusion": masses of men in uniform deceived by manipulators in high places, who engaged and perverted religion, family, and love to the services of a mindless nationalism and a false definition of masculinity. To this image of the soldier as victim, some veterans added a variant: the soldier as comrade. In this construction men found in wartime relationships a deeper effect than they had ever experienced in the artificial constraints of civilian life, and were ultimately willing to stand and die for those relationships.

More recent interpretations develop a point first made by Ernst Jünger and developed by Sigmund Freud. The taboo breaking sanctioned by war, the violence, and even—or especially—the killing could be attractive to men whose behaviors had been compulsively restrained by industrial civilization. From the opposite perspective, a school of military social history stresses the importance of routine. The nature of trench warfare meant that men and units were in the lines only a limited part of the time. Most frontline duty itself was routine, as opposed to participation in major operations. It involved occupying the same stretches of trench in familiar sectors. Behind the lines as well, armies as a rule sustained a "culture of competence," with food, mail, and medical care provided in predictable fashions, and with the average soldier's life predictable enough to be bearable. Units also developed as "niche societies," in which all but the most extreme personalities and behavior patterns could find a place. Adolf Hitler was more at home during his four years in the Sixteenth Bavarian Reserve Regiment than at any other time in his life.

Finally there was discipline. The number of capital cases on the Western Front was extremely limited relative to the size of the armies, and a high proportion of those charges involved offenses punishable in civil life as well, such as rape or murder. The punitive machinery of the armies, however, was omnipresent—along with its reverse side: the soldier who "kept his nose clean," who obeyed orders and avoided drawing attention to himself, was likely to be ignored most of the time by the system.

When all the factors are collated, the frontline cohesion of the armies of the Great War may remain a subject of controversy, but is hardly the stuff of mystery. Each man had his own reasons to stand—and by standing, to sustain the conflict.

Viewpoint:
The essential reason why millions of soldiers continued to fight was consent, derived from love of country, hatred of the enemy, and a crusading spirit.

Soldiers of the Great War were motivated by an idealistic and crusading patriotism that is best captured in the phrase *dulce et decorum est pro patria mori* (sweet and fitting it is to die for one's country). Together with an often intense hatred of a traditional enemy, patriotism kept soldiers fighting under the horrendous conditions and unprecedented strains of trench warfare on the Western Front, the snow and bitter cold of the Isonzo (1915–1917), the heat and stench of Gallipoli (1915–1916), and many other brutal theaters. Soldiers fought not simply because their commanders ordered them to or for their buddies, but because they believed in the righteousness of their nation's cause.

In defending the cause, soldiers found affirmation in compliance rather than resistance. This claim may initially seem implausible. After all, did not the Oxford Union famously declare in 1933 that "this House will in no circumstances fight for its King and Country"? And did not Paul Baumer, the thoughtful and somewhat fatalistic German soldier in the 1930 movie version of Erich Maria Remarque's *All Quiet on the Western Front* (1929), intone that, "It's dirty and painful to die for your country. When it comes to dying for your country it's better not to die at all"? Yet, these were postwar intonations. Widespread disillusionment and confusion following an inconclusive Versailles Treaty (1919) irrecoverably changed war memories. Veterans concluded that the results of the war failed miserably to redeem the ultimate price paid by millions of their comrades.

Nevertheless, postwar disillusionment and irony—powerful as they were—should not obscure the enthusiastic patriotism exhibited by soldiers in nearly every country in 1914. While initial war enthusiasm can be overstressed, the ecstatic faces in the Odeonplatz in Munich, including a young and beaming Adolf Hitler, tell a story of national elation that is not easily dismissed. Many joined Hitler in seeing war as a glorious test of national fitness, an antidote to a modern world made impersonal and devoid of spiritual meaning by widespread mechanization and oppressive factory systems. The men of 1914 expected war and even considered it to be inevitable. As millions of men marched to their respective national colors, they both exhibited and stimulated intense outpourings of national pride. The belief that each army was engaged in a defensive crusade against unappeasable aggression reinforced such outpourings. Thus Sigmund Freud gushed: "All my libido goes with Austria." Of course, this initial burst of enthusiasm drew strength from a shared belief that the worst of the fighting was to be over in a matter of weeks.

Thus soldiers marched to war singing national songs such as "God Save the King" and "La Marseillaise," not the Communist Internationale. Prewar fears of violent and pan-national socialist uprisings proved unfounded as workers discovered they had more in common with their own countrymen—even those among the privileged classes—than workers of other countries. Putative worker solidarity vanished as World War I became a war of imperial self-assertion and personal self-definition.

Not every soldier served unstintingly or even willingly, of course. As the war dragged on into 1915 and 1916, many conscripts answered the call reluctantly. Yet, answer it they did. Their actions affirmed their belief in the validity of contractual obligations to the nation-state and to their fellow citizens. As Michael Geyer has noted, "To be German or to be French always also meant to be militarily prepared and, that is, to be conscripted." Defending the state was a sacred trust and obligation that was further entangled in powerful and inextricable ways with notions of masculinity and self-identity. Not many men wanted to face the interrogative challenge of "What did you do in the war, Daddy?" without rifles in their hands and war chests replete with stories of frontline derring-do.

Such challenges were not just propagandistic poster slogans—they cut to the core of a man's being. Naked and coercive applications of state power were unnecessary and counterproductive when men had been taught virtually from the cradle that their duty as honorable males was to fight for their communities and nations when called upon. If one died while fighting, the state would live up to its share of the contract by memorializing, remembering, and honoring the dead and caring for his widow and family. Reminiscent of the Funeral Oration of Pericles, state-sanctioned representations of heroic citizen-soldiers were alive, well, and remained powerfully persuasive throughout the Great War.

Manifestations of these representations varied by country. In France, *poilus* saw themselves as republican citizens defending the honor and integrity of France against the traditional enemy. Frenchmen fought to expel the hated "Hun" invader and to safeguard the inalienable rights granted to them by a republic that, by enshrining these rights, made itself worthy of selfless service and devotion. Despite initial failure in August

A London street tribute to neighborhood men at the front, including a framed list of soldiers' names

(from The Illustrated War News, 12 July 1916, page 17, Joseph M. Bruccoli Great War Collection, Thomas Cooper Library, University of South Carolina)

1914, the French army remained the school of the nation and its foremost symbol of spiritual revival and republican vigor.

The so-called mutinies of 1917 were exceptions that actually highlighted the rule of patriotic devotion. *Poilus* did not mutiny because they disagreed with French war aims. Rather, they rebelled as comrades, and in spite of coercion, to stop futile and suicidal offensives. Refusing to launch more frontal assaults, they nevertheless remained on duty in their trenches to deter German attacks. Indeed, the mutineers overwhelmingly kept their work stoppage a private matter, taking care not to alert the Germans to disaffection within French ranks.

Recognizing the patriotic passion and zeal of his soldiers, General Philippe Pétain proffered liberal terms of forgiveness. Of the 23,385 verdicts of "guilty" handed down during the mutiny, a mere 49 soldiers were executed. Recovering quickly from the republican-inspired rebelliousness of 1917, *poilus* served the state with renewed fervor throughout 1918.

The French army began and remained a mass conscript army of politicized and patriotic citizen-soldiers. In contrast, the British Expeditionary Force (BEF) of 1914 was a small professional force of six divisions. The destruction of this highly proficient force by early 1915 led to the creation of the first million-man British army and Lord Horatio Kitchener's famous "Pals" battalions. Near-universal respect for the nobility of voluntary military service meant that the demands of war fell evenly across class lines in Britain. Members of the BEF did not take college deferments, as did many American men during the Vietnam War (ended 1975). Deeply held duties of noblesse oblige and national service, informed by values of gallantry, impelled Oxbridge students and members of the peerage to volunteer; they died in battle at nearly twice the rate of plebian rankers. Female Oxbridge students also answered the call of duty and enlisted as nurses, most famously Vera Brittain. Officers and rank-and-filers alike shared a view that German militarism and drive for *Weltpolitik* posed a dire threat to the British Empire, and possibly even to the Home Islands. For the average Tommy, the Germans were overbearing, militaristic, even criminal bullies who needed to be taught a lesson. British Tommies voted with their feet as the BEF rapidly mushroomed from six divisions in 1914 to seventy in 1916.

The subsequent disaster of the Somme campaign (1916) led to a decline in idealism, but not in devotion to opposing German militarism and the Kaiser's drive for power. Despite horrendous losses on the battlefield, the BEF continued to contest the Kaiser's challenge to liberal democracy in Europe and the British parliamentary system. While rank-and-filers' daily concerns of getting a hot meal or surviving the latest artillery barrage often obscured intangibles such as love of country or empire, they nevertheless tacitly acknowledged the worthiness and even sacredness of the Empire. Recognition, respect, and responsibility to a patriotic cause, along with reckless bravado in battle, were not the exclusive preserves of the educated and reflective classes. Only honestly held (if sometimes ill-defined and critical) belief in the Empire and its institutions can explain the superhuman endurance of British Tommies and their Dominion comrades in the face of disastrous offensives launched by Douglas Haig in 1916 and 1917.

Sincere affection for the Empire as well as strong manifestations of national self-identity were famously displayed by Canadian, Australian, and New Zealand soldiers. Less well-known is the equally impressive devotion to Empire and national identity demonstrated by Indian soldiers. As one Sikh soldier boasted to his brother back in India, "Our people have exalted the name of our country. . . . We shall never get such another chance to exalt the name of race, country, ancestors, parents, village and brothers, and to prove our loyalty to the government." Other letters sent home by Indian soldiers included clear expressions of support for the King as sovereign of the Empire.

Tsarist Russia provided further confirmation of love of sovereign and country. Traditionally held in semireligious awe as the father of his people, Tsar Nicholas II exploited an ethos of devotion to and love of Mother Russia. Russian soldiers fell on their knees to kiss his boots as the Tsar handed them religious icons to inspire and protect them in battle. Russian intellectuals revived memories of the war against Napoleon Bonaparte to remind Russians that they had saved Europe from naked aggression and overweening ambition before and would do so again. Under Aleksey Brusilov, Russian soldiers showed élan and national pride in attacking Austria-Hungary in 1916. Where the Tsar and his circle of lackeys erred was in not trusting the patriotism of Russian soldiers enough. Incompetence, betrayal, and coercion led to revolution.

With respect to the Central Powers, one might expect that the multiethnic Austro-Hungarian Empire was forced to resort wholesale to coercion to maintain the cohesion of its combat units. Not until 1918 was large-scale coercion necessary, however. Until then, Austro-Hungarian units loyally served the Emperor and fought with considerable staying power against Italy and Russia. Italians, too, fought admirably along the Isonzo River, motivated in part by the traditional struggle against Austria but also by a tenuous, if nevertheless telling, allegiance to Italian national identity.

Turning to Germany, there was no lack of love of country in a Second Reich whose most visible and respected institutional symbol was the army. The Kaiser's statement at the outset of war that he knew no parties, only Germans, was universally applauded and accepted. Pursuit of glory and confirmation of masculinity by feats of arms served to reinforce love of country and Kaiser. The perception that Germany was encircled by a hostile coalition bent on keeping Germans in their place turned the war into a struggle for national existence, at least in German eyes. Draconian disciplinary measures were rarely required: fewer than fifty soldiers were executed during the war. Even in the blackest days of 1918, German forces largely maintained their cohesion and combat effectiveness. Comradeship was an important factor, but so too was resoluteness born of a belief in the worthiness of the German cause.

This belief eventually collapsed, however, under the dual strain of war and perceived national betrayal. The Second Reich, Dennis E. Showalter concludes, "ultimately failed to keep its promises to the men who wore its uniform." Erich von Falkenhayn's Verdun Offensive (1916) and Erich Ludendorff's Spring Offensive (1918) lacked any clear sense of national purpose, undermining the social contract that cemented German soldiers to national institutions. Thus Germany lost—not because of inadequate coercion or lack of comradeship within the ranks, but because of perceptions of betrayal of the cause for which soldiers ostensibly fought. By betting on a virtual military dictatorship in 1918, Germany eroded the national institutions from which its soldiers drew sustenance. The ultimate collapse of the Central Powers in 1918, and subsequent rise of the fascist nations of the interwar period, served to highlight the power of nationalism and love of country to energize and impel soldiers to brave the "storm of steel" in defense of their nation.

—WILLIAM J. ASTORE, U.S. AIR
FORCE ACADEMY

Viewpoint:
Comradeship and coercion ultimately kept soldiers at their posts.

During the heady beginning stages of World War I, men from every European nation rallied to their flags. They willingly and patriotically served in their national armed services. Their initial motivations included love of country, hatred of the enemy, and a crusading spirit. These derivations of the "consent thesis" worked as incentives until the casualties mounted. By 1916, however, many soldiers had lost their fervor and instead remained at their posts because of comradeship and coercion.

As the European nations mobilized for World War I, national leaders worried that some political factions such as union members, socialists, or ethnic minorities would not support the war effort. The war, after all, could have been portrayed according to a Marxist critique as a conflict between nations in which bourgeois (middle- and upper-class) goals would be achieved by spilling proletarian (working-class) blood. Those laborers who were attempting to secure more rights and privileges for themselves might also have resisted military service. The ethnic minorities and political inferiors in the Austro-Hungarian Empire also might have refused to fight for their Austrian and Hungarian overlords. However, none of these fears came to fruition at the outset of hostilities in 1914. Class and ethnic distinctions withered away, at least in the short term. Only a few pacifists and radicals objected to the coming of war.

Every European government took this opportunity to shape its rationales for war as a

BEAUMONT HAMEL

In this excerpt from Tender Is the Night *F. Scott Fitzgerald describes the battlefield near Beaumont Hamel, a village in northeastern France and the scene of bitter fighting in 1916:*

'See that little stream—we could walk to it in two minutes. It took the British a month to walk to it—a whole empire walking very slowly, dying in front and pushing forward behind. And another empire walked very slowly backward a few inches a day, leaving the dead like a million bloody rugs. No Europeans will ever do that again in this generation.'

'Why, they've only just quit over in Turkey,' said Abe. 'And in Morocco—'

'That's different. This Western Front business couldn't be done again, not for a long time. The young men think they could do it but they couldn't. They could fight the First Marne again but not this. This took religion and years of plenty and tremendous sureties and the exact relation that existed between the classes. The Russians and Italians weren't any good on this front. You had to have a whole-souled sentimental equipment going back further than you could remember. You had to remember Christmas, and postcards of the Crown Prince and his fiancée, and the little cafés in Valence and beer gardens in Unter den Linden and weddings at the mairie, and going to the Derby, and your grandfather's whiskers.'

'General Grant invented this kind of battle at Petersburg in sixty-five.'

'No, he didn't—he just invented mass butchery. This kind of battle was invented by Lewis Carroll and Jules Verne and whoever wrote "Undine," and country deacons bowling and marraines in Marseilles and girls seduced in the back lanes of Württemberg and Westphalia. Why, this was a love battle—there was a century of middle-class love spent here. This was the last love battle.'

Source: *F. Scott Fitzgerald,* Tender Is the Night *(New York: Scribners, 1934).*

just cause, a defensive action, or a last resort. Active-duty soldiers began moving toward the future battle fronts. Reservists willingly answered their call to active duty. New recruits entered military service. In every capital city in Europe, civilian crowds cheered, prayed, and sang as they celebrated the start of World War I. The war was to be a means to achieve glory, territorial expansion, vengeance, or national validation. For the soldiers themselves, the conflict represented a way to achieve a sense of meaning in life, to satisfy a longing for comradeship, and to achieve a level of adulthood. As mobilization and war plans leaped into high gear, a feeling of euphoria gripped Europe.

The initial movement of men and matériel in August 1914 was astounding. Britain acquired 165,000 cavalry and draft horses during its initial mobilization phase. The Austrians mobilized 600,000 men, the Germans some 700,000 men, and the Russians more than 1 million. Eventually, militaries swelled into the millions. Germany alone sent more than 2,000 trains with 50 railroad cars each eastward across the Rhine in August 1914 alone. The soldiers departing on their trains left their loved ones not with sorrowful tears but with joy and anticipation. As the soldiers left, the national industries retooled to produce the weapons, ammunition, and other matériel to support the war effort.

By the time the Battles of the Somme and Verdun were fought in 1916, public support for the war decreased. Many soldiers' enthusiasm for God and country also waned. Casualties included those soldiers killed, wounded, or missing. At the battle of the Somme, the German and British casualties amounted to 415,000 and more than 650,000 men, respectively. In the battle of Verdun, German and French losses exceeded 325,000 each. British casualties numbered more than 3 million, or 36 percent, of that total British military force of 9 million. French casualties numbered more than 6 million, or 73 percent, of its military strength of 8.5 million. German casualties numbered more than 7 million, or 66 percent, of total military strength of 11 million. Russian casualties numbered 9 million, or 75 percent, of the total military strength of 12 million. The Austro-Hungarian casualties numbered 6.7 million, or 86 percent, of the total military manpower of 8 million. And, because the United States did not enter the conflict until spring 1917, its casualties numbered 260,000, or 6 percent, of the total military strength of 4 million. Of these American soldiers, however, only 1 million actually saw combat.

As these casualties rose, and as the war appeared to be more meaningless after 1916, the soldiers went through a transformation as they were exploded and exploited. They pulled still closer together into cohesive groups. Comrades in arms understood one another's sacrifice. As gender theorist Jean Bethke Elshtain argues, in *Women and War* (1987), combat experience caused a shift from the individual soldier thinking of himself before everyone else to that individual soldier thinking of the collective good of his small unit before himself. Moreover, such male bonding erased artificial social barriers because soldiers shared a common destiny, a common status, a united purpose, and an equality of condition. Indeed, this camaraderie among soldiers served as a symbol

for national unity, at least for the first two years of the conflict. Even when disillusionment increased as the hoped-for short conflict dragged on for years, the soldiers remained loyal to their comrades. It was they who were worth fighting, killing, and dying for, rather than God and country.

Even with small-unit cohesion and male bonding, many soldiers in World War I, perhaps as high as 30 percent of casualties, experienced some form of shell shock; men with this condition refused to fight, dropped into a catatonic state, ran away from the battlefield, or trembled and sobbed uncontrollably during the fighting. Likewise, following the end of the conflict, veterans reacclimated themselves to civilian life only with great difficulty; some veterans could never really heal the psychological wounds of war. Later in the twentieth century, this condition would be diagnosed as post-traumatic stress disorder.

Following the bloody battles of the Somme and Verdun, discipline within most of national militaries began to falter. Maintaining high levels of morale also posed problems for the military leadership of Europe. Coercion became more and more necessary to facilitate military action. As soldiers climbed over the top and charged across "no man's land" against enemy trenches, some officers and noncommissioned officers remained behind to force stragglers to join in the assault. Desertion and other infractions could be dealt with harshly. Admittedly, however, it was easier to coax soldiers to defend themselves against an enemy attack; defense offered much more safety and entailed much less risk than the assaulting forces enjoyed.

Despite efforts to the contrary, the increasing strains of total war caused breakdowns in several instances, indicating the low level to which discipline and morale had fallen. In fact, several nations experienced mutinies and revolutions in 1917 and 1918.

The Russian Revolutions of 1917 revealed the decreasing support for the war effort among the Russian people and soldiers. Germany had defeated the ill-prepared, ill-equipped Russian military forces in 1914 in battles such as Tannenberg and Masurian Lakes. Because Czar Nicholas II exercised direct command over his military forces, he bore the brunt of resentment among soldiers and civilians for keeping the nation in a conflict with no hope of victory. In March 1917 munitions workers in St. Petersburg went on strike because of ever-worsening living conditions; Russian army units joined them in the streets. The resistance spread to other areas. Without the support of the armed forces, Nicholas II abdicated that month. The provisional government replacing him made a critical error in remaining in World War I. As a result, a second revolution, the so-called Bolshevik Revolution, occurred in November 1917. By pulling Russia out of World War I, the new Bolshevik regime gained credibility with the people and military.

France also faced discipline problems late in the war in 1917. General Robert Nivelle took over command of the French army in 1916. As with many World War I commanders, he failed to grasp the firepower advantage enjoyed by forces defending the trenches. Despite the killing efficiency of the machine gun and other weapons, Nivelle ordered the French army to attack the Germans in the Second Battle of the Aisne, otherwise known as Nivelle's Offensive, in spring 1917. He hoped in vain to achieve a decisive victory in this battle. After the battle, more than half the French army mutinied. The soldiers resented the bloody battles ordered by what they believed to be incompetent commanders; they hated the living conditions on the front lines; and they desired more leave to return to the home front. Those soldiers in the enlisted ranks refused to return to their own trenches or to attack German trenches. The crisis crippled the French army for months. Twenty-three leaders of these mutinies were executed, and thousands of other French soldiers were court-martialed. Even after summer 1917, the French army existed as little more than a defensive force for at least a year.

Even Germany was not immune to breakdowns in military discipline. In late 1918 the German High Seas Fleet was ordered to sail from its base at Kiel against the British Royal Navy in a glorious final mission. Because of low morale, poor conditions, and the expectation of certain death in the suicidal mission, German sailors mutinied. Their refusal to obey orders set off a revolution that spread across Germany.

In spring 1917 the United States entered World War I. For American soldiers, the conflict represented an opportunity to conquer another frontier. Going "over there" to fight the evil Hun played into the American male's psyche as an opportunity to be crusader, adventurer, and civilizer of frontiers. The same euphoria and patriotism in Europe back in 1914 replayed in the American public and military in 1917. Because Americans entered the war so late and suffered so few casualties, their combat experience of World War I did not cause as significant a level of disillusionment among veterans following the end of the conflict as it did in Europe. Certainly no revolutions or mutinies occurred among U.S. soldiers and sailors. Still, some cases of shell shock and post-traumatic stress disorder occurred in the American military during and after World War I.

Millions of European and American soldiers went to war because of the "consent thesis" derived from love of country, hatred of the enemy, and a crusading spirit. After the initial shock of combat, the consent thesis was not enough to keep these combat veterans on the front. Comradeship and coercion proved to be more effective in keeping soldiers in their place. Even these factors, however, did not stop mutinies and revolutions as the war dragged on for years.

–DAVID J. ULBRICH,
TEMPLE UNIVERSITY

References

Michael C. C. Adams, *The Great Adventure: Male Desire and the Coming of World War* I (Bloomington: Indiana University Press, 1990).

Tony Ashworth, *Trench Warfare, 1914–1918: The Live and Let Live System* (London: Macmillan, 1980; New York: Holmes & Meier, 1980).

Stéphane Audoin-Rouzeau, *Men at War, 1914–1918: National Sentiment and Trench Journalism in France during the First World War*, translated by Helen McPhail (Providence: Berg, 1992).

Audoin-Rouzeau and Annette Becker, *14–18: Retrouver la Guerre* (Paris: Gallimard, 2000).

Vera Brittain, *Testament of Youth: An Autobiographical Study of the Years 1900–1925* (London: Gollancz, 1933; New York: Macmillan, 1933).

John Ellis, *Eye-Deep in Hell: Trench Warfare in World War I* (London: Croom Helm, 1976).

Jean Bethke Elshtain, *Women and War* (New York: Basic Books, 1987).

Paul Fussell, *The Great War and Modern Memory* (New York: Oxford University Press, 1975).

Michael Geyer, "Comment on Paret and Howard," *Journal of Military History,* 57 (October 1993): 145–163.

Michael Howard, *War in European History* (London & New York: Oxford University Press, 1976).

John Keegan, *The Face of Battle* (London: Cape, 1976; New York: Viking, 1976).

Keegan, *The First World War* (London: Hutchinson, 1998).

David M. Kennedy, *Over Here: The First World War and American Society* (New York: Oxford University Press, 1980).

Eric J. Leed, *No Man's Land: Combat and Identity in World War* I (Cambridge & New York: Cambridge University Press, 1979).

George L. Mosse, *Fallen Soldiers: Reshaping the Memory of the World Wars* (New York: Oxford University Press, 1990).

David Omissi, ed., *Indian Voices of the Great War: Soldiers' Letters, 1914–18* (Basingstoke, U.K.: Macmillan; New York: St. Martin's Press, 1999).

Guy Pedroncini, *Les Mutineries de 1917* (Paris: Presses Universitaires de France, 1967).

G. D. Sheffield, *Leadership in the Trenches: Officer-Man Relations, Morale, and Discipline in the British Army in the Era of the First World War* (Houndmills, Basingstoke, Hampshire, U.K.: Macmillan; New York: St. Martin's Press in association with King's College, London, 2000).

Dennis E. Showalter, "The Hun: German Soldiers in the First World War," in *The German Empire and Britain's Pacific Dominions,*

1871–1919: Essays on the Role of Australia and New Zealand in World Politics in the Age of Imperialism, edited by John A. Moses and Christopher Pugsley (Claremont, Cal.: Regina, 2000), pp. 317–393.

Leonard V. Smith, *Between Mutiny and Obedience: The Case of the French Fifth Infantry Division during World War* I (Princeton: Princeton University Press, 1994).

David J. Ulbrich, "A Male-Conscious Critique of *All Quiet on the Western Front,*" Journal of Men's Studies, 3 (February 1995): 229–240.

Jeffrey Verhey, *The Spirit of 1914: Militarism, Myth and Mobilization in Germany* (Cambridge & New York: Cambridge University Press, 2000).

H. L. Wesseling, *Soldier and Warrior: French Attitudes toward the Army and War on the Eve of the First World War,* translated by Arnold J. Pomerans (Westport, Conn.: Greenwood Press, 2000).

SOLDIERS' MOTIVATIONS

Were the British doomed in the Battle of the Somme (1916) by the decision to seek a decisive breakthrough?

Viewpoint: Yes. Sir Douglas Haig's decision to seek a decisive breakthrough damaged his army's ability to sustain itself in the later stages of the operation.

Viewpoint: No. The problems experienced by the British Expeditionary Force (BEF) at the Somme reflected inexperience in planning for such an offensive.

One of the more controversial engagements of the Great War, the Somme (1916) was conceptualized as a breakthrough, but it was fought as a battle of attrition. Even today it is viewed as one of those experiences that defines a nation and a people. Initial plans for a joint Franco-British general offensive in the summer of 1916 were thwarted by the German attack at Verdun, which reduced French contributions to little more than a token force. The burden fell on the British Expeditionary Force (BEF), whose commander, Sir Douglas Haig, expected to blast open the German positions with a previously unprecedented artillery preparation. The infantry was correspondingly expected to have a walkover, and many of the assault formations, were from Horatio Kitchener's New Armies: men who had never worn a uniform before 1914. Many of the Kitchener units in turn were "Pals" formations, recruited from particular localities or occupations. When the attack went in on 1 July 1916 and the principal German positions proved to be essentially intact, the Pals suffered a high proportion of the approximately sixty thousand British casualties.

Their sacrifice has become a trope for unimaginative British leadership, which sacrificed the best and bravest of their country in an endeavor doomed from the start. Haig and his staff certainly exaggerated the power of modern artillery. Hindsight makes it clear that the BEF had neither enough guns, enough ammunition, nor the kind of fire-control system to produce the results expected. Moreover, 1 July was only the first day of a campaign that included twelve separate battles before finally being terminated in mid November. The ground captured was less important than the institutional results. Scholars of operational history make a solid case that the BEF learned its craft on the Somme and thereafter became an increasingly formidable instrument of war. Students of the German army stress the heavy casualties it suffered, especially among its irreplaceable prewar cadres of professionals. British tactics to the end of the campaign, however, too often involved hammering into the same heavily defended sectors with too little fire support, too little tactical preparation, and too little thought beyond "sticking it." British staff work was too often amateurishly ham-handed. British command methods were too often predicated on morale overcoming barbed wire. The Somme may have been a learning experience, but the tuition was unconscionably, unnecessarily high.

Viewpoint:
Yes. Sir Douglas Haig's decision to seek a decisive breakthrough damaged his army's ability to sustain itself in the later stages of the operation.

British Expeditionary Force (BEF) commander in chief Sir Douglas Haig was at bottom a simple man. That assessment must not be read as a polite euphemism for simpleminded. In terms of character and personality, however, Haig had no hidden depths, none of that ability to see the fourth side of a three-sided question that delights intellectuals in general and military historians in particular. Allied plans for 1916 proposed a major combined offensive, in midsummer, at the junction of the two armies: the Somme River. The original intention—shared by French and British staffs—was to break open twenty miles of German front, drive their mobile forces through the gap and into open country, and decide the war by autumn.

The decisive blow would be delivered not by the "poor bloody infantry," sacrificed in tens of thousands during the futile attacks of 1915, but rather by the artillery. Instead of collapsing under the strain of prolonged war, societies were still sending their sons to training camps and working overtime to manufacture guns and shells. Since August 1914 the artillery of both the British and French armies had increased in numbers of weapons and sheer size of guns and had improved techniques of fire control and ammunition supply to levels unthinkable a decade earlier. One of the overlooked paradigms of World War I is the relative ease with which generals and their staffs converted from an emphasis on maneuver to an acceptance of mass force as a norm—a desirable norm.

Haig was no stranger to mass war. As an army commander in 1915 he showed no reluctance to send waves of men against defended positions, but he also recognized, more quickly than some of his counterparts, that in the constricted tactical conditions of the Western Front, numbers of infantrymen served primarily to perplex and embarrass, to get in each other's way, and increase the casualty lists. For the 1916 campaign Haig correspondingly turned to the guns: piling up the tubes and shells, he expected to blow away German positions in his sector of the attack front before the British infantry ever left its trenches.

He retained that mind-set even after the German offensive at Verdun made clear that French participation in the offensive would be minimal. Less important than the number of divisions was the number of guns, most of them as yet old pieces—obsolete field guns or dismounted fortress weapons. The French nevertheless had made increasingly effective use of them as "position weapons," difficult to place forward but valuable in the initial artillery preparation. The British had nothing like this reserve of old equipment—and now would have no more of the French guns than their allies could decently get away with providing.

Haig remained confident that the exponentially increasing BEF artillery by itself could open the way for his infantry and mounted troops—first Bapaume, then "into the blue." That confidence, however, overlooked the infantry's experiences of 1915. From Neuve Chapelle to Loos, the evidence was clear: enough shells relative to a given target zone could indeed enable a successful infantry assault. Breaking in, however, was not the same as breaking through—and breaking through was not the same as breaking out. British infantry had achieved its most significant local successes by using modified prewar tactics emphasizing "fire and movement" by small units: companies and platoons supporting each other, taking advantage of opportunities as they developed. The argument familiar at higher headquarters that the citizen soldiers that by now filled the ranks were incapable of maneuver on any level was only partly valid. Neither the junior officers nor their men were practiced veterans in small-unit tactics. "Fire and maneuver" was nevertheless the principal kind of field training most formations of Horatio Kitchener's "New Armies" had received from their "dugout" senior officers, who had retired after the Boer War (1899–1902).

Haig, however, was not impressed by the arguments of his subordinates, in particular Sir Henry Rawlinson, whose Fourth Army was to make the attack. This concern was not simple stubbornness. Haig emphasized control. He wanted his first waves to strike the disrupted German positions with the force of a sledgehammer—not dissipate their energies seeking weak spots. The question was further complicated by logistics. Previous operations had also shown attacking forces that reached their objectives failed to hold them because the survivors ran out of ammunition, bombs, and water before supplies could be brought across the moonscape of "no man's land" after the barrages and counterbarrages had done their work. It was little wonder that the developing staffs at all BEF levels produced increasingly elaborate lists of material needed to consolidate captured positions, inform higher headquarters of events, and prepare for the next stage of the advance. It was no wonder at all that the loads fell on the infantry.

Rawlinson, evaluating the same evidence, argued for a "bite and hold" approach: using the initial barrage to penetrate the German defense system, then prepare a second push, and so on. Haig's rejection of the idea reflected to a degree its provenance from outside his headquarters. It reflected as well his conviction that Rawlinson was the kind of officer too clever for everyone else's good. At bottom, however, Haig believed in the BEF—that even the green divisions that made up the bulk of the assault force could get forward under the fire of the five hundred heavy guns that had savaged the German lines for a week. He believed even the best-prepared positions would crumble and their defenders die or go mad.

Haig's faith was unrequited. The German dugouts and their supporting trench systems remained intact. Enough Germans remained alive to man the machine guns that covered the largely uncut wire. Overloaded infantrymen lost touch with barrages scheduled by timetables. At the end of the first day, sixty thousand British were dead, wounded, or missing. A dozen of the best and most promising BEF divisions had been shattered—some so badly that they could never again be trusted in anything but quiet sectors. The disaster, serious enough in itself, did not create paralysis. If anything it inspired at unit levels a determination to learn what was necessary and to do better in the next "show." Compared to expectations, however, the events of 1 July 1916 created a situation in which the rest of the Somme campaign depended on improvisation at all levels: tactical, operational, and strategic. Improvisation was a strong point of neither the BEF nor its commanding general. The results speak eloquently for themselves—in the dozens of cemeteries that remain sites of memory and mourning almost a century later.

−DENNIS SHOWALTER,
COLORADO COLLEGE

Viewpoint:
No. The problems experienced by the British Expeditionary Force (BEF) at the Somme reflected inexperience in planning for such an offensive.

On 1 July 1916 the British army commenced one of the greatest battles in its history. Its objective was nothing less than the decisive defeat of the German army and victory on the Western Front. However, the day ended as one of the most tragic failures for the British Expeditionary Force (BEF), costing about 57,000 casualties, including almost 20,000 dead. The British commander, General Douglas Haig, continued the attack into November, admittedly on a spasmodic and less intensive scale, but decisive victory remained elusive and the battle instead became an attritional struggle, wearing down both sides until exhaustion and the approach of winter brought it to a halt.

Haig has been criticized for insisting that his troops push straight through the German defenses to the open fields beyond and for rejecting an alternative plan proposed by his subordinate, General Henry Rawlinson, who was the commander of the British Fourth Army and the officer directly responsible for the planning and conduct of the battle. Rawlinson had proposed to Haig that the British employ a "bite and hold" method of attack; his initial plan for the Somme drew upon several related observations he made on the battles of 1915. He concluded that while the British could routinely seize the enemy's first line, the attacking troops encountered great difficulty and casualties when they attempted a greater penetration of their defenses. Rawlinson also recognized the superiority of defensive firepower and the ability of the defense to inflict greater casualties on the attacker than they could inflict on the defender. For the Somme, Rawlinson proposed attacking in a series of stages, each time seizing a small piece of enemy ground and then using British defensive firepower to crush the inevitable German counterattack. In effect, Rawlinson was proposing a British version of the tactics the Germans had themselves employed during their battle with the French at Verdun (1916). He wanted to force the enemy to counterattack at a disadvantage and thereby incur greater losses than the British, leading to the collapse of the German army. Haig rejected these proposals and insisted that the Fourth Army plan to break through the enemy's lines in one great push.

While the tactics proposed by Haig and Rawlinson appear to be different, the differences are in fact superficial. Despite Rawlinson's preference for "bite and hold" tactics, his operational objective was the same as that of Haig, the destruction of the German army in a decisive battle. Instead of one great push, he simply called for a more deliberate approach. After the failure of the first day, subsequent British efforts became more limited in their scale and objective, but despite more modest goals the British never intended to lure the German army into a disadvantageous defensive slaughter. Rather, Haig continued to hope for a breakthrough and the rapid collapse of the enemy. Moreover, it is not clear that Rawlinson's "bite and hold" method would have resulted in fewer casualties for the British over the course of the battle. The German example of Verdun illustrates the difficulty of such a task. The Verdun battle lasted from February until the Germans broke off the attack when the assault at Somme began. Yet, despite six months of effort, German troops suffered almost as much as the French. At no point in the battle did the Germans establish a rate of attrition favorable enough to destroy the French army without also consuming their own.

Nevertheless, Haig's reluctance to adopt Rawlinson's tactics does not account for the tactical fail-

"THEY CAN HAVE ALL THEY WANT AT THE SAME PRICE"

On 15 September 1916 Bavarian general Prince Rupprecht, who commanded the Sixth Army in the defense of Lorraine (1914), reported on the Allied attack on the Somme:

Sunday, Monday, and Tuesday, September 9th, 10th, and 11th marked the culmination thus far of the first desperate effort of the Entente to force our positions. My officers will tell you the result as we see on this side see it. Our losses in territory may be seen on the map with a microscope. Their losses in that far more precious thing—human life—are simply prodigious.

Amply and in full coin have they paid for every foot of ground we sold them. They can have all they want at the same price. We have a reserve, constituted of trained officers and trained men, which has not yet been drawn upon. We are not, like the Entente Generals, forced to throw raw, untrained recruits into the very front of the fighting.

Whether this will be the last effort we cannot know. We have taken measure of their strength at its maximum tide and are prepared for anything they can deliver. For the sake of the thousands whom new attacks will slay in vain we hope they have learned a lesson. So far as the interests of the Fatherland are concerned, we are indifferent; indeed, inclined to welcome any further folly they may indulge in.

It saddens us to exact the dreadful toll of suffering and death that is being marked up on the ledger of history, but if the enemy is still minded to possess a few more hectares of blood-sodden soil, I fear they must pay a bitter price.

On 28 September Rupprecht added:

This Somme offensive brings an attack of unusual violence every six days on the average. I know this country well from the fighting of 1914. At that time we had moving warfare, while we are now in a position of siege.

In his attacks, beginning in July, the enemy has gained some ground, but a decision of the situation is not to be thought of. One cannot prophesy how things will go here, but one thing is certain: Everything has now been so well provided for by us that one can quietly await coming events, be they what they may.

The offensive will certainly not be at an end very soon. One may well look forward to an offensive of great endurance, with very violent attacks, prepared for by a colossal expenditure of ammunition. We have, however, taken all necessary measures.

Our artillery has been strengthened and our flyers also. In the last few days our flyers have again had some good successes after their hard fight against the enemy flyers. The fact that our flyers are getting the upper hand is of prime advantage to our artillery.

Our troops have given their all and the nut was too hard for the enemy to crack. I am of the opinion that the enemy is seeking a decision here and this year, and in this he has failed.

Source: Charles F. Horne, ed., Source Records of the Great War, volume six (Indianapolis: American Legion, 1930), pp. 251–253.

---

ure of the first day of battle. Rather, the British failed to meet Haig's goals because the soldiers did not have the required skills to achieve a decisive victory at that time, whether by breakthrough or "bite and hold." The enormous losses were a result of the failure of the Fourth Army to control the battlefield and neutralize German defensive firepower. The Somme was the largest and most complex battle the British had attempted to that date in World War I. Its successful waging was beyond the scope of the abilities of the British army in 1916.

The British army faced several tactical and technological impediments that greatly handicapped its performance during the battle. Rawlinson did not draw up a unified plan for the attack of the Fourth Army. Rather, following British army policy, he devolved this responsibility onto his corps commanders, who then passed the task on their divisional subordinates. Within the eleven divisions participating in the opening phase of the battle, each brigade, and even battalion, designed their own battle plan. Therefore, the Fourth Army lacked any uniformity of planning at any level. Of the eleven divisions attacking on 1 July, seven were recently raised "New Army" formations and most of the soldiers were about to experience battle for the first time. The lack of central planning meant that the new men could not learn from veterans and had to discover the best way to fight on their own.

While the absence of central direction helps to justify some of the variations in degree of success achieved by individual units, it does not explain the overall failure of the first day, because the critical arm of the battle was not the infantry but rather the artillery. While the task of the infantry was to advance through the enemy's lines, they would do so behind the fire of the artillery of the Fourth Army, which had previously destroyed or suppressed the German defenders. To this end, Rawlinson's gunners planned a preliminary bombardment of five days (extended to seven because of poor weather), a rolling barrage in front of the infantry, and a counterbattery bombardment on the enemy's battery locations. The responsibility for the casualties on the first day was primarily the result of the failure of Fourth Army artillery in all three missions.

The Fourth Army had no shortage of guns or ammunition for its tasks. Rawlinson had at his disposal more than 1,400 guns, including 233 howitzers and 1.6 million shells. However, a consideration of numbers alone exaggerates the true weight of the British bombardment. Robin Prior and Trevor Wilson, in *Command on the Western Front: The Military Career of Sir Henry Rawlinson, 1914–18* (1991), have pointed out that the more critical measurement is the ratio of number of shells per target area. Seen from this perspective, the bombardment by the Fourth Army was actually less than half the strength that the British had employed the previous year at the Battle of Neuve Chapelle.

Further weakening the bombardment was the fact that the Fourth Army had a relatively small proportion of heavy guns. In 1916 the British army still suffered from the prewar preference for the light 18-pounder rather than guns of larger caliber. The shrapnel shell from this gun was well suited for the destruction of German wire, but it had no effect on enemy soldiers who waited out the maelstrom of falling shells in the safety of their deep dugouts. Moreover, much of the ammunition provided for the heavy guns, the only weapons capable of reaching the enemy's dugouts, proved defective and buried itself in the ground without exploding. Fuses were also a problem for some calibers, thereby weakening the barrage further. For example, the 9.2-inch howitzer fuse tended to fall off in flight. When the bombardment ended, sufficient numbers of the enemy's front-line troops still survived to pour fierce rifle and machine-gun fire into the British infantry struggling across "no man's land."

The low technical quality of the British counterbattery fire also impaired the effectiveness of the bombardment. Much of the counterbattery fire of the Fourth Army depended on the obsolete 4.7-inch gun, a weapon whose barrels were largely worn out by the time of the Battle of Loos the previous year. The British also had trouble locating enemy battery positions from the air, and the key techniques of sound-ranging and flash-spotting were still too primitive to assure accuracy. Even when the British fixed the enemy's position, the gunner's slowness to appreciate the vital role played by survey, calibration, and meteorological conditions prevented them from achieving accuracy of fire. As a result, when the battle began, most German batteries were able to fire their defensive barrages.

Without a successful artillery plan any advance on the Western Front was doomed before it started. The infantry could only survive the crossing of "no man's land" when friendly artillery had neutralized the enemy's defensive firepower. At the Somme the British gunners had comprehensively failed at this task. The result was catastrophe. However, the gunners learned quickly from their mistakes. The 15 September attack of the Somme campaign was the first battle for which the British developed a coordinated counterbattery plan. In November 1916 Third Corps established the first Counter-Battery Staff Office in the army. By early 1917 each corps had one. This agency proved to be the turning point in the development of skills to coordinate counterbattery fire, and the British exploited its advantages to subdue the enemy's artillery in subsequent campaigns. In 1917 the artillery received the highly effective 106 fuse, and the 6-inch howitzer came into wider service in the counterbattery role. Moreover, the Ministry of Munitions moved to eliminate defects from artillery ammunition.

Haig's hopes for the Somme offensive were certainly too ambitious, especially for an army with the capabilities that the British possessed in July 1916. He could partially justify the battle on political grounds, that is, the need to relieve German pressure on the French at Verdun. Yet, even if the requirement to support a coalition partner is discounted, the battle was still essential and its outcome important. The Battle of the Somme was a critical moment in the development of the British army in World War I. Even while it still raged, the British began to learn its lessons and incorporate the solutions that it had suggested into their operations. More than two years passed before the British achieved victory in 1918, but the legacy of the Battle of the Somme was reflected in the gradual improvement in the force of arms of the British army. By mid 1918 the British army had matured into a military force able to defeat the German army on the field of battle.

–ALBERT PALAZZO,
UNIVERSITY OF NEW SOUTH WALES
AT THE AUSTRALIAN DEFENCE
FORCE ACADEMY

References

Paddy Griffith, *Battle Tactics of the Western Front: The British Army's Art of Attack, 1916–18* (New Haven: Yale University Press, 1994).

Griffith, ed., *British Fighting Methods in the Great War* (London & Portland, Ore.: Cass, 1996).

Albert Palazzo, "The British Army's Counter-Battery Staff Office and Control of the Enemy in World War I," *Journal of Military History*, 63 (January 1999): 55–74.

Robin Prior and Trevor Wilson, *Command on the Western Front: The Military Career of Sir Henry Rawlinson, 1914–18* (Oxford, U.K. & Cambridge, Mass.: Blackwell, 1991).

G. D. Sheffield, "The Indispensable Factor: The Performance of British Troops in 1918," in *1918 Defining Victory*, edited by Peter Dennis and Jeffrey Grey (Canberra: Department of Defense, 1999), pp. 72–95.

Tim Travers, *How the War Was Won: Command and Technology in the British Army on the Western Front, 1917–1918* (London & New York: Routledge, 1992).

THE SOMME

TREATY OF VERSAILLES

Did the Treaty of Versailles in 1919 provide the framework for a durable peace?

Viewpoint: Yes. The Versailles settlement was purposely designed to establish lasting international stability. It was no harsher than comparable treaties and was entirely appropriate for the political environment of 1919.

Viewpoint: No. The Treaty of Versailles was disastrous because it embittered Germany and fostered political radicalism in that country.

The Great War left the international relations of the world in a dysfunctional state. The much-maligned Treaty of Versailles (1919) and its counterparts were, however, less responsible for that condition than their reputation would have it. The Versailles settlement was worked out quickly. Armies needed to be demobilized. Food had to be shipped to countries previously blockaded. Revolutionary movements demanded containment. The negotiating processes were highly bureaucratized by earlier standards. They were also highly publicized. The discussions made corresponding demands on the diplomatic and political skills of all the participants. It is scarcely surprising that the results of the conference did not meet long-range needs, either in Europe or elsewhere in a world increasingly resentful of Euro/Western hegemony.

At the same time, however, the Versailles settlement was flexible, incorporating the possibility of future modification. None of the participants regarded it as anything but a work in progress. By the mid 1920s the Rhineland occupation had come to an end. Germany was a member of the League of Nations. Even the issue of reparations was in the process of being negotiated.

The Versailles settlement was undermined not by its intrinsic weaknesses but by the general lack of restraint that emerged in Europe after 1914 and persisted as an independent consequence of the war. Low- and mid-level armed conflict persisted into the mid 1920s: Russia and Poland, Turkey and Greece, and France and Spain in Morocco—that last conflict, in passing, far more costly than any nineteenth-century imperialist war. The Little Entente, the French network of eastern European alliances, and the Balkan ambitions of Italy encouraged unstable successor states to threaten each other with armies they could not afford. Postwar European economic relationships developed in zero-sum contexts well before the Great Depression. Great-power policy became the conduct of war by other means. The new Soviet Union regarded itself in a state of war with its capitalist counterparts. Germany and Russia were entirely excluded from the peace negotiations. The allies blockaded Germany for a year after the armistice. Even the League of Nations developed into a forum for expressing antagonisms. President Woodrow Wilson's principle of "open covenants openly arrived at" too often became "overt hostilities publicly expressed." International agreements are only as good as the will to implement them. After 1918 that will increasingly eroded in Europe and the world.

Viewpoint:
Yes. The Versailles settlement was purposely designed to establish lasting international stability. It was no harsher than comparable treaties and was entirely appropriate for the political environment of 1919.

Few people today would argue that the Treaty of Versailles, signed in 1919, was a good or lasting peace. Saying that the treaty failed to establish lasting peace in Europe, however, is different from saying that the treaty was designed to be so harsh that it would inevitably fail. Whatever faults were contained within the final treaty (and there were many), the framers of Versailles entered into the peace negotiations intent on creating what British diplomat Harold Nicolson called "eternal peace." "We were," he said, "bent on doing great, permanent, and noble things."

That they failed is beyond question, but they did not fail because the treaty they wrote was unduly harsh. Although it was significantly larger in scope than most European peace treaties, one must bear in mind that the war it followed was also significantly larger in scope than any conflict in history. Moreover, none of the provisions of the treaty were particularly novel. Virtually all of them, including indemnities and intentional humiliations, had been common features of European peace agreements for decades. The Germans used many of them against France following the Franco-Prussian War (1870–1871). Europeans were quite familiar with the Latin phrase *Vae Victis* (Woe to the conquered). While one can argue that the conferees could or should have been magnanimous in victory, one cannot argue that they were breaking significant new ground by not doing so.

The men who gathered in Paris had before them a truly historic opportunity. They had obtained from Germany an armistice that left the Germans with virtually no means of defending themselves against whatever treaty the Allies might wish to write. Not since 1815 had the powers of Europe held such power to redesign the Continent. At that conference the British delegation had involved fourteen diplomats. The British delegation of 1919, by contrast, occupied five entire Parisian hotels. At the height of the conference, more than one thousand diplomats from more than thirty nations were in attendance. The conferees had before them the power to redraw the map of Europe and settle the many disputes that representatives of virtually every nation and aspiring nation in the world brought before them.

In the end they failed because they simply tried to do too much. No group of men could have accomplished the goals that these men set before themselves. The three most important nations were represented by men who largely avoided their own staffs and tried to make all decisions themselves. French premier Georges Clemenceau, British prime minister David Lloyd George, and U.S. president Woodrow Wilson met behind closed doors more than two hundred times (sometimes with Italian prime minister Vittorio Orlando, sometimes without him) and fought among themselves to push their own ideas. The stress caused Wilson to fall seriously ill and Clemenceau risked his life by working on, even after surviving an assassination attempt that left a bullet lodged near his lungs.

National rivalries and the egos of forceful personalities produced a treaty that was unfavorable to Germany, but it was largely in line with comparable recent agreements. The precedent on the minds of most Frenchmen was the Treaty of Frankfurt (1871) that had ended the Franco-Prussian War. Under the terms of that treaty, Prussia forced France to cede the disputed and resource-rich territories of Alsace and Lorraine and to pay a punitive indemnity of 5 billion francs (about $1 billion). This indemnity amounted to more than twice the total German costs for the war. A German army of occupation remained in France until the French government paid the debt in 1873 by increasing taxes and promoting "liberation loans." To underscore French humiliation, the Prussians forced the French to accept a victors' march through Paris. Intending to rub even more salt in French wounds, the Prussians declared the founding of the Second Reich at Versailles, the palace built by Louis XIV as a symbol of French power.

Europeans fully understood that winners write the terms and losers sign them. The peace agreements of World War I that preceded Versailles were no exceptions. In December 1916 the Germans defeated Romania and as a consequence seized the majority of Romanian grain and oil fields. German forces occupied the Romanian capital, Bucharest, and German diplomats approved the transfer of the southern Romanian region of Dobruja to Bulgaria, one of the Central Powers, and therefore an ally of Germany.

The treaty Germany signed with Bolshevik Russia was arguably the harshest in modern European history. On 3 March 1918 Russia formally withdrew from the war after signing the Treaty of Brest-Litovsk. In that treaty, Germany forced Russia to give up all claims to Poland, Belarus, the Baltic States (where the Germans confidently expected to place German princes

WAR GUILT AND REPARATION

The following articles are part of the Treaty of Versailles (1919):

ARTICLE 231.

The Allied and Associated Governments affirm and Germany accepts the responsibility of Germany and her allies for causing all the loss and damage to which the Allied and Associated Governments and their nationals have been subjected as a consequence of the war imposed upon them by the aggression of Germany and her allies.

ARTICLE 232.

The Allied and Associated Governments recognise that the resources of Germany are not adequate, after taking into account permanent diminutions of such resources which will result from other provisions of the present Treaty, to make complete reparation for all such loss and damage.

The Allied and Associated Governments, however, require, and Germany undertakes, that she will make compensation for all damage done to the civilian population of the Allied and Associated Powers and to their property during the period of the belligerency of each as an Allied or Associated Power against Germany by such aggression by land, by sea and from the air, and in general all damage as defined in Annex I hereto.

In accordance with Germany's pledges, already given, as to complete restoration for Belgium, Germany undertakes, in addition to the compensation for damage elsewhere in this Part provided for, as a consequence of the violation of the Treaty of 1839, to make reimbursement of all sums which Belgium has borrowed from the Allied and Associated Governments up to November 11, 1918, together with interest at the rate of five per cent (5%) per annum on such sums. This amount shall be determined by the Reparation Commission, and the German Government undertakes thereupon forthwith to make a special issue of bearer bonds to an equivalent amount payable in marks gold, on May 1, 1926, or, at the option of the German Government, on the 1st of May in any year up to 1926. Subject to the foregoing, the form of such bonds shall be determined by the Reparation Commission. Such bonds shall be handed over to the Reparation Commission, which has authority to take and acknowledge receipt thereof on behalf of Belgium.

ARTICLE 233.

The amount of the above damage for which compensation is to be made by Germany shall be determined by an Inter-Allied Commission, to be called the Reparation Commission and constituted in the form and with the powers set forth hereunder and in Annexes II to VII inclusive hereto.

This Commission shall consider the claims and give to the German Government a just opportunity to be heard.

The findings of the Commission as to the amount of damage defined as above shall be concluded and notified to the German Government on or before May 1, 1921, as representing the extent of that Government's obligations.

The Commission shall concurrently draw up a schedule of payments prescribing the time and manner for securing and discharging the entire obligation within a period of thirty years from May 1, 1921. . . .

ARTICLE 235.

In order to enable the Allied and Associated Powers to proceed at once to the restoration of their industrial and economic life, pending the full determination of their claims, Germany shall pay in such installments and in such manner (whether in gold, commodities, ships, securities or otherwise) as the Reparation Commission may fix, during 1919, 1920 and the first four months of 1921, the equivalent of 20,000,000,000 gold marks. Out of this sum the expenses of the armies of occupation subsequent to the Armistice of November 11, 1918, shall first be met, and such supplies of food and raw materials as may be judged by the Governments of the Principal Allied and Associated Powers to be essential to enable Germany to meet her obligations for reparation may also, with the approval of the said Governments, be paid for out of the above sum. The balance shall be reckoned towards liquidation of the amounts due for reparation. Germany shall further deposit bonds as prescribed in paragraph 12 (c) Of Annex II hereto.

Source: "The Versailles Treaty," *Internet website, http://history.acusd.edu/gen/text/versaillestreaty/ver231.html*

on thrones), Finland, Bessarabia, Ukraine, and the Caucases. In all, Russia lost territory three times larger than Germany itself (a grand total of 750,000 square kilometers), including one-third of its prewar population, one-third of its arable land, and 90 percent of its coal fields. Germany seized all Russian naval bases in the Baltic except one and disarmed the Russian Black Sea Fleet.

German plans for the West were scarcely less harsh. Before the war, Germany had developed the so-called September Program to guide the victors' peace that they planned to dictate to France and Britain. If victorious, Germany envisioned a peace with four primary features: first, a heavy war indemnity on France would prevent that country from rearming. This time, the Germans planned to take French overseas colonies as well. Second, the Germans would create and dominate an economic union including wartime enemies such as France, Belgium, and Italy but also including neutrals such as Holland, Norway, Sweden, and Denmark. A German-dominated Poland and ally Austria-Hungary were also to be included. Third, Germany would enlarge its Central African empire at the expense of Belgium, Britain, and France. Fourth, Germany would annex neutral Holland into the German Reich. As the war progressed, the costs of the war led German leaders to expect to receive even more spoils should they emerge victorious. Total war would now call for total peace.

Brest-Litovsk and the September Program set the tone for future peace treaties. As German armies began to retreat in 1918, they destroyed fields, wells, mines, bridges, canals, and anything else that the Allied armies might use to speed up their drive east. Now someone would have to pay to rebuild those devastated areas and, in true European fashion, the winners presented a bill to the losers. Calls such as "Le Boche Payera" in France and "squeeze the Germans like a lemon until the pips squeak" in Britain, however, were more rhetoric than reality. The conferees agreed not to set a total amount, establishing instead a commission to determine the totals. In theory, this commission might have set increasingly unrealistic debts. In reality, Allied postwar programs such as the Dawes Program were dedicated to reducing and refinancing overall German debt, not enlarging it.

Much recent scholarship has emphasized the role of Germany in exacerbating the debt crisis. Germany did not raise taxes or support loans to pay the reparations, as France did from 1871 to 1873. Niall Ferguson, in an essay in Manfred F. Boemke, Gerald D. Feldman, and Elisabeth Glaser's *The Treaty of Versailles: A Reassessment After 75 Years* (1998) argues that German leaders were more interested in using the debt to play

domestic politics than they were in paying it off. In short, the postwar financial crisis in Germany owes as much to the actions of Weimar Germany as it does to the terms of the Treaty of Versailles.

Neither was the War Guilt Clause exceptional. Although most Europeans understood that blaming Germany exclusively for the outbreak of the war was patently ridiculous, the guilt clause was typical of the kinds of humiliations normally visited upon the vanquished. Indeed, the clause substituted an official stigma for an Allied victory parade through Berlin, something the Germans opposed even more strongly than they opposed the guilt clause. Some scholars have argued that the absence of a victory march was one of the greatest mistakes of the Allies. The war in the West had been fought in France and Belgium; Germany was still intact. Without a victors' march, the German army (which itself paraded through Berlin as President Friedrich Ebert hailed it as "unvanquished from the field") could reject the guilt clause and make the fallacious claim that it had not been defeated on the battlefield. A triumphal march such as the German one down the Champs Elysées in 1871 would have laid bare that fiction and made it much more difficult for future German leaders to claim that they had been stabbed in the back.

The idealism of President Wilson and his Fourteen Points made the eventual treaty look exceedingly severe. It is important to keep in mind, however, that for all its harshness, the treaty was not nearly as harsh as some in Europe had wanted. As noted, there was no march through Germany and no Allied occupation of Germany similar to their occupation of northeastern France from 1871 to 1873. The Allies did not, as the French military had publicly and loudly demanded, create bridgeheads across the Rhine River. Nor did the Allies attempt to separate the Rhineland from Germany as many French industrialists had demanded. Even the vast majority of Germans understood that the Rhineland would be demilitarized and that France would take back Alsace and Lorraine (though some Germans unrealistically believed they could demand a plebiscite), but the Allies made no further territorial demands in the West. They also did not encourage a nascent separatist movement in Bavaria, nor did the conferees take seriously the arguments of those on the French Right who thought that Germany should be returned to its 1870 borders.

Prime Minister Lloyd George was especially concerned to limit the reach of the treaty for fear of creating future areas of dispute such as Alsace-Lorraine. Largely thanks to his efforts, the final treaty did not give Danzig to Poland outright nor did it demilitarize East Prussia. Both of these features had been contained in the initial report of the Commission on Polish Affairs. It is thus misleading to view the treaty as a product of the unchecked demands of the Great Powers.

In fact, by the end of the conference there were many thoughtful people in Europe who believed that the treaty had been too soft. French Marshal Ferdinand Foch made his famous statement, "This is not peace. It is an armistice for twenty years," in frustration at what he perceived as the softness of the treaty, particularly the failure to create Allied military bridgeheads across the Rhine. Versailles was no peace with honor, but neither was it the Carthaginian peace that many Germans later claimed it was. In its principal features, Versailles was perfectly in line with recent European tradition. It is more accurate to say that Germany perceived the treaty as unduly harsh, even though it was no worse than what the Germans had planned for their enemies. That perception, much more than realities, brought war to Europe again almost twenty years to the day after Foch's chilling prophecy.

–MICHAEL S. NEIBERG, U.S. AIR FORCE ACADEMY

Viewpoint:
No. The Treaty of Versailles was disastrous because it embittered Germany and fostered political radicalism in that country.

A recent revisionist argument has suggested that the provisions of the Paris Peace Settlement—specifically the terms of the Treaty of Versailles (1919) signed with Germany—created a rational framework for postwar Europe and promised long-term international stability. The traditional historical analysis, however, is much more correct in its assessment of the post–World War I peace settlement as a disaster for European stability. The Treaty of Versailles violated the spirit of a promised democratic peace; placed the entire burden of responsibility for the war on the shoulders of Germany; required it to pay symbolically offensive, yet ultimately insignificant, reparations to the Allies; and deprived it of its great power status in an unrealistic and unsustainable fashion. The cumulative effect of these factors created widespread sentiments of anger and betrayal among the German people, undermined the stability of the postwar moderate republican government of Germany, legitimized extreme political movements in the eyes of the centrist and traditional right-wing mainstream, and catalyzed a foreign policy centered on recovering losses and pursuing the hegemony that

had eluded Imperial Germany. The rise of Adolf Hitler and the genesis of World War II were in many ways a direct result of the harsh peace forced upon Germany in 1919.

The first and perhaps most important flaw in the Versailles settlement—and the one most overlooked by historians—is that the request by Germany for an armistice stemmed from its leaders' impression that the peace would be fair, equitable, and democratic. Concretely, they expected a peace settlement that would follow the guidelines of President Woodrow Wilson's famous "Fourteen Points." Presented to Congress on 8 January 1918, Wilson's terms called for a postwar world dominated by open diplomatic relations, multilateral disarmament, free trade, freedom of the seas, and the settlement of disputes by international representative organizations. They also involved several provisions for the revision of European borders along ethnic lines, including but not limited to the evacuation of the wartime conquests of Germany, the return of Alsace-Lorraine to France, national self-determination for the peoples of the Habsburg and Ottoman Empires, and the resurrection of a Polish state with access to the sea. In subsequent public addresses Wilson restated his points and added that their provisions could be modified on a case-by-case basis. When Germany, finally convinced of its inability to win the war, approached the Allies for an armistice in October 1918, Wilson replied with a series of diplomatic notes declaring that he would only negotiate with a democratic German government free from its "military masters and the monarchical autocrats."

No responsible German officials believed that a peace treaty drafted on this basis would turn into the Carthaginian peace that the Allies presented to their country the following year. In the last weeks of the war, Germany accepted all of Wilson's terms in principle. None of them were judged too severe, at least from the perspective of Berlin. The return of Alsace-Lorraine, a largely French region that had a long history of being passed back and forth between Germany and France, and had not been well integrated into the German Empire anyway, was not a serious loss. Re-creating a Polish state with sea access was also a minimal threat, since the Empire contained far fewer Poles than either Russia or Austria and had already proclaimed a new Polish state in November 1916. Wilson's call for Polish "access to the sea" did not strictly involve massive territorial transfers from Germany, as access could easily be granted either by giving up only the Baltic port of Danzig or allowing Polish commerce to cross German territory free of customs duties. Both measures had historical precedents. Abandoning the strong military presence of the Empire in the East was acceptable because a broad segment of German political opinion opposed direct territorial annexation, while the

Imperial government itself had established friendly national states that could potentially continue to exist without a German military presence. Wilson's last demand, for political reform, actually coincided with the long-standing goals of many German politicians. In late October 1918 even Kaiser William II became a convert to liberalization and consented to the creation of constitutional monarchy. When the popular mood nevertheless forced his abdication, the unexpected advent of a democratic republic represented an even greater fulfillment of Wilson's conditions.

As negotiations for an armistice entered their last phase in the first week of November 1918, the Germans had no reason to believe that the price of peace would amount to anything more than the terms outlined by Wilson. The only inkling that this arrangement would not in fact be the case came from the extremely limited German understanding of Allied reservations to Wilson's peace program. The joint Allied terms for the armistice presented on 5 November contained language that left the concept of "freedom of the seas" open for interpretation and alluded to indemnity payments for damage to civilian property. Neither codicil appeared to contradict the spirit—or most of the letter—of Wilson's program, but in truth Allied objections applied voluminously to each of the Fourteen Points, and the American president could only preserve a unified approach by secretly conceding on each of them and not telling the Germans. Through no fault of their own, German leaders were duped into accepting a punitive peace that departed radically from both their own expectations and Wilson's original intentions. Their position was made worse by the extreme last-minute military provisions of the armistice, crafted by Marshal Ferdinand Foch of France. Sensing the unwillingness of Germany to continue the war and not wanting to leave it any military leverage in the peace negotiations, Foch insisted on the complete withdrawal of German forces not only from their existing positions on the western front but from German territory west of the Rhine. Germany was also supposed to surrender its fleet, much of its heavy artillery, and a large number of railway cars vital for mobilization and rapid troop movements. In other words, Germany had to surrender its material means of continuing the war even before the peace negotiations began. Although they were not without suspicion, the new leaders of Germany knew they had little choice and, trusting that the negotiations would be fair nevertheless, agreed to Foch's terms.

From literally the first moment of the peace conference, it was clear that the peace settlement would be the *Diktat*—or dictation—that its critics later described. Revenge was a prominent theme even in the scheduling of the talks. They were delib-

erately postponed until the symbolic date of 18 January 1919, the anniversary of the proclamation of the German Empire in 1871. Germany and its allies were not allowed to attend. Rumors that the meetings were only a preliminary series of inter-Allied discussions for a large and inclusive peace conference were circulated to fool the Germans into thinking that they would ultimately be heard and permitted to negotiate. These rumors, however, never materialized into fact and were later disavowed. The details of the peace treaty were decided in secret, first by a working group of the American, British, French, Italian, and Japanese heads of government and foreign ministers—the "Council of Ten"—and later by a de facto triumvirate of Wilson, British prime minister David Lloyd George, and French premier Georges Clemenceau.

Wilson was hard put to maintain his original sense of justice in the peace treaty. Lloyd George and Clemenceau correctly took him for a foreign-policy neophyte whom they could outmaneuver, and they secretly agreed to support each other's goals in talks with him. They frequently invoked diplomatic technicalities, employed rhetorical tricks, and made dramatic appeals in order to impose many of their views on the American president. Wilson, of course, had already conceded on many issues in order to persuade them to accept the armistice. Nevertheless, through compromise and some clever negotiating of his own he managed to preserve some of his original ideas and soften some of the more extreme British and French demands. Lloyd George and Clemenceau, for example, accepted the League of Nations as an institution to arbitrate international disputes. Clemenceau was also persuaded to give up the territorial dismemberment of Germany for strategic and economic reasons, and to accept a reduced figure for war reparations.

Yet, overall, Wilson's provisions for a moderate peace were distorted and no room was left for bargaining. When the Treaty of Versailles—a book-length document of 440 separate articles—was presented to a German diplomatic delegation on 7 May 1919 (the fourth anniversary of the sinking of the passenger liner *Lusitania*), the visibly disturbed German delegation understood that none of it was negotiable and that, in plain language, their country had been had. To list the most important of the unexpected terms, Germany had to accept full responsibility for the war (under the "War Guilt Clause," Article 231), even though that degree of responsibility was at the time, and has ever since, remained highly questionable. All of the colonies of Germany were taken away, a substantial part of its eastern provinces were ceded to Poland (despite the earlier ambiguity about the meaning of "access to the sea" and the inclusion of territory that had nothing to do with sea communica-

tions), and other border areas were to be ceded to Belgium, Denmark, and Lithuania on the basis of national self-determination. For ethnic Germans, however, national self-determination was expressly denied first by a French-inspired clause that forbade any political or customs union between Germany and Austria, and later by Allied recognition of the new Polish, Italian, and Czechoslovakian frontiers, all of which contained large German minority populations.

Germany was also restricted by astonishingly severe limitations on its military power. Its army could field no more than one hundred thousand troops—or about 20 percent of its pre-war total. Its offensive capacity was for all practical purposes abolished by prohibitions on tanks, planes, and an army general staff. The navy was forbidden to maintain capital ships (of more than ten thousand tons displacement) or submarines. The west bank of the Rhine and a fifty-kilometer zone to the east of the river were placed under Allied occupation for a maximum period of fifteen years and were to remain permanently demilitarized thereafter. The industrial Saar region was to be placed under French sovereignty for fifteen years and was then subject to a referendum to determine its future. From a strategic perspective, Germany was barely left with a

self-defense capability and was effectively removed from the ranks of the great powers.

The most onerous provision of all, however, was the requirement of Germany to pay heavy reparations to the Allies. Following from its acceptance of war guilt, the reparations were to include compensation for war damage, as well as military pensions and pensions for the families of dead Allied soldiers. In 1921 their full amount was fixed at $33 billion—an impossibly high sum for the era, yet actually less than Clemenceau had initially wanted. The transfer of German territory, military equipment, and colonial possessions was not to be credited against the sum. One of Lloyd George's assistants had characterized the British approach to reparations as squeezing a lemon "until the pips squeak." Despite the outrageousness of these provisions—recognized even by members of the Allied delegations, including several American members who resigned in protest—the German delegation could only submit. In another stinging jab of irony, the signing ceremony was held in the Hall of Mirrors in the Palace of Versailles, a location chosen because it had been the site of the proclamation of the German Empire in 1871.

As soon as word of the full dimensions of the Versailles Treaty became known to the German public, it provoked a sense of bitterness and out-

David Lloyd George, Vittorio Orlando, Georges Clemenceau, and Woodrow Wilson (l.–r.) at the Paris Peace Conference in 1919

(Roger Viollet)

rage that lasted for many years. The treaty represented complete betrayal of what was expected to have been a just and honorable peace. German conservatives viewed the left-wing politicians who had ultimately signed the armistice and accepted the treaty as the "November criminals" who had "stabbed Germany in the back." Many Germans remembered that their armies were still standing on foreign soil in November 1918 and felt that the honor of their nation and its institutions had been stained not only by foreigners but by their own leaders. Right-wing extremists, including Hitler, made the ugly insinuation that Germany had been the victim of an international Jewish conspiracy and found many sympathetic listeners. Naturally these people were forgetting that the German High Command and Imperial government had recognized their inability to win the war and set the armistice in motion, but it was the new democratic government—the Weimar Republic—that bore political responsibility for the harsh peace. Over time the legitimacy of the German democracy was corroded by association. Had the new democratic state been given the just peace that it had believed in, was promised, and expected, that would not have been so.

The most significant long-term consequence of the peace, however, was that none of the provisions that created so much outrage in Germany had any lasting practical significance. Even the War Guilt Clause, the fundamental article of the treaty that formed the basis for its other harsh terms, became unsustainable. It goes without saying that German public opinion rejected it in principle. For decades before the war, the Germans had believed that their country had long been denied its place in the sun by the machinations of foreign governments and that its justified place among the great powers had been constricted and destroyed by its jealous neighbors. The dominant German opinion was that the growth of the Empire had been unjustly blunted by the Entente powers and that it was thus provoked into lashing out. This thesis was not seriously challenged in German historiography until Fritz Fischer in the 1960s published his comprehensive study of Imperial German war aims.

As war memories faded and the propagandistic view of German aggression receded, many in the West came to share the German public's view of the war. "Revisionist" historians such as American Charles Beard argued in the 1920s and 1930s that Germany had been the victim of insecure hegemonic neighbors that essentially forced it to fight World War I, an argument that still circulates today. Others made the popular, though invalid, argument that the war was really no one's fault and had been the inevitable consequence of opposing alliance systems and imperial ambitions. A congressional committee chaired by Senator Gerald Nye (R–North Dakota), commissioned in 1934 to investigate U.S. entry into World War I, reported that the United States had been pushed into the conflict by ruthless bankers and arms merchants for their own profit. The British leadership developed the widespread view that their erstwhile German opponents were honorable men of a proud tradition who should not have to feel perpetual guilt. In the 1930s a wide body of elite opinion in Britain believed that the Treaty of Versailles could be replaced by a framework of revisionist agreements favorable to Hitler's Germany.

The territorial provisions of the Versailles settlement also proved ultimately unsustainable. German colonies were gone forever, but the situation in Europe remained highly unstable. The drastic changes of borders and limitations on self-determination rights remained contentious debates in which even many Allied leaders came to sympathize with the German side. As early as 1921 the changes to the Polish and Danish frontiers of Germany were minimized with Allied acquiescence. Over the next two decades neither Britain nor the United States were willing to commit themselves to defend the borders established by the Versailles settlement, and even many French leaders considered them to be transient. In 1925, when the centrist German foreign minister Gustav Stresemann successfully negotiated the Locarno Pact, a West European nonaggression pact that also guaranteed the security of the frontiers, the British government conceded that the eastern borders of Germany might be open to revision at a later date. When Hitler remilitarized the Rhineland in March 1936, many British and French leaders wondered aloud whether they should worry about the dictator invading "his own back yard." Two years later, the coerced union of Nazi Germany with Austria—illegal under the Treaty of Versailles—was unopposed. In September 1938 the British and French governments agreed to Hitler's annexation of German-populated border districts in Czechoslovakia as a peace-preserving measure, even though none of the territory in question had ever belonged to Germany. Nor did they take action when Hitler occupied much of the rest of Czechoslovakia in March 1939, or when he reincorporated the port of Memel from Lithuania into the Reich the same year. Only Hitler's invasion of Poland in September 1939 prompted declarations of war from the arbiters of the Treaty of Versailles.

The military provisions of Versailles, which were intended to eliminate Germany as a threat to European security, proved to have no teeth. Although the limits on the size and offensive capacity of the German army were initially respected, the Allies failed to establish any long-term mechanism to ensure the permanent compliance of the Germans. In addition to their failure to form a lasting postwar alliance, there were no international inspection teams (apart from a powerless disarmament commission) or unilateral national efforts to make sure that Germany was keeping its armed forces in line with the restrictions. Even the democratic and nonmilitaristic Weimar Republic systematically violated them. While it would have been hard to hide an army that exceeded the one-hundred-thousand-man limit, the new government employed a large number of combat veterans in so-called *Freikorps* (free corps), armed militias ostensibly needed to maintain public order. The traditional General Staff structure was only superficially abandoned; many of its personnel were retained in a so-called *Truppenamt* (troop office) that duplicated most of the functions of the banned General Staff. A secret agreement with the Soviet Union allowed the Germans to train combat pilots and tank crews on Soviet soil in exchange for training the Red Army by German officers. Major naval construction was difficult to hide, but the Weimar government illegally contracted out submarine construction to shipyards in the Netherlands and Finland. If the guarantors of Versailles knew the full implications of these developments in the 1920s, they never said anything.

After Hitler came to power, German violations of the military provisions of Versailles not only continued but also grew bolder and became more public. In March 1935 Hitler unilaterally renounced the military provisions of Versailles and reintroduced a peacetime draft. At almost the same time his government publicly acknowledged the development of an air force with more than three hundred planes. Again nothing was done. On the contrary, in June 1935 the British government accepted Hitler's offer to renegotiate the Versailles prohibition on the development of capital ships by Germany and signed an agreement that allowed Hitler to build a fleet up to 35 percent the size of the Royal Navy. The limitations of the Treaty of Versailles on German armed forces were meaningless in the long run.

The reparations issue, finally, proved to be the biggest farce of all. The enormous $33 billion bill presented to Germany in 1921 was simply unpayable. Honest remittance would have crippled even a healthy, prosperous economy. Germany had just emerged from the costliest war in history up to that time and had also lost a significant portion of its industrial base to territorial changes and foreign occupation. The dislocation caused by altered frontiers and the demobilization of almost its entire army damaged its economy further. Clearly the German government was in no position to pay, and it defaulted within fifteen months. When France and Belgium occupied the industrial Ruhr region in retaliation in January 1923, the German government resorted to hyperinflation to subsidize passive resistance among workers in the region so that the French

could not collect compensation directly. The frustrated French were unable to secure British and American support for their action and had to withdraw in September 1924. A subsequent renegotiation of reparations payments, conducted by the American financier Charles Dawes, indexed them to the economic prosperity of Germany. Another renegotiation in 1929, devised by the American financier Owen Young, reduced the principal amount to just $9 billion and extended German payments out until the improbable year of 1988. The entire concept was soon made irrelevant by the world economic crisis, however, and in 1931 President Herbert Hoover declared a moratorium on the repayment of the World War I debts by the Allies if they would agree to a moratorium on German reparations payments. When Hitler came to power in 1933, he unilaterally repudiated reparations payments forever. The Allied reparations commission calculated that it received less than 15 percent of the amount decreed in 1921. At the same time, however, the German people suffered related economic privation, the indignity of Franco-Belgian occupation in the Ruhr, and the continuing burden of war guilt. While they paid relatively little when all was said and done, they were even more embittered by the Treaty of Versailles.

The peace settlement that ended World War I was a disaster. It fundamentally ignored the continued standing of Germany as a viable world power and violated the honest trust that democratic-minded German politicians had placed in Wilson's professed desire for an honest peace. At the same time, it created far-ranging provisions that could not have been sustained without a long-term Allied commitment to police German foreign, military, and economic policies. No Allied power was willing to take up that commitment, and eventually the victors of World War I conceded on virtually every limitation and debility they had forced on Germany in 1919. While the terms of the Treaty of Versailles had little lasting effect, they nevertheless embittered a generation of Germans who became hostile to the West, supported dangerous political radicalism, and realized that their country still had the strength to refashion the international order.

–PAUL DU QUENOY,
GEORGETOWN UNIVERSITY

References

Manfred F. Boemke, Gerald D. Feldman, and Elisabeth Glaser, eds., *The Treaty of Versailles: A Reassessment After 75 Years* (Washington, D.C.: German Historical Institute; Cambridge & New York: Cambridge University Press, 1998).

Karl Dietrich Bracher, *The German Dictatorship: The Origins, Structure, and Effects of National Socialism*, translated by Jean Steinberg (New York: Praeger, 1970).

Edward Mandell House and Charles Seymour, eds., *What Really Happened at Paris: The Story of the Peace Conference, 1918–1919* (New York: Scribners, 1921).

Walter LaFeber, *The American Age: Foreign Policy at Home and Abroad*, volume 2, *Since 1896*, second edition (New York: Norton, 1994).

Melvyn P. Leffler, *The Elusive Quest: America's Pursuit of European Stability and French Security, 1919–1933* (Chapel Hill: University of North Carolina Press, 1979).

Etienne Mantoux, *The Carthaginian Peace, or, the Economic Consequences of Mr. Keynes* (London & New York: Oxford University Press, 1946).

Sally Marks, *The Illusion of Peace: Europe's International Relations, 1918–1933* (London: Macmillan, 1976; New York: St. Martin's Press, 1976).

Arno J. Mayer, *Politics and Diplomacy of Peacemaking: Containment and Counterrevolution at Versailles, 1918–1919* (New York: Knopf, 1967).

Charles L. Mee Jr., *The End of Order: Versailles, 1919* (New York: Dutton, 1980).

Julius William Pratt, *A History of United States Foreign Policy* (New York: Prentice-Hall, 1955).

Alan Sharp, *The Versailles Settlement: Peacemaking in Paris, 1919* (Basingstoke, U.K.: Macmillan Education, 1991; New York: St. Martin's Press, 1991).

Marc Trachtenberg, *Reparation in World Politics: France and European Economic Diplomacy, 1916–1923* (New York: Columbia University Press, 1980).

U.S. State Department, *Papers Relating to the Foreign Relations of the United States: The Paris Peace Conference, 1919*, thirteen volumes (Washington, D.C.: Government Printing Office, 1942–1947).

Richard M. Watt, *The Kings Depart: The Tragedy of Germany: Versailles and the German Revolution* (New York: Simon & Schuster, 1968).

UNRESTRICTED SUBMARINE WARFARE

Was the German policy of unrestricted submarine warfare a commitment to total war?

Viewpoint: Yes. By targeting all shipping and sinking vessels without warning, Germany practiced a form of total war on its enemies.

Viewpoint: No. Although the desire to remove Great Britain from the conflict was great, Germany was incapable of accomplishing such a task.

Prior to the outbreak of World War I, submarines were generally considered a major threat to large warships. The point was corroborated in September 1914, when a single German U-boat sank three old British cruisers in minutes and the entire Grand Fleet shifted its anchorage. The implications of undersea war against commerce were slower to develop, though British subs had some successes in the Baltic and in Turkish waters during the Dardanelles campaign. Germany, however, systematically initiated undersea operations against merchant shipping in 1915, partly in an effort to lure the Grand Fleet from its anchorage and partly as a way of striking against what seemed to the planners in Berlin the jugular vein of the British Empire.

The Germans began with a small number of short-range, slow, and poorly armed boats. From the beginning they pursued a policy of unrestricted warfare: sink at sight, sink without warning. Sometimes described as reflecting the physical difficulties of implementing conventional rules of search and seizure, the decision instead reflected a commitment to ending the war by escalating it. Lack of success in terms of tonnage sunk did as much as widespread denunciation of the practice by neutral powers to lead to the suspension of unrestricted submarine warfare in the spring of 1916. It led as well to the recall of all submarines operating outside of the English Channel and the Mediterranean, because of the conviction of the naval high command that submarines could not operate effectively under conventional rules of prize taking.

In the next months a series of memoranda argued that unrestricted submarine warfare, consequently pursued, could force Britain from the war in half a year by shutting off vital imports and otherwise disrupting an economy already strained to its limits. The arguments proved convincing; on 9 January 1917 unrestricted submarine warfare was again authorized. The risks of that policy bringing the United States into the conflict were considered acceptable. Before the United States could mobilize, submarine proponents hoped, the war would be over. Even if it still continued, the U-boats would prevent shipping any significant forces to Europe.

In April the United States declared war on Germany. In the first half of 1917 the U-boats accounted for almost 2,800,000 tons of British and Allied shipping. Despite the panic that figure caused in the Admiralty, however, the British war effort was never seriously endangered. The introduction of convoys and aircraft escorts, increased use of depth charges and mines against submarines, and improved shipbuilding programs on both sides of the Atlantic brought the undersea offensive to a virtual standstill by the turn of the year. Another of the high-risk gambits by the Second Reich proved a fiasco.

Viewpoint:
Yes. By targeting all shipping and sinking vessels without warning, Germany practiced a form of total war on its enemies.

If one accepts the basic definition of "total war" as making war not only on an enemy's armed forces but also on the opponent's economy, morale, and society, then it is easily argued that U-boats waged total war both directly and indirectly. German submarine policy vacillated throughout the war, eventually calling for U-boats to attack both British and neutral merchant vessels, and culminated in the unrestricted U-boat warfare method—attacking without warning—that brought the United States into the war in 1917.

The Imperial German Navy initially planned to use its submarine force in conjunction with the High Seas Fleet of dreadnought battleships. On occasion throughout the war, it would revert to the tactic of setting submarine "traps" for approaching British warships—usually unsuccessfully. These submarine ambushes were designed to whittle away the strength of the British Grand Fleet in order that the numerically inferior High Seas Fleet would stand a chance in a pitched naval engagement. One amazing and unequaled success for the U-boats occurred early in the war when on 22 September 1914 the *U-9* dispatched the heavy cruisers *Aboukir, Cressy,* and *Hogue* off the Dutch coast.

The High Seas Fleet, however, remained ineffective and hid outnumbered in its bases in northern Germany. Frustrated and overshadowed by the costly land war, the Navy sought a strategy by which it could counter the British blockade or at least make some contribution to the war effort. A war on British commerce using submarines was one possible way to engage German naval forces to help win the war. Even the commander of the High Seas Fleet, Admiral Friedrich von Ingenohl, stated:

> We can wound England most seriously by injuring her trade. . . . The whole British coast, or anyway a part of it, must be declared to be blockaded, and at the same time the aforesaid warning (to neutrals) must be published. . . . The gravity of the situation demands that we should free ourselves from all scruples which certainly no longer have justification.

The idea was quite simple: German submarines would not only sink British merchant vessels but also scare away any neutral shipping trading with England. Attacks would be made without warning to enhance the moral effect. The combination of these forces would serve to destroy the British economy and, hence, its war effort. Wary of the diplomatic effect on neutral nations, the German government opposed such proposals. Prewar studies had concluded that the German submarine force would require more than two hundred U-boats to be successful in such a campaign. The fact that Germany possessed only twenty-eight functioning U-boats by December 1914 challenged the logic of this proposed strategy.

Early in the Great War, submarine and "surface raider" captains normally accepted prize law, which dictated that a warship must first search a merchant vessel and subsequently provide for the safety of its passengers and crew, as the governing rules of conduct. Merchant vessels were stopped, boarded, and inspected; if found carrying contraband, the crew would be ushered into lifeboats and the ship sunk with timed explosive charges or shellfire from the deck gun. Since early U-boats carried only a handful of torpedoes, skippers usually saved these weapons for stealthy, submerged attacks on warships or armed merchantmen. Sinking the merchant vessel was a necessity, since the efficiently manned submarine (of thirty to forty crew members) could not afford to give up even the smallest prize crew and British patrols would probably intercept the vessel as it approached a German port.

By February 1915 the German admirals had finally persuaded the Kaiser and his cabinet to attempt a submarine counterblockade, and the Germans launched their first U-boat campaign against British trade. While publicly declaring the waters around Great Britain a "war zone" and warning neutral merchantmen of the dangers of sailing therein, German submarines attacked without warning and succeeded in sinking nearly 100,000 tons of merchant shipping per month. It was extremely difficult to discern the difference between a British merchant ship and that of a neutral vessel through the view of a periscope, so none would be spared. The sinking of the *Lusitania* in May and the *Arabic* in August brought unbearable pressure on German diplomats when the United States loudly protested the attacks. In September the Kaiser ordered all submarine captains not to attack passenger liners. The lack of seaworthy U-boats led to the waning of this first campaign—the Germans were able to maintain only three or four U-boats at sea at any one time during the last three months of 1915. Since the start of the war, U-boats had accounted for 800,000 tons of shipping, which was only "a mere fraction of the 12.4 million tons available to Britain and the Empire" in August 1914.

THEY KEPT THE
SEA LANES
OPEN

INVEST IN THE
VICTORY LIBERTY LOAN

Still, the U-boats continued to attack merchant vessels without warning. In March 1916 the *UB-29* torpedoed the channel packet *Sussex*. The death of twenty-five Americans brought sharper protests and an ultimatum from President Woodrow Wilson, promising the severance of diplomatic ties if the unrestricted attacks continued. On 24 April the German government ordered the navy to cease attacks without warning and revert to the prize-rule standard. U-boat attacks without prior warning accounted for 21 percent of all sinkings in 1915, while 29 percent of ships sunk in 1916 were performed without warning.

In January 1917 there was a major shift in the balance of the U-boat war. The German High Seas Fleet had won a tactical victory against the British at the Battle of Jutland on 31 May 1916, but it was still strategically trapped in its bases. The navy had to do something to help the war effort, especially since the German army had sustained immense casualties during the Somme Offensive (July–November 1916). By January there were one hundred German submarines available for service. The situation was ripe for a new submarine offensive.

The German Chief of the Admiralty Staff, Admiral Henning von Holtzendorff, argued

for an all-out unrestricted U-boat offensive against Britain in order to end the war by breaking the economic foundation of British power—her merchant fleet. If the campaign could be launched by 1 February 1917, he argued, the war could be over by 1 August—before the Allies could bring in their next harvest to ensure a sufficient supply of food. Chancellor Theobald von Bethmann Hollweg feared that such a campaign would certainly bring America into the war, but the naval leaders argued that the war would be over before the United States could mobilize and have any effect on the land war. Holtzendorff calculated that the U-boats could sink 3.6 million of the 11 million tons of British shipping in six months (or 600,000 tons per month). Scaring away a few more million tons of neutral shipping would add to the loss and certainly force Britain—relying on imports for foodstuffs—into a decision of accepting either surrender or famine.

The Kaiser was won over and Bethmann Hollweg acquiesced; the campaign began on 1 February 1917 and produced immediate results. Two days later, the United States severed diplomatic ties with Germany. In April U-boats had sunk 881,000 tons of Allied ship-

Poster dramatizing the threat of submarine warfare

(Joseph M. Bruccoli Great War Collection, Thomas Cooper Library, University of South Carolina)

UNRESTRICTED SUBMARINE WARFARE

ping (compared with 386,000 tons in January 1917) and the Americans declared war. It was not until the adoption of the convoy system and the entrance of the U.S. merchant fleet and shipbuilding industry that the U-boat offensive would be turned back. Grain reserves in Australia, Canada, South America, and the United States provided excess to the losses at sea. Finally, the Germans lacked the numbers of U-boats to do the job thoroughly; the hundred or so vessels available in February did not provide adequate numbers when one considers that many had to be in overhaul or in transit to and from the shipping lanes. Perhaps thirty boats were on patrol on any given day.

There is one final element of proof that the use of the submarine in the Great War was an example of total war. When the United States entered the conflict, it first had to build an army and then transport it to France. At the peak of its efforts during the summer of 1918, the United States was depositing ten thousand soldiers on French soil per day. When offered the choice of sinking troop transports, which may have affected the land war to the advantage of Germany, or of continuing to attack British commerce, the German Navy chose trade. Thus, not a single inbound troopship, with a few thousand American soldiers onboard, was lost to a submarine.

–JOHN ABBATIELLO,
U.S. AIR FORCE ACADEMY

Viewpoint:
No. Although the desire to remove Great Britain from the conflict was great, Germany was incapable of accomplishing such a task.

On 1 February 1917 Germany unleashed its second unrestricted submarine campaign during World War I in a desperate bid to win a decisive victory before total exhaustion set in. This campaign, which the Germans called their "last card," involved the sinking, without warning, of all Allied and neutral shipping that entered the waters around Great Britain. The Germans hoped to be able to sink enough British ships and to frighten enough neutral ships off the seas to starve Britain out of the war. This decision proved to be one of the decisive events of the entire conflict. The plan ultimately failed in its objective, to knock Great Britain out of the war,

and brought a fresh opponent, the United States, into the field against the Central Powers.

The submarine campaign, like the extended battles in the trenches, was something new in warfare. Prior to the war most naval strategists were convinced that the next naval war would be decided in one large battle between opposing fleets of battleships. The submarine was seen as a purely auxiliary weapon that might, at best, be able to whittle away at one or both of the battle fleets. Virtually no one envisioned its use in a *guerre de course* because it could not operate by the accepted rules of naval warfare, which meant that merchant vessels were to be stopped and searched and only sunk if they were found to be carrying contraband. Given the vulnerability of early submarines to gunfire, that operational plan was simply not feasible. Hence the Germans, once they decided to use the submarines against enemy shipping, were forced to attack and sink merchant vessels without warning. This policy meant by its very nature that German submarines would be attacking civilians, which has led to a debate over whether the unrestricted submarine campaign could be considered an instance of "total war."

Before one can really begin to examine the campaign itself, the issue of total war must be addressed. Just what exactly is it? There are several definitions for the term. One can isolate three key factors that separate total war from "traditional" war. First of all, total war involves the mobilization of an entire society and its economy for the war effort. In more traditional warfare the armies and navies of the belligerents carried on the war while the remainder of society tried to exist much as it had in peacetime. In the age of total war this arrangement becomes impossible. Since the state sees itself engaged in a life or death struggle, it must mobilize all its productive resources for the conflict. This strategy leads directly to the second characteristic of total war: its aims. In total war there are only two possible outcomes, total victory or total defeat. A compromise peace is ruled out. This inflexibility stems almost naturally from the total mobilization of a society for war. In order to mobilize society the struggle must be portrayed as black and white, survival versus destruction. This dichotomy by its nature closes off paths for the statesmen seeking an end to the conflict. Total war, therefore, feeds upon itself. In order for the state to achieve its goals it must mobilize its civilian population, which therefore expands the war aims of the state. The third characteristic of total war also stems directly from the first. It stands to reason that if an entire society is being mobilized for the war effort, then that entire society becomes a legitimate target for the enemy's war effort. Therefore, in a total war, the old distinc-

THE UNITED STATES TAKES A STAND

On 19 April 1916 President Woodrow Wilson addressed the U.S. Congress on the issue of German submarine warfare:

In pursuance of the policy of submarine warfare against the commerce of its adversaries, announced and entered upon by the Imperial German Government, despite the solemn protest of this Government, the commanders of German undersea vessels have attacked merchant ships with greater and greater activity, not only upon the high seas surrounding Great Britain and Ireland, but wherever they could encounter them, in a way that has grown more and more ruthless, more and more indiscriminate, as the months have gone by, less and less observant of restraints of any kind; and they have delivered their attacks without compunction against vessels of every nationality and bound upon every sort of errand. Vessels of neutral ownership, even vessels of neutral ownership bound from neutral port to neutral port, have been destroyed along with vessels of belligerent ownership, in constantly increasing numbers. Sometimes the merchantman attacked has been warned and summoned to surrender before being fired upon or torpedoed; sometimes passengers or crews have been vouchsafed the poor security of being allowed to take to the ship's boats before she was sent to the bottom. But again and again no warning has been given, no escape even to the ship's boats allowed to those on board. What this Government foresaw must happen has happened. Tragedy had followed tragedy on the seas in such fashion, with such attendant circumstances, as to make it grossly evident that warfare of such a sort, if warfare it be, cannot be carried on without the most palpable violation of the dictates alike of right and of humanity. Whatever the disposition and intention of the Imperial German Government, it has manifestly proved impossible for it to keep such methods of attack upon the commerce of its enemies within the bounds set by either the reason or the heart of mankind. . . .

I have deemed it my duty, therefore, to say to the Imperial German Government that if it is still its purpose to prosecute relentless and indiscriminate warfare against vessels of commerce by the use of submarines, notwithstanding the now demonstrated impossibility of conducting that warfare in accordance with what the Government of the United States must consider the sacred and indisputable rules of international law and the universally recognized dictates of humanity, the Government of the United States is at last forced to the conclusion that there is but one course it can pursue and that unless the Imperial German Government should now immediately declare and effect an abandonment of its present methods of warfare against passenger and freight-carrying vessels, this Government can have no choice but to sever diplomatic relations with the German Empire altogether.

The decision I have arrived at with the keenest regret; the possibility of action contemplated I am sure all thoughtful Americans will look forward to with unaffected reluctance. But we cannot forget that we are in some sort and by the force of circumstances the responsible spokesmen of the rights of humanity, and that we cannot remain silent while those rights seem in process of being swept utterly away in the maelstrom of this terrible war. We owe it to a due regard for our own rights as a nation, to our sense of duty as a representative of the rights of neutrals the world over, and to a just conception of the rights of mankind to take this stand now with the utmost solemnity and firmness.

I have taken it, and taken it in confidence that it will meet with your approval and support. All sober-minded men must unite in hoping that the Imperial German Government, which has in other circumstances stood as the champion of all that we are now contending for in the interest of humanity, may recognize the justice of our demands and meet them in the spirit in which they are made.

Source: *Charles F. Horne, ed.,* Source Records of the Great War, *volume 4 (Indianapolis: American Legion, 1930), pp. 89–90.*

tion between combatant and civilian is largely done away with and civilians become just another asset of the state. Furthermore, if the will of the civilian population to continue the conflict can be broken, the war can be won even if the opposing armed forces are not completely defeated. Given this working definition, was the unrestricted submarine campaign an example of total war? To truly answer this question one needs to look at three factors: the goals of the campaign, the materials at hand, and the actual accomplishments of the campaign.

When discussing the goals of German unrestricted submarine war one needs to make a distinction between the first and second campaigns. The original unrestricted campaign was started in February 1915. When this campaign began the Germans only had thirty submarines available, only one-third of which could be on station at any one time. This shortfall meant they had in effect only ten to twelve submarines usually on patrol. This number was hardly sufficient to force Britain to sue for peace. In fact, the goal of the first unrestricted campaign was not to force Britain to surrender but rather to compel them to lift the blockade of Germany. The first campaign was largely a spur-of-the-moment reaction to what the Germans perceived to be British violations of neutral trading rights. Since the British declined to risk their High Seas Fleet in direct confrontation with the full Grand Fleet, the Germans were forced to turn to the submarines as retaliation for the British blockade.

The first unrestricted campaign did not succeed. The Germans simply did not possess enough submarines. In fact, according to Paul G. Halpern, in *A Naval History of World War I* (1994), instead of having ten to twelve submarines on station, the average number on patrol was actually only six. The damage done by these few boats was so negligible that the British never seriously considered trading an end to their blockade for an end to the submarine campaign. Not only did the campaign fail, but it had resoundingly negative diplomatic consequences as a result of the sinking of passenger liners. The most famous incident, of course, was the sinking of the *Lusitania* on 7 May 1915. That event seriously soured relations between Germany and the United States because 178 Americans lost their lives. Other neutrals were angered as well and the Germans, by June 1915, were forced to limit the operations of their submarines. From this point on through 1916 the Germans waged what was called "restricted submarine warfare," during which they attempted to spare neutral vessels while continuing their attacks against British shipping. The submarine war was continued not in the hopes of defeating Britain but largely for the lack of any better strategy. The campaign was discontinued briefly when the new commander of the High Seas Fleet, Admiral Reinhard Scheer, in May 1916, recalled all German submarines in the North Atlantic from their war on commerce in order to have them lay a submarine trap for the Grand Fleet, when he began the operations that would lead to the Battle of Jutland (31 May). The submarines, though, proved to be ineffective in this role and after the battle returned to their restricted campaign.

Up to this point the submarine campaign had fallen far short of the criteria for total war.

In terms of its goals, at least, that situation soon changed. During 1916 Admiral Henning von Holtzendorff, head of the German Naval Staff, and a select committee of advisers worked on a study that would, ostensibly, prove that a renewed submarine campaign would force Great Britain to surrender within six months. Following the disastrous "turnip winter" of 1916–1917, when the bulk of the German potato crop failed, Holtzendorff presented this plan to the chancellor, Theobald von Bethmann Hollweg, and the new head of the General Staff, Paul von Hindenburg. This famous memorandum listed the amount of shipping available to Great Britain, about ten million tons, and argued that the existing German submarine force could destroy roughly six hundred thousand tons of shipping per month if all restrictions were lifted. Holtzendorff contended that after six months the loss of roughly one third of all its merchant shipping would cause such shortages that the British population would demand an end to the war. The mathematical certainty with which Holtzendorff made his case proved to be more persuasive than the objections put forward by Bethmann Hollweg, that a renewed submarine campaign would mean war with the United States. Holtzendorff's response to Bethmann Hollweg's warnings was that war with the United States would not matter since Britain would be forced to sue for peace before the Americans could become a factor. Clearly, the goal of the second unrestricted campaign was to force Britain out of the war by destroying the will to fight of the British civilians. In this sense, at least, the second unrestricted campaign qualifies as total war, but questions remained. Could the Germans achieve their aims? Did they have the requisite materials?

When the new campaign began in early 1917 the Germans had only 105 operational submarines. Of these, 23 were concentrated in the Mediterranean, 10 in the Baltic, and 3 in the Black Sea. That left 69 available for use in the decisive waters around Great Britain. However, 23 of those 69 were smaller boats known as UB- and UC-class submarines. These small craft were really only useful in coastal waters and were lightly armed. In fact, the UC class were essentially minelaying submarines that could not really be used on merchant patrols at all. Therefore, only 46 submarines were available to carry on the commercial war, barely more than had been available in 1915.

Furthermore, the U-boats of World War I were not true submarines but rather submersibles. They were extremely slow while submerged, averaging five to six knots, with some being able to make as many as ten knots, which meant that they were too slow to keep up with most merchant ships unless they were on the surface. That situation, however, posed another problem, since they were unarmored and extremely vulnerable to gunfire, while only being lightly armed themselves, usually with a 3.4-inch gun. Their ability to attack while submerged was also limited by the small number of torpedoes they carried. Even the larger class of German submarines generally carried only four torpedoes. This lack of firepower meant that most ships sunk by submarines were holed by the deck gun. Taken together, the German submarine force was effective against merchant shipping while being extremely vulnerable to enemy naval vessels. For the first five months of the new campaign this shortcoming did not matter, but after May 1917, when the British began to implement the convoy system, it became decisive.

The implementation of the convoy system forced the Germans to attack while submerged, which had several effects. First of all, it limited the number of ships they could sink to the complement of torpedoes the submarines carried. Furthermore, once a submarine attacked a ship in convoy, it would be attacked in turn by the escorts. Even if the submarine was not destroyed, the escorts would force it to break off contact with the convoy, which could then escape. The convoy system drastically limited the effectiveness of the submarine campaign.

Clearly, the material resources possessed by the Germans were limited. The German submarine force could only hope to win a decisive victory against Great Britain if the British persisted, as they did until May 1917, in their refusal to implement a convoy system. Once British merchant shipping was protected by warships the German submarine force was reduced to nothing more than a nuisance. Despite their lofty objective the Germans were not equipped to wage a total submarine war in 1917. That circumstance, however, is not to say they did not have success. In fact, they reached the numbers von Holtzendorff projected for them.

The beginning of the unrestricted campaign provided the greatest successes to date for the Germans. According to Halpern, in February the submarines destroyed 520,412 tons of shipping; in March, 564,497 tons; and in April, a record (not even reached by Karl Dönitz's infamous wolfpacks during World War II) of 860,334 tons. In May the shipping destroyed dropped to 616,316 tons, still above Holtzendorff's projected numbers, and they rose in June to 696,725 tons. In July, once convoys had been fully implemented, the numbers fell to 555,514 tons and then continued to decline. The submarines, though, reached the goals set for them. They destroyed a total of 3,813,798 tons over the course of those six months, averaging 635,633 tons each month. This success exceeded Holtzen-

dorff's predictions, yet the British did not sue for peace in July.

The basic problem came from Holtzendorff's analysis. He assumed that the submarine campaign would destroy the British will to resist, but his analysis was based on faulty assumptions of their "national character." Ironically, even though he was thinking in terms of total war, Holtzendorff and the rest of the German leadership could not conceive of the British responding in the same way. The Germans assumed that the British would never implement rationing, or if they did, that there would be a revolt. In the final analysis, they did not believe that the British people would be capable of withstanding the type of privations that German citizens had endured for more than two years. It is true that panic did begin to seep in to the Admiralty in April 1917 with the First Sea Lord, John Jellicoe, in particular, becoming convinced that there was no answer to the submarine menace and that the war was lost, but there is no evidence of panic in Britain as a whole. Some rationing was introduced, but the major crisis hoped for by the Germans never emerged. Furthermore, after August 1917 the submarines were largely contained by the convoys. The amount of shipping lost dropped below four hundred thousand tons in September and remained at or below that level for the remainder of the war. In sum, despite reaching their tonnage goal, the German submariners never came close to knocking Britain out of the war.

So, was the German unrestricted submarine campaign an example of total war? It was first conceived as a response to the British blockade of Germany, not as an attempt to really starve out Great Britain. Certainly, the goal of the second campaign, to knock Britain completely out of the war, fits under the rubric of total war but, given the materials at hand, it was unattainable. Holtzendorff's memorandum neglected the reality of the situation for Germany. In an effort to provide the navy with a major role in the war effort, Holtzendorff and his advisers crafted a memorandum that seemed to demonstrate with mathematical certainty that winning the war was a simple matter of destroying shipping. It was based on faulty assumptions that had little or no grounding in reality. In fact, it is difficult to escape the conclusion that Holtzendorff's reasoning was based not on reality but simply on wishful thinking. Since a compromise peace was unthinkable there had to be a way for Germany to win the war before another winter exhausted all the combatants. The army was clearly incapable of accomplishing that task; if Germany was to attain its extensive war aims, the navy had to win the war and the only weapon they had were the submarines. Therefore, it had to be possible for the submarines to defeat Britain and Holtzendorff's mission was to figure out how that could be done. The fact that the relatively small number of boats and their limited technical capacities made a truly total submarine war impossible was pushed to the background, as were any thoughts that British civilians might be able to withstand serious privations in food and other materials as long as the German population had. Even had the Germans been able to maintain their level of sinking ships at or near six hundred thousand tons per month for the remainder of the war, it is unlikely that the outcome would have been much different. Quite simply put, in 1917 the German submarine arm was incapable of destroying the will of Great Britain to fight. Their aims may have been total, but their capacities were not. German submariners were trying to carry out a real-life "Mission Impossible."

–MARK KARAU,
SANTA FE COMMUNITY COLLEGE

References

Roger Chickering and Stig Förster, eds., *Great War, Total War: Combat and Mobilization on the Western Front, 1914–1918* (Washington, D.C.: German Historical Institute, 2000; Cambridge & New York: Cambridge University Press, 2000).

Fritz Fischer, *Griff nach der Weltmacht,* translated as *Germany's Aims in the First World War* (New York: Norton, 1967).

Paul G. Halpern, *A Naval History of World War* I (Annapolis, Md.: Naval Institute Press, 1994).

Holger H. Herwig, *The First World War: Germany and Austria-Hungary, 1914–1918* (London & New York: Arnold, 1997).

Herwig, "A Total Rhetoric, Limited War: Germany's U-boat campaign, 1917–1918," in *Great War, Total War: Combat and Mobilization on the Western Front, 1914–1918,* edited by Chickering and Förster (Washington, D.C.: German Historical Institute, 2000; Cambridge & New York: Cambridge University Press, 2000), pp. 192–199.

Gerhard Ritter, *The Sword and the Sceptre: The Problem of Militarism in Germany,* 3 volumes, translated by Heinz Norden (Coral Gables, Fla.: University of Miami Press, 1969–1973).

Eberhard Rössler, *The U-Boat: The Evolution and Technical History of German Submarines,* translated by Harold Erenberg (Annapolis, Md.: Naval Institute Press, 1981).

William Sowden Sims, *The Victory at Sea* (Garden City, N.Y.: Doubleday, Page, 1920).

John Terraine, *Business in Great Waters: The U-boat Wars, 1916–194*5 (London: Cooper, 1989).

UNRESTRICTED
SUBMARINE WARFARE

THE WAR AND AMERICA

Did the Great War have a positive impact on the United States?

Viewpoint: Yes. The war provided focus for the United States and introduced the nation to the nature of its responsibilities as a great power.

Viewpoint: No. World War I highlighted and exacerbated internal ethnic, social, and economic tensions, while militarizing the country to a far greater degree than even the Civil War.

The entry of the United States into the Great War represented the apotheosis of a Progressive movement that had shaped the political and social structures of the country for a quarter century on both sides of the Democrat-Republican line. Woodrow Wilson might have campaigned successfully for reelection to the presidency in 1916 behind the slogan: "He kept us out of war," but his decision to initiate hostilities with the Central Powers in April 1917 was widely supported by those Americans, both intellectuals and ordinary folks, who believed that U.S. participation was the key to a brave new world.

Abroad, Wilson sought a peace that would protect democracy and free trade through encouraging the self-determination of free peoples. He advocated a League of Nations as a clearinghouse for grievances and a focal point for collective security against challenges to the liberal/capitalist status quo he postulated as the norm. Domestically the war fostered the mobilization of power behind public authority. Government propaganda supported the introduction of conscription while federal agencies regulated private profit and monitored loyalty. At the same time, pressure groups and interest groups of all kinds, suffragettes and civil-rights advocates, trade unionists and businessmen, sought to turn that now-focused power to their advantage.

Had American participation in the war lasted longer, perhaps a more decisive sorting of winners and losers might have been possible. As it was, the unexpectedly rapid collapse of Germany and its allies in the fall of 1918 created a cluster of loose ends. Voters turned unexpectedly against both the wartime regulatory state and Wilson's minatory moralizing, returning a Republican majority to Congress in the 1918 elections. The League of Nations and the Versailles Treaty (1919) both failed to pass a Congress alienated by Wilson's arrogance. Labor unrest flourished, fueled in many states by the hostility of returned veterans to what they regarded as left-wing agitators. Socialists and immigrants were targets of a "red scare" reflecting fear of the emergence of Bolshevism in Russia. If one constitutional amendment, the Nineteenth (1920), enacted women's suffrage, another, the Eighteenth (1919), legalized national prohibition.

Yet, the Great War was not entirely without long-term consequences. The balance of financial power shifted from Britain to the United States, from London to New York. Wilson's internationalism faded, but it never disappeared from an America no longer able to feel entirely safe behind its oceans. Democracy became a concept to be extended downward as well as outward, incorporating previously excluded groups at least into the fringes of the U.S. polity. For the United States, as well as for Europe, World War I was a watershed.

Viewpoint:
Yes. The war provided focus for the United States and introduced the nation to the nature of its responsibilities as a great power.

By 1918 World War I provided a rallying cause for the diverse peoples of the United States. The sectional divisions of the Civil War (1861–1865) and the new problems of large-scale immigration and urbanization melted away as the nation unified for its second foreign war (the first being the Spanish-American War, 1898). Support for the Allied war effort soared as American businesses flourished, skilled and unskilled workers saw a real rise in income and standards of living, and women and minorities found better-paying and more-fulfilling work. By the end of the war, America had emerged not only as a victor, but as the one nation still able to drive a new world peace. The prewar mismatch of the great economic but weak military might of the United States dissolved as America achieved military parity and even supremacy over the older nations of Europe. The Great War provided the catalyst for rapid change in the United States, both domestically and internationally, from a fragmented, isolated nation into the leader of postwar peace.

For most Americans, events in Europe in 1914 elicited only vague curiosity. However, as the war expanded, American economic and psychological involvement on the side of the Allies became increasingly difficult to hide. Exacerbating tensions on the eastern seaboard was the German declaration of unrestricted, unannounced U-boat operations on 1 February 1917. Shortly afterward, antiwar sentiment in the Southwest shifted at the news of the Zimmermann telegram, in which the Germans invited the Mexicans to regain their lost territories in the United States. Broadened anti-German feeling made President Woodrow Wilson's decision for war acceptable, and even welcomed, by many Americans. Those who were not already convinced of the sagacity of Wilson's decision were swayed by his eloquent declaration of war on 2 April 1917, in which he insisted, "The world must be made safe for democracy. Its peace must be planted upon the tested foundations of political liberty." The Senate approved the war resolution 82 to 6 on 4 April and the House approved it 373 to 50 on 6 April. Opposition to the war became an unpopular minority position.

To consolidate and direct public opinion, Wilson appointed George Creel to head the Committee on Public Information (CPI). With perhaps misplaced ideology, Creel nevertheless encouraged Americans to drop their Old World

identities and become "unhyphenated Americans" united in German-bashing. The specter of propaganda-enhanced, barbaric Huns in popular culture turned many Americans away from the British as a common target to the Germans, creating a homogenized, patriotic citizenry.

Wartime mobilization helped to break down long-standing economic barriers among Americans and directed economic power at a national goal. The enormously unpopular Civil War–era draft was scrapped in favor of the new Selective Service Act (18 May 1917), which still required young men to sign up for the draft, but removed the provision that a willing substitute or money would be accepted in lieu of military service. Women also enlisted in the armed services for the first time in important auxiliary roles. Americans were so willing to support the war effort, as a whole, that they purchased $23 billion in Liberty Bonds in addition to paying $10 billion in new taxes. Other monies were borrowed from the newly established Federal Reserve banks, which were ordered to expand the money supply.

The most telling evidence of the positive influence of the Great War on America was the phenomenal growth in the business and labor sectors. Bernard Baruch's War Industries Board (WIB) did more than any other organization to foster a cooperative attitude between the government and industry. Baruch persuaded U.S. Steel to lower prices and Henry Ford to limit production of consumer automobiles, leading the state and big business into unprecedented partnerships. The WIB ensured the smooth operation of business so much that some cried out against the infiltration of the government by executives. The subsidization, regulation, and organization of many wartime industries continued after the war, leading some historians to point to World War I as the beginning of the modern bureaucratic American state. Businesses saw expansion and high profits during the wartime years, leading to a rise in manufacturing capital expenditure from $600 million in 1915 to $2.5 billion in 1918. *Average* corporate profits nearly tripled between 1914 and 1919. Farm production increased from 30 to 40 percent as a result of expanded acreage and availability of farm machinery.

Several factors, including economic expansion, army mobilization, and a reduction in European immigration increased real wages and the standard of living for working people (many of them immigrants). The labor movement, which had stalled before the war, saw rapid increases in union membership (labor unions increased by 1.5 million members between 1917 and 1919) and major improvements in labor conditions. The formation of the National War

RESTRICTIONS ON ALIENS

On 6 April 1917 President Woodrow Wilson issued the following twelve regulations regarding individuals declared "alien enemies":

[1] An alien enemy shall not have in his possession, at any time or place, any firearm, weapon or implement of war, or component part thereof, ammunition, maxim or other silencer, bomb or explosive or material used in the manufacture of explosives;

[2] An alien enemy shall not have in his possession at any time or place, or use or operate any aircraft or wireless apparatus, or any form of signalling device, or any form of cipher code, or any paper, document or book written or printed in cipher or in which there may be invisible writing;

[3] All property found in the possession of an alien enemy in violation of the foregoing regulations shall be subject to seizure by the United States;

[4] An alien enemy shall not approach or be found within one-half of a mile of any Federal or State fort, camp, arsenal, aircraft station, Government or naval vessel, navy yard, factory, or workshop for the manufacture of munitions of war or of any products for the use of the Army or Navy;

[5] An alien enemy shall not write, print, or publish any attack or threats against the Government or Congress of the United States, or either branch thereof, or against the measures or policy of the United States, or against the person or property of any person in the military, naval, or civil service of the United States, or of the States or Territories, or of the District of Columbia, or of the municipal governments therein;

[6] An alien enemy shall not commit or abet any hostile act against the United States, or give information, aid, or comfort to its enemies;

[7] An alien enemy shall not reside in or continue to reside in, to remain in, or enter any locality which the President may from time to time designate by Executive Order as a prohibited area in which residence by an alien enemy shall be found by him to constitute a danger to the public peace and safety of the United States, except by permit from the President and except under such limitations or restrictions as the President may prescribe;

[8] An alien enemy whom the President shall have reasonable cause to believe to be aiding or about to aid the enemy, or to be at large to the danger of the public peace or safety of the United States, or to have violated or to be about to violate any of these regulations, shall remove to any location designated by the President by Executive Order, and shall not remove therefrom without a permit, or shall depart from the United States if so required by the President;

[9] No alien enemy shall depart from the United States until he shall have received such permit as the President shall prescribe, or except under order of a court, judge, or justice, under Sections 4069 and 4070 of the Revised Statutes;

[10] No alien enemy shall land in or enter the United States, except under such restrictions and at such places as the President may prescribe;

[11] If necessary to prevent violations of these regulations, all alien enemies will be obliged to register;

[12] An alien enemy whom there may be reasonable cause to believe to be aiding or about to aid the enemy, or who may be at large to the danger of the public peace or safety, or who violates or attempts to violate, or of whom there is reasonable ground to believe that he is about to violate, any regulation duly promulgated by the President, or any criminal law of the United States, or of the States or Territories thereof, will be subject to summary arrest by the United States Marshal, or his deputy, or such other officer as the President shall designate, and to confinement in such penitentiary, prison, jail, military camp, or other place of detention as may be directed by the President.

Source: *"Alien Enemy Presidential Proclamations," Internet website, http://www.staff.uiuc.edu/~rcunning/presproc.htm.*

Labor Board (NWLB), far from crushing working people, actually supported the right of workers to organize unions, furthered the acceptance of the eight-hour day, backed time-and-a-half pay for overtime, and supported equal pay for women. The Industrial Workers of the World (IWW, but better known as the Wobblies), the more-radical and disruptive element of the labor movement, saw the destruction of their support base as the labor movement achieved many of its prewar aims without violence or the overthrow of capitalism.

Women made many labor gains during World War I. About one million women entered the workforce and many more moved out of low-paying drudgery, such as domestic service, to higher-paying industrial work. One manufacturer said, "One of the lessons from the war has been to show that women can do exacting work." A new government organization, Women in Industry Service (WIS), was ordered to be formed to respond to women laborers' needs. The WIS instructed employers to give women rest periods, a minimum wage, meal breaks, restroom facilities, and to prohibit night work. These instructions were widely ignored and not enforced, but the agency soon grew to a permanent postwar division of the Labor Department called the Women's Bureau, which continued the work of education and investigation of women laborers' grievances.

Women as laborers did not immediately advance to the status of men, but women as citizens did. After more than a century of battle for the vote, women finally succeeded in pushing through an amendment to the Constitution assuring their enfranchisement. The struggle was finally won as a result, in part, of women's contributions to the American wartime effort. Carrie Chapman Catt's moderate policy of Congressional persuasion combined with Alice Paul's more-radical methods encouraged Wilson to push for amendment adoption as "vital to the winning of the war."

Minorities also reaped the benefits of wartime service and a wartime economy at home. Although African American troops were still segregated from white troops during the Great War, these all-black units entered combat and often served gallantly. The 369th Infantry experienced the longest service of any American regiment deployed in a foreign army, serving in the trenches for 191 days. The entire unit received the *Croix de Guerre* from the French government and 171 officers and enlisted men received individual commendation for bravery. The Great Migration occurred shortly after the end of World War I as blacks found higher-paying jobs and better living conditions in the North. Other underutilized people in the South and West,

including large groups of Mexicans, found jobs in agriculture during the wartime mobilization.

America also benefited internationally. By 1917 U.S. gold stock had nearly doubled as the European Allies purchased American exports, increasing not only monetary wealth in the United States but also trade in previously closed markets. Americans became so dominant in the postwar global economy, according to David M. Kennedy in *Over Here: The First World War and American Society* (1980), that one British official, lamenting the loss of Latin American markets, stated, "What can actually be done when we are so immensely beholden to the Americans for their cooperation in the war?"

Militarily, America survived the war with the only modern, industrialized army and navy left intact. Military reforms made by Secretary of War Elihu Root during his term in office (1899–1904) had finally paid off. The country could finally summon, train, equip, and deploy overseas a significant military force—a task that had eluded Americans since the founding of the nation. The European powers often mocked the inexperience of American farm boys in the trenches, but the sheer numbers of troops committed by the United States more than compensated for lack of combat sophistication. For the first time, foreign powers looked upon America as both an economic and military powerhouse, capable of immense power projection.

Wilson, the architect of the Treaty of Versailles, assured the diplomatic presence of America in all future European settlements. His Fourteen Points, though rejected in many ways by the Allies, became the backbone for his new world order. The Washington Conference (1922) to limit naval building, the Dawes Plan (1924) to schedule German reparations, the Kellogg-Briand Pact (1930) to renounce war, and the League of Nations were all American constructs. Although the United States did not join the League, the idea of global cooperation (later embodied in the United Nations) stemmed from American ideology and political roots. By intervening in World War I, America ensured lasting involvement in the international landscape, usually in a leadership role.

The Great War greatly increased the standing of the United States as a world power. The nation, though divided because of its varied ethnic populations, found the war to be a great unifier economically, culturally, and morally. Recent immigrants enthusiastically bought war bonds, planted Liberty Gardens, and volunteered for military service just as other Americans did. Business boomed and continued to grow throughout the 1920s. Labor rights were negotiated so generously that radical labor groups lost their platforms. Women and minorities found respect and higher wages performing work for absent servicemen. The economic standing of America was so great that the country underwent the so-called Second Industrial Revolution in the 1920s, leading to a 75 percent increase in the output of the average worker from 1919 to 1929. As Wilson assumed leadership at the ultimately doomed Versailles Conference (1919), America had unquestionably risen in economic, military, and diplomatic power as compared to the great European nations. The Great War fueled the transformation of the United States from a parochial, peripheral nation to a major world power.

–KRISTI L. NICHOLS, U.S. AIR FORCE ACADEMY

Viewpoint:
No. World War I highlighted and exacerbated internal ethnic, social, and economic tensions, while militarizing the country to a far greater degree than even the Civil War.

One of the most important changes between the Civil War (1861–1865) and the entry of the United States into World War I (1917) was the shifting demographic makeup of American society. In this period large numbers of eastern and southern Europeans came to the United States in response to the tremendous need for labor during its great industrial expansion. Immigration peaked between 1906 and 1915, after which World War I effectively shut off the flow of people from Europe. In those years, almost 9,500,000 immigrants came to the United States, most of whom crowded into cities in the East and Midwest. Media depictions of urban ghettos generated negative images and stereotypes of these new Americans.

As a reflection of American nativism, military suspicion of these new arrivals ran deep. Many new immigrants did not speak English, and Protestants were a minority among them. Many Americans, especially those at the top of the civilian and military power structures, believed in the hierarchy of races preached by Social Darwinists. They feared that the infusion of blood from these new races might dilute the American national character. Military officials also suspected that the new migrants were infected with dangerous old-world ideologies such as socialism, communism, and anarchism. As early as 1894 the U.S.

Army had banned foreign-born Americans from first-term enlistments.

The war did little to ease official suspicions of the new arrivals. Many of them were either from Germany or from parts of the Austro-Hungarian Empire. Incorporation of these men presented legitimate security issues, but Americans largely failed to understand that most newcomers posed no risk at all. Furthermore, many of these immigrants left precisely because of their opposition to the regimes in Germany and Austria-Hungary (as well as the tsarist system in Russia). American Slovaks, Poles, and Czechs, for example, had little love for the Austro-Hungarian Empire. Many hoped that the war would produce independence for their native nations. Other immigrants felt strong connections to Allied nations such as Greece, Serbia, and Romania. Many new arrivals would have gladly returned to fight in the old world if the army had allowed them to do so. At Camp Gordon, Georgia, 92 percent of men from Slavic, Italian, and Russian-Jewish backgrounds volunteered to go overseas immediately.

To most native-born Americans, ethnic loyalties seemed incompatible with the "100% Americanism" demanded by the government. The pressures to Americanize, what Bruce White, in an article in *Anticipating Total War: The German and American Experiences, 1871–1914*, edited by Manfred F. Boemeke, Roger Chickering, and Stig Förster (1999), called "the ultimately ominous side of *e pluribus unum*," could take extreme forms. Many regions of the United States banned the teaching of German and several Slavic languages. In Iowa the governor forbade the speaking of German in public places or over the telephone. The city of Pittsburgh added an *h* to the end of its name in order to appear less German, even though the city was the only one in the nation named for a British prime minister. Federal legislation targeted new arrivals as well. The Trading with the Enemy Act (1917) required all foreign-language publications to submit English translations in order to maintain mailing rights. The Espionage Act (1917) further enabled the government to censor all such publications. As a result, an editorially independent foreign-language press virtually ceased to operate for the duration of the war. The Espionage Act also enabled the post office to open and censor mail going to and coming from foreign countries.

In addition, the newly created government propaganda ministry, the Committee for Public Information, stressed the need for immigrants to abandon their old-world cus-

THE WAR AND AMERICA

THE WAR AND AMERICA

toms in favor of nominally "American" ones. English language and Americanization classes proliferated across the country, as did highly publicized Americanization trips to heritage sites such as Mount Vernon, where representatives of thirty-three ethnic groups paraded past the grave of the first U.S. president. Suspicion of immigrants also led to two landmark congressional decisions. The first, in 1917, mandated a literacy test for new arrivals. The

second, passed in 1921, but largely conceived during the war, placed a numerical ceiling on immigration for the first time.

Despite the dominant image of the immigrant as potential enemy, the numerical realities of preparing the American Expeditionary Force (AEF) meant that immigrants would necessarily become a part of the U.S. Army. By some estimates, as many as one recruit in five was foreign-born. The members of the

AEF spoke fifty languages. At first, the army planned to use immigrants as they were then using African Americans, in separate units devoted mainly to manual labor. American politicians then began to argue for using the army as a tool to teach Americanism. Immigrants soon found themselves not in the Meuse-Argonne, but in special "development battalions" learning English, American history, and the dangers of unionization. Henry Breckenridge, a former assistant secretary of war, praised Universal Military Training as "the only way to yank the hyphen out of America."

Changes in American government gave federal authorities new powers to regulate all spheres of society, including the military. The Progressives were a large and diverse group with various interests. They nevertheless shared a general consensus that local governments were less efficient and more prone to machine-style corruption than state and federal governments. As a result, they centralized many features of American society and fundamentally changed the traditional local basis of most American lives.

These changes influenced the military as well. Centralization began in 1877 with the passage of the National Guard Act, which mandated federal standards for Guard units and made those units subject to federalization in the event of national emergency. These measures were primarily designed to make the Guard an effective fighting force in the wake of the violent railroad strike that had occurred earlier that year. These strikes, moreover, relate to the changes described above. Most of the strikers were first- and second-generation immigrants. The Guard, on the other hand, was constituted disproportionately of native-born Protestants. Most government and business leaders looked to the Guard as the most effective antistrike force available to law enforcement. The 1877 strike was national, affecting cities from Baltimore to Pittsburgh and from St. Louis to San Francisco. Federalization seemed a logical response to strikes that now spread quickly along railroad lines.

A second step occurred in 1903 with the passage of the General Staff Act. Progressives and army modernizers had long advocated the creation of a general staff along European lines. The chaotic and localized mobilization for the Spanish-American War (1898) seemed to them to argue for the creation of a central body to organize planning and strategy. The General Staff linked various national and local agencies into something like a coherent whole, though the American system fell far short of the near-total control exercised by many European staffs.

The main point here is that the federal government had at its disposal several more mechanisms with which to control war fighting than it had possessed in 1861 or 1898. The government had more authority with which to issue legislation governing domestic events and more power to enforce that authority. The result was a flurry of legislation that led to a centralization of military effort that was unprecedented in American history. That legislation included the Sedition Act (1917), which made speaking out against the war a crime. Judge Kenesaw Mountain Landis gained such national prominence for his vigorous interpretation and enforcement of the act that he was named commissioner of Major League Baseball shortly after the war (1920) and was asked to root out gambling in the sport. The Lever Act (1917) gave the government control over essential war resources such as coal and food. The United States also abandoned its traditional belief in volunteerism and used a complex system of selective service to access, categorize, psychologically test, and train 2.8 million men.

The government used formal and informal authority to control and influence other aspects of the war effort as well. The National War Labor Board used a combination of rewards and threats of punishments to reduce labor unrest (and therefore control politically suspect immigrants) and lessen the occurrence of strikes. The War Industries Board regulated the production of natural resources and manufactured goods at prices set by government boards. The United States Employment Service centralized efforts to move women and African Americans into factory employment. All of these efforts were rooted in prewar Progressive ideals about the utility of government in coordinating national efforts.

While World War I largely marks the end of the Progressive period in American history, it does not mark the end of the influence of Progressive ideals. Many Progressive economic and political ideas reappeared in the New Deal era (1933–1941). Nor did World War I signal the end of attempts to reduce ethnic influences in the United States. In the 1920s a new nativism appeared in the United States, resulting in legislation that virtually banned immigration from Asia and southern and eastern Europe. The famous Sacco and Vanzetti case (the two men were executed in 1927; they were convicted in 1921 on questionable evidence for the 1920 murder of a paymaster in Massachusetts) attracted worldwide attention to American social problems.

The 1920s were a time of tense ethnic relations, reflecting the tensions and problems that remained from American participation in World War I.

–MICHAEL S. NEIBERG, U.S. AIR
FORCE ACADEMY

References

David Goldfield, and others, *The American Journey: A History of the United States,* volume two, second edition (Upper Saddle River, N.J.: Prentice Hall, 2001).

Carol S. Gruber, *Mars and Minerva: World War I and the Uses of Higher Learning in America* (Baton Rouge: Louisiana State University Press, 1975).

Meirion and Susie Harris, *The Last Days of Innocence: America at War, 1917–1918* (New York: Random House, 1997).

Peter Karsten, "Armed Progressives," in *The Military in America: From the Colonial Era to the Present,* edited by Peter Karsten (New York: Free Press, 1980), pp. 239–274.

David M. Kennedy, *Over Here: The First World War and American Society* (New York: Oxford University Press, 1980).

Ronald Schaffer, *America in the Great War: The Rise of the War Welfare State* ((New York: Oxford University Press, 1991).

Bruce White, "War Preparations and Ethnic and Racial Relations in the United States" in *Anticipating Total War: The German and American Experiences, 1871–1914,* edited by Manfred F. Boemeke, Roger Chickering, and Stig Förster (Cambridge & New York: Cambridge University Press, 1999), pp. 97–124.

REFERENCES

1. AFRICA

Boahen, A. Adu. General History of Africa. Volume 7. Africa under Colonial Domination 1880-1935. London: Heinemann; Berkeley: University of California Press, 1985.

Farwell, Byron. The Great War in Africa, 1914-1918. New York: Norton, 1986.

Gardner, Brian. German East: The Story of the First World War in East Africa. London: Cassell, 1963.

Hodges, Geoffrey. The Carrier Corps: Military Labor in the East African Campaign, 1914-1918. New York: Greenwood Press, 1986.

Hoyt, Edwin P. Guerilla: Colonel von Lettow-Vorbeck and Germany's East African Empire. New York: Macmillan, 1981.

Miller, Charles. Battle for the Bundu: The First World War in East Africa. New York: Macmillan, 1974.

Mosley, Leonard Oswald. Duel for Kilimanjaro: An Account of the East African Campaign, 1914-1918. London: Weidenfeld & Nicolson, 1963.

Page, Melvin E., ed. Africa and the First World War. London: Macmillan, 1987; New York: St. Martin's Press, 1987.

2. ARMORED WARFARE

Childs, David J. A Peripheral Weapon?: The Production and Employment of British Tanks in the First World War. Westport, Conn.: Greenwood Press, 1999.

Citino, Robert M. Armored Forces: History and Sourcebook. Westport, Conn.: Greenwood Press, 1994.

Smithers, A. J. A New Excalibur: The Development of the Tank, 1909-1939. London: Cooper, in association with Secker & Warburg, 1986.

3. BIOGRAPHIES

Abraham, Richard. Alexander Kerensky: The First Love of the Revolution. New York: Columbia University Press, 1987.

Bond, Brian and Nigel Cave, eds. Haig, A Reappraisal 70 Years On. London: Cooper, 1999.

Cooke, James J. Pershing and His Generals: Command and Staff in the AEF. Westport, Conn.: Praeger, 1997.

Gilbert, Bentley Brinkerhoff. David Lloyd George, A Political Life. Volume 2. The Organizer of Victory, 1912-16. London: Batsford, 1992.

Hantsch, Hugo. Leopold Graf Berchtold: Grandseigneur und Staatsman. 2 volumes. Graz: Verlag Styria, 1963.

Mango, Andrew. Atatürk: The Biography of the Founder of Modern Turkey. Woodstock, N.Y.: Overlook Press, 2000.

Owen, Frank. Tempestuous Journey: Lloyd George, His Life and Times. London: Hutchinson, 1954.

Powell, Geoffrey. Plumer: The Soldier's General: A Biography of Field-Marshal Viscount Plumer of Messines. London: Cooper, 1990.

Prior, Robin and Trevor Wilson. Command on the Western Front: The Military Career of Sir Henry Rawlinson, 1914-18. Oxford, U.K. & Cambridge, Mass.: Blackwell, 1991.

Robertson, William. Soldiers and Statesmen, 1914-1918. 2 volumes. London: Cassell, 1926; New York: Scribners, 1926.

Rowland, Peter. David Lloyd George: A Biography. New York: Macmillan, 1975.

4. COMBAT EXPERIENCE

Ashworth, Tony. Trench Warfare, 1914-1918: The Live and Let Live System. London: Macmillan, 1980; New York: Holmes & Meier, 1980.

Audoin-Rouzeau, Stéphane. Men at War, 1914-1918: National Sentiment and Trench Journalism in France during the First World War. Translated by Helen McPhail. Providence: Berg, 1992.

Audoin-Rouzeau and Annette Becker. 14-18: Retrouver la Guerre. Paris: Gallimard, 2000.

Cecil, Hugh and Peter H Liddle, eds. Facing Armageddon: The First World War Experienced. London: Cooper, 1996.

Chickering, Roger and Stig Förster, eds. Great War, Total War: Combat and Mobilization on the Western Front, 1914-1918. Washington, D.C.: German Historical Institute, 2000; Cambridge & New York: Cambridge University Press, 2000.

Ellis, John. Eye-Deep in Hell: Trench Warfare in World War I. London: Croom Helm, 1976.

Griffith, Paddy, ed. British Fighting Methods in the Great War. London & Portland, Ore.: Cass, 1996.

Keegan, John. The Face of Battle. London: Cape, 1976; New York: Viking, 1976.

Leed, Eric J. No Man's Land: Combat and Identity in World War I. Cambridge & New York: Cambridge University Press, 1979.

Liddell Hart, B. H. The Real War, 1914-1918. Boston: Little, Brown, 1930.

Marks, Thomas Penrose. The Laughter Goes from Life: In the Trenches of the First World War. London: Kimber, 1977.

5. DIPLOMACY AND INTERNATIONAL RELATIONS

Boemke, Manfred F., Gerald D. Feldman, and Elisabeth Glaser, eds. The Treaty of Versailles: A Reassessment After 75 Years. Washington, D.C.: German Historical Institute; Cambridge & New York: Cambridge University Press, 1998.

House, Edward Mandell and Charles Seymour, eds. What Really Happened at Paris: The Story of the Peace Conference, 1918–1919. New York: Scribner's, 1921.

Kennan, George. Soviet-American Relations, 1917–1920. Volume 1. Russia Leaves the War, 1917–1920. Princeton: Princeton University Press, 1956.

LaFeber, Walter. The American Age: Foreign Policy at Home and Abroad. Volume 2. Since 1896. Second edition. New York: Norton, 1994.

Leffler, Melvyn P. The Elusive Quest: America's Pursuit of European Stability and French Security, 1919–1933. Chapel Hill: University of North Carolina Press, 1979.

Mantoux, Etienne. The Carthaginian Peace, or, the Economic Consequences of Mr. Keynes. London & New York: Oxford University Press, 1946.

Marks, Sally. The Illusion of Peace: Europe's International Relations, 1918–1933. London: Macmillan, 1976; New York: St. Martin's Press, 1976.

Mayer, Arno J. Politics and Diplomacy of Peacemaking: Containment and Counterrevolution at Versailles, 1918–1919. New York: Knopf, 1967.

Mee Jr., Charles L. The End of Order: Versailles, 1919. New York: Dutton, 1980.

Pratt, Julius William. A History of United States Foreign Policy. New York: Prentice-Hall, 1955.

Sharp, Alan. The Versailles Settlement: Peacemaking in Paris, 1919. Basingstoke, U.K.: Macmillan Education, 1991; New York: St. Martin's Press, 1991.

Trachtenberg, Marc. Reparation in World Politics: France and European Economic Diplomacy, 1916–1923. New York: Columbia University Press, 1980.

U.S. State Department. Papers Relating to the Foreign Relations of the United States: The Paris Peace Conference, 1919, 13 volumes. Washington, D.C.: Government Printing Office, 1942–1947.

6. EASTERN FRONT

Fedyshyn, Oleh S. Germany's Drive to the East and the Ukrainian Revolution, 1917–1918. New Brunswick, N.J.: Rutgers University Press, 1971.

Reshetar Jr., John S. The Ukrainian Revolution, 1917–1920: A Study in Nationalism. Princeton: Princeton University Press, 1952.

Wheeler-Bennett, John W. Brest-Litovsk: The Forgotten Peace, March 1918. London: Macmillan, 1938.

7. FRANCE

Agulhon, Maurice. The French Republic: 1879–1992. Translated by Antonia Nevill. Oxford, U.K. & Cambridge, Mass.: Blackwell, 1993.

Becker, Jean-Jacques. 1914, comment les Français sont entrés dans la guerre: contribution à l'étude de l'opinion publique printemps-été 1914. Paris: Presses de la Fondation nationale des sciences politiques, 1977.

Benbassa, Esther. The Jews of France: A History from Antiquity to the Present. Translated by M. B. DeBevoise. Princeton: Princeton University Press, 1999.

Cole, Ronald H. "'Forward With the Bayonet': The French Army Prepares for Offensive War, 1911–1914." Dissertation, University of Maryland, 1975.

Doise, Jean and Maurice Vaïsse. Diplomatie et outil militaire, 1871–1991. Paris: Editions du Seuil, 1992.

Foch, Ferdinand. De la Conduite de la Guerre: La Manœuvre pour la Bataille avec 13 cartes et croquis. Paris: Berger-Levrault, 1915.

Gorce, Paul-Marie de la. The French Army: A Military Political History. Translated by Kenneth Douglas. London: Weidenfeld & Nicolson, 1963; New York: Braziller, 1963.

Goutard, Adolphe. La Marne: Victoire Inexploitée. Paris: Laffont, 1968.

Hyman, Paula. From Dreyfus to Vichy: The Remaking of French Jewry, 1906–1939. New York: Columbia University Press, 1979.

King, Jere Clemens. Foch Versus Clemenceau: France and German Dismemberment, 1918–1919. Cambridge, Mass.: Harvard University Press, 1960.

King. Generals & Politicians: Conflict between France's High Command, Parliament, and Government, 1914–1918. Berkeley: University of California Press, 1951.

Mangin, Charles. Comment Finit la Guerre: Avec Onze Cartes. Paris: Plon-Nourrit, 1920.

Palat, Barthélemy. La Grande Guerre sur le Front Occidental. 14 volumes. Paris: Chapelot, 1917–1929.

Pedroncini, Guy. Les Mutineries de 1917. Paris: Presses Universitaires de France, 1967.

Porch, Douglas. The March to the Marne: The French Army, 1871–1914. Cambridge & New York: Cambridge University Press, 1981.

Ralston, David B. The Army of the Republic: The Place of the Military in the Political Evolution of France, 1871–1914. Cambridge, Mass.: M.I.T. Press, 1967.

Shirer, William L. The Collapse of the Third Republic: An Inquiry into the Fall of France in 1940. New York: Simon & Schuster, 1969.

Smith, Leonard V. Between Mutiny and Obedience: The Case of the French Fifth Infantry Division during World War I. Princeton: Princeton University Press, 1994.

Weber, Eugen. France, Fin de Siècle. Cambridge, Mass.: Belknap Press of Harvard University Press, 1986.

Weber. The Hollow Years: France in the 1930s. New York: Norton, 1994.

Wesseling, H. L. Warrior and Soldier: French Attitudes Toward the Army and War on the Eve of the First World War. Translated by Arnold J. Pomerans. Westport, Conn.: Greenwood Press, 2000.

Wright, Gordon. France in Modern Times: From the Enlightenment to the Present, fifth edition. New York: Norton, 1995.

Zuccotti, Susan. The Holocaust, the French, and the Jews. New York: BasicBooks, 1993.

8. GENERAL HISTORIES

Eksteins, Modris. The Rites of Spring: The Great War and the Birth of the Modern Age. New York: Houghton Mifflin, 1989.

Fussell, Paul. The Great War and Modern Memory. New York: Oxford University Press, 1975.

Gilbert, Martin. The First World War: A Complete History. New York: Holt, 1994.

Gilbert. The Jews in the Twentieth Century: An Illustrated History. New York: Schocken Books, 2001.

Horne, John, ed. State, Society, and Mobilization in Europe During the First World War. Cambridge & New York: Cambridge University Press, 1997.

Howard, Michael. War in European History. London & New York: Oxford University Press, 1976.

Johnson, Paul. A History of the Jews. New York: Harper & Row, 1987.

Keegan, John. The First World War. London: Hutchinson, 1998.

Kennedy, Paul. The Rise and Fall of the Great Powers: Economic Change and Military Conflict from 1500 to 2000. New York: Random House, 1987.

Liddell Hart, B. H. The Real War, 1914–1918. Boston: Little, Brown, 1930.

Liddell Hart. Reputations: Ten Years After. Boston: Little, Brown, 1928.

Maier, Charles S. Recasting Bourgeois Europe: Stabilization in France, Germany, and Italy in the Decade After World War I. Princeton: Princeton University Press, 1975.

Mosier, John. The Myth of the Great War: A New Military History of World War I. New York: HarperCollins, 2001.

Mosse, George L. Fallen Soldiers: Reshaping the Memory of the World Wars. New York: Oxford University Press, 1990.

Paschall, Rod. The Defeat of Imperial Germany, 1917–1918. Chapel Hill, N.C.: Algonquin, 1989.

Pound, Reginald. The Lost Generation of 1914. New York: Coward-McCann, 1964.

Roshwald, Aviel and Richard Stites, eds. European Culture in the Great War: The Arts, Entertainment, and Propaganda, 1914–1918. Cambridge & New York: Cambridge University Press, 1999.

Sachar, Howard Morley. The Course of Modern Jewish History. Cleveland: World, 1958.

Strachan, Hew, ed. World War I: A History. Oxford & New York: Oxford University Press, 1998.

Terraine, John. To Win a War: 1918, the Year of Victory. London: Sidgwick & Jackson, 1978.

Tuchman, Barbara W. The Guns of August. New York: Macmillan, 1962.

Vital, David. A People Apart: The Jews in Europe, 1789–1939. Oxford & New York: Oxford University Press, 1999.

9. GERMANY & AUSTRIA-HUNGARY

Alff, Wilhelm, ed. Deutschlands Sonderung von Europa, 1862-1945. Frankfurt & New York: Peter Lang, 1984.

Armeson, Robert B. Total Warfare and Compulsory Labor: A Study of the Military-Industrial Complex in Germany during World War I. The Hague: Nijhoff, 1964.

Asprey, Robert B. The German High Command at War: Hindenburg and Ludendorff Conduct World War I. New York: Morrow, 1991.

Balfour, Michael. The Kaiser and His Times. London: Cresset, 1964; New York: Houghton Mifflin, 1964.

Berghahn, V. R. Germany and the Approach of War in 1914, second edition. New York: St. Martin's Press, 1993.

Bittner, Ludwig and Hans Uebersberger, eds. Österreich-Ungarns Aussenpolitik von der bosnischen Krise 1908 bis zum Kriegausbruch 1914: Diplomatische Aktenstücke des österreichisch-ungarischen Ministeriums des Aussern, 9 volumes. Vienna: Österreichischer Bundesverlag, 1930.

Bracher, Karl Dietrich. The German Dictatorship: The Origins, Structure, and Effects of National Socialism. Translated by Jean Steinberg. New York: Praeger, 1970.

Bucholz, Arden. Moltke, Schlieffen and Prussian War Planning. New York: Berg, 1991.

Chickering, Roger. Imperial Germany and the Great War, 1914–1918. Cambridge & New York: Cambridge University Press, 1998.

Conze, Werner. The Shaping of the German Nation: A Historical Analysis. Translated by Neville Mellon. New York: St. Martin's Press, 1979.

Farrar Jr., L. L. The Short-War Illusion: German Policy, Strategy and Domestic Affairs, August-December 1914. Santa Barbara, Cal.: ABC-Clio, 1973.

Fischer, Fritz. Griff nach der Weltmacht. Translated as Germany's Aims in the First World War. New York: Norton, 1967.

Feldman, Gerald D. Army, Industry, and Labor in Imperial Germany, 1914–1918. Princeton: Princeton University Press, 1966.

Foley, Robert T. "Attrition: Its Theory and Application in German Strategy, 1880–1916." Dissertation, Kings College, 1999.

Friedrich, Otto. Blood and Iron: From Bismarck to Hitler, the von Moltke Family's Impact on German History. New York: HarperCollins, 1995.

Gay, Peter. Weimar Culture: The Outsider as Insider. New York: Harper & Row, 1968.

Herwig, Holger H. The First World War: Germany and Austria-Hungary, 1914–1918. London & New York: Arnold, 1997.

Hillgruber, Andreas. Germany and the Two World Wars. Translated by William C. Kirby. Cambridge, Mass.: Harvard University Press, 1981.

Holborn, Hajo. A History of Modern Germany, volume 3, 1840-1945. New York: Knopf, 1969.

Johnson, Lonnie R. Central Europe: Enemies, Neighbors, Friends. New York: Oxford University Press, 1996.

Kitchen, Martin. The Silent Dictatorship: The Politics of the German High Command Under Hindenburg and Ludendorff, 1916-1918. New York: Holmes & Meier, 1976; London: Croom Helm, 1976.

Kocka, Jürgen. Facing Total War: German Society, 1914–1918. Translated by Barbara Weinberger. Cambridge, Mass.: Harvard University Press, 1984.

Pulzer, Peter. Jews and the German State: The Political History of a Minority, 1848-1933. Oxford, U.K. & Cambridge, Mass.: Blackwell, 1992.

Ritter, Gerhard. The Schlieffen Plan: Critique of a Myth. Translated by Andrew and Eva Wilson. London: Wolff, 1958.

Ritter. The Sword and the Sceptre: The Problem of Militarism in Germany, 3 volumes. Translated by Heinz Norden. Coral Gables, Fla.: University of Miami Press, 1969-1973.

Rothenberg, Gunther E. The Army of Francis Joseph. West Lafayette, Ind.: Purdue University Press, 1976.

Sheehan, James J., ed. Imperial Germany. New York: New Viewpoints, 1976.

Smith, Woodruff D. The Ideological Origins of Nazi Imperialism. New York: Oxford University Press, 1986.

Tunstall Jr., Graydon A. Planning for War Against Russia and Serbia: Austro-Hungarian and German Military Strategies, 1871-1914. Boulder, Colo.: Social Science Monographs; New York: Columbia University Press, 1993.

Verhey, Jeffrey. The Spirit of 1914: Militarism, Myth and Mobilization in Germany. Cambridge & New York: Cambridge University Press, 2000.

Watt, Richard M. The Kings Depart: The Tragedy of Germany: Versailles and the German Revolution. New York: Simon & Schuster, 1968.

Wheeler-Bennett, John W. Wooden Titan: Hindenburg in Twenty Years of German History, 1914-1934. New York: Morrow, 1936.

Williamson Jr., Samuel R. Austria-Hungary and the First World War. Houndmills, Basingstoke, Hampshire: Macmillan, 1991.

10. GREAT BRITAIN AND THE EMPIRE

Bourke, Joanna. Dismembering the Male: Men's Bodies, Britain and the Great War. Chicago: University of Chicago Press, 1996.

French, David. The Strategy of the Lloyd George Coalition, 1916–1918. Oxford: Clarendon Press, 1995; New York: Oxford University Press, 1995.

Harper, Glyn. Massacre at Passchendaele: The New Zealand Story. Auckland: HarperCollins, 2000.

Harris, J. P. and Niall Barr. Amiens to the Armistice: The BEF in the Hundred Days' Campaign, 8 August–11 November 1918. London & Washington, D.C.: Brassey's, 1998.

Macdonald, Lyn. They Called it Passchendaele: The Story of the Third Battle of Ypres and of the Men Who Fought In It. London: Joseph, 1978.

Moses, John A. and Christopher Pugsley, eds. The German Empire and Britain's Pacific Dominions, 1871–1919: Essays on the Role of Australia and New Zealand in World Politics in the Age of Imperialism. Claremont, Cal.: Regina, 2000.

Prior, Robin and Trevor Wilson. Passchendaele: The Untold Story. New Haven: Yale University Press, 1996.

Sheffield, G. D. Leadership in the Trenches: Officer-Man Relations, Morale, and Discipline in the British Army in the Era of the First World War. Houndmills, Basingstoke, Hampshire, U.K.: Macmillan; New York: St. Martin's Press, in association with King's College, London, 2000.

Simkins, Peter. Kitchener's Army: The Raising of the New Armies, 1914–16. Manchester & New York: Manchester University Press, 1988.

Steel, Nigel and Peter Hart. Passchendaele: The Sacrificial Ground. London: Cassell, 2000.

Terraine, John. The Road to Passchendaele: The Flanders Offensive of 1917: A Study in Inevitability. London: Cooper, 1977.

Travers, Tim. How the War Was Won: Command and Technology in the British Army on the Western Front, 1917–1918. London & New York: Routledge, 1992.

Travers. The Killing Ground: The British Army, the Western Front, and the Emergence of Modern Warfare, 1900–1918. London & Boston: Allen & Unwin, 1987.

Turner, John. British Politics and the Great War: Coalition and Conflict, 1915–1918. New Haven: Yale University Press, 1992.

Wilson. The Myriad Faces of War: Britain and the Great War, 1914–1918. Cambridge: Polity Press, 1986; Oxford & New York: Blackwell, 1986.

Winter, Denis. Haig's Command: A Reassessment. London & New York: Viking, 1991.

Wolff, Leon. In Flanders Fields: The 1917 Campaign. New York: Viking, 1958.

Woodward, David R. Lloyd George and the Generals. Newark: University of Delaware Press, 1983; London: Associated University Presses, 1983.

11. INTERNET WEBSITES

Encyclopaedia of the First World War
http://www.spartacus.schoolnet.co.uk/FWW.htm

The Great War (1914–1918)
http://www.pitt.edu/~pugachev/greatwar/www1.html

The Great War and the Shaping of the 20th Century
http://www.pbs.org/greatwar/

The World War I Document Archive
http://www.lib.byu.edu/~vdh/wwi/

World War I: Trenches on the Web
http://www.worldwar1.com/

12. IRELAND

Hennessey, Thomas. Dividing Ireland: World War I and Partition. London & New York: Routledge, 1998.

McCaffrey, Lawrence J. Ireland: From Colony to Nation-State. Englewood Cliffs, N.J.: Prentice-Hall, 1979.

Ward, Alan J. Ireland and Anglo-American Relations, 1899–1921. London: Weidenfeld & Nicolson, 1969.

13. LIBRARY HOLDINGS

Herbert Hoover Presidential Library, West Branch, Iowa

Imperial War Museum, London

The Joseph M. Bruccoli Great War Collection, Special Collections Department, Alderman Memorial Library, University of Virginia

The Joseph M. Bruccoli Great War Collection, Thomas Cooper Library, University of South Carolina

14. MEMOIRS & AUTOBIOGRAPHIES

Adams, Bernard. Nothing of Importance: A Record of Eight Months at the Front with a Welsh Battalion, October, 1915, to June, 1916. London: Methuen, 1917.

Barbusse, Henri. Under Fire: The Story of a Squad. London & Toronto: Dent, 1917; New York: Dutton, 1917.

Binding, Rudolf. A Fatalist at War. Translated by Ian F. D. Morrow. Boston & New York: Houghton Mifflin, 1929.

Brittain, Vera. Testament of Youth: An Autobiographical Study of the Years 1900–1925. London: Gollancz, 1933; New York: Macmillan, 1933.

Carstairs, Carroll. A Generation Missing. London: Heinemann, 1930; Garden City, N.Y.: Doubleday, Doran, 1930.

Chapman, Guy. A Passionate Prodigality: Fragments of Autobiography. London: Nicolson & Watson, 1933.

Conrad von Hötzendorf, Aus Meiner Dienstzeit, 1908–1918. 5 volumes. Vienna: Rikola Verlag, 1921–1925.

Croney, Percy. Soldier's Luck: Memoirs of a Soldier of the Great War. Ifracombe, U.K.: Stockwell, 1965.

Dos Passos, John. Three Soldiers. New York: Doran, 1921.

Eyre, Giles E.M. Somme Harvest: Memories of a P.B.I. in the Summer of 1916. London: Jarrolds, 1938.

Ferguson, Niall. The Pity of War. New York: BasicBooks, 1999.

Foch, Ferdinand. The Memoirs of Marshal Foch. Translated by T. Bentley Mott. Garden City, N.Y.: Doubleday, Doran, 1931.

Gordon, Huntly. The Unreturning Army: A Field-Gunner in Flanders, 1917–18. London: Dent, 1967.

Graves, Robert. Good-bye to All That: An Autobiography. London: Cape, 1929.

Groener, Wilhelm. Lebenserinnerungen: Jugend, Generalstab, Weltkrieg. Göttingen: Vandenhoeck & Ruprecht, 1957.

Joffre, Joseph. The Personal Memoirs of Joffre, Field Marshal of the French Army. Volume 1. Translated by Mott. New York & London: Harper & Row, 1932.

Kerensky, Alexander F. The Catastrophe: Kerensky's Own Story of the Russian Revolution. New York & London: Appleton, 1927.

Knyvett, R. Hugh. "Over There" with the Australians. London: Hodder & Stoughton, 1918; New York: Scribners, 1918.

Lafond, Georges. Covered with Mud and Glory. Boston: Small, Maynard, 1918.

Lettow-Vorbeck, Paul Emil von. My Reminiscences of East Africa. London: Hurst & Blackett, 1920.

Lloyd George, David. War Memoirs of David Lloyd George. 6 volumes. London: Nicolson & Watson, 1933-1936; Boston: Little, Brown, 1933-1936.

Ludendorff, Eric. My War Memories, 1914-1918, 2 volumes. London: Hutchinson, 1919.

Martin, Bernard. Poor Bloody Infantry: A Subaltern on the Western Front, 1916-1917. London: Murray, 1987.

Miliukov, Paul. Political Memoirs, 1905-1917. Edited by Arthur P. Mendel. Translated by Carl Goldberg. Ann Arbor: University of Michigan Press, 1967.

Pershing, John J. My Experiences in the World War. 2 volumes. New York: Stokes, 1931.

Rommel, Erwin. Infanterie Greift An. Potsdam: Voggenreiter, 1941. Translated as Attacks. Vienna, Va.: Athena Press, 1979.

Sassoon, Siegfried. Memoirs of an Infantry Officer. London: Faber & Faber, 1930.

15. MIDDLE EAST

Alangari, Haifa. The Struggle for Power in Arabia: Ibn Saud, Hussein and Great Britain, 1914-1924. Reading, U.K.: Ithaca Press, 1998.

Bullock, David L. Allenby's War: The Palestine-Arabian Campaigns, 1916-1918. London & New York: Blandford Press, 1988.

Bush, Eric Wheler. Gallipoli. London: Allen & Unwin, 1975; New York: St. Martin's Press, 1975.

Darwin, John. Britain, Egypt, and the Middle East: Imperial Policy in the Aftermath of War, 1918-1922. New York: St. Martin's Press, 1981.

Hickey, Michael. Gallipoli. London: Murray, 1995.

James, Lawrence. The Golden Warrior: The Life and Legend of Lawrence of Arabia. London: Weidenfeld & Nicolson, 1990.

Kedourie, Elie. England and the Middle East: The Destruction of the Ottoman Empire, 1914-1921. London: Mansell; Boulder, Colo.: Westview Press, 1987.

Kinross, Lord. The Ottoman Centuries: The Rise and Fall of the Turkish Empire. New York: Morrow, 1977.

Laffin, John. Damn the Dardanelles!: The Story of Gallipoli. London: Osprey, 1980.

Lawrence, T. E. Seven Pillars of Wisdom: A Triumph. London: Oxford, 1926.

Macfie, A. L. The End of the Ottoman Empire, 1908-1923. London & New York: Longman, 1998.

Miller, Geoffrey. Straits: British Policy Towards the Ottoman Empire and the Origins of the Dardanelles Campaign. Hull, U.K.: University of Hull Press, 1997.

Moorehead, Alan. Gallipoli. New York: Harper, 1956.

Palmer, Alan. The Decline and Fall of the Ottoman Empire. New York: M. Evans, 1992.

Penn, Geoffrey. Fisher, Churchill, and the Dardanelles. Barnsley, South Yorkshire, U.K.: Cooper, 1999.

Robertson, John. Anzac and Empire: The Tragedy and Glory of Gallipoli. London: Cooper, 1990.

Shaw, Stanford. History of the Ottoman Empire and Modern Turkey. Cambridge & New York: Cambridge University Press, 1976.

Steel, Nigel and Peter Hart. Defeat at Gallipoli. London: Macmillan, 1994.

Turfan, Naim. The Rise of the Young Turks: Politics, The Military and Ottoman Collapse. London: Tauris, 1999.

16. NAVAL OPERATIONS

Alexander, Roy. The Cruise of the Raider "Wolf." New York: Yale University Press, 1939.

Beeler, John F. British Naval Policy in the Gladstone-Disraeli Era, 1866-1880. Stanford., Cal.: Stanford University Press, 1997.

British Admiralty Staff Study. Review of German Cruiser Warfare, 1914-1918. Unpublished, London, 1940.

Brodie, Bernard. Sea Power in the Machine Age. Princeton: Princeton University Press; London: Oxford University Press, 1941.

Halpern, Paul G. A Naval History of World War I. Annapolis, Md.: U.S. Naval Institute Press, 1994.

Herwig, Holger H. "Luxury" Fleet: The Imperial German Navy, 1888-1918. London & Boston: Allen & Unwin, 1980.

Lochner, R. K. The Last Gentleman-of-War: The Raider Exploits of the Cruiser Emden. Translated by Thea and Harry Lindauer. Annapolis, Md.: U.S. Naval Institute Press, 1988.

Marder, Arthur J. From the Dreadnought to Scapa Flow: The Royal Navy in the Fisher Era, 1904-1919. 5 volumes. London & New York: Oxford University Press, 1961-1970.

Massie, Robert K. Dreadnought: Britain, Germany, and the Coming of the Great War. New York: Random House, 1991.

O'Connell, D. P. The International Law of the Sea. Volume 2. Edited by I. A. Shearer. Oxford & New York: Clarendon Press, 1984.

Rössler, Eberhard. The U-Boat: The Evolution and Technical History of German Submarines. Translated by Harold Erenberg. Annapolis, Md.: U.S. Naval Institute Press, 1981.

Schmalenbach, Paul. German Raiders: A History of Auxiliary Cruisers of the German Navy, 1895-1945. Translated by Keith Lewis. Cambridge: Patrick Stephens, 1979.

Sims, William Sowden. The Victory at Sea. Garden City, N.Y.: Doubleday, Page, 1920.

Terraine, John. Business in Great Waters: The U-boat Wars, 1916-1945. London: Cooper, 1989.

Wallin, Jeffrey D. By Ships Alone: Churchill and the Dardanelles. Durham, N.C.: Carolina Academic Press, 1981.

17. ORIGINS OF WORLD WAR I

Adams, Michael C. C. The Great Adventure: Male Desire and the Coming of World War I. Bloomington: Indiana University Press, 1990.

Joll, James. The Origins of the First World War. Second edition. London & New York: Longman, 1984.

Keiger, John V. F. France and the Origins of the First World War. London: Macmillan, 1983; New York: St. Martin's Press, 1983.

Kennedy, Paul M. The Rise of the Anglo-German Antagonism, 1860-1914. London & Boston: Allen & Unwin, 1980.

Kennedy, ed. The War Plans of the Great Powers, 1880-1914. London & Boston: Allen & Unwin, 1979.

Lee, Dwight E., ed. The Outbreak of the First World War: Causes and Responsibilities. Fourth edition. Lexington, Mass.: D.C. Heath, 1975.

Mombauer, Annika. Helmuth von Moltke and the Origins of the First World War. Cambridge & New York: Cambridge University Press, 2001.

Stevenson, David. Armaments and the Coming of War: Europe, 1904-1914. Oxford & New York: Clarendon Press, 1996.

18. PAPERS, DOCUMENTS & DIARIES

Browder, Robert Paul and Alexander F. Kerensky, eds. The Russian Provisional Government, 1917: Documents. Volume 2. Stanford, Cal.: Stanford University Press, 1961.

Brown, Malcolm, ed. The Imperial War Museum Book of the First World War: A Great Conflict Recalled in Previously Unpublished Letters, Diaries, Documents, and Memoirs. London: Sidgwick & Jackson, 1991.

Dunn, J. C. The War the Infantry Knew, 1914–1919: A Chronicle of Service in France and Belgium with the Second Battalion, His Majesty's Twenty-third Foot, the Royal Welch Fusiliers: Founded on Personal Records, Recollections and Reflections. London: P. S. King, 1938.

Geiss, Imanuel, ed. July 1914: The Outbreak of the First World War; Selected Documents. Translated by Henry Meyric Hughes and Geiss. London: Batsford, 1967.

Hitchcock, F. C. Stand To: A Diary of the Trenches, 1915–18. London: Hurst & Blackett, 1937.

Hoffmann, Max. War Diaries and Other Papers. Translated by Eric Sutton. London: Secker, 1929.

Jünger, Ernst. Copse 125: A Chronicle from the Trench Warfare of 1918. Translated by Basil Creighton. London: Chatto & Windus, 1930.

Jünger. The Storm of Steel: From the Diary of a German Storm-Troop Officer on the Western Front. London: Chatto & Windus, 1929; Garden City, N.Y.: Doubleday, Doran, 1929.

Omissi, David, ed. Indian Voices of the Great War: Soldiers' Letters, 1914–18. Basingstoke, U.K.: Macmillan; New York: St. Martin's Press, 1999.

Powers, Lyall H., ed. Henry James and Edith Wharton: Letters, 1900–1915. New York: Scribners, 1990.

Roy, Reginald H., ed. The Journal of Private Fraser, 1914–1918: Canadian Expeditionary Force. Victoria, B.C.: Sono Nis Press, 1985.

Stevenson, Frances. Lloyd George: A Diary. Edited by A. J. P. Taylor. London: Hutchinson, 1971; New York: Harper & Row, 1971.

Vaughn, Edwin Campion. Some Desperate Glory: The Diary of a Young Officer, 1917. London: Warne, 1981.

West, Arthur Graeme. The Diary of a Dead Officer, Being the Posthumous Papers of Arthur Graeme West. London: Allen & Unwin, n.d.

19. RELIGION

Abrams, Ray H. Preachers Present Arms. New York: Round Table Press, 1933.

Bailey, Charles E. "Gott Mit Uns: Germany's Protestant Theologians in the First World War." Dissertation, University of Virginia, 1978.

Homan, Gerlof D. American Mennonites and the Great War, 1914–1918. Waterloo, Ontario & Scottsdale, Penn.: Herald Press, 1994.

Hoover, Arlie J. God, Germany, and Britain in the Great War: A Study in Clerical Nationalism. New York: Praeger, 1989.

Marrin, Albert. The Last Crusade: The Church of England in the First World War. Durham, N.C.: Duke University Press, 1974.

Piper Jr., John F. The American Churches in World War I. Athens: Ohio University Press, 1985.

20. RUSSIA

Acton, Edward, and others, eds. Critical Companion to the Russian Revolution, 1914–1921. Bloomington: Indiana University Press, 1997.

Figes, Orlando. A People's Tragedy: The Russian Revolution, 1891–1924. London: Cape, 1996.

Figes and Boris Kolonitskii. Interpreting the Russian Revolution: The Language and Symbols of 1917. New Haven: Yale University Press, 1999.

Frankel, Edith Rogovin, and others, eds. Revolution in Russia: Reassessments of 1917. Cambridge & New York: Cambridge University Press, 1992.

Pipes, Richard. The Russian Revolution. New York: Knopf, 1990.

Stockdale, Melissa Kirschke. Paul Miliukov and the Quest for a Liberal Russia, 1880–1918. Ithaca, N.Y.: Cornell University Press, 1996.

Wade, Rex A. The Russian Revolution, 1917. Cambridge & New York: Cambridge University Press, 2000.

Wildman, Alan K. The End of the Russian Imperial Army. 2 volumes. Princeton: Princeton University Press, 1980, 1987.

21. STRATEGY, LOGISTICS, TACTICS

Bonham-Carter, Victor. The Strategy of Victory, 1914–1918: The Life and Times of the Master Strategist of World War I: Field-Marshal Sir William Robertson. New York: Holt, Rinehart & Winston, 1963.

Creveld, Martin van. Supplying War: Logistics From Wallenstein to Patton. Cambridge & New York: Cambridge University Press, 1977.

French, David. The Strategy of the Lloyd George Coalition, 1916–1918. Oxford: Clarendon Press; New York: Oxford University Press, 1995.

Griffith, Paddy. Battle Tactics of the Western Front: The British Army's Art of Attack, 1916–18. New Haven: Yale University Press, 1994.

Gudmundsson, Bruce I. Stormtroop Tactics: Innovation in the German Army, 1914–1918. New York: Praeger, 1989.

Johnson, Hubert C. Breakthrough! Tactics, Technology, and the Search for Victory on the Western Front in World War I. Novato, Cal.: Presidio Press, 1994.

Luttwak, Edward N. Strategy: The Logic of War and Peace. Cambridge, Mass.: Belknap Press of Harvard University Press, 1987.

Paret, Peter, ed. Makers of Modern Strategy: From Machiavelli to the Nuclear Age. Princeton: Princeton University Press, 1986.

Snyder, Jack L. The Ideology of the Offensive: Military Decision Making and the Disasters of 1914. Ithaca, N.Y.: Cornell University Press, 1984.

Wallach, Jehuda L. The Dogma of the Battle of Annihilation: The Theories of Clausewitz and Schlieffen and Their Impact on the German Conduct of Two World Wars. Westport, Conn.: Greenwood Press, 1986.

Weigley, Russell F. The American Way of War: A History of United States Military Strategy and Policy. New York: Macmillan, 1973.

Williamson Jr., Samuel R. The Politics of Grand Strategy: Britain and France Prepare for War, 1904–1914. Cambridge, Mass.: Harvard University Press, 1969.

22. TECHNOLOGY AND SCIENCE

Bidwell, Shelford and Dominick Graham. Fire-Power: British Army Weapons and Theories of War, 1904–1945. London & Boston: Allen & Unwin, 1982.

Ellis, John. A Social History of the Machine Gun. New York: Pantheon, 1975.

Haber, Ludwig F. The Poisonous Cloud: Chemical Warfare in the First World War. Oxford & New York: Oxford University Press, 1986.

Hartcup, Guy. The War of Invention: Scientific Developments, 1914–18. London & Washington, D.C.: Brassey's, 1988.

Murray, Williamson and Allan R. Millett, eds. Military Innovation in the Interwar Period. Cambridge & New York: Cambridge University Press, 1996.

Showalter, Dennis. "Mass Warfare and the Impact of Technology." In Great War, Total War: Combat and Mobilization on the Western Front, 1914–1918. Edited by Roger Chickering and Stig Förster. Cambridge & New York: Cambridge University Press, 2000, pp. 73–93.

Travers, Tim. How the War Was Won: Command and Technology in the British Army on the Western Front, 1917–1918. London & New York: Routledge, 1992.

23. UNITED STATES: HOME FRONT

Boemeke, Manfred F., Roger Chickering and Stig Förster. Anticipating Total War: The German and American Experiences, 1871–1914. Cambridge & New York: Cambridge University Press, 1999.

Gruber, Carol S. Mars and Minerva: World War I and the Uses of Higher Learning in America. Baton Rouge: Louisiana State University Press, 1975.

Harris, Meirion and Susie, The Last Days of Innocence: America at War, 1917–1918. New York: Random House, 1997.

Karsten, Peter, ed. The Military in America: From the Colonial Era to the Present. New York: Free Press, 1980.

Kennedy, David M. Over Here: The First World War and American Society. New York: Oxford University Press, 1980.

Schaffer, Ronald. America in the Great War: The Rise of the War Welfare State. New York: Oxford University Press, 1991.

24. U.S. FORCES IN EUROPE

American Battle Monuments Commission. American Armies and Battlefields in Europe: A History, Guide, and Reference Book. Washington, D.C.: U.S. Government Printing Office, 1938.

Braim, Paul F. The Test of Battle: The American Expeditionary Forces in the Meuse-Argonne Campaign. Newark: University of Delaware Press; London: Associated University Presses, 1987.

Coffman, Edward M. The War to End All Wars: The American Military Experience in World War I. New York: Oxford University Press, 1968.

Cooke, James J. The All-Americans at War: The 82nd Division in the Great War, 1917–1918. Westport, Conn.: Praeger, 1999.

Grotelueschen, Mark E. Doctrine Under Trial: American Artillery Employment in World War I. Westport, Conn.: Greenwood Press, 2001.

Hallas, James H., ed. Doughboy War: The American Expeditionary Force in World War I. Boulder, Colo.: Lynne Rienner, 1999.

Harbord, James G. The American Army in France, 1917–1919. Boston: Little, Brown, 1936.

Jamieson, Perry D. Crossing the Deadly Ground: United States Army Tactics, 1865–1899. Tuscaloosa: University of Alabama Press, 1994.

Johnson II, Douglas V. and Rolfe L. Hillman Jr. Soissons, 1918. College Station: Texas A&M University Press, 1999.

Trask, David F. The AEF and Coalition Warmaking, 1917–1918. Lawrence: University Press of Kansas, 1993.

Zieger, Robert H. America's Great War: World War I and the American Experience. Lanham, Md.: Rowman & Littlefield, 2000.

25. WOMEN & GENDER

Anderson, Bonnie S. and Judith P. Zinsser. A History of Their Own: Women in Europe From Prehistory to the Present. Revised edition. Volume 2. New York: Oxford University Press, 2000.

Braybon, Gail. Women Workers in the First World War: The British Experience. London: Croom Helm, 1981; Totowa, N.J.: Barnes & Noble, 1981.

Condell, Diana and Jean Liddiard. Working for Victory?: Images of Women in the First World War, 1914–18. London: Routledge & Kegan Paul, 1987.

Daniel, Ute. The War from Within: German Working-Class Women in the First World War. Translated by Margaret Ries. Oxford & New York: Berg, 1997.

Darrow, Margaret H. French Women and the First World War: War Stories from the Home Front. Oxford & New York: Berg, 2000.

Elshtain, Jean Bethke. Women and War. New York: Basic Books, 1987.

Gavin, Lettie. American Women in World War I: They Also Served. Niwot: University Press of Colorado, 1997.

Goldstein, Joshua S. War and Gender: How Gender Shapes the War System and Vice Versa. Cambridge: Cambridge University Press, 2001.

Greenwald, Maurine Weiner. Women, War, and Work: The Impact of World War I on Women Workers in the United States. Westport, Conn.: Greenwood Press, 1980.

Higonnet, Margaret Randolph, and others, eds. Behind the Lines: Gender and the Two World Wars. New Haven: Yale University Press, 1987.

Mosse, George L. The Image of Man: The Creation of Modern Masculinity. New York: Oxford University Press, 1996.

Ouditt, Sharon. Fighting Forces, Writing Women: Identity and Ideology in the First World War. London & New York: Routledge, 1994.

Woollacott, Angela. On Her Their Lives Depend: Munitions Workers in the Great War. Berkeley: University of California Press, 1994.

CONTRIBUTORS' NOTES

ABBATIELLO, John: An Air Force pilot since graduation from the U.S. Air Force Academy in 1987, he completed in 1995 a master's degree at King's College, London, and subsequently taught military history as a member of the faculty at the Academy. He recently returned to King's, where he is pursuing a doctorate; his studies focus on naval aviation in World War I.

ASTORE, Lieutenant Colonel William J.: Associate professor and director of international history at the U.S. Air Force Academy; earned his doctor of philosophy degree from the University of Oxford in 1996; author of Observing God: Thomas Dick, Evangelicalism, and Popular Science in Victorian Britain and America (2001).

BRUCE, Robert B.: Sam Houston State University.

BUTCHER, Daniel Lee: Doctoral candidate in history at Kansas State University.

CITINO, Robert M.: Professor of History at Eastern Michigan University; author of The Evolution of Blitzkrieg Tactics: Germany Defends Itself Against Poland, 1918–1933 (1987) and The Path to Blitzkrieg: Doctrine and Training in the German Army, 1920–1939 (1999).

COOKE, James J.: University of Mississippi.

CORUM, James S.: Professor of Comparative Military Studies at the USAF School of Advanced Airpower Studies; author of The Roots of Blitzkrieg: Hans von Seeckt and German Military Reform (1992), The Luftwaffe: Creating the Operational Air War, 1918–1940 (1997), and, with Richard Muller, The Luftwaffe's Way of War (1998).

DINARDO, Richard L.: Associate professor for National Security Affairs at the U.S. Marine Corps Command and Staff College, Quantico, Virginia; author of Mechanized Juggernaut or Military Anachronism?: Horses and the German Army of World War II (1991), Germany's Panzer Arm (1997), and "The Dysfunctional Coalition: The Axis Powers and the Eastern Front," Journal of Military History (1996).

ECHEVARRIA, Antulio: Strategic Studies Institute.

ERICKSON, Lieutenant Colonel (Ret.) Edward J.: Doctoral candidate in history at the University of Leeds, Yorkshire, United Kingdom; teaches world history at Norwich High School, Norwich, New York; author of Ordered to Die: A History of the Ottoman Army in the First World War (2001); and co-author, with Frederick M. Lorenz, of The Euphrates Triangle: Security Implications of the Southeast Anatolia Project (1999).

FOLEY, Robert T.: Completed his doctorate in German strategic thought before and during World War I at the Department of War Studies, King's College, London; lecturer, assigned to the Joint Services Command and Staff College in the Defense Studies Department of King's College; editor and translator of Alfred von Schlieffen's Military Writings (forthcoming).

FORSTCHEN, William R.: Assistant professor of history at Montreat College; author of The Lost Regiment series.

GILTMER, Philip: U.S. Military Academy.

GREGORY, Adrian: Oxford University.

GROTELUESCHEN, Mark E.: Doctoral student at Texas A&M University, College Station; active-duty officer in the U.S. Air Force; and author of Doctrine Under Trial: American Artillery Employment in World War I (2001). He has degrees from the U.S. Air Force Academy (1991) and the University of Calgary (1998) and has served as an assistant professor of History at the U.S. Air Force Academy.

HABECK, Mary: Yale University.

HELM, Lawrence A.: Holds a B.A. and M.A. in East European History from The George Washington University; directs Information Technology development at NASA Headquarters, Washington, D.C.; and is author of "Soviet Special Forces" in The New Face of War (1991) and two articles in the History in Dispute series on Hungary and Yugoslavia in the Cold War (2000).

KARAU, Mark: Santa Fe Community College.

KAUTT, Captain William: U.S. Air Force, San Antonio, Texas; former assistant professor of History at the U.S. Air Force Academy; author of The Anglo-Irish War, 1916–1921: A People's War (1999).

KIESLING, Eugenia C.: Associate professor of history at the U.S. Military Academy; author of Arming Against Hitler: France and the Limits of Military Planning (1996).

MARBLE, Sanders: www.ehistory.com.

McCARTNEY, H. B.: Lecturer in Defense Studies for King's College, London, based at the Joint Services Command and Staff College; contributor to "Post Combat Syndromes from the Boer War to the Gulf," British Medical Journal (forthcoming); writing a book about the British Territorial Force and World War I.

McJIMSEY, Robert: Professor of history at Colorado College; author of "A Country Divided?: English Politics and the Nine Years' War," Albion, 23 (Spring 1991) and "Crisis Management: Parliament and Political Stability, 1692–1719," Albion (forthcoming).

MOYD, Michelle: Cornell University.

NEIBERG, Michael S.: Assistant professor of history at the U.S. Air Force Academy; author of Making Citizen Soldiers: ROTC and the Ideology of American Military Service (2000) and Warfare in World History (2001).

NICHOLS, Kristi L.: U.S. Air Force Academy.

OLIVIER, David H.: B.A. from York University and an M.A. from the University of Toronto; completed his Ph.D. at the University of Saskatchewan. His dissertation was on German theories of commerce-raiding in the nineteenth century.

PALAZZO, Albert: Research Fellow in the School of History, University of New South Wales at the Australian Defence Force Academy; completed his B.A. and M.A. at New York University and Ph.D. at Ohio State University; author of Seeking Victory on the Western Front: The British Army and Chemical Warfare in World War I (2000), The Australian Army: A History of Its Organisation From 1901 to 2001 (2001), and The History of the Royal Australian Corps of Transport, 1973–2000 (forthcoming).

QUENOY, Paul du: Doctoral candidate in history at Georgetown University.

SANBORN, Josh: Assistant professor of Russian and East European history at Lafayette College. He has written several articles on the impact of war on Russian society and has a book forthcoming on the relationship between military conscription and Russian nationalism.

SHOWALTER, Dennis: Professor of history at Colorado College; president of the Society for Military History; visiting professor at the U.S. Military Academy and U.S. Air Force Academy; author and editor of many books; joint editor of War in History.

SPIRES, David N.: Holds a Ph.D. in military history from the University of Washington and teaches history at the University of Colorado at Boulder. As a career Air Force officer, he served on the faculty of the Air Force Academy; in intelligence assignments in Vietnam, Europe, and Turkey; and as staff historian at Headquarters United States Air Forces in Europe. His publications include articles and presentations on the German Army and Air Force Space issues, and books on the pre-Hitler German Army, U.S.-Greek military relations, and strategic defense issues. He is the author of Beyond Horizons: A Half Century of Air Force Space Leadership (1997) and Air Power for Patton's Army: The XIX Tactical Air Command in the Second World War (forthcoming). He edited Key Documents in Air Force Space History (forthcoming), a collection of important documents from the U.S. military space program.

TUNSTALL, Graydon A.: University of South Florida.

ULBRICH, David J.: Doctoral student in military history at Temple University; author of "Henry S. Aurand: Student, Teacher, and Practitioner of U.S. Army Logistics, 1920–1995," in The Human Tradition in America Between the Wars, 1920–1945 (2001).

WHEATLEY, John: Independent scholar, Brooklyn Center, Minnesota.

INDEX

A

A-10 tank buster VI 173
Abbott, Lyman VIII 204
ABM Treaty. *See* Anti-Ballistic Missile Treaty
Aboukir (British ship) VIII 288
abortion II 80, 220–226, 284
Abraham Lincoln Brigade VI 154, 176
Acheson, Dean I 27–30, 58–59, 69, 89, 160, 174, 220,
     286, 294; II 45, 134, 206; VI 75, 147–150
    McCarthy attacks on II 211
Acheson-Lilienthal Report I 27, 29–31, 220–221
    "Atomic Development Authority" I 29
acquired immunodeficiency syndrome (AIDS) II 224
activists, antiwar II 10
Adana Declaration VII 79
Addams, Jane III 165, 168, 171, 201
    campaign against cocaine III 134
    Hull House III 166, 208
Adenauer, Konrad I 255, 257; VI 207, 210
Administration Floodplain Management Task Force
    VII 214
Admirals' Revolt (1949) I 3–9
Aegean Sea VIII 117, 212
Aegis class warships VI 109
Aehrenthal, Alois VIII 45
affaire des fiches VIII 151
affirmative action II 143, 183, 167
Afghanistan I 95, 105; II 62; VI 4, 44, 50, 110, 113,
    165, 188, 194, 217, 221, 224, 226, 229, 232,
    236, 241, 261, 272; VIII 31, 35
    1978 coup in VI 166
    imperialism I 151
    Muslim fanaticism in VI 165
    opium trade I 15
    Soviet invasion of I 10–16, 71, 101, 183, 185–186,
        217–218, 289; II 56; VI 2, 30, 35, 42–44,
        66, 68, 107, 133, 162, 165–166, 222, 225,
        226, 232, 237, 241, 246, 261, 270
    Soviet troops withdrawn VI 45
    tensions with Iran I 15
    war with Soviets I 196
AFL. *See* American Federation of Labor
Africa VI 41, 50, 63, 77, 83, 164, 189, 209, 246, 249,
    264, 267; VIII 33, 109
    AIDS in VII 244
    dams in VII 1–9, 236–246, 287
    deep-water sources in VII 62–68
    drinking water in VII 2
    genocide in VI 216
    German interests in VIII 100
    hydroelectric power in VII 2, 5
    independence of colonies in VI 13

    influenza epidemic in VIII 89
    Soviet activities in VI 2
    U.S. policy in VI 87
    water shortage in VII 280
    World War I VIII 84–90
Africa, Southern VII 63–68
African Americans
    socio-economic divisions III 118
    World War I VIII 298, 301
    World War II III 213–219
African National Congress (ANC) VI 5; VII 239, 286
Afrika Korps (Africa Corps) V 123, 181, 226, 232
Afrikaner Nationalist Party VII 239
Agadir, Morocco VIII 33
Age of Sail VIII 136
Agrarian Reform Law (1952) I 93, 123, 126
Agricultural Adjustment Act (1933) III 27, 30, 62, 66,
    156–163
    Supreme Court ruling III 25
Agricultural Adjustment Administration (AAA,
    1933) III 154, 157; VI 124
agricultural revolution III 2
agricultural science II 83–85
agricultural technology III 1–8
    Global Positioning Satellites (GPS) III 5
    history III 2, 5
    impact of tractors III 6
    post–World War II mechanization III 3
    time management III 4
Agua Caliente Reservation VII 170
Aid for Families with Dependent Children (AFDC) II
    278
Airborne Warning and Control System (AWACS) VI
    173
aircraft carrier
    defeat of U-boats IV 4
    role in World War II I 4; IV 1–7
airplanes VIII 17
Akhmerov, Yitzhak VI 126
Akosombo Dam (Ghana) VII 4
Akron v. *Akron Center for Reproductive Health* (1983) II
    222
Alamo Canal VII 152, 154–155, 157, 159
Alabama (Confederate ship) VIII 136–137
Alaska VII 197
    salmon range VII 196
Albania I 294; VI 134, 175, 181, 261, 275, 280–281;
    VIII 212
    lack of environmental control in VII 145
    Soviet domination until 1968 I 107
Albanian Communist Party VI 280
Alessandri Rodríguez, Jorge I 124, 127
Alexander (Serbian king) VIII 45
Alexander, Harold IV 149, 181; V 73, 125
    Italian campaign IV 144

Alexandria, Egypt VII 147
    construction of sewage plants in VII 148
Algeciras, Spain, conference in (1906) VIII 32
Algeria I 151, 281; VI 83, 103, 106–107, 188; VII 82
    colonial policy of French VI 80, 136
    coup in (1958) VI 106
    environmental law in VII 145
    independence from France I 278
Algiers Conference (1973) VI 268
al-Husayni, Muhammed Amin VII 137
All Quiet on the Western Front (1929) VIII 55, 59, 188,
    264
All-American Canal VII 154–155
Allen, Richard VI 229, 231
Allenby, Edmund VIII 37, 39, 41, 121, 213, 216
Allende Gossens, Salvador I 26, 68, 123–125, 127–
    140; VI 64, 86–87, 265
Alliance for Progress I 17–26, 126, 132; II 115
Allied Expeditionary Force (AEF) V 20, 23, 25
Allied Mediterranean Expeditionary Force VIII 119
Allies IV 208–215; V 27–33
    relationship of IV 209; V 34–47
    strategy IV 143–150; V 19–26
All-Russian Council of Soviets VIII 171
Alpine Regional Hydroelectric Group VII 98
Alps VII 229, 231
Alsace-Lorraine VIII 71–72, 76, 151, 180, 226, 232,
    234–237, 280–281
Altmühl River VII 204–207
Amalgamated Clothing Workers Union III 191
Amazon River VII 235
Ambrose, Stephen I 214, II 50
America First movement V 135–136
American Civil Liberties Union (ACLU) II 283; III
    39; V 224
    Scopes Trial III 33
    Scottsboro case III 185
American Coalition of Life Activists (ACLA) II 223
American Communist Party III 221, 223–226
American culture
    frontier and exploration as symbols of II 245
    hegemony II 213
    spread of II 213
American Eugenics Society III 21–22
American Expeditionary Force (AEF) VIII 10–25, 182,
    300
    Catholics in VIII 205
    effect of gas on VIII 239
    women nurses in VIII 130
American Farm Bureau Federation III 159
American Federation of Labor (AFL) II 188; III 183
    attitudes toward opium III 134
    reasons for decline III 195
American Federation of Labor-Congress of Industrial
    Organizations (AFL-CIO) II 190; VI 237
American Federation of State, County, and Municipal
    Employees (AFSCME) II 190–191
American Federation of Teachers II 190
American Independent Party II 180
American Indian Defense Association (AIDA) III 141
American Institute of Public Opinion (AIPO) III 66
American Jewish Committee II 24
American Labor Party II 197
American Management Association III 68
American Medical Association (AMA) II 221
American Party
    1968 presidential race II 281
American Revolution (1775–1783) I 88
American River VII 29
Amin, Hafizullah I 10–12, 15; VI 165–166
Amin, Idi VI 83
Amnesty International I 146
Amphibians VII 216–217
Anatolian Plain VII 10
Anarchism VIII 254
Anarcho-Syndicalism VIII 254
Anatolia VIII 189, 211–214
    Christians in VIII 211

Islamic rule in VIII 211
Anderson, Sherwood III 177
Andre, Louis VIII 151
Andropov, Yuri I 13; II 60; VI 111, 116, 226, 239
    domestic programs I 197
    foreign policy I 186
    views on Afghan war I 13
Angleton, James Jesus I 66
Anglican Church, in World War I VIII 202
Anglo-American Corporation VII 5
Anglo-American Financial Agreement (1945) VI 79
Anglo-American Mutual Aid Agreement (1942) VI 78
Anglo-Boer War (1899–1902) VIII 34, 73, 103, 200,
    272
    opposition to VIII 77
Anglo-German naval rivalry VIII 29–36
Anglo-Iranian Oil Company I 69; VI 255
Anglo-Irish Treaty (1921) VIII 158, 160
Angola I 95, 105, 152; II 56; VI 7, 44, 50, 65–66, 83,
    87, 165, 178, 188, 194, 221–222, 241, 256,
    261, 265; VII 236, 239
    Cuban troops in VI 41, 43
    Portuguese immigration to VII 237
    Soviet support I 185
    withdrawal of Cuban troops VI 7
Annie Hamilton Brown Wild Life Sanctuary VII 277
Anschluss (political union, 1938) IV 19–20, 126, 191,
    224; V 293
    European reactions to IV 127
Anthony, Susan B. II 74; III 199
Anti-Ballistic Missile (ABM) Treaty (1972) I 199, 200,
    227, 231; II 61, 171; VI 18, 30, 35, 43
anti-ballistic missiles (ABMs) VI 17
Anti-Comintern Pact (1936) V 115, 229
anticommunism V 114
    as concensus builder II 211
    domestic II 211
    impact on labor movement II 189
    influence on foreign policy II 205
    legislation II 131
    propaganda II 130
anti-nuclear weapons protests VI 15, 22
    impact on Soviet policy VI 17
Anti-Saloon League III 262
anti-Semitism III 252, 254; IV 137, 139; VI 88; VIII
    61
    impact on Nazi collaboration IV 131
Anti-Submarine Detection Investigation Committee
    VIII 196
Anti-Tactical Ballistic Missiles (ATBM) I 195
Anti-Tank Guided Missiles (ATGMs) VI 172
antiwar movement II 159, 161
    demonstrations II 3
    impact on American politics II 3
Apache helicopter VI 173
apartheid II 20, 100; VI 6; VII 5, 7
Appolinaire, Guillame VIII 191
Apollo 8 (1968) II 257–258
Apollo 11 (1969) II 258
Apollo 12 (1969) II 259
Apollo Theatre III 188
appeasement I 300; IV 16–21
Arab-American Corporation (ARAMCO) II 145
Arab Higher Committee for Palestine VII 137
Arab-Israeli War (1967) II 142, 148, 150; VI 31
Arab-Israeli War (1973) VII 136
Arab League VI 135, 161
Arab nationalism VI 161, 163
Arab oil embargo (1973) VI 107
Arab Revolt (1916) VIII 37–42, 214
Arabia VIII 37, 41, 212
Arabian peninsula VIII 38
Arabic (British ship), sinking of VIII 288
Arafat, Yasser I 159
Aravalli Mountains VII 125
Arbenz Guzmán, Jacobo I 24, 49, 66, 93, 123–126,
    129–131, 211
    Guatemala I 70

overthrow of government in Guatemala III 53
Arcadia Conference (1941-1942) IV 209, 212; V 38
Arendt, Hannah I 135; III 103; V 166
Arévalo, Juan José I 24, 123, 126
Argentina I 24, 54, 94; VI 194, 266
    Communist guerrilla movements I 125
    human rights record I 143
    in War of the Triple Alliance I 125
    military coups I 26
    nuclear nonproliferation I 224
    nuclear weapons development I 219, 223
    reduction of U.S. military aid I 141
    war with Great Britain VI 8, 13
Arias, Oscar VI 191
Arias peace process VI 194
Arizona VII 211-212, 214-216
    water policy in VII 108-115, 152-153
Arizona v. *California* (2000) VII 168, 290-303
Arkansas River VII 10-16
Arkhipov, Ivan VI 44
Arlington Dam (United States) VII 54
Armenia VIII 41, 208, 212, 214, 216
    mandate in VIII 12
    massacres in VIII 216
    occupies Caucasia VIII 217
    Soviet Republic VIII 214
    war against populace VIII 213
arms race I 180-187, 262; II 49, 56, 65
Armstrong, Louis "Satchmo" II 218; III 79
Armstrong, Neil II 257, 259
Army of Northern Virginia VIII 49
Army of the Republic of Vietnam (ARVN) VI 98-99
Army War College, Carlisle Barracks, Pennsylvania VIII 16
Arnold, Henry Harley "Hap" V 5, 51, 88, 91, 98-99
Arrowrock Dam (United States) VII 26
artillery VIII 52, 56, 61, 68, 110, 112-115, 180, 220, 272, 275
    boring of VIII 199
    Prussian VIII 67
    United States VIII 16-17
Arun Dam (Nepal) VII 9
Asia VI 77, 79, 189, 201, 264, 271
Askaris VIII 84-85, 87, 90
Asmal, Kader VII 9
Aspinall, Wayne Norviel VII 114
Asquith, Herbert VIII 77-78, 81-82, 103-104, 106, 155, 161-162
Assad, Hafiz al- I 163, 314
Association of Professional NGOs for Social Assistance in Baia Mare (ASSOC) VII 252
Association of South-East Asian Nations (ASEAN) VI 271
Astoria, Oregon VII 53
Aswan Dam II 146, 148
Aswan High Dam (Egypt) VII 3
Ataturk, Kemal VIII 118, 211-214
Atchafalaya River VII 161
Atkins, J. D. C. VII 56
Atlanta Exposition (1895) III 268, 271
Atlantic Charter (1941) I 301; II 99; V 45, 146-149; VI 9, 78-79
atmospheric nuclear testing VI 16
atomic bomb II 228; III 10, 16; V 48-55; VI 20, 57, 136, 154, 254-255; VIII 195
    American I 260, 262-263
    Anglo-American cooperation on VI 10
    data passed to Soviet Union II 231
    development V 44
    Hiroshima and Nagasaki III 10
    impact on World War II II 268; III 11
    introduction I 4
    Soviet Union development of II 229
    "Stockholm Appeal" II 47
Atomic Energy Act (1946) I 220-221
Atomic Energy Act (1954) VII 175
Atomic Energy Commission (AEC) I 27, 29-31, 214, 220; II 82; VII 174-175, 178

Atoms for Peace I 216-217, 221; II 51
Attaturk Dam (Turkey) VII 82
Attlee, Clement VI 11, 250
Attorney General's List I 76
Auchinleck, Sir Claude John Eyre V 76, 172
Audubon Society VII 31, 258
Auden, Wystan VIII 191
Aufmarschplan I (Deployment Plan I) VIII 247
Aufmarschplan II (Deployment Plan II) VIII 247-248
August Revolution (1945) V 146
Aurul SA cyanide spill (Romania) VII 248-250, 252-255
Auschwitz I 138; III 253-254, 256; V 54, 56-57, 60, 158, 160-163, 219; VIII 94
    theories of formation V 156
Australia VI 136; VIII 33, 133, 137, 160-161, 208
    grain reserves VIII 290
    motivation of soldiers VIII
    World War I VIII 54, 117-123, 220
Australia (Australian ship) VIII 137
Australian and New Zealand Army Corps (ANZAC) VIII 121-122
Austria I 253, 293; VI 136; VIII 18, 82, 106, 251-252, 266, 281
    alliance with Germany (1879) VIII 35
    Central European Model I 108
    contribution of Jews in VIII 167
    customs union with Germany forbidden VIII 283
    dam agreement with Hungary VII 101
    dams in VII 101
    East German emigration through VI 118, 121
    occupation I 108
    pre-World War I alliances VIII 225-231
    Socialists in VIII 260
    supports Slovak anti-nuclear activists VII 103
    union with Nazi Germany VIII 284
Austria-Hungary VIII 76, 95, 98, 104, 172, 178, 226, 228, 230, 266-267, 280, 299
    army, size of VIII 69
    collapse of VIII 216-217
    invades Poland VIII 72
    invades Serbia VIII 72
    relations with Germany concerning Slavic lands VIII 94
    Socialists in VIII 257, 261
    World War I VIII 11, 43-49
        casualties VIII 125, 268
        defense budget VIII 44
        Jews in VIII 164
        mobilization in VIII 125
        motivation of soldiers VIII 266
        war against the United States VII 11
Auténtico Party I 91
automobile
    impact on interstate highway development II 106
    impact on United States II 109
    recreation II 108
Axis I 3; V 62-67
    defeat in Tunisia IV 144
    North African campaign V 66
    parallel war theory V 63-65
Azerbaijan VI 255; VIII 96, 216

B

B-1 bomber I 191; II 57
B-1B "Lancer" supersonic nuclear bomber VI 109, 234
B-17 bomber V 4, 5, 6, 98
B-17C bomber V 5
B-17E bomber V 5
B-24 bomber V 7, 98
B-26 bomber V 5
B-29 bomber V 3, 7, 49, 52,
B-36 bomber I 3- 8
B-52 I 189, 193
B-58 I 193

Babbitt (1922) II 109; III 177
Baby Boomers VI 24–25
Baby M II 80
Back to Africa movement III 121
Backfire bomber VI 259
Bacon, Francis VI 195
Badoglio, Marshall Pietro V 178
    Italian campaign IV 144
Baghdad Pact (1955) I 161, 277; II 146
    Iraq I 277
    Turkey I 277
Baghdad Railway VIII 212
Baia Mare Environmental Protection Agency VII 248,
    253
Baia Mare Task Force VII 248, 252, 254
Baia Mare, Romania VII 247, 249, 253, 255
Baker v. Carr (1962) II 139, 281–282, 286
Baker, Newton VIII 17–18
Bakunin, Mikhail Aleksandrovich VI 179
Bakuninist anarchists VI 178
balance of power VI 45
Balcones Escarpment VII 70
Baldwin, James II 90–91; III 82
Baldwin, Prime Minister Stanley V 120; VIII 168, 190
Balfour Declaration (1917) VIII 37, 41, 163, 166, 168,
    208
Balfour, Arthur VIII 16, 168
Balkan League VIII 212
Balkan Wars VIII 39, 43–45, 117, 211, 214, 230
Balkans I 289; V 68–78; VI 50, 272; VII 82; VIII 76,
    80, 95, 106, 226, 228, 252
    as second front V 75– 76
    Christians in VIII 211
    genocide in VI 216
    Islamic rule in VIII 211
    Soviet influence I 304
    World War I VII 43–49
Ballistic Missile Defense (BMD) I 186, 195–203, 225
    technological problems I 199–200
Baltic Sea VII 18, 148; VIII 75
    salmon populations in VII 90
    submarines in VIII 292
Baltic States VI 133, 218, 251
Bandung Conference (1955) VI 267, 269
Banking Act (1935) III 59
Bao Dai I 290; V 146, 148; VI 98
Barada River VII 81
Barbusse, Henri VIII 59, 188
Barcelona Convention VII 143–145
Bargi Project (India) VII 132
Barmen Declaration (1934) IV 189
Barnes, Michael D. VI 193
Baruch, Bernard I 27, 29–30, 220; VIII 296
Baruch Plan (1946) I 27– 32, 216, 220, 258
Basic Principles of Relations (U.S.-Soviet) VI 43
Basie, Count II 214
Basutoland VII 237, 241
Bataan Death March (1942) V 152, 183
Batista y Zaldívar, Fulgencio I 49, 91–92, 121, 275; II
    266; III 51; VI 63, 141
Battles—
    —Amiens (1918) VIII 54, 56–57, 194
    —Antietam (1862) VIII 67
    —the Atlantic (1939–1945) IV 261; V 46, 79–82,
        131, 176, 180; V 85
    —Anzio (1944) VIII 223
    —Argonne Forest (1918) VIII 10, 20, 25
    —Arras (1917) VIII 223
    —Artois (1915) VIII 110
    —Atlanta (1864) VIII 68
    —Austerlitz (1805) VIII 67
    —Avranches (1944) V 125
    —Belleau Wood (1918) VIII 27
    —Bolimov (1915) VIII 242
    —Britain (1940) IV 168; V 4, 80, 106, 124, 135,
        152, 176, 261; V 96
    —Broodseinde (1917) VIII 220

    —the Bulge (1944–1945) IV 44, 51, 64, 184; V 2,
        13, 21–23, 129
    —Cambrai (1917) VIII 52–53, 56, 112–113, 221
    —Cannae (216 B.C.E.) VIII 72, 179, 249
    —Cantigny (1918) VIII 15
    —Caporetto (1917) VIII 52, 221
    —Caucasia (1914) VIII 216
    —Champagne (1915) VIII 110
    —Chemin des Dames (1917) VIII 104, 149
    —Cold Harbor (1864) VIII 67
    —Coral Sea (1942) IV 2, 6
    —Coronel (1914) VIII 133, 135, 137
    —Cuito Cuanavale (1987) I 96; VI 7
    —Dien Bien Phu (1954) I 70; II 266; VI 106, 136
    —El Alamein (1943) IV 180; V 176, 179, 181
    —Falkland Islands (1914) VIII 133, 137
    —Flanders Offensive (1917) VIII 77
    —Franklin (1864) VIII 60
    —Fredericksburg (1862) VIII 77
    —Gallipoli (1915) VIII 38, 40, 104, 106, 117–123,
        162, 166, 213, 216, 264
    —Gettysburg (1863) VIII 67–68
    —Guadalcanal (1942-1943) V 132, 196, 199
    —Hamel (1918) VIII 57
    —Isandhlwana (1879) VIII 200
    —Isonzo (1915–1917) VIII 113, 125, 264
    —Iwo Jima V 52, 199; VIII 60
    —Jutland (1916) VIII 72, 289, 292
    —Kasserine Pass (1942) V 124
    —Khalkin Gol (1938) V 136
    —Kut-al-Amara (1916) VIII 216
    —Le Cateau (1914) VIII 252
    —Loos (1915) VIII 239, 243, 272, 276
    —Lorraine (1914) VIII 179–185, 274
    —Ludendorff Offensive (1918) VIII 55, 112
    —Malvern Hill (1862) VIII 67
    —Marengo (1800) VIII 67
    —Marne (1914) VIII 20, 114, 180, 182, 184, 199,
        246, 253
    —Mars-la-Tour (1870) VIII 75
    —Masurian Lakes (1914) VIII 114, 252, 268
    —Meggido (1918) VIII 41, 216
    —Menin Road (1917) VIII 219
    —Messines (1917) VIII 219
    —Metz (1870) VIII 71
    —Meuse-Argonne (1918) VIII 17, 19, 23, 25, 27,
        114, 301
    —Midway (1942) IV 2, 6; V 5, 132, 196
    —Mons (1914) VIII 252
    —Moscow (1941–1942) VI 40
    —Mukden (1905) VIII 75
    —North Africa (1940–1943) V 80
    —Neuve-Chapelle (1915) VIII 110, 242, 272, 276
    —Nivelle Offensive (1917) VIII 107, 114, 218, 223,
        269
    —Okinawa (1945) V 52; VIII 60
    —Papua, New Guinea V 199
    —Passchendaele (1917) VIII 80, 102, 104, 104,
        111, 186, 218–224
    —Petersburg (1864) VIII 23, 68
    —the Philippines V 199
    —Polygon Wood (1917) VIII 219
    —Riga (1917) VIII 52, 112
    —Salonika (1918) VIII 104, 149, 212, 216
    —Sarikamish (1914) VIII 216
    —Second Aisne (1917) VIII 114
    —Second Ypres (1915) VIII 200
    —Sedan (1870) VIII 67
    —Soissons (1918) VIII 17, 27, 54–55
    —Somme (1916) VIII 14, 19, 52, 56, 61, 67, 78, 80,
        103, 106, 111, 113–114, 125, 128–129, 143,
        158, 186–187, 200, 203, 218, 223–224, 239,
        266, 268, 271–276, 289
    —Spring Offensive (1918) VIII 201, 241, 244, 266
    —St. Mihiel (1918) VIII 17, 19, 25
    —Saipan V 52
    —Stalingrad (1942–1943) V 132, 179; VIII 139
    —Suez Canal (1915) VIII 213, 216

INDEX

—Tanga (1914) VIII 85, 89
—Tannenberg (1914) VIII 114, 268
—Third Gaza (1917) VIII 121
—Third Ypres (1917) VIII 52, 104, 107, 111, 187, 203, 218–224, 240 *see also* Passchendaele
—Trafalgar (1805) VIII 33, 196
—Verdun (1916) VIII 19, 60–61, 67, 106, 110–111, 113–114, 125, 128–129, 143, 186–187, 191, 224, 239–240, 266, 268, 272–273
—Wagram (1809) VIII 67
—Waterloo (1815) VIII 67–68, 160
—Ypres (1914–1915) VIII 67, 182, 239, 242
Bautista Sacasa, Juan VI 190
Bavaria VII 204–205; VIII 209
    Ministry for Development and Environmental Issues VII 206
    separatist movement in VIII 280
Bay of Bengal VIII 133, 137
Bay of Biscay V 238
Bay of Pigs (1961) I 66, 70, 89, 92, 94, 129; II 115, 247, 266; VI 64, 66, 71, 131, 139, 141
Beard, Charles VIII 284
Beas River VII 130
the Beatles
    "Beatlemania" II 18
    "Rubber Soul" II 215
    Bob Dylan as influence II 215
Bechuanaland Protectorate VII 34
Beckmann, Max VIII 188, 191
Beef Protocol VII 34, 37
Begin, Menachem VI 163
Beirut, Lebanon VII 81
Bekáa Valley VII 79, 81
Belarus VI 54, 215, 218; VIII 97, 278
    surrender of nuclear weapons to Russian Federation I 220
    U.N. I 285
Belgian Relief Commission VIII 98
Belgium VI 77, 183, 188, 264; VIII 24, 67, 71, 97, 110, 155, 162, 179, 182–184, 203, 205, 208, 230, 235, 237, 245–246, 248, 251, 280, 283
    Army VIII 184
    Brussels Treaty I 208
    German invasion of VIII 72, 110, 203, 206, 232, 238
    loss of African colonies VIII 280
    occupies Ruhr VIII 285
    postwar influence of Communist parties I 174
    submarine bases in VIII 134
    troops in Africa, World War I VII 84, 86
Belgrade VII 248
Belgrade Conference for Foreign Ministers (1978) VI 268
Bellevue, Washington VII 189, 191
Bellotti v. *Baird* (1979) II 222
Belorussia
    U.N. membership I 300
Benelux countries VI 275
Benedict XV VII 206, 209
Ben-Gurion, David I 278, 281
Beria, Lavrenty I 38; VI 255
    nuclear spying I 184
    Soviet nuclear weapons development I 238, 245
Berchtold, Leopold VIII 46, 228
Berlin I 33, 119–120; II 171; VI 73, 142, 169, 252
    airlift (1948) II 42, 264; V 149; VI 9
    blockade of (1948) II 36, 66; VI 49, 133, 141, 173, 177, 252, 255
    bombing of V 5
    German attack on (1945) VI 169
    Soviet capture of VI 251
Berlin Crisis (1958–1959) I 33–39, 168 169; VI 104
Berlin Crisis (1961) I 171
Berlin Wall I 120; II 66; VI 51, 64, 104, 115, 118, 122, 142, 235
    erection I 34
    fall of VI 51, 111
    last E. German fugitive killed at VI 118

Berlin West Africa Conference (1885) VI 267
Bermuda Conference (1943) III 252
Bessmertnykh, Alexander A. VI 223
Bethmann Hollweg, Theobald VII 143, 164, 289,
Betts v. *Brady* (1942) II 290
Bevin, Ernest VI 101
Bhakhra Dam (India) VII 130
Bhopal, India (1984) II 86
Bidault, Georges I 175, 273; VI 101
Biddle, Francis V 187–188, 224
Big Bend Dam (United States) VII 31
Big Brother and the Holding Company II 219
Billboard II 217
    charts II 214
    classifications of music II 214
    music categories II 218
Biltmore Conference (1942) II 145
bioengineering II 83–85
bipartisanship II 195
    vs. concensus II 205
bipolarity VI 213
birds—
    bald eagle VII 215, 220, 234
    Black Capped Vireo VII 72
    brown-headed cowbird VII 216
    ducks VII 277
    European Starling VII 216
    Golden Cheeked Warbler VII 72
    in Pacific flyway VII 151
    in the Atlantic flyway VII 277
    kingfisher VII 205
    southwestern willow flycatcher VII 211, 216
    spotted owl VII 226
    western yellow-billed cuckoo VII 215
    white-tailed sea eagle VII 252–253
    Yuma clapper rail VII 215
birth control pill II 224–240
Biscayne Bay VII 266
Bismarck, Otto von VI 9; VIII 35, 137, 207, 226, 249
Bizonia VI 101
Black, Hugo II 280, 284; III 105
Black Death (1347–1351) VIII 61, 189
Black Manhattan (1930) III 122
black nationalism II 89, 93; III 120
Black Panthers II 89, 165, 197
    demonstration at the California State Assembly (1967) II 94
    Party for Self-Defense II 94
Black Power II 24, 93–95, 162
Black Power conference (1966) II 93, 95
Black Power movement III 120
Black Sea VII 104, 148, 204–205, 210, 247
    submarines in VIII 292
    time needed to flush pollution from VII 142
Black Sea Fleet VIII 33, 280
Black Sharecroppers Union II 197
Black Student Union II 94
Blackboard Jungle (1955) II 214, 219
Blackman, Harry A. II 221, 225
Blanco River, Texas VII 72
Blanquistes VI 178
Blatnik, John Anton VII 258, 268
Bletchley Park IV 261, 263
Blitzkrieg (lightning war) IV 23–32, 54, 56, 100, 105, 167, 282; V 102, 118, 228
Bloomer, Amelia III 167
Blue Gold Report VII 285
Blunt, Anthony VI 11
Bohr, Niels
    Soviet nuclear spying I 241–242, 247–248
Bokassa, Jean Bédel VI 83
Boland Amendments I 54; VI 58, 61, 193, 195, 231
Boland, Edward Patrick VI 61
Boldt, George VII 199
Bolivia I 21, 95, 125–126; VI 50, 178
Bolling v. *Sharpe* (1950) II 137
Bolshevik Revolution (1917) I 73; VIII 82, 98, 223

Bolsheviks VI 244, 247; VIII 95, 171, 173, 175–176, 178, 255, 258, 260–261, 269, 278
Bolshevism VIII 209, 295
Bomber gap I 188–189, 191, 193; VI 35
bomber offensive V 86–92
    Battle of Hamburg (1943) V 87–88
    Dresden raids (1945) V 92
    Pacific theater V 89, 91–92
Bonaparte, Napoleon I 167; VIII 30, 47, 49, 66–67, 71, 132, 194, 196, 199, 233–234, 237, 266
Bonneville Dam (United States) VII 29, 31, 53, 57, 60, 198
Bonneville Power Administration VII 55, 202, 223
bore-hole technology VII 34, 62–68
Bosch, Hieronymus VIII 204
Bosch Gavíño, Juan I 24, 71
Bosnia VI 51, 53, 213, 217, 225; VIII 11, 44, 230
    lack of environmental control in VII 145
Bosnian Crisis (1908) VIII 43–45, 226, 228
Bosporus Straits VI 255; VIII 214, 216
Bossert, Wayne VII 187
Boston VII 256, 261–262
Boston Tea Party (1773) III 219
Botswana VI 83; VII 236, 243
    fences in VII 33–39
Botswana Meat Commission (BMC) VII 33
Boulanger, Georges VIII 147, 152
Boulder Dam (United States) VII 28–29, 109
Boundary Waters Treaty (1909) VII 116–117, 120
Bowker, W. K. VII 158
Bowman, Isaiah VII 47
Boxer Rebellion (1900) III 136; VIII 87
Bradley armored personnel carrier VI 241
Bradley, Omar N. I 6; V 15, 21, 23, 102, 125–126, 129, 136
Brandeis, Justice Louis D. II 280; III 25–27, 207
Brandenberg v. *Ohio* (1969) II 281
Brandt, Willy I 35; VI 59, 206–208, 210–211
    treaty with Soviets I 185
    visit to Moscow VI 207, 211
Brauchitsch, Walter von V 127, 143
Brazil I 15, 20, 25, 125, 143, 219, 223; VI 215, 266
Brazzaville Conference (1944) V 171
Brecht, Berthold VI 229
Breckenridge, Henry VIII 301
Bredehoeft, John VII 182
Brennan, William II 221, 282
Bretton Woods Conference (1944) VI 78, 144
Bretton Woods finance system VI 204
Brezhnev Doctrine I 10–11; VI 43, 118
Brezhnev, Leonid I 104, 151, 153, 197; II 69, 169; VI 21, 43, 68, 75, 111, 116, 163, 184, 226, 239
Brezhnev-Nixon summit (1972) II 170
Briand, Aristide VIII 255
Bridge Canyon Dam (United States) VII 30, 109
Brissenden, Richard B. VII 158
Bristol Bay, Alaska VII 197
British Expeditionary Force (BEF) VIII 71, 77, 79, 102–103, 106, 110, 219–224, 252, 265, 271–276
    chaplains in VIII 203
    use of tanks VIII 51–58
British Guiana I 15, 24, 125; VI 96
British North America Act (Constitution Act, 1867) VII 117
British-United States Agreement (BRUSA) VI 11
Brittain, Vera VIII 266
Brodie, Bernard I 165; II 65
Brooke, Sir Alan Francis V 43, 76
Brooke, Rupert VIII 188
Brooks, William K. VII 40, 43, 46–47
Broom and Whisk Makers Union II 191
Brotherhood of Sleeping Car Porters II 189, 217–218
Brower, David Ross VII 110, 112
Brown, Harold VI 42–43
Brown v. *Board of Education of Topeka, Kansas* (1954) II 20, 23–24, 26, 45, 80, 90–91, 136–143, 270, 280, 286, 293, 295; III 27, 185

Brusilov, Aleksey VIII 266
Brussels Treaty (1954) I 208; VI 101
Bryan, William Jennings III 32, 34, 36–37; VIII 204
    Scopes Trial III 33
Brzezinski, Zbigniew I 135, 143, 146; VI 42, 166, 256, 263
Buchenwald V 57
    German people's reaction V 215
Buck v. *Bell* (1927) III 18, 21
Buddhist monks, immolation of VI 23
Bulganin, Nikolai A. VI 135
Bulgaria I 107, 294; II 39, 153; VI 251–252, 261, 274, 276, 280; VIII 11, 14, 44, 46, 95, 212, 216–217, 230
    ally of Germany VIII 278
    U.S. push for greater freedoms I 110
    U.S. recognizes communist government I 303
Bull Moose Party III 243
Bund Deutscher Mädel (German Girls' Organization) IV 191
Bund Naturschutz in Bayern (BUND) VII 206, 210
Bundestag (Federal Diet) VI 102
Bundy, McGeorge I 29, 294; II 6
    flexible response I 120
    use of nuclear weapons policy I 171
Bureau of Indian Affairs (BIA) III 141, 143; VII 55–56, 59, 166–167, 169, 172
Burger, Justice Warren E. II 182, 221, 284
Burgess, Guy I 243, 245; VI 11
Burma VIII 35
    fall of V 197
    opium trade I 15
Burundi II 101, 155
Bush, George VI 28, 51, 58, 61, 191, 195, 205, 226, 229, 242, 257
    Africa policy VI 7
    civil war in Somalia II 155
    foreign policy "balance of power" II 155
    international political experience II 152
    New World Order II 152–158
    nuclear nonproliferation policy I 224
    Panama intervention II 155
    Persian Gulf crisis II 153
    relationship with former Yugoslavia II 155
    role of United States II 155
    U.S. spying on Soviet Union I 191
    unilateral U.S. foreign policy II 156
Bush, George W. VII 224
Bush (George Sr.) administration II 100; VI 120
    arms-control agreements VI 20
    defense spending VI 224
    envisionment of New World Order II 155
    nuclear-nonproliferation policy I 217
    policy on Afgahnistan I 14–16
Bushido code III 13
Butler, Justice Pierce III 25
Byrnes, James F. I 28, 31, 263, 304; II 206; V 51, 53

C

Cabora Bassa Dam (Mozambique) VII 237, 239, 240
Cairncross, John VI 11
    Soviet nuclear spying I 243–245
Cairo Conference (1943) VI 146
California VII 180, 201
    dams in VII 27, 29
    Department of Fish and Game VII 178
    environmental activism in VII 174
    flood control in VII 273
    pollution control in VII 264
    receives federal swamplands VII 272
    water policy in VII 153
California Aqueduct VII 179
California Coastal Commission VII 175, 179
California Development Company (CDC) 155
Calueque Dam (Angola) VII 239
Cambodia I 40–47, 145, 289, 299; II 6, 177; VI 4, 44, 60, 63, 65, 68, 83, 93, 188, 194, 203, 221

as a colony of France I 290
 Khmer Rouge movement I 15; VI 271
 spread of communism I 297
 supply lines through VI 60
 U.S. bombing of I 183, 291; VI 86
 U.S. invasion of I 291; VI 23, 26, 165, 284
 Vietnam invasion of VI 44
Camp David agreement (1978) I 159
Camp Gordon, Georgia VIII 23, 299
Canada I 30–31; VI 101, 136; VII 182; VIII 33, 83,
    160–161, 208
 Atomic Energy Act I 221
 charter member of NATO I 208
 criticism of Libertad Act I 98
 Cuban investment I 97
 discussion of nuclear weapons I 28
 fish hatcheries in VII 202
 fishing rights in VIII 35
 grain reserves VIII 290
 motivation of World War I soldiers VIII 266
 policy on cleaning Great Lakes VII 116–124
 relations with United States VII 116–124
 social programs in VI 187
 World War I VIII 220
Canada Water Bill (1969) VII 119–120
Canada-Ontario Agreement (COA) VII 120
Cape Colony VIII
capitalism II 30–31, 34, 56–57, 60; III 63, 191, 194–195
 capitalist encirclement II 39
 capitalist system III 190
Cárdenas, Lazaro VII 155
 expropriates lands of Colorado River Land
     Company VII 152
 pushes against agricultural production VII 153
Cardozo, Justice Benjamin III 25, 28
Carmichael, Stokely II 79, 93, 95, 165
Carnegie Endowment for International Peace VI 123–
    124, 129
Carpathian Ruthenia VI 244
Carranza, Venustiano III 126–129
Carriage Workers Union II 191
Carribean VI 103
 British interests in VIII 33
 Soviet influence in VI 261
 U.S. policy in VI 140
Carson, Edward VIII 161–162
Carson, Rachel VII 86, 160, 162, 278
Carter, Jimmy I 48–52, 101, 106, 141, 317; II 57–58,
    97–98, 199, 204, 278; III 48; VI 20, 30,
    109, 166, 193, 222, 226, 229, 232, 236, 241,
    256, 270
 Africa policy VI 1
 China policy VI 42–43
 emphasis on human rights II 100–101
 grain embargo against Russia VI 241
 human-rights policy VI 190
 mediator between Egypt and Israel I 159
 post-presidential career II 100
 response to Soviet invasion of Afghanistan I 11
 support to El Salvador VI 193
 suspends aid to Pakistan I 218
 withdrawal of SALT II Treaty I 10, 12
Carter administration I 50; II 67, 103; VI 2, 35, 56,
    229, 261, 263
 Central America policy I 54
 Chile I 141
 China policy VI 41
 containment policy I 13
 defense cuts VI 201
 détente I 102
 emphasis on human rights I 140–146
 foreign policy I 52, 57
 human rights I 52; VI 43
 Iran crisis VI 166, 226
 Iran embassy rescue disaster VI 232
 limited-nuclear-war doctrine I 171
 military spending VI 222
 military under VI 232

Nuclear Nonproliferation Act (1978) I 223
 nuclear-nonproliferation policy I 216
 Olympic boycott VI 107
 Pershing II missile deployment VI 20
 policy on Afghanistan I 10, 12, 15–16
 policy on Nicaragua VI 190, VI 191
 policy on Pakistan I 15, 223
 Presidential Directive (PD) 59 I 171
 reaction to Soviet invasion of Afghanistan VI 44,
     133, 237
 reaction to Team B VI 256
 SALT II I 191
Carter Doctrine VI 166, 270
Casablanca Conference (1943) IV 144, 214; V 46, 85,
    252, 270, 272, 275
Cascades Canal VII 52
Cascades Mountains VII 52, 56, 189
Casey, William I 50–51, 54; II 57; VI 231, 239
Caspian Sea VIII 91, 216
Castillo Armas, Carlos I 123, 126
Castro, Fidel I 49, 89, 91–96, 121, 283; II 120, 260,
    266; VI 4, 7, 24, 63–68, 71, 139–142, 185,
    192
 Bay of Pigs II 115
 Cuban Missile Crisis II 116
 Cuban revolution I 275
 relationship with Soviet Union II 116
 support for communist uprising in Bolivia I 126
 takeover in Cuba I 17
Castro Ruz, Raul VI 70
Catholic Church I 305; VI 170; VIII 202–203, 205,
    208–209
 criticism of communism I 271
 influence on society II 164
 opinion of/relationship with Hitler IV 187, 190
 relationship with Nazi Party IV 33–39
 Second Vatican Council (1963) II 164
Caucasus Mountains VIII 96, 212–213, 280
Ceauçescu, Nicolae VI 51, 88, 265; VII 250, 254
Celilo Falls, Oregon VII 29, 55, 60
Center for International Environmental Law VII 9
Central African Empire VI 83; VIII 280
Central America I 48–57; VI 131, 265, 283
Central Arizona Project (CAP) VII 108–109, 112, 114
Central Asia VI 109, 162, 165, 248
Central Committee of the French Communist Party VII
    97
Central Europe
 impact of anticanal protest VII 206
 Rhine-Main-Danube Canal VII 204–210
Central High School, Little Rock, Arkansas II 20–52
Central Intelligence Agency (CIA) I 49, 64–71, 92, 94,
    119, 191, 211, 263; II 5, 52, 54, 57, 63, 69,
    103, 115, 152, 178, 260; VI 6, 24, 57, 61, 64,
    96, 133, 151, 188, 231, 260
 anti-Sandinista forces I 54
 assessment of Soviet military strength VI 257,
     259
 covert operations in British Guiana I 24
 covert operations in Chile I 124, 131; VI 86–87
 covert operations in Guatemala I 123, 131
 covert operations in Latin America I 26
 Operation Mongoose II 120
 origins I 64, 74
 plot to overthrow Castro I 275
 Rosenberg records II 230
 supply of Angolan rebels VI 1
 support of contras VI 237
 training of anti-Castro Cubans in Guatemala VI
     141
Central Powers VI 176; VIII 18, 22, 117, 133, 172–
    173, 221, 242, 251, 278, 290, 295
 collapse of VIII 267
 motivation of World War I soldiers VIII 266
Central Utah Project (CUP) VII 31
Central Valley Project VII 29
Ceyhan River VII 79
Chaco War (1932–1935) I 125

Chagall, Marc VIII 191
Chamberlain, Neville IV 17, 20, 125; V 117, 169
    appeasement policy IV 18
    Ten Year Rule IV 21
Chambers, Whittaker II 130; III 34; VI 123–129
Chamorro, Violeta Barrios de VI 191, 195
Chandelier Workers Union II 191
Charter 77 movement VI 237
Chechnya
    Soviet operations in VI 169, 218
Chemical warfare V 101–107
    in World War I VIII 239–244
Chernenko, Konstantin I 197; II 60; VI 111, 226
    succeeded by Gorbachev VI 14
Chernobyl (1986) II 86; VII 18, 20, 22, 247
Chesapeake Bay oysters in VII 40–50
Chesapeake Bay 2000 Agreement VII 49
Chesapeake Biological Laboratory VII 47–48
Chetniks VI 275, 277
Chiang Kai-shek I 40, 58, 61, 86, 265–266, 268, 275,
        303–304; II 133, 211; V 191, 194–196; VI
        38, 146, 158, 254
Chicago VII 116, 122, 262
    water supply system in VII 283
Chicano Power II 94
Chief Joseph Dam (United States) VII 53
Chile I 123–128, 140, 152; VI 64, 87, 194, 265–266
    access to Import-Export Bank I 53
    Allende government I 26
    CIA activites in VI 86–87
    coup of 1960s I 26
    human rights record I 143
    U.S. intervention (early 1970s) I 15, 123–133
China I 41, 44, 54, 59, 86–91, 141, 277, 287–288, 292;
        II 4, 9, 36, 39–40, 47, 119, 168, 171; VI 10,
        35, 42, 49, 53, 56, 59, 90, 107, 121, 136, 147,
        154, 175, 178, 181, 199, 201, 203, 213–214,
        243, 265, 271
    accuses Soviets of aiding Vietnam VI 44
    as balance to U.S.S.R VI 201
    attacks on Quemoy and Matsu I 265–270, 275
    attacks Vietnam VI 43
    blue-water navy of VI 53
    bombing of embassy in Belgrade VI 54
    border clashes with Soviet Union VI 40, 43
    defense spending of VI 54
    economy VI 53, 219
    German interests in VIII 31, 137
    human-rights in VI 219
    influence on North Vietnam I 296–297
    Korean War I 273–275
    meeting with United States in Warsaw (1969) VI
        43
    Nationalists I 61
    nuclear espionage of VI 219
    Nuclear Non-Proliferation Treaty I 218
    nuclear proliferation I 222–224
    nuclear weapons development I 222, 239
    purchase of Western military hardware VI 42
    rapprochement with the United States VI 38–45
    relations with Russia VI 53
    relations with Soviet Union VI 38, 113, 203
    Russian threat to British interests in VIII 33
    Soviet role in postwar VI 254
    support for Afghan resistance VI 166
    support for FNLA and UNITA VI 1
    Taiwan-U.S. mutual-security treaty I 268
    Tiananmen Square Massacre (1989) VI 54, 113,
        121
    U.N. Security Council membership I 300
    U.S. intelligence sites in VI 43
    U.S. Ping-Pong team trip VI 43
    U.S. relations with VI 4, 88
China Hands I 58–63; VI 158
Chinese Civil War VI 150
Chinese Communist Party (CCP) VI 181
Chinese Cultural Revolution (1966–1976) VI 40
Chinese Revolution (1949) VI 177

Chlorine gas, effects of VIII 239
Chou En-lai I 266, 269, 277
Christian Democratic Party (CDP)
    in Chile I 124, 127–130
Christmas bombing (1972) VI 28
Christian Church, evangelization of VIII 203
Christmas Truce (1914) VIII 62–63
Chunuk Bair VIII 117–118, 123
Church, Frank VI 61
Church of England
    World War I VIII 203, 208
    World War I chaplains VIII 203
Churchill, Winston I 31, 154, 201, 231, 305; II 32, 39;
        IV 19, 40–45, 144, 148, 210, 213; V 25, 34–
        46, 85, 102, 104, 109, 118, 123, 135–136,
        146, 152, 168, 176, 221–222, 236; VI 8, 78,
        104, 146, 173, 267, 280; VIII 33, 79, 104,
        117–118, 122
    "balance of terror" VI 15
    Balkans V 46, 69–72, 75
    "Iron Curtain" speech (1946) I 286; VI 9, 49,
        250
    military background IV 41–42
    opposition to Operation Anvil/Dragoon V 238–
        241
    Tehran Conference (1943) I 259
    Yalta Agreement (1945) I 300–304
    Yalta Conference (1945) V 309–315
CIA. See Central Intelligence Agency
CIO. See Congress of Industrial Organizations
civil liberties I 73–81
Civil Rights Act (1964) II 25–26, 91, 141, 162, 164,
        192, 277–278, 293
Civil Rights movement II 19–28, 42–48, 80, 89–96,
        159, 162–163, 165, 180, 257; III 181–189,
        268; VI 25, 140
    affirmative action II 143
    connections to labor movement II 189
    March for Jobs and Freedom (1963) II 27
    March on Washington (1963) II 25, 91–92
    media coverage of II 20–22
    President's Committee on Civil Rights (1946) II
        42
    relationship with labor movement II 192
    resistance to II 25, 140
    Scottsboro case III 188
    "separate but equal" doctrine II 137
    use of civil disobedience II 140
    voter registration II 27
Civil War (1861–1865) VI 26, 28, 57; VIII 14, 18, 23,
        25, 68, 136, 149, 199, 226, 296, 299
Civil Works Administration (CWA, 1933) III 154
Civilian Conservation Corps (CCC, 1933) III 154
Clark, Mark W. IV 146; V 125–126, 187
    Italian campaign IV 144
Clark, William P. VI 231
Clark Amendment (1975) VI 1–4
Clay, Lucius I 35–36
Clausewitz, Carl von VIII 16, 71, 112–113, 199
Clean Air Act Amendments (1970) II 183
Clean Water Act (1972) VII 256, 258, 262–264, 267–
        269, 274, 303–305
    reauthorization VII 274
Clemenceau, Georges VIII 11, 19, 78, 147, 149–150,
        256, 278, 283–283
    assassination attempt upon VIII 278
Cleveland VII 116, 122–123, 262, 265
Clifford, Clark M. I 160; II 6, 205
Clifford-Elsey report II 205, 208
Clinton, Bill I 97–98; II 80; VI 8, 58, 61, 231, 235;
        VII 224; VIII 11
    abortion legislation II 223
    and dam protests VII 221
    Dayton accords VI 154
    impact of 1960s on presidency II 163
    Israel I 159
    Lewinsky scandal VI 231
    pro-choice stand II 223

re-election of II 200
Clinton administration
    arms-control agreements VI 20
    defense spending VI 220
    foreign policy of VI 58
    nuclear nonproliferation I 224
    on flood control VII 214
CNN Cold War television series VI 66
Coastal Zone Management Act (1972) II 183
Cobra helicopter VI 173
Colautti v. *Franklin* (1979) II 222
Colby, William E. VI 257
Cold War I 27–32, 82–90, 101–106, 115–122, 148–155,
    165–203, 216–224, 271–276, 300–303; II 4,
    9, 30–63, 68, 104, 163; III 10, 48; V 46, 119,
    145, 149, 191, 199; VI 1–6, 8–11, 30–33,
    108–115, 130–133, 160–162, 168–172, 175–
    178; VII 31, 53, 97, 174, 188
    casualties in VI 50
    causes of VI 252
    conclusion of VI 47–51, 213–216
    dam building in VII 29
    effect of nuclear weapons I 250–257
    end of VI 150, 214
    impact on development of space programs II 241
    impact on federal highway development II 107
    impact on U.S. space program development II
        257
    late 1970s intensification II 172
    military buildup II 43
    mutual assured destruction (MAD) I 251–252
    origins of I 258–264; II 30
    Reagan's role in ending VI 221–241
    Stalin's role in starting VI 250–252
    vindicationist interpretation VI 155
Cole v. *Young* I 80
Collier, John, Commissioner of Indian affairs III 141–
    142
Collins, J. Lawton I 6; V 122
Colorado VII 10, 13, 112, 181, 182
    farmers' use of water in VII 13
    production of crops on irrigated land in VII 11
Colorado River VII 27, 31, 151–153, 155, 168, 211, 214
    dams on VII 108–115, 152
Colorado River Compact (CRC) VII 152–153
Colorado River Irrigation District VII 157
Colorado River Land Company VII 152
Colorado River Storage Project (CRSP) VII 27, 112
Columbia Basin VII 29
    dams in VII 196
Columbia Basin Project VII 202
Columbia River VII 25, 27–28, 31, 51–61, 197, 199,
    202, 219–220, 222, 225, 227
    as salmon producer VII 53
    first major navigation project on VII 52
    hydroelectric dams on VII 198
Columbia River Fisherman's Protective Union VII 53
Columbia River Highway VII 57
Columbia River Inter-Tribal Fish Commission VII 61
Columbia River Packers Association VII 53
Comal River VII 70
combat effectiveness
    Germany V 282, 284
    Japan V 281–282
    Leyte campaign V 281
    Normandy invasion V 282
    psychological limits IV 47–52
    United States V 278–286
Combined Chiefs of Staff (CCS) V 20, 23, 25, 38, 42–
    45
Commission on Polish Affairs VIII 281
Commission on Presidential Debates II 196, 199
Committee on Public Information (CPI) VIII 296
Committee on the Present Danger VI 256, 262
Committee to Re-Elect the President (CREEP) II 177;
    VI 24
Commonwealth of Independent States (CIS) VI 54
Commonwealth of Nations VI 13

communism I 148–155; II 31–32, 56–57, 160; VI 49
    atheism of VI 176
    attraction for women VI 49
    China II 267
    collapse of II 153
    global II 130
    ideology I 258–262; VI 49
    infiltration of federal government II 133
    world domination VI 175–182
Communist Control Act (1954) I 74, 77
Communist Information Bureau (Cominform) I 36–
    113; VI 179, 246
Communist International (Comintern) I 113; III 224,
    226; IV 80; VI 178, 254, 277
Communist Manifesto (1848) VI 178
Communist Party I 74; III 182, 221
    in Chile I 124
    in Guatemala I 123
    of the Soviet Union III 224; VI 179, 276
    of Yugoslavia (CPY) VI 273–278, 280–281
Communist Party of the United States of America
    (CPUSA) II 46–48; III 237; VI 123, 154,
    157
    1932 presidential candidate III 182
    Federation of Architects, Engineers, Chemists and
        Technicians II 228
    history of III 224
    organization of Southern Tenant Farmers
        Unions II 189
Community Action Programs (CAP) II 270–276
Compañía de Terrenos y Aguas de la Baja California,
    S.A. VII 155
Comprehensive Immigration Law (1924) III 233
Comprehensive Test Ban Treaty (CTBT) I 224; VI 58
Comprehensive Wetlands Management and
    Conservation Act VII 274
Concert of Europe VI 203
Conference on Environmental Economics at Hyvinkää
    (1998) VII 89
Congregational Church VIII 204
Congress of African People (1970) II 95; III 193, 195
Congress of Industrial Organizations (CIO) II 188,
    197; III 183–184, 191, 195
Congress on Racial Equality (CORE) II 161; III 219
Connally, John VI 257
Connolly, Thomas T. II 208; III 31; VI 151
Conrad von Hotzendorf, Franz VIII 46–47, 49, 252
Conservation in Action Series (1947) VII 278
Conservative Party (Great Britain) VI 13
Conscription Crisis (1917) VIII 158–159
Constantinople VIII 117–118, 122, 173, 212, 214–215,
    228
Contadora peace process VI 194
containment I 142, 144, 154, 158, 160, 183–184, 187,
    262, 271–272, 274, 288, 293; II 30–31, 58,
    269; VI 59, 80, 83, 203
    Dulles criticism of I 273
    during Carter administration I 13
    strongpoint I 82–86
    universal I 82–90
Contras VI 57, 61, 191–196, 237, 241
Convention on the Protection of the Mediterranean Sea
    against Pollution VII 143–144, 305–310
conventional warfare IV 46–52
convergence theory VI 241
Coolidge, Calvin III 22, 25, 47, 176, 178, 226
Coolidge administration
    authorizes Boulder Dam VII 28
Cooper v. *Aaron* (1958) II 286
Cooper, John Sherman VI 61
Cooper-Church amendment (1970) I 44; VI 60
Coordinating Unit for the Med Plan VII 145
Coppola, Francis Ford VI 222
Cordier, Andrew VI 75
Costa Rica I 53
    invasion threats from Nicaragua (1949, 1955) I
        125
    U.S. intervention in mid 1950s I 15

Council of Ten VIII 282
Council on Environmental Quality Rainfall VII 214, 224
Council on Foreign Relations VI 199, 203
Coventry (1940 bombing raid) V 6, 96
credibility gap VI 23
Creel, George VIII 296
Crete VIII 212
Croatia VI 276; VIII 95
Crocker, Chester A. VI 4
Cuba I 51, 53, 68, 89, 91, 94, 96, 98, 125, 292; VI 35, 50, 63–68, 77, 141–142, 182, 188, 213, 246, 249, 261, 271
    Bay of Pigs invasion (1961) I 66, 70, 89, 92, 94, 129; II 115, 247, 266; VI 131
    blockade of VI 72
    Castro takeover I 17
    exiles VI 64
    exports to Soviet Union VI 249
    imperialism I 151
    nuclear missiles in VI 70–71
    policy in Angola VI 165
    receives aid from Soviet Union I 275
    relations with the United States VI 70–76
    revolution of 1959 I 18, 20, 125; VI 63
    Soviet subsidies VI 249
    Soviet troops in VI 70
    support for the MPLA VI 1
    support for revolutions VI 64
    support for Third World VI 63
    threat to stability in Central America I 49
    troops in Africa VI 2, 4, 249
    troops in Angola VI 1, 7, 41, 43
    troops in Ethiopia VI 41
    troops on Grenada VI 221
    troops overseas VI 65
    U.S. intervention (1898) I 125
Cuban Communist Party I 91–93
Cuban Liberty and Democratic Solidarity (Libertad) Act
    See Helms-Burton bill
Cuban Missile Crisis (1962) I 49, 92–94, 98, 102, 125, 131, 168, 183–184, 230, 294; II 66, 117, 120, 257, 265; VI 30–31, 36, 42, 50, 64, 66, 70–76, 101–104, 139, 142, 174, 262
Cuito Canavale, battle of (1987) VI 7
Cullen, Countee III 79, 234–236
Cunene River VII 236–237, 239, 240, 242
Curagh Mutiny (1914) VIII 161
Cuyahoga River VII 116, 118, 123, 265
cyanide effects VII 247, 253
Cyprus I 135
Czech Republic VI 217
Czechoslovakia I 109–110, 112, 277, 293–294, 303; II 9; VI 103, 110, 119, 131, 133, 165–166, 178, 217, 227, 237, 246, 249, 251–252, 261, 274, 276
    appeal of Marshall Plan I 178
    arms shipment to Guatemala (1954) I 49, 123, 126
    atttempted alliance with France VI 255
    dams in VII 100
    frontiers recognized VIII 283
    Germany annexes border districts VIII 284
    human rights abuses I 146
    Munich Agreement (1938) I 300
    occupation of VIII 284
    political changes in VII 101
    Soviet coup (1948) I 173, 182, 185
    Soviet invasion (1968) I 11–12, 218; VI 43, 116, 182, 249

D

Daladier, Edouard V 116
    appeasement policy IV 20
Damascus VIII 39, 41
Damodar Valley VII 130, 132
Damodar Valley Corporation VII 127, 132

Dams VII 1–9, 14, 25–32, 51–61, 100–107, 125–134, 196, 236–246
    and fish VII 53, 196–203
    benefits of VII 1, 28
    breaching of VII 31, 221, 224, 226
    hydroelectric energy VII 226
    political economy of VII 129
Danube River VII 100, 101–104, 106, 204–207, 209–210, 247, 250, 253, 255
Danzig VIII 280–281
Dardanelles VIII 38, 80, 117–123, 212, 214, 216
Darrow, Clarence III 32–34, 37–39
    relationship with NAACP III 186
    Scopes Trial III 33
Darwin, Charles III 32–33; VIII 93
Davies, John Paton VI 158
Dawes, Charles VIII 285
Dawes Plan (1924) IV 270; V 119; VIII 298
Dawes Severalty Act (1887) III 140–143; VII 166, 167, 168, 171
Dayton Accords (1995) II 100, 154
D-Day (6 June 1944) VI 168, 251
Declaration of Independence VI 9
De Witt, John L. V 184, 187
Debs, Eugene V. II 196; III 151, 175, 208, 222–223, 234
Declaration of PAris (1856) VIII 136
Declaration of Punta del Este (1961) I 17
Decolonization VI 264
    effects of on Third World VI 83
Defense Intelligence Agency (DIA)
    NIE reports VI 257
    Soviet military strength VI 259
Defense of the Realm Act (1914) VIII 158
Defense Readiness Condition (DEFCON) VI 163
Democratic Party II 49, 162–165, 180, 194–195, 198, 257; III 191–195
    association with labor movement II 187–192
    Democratic National Convention (1964) II 28, 161–163
Democratic National Convention (1968) II 162, 180; VI 25
    Mississippi Freedom Democratic Party II 28, 161, 197
    relationship with African Americans III 118
Democratic National Committee (DNC)
    headquarters broken into VI 24
Democratic Republic of Vietnam. See North Vietnam
Deng Xiaoping VI 4, 42, 44, 204
    visits United States VI 43
Dennis v. United States I 78–79
Denmark VIII 280, 283–284
deoxyribonucleic acid (DNA) II 82–85
Department of Commerce and Labor, Bureau of Corporations III 242
Department of Defense I 74, 83
Department of Energy VI 257
Department of State I 83
Desert Storm (1991) VI 28
d'Estaing, Valéry Giscard VI 104
détente I 11, 52, 101–106, 140–143; II 56, 60, 63, 118, 168, 170–174; VI 2, 21, 32–33, 35, 41, 65, 68, 88, 103, 112, 116, 164–166, 202–204, 209, 229, 232, 237–238, 256–257, 270
deterrence theory VI 31
Detroit riots VI 141
Dewey, Thomas E. I 60, 272; II 280
DeWitt, John L. III 103, 106, 109
Diablo Canyon VII 178
Díaz, Porfirio III 125, 127
dichlorodiphenyltrichloroethane (DDT) VII 147, 234
Dien Bien Phu (1954) I 70; II 266
Dimitrov, Georgi Mikhailovich VI 275, 280
Dinosaur National Monument, Colorado VII 27, 29, 112
Disraeli, Benjamin VIII 168
District of Columbia

signed the Chesapeake Bay 2000 Agreement VII 49

Dixiecrats VI 142

Djilas, Milovan VI 275, 278, 280–281

Dobrynin, Anatoly VI 41, 163

Dodacanese Islands VIII 212

Dodd, Christopher J. VI 194

Dominican Republic I 15, 24, 71, 91, 94, 125; III 247; VI 66, 140, 266
    rumored coup in VI 140
    U.S. troops in (1965) VI 140, 165–166

domino theory I 130, 266–267, 295–299; II 119, 266–267

Dongamusi area, Zimbabwe VII 64

Dönitz, Karl V 3, 79–85, 143, 256–257, 262

Donzère-Mondragon Dam (France) VII 93, 95

Doolittle Raid (1942) V 3

Doolittle, James C. "Jimmy" V 92, 98–99

Dos Passos, John III 182, 234–237

Douglas, William O. II 284; III 105

Downey, Sheridan VII 153, 156

Dr. Strangelove or How I Learned to Stop Worrying and Love the Bomb (1964) I 236; VI 31

draft resistance movement II 4, 6

Drakensburg Mountains VII 236

Dred Scott v. *Sandford* (1857) II 280; III 28

Dresden (German ship) VIII 133, 137

Dresden bombing V 5, 54, 88, 221

Dresdner Bank VII 250

Dreyfus, Alfred VIII 68, 147, 149, 168

Dreyfus Affair (1894–1898) VI 136; VIII 68, 146–147, 149, 151–152, 164

Dubcek, Alexander VI 119

Du Bois, W. E. B. II 44, 46, 137; III 84, 117–118, 120–123, 182, 267–274

Dual Alliance VIII 73

Dual Monarchy VIII 43–47, 76

Dulles, Allen I 71, 130; II 50
    ties to United Fruit Company I 126

Dulles, John Foster I 49, 69, 130, 149, 267–274, 278, 282; II 50–51, 135, 168, 208; VI 130, 153, 221, 268
    "massive retaliation" policy I 192, 211, 213
    New Look policy I 117, 211, 214
    U.S. policies in Europe I 208

Dunkirk evacuation (1940) V 123

Dunkirk Treaty (1947) I 208; VI 210

Durance River VII 98

Dust Bowl VII 181, 183, 185

Dutch East Indies VIII 137

Duwamish River VII 189, 191

Dwight D. Eisenhower System of Interstate and Defense Highways II 109

E

Eaker, Ira C. V 5, 98

Earth Day VII 123, 265

East Africa VIII 193

East Germany I 107, 274; VI 110–111, 115–122, 141, 178, 182, 206–212, 217, 246, 249, 251, 261, 276
    defectors VI 170
    dissidents in VI 117, 121, 211
    Dulles acceptance of Soviet influence I 273
    flight of citizens VI 141
    political parties in VI 121
    reforms I 154
    relations with Soviet Union I 253
    revolt against totalitarianism (1953) I 254
    shift in leadership VI 117
    Soviet suspicion of I 185
    strategic importance I 109

East Prussia VIII 249, 252, 280

Easter Rising (1916) VIII 154–162, 209

East Timor, Indonesian invasion of VI 270

Eastern Europe VI 116, 120, 131, 148, 181, 201, 207–208, 221, 224, 226, 236, 251, 267, 281; VII 250
    collapse of communist regimes in VII 101
    collapse of Soviet control in VI 216
    dissident movements in VI 229
    environmental crisis in VII 17–24
    German occupation (World War I) VIII 91–101, 176
    German occupation (World War II) VIII 91–101
    NATO expansion in VI 54
    political repression in VII 18
    removal of Soviet forces VI 110
    Soviets in VI 244–245, 250, 252
    Soviets block Marshall Plan to VI 255
    treatment of refuges VI 251
    U.S. support of dissidents in VI 3
    voter apathy on environmental issues VII 20

Eastern Front IV 53–60
    casualties IV 55
    Soviet advantages IV 55

Eastern Orthodox Church VIII 207

Ebert, Friedrich VIII 257, 280

Ebro River VII 147

Echo Park Dam (United States) VII 27, 29, 30–31

Economic Commission for Latin America (ECLA) I 20–22

Economic Opportunity Act (1964) II 276

Economic Opportunity Act (1965) II 272

Eden, Anthony I 272, 280; V 41, 290, 312; VI 11

Edison, Thomas Alva VIII 197

Edmondson, W. T. VII 189, 192

Edwards Aquifer VII 69–75

Egypt I 308–312, 273, 283; II 53; VI 11, 83, 137, 162–164, 172, 246, 271–27; VII 29, 82, 135, 149; VIII 31–32, 38, 168, 213
    Arab-Israeli War (1967) II 150
    Aswan High Dam VII 3
    attack on Israel VI 10, 161, 163
    conflict with Israel I 159
    deportation of Jews VIII 166
    environmental control in VII 145
    Free Officers' regime II 148
    Great Britain in VIII 35
    Kafara Dam VII 3
    nuclear weapons development I 219
    Soviet alliance I 161; II 146; VI 43, 81
    Soviet-Egyptian Pact (1955) I 162
    Suez Canal I 308, 316
    Suez Crisis I 289; VI 135, 270
    Suez War I 277, 280
    U.S. resistance to return of Soviet troops VI 163
    Western Desert Project VII 2
    World War I VIII 37–42

Ehrlichman, John D. VI 24

Einsatzgruppen (special action commandos) IV 88, 131, 134, 141; V 161

Einstein, Albert VIII 167

Eisenhower, Dwight D. I 35, 64, 71, 92, 102, 210–215, 274, 292, 297, 306; II 38, 45, 49–55, 64, 67, 105–106, 112, 135, 137, 200, 229, 232, 260, 280; IV 183; V 314, 92, 69, 281, 284; VI 11, 17, 35, 64, 86, 96, 130, 133, 136, 139, 153, 155, 231
    appeal to Soviets VI 135
    as NATO commander-general I 208
    Atoms for Peace I 216–217; II 49, 53
    Battle of the Bulge IV 64
    Bay of Pigs invasion II 52, 54, 115
    Berlin crisis I 69
    "Chance for Peace" speech II 53
    dealings with de Gaulle VI 105
    Eisenhower Doctrine (1957) I 280–282; II 148
    foreign policy of VI 141
    Interstate Highway Act II 105
    Korea VI 146
    military career IV 65
    1952 presidential campaign I 274

Open Skies policy II 51, 54; VI 20, 35
planning D-Day invasion IV 68
restraint in use of nuclear weapons I 236–237
rollback policy I 72
sends envoy to mediate Middle East water dispute
    VII 138
space program II 242, 260
Suez Crisis VI 80
summit with Macmillan VI 10
support of U.S. involvement in Korea II 211
Supreme Allied Commander II 50
Taiwan policy I 68
vetos rivers-and-harbors legislation VII 259
World War I service VIII 192
WWII strategy in Germany VI 169
Eisenhower administration I 49, 66, 94, 110, 117, 281;
    VI 30, 56, 81, 92, 95, 139, 149, 238; VII
    259
    "atomic diplomacy" I 211, 213, 267
    Atoms for Peace policy I 216
    concern over Soviet Middle East policy VI 239
    containment policy I 184
    defense spending VI 144
    Dulles, John Foster I 278
    East Germany policy I 271
    Eisenhower Doctrine I 282
    Hungarian uprising VI 13
    Middle East policy I 161
    military spending I 69, 192
    New Look policy I 210–215, 266
    Nixon as vice president VI 203
    policy on Cuba VI 141
    refuses to recognize Castro VI 64
    rejection of arms control I 230
    "rollback" strategy VI 221
    Social Progress Trust Fund I 20
    Suez Crisis VI 11
    Taiwan policy I 266, 268, 270
    Vietnam policy I 293, 297; VI 10
El Niño VII 201–202, 212
El Salvador I 48, 51, 53, 56, 94, 141; II 58, 103; VI
    190, 194, 221, 266, 270
    CIA covert operations I 26
    human rights violations in VI 241
    marxist guerrillas in VI 193
    relations with Nicaragua I 50, 54
    U.S. role in I 15
Elbe River VI 251
Elizabeth I VIII 168
Ellington, Duke II 214; III 78–79
Ellsberg, Daniel VI 24, 26
Emden (German ship) VIII 132–136
Endangered Species Act VII 202, 211, 215, 223, 226
Endangered Species Committee VII 224, 227
Endrin VII 160–165
Engel v. Vitale (1962) II 281
Engels, Friedrich VI 176, 281
English Channel VIII 29, 35, 75, 134, 182, 287
Enola Gay V 50–53
Entente Cordiale (1904) VIII 33, 35, 226
Environmental Defense Fund VII 274
environmental impact assessment (EIA) studies VII 128
environmental movement
    contribution to collapse of Soviet bloc VII 17–24
    in Estonia VII 17–24
    in Poland VII 17–24
    in the United States VII 31
environmental policy VII 175
Environmental Protection Agency (EPA) II 183; VII
    123, 263, 266
environmentalists
    fight U.S. dams VII 113
Epupa Dam (Namibia) VII 237, 239, 242–143
Equal Employment Opportunity Commission
    (EEOC) II 182
Equal Pay Act (1963) II 192
Equal Rights Amendment (ERA) II 72, 78–80, 163,
    224

Equatorial Africa VIII 31
Esmeralda (mining company) VII 248, 250, 254
Erhard, Ludwig VI 210
Eritrea VI 165
Escobedo, Danny II 284
Escobedo v. Illinois (1964) II 281
Espionage Act (1917) III 223, 229, 234
Estonia VI 178; VIII 93–94, 96–97
    annexed by Soviet Union VII 22
    environmental activism in VII 17–24
    first national park VII 22
Estonian Nature Conservation Society VII 22
Estonian Writers' Union VII 23
Ethiopia VI 4, 63, 68, 188, 261, 271
    claim to Ogaden VI 165
    Cuban troops in VI 41
    relations with Soviet Union VI 165
    Somalia attack on VI 165
Ethiopian-Somali crisis VI 166
ethnic cleansing VI 211
eugenics movement III 17–23
Eugenics Record Office (1910) III 18, 21
Euphrates-Tigris Basin VII 76–84
Eurasia
    introduction of species from VII 217
Eureka, California VII 178
Europe VII 206, 229
    as market for African beef VII 33
    backs Zionist settlements in Israel VII 136
    capitalism in VI 49
    demographic impact of World War I VIII 189
    patriarchal society in VIII 129
    support for World War I in VIII 125
    U.S. troops in VI 251
European Bank for Construction and Development VI
    120
European Community (EC) I 108, 209
European Court VII 250
European Economic Community (EEC) VI 13, 106,
    209; VII 33, 36
European Free Trade Association (EFTA) I 108
European Recovery Plan. See Marshall Plan
European Union (EU) VI 51, 53, 216–217, 219; VII
    34, 37, 83, 100, 106, 143, 146–148, 207, 248,
    250
eutrophication VII 90, 148, 265
Everglades VII 271
Executive Committee of the National Security Council
    (ExComm) VI 70, 73
Executive Order 9066 III 105; V 183, 188–189
Exxon Valdez oil spill (1989) II 86

F

F-16 fighter VI 223
Fair Employment Practices Committee (1941) IV 218
Faisal I VIII 37–39, 214
Falin, Valentin VI 117, 119
Falkenhayn, Erich VIII 114, 213, 252, 266
Falkland Islands VI 13
Falklands War (1983) VI 8
Fall, Albert III 127, 141, 178
Farmer Labor Party II 197
Fascism IV 77–84
Fashoda Incident (1898) VIII 33
Faubus, Orval II 20, 137, 140
FB 111 bomber VI 259
FBI. See Federal Bureau of Investigation
February Revolution (1917) VIII 171–173
Federal Aid Highway Act (1956) II 109
Federal Aid Road Act (1916) II 106
Federal Bureau of Investigation (FBI) I 76, 292; II 5,
    47; III 107; VI 24, 157, 257
    communist spy investigations II 131
    NIE reports VI 25
    Rosenberg files II 228, 231
    treatment of spies II 231
    wiretapping I 77

Federal Bureau of Public Roads II 109
Federal Communications Commission (FCC) II 123, III 55
Federal Deposit Insurance Corporation (FDIC) III 62, 152
Federal Emergency Management Agency VII 214
Federal Emergency Relief Administration (FERA, 1933) III 149, 159
Federal Occupational Safety and Health Act (1970) II 192
Federal Oil Pollution Control Act (1924) VII 41
Federal Power Commission VII 53
Federal Republic of Germany. *See* West Germany
Federal Reserve Board (FRB) III 57, 152, 207, 211
Federal Water Pollution Control Administration VII 175
Federation of Bird Clubs of New England VII 277
Feklisov, Aleksandr II 228–229
    Soviet nuclear spying I 242
feminism II 72–81, 163–164
Fenian Rebellion (1867) VIII 161
Ferdinand, Franz VIII 43–44, 46, 49, 228
Field, Noel VI 125–126
Fifth Amendment II 132, 134, 281–282
fifth column III 103–107, 252
Final Solution IV 137–139; V 57–60
    response of German churches IV 188
Finland I 110–112; II 34; VI 244, 255; 97, 101, 280
    Äänekoski mills VII 86–88
    environmental policies in VII 85–91
    German submarine construction in VIII 285
    National Board of Waters VII 85
Finlandization I 107–113, 151
Finnish Association for Nature Conservation (FANC) VII 86
First Amendment II 166
First Balkan War (1912) VIII 118
First Indochina War (1946-1954) VI 98. *See* Vietnam War
First International Meeting of People Affected by Dams, Curitiba, Brazil VII 105
Fish VII 215–216, 252
    hatcheries programs VII 201
    impact of dams on VII 219–228
    salmon VII 27, 29, 31, 51–61, 86, 90, 191, 196–203, 209, 219–228, 235
    trout VII 31, 87, 216, 219, 223, 230, 234
Fish ladders VII 29
Fish Passage Center VII 223
Fisher, John VIII 30–31, 122, 137
Fitin, Pavel VI 127
Fitzgerald, F. Scott III 54, 78, 83, 182; VIII 191
Fitzgerald, John F. III 262
Five-Power Naval Limitation Treaty (1921) V 203
Flanders, Ralph E. VI 156
Flathead Irrigation Project VII 167–169, 171–172
Flerov, Georgy N. I 244–248
flexible response policy I 115–122; II 118; VI 9, 66, 141
Fliegerkorps (Air Corps) IV 167
Flood Control Acts VII 29, 54
Flood Defense Plan VII 232
flu epidemic (1919) III 96–97
Flying Tigers (U.S.) V 199
Foch, Ferdinand VIII 55, 57, 103, 114, 150, 184, 204, 219, 221, 234, 236, 281–282
Ford, Gerald R. I 101; II 179, 278; VI 1, 58, 87, 229, 256–257
    criticized by Reagan I 52
    human rights I 141
    policy toward Pakistani nuclear program I 223
    sale of military hardware to China VI 4
Ford administration VI 1, 56, 199–200, 260
    détente I 102
    London Suppliers' Group I 19
    nuclear nonproliferation policy I 216, 223
Ford, Henry VIII 296
Formosa Straits VI 147

Forrestal, James V. I 4–5, 159; II 206
Foster, John VI 257
Foster Bill (1910) III 137
Fort Peck Dam (U.S.) VII 28, 170
Four-Power Pact (1921) V 120, 203, 206
Four-Square Gospel Temple III 177
Fourteen Points (1918) II 99, 101, 145; VI 77; VIII 280–282, 298
Fourteenth Amendment II 20, 138, 224, 282, 284
    due process clause II 281
    equal protection clause II 138–139, 141, 221
Fourth Amendment II 281
France I 34, 151, 278, 280, 283, 289, 293, 305; II 153, 264; VI 11, 76, 97, 100–107, 137, 178, 183, 189, 201, 209, 214, 234, 246–247, 264; VIII 30, 44, 71, 76, 82, 104, 172, 176, 182, 212, 245–246, 249, 251–252, 280
    aftermath of World War II I 173; VI 49
    alliance with Russia (1893) VIII 35, 212
    anti-Catholic sentiment VIII 204
    anti-Semitism in VIII 168
    Army 17, 69, 179, 185, 232–238
        in World War I VIII 218
            mutiny of VIII 67, 223, 269
            offensive tactics of VIII 71
    artillery VIII 199, 272
    as arm supplier VI 107
    attack on Germany VIII 72
    attempted alliance with Czechoslovakia VI 255
    Catholics in World War I VIII 207
    colonial policy of VI 93; VII 81, 135
    communist party in I 204, 208
    Cuban Missile Crisis VI 102
    decolonization policy VI 77–83
    Dunkirk Treaty I 208
    ecological policy VII 92–99
    fall of IV 70–76; V 35, 36
    Fifth Republic I 283; VI 106
    first nuclear test VI 106
    Fourth Republic I 283; VI 80
    German invasion of VIII 110, 278
    Grand Armee VIII 49, 233
    inability to hold Vietnam II 266
    in Algeria VI 80, 106, 136
    in Indochina VI 106
    in Middle East VI 161; VIII 37
    in Morocco VIII 277
    in Southeast Asia II 264
    in Vietnam VI 102
    Jews in VIII 164, 168
    Med Plan VII 145
    Ministry of the Interior VIII 255
    Munich Agreement (1938) I 300
    nuclear arsenal VI 103, 106, 187
    Nuclear Non-Proliferation Treaty I 218
    opposition to rearming Germany VI 9
    pays Germany indemnity VIII 278
    postwar decline I 285
    refuses to sign NPT VI 106
    relations with Great Britain VIII 32
    relations with Soviet Union VI 145
    relations with the United States VI 104
    reluctance to declare war on Germany IV 117–120
    Socialists VIII 254–256, 260–261
    Suez Crisis I 277; VI 135–136, 270
    Third Republic VIII 146–147, 151–152
    vetos British EEC membership VI 13
    war with Vietnam I 213, 290
    withdrawal from NATO VI 81, 103, 106, 145, 209
    World War I VIII 11–17
        access to U.S. products VIII 18
        African American troops in VIII 298
        casualties VIII 125, 187, 191
        control of U.S. troops VIII 17
        mobilization in VIII 125

motivation of soldiers VIII 264–265
planning VIII 232–238
prewar alliances VIII 225–231
prewar realtions between army and government VIII 146–152
religion during VIII 203
response of population VIII 255
size of army VIII 75
U.S. pilots in VIII 23
wartime manufacturing VIII 16
women in manufacturing VIII 129
Francis Joseph I VIII 47
Franco, Francisco I 209; II 97; IV 224–231
abandonment of Axis IV 227
rise to power IV 224, 226
Franco-Prussian War (1870–1871) VIII 35, 67, 73, 114, 146–147, 234
Franco-Russian alliance VIII 234
Frankenstein, or, the Modern Prometheus (Shelley) II 86
Frankfurter, Justice Felix II 280–283; III 27, 103, 228, 234–235
Sacco and Vanzetti III 232
Frazier-Lemke Farm Bankruptcy Act (1934) III 30, 162
Free French Forces IV 276; V 241
Free Officers Committee I 277
Free Speech movement II 159; VI 25
Freedom of Information Act II 125
Freedom Rides (1961) VI 25
Freedom Summer (1964) II 161; VI 25
Freikorps (volunteer paramilitary units) IV 80; VI 176; VIII 285
French, John VIII 103
French Communist Party VI 179, 245; VIII 256
French Equatorial Africa VI 83
French Foreign Office. *See* Quai d'Orsai
French Indochina (Vietnam) VIII 35
French Morocco VIII 32, 35
French Revolution (1789–1799) VIII 149
French Socialist Party VIII 169, 256
Frente Sandinista de Liberación (FSLN, or Sandinista National Liberation Front) VI 190–191
Freud, Sigmund VI 90; VIII 167, 263–264
Front de Libération Nationale (Front Liberation National, FLN) I 277; VI 106
Frying Pan/Arkansas Transmountain Water Project VII 10, 13
Fuchs, Karl/Kluas I 242–249; II 130, 228, 231; VI 158
Fuller, J. F. C. VIII 53–54, 56, 112, 195, 241
fundamentalist movement III 32–42

G

G.I. Bill of Rights II 189
Gabcikovo Dam (Slovakia) VII 100—107
Gabrielson, Ira VII 277—278
Gaddis, John Lewis I 83, 154, 252, 256, 273; II 31, 37, 156, 204
Gadhafi, Mu'ammar I 159, 223, 314; VI 268, 270
Gaelic League VIII 161
Gagarin, Yuri II 68, 257, 260
Gandhi, Indira VI 271
Gaither report I 190–194
Galicia VIII 72
Galvin, Robert VI 257
Gamasy, Abd al-Ghani al- I 309, 313
Gandhi, Mohandas II 22; III 219
Gariep Dam (South Africa) VII 237, 240, 242—243
Garrison Dam (U.S.) VII 29, 31
Garvey, Marcus II 90; III 79, 117–123
de Gaulle, Charles I 283; V 171, 247; VI 11, 79, 81, 97, 100–104, 106, 145, 209
critic of U.S. Vietnam policy VI 107
Free French Forces IV 76
seeking independent role for France VI 105
vetos British membership in EEC VI 106

vision for Europe VI 106
visit to Algeria VI 106
World War I service VIII 192
Gates, Robert VI 259
Gaza VIII 216
Geheime Staatspolizei (Gestapo, Secret State Police) V 213–216
Gelman, Harry VI 41
General Agreement on Tariffs and Trade (GATT, 1944) VI 78
genetic engineering II 85–88; III 17, 23
Geneva Accords I 41, 297; II 266–267; VI 142, 216
Geneva Conference (1925) V 103
Geneva Conference (1978) VI 164
Geneva Convention (1929) I 170, V 187, 222, 264
Geneva General Disarmament Conference (1932–1933) V 204
Geneva Summit (1985) VI 36, 224
Gerisamov, Gennadi VI 117
German Communist Party VI 274; VIII 257
German East Africa VIII 84–90, 133, 137
German High Command VIII 172–173
German High Seas Fleet, mutiny VIII 269
German Imperial Navy VIII 288
German Independent Social Democrats VIII 260
German Military Mission VIII 119
German Protestant League VIII 204
German reunification VI 120, 207
German Social Democrats VIII 256
German Wars of Unification (1864–1871) VIII 73
Germany I 85–86, 89, 110, 112, 134–136, 149, 176, 245, 263, 285, 288, 293, 305; II 31–32, 36, 38, 40, 153; III 10; VI 101, 104, 136, 151, 169, 176, 179, 254; VII 81, 229, 250; VIII 18, 44, 48, 76–77, 82, 192, 216, 299
aftermath of World War II I 173
alliance with Austria VIII 35, 43
anti-Semitism in VIII 165–166, 169
Army VIII 18, 224, 234
Irish Brigade VIII 158
modern weapons VIII 75
size of VIII 69
"storm tactics" VIII 68
Auxiliary Service Law VIII 140, 143
canals VII 210
Catholic Center Party VIII 165, 257
chaplains in army VIII 202
colonial rule in Africa VII 236
colonialism VIII 30–31
compulsory labor draft VIII 257
contributions of Jews VIII 167
customs union with Austria forbidden VIII 283
dams VII 101
debt crisis VIII 280
defeat of Romania VIII 278
division of I 300
economic consolidation of occupation zones I 113
environmental movement 204—210
exclusion from League of Nations I 206
execution squads in Russia VIII 99
fear of communism in VI 49
"field grey socialism" VIII 144
Four Year Plan (1936) IV 96
Hindenburg Program 140, 143
Hindenburg-Ludendorff plan VIII 139–145
Imperial German General Staff VIII 92
Independent Social Democrats VIII 257, 260
inmportation of foreign labor VIII 144
in the Mediterranean theater IV 144
invasion of the Soviet Union I 107, 260; IV 141, 209; V 226–234
League of Nations VIII 277
Munich Agreement (1938) I 300
National Socialism VIII 209
Navy VIII 29–36
East Asian Squadron VIII 132, 137

surface commerce raiders VIII 132–135
Nazis VI 251–252
non-aggression pact with Poland (1935) IV 125
occupation by Allies VI 267
occupation of Czechoslovakia VIII 284
occupation of Eastern Europe (World War I) VIII 91–101
occupation of Eastern Europe (World War II) VIII 91–101
occupation of France VIII 278
partition I 252–257
postwar occupation I 33–39
Race and Settlement Office VIII 94
rearmament I 208
remilitarization IV 96
reparation payments IV 270
Second Naval Law VIII (1900) 31, 33
Second Reich VIII 29, 184,
Socialists VIII 261
Soviet invasion of (1945) VI 16
Third Reich VIII 92, 95–96
Turnip Winter (1916–1917) VIII 144
War Ministry VIII 144
War Raw MAterials Department VIII 140
war reparations I 300
Weimar Germany I 137
World War I VIII 11–17, 271–276
    armistace VIII 278
    atrocities in VIII 203, 208
    blockade of VIII 140, 277
    casualties VIII 125, 187, 268
    Catholics in VIII 207
    chemical warfare VIII 239–244
    economic mobilization VIII 139–145
    excluded from peace negotiations VIII 277
    in Africa VIII 84–90
    indemnities imposed VIII 283
    invasion of Belgium VIII 72, 110
    Jews in VIII 163–164
    military gap VIII 249
    mobilization VIII 125, 268
    motivation of soldiers VIII 266
    pilots trained in Soviet Union VIII 285
    planned annexation of Holland VIII 280
    planning VIII 245–248
    prewar alliances VIII 225–231
    prewar consumption VIII 140
    religion VIII 203–204
    shipbuilding VIII 35
    submarine warfare VIII 77, 82, 172, 204, 287–294
    taxes VIII 280
    treaty with Russia VIII 278
    U.S. occupation VIII 24
    women VIII 130
World War II
    economy IV 96–98
    submarine warfare VIII 293
Gero, Erno VI 134
Ghana I 277; II 42, 45; VII 237
    Akosombo Dam VII 4
    nonaligned movement I 110
Gibbons, Cardinal James VIII 205
Gibraltar VIII 134, 204
Gibson, Charles Dana III 170
    Gibson girl III 167, 171
Gideon v. Wainwright (1963) II 281, 290
glasnost I 13–14; II 58–60; VI 17, 114, 212, 245
Glasser, Harold VI 126
Glass-Steagall Banking Act (1933) III 152
Glavnoye Razvedyvatelnoye Upravleniye (GRU, or Central Intelligence Office) VI 124
Glen Canyon Dam (U.S.) VII 27, 29–31, 110, 112, 152

Global Resource Action Center for the Environment (GRACE) VII 283
Global warming VII 225
Global Water Partnership VII 280
Godesburg Declaration (1939) IV 190
Goebbels, Josef IV 139, 141; V 154, 164
Gold Act (1933) III 28
Gold, Harry I 242–243; II 228, 231; VI 154
Goldwater, Barry VI 203
Goldwater-Nichols Department of Defense Reorganization Act (1986) VI 234
Gomulka, Wladyslaw VI 130, 134
Gorbachev, Mikhail I 13, 101, 152, 257; II 56–62; VI 1, 4, 17, 31, 33, 36, 46, 50, 103, 114, 188, 211, 223, 226, 228–229, 232, 239, 242, 245, 261; VII 20, 23–24
    fall of VI 113
    nuclear nonproliferation policy I 224
    perestroika/glasnost I 224; II 58–60
    plans for economic change I 152
    policy on East Germany VI 115–122
    political reforms of VI 44
    Soviet defense spending I 184
    strategic arms negotiations I 197
    views on Afghanistan I 13–15
    visit to China VI 45
Gordievsky, Oleg VI 126
Göring, Marshal Hermann IV 27, 163; V 14, 133, 152, 221, 223
Gough, Hubert VIII 219, 222, 224
Goulart, João I 24–26
Gove Dam (Angola) VII 239
Grand Canyon VII 29–31, 109, 111–112
    dams in VII 108–115
Grand Coalition V 27–33; VI 207
Grand Coulee Dam (U.S.) VII 27–29, 53, 198, 223
Grandmaison, Louis de VIII 73, 234
Grant, Ulysses S. VI 26; VIII 23, 67
Graves, Robert VIII 186, 188, 191
Gray v. Sanders (1963) II 139
Great American Desert VII 181–187
Great Britain I 14, 30, 34, 85, 277–278, 280, 288, 305; II 35, 264; VI 101, 106, 137, 183, 189, 264, 274, 250; VIII 44, 172, 212, 249
    access to U.S. products, World War I, VIII 18
    aftermath of World War II I 173; VI 49
    Air Inventions Committee VIII 196
    alliance with Japan (1902) VIII 34
    antinuclear protest in VI 16
    anti-Semitism in VIII 168
    Army
        Counter Battery Staff Office VIII 276
        Imperial General Staff VIII 102–108, 221
        Irish soldiers in VIII 158–159, 161
        tanks VIII 113
    Asian colonies of VI 9
    atomic bomb VI 187
    Baghdad Pact I 161
    balance of power in Europe I 254
    "blue water" strategy VIII 82
    Board of Invention and Research VIII 196
    Board of Trade VIII 81
    Catholic Church in VIII 208
    Chancellor of the Exchequer VIII 78
    colonial power I 259; II 32; VII 4, 135, 236–237
    Conservative Party VIII 82
    cooperation with U.S. intelligence VI 11
    decline as world power I 83
    decolonization policy VI 77–83
    Dunkirk Treaty I 204, 208
    economic policies in VI 13
    EEC membership vetoed VI 13
    House of Commons VIII 103, 161
    House of Lords VIII 77
    importance of navy to VIII 30
    in Middle East VI 161; VIII 35, 37–42
    Indochina peace conference VI 10

Irish independence VIII 154–162
Labour Party I 285; VIII 255
Liberal Party VIII 78, 81
Ministry of Munitions VIII 106, 276
Munich Agreement (1938) I 300
Munitions Inventions Department VIII 196
National Service Projects VIII 203
National Shell Filling Factories VIII 129
Nuclear Non-Proliferation Treaty I 218
People's Budget (1909) VIII 77, 81
postwar recovery I 177
relations with France VIII 32
relations with Soviet Union V 28–33; VI 9
relationship with United States V 28–33; VI 8, 14
resistance to standing army VIII 30
role in Europe VI 13
Royal Navy VIII 29–36, 117, 160
Royal Ordinance Factories VIII 129
Socialists VIII 255, 261
Soviet espionage in VI 25
Suez Crisis I 277; VI 135–136; 270
War Committee VIII 82, 104
water issues VII 234, 240, 286
Women's Army Auxiliary Corps (WAAC) VIII 129
Women's Land Army VIII 130
Women's Police Volunteers VIII 130
Women's Royal Air Force (WRAF) VIII 129
Women's Royal Naval Service (WRNS) VIII 129
women suffrage VIII 128
World War I VIII 11–17, 117–123, 218–224, 271–276
    Arab and Jewish policy during VIII 163
    Allied cooperation VIII 11
    artillery VIII 272
    battleships in VIII 29–36
    casualties VIII
    chaplains in VIII 202
    impact of German subs upon VIII 69, 287–294
    in Africa VIII 84–90
    Jews in VIII 164, 168
    mandates VIII 12, 214
    mobilization in VIII 125, 268
    motivation of soldiers VIII 266
    prewar alliances VIII 225–231
    production of tanks in VIII 56
    religion and VIII 203
    strategic policy VIII 102–108
    submarines VIII 287
    surface commerce raiders agaisnt VIII 132–135
    U.S. pilots in VIII 23
    wartime manufacturing VIII 16
    Western Front VIII 81–82
Yalta Agreement (1945) I 300–301, 306
Great Depression I 88, 180; II 46, 86, 160; III 38, 50, 54–60, 62–68, 148, 182, 194; VI 78, 158, 176; VII 25, 28, 53, 157, 202; VIII 59, 167, 277
    attraction of communism during VI 49
    cause of end III 62
    impact on automobile industry II 106
    impact on labor movement II 191
    impact on New Deal III 151
The Great Gatsby (Fitzgerald) II 109; III 54
Great Lakes VII 116–124
Great Lakes Water Quality Agreement (1972) VII 120, 124, 310–317
Great Leap Forward (1958–1960) VI 181
Great Plains VII 10–16; VIII 27–28
Great Society VI 140, 144
Great Terror (1936–1938) I 137–138
Great War, *see* World War I
Greater East Asia Co-Prosperity Sphere IV 258

Grebe, Reinhard VII 206–207
Grechko, Andrei VI 165
Greco-Turkish War (1920–1922) VIII 214
Greece I 87, 89, 294; II 39, 207; VI 148, 161, 182, 244, 250–255, 275, 280; VII 82, 148–149; VIII 212, 216, 230, 277
    British support for VI 11
    civil war in I 82, 110; VI 274
    First Balkan War VIII 118
    invades Smyrna VIII 214, 217
    Soviet intervention I 73–74, 258
    U.S. role in 1967 coup I 15
    water issues VII 146–147
Greek Communist Party VI 274
Green v. School Board of New Kent County (1968) II 293
Greenback Party II 196, 199
Greenglass, David II 228–231
    Soviet nuclear spying I 241, 243, 246–248
Grenada I 56–57; II 44, 58; VI 83, 165, 194, 221–222, 234, 237, 261, 270
Griswold v. Connecticut (1965) II 281–283, 286
Groener, Wilhelm VIII 96, 143, 246
Gromyko, Andrey VI 75, 116
Groves, Leslie I 28, 235, 247
Group for Environmental Monitoring (GEM) VII 238
Group of 77 (G-77) VI 271
Guantanamo Bay VI 64
Guatemala I 54–56, 70, 89, 94, 122–133; II 40, 103; VI 21, 131, 194, 266
    1954 coup I 128
    Agrarian Reform Law (1952) I 123, 126
    CIA involvement I 211
    CIA trained anti-Castro Cubans in VI 141
    coup of 1954 I 123
    human rights violations in VI 241
    Marxist guerrillas in VI 193
    military coup of 1963 I 24
    United Fruit Company I 70
    U.S. intervention (1954) I 15, 123–133
Guderian, Heinz W. IV 282; V 123–127
Guevara, Ernesto "Che" I 93; II 160, 215; VI 70
    death I 126
    role in communist revolution in Bolivia I 126
gulag archipelago VI 250
Gulf of Sidra VI 165, 234
Gulf of Tonkin incident (1964) I 291; VI 144
Gulf of Tonkin Resolution (1964) I 91; II 7; VI 139, 284, 287
gunboat diplomacy VI 166
Gurion, David Ben I 216
Guyana. *See* British Guiana
Gypsies, murder of VIII 94–95

H

Habeas Corpus VI 9
Haber, Fritz VIII 241–242
Habib, Philip Charles VI 229
Habitat Patch Connectivity Project VII 232
Habsburg Empire VI 217; VIII 43, 257, 281
Hafiz El Assad II 146
Hague Conference (1911–1912) III 137; VIII 240
Hague Conventions (1907) V 222, 264; VIII 244
Haig, Alexander M. I 56; II 179; VI 44, 225, 229, 231
Haig, Douglas VIII 52, 56, 77, 79, 103–104, 106, 108, 114, 218–221, 223, 26, 271–273
Hainburg Dam Project (Austria) VII 105
Haiti I 51, 125; II 100; III 50; VI 58, 194, 213, 217, 283
Haldeman, Harry R. VI 24
Halder, Franz V 126–127, 227
Hallstein Doctrine VI 208, 210
Halsey Jr., William F. IV 173
Haman Act VII 47
Hamilton, Ian VIII 118–119, 122
Hankey, Maurice VIII 79
Hannibal VIII 179, 249
Hanoi I 41–47

Hardin, Garrett VII 47, 70, 72–73
Harding, Warren G. III 25, 69, 175–178
Harlan, John Marshall II 23, 282–283
Harlem Renaissance III 78–84, 118–120, 184
Harkin, Thomas R. VI 194
Harriman, W. Averell I 306; II 264; V 312
Harris, Sir Arthur "Bomber" V 87, 91
Harrison Act (1914) III 133, 137
    narcotics legislation III 137
Hart, Sir Basil Henry Liddell V 23, 102
Harvard University VI 90, 129, 199, 203, 258
Hashemite Arabs VIII 40–41
Hatch Act (1939) III 11
Hauptmann, Bruno III 110–116
Hayden, Carl Trumbull VII 109, 112, 154, 155
Hayes, James Allison VII 274
Heady, Earl O. VII 187
Heeringen, Josias von VIII 180, 184
Heine, Heinrich VI 121
Hells Canyon Dam (United States) VII 55
Helsinki Conference (1975) I 142
Hendrix, Jimi II 219
Helms, Richard M. VI 24
Helms-Burton Bill I 97–98
Helsinki Accords VI 200
Hemingway, Ernest VIII 186, 188, 191
Henry VIII, founds Royal Navy VIII 30
Hepburn Act (1906) III 243, III 245
Herero/Nama Rebellion (1904) VIII 87
Hess, Rudolf V 223–224
Hezbollah VI 234
Hideki Tojo V 112; VI 75
Highway Act (1987) II 112
Highway Revenue Act (1956) II 107
Himmler, Heinrich I 305; IV 131; V 154, 162
Hindenburg, Paul von V 114–115, 120; VIII 54, 93, 95–
    96, 140, 143, 252, 292
Hindenburg Line VIII 27, 53, 57
Hinton, Harold VI 41
Hirabayashi v. *United States* (1943) III 103, 105–106; V
    188
Hirabayashi, Gordon V 188–189
Hirakud Dam (India) VII 130
Hirohito, Emperor V 49, 108–113; VIII 95
Hiroshima I 30, 230, 239, 242–246, 249; II 268; III 12,
    15, 216; V 1, 3, 8, 49, 50, 52, 55, 111, 154, 192,
    221; VI 31, 254
Hiss, Alger II 130–133, 229; III 34; VI 123–129, 154,
    156, 158
    conviction for perjury VI 124
    Pumpkin Papers VI 127, 129
    trip to Moscow VI 126
Hiss, Priscilla VI 124
Hitler, Adolf I 150, 235, 239, 256, 274, 288, 293, 300,
    305; II 156; III 38, 250–257; IV 17–19; V 14,
    35, 57–58, 61, 79, 81, 84, 93, 96, 98, 104, 107–
    109, 122–125, 152–158, 173, 221, 226; VI 49,
    61, 158, 176, 178, 251, 254, 275, 277, 281;
    VIII 30, 58, 92, 94–97, 99, 166, 186, 241, 263–
    264, 281, 284
    annexation of Sudentenland IV 19; VIII 284
    appeasement of I 276
    declaration of war on U.S. V 131–136
    failure as war leader IV 108
    foreign policy IV 122–128
    German rearmament IV 116–117
    goals of foreign policy IV 123
    Hitler and Stalin I 134–139
    influence on the *Wehrmacht* V 137–144
    invasion of the Rhineland IV 115
    invasion of Soviet Union IV 111
    responsibility for World War II IV 114–120
    remilitarizes the Rhineland VIII 284
    rise to power V 114–121
    war leader IV 104–112
Ho Chi Minh I 46, 183, 290, 294, 296, 297, 298; II 97,
    263–264, 266, 267; V 145–150, 174; VI 28,
    80, 92–93, 98, 107, 203

Ho Chi Minh Trail VI 142
Hoffmann, Max VIII 93, 252
Hokkaido VI 147
Holland VIII 72, 245, 261, 280
Holmes, Justice Oliver Wendell II 280–281, 284; III 17–
    18; VI 123
Holocaust III 251–257; IV 129–142; V 56–61, 151–166;
    VIII 166
    collaboration IV 129–135
    role in twentieth-century history V 163
    theories IV 136–141
Holtzendorff, Henning von VIII 289, 292–293
Home Rule Bill (1914) VIII 155, 158, 161
Home Rule Party VIII 158
Homer VIII 117
Honduras VI 193–194
Honecker, Erich VI 117–118, 120–121, 211
Hoover Dam (United States) VII 27, 29, 94, 109, 152
Hoover, Herbert I 285; II 49, 86; III 25–26, 50, 66,
    VIII 285
    goodwill trip to South America (1928) III 46
    Prohibition III 174
    Reconstruction and Finance Corporation II 209
    signs the Colorado River Compact VII 152
Hoover administration
    Native American policies III 144
    Reconstruction Finance Corporation (RFC) III 154
Hoover Dam II 257
Hoover, J. Edgar I 76, 292; II 232; III 107, 233; VI 24,
    158
Hopkins, Harry L. I 306; V 196; VI 155
horizontal escalation VI 221
Horn of Africa VI 42, 164, 256
Hortobagy National Park VII 253
House, Edward VIII 228
House Un-American Activities Committee (HUAC) I 77,
    79, 306; II 130–134, 207; VI 124, 127, 129,
    178
Houston, Charles Hamilton II 19, 22, 137–138
How the Other Half Lives (Riis) III 260
Hoyos Mission (1914) VIII 47
Hoxha, Enver VI 181
Hudson River VII 256, 261
Hughes, Justice Charles Evans III 25–27, 179; V 205
Hughes, Langston III 79, 83, 182
Hull, Cordell III 47, 50; V 264, 312; VI 78–79
human rights I 140–146; II 97–102; VI 51, 208
    in U.S. history II 98
    influence on U.S. foreign policy II 101
Humphrey, Hubert H. II 162, 177, 197; VI 85–86
Hungarian Revolutionary Committee VI 134
Hungarian uprising (1956) VI 130–137
Hungary I 109, 112, 119, 152, 274, 294; II 36, 52; VI 8,
    103, 110, 116, 118, 165, 178, 181, 217, 246, 249,
    251, 261, 274; VII 247–249, 253–254
    attempted coup against communists (1956) I 276;
    VI 130, 270
    dams in VII 100–??
    East German emigration through VI 118, 121
    environmental groups in VII 103
    Ministry for Environmental Protection VII 247–
    248, 250
    Ministry of Water and T ransportation VII 250
    Soviet invasion of VI 182
Hunt, E. Howard VI 24
Huntington, Samuel P. VI 198
Hurston, Zora Neale II 137; III 78–82, 184
Husayn ibn 'Ali (King Hussein) VIII 37–40
Hussein (King of Jordan) I 156, 314, 317; II 147; VI 201;
    VIII
Hussein, Saddam I 159, 163, 224; II 153, 156; VI 54, 58,
    61, 217, 225
Hutier, Oskar von VIII 112, 240

I

Ice Harbor Dam (United States) VII 31, 55
"Ichi-Go Offensive" (1944) V 151

Ickes, Harold L. II 211; III 150
Idaho VII 201, 220, 224
    dams in VII 26, 29
    salmon in VII 196
Idaho Fish and Game Department VII 53
Idaho Rivers United VII 221
Immigration Act (1924) III 22, 229
Immigration and Nationality Act (1952) I 77
Imperial Economic Conference (1932) VI 78
Imperial Irrigation District (IID) VII 152, 154–155
Imperial Valley VII 151, 154–155
Imperial Presidency VI 56–57
Import-Export Bank I 53; III 47
Incidents at Sea Agreement (1972) VI 31
Independence Party II 199
India I 151, 277; II 85, 117; VI 50, 53, 79, 136, 188,
        214–215, 219, 271; VII 125; VIII 32–33, 83,
        103, 133, 168, 208
    agriculture in VII 130, 133
    Army VIII 38
    British in VI 161
    British rule in VII 125
    Central Ministry of Environment and Forests VII
        133
    dams in 9, 125–134
    Ministry of Environment and Forests VII 128
    Moghul canals in VII 125
    nuclear test (1974) I 216, 223
    nuclear weapons development I 219–223, 228; VI
        53
    policy toward Soviet Union VI 81
    World War I VIII 216
        motivation of soldiers in VIII 266
Indian Ocean VIII 137
Indian Reorganization Act (IRA, 1934) III 139–146,
        151, 162; VII 167
Indian Self-Determination Act (1975) VII 172
Indochina I 44–46, 86, 290; VI 59, 81, 103, 106, 141,
        188, 203, 209, 283; VIII 233
Indonesia I 269, 273, 277, 295; II 40, 117; VI 81, 188;
        VIII 137
    invasion of East Timor VI 270
Industrial Revolution VIII 136
Industrial Workers of the World (IWW) VIII 298
Inland Empire Waterways Association VII 53, 55
in loco parentis VI 25
Institute for Water Resources (IWR) VII 262
Integrated River Basin Development VII 1
integration II 24, 90, 92, 136, 292
Intercontinental Ballistic Missile (ICBM) I 49, 189,
        192, 230; II 118; VI 50, 110, 144, 202, 260
Intergovernmental Maritime Consultative Organization
        VII 143
Intermediate Range Ballistic Missile (IRBM) I 193
Intermediate Range Nuclear Forces (INF) Treaty VI
        17–18, 44, 224, 232, 242
    Soviets walk out of VI 44
INS v. Chadha VI 286
Internal Security Act (1950) I 74–77; II 131
International Bank for Reconstruction and
        Development (IBRD, or World Bank) VI
        78
International Boundary and Water Commission
        (IBWC) VII 154–155, 157
International Coalition for the Restoration of Rivers
        and Communities Affected by Dams VII 131
International Commission for the Scientific
        Exploration of the Meditteranean Sea
        (CIESM) VII 143
International Commission on Large Dams VII 126,
        130
International Court of Justice (ICJ) VII 100, 103, 106
International Day of Action Against Dams and for
        Rivers, Water & Life VII 96
International Forum on Globalization (IFG),
        Committee on the Globalization of Water,
        VII 285

International Joint Commission (IJC) VII 116–117,
        123
International Labor Defense (ILD) III 186, 236
International Ladies Garment Workers Union
        (ILGWU) III 191
International Law Commission of the United Nations
        VII 79
International Military Tribunal (IMT) V 221, 224
International Monetary Fund (IMF) I 22; VI 53, 78,
        120
International Rivers Network VII 9, 238
International Workers of the World (IWW) III 223
International Working Men's Association (First
        International, 1864) VI 178
Interstate Commerce Commission (1887) III 10
Interstate Highway Act (1956) II 105–113
interwar naval treaties V 201–209
Iran I 15, 82, 87–89, 110, 113, 141, 145, 263, 294; II
        34, 103, 144, 153; VI 21, 54, 113, 131, 162,
        165–166, 195, 201, 215–217, 231–232, 266;
        VIII 35, 82
    arms sales I 51
    CIA involvement I 211
    crucial to U.S. security I 85
    hostage crisis in VI 107, 166, 226, 232, 268
    sale of U.S. missiles to VI 196
    Soviet interests in VI 255
    Soviet occupation of VI 165
    Soviet withdrawal from VI 161
    tensions with Afghanistan I 15
    territorial concessions I 288
    war with Iraq I 54
    Western interest in VI 255
Iran-Contra Affair VI 3, 57–58, 191–196, 231–232
Iran-Iraq War (1980-1988) VI 162, 271
Iraq I 202; II 144, 153; 54, 58, 107, 162–163, 213, 215,
        217, 219, 261, 268, 271
    ancient irrigation in VII 11
    Gulf War I 163; VI 225
    invasion of Kuwait I 289
    Kurds in VI 54, 61, 217
    nuclear reactor at Osiraq VI 106
    overthrow of Faisal II (1958) I 282
    Pan-Arab campaign I 281
    Shiites in VI 61, 217
    water policy in VII 135–141
Ireland VIII 83
    British rule in VIII 154–162
    Catholic condemnation of Easter Rising VIII 209
    Council of Bishops VIII 209
    Easter Rising VIII 154–162, 209
    famine in VIII 189
    Home Rule 154–162
    World War I
        conscription in VIII 158
        impact upon country VIII 154–162
        religion in VIII 208
Irish Citizen Army VIII 158
Irish Parliamentary Party VIII 155–156
Irish Republican Army VIII 158
Irish Republican Brotherhood VIII 155–156
Irish Unionists VIII 161
Irish Volunteers VIII 158, 161
Iron Curtain VI 49, 118, 173, 206
Iron Curtain speech (1946) VI 250
Isma'il, Hafiz I 309–312
Israel I 56, 162–164, 278, 283, 309, 316–317; VI 43,
        83, 164, 172, 188, 200–201, 215, 246, 261,
        271
    Arab opposition to VI 160
    attacked by Egypt and Syria VI 163
    founding of IV 160
    invasion of Lebanon I 196
    Iraqi bombing of I 195
    military I 163, 278, 308
    nuclear weapons development I 218, 222
    preemptive strikes against Egypt and Iraq I 239

Suez Crisis I 192, 277, 280, 289; VI 11, 106, 135, 270
Israeli Air Force (IAF) VI 172
Israeli Defense Forces (IDF) VI 161
Italian Communist Party VI 179, 245
Italy I 293; II 39; VI 178, 246–247, 251, 267, 274; VII 149; VIII 47, 95, 104, 106, 192, 212, 221, 233, 261, 266, 277, 280, 283
    aftermath of World War II I 173
    alliance with Germany VIII 35
    antinuclear protest in VI 16
    Army, size of VIII 69
    cost of Med Plan to VII 146
    hindering the Axis effort V 175–182
    invades Libya VIII 212
    navy VIII 212
    pollution from industrial centers in VII 147
    postwar influence of Communist parties I 174, 176
    Socialists VIII 254, 261
    World War I
        airplanes given to United States VIII 19
        prewar alliances VIII 225–231
        refuses mandate for Armenia VIII 12
    Yalta Agreement (1945) I 301, 306
Itezhitezhi Dam (Zambia) VII 240
Izaak Walton League of America VII 53, 122

J

Jackson, Justice Robert H. III 27; V 188, 222–224
Jackson, Thomas (Stonewall) VIII 23
Jackson State College VI 23
Jackson-Vanik Amendment I 140, 142
James, Henry VIII 203
Japan I 30, 85, 88, 259, 285, 288; II 35, 39–40, 264; III 10, 12, 108; VI 53, 113, 147, 149, 151, 204, 217, 254, 266–267; VIII 230
    atomic bombing of I 4, 183, 239, 263; VI 71, 255
    British alliance with (1902) VIII 34
    domino theory I 266
    economic problems in VI 219
    Greater East Asia Co-Prosperity Sphere IV 258
    industrialization of IV 254
    interest in Arab oil I 162
    invasion of China IV 254
    Manchurian occupation I 59
    military conduct IV 151–156
    military tradition in VI 27
    mutual defense relationship with United States VI 54
    occupation of Korea VI 146
    postwar recovery of I 263, VI 59
    postwar occupation I 3
    Soviet war against VI 251
    surrender III 11, 15; VI 49
    treatment of prisoners of war IV 152
    wars with Russia I 263
    women in World War II V 305
    World War I, entry into VIII 137
    WWII peace terms VI 146
Japanese Americans
    internment of III 102–109; V 183–190; VI 57
Japanese death marches
    Bataan (1942) IV 152
    Sandakan (1945) IV 152
Jaures, Jean VIII 151, 255
Javits, Jacob K. VI 285
Jellicoe, John VIII 293
Jews
    murder of VIII 94–95
    World War I, participation in VIII 164–169
Jerusalem VIII 41, 216
JFK (1991) VI 138
Jim Crow II 23–28, 43–45, 90, 140–142, 163
Jocko Valley VII 167, 169
Jodl, Alfred V 3, 22, 127, 224

Joffre, Joseph VIII 11, 16, 71, 114, 129, 147–149, 182–183, 232, 234, 236–237, 252
Johannesburg, South Africa VII 4, 7
John Day Dam (United States) VII 53–54
John Martin Dam (United States) VII 13–14
Johnson Administration VII 259
    liberal activism of VII 123
Johnson, Andrew VI 57
Johnson, Louis A. I 3–8
Johnson, Lyndon B. I 8, 64, 66, 89, 119, 130, 159, 291; II 5–7, 45, 93, 114–115, 141, 161; III 31; VI 23, 28, 66, 86, 95, 138–145, 185, 201, 284
    criticism of Eisenhower administration I 193
    decides not to run for reelection VI 145
    defense spending VI 144
    Great Society I 292; II 162, 175, 181, 270–271, 276
    Gulf of Tonkin incident I 291
    opinion of space program II 247, 260
    opposition to VI 24
    Philadelphia Plan II 182
    signs Central Arizona Project bill VII 110
    Vietnam War I 292, 296; II 4, 266; VI 59
    views on Latin America I 18
    War on Poverty II 166, 270–279
Johnson administration I 68; II 4, 163; VI 26, 28, 59, 103, 138–145, 199, 204; VII 259
    arms control VI 33
    arms race I 190
    atmospheric-testing bans VI 20
    Central Intelligence Agency I 64
    liberal activism of VII 123
    policies on Latin America I 18, 24
    responsibility for Vietnam War VI 99
    tension with Great Britain VI 10
    Vietnam policy I 41, 293; VI 103, 202
Johnson v. *Virginia* (1963) II 138
Johnston Eric VII 137–138
Joint Chiefs of Staff I 201; VI 151
Joint Technical Committee (JTC) VII 79
Jones, Robert Emmett Jr. VII 269
Jordan VI 201; VII 78–79, 82, 135, 138; VIII 39, 41
    fundamentalist movements in I 163
    mandate in VIII 168
    Pan-Arab campaign I 281
    support of U.S. I 158
    West Bank captured by Israel I 156
Jordan River Basin VII 137–138
Joyce, James VIII 191
Jünger, Ernst VIII 59, 64, 263
Jupiter missiles VI 71

K

Kádár, János VI 130, 134
Kafara Dam (Egypt) VII 3
Kafue Dam (Zambia) VII 137, 240
Kafue River VII 2, 5, 137
Kahn, Agha Mohammad Yahya VI 88
Kalahari Desert VII 33–34, 36–37, 236
    lack of surface water in VII 38
kamikaze VIII 60
Kampuchia VI 165
Kansas VII 10–11, 13, 181–182, 185, 187
    alfalfa production in VII 13
    sugar-beet production in VII 13
    water diverted from VII 13
    water policy in VII 185
Kapp Putsch (1920) IV 271
Kardelj, Edvard VI 281
Kariba Dam VII 1, 4–5, 8, 239, 242–243
Kariba George VII 1, 237, 239, 245
Karl I VIII 257
Karmal, Babrak I 10–15; VI 238
Katse Dam (Lesotho) VII 7, 237, 241, 244
Kattenburg, Paul VI 96
Kaufman, Irving R. II 131, 230, 232
Kazakhstan VI 109, 215

Keating, Kenneth B. VI 73
Keitel, Wilhelm V 3, 127, 142–143, 223–224
Kelheim VII 204, 209
Kellogg-Briand Pact (1928) III 179; V 115; VIII 298
Kellogg, James L. VII 49
Kennan, George F. I 22, 31, 75, 82, 138, 148, 150, 154,
    159, 284–285, 288; II 8, 60, 267; VI 188
    "Long Telegram" I 261; II 34, 205, 264; VI 9
    containment policy I 110, 274
    domino theory I 266
    later view of containment I 183
    Marshall Plan I 176
    Mr. X II 206
    rules for handling relations with the Soviet
      Union I 186
Kennedy, John F. I 23, 64, 68, 89, 92, 94, 119–121,
    130, 257, 291–292; II 8, 45, 52, 67–68, 93,
    114–120, 160; III 48; VI 64, 66, 70, 73, 93,
    96, 102–103, 138–145, 188
    Alliance for Progress I 17, 20, 23; II 115
    assasssination I 18; II 180; VI 138, 142
    Bay of Pigs I 71; II 115, 119
    Camelot mystique II 117
    Cold War policies II 117
    compared with Franklin D. Roosevelt II 115
    criticism of Eisenhower administration I 193; VI
      141
    critiques of performance in Cuban Missile
      Crisis VI 73
    Cuban Missile Crisis II 116, 120, 265
    decolonization policy VI 81
    Food for Peace II 116
    foreign policy II 117
    Inauguration Address I 23
    and Jimmy Hoffa II 190
    Johnson as vice president running mate VI 142
    limited-nuclear-war doctrines I 169
    Nuclear Test Ban Treaty (1963) II 118
    Peace Corps II 116
    plot to overthrow Castro I 276
    presidential campaign I 17
    promotion of space program II 260
    Roman Catholicism of VI 142
    State of the Union address (1961) VI 140
    strategy in Southeast Asia VI 95
    support of British VI 11
    supports coup against Diem VI 98
    United Nations II 115
    Vietnam policy I 183
Kennedy, Robert F. II 9; VI 75, 96
    assassination of II 162, 180
    civil-rights issues II 22
    Cuban Missile Crisis VI 70–76
    nuclear disarmament in Turkey I 121
    U.S. Attorney General II 22
    War on Poverty involvement II 272
Kennedy administration VI 26, 56, 72, 92, 99, 138–
    145, 238
    Alliance for Progress I 17–26
    and civil rights II 26
    attempts to overthrow Fidel Castro I 24
    Berlin Wall Crisis I 119–120
    Cuban Missile Crisis I 120
    Cuban policy I 67
    "flexible response" I 115, 214
    Latin America policy I 17–26
    liberal activism of VII 123
    limited-nuclear-war doctrines I 171
    policy on Berlin VI 141
    policy on Castro VI 71
    responsibility for Vietnam War VI 99
    scraps Skybolt missile VI 11
    Vietnam policy I 293–294
Kerensky, Aleksandr VIII 170–178, 223, 258
Kern County Water Agency VII 179
Kerouac, Jack II 74, 160
Kerr Dam (Unted States) VII 169
Kent State University VI 23

Kenya VI 188
Key West Agreement I 5–8
Keynes, John Maynard III 54–55; VIII 191
Khan, Genghis VI 40
Khariton, Yuly Borisovich
    Soviet nuclear weapons development I 244–248
Khmer Rouge I 15, 41, 44, 46, 295; VI 271
Khomeini, Ayatollah Ruhollah I 11, 141, 158; VI 165,
    268, 270
Khrushchev, Nikita S. VI 17, 21, 31, 35, 64, 68, 70–71,
    73, 81, 93, 111, 133, 141–142, 178, 184, 226,
    246; I 33–38, 66, 94, 102, 120–121, 151,
    256, 294; II 35, 40, 54–57, 66, 68, 115–117,
    229
    arms race I 182
    Berlin I 38, 120, 168
    role in Cuban Missile Crisis II 120
    secret speech (1956) I 66; VI 133, 181, 186, 188,
      264
    Soviet nuclear capabilities I 194
    threats to use nuclear weapons I 192
Kiel Mutiny (1918) VIII 269
Kienthal Conference (1916) VIII 256, 261
Kim Il-Sung I 294; II 37; VI 147, 150
    invasion of South Korea I 182
Kiessinger, Kurt VI 210;
King, Ernest J. V 39, 44, 188, 258
King Michael VI 252
King, Martin Luther, Jr. II 19, 22–24, 26–27, 42–44,
    48, 89, 91–95, 162, 165, 197; III 120, 182 ;
    VI 25
    assassination of II 180
    "Man of the Year" II 22
    press coverage of II 22
Kinzig River VII 230
Kinzua Dam (United States) VII 29
Kirkland, Washington VII 189, 191
Kitchener, Horatio VIII 78, 103, 203, 266, 271–272
Kitzhaber, John A. VII 222, 224
Kirchenkampf (Church Struggle) IV 38, 188, 191; V 215
Kirkpatrick, Jeane J. I 50–56; II 101; VI 261
Kissinger, Henry I 40, 45–47, 53, 101–102, 104, 119,
    140–141, 159, 162, 272, 292, 317; II 169–
    172, 179; VI 30, 35, 38, 41–42, 51, 53, 61,
    65, 162–163, 206, 209, 229, 237, 257, 267
    ABM Treaty I 199
    détente policy I 52
    diplomatic campaign I 317
    foreign policy approach of VI 85–91, 198–205
    limited-nuclear-war doctrines I 170
    negotiations with North Vietnamese I 291
    nuclear proliferation policy I 222–223
    on multipolar world VI 199
    realpolitik I 149
    secret mission to China II 170; VI 38, 43
    shutting the Soviets out of the Middle East I 105
Kohl, Helmut VI 54, 117, 120, 208
Komitet gosudarstvennoy bezopasnosti (Committee for
    State Security, KGB) I 12, 66, 70, 93, 242; II
    63; VI 18, 21, 239
    recruitment of the Rosenbergs II 228
Konar Dam (India) VII 130
Königsberg VI 244
Königsberg (German ship) VIII 90, 133, 137
Korea I 89, 288, 293; II 4, 40, 50; VI 56, 270, 272
    division of I 275; VI 146
    Eisenhower policy I 271
    independence of VI 146
    proposal for U.S. troops in I 262
    strategic importance of VI 147
    U.S. troops sent (1950) I 211
Korean War (1950–1953) I 69, 87, 89, 102, 158, 170,
    182, 192, 265–266, 273; II 9, 36–37, 42, 52,
    66, 131, 134, 146, 211, 230; V 32; (1950–
    1953) VI 8–9, 36, 50, 57, 102, 106, 136, 144,
    146–151, 154, 173, 177, 261, 284–285
    effect on demand for Latin American imports I 21
    Eisenhower administration I 211

INDEX

Geneva negotiations II 264
impact on McCarthyism II 131
outbreak I 3, 7
Truman administration policy I 275
U.S. and Soviet pilots in VI 50
U.S. troops in VI 165
Korean Air Lines 007 VI 44, 261
Korematsu, Fred V 188–189
Korematsu v. *United States* (1944) III 103; V 188
Kornilov, Lavr VIII 176
Kosovo VI 53–54, 225
Kosovo Crisis (1999) VI 61, 283
Kraków VII 21
smog in VII 18
Krenz, Egon VI 1118, 122
Kriegsakademie (German Military Academy) V 126
Kriegsmarine (German Navy) IV 4, 264; V 79– 80, 82, 83, 131, 133, 135, 136, 255, 257
Kristallnacht (Night of Broken Glass, 1939) III 256; IV 137, 141; V 216
Krueger, Walter V 99, 126
Ku Klux Klan (KKK) II 25; III 78, 90, 123, 174
kulaks, destruction of VI 274
Kurchatov, Igor Vasilyevich I 244–248
Kuwait II 153, 156; VI 225; VII 79, 81
Iraqi invasion I 289
Kvitsinsky, Yuli VI 117
Kyushu III 14–15

L

La Follette, Robert M. III 178, 184, 210
labor movement II 187–193; III 181, 190–195
labor unions II 187–193; III 183; VI 49
Labour Party (Britain) V 46; VI 11, 13, 20
LaGuardia, Fiorello II 197; III 219
Lahemas National Park VII 22
Lahn River VII 230
Lakes—Celilo
Constance VII 231–232
Erie VII 116, 118, 122–123, 265, 269
Hulch VII 136
Kariba VII 4
Mead VII 31
Michigan VII 265
Ontario VII 118
Päijanne VII 86–87
Powell VII 30–31, 110, 112
Solitude VII 29
Superior VII 266–277
Titicaca VII 74
Washington VII 188–195
Landrum-Griffin Act II 192
Landis, Kennesaw Mountain VIII 301
Laos I 41, 46, 68, 299; II 6, 54, 260; VI 60, 93, 188, 203
as a colony of France I 290
Imperialism I 151
spread of communism I 297
U.S. bombing of I 183
Lateran Treaty (1928) VIII 208
Latin America I 52– 56; VI 141, 264, 267
agricultural output I 21
human rights I 146
land reform I 21
legacy of Reagan's Policies I 56
revolutionaries in VI 80
U.S. military aid I 19
U.S. relations with II 99
U.S. troops in VIII 14
World War II III 51
Latvia VI 178; VIII 93–94, 96
Law of the Non-Navigational Uses of International Watercourses (1997) VII 79
Lawrence, Thomas (Lawrence of Arabia) VIII 37–39, 87, 214
Lebanon VII 81, 138
lack of environmental control in VII 145

Le Duc Tho VI 40
League of Nations I 30, 206, 284–285; II 145, 156, 175, 180, 207, 211; IV 17–18, 267; V 115, 117, 119, 169, 202, 206, 228, 292; VI 57; VIII 13, 20, 156, 168, 277, 282, 295, 298
American involvment I 286, V 292
failure to prevent World War II IV 115
League of Women Voters III 171
Leahy, William D. I 5; III 15; V 52
Lebanon I 282; VI 270; VIII 37, 213
American hostages in I 54
bombing of U.S. Marines barracks VI 234
civil war in VI 43
deployment of Marines to I 157; VI 66, 222
French role in VI 103
Israeli invasion of I 196
intervention in VI 103
U.S. troops, 1958 II 52
Lebensraum (living space) IV 54, 80, 96, 109, 123, 138 141
Ledbetter, Huddie "Leadbelly" II 214
Lee, Robert E. VIII 23
Leffler, Melvyn I 174, 262
Legal Defense Fund (LDF) II 19, 137–138, 141
Legislative Reference Service (LRS) VII 258
Leipzig VI 118, 122
LeMay, Curtis E. I 188; III 216; V 89–99; VI 71
Lend Lease Act (1941) I 301; II 32–35; IV 55, 58, 157–162; V 5; VI 78, 255
Lend-Lease Agreement (French, 1945) VI 79
Lenin, Vladimir I 135, 139, 149, 151, 294; II 56–57; VI 81, 108, 175–176, 178–179, 196, 243–244, 248, 274–275, 281; VIII 95, 97, 173–174, 176, 258, 260–261
Lennon, John II 216
Leopold, Aldo VII 226, 278
Lesotho (Africa) VII 2, 4, 7, 236, 241, 243
Lesotho Highlands Development Authority (LHDA) VII 1–2, 4, 237, 243
Lettow-Vorbeck, Paul von VIII 84–90
the Levant VI 103
Levitt, Abraham II 110, 252
Levitt, William II 110
Levittown, N.Y. II 110, 249
Lewis, C. S. VIII 61
Lewis, John L. II 22, 90–91, 161; III 192
Libertad Act. *See* Helms-Burton bill
Liberty Bonds VIII 204, 296
Liberty Union Party II 197
Libya I 152, 159, 28; VI 54, 107, 163, 165, 217, 271; VIII 39
Imperialism I 151
Italian invasion of VIII 212
lack of environmental control in VII 145
nuclear weapons development I 219
revolution I 158
U.S. air strikes on VI 107, 222, 234
Liddell Hart, B. H. VIII 71, 196
Lieberthal, Kenneth VI 41
Likens, Gene E. VII 262
Lilienthal, David E. I 27–31
Liman von Sanders, Otto VIII 120–121
Limited Nuclear Test Ban Treaty (1963) VI 18, 33
Limited-nuclear-war doctrines I 165–172
Limpopo River VII 33
Lincoln, Abraham VI 57
Lindbergh, Charles A. III 110–116; V 135
Lindbergh kidnapping III 110–116
Lippmann, Walter II 8, 59; III 34, 207; VI 75
Lithuania VI 178; VIII 93–94, 96, 283–284
Little Goose Dam (United States) VII 31
Livonia VIII 97
Ljubljana Gap V 72–74
Lloyd George, David III 99; VIII 11, 20, 57, 77–83, 102–108, 155–156, 219–223, 278, 280, 282– 283
industrial mobilization by VIII 78
Minister of Munitions VIII 78

Minister of War VIII 78
thoughts on Germany VIII 81
Locarno Pact (1925) VIII 284
Lochner v. *New York* (1905) II 280–281
Lodge, Henry Cabot I 290, 298, 306; II 208; III 247;
VI 95–96, 196
Lomé Convention (1975) VII 33
London Charter (1945) V 222
London Conference (1930) V 204
London Naval Conference (1930) V 207
London Recommendations (1 June 1948) VI 101
London Suppliers' Group I 219, 223
Long, Huey III 28, 86–94, 210
Los Alamos I 242–243
Los Angeles Department of Water and Power (LADWP)
VII 178
Los Angeles Olympics (1984) VI 242
Louis XIV VIII 81, 278
Louisiana Stream Control Commission VII 161, 165
Loving v. *Virginia* (1967) II 139
Lower Granite Dam (United States) VII 31
low-intensity conflicts (LIC) VI 3, 131, 229
Lower Monumental Dam (United States) VII 31
Loyettes project (France) VII 93
Luce, Clare Booth VI 257
Ludendorff, Erich V 157; VIII 12, 49, 54–55, 91, 93–
97, 100, 114–115, 140, 143, 220, 240, 252,
257, 266
Ludwig Canal VII 204–205
Luftwaffe (German Air Force) IV 6, 14, 19, 107, 125,
163–169, 264, 282; V 1–2, 4–5, 7, 14, 60, 69,
72, 93, 95, 96, 123, 133, 179, 181, 223, 230,
231–233, 257
Lusitania (British ship), sinking of VIII 204, 288, 292
Luther, Martin VIII 204
Lutheran Church, and World War I VIII 208
Luxembourg VIII 24, 72, 232, 246, 248
Luxemburg, Rosa VIII 257
Lvov, Georgy VIII 170, 174, 177
lynching III 186, 268, 274

M

Maastricht Treaty (Treaty of European Union) VI 217
MacArthur, Douglas I 89; II 50; III 15, 28; IV 7,
171–176; V 3, 16, 109, 126, 136, 192, 254,
296, 299; VI 146–147, 151
image IV 175
in Pacific theater IV 176
military career background IV 172
Philippines campaign IV 176
South Pacific Area Command (SWPA) IV 173
Tokyo trials V 264–265
Machel, Samora Moisés VI 2, 4–5
Macmillan, Harold VI 10–11
MAD. *See* Mutual Assured Destruction
Madikwe Game Reserve, South Africa VII 38
Madsen v. *Women's Health Center* (1994) II 79
Maginot Line VIII 197
Mahan, Alfred Thayer VIII 31, 67, 72
Maheshwar project (India) VII 132
Main River VII 206, 209, 210, 230
Maji Maji Rebellion (1905) VIII 89
Malcolm X II 89, 93, 96, 197, 298; III 121, 182
Malenkov, Georgy I 38, 184, 192
Malta summit (1989) VI 51
Manhattan Project I 28, 235, 239, 241–249; II 228,
231; V 44, 50; VI 154, 177; VIII 197
Mann Doctrine I 24
Mann-Elkins Act (1910) III 45
Manstein Plan IV 107
Manstein, Fritz Erich von IV 282; V 15, 123, 126, 221
Mao Tse-tung I 59, 61, 73, 82–83, 86, 89, 134, 141,
265–266, 268, 303–304; II 36, 97, 169, 172,
264, 269; V 147–148, 191, 194; VI 40, 43,
150, 158, 181, 203
alliance with the Soviet Union I 184

view of Khrushchev I 294
Mapp v. *Ohio* (1961) II 281, 286
Marbury v. *Madison* (1803) II 286
March on Washington (1941) III 218
March on Washington (1963) I 192
Marshall, George C. I 34, 60, 159, 304; II 36; III 15,
218; IV 65, 176, 213, 221; V 25, 39, 42–43,
46, 51, 126–127, 136, 188, 196, 258, 279,
314; VI 90, 153, 255
Balkans campaign V 72
Marshall Plan I 173
purpose of Marshall Plan I 177
Soviet participation in Marshall Plan I 176
Marshall, Justice Thurgood II 19–20, 22, 42, 91, 137–
138, 141, 289
Marshall Plan I 18, 22, 36, 75, 86, 88, 107–109, 112–
113, 151, 173–179, 181–182, 208, 258, 288;
II 36, 40, 42, 100, 132, 209, 264; III 53; VI
9, 101, 104, 148, 211, 255, 267
list of countries recieving monatery aid I 174
opposition I 80
Maryland VII 274
Maryland Oyster Commission VII 46
Marx, Karl I 139, 149; II 56–57, 74; VI 122, 176, 178,
187, 274–275, 281; VIII 254–258, 260
Marxist Popular Movement for the Liberation of
Angola (*Movimento Popular de Libertação de
Angola* or MPLA) VI 1, 6, 87, 165
Massachusetts Audubon Society VII 277
mass media II 121–128, 166
ability to segment American society II 125
impact on American society II 122
and politics II 127
populist strain, 1990s II 124
revolution of print culture II 122
studies of II 124
massive retaliation policy I 115–117; II 30–31, 51, 118
Matsu I 211, 275; II 52
Chinese attack I 265–270
Eisenhower administration I 213
Mayor's Citizens Committee on Water (MCCW)
VII 74
McCarran Act (1950) I 77, 79–81
McCarthy, Eugene II 162, 198
McCarthy, Joseph R. I 58, 62, 75, 77–80, 87, 197, 272,
274, 295; II 129–135, 207, 211, 229; V 197;
VI 139, 150, 153–159, 178
anticommunism as ideological war II 131
anticommunist hysteria I 236
attacks George C. Marshall II 134
censure of II 132; VI 153, 156
death VI 153
supporters II 154
Wheeling speech (1950) VI 153–154
McCarthyism I 75, 304, 306; II 47–48; 129–135, 160
and the Cold War II 132
and the New Deal II 132
beginnings of II 30
"red baiting" I 75
Red Scare II 133
McCormack Act (1938) III 11
McFarland, Ernest William VII 109, 153
McGovern, George VI 26, 88
McKinley, William III 241, 272
McMahon Act (1946) VI 10
McNair, Lesley J. IV 246, 248; V 126
McNamara, Robert S. I 41, 166, 294, 296; II 9; VI 59,
75, 95, 103, 144
McNary Dam (United States) VII 53
McPherson, Aimee Semple III 33, 39
McReynolds, Justice James III 25–26, 28
Mediterranean Action Plan VII 142–150
Mediterranean Agreements (1887) VIII 226
Mediterranean Sea VIII 106, 134–135, 287
beach closings along VII 147
British interests in VIII 33
pollution control in VII 142–150
submarines in VIII 292

INDEX

Mein Kampf (1925-1927) IV 111, 123, 137, 186, 227; V 132; VIII 99

Meir, Golda VI 163

Mencken, H. L. III 32, 37, 78, 98, 128, 175
    flu epidemic III 101

Mensheviks VIII 258

Merrill's Marauders V 198

Mesopotamia VIII 39-40, 121, 193, 212-213, 216
    mandate in VIII 168

Metro Action Committee (MAC) VII 191

Metropolitan Problems Advisory Committee VII 190

Mexicali Valley VII 151-154, 157

Mexican Revolution III 124-131

Mexican Water Treaty VII 151-159

Mexico III 124-131; VII 197; VIII 296, 298
    cientificos (scientific ones) III 125
    criticism of Libertad Act I 98
    Cuban investment I 97
    departure of French army (1867) I 125
    land reform I 21
    mining industry III 125
    nationalization of U.S. businesses, 1930s I 130
    relations with the United States VIII 16, 18, 22
    salmon range VII 196
    water policy in VII 151-159

Michel, Victor VIII 234-235

Middle East I 157-158, 161, 277; VI 53, 79, 90, 135-136, 162, 171, 188, 266, 268, 271; VIII 109, 211, 228
    Arab-Israeli conflict II 145
    infrastructure I 158
    peace process I 289
    relations with United States I 278
    Soviet influence VI 160-167, 261
    Suez Canal Zone II 146
    U.S. interests I 162; VI 61
    water crisis in VII 135-141
    water policy in VII 76-84
    water shortage in VII 280
    World War I 37-42

Migratory Bird Conservation Act (1929) VII 277

Mihajlovic, Draza VI 275, 277-278

Mikva, Abner Joseph VII 121

military gap between U.S. and Soviet Union I 188-194

Military Intelligence Service (MIS) III 14-15

Millerand, Alexandre VIII 152, 255

Milliken v. *Bradley* (1974) II 293, 298

Milne, George VIII 214, 216

Milyukov, Pavel VIII 173-174

Minow, Newton II 121, 23

Miranda, Ernesto II 284

Miranda v. *Arizona* (1966) II 281, 284, 286

Missao do Fomento e Powoamento dio Zambeze (MFPZ) VII 240

missile gap I 182-194; II 260; VI 21, 141

Mississippi River VII 27, 29, 31, 182, 211

Mitchell Act (1938) VII 202

Mitchell, William A. (Billy) IV 2; V 3, 14, 126

Mitterand, François-Maurice VI 102, 104

Mobutu Sese Seko VI 81

Mohammad Reza Pahlavi (shah of Iran) I 11, 141-146; II 97

Molotov, Vyacheslav I 36, 113, 175, 177, 238, 303; II 35; VI 101, 255, 280
    Molotov Plan I 178; II 40
    Soviet nuclear spying I 245

Molotov-Ribbentrop Pact I 110

Moltke, Helmuth von (the Elder) VIII 73, 75, 184, 248-249, 252

Moltke, Helmuth von (the Younger) VIII 72, 114, 179-180, 182, 184, 226, 248

Monroe Doctrine (1823) I 124-125, 132; II 98, 156, 257; III 45-46, 243, 247; VI 75
    as applied to Cuba VI 71
    Roosevelt Corollary (1904) III 46

Montgomery bus boycott II 22-24, 90, 140

Montgomery, Field Marshal Bernard Law II 50; IV 64, 66, 144, 177-184; V 16, 19-25, 28, 34, 42, 44, 122-125, 129

Morelos Dam (Mexico) VII 152, 155, 157-159

Morgenthau, Hans J. I 266; II 8

Morgenthau, Henry III 257
    Morgenthau Plan (1944) II 210

Morrill Act (1862) III 2

Morocco VIII 32, 152, 227

Moroccan Crisis (1905) VIII 35

Mosaddeq, Mohammad I 66, 69, 211; II 146; VI 131

Moscow Conference (1944) V 311

Moscow Olympics (1980) VI 166, 237
    U.S. boycott VI 43

Mountbatten, Lord Louis V 42, 196

Movimiento de Izquierda Revolucionaria (MIR) I 127,130

Movimiento Nacionalista Revolucionario (MRN) I 125-126

Moynihan, Daniel Patrick II 166, 271, 276

Mozambique VI 1-7, 188, 221, 256, 261; VII 236-237, 239-240
    aid from Soviet Union VI 2
    independence VI 2
    Porgtuguese immigration to VII 237

Mozambique Liberation Front (*Frente da Libertação de Moçambique* or FRELIMO) VI 2, 6; VII 239

Mozambique National Resistance Movement (*Resistência Nacional Moçambicana* or RENAMO) VI, 2, 4, 6

Mubarak, Hosni I 163, 317

Mudros Armistice (1918) VIII 217

mujahidin (mujahideen) I 10-16; VI 2, 133, 165, 238
    U.S. support VI 229

Mundt, Karl E. I 74, 306; II 131, 211

Mundt-Nixon Bill I 74

Munich Agreement (1938) I 293, 300

Munich Conference (1938) IV 127

Municipality of Metropolitan Seattle (Metro) 188-195

Murphy, Charles Francis III 262

Murphy, Justice Frank V 188

music
    "folk revival" II 214
    as political force II 214

music industry
    impact of television II 218
    record companies at Monterey Music Festival II 219
    sheet music production II 217
    technological advances II 216
    youth market II 219

Muskie, Edmund Sixtus VII 176, 261, 263-264, 268

Mussolini, Benito I 134; IV 14, 80; V 36, 108-109, 117, 135, 169, 175-177, 226, 233; VIII 95
    alliance with Hitler V 179
    downfall V 2
    invasion of Ethiopia V 118, 120
    proposal of the Four Power Pact V 120
    removal from power V 178, 179
    support of Franco IV 224, 226

Muste, A. J. II 7; III 184

Mutual Assured Destruction (MAD) I 154, 169-171, 191, 198, 202, 226-227, 230-232, 251-252; II 67; VI 31, 168, 174

Mutual Defense Assistance Act (1949) I 59

Mutual Security Act I 175

Mutual Security Program (MSP) I 175

MX missile VI 17-18

N

Nader, Ralph VII 178, 265, 269

Nagasaki I 30, 230, 239, 242-245, 249, 268; III 12, 15; V 3, 8, 49, 52, 111, 154, 192; VI 31; VII 174

Nagy, Imre VI 130-131, 134, 270

Nagymaros Dam (Hungary) VII 100-101, 104

Namibia VI 1 6; VII 7, 38, 236-237, 240-242
    as U.N. Trust Territory 236

withdrawal of South African troops VI 7
Nanking Massacre (1937) V 151
Napoleonic Wars (1803–1815) I 166, 259; VIII 233–234
narcotics III 133–137
    Boxer Rebellion III 136
    Foster Bill (1910) III 137
    Harrison Act (1914) III 137
    history of legal regulation III 133
    progressive movement III 135
Narmada (Sardar Sarovar) Project (India) VII 127, 132
Narmada River 9, 134
Narodny Kommissariat Vnutrennikh Del (People's
    Commissariat for Internal Affairs,
    NKVD) IV 50; V 233; VI 275, 278
Nassau Agreement (1962) VI 11, 13
Nasser, Gamal Abdel I 110, 162, 273, 277–278, 283,
    314; II 117, 146–147; VI 11, 80–81, 106, 161,
    246, 268, 270; VII 3
    challenges Britain I 280
    pan-Arab campaign I 281
    "positive neutrality" II 148
Nation of Islam II 93–95
National Aeronautics and Space Administration
    (NASA) II 246, 258, 260
    creation of II 242
    funding of II 261
National Association for the Advancement of Colored
    People (NAACP) II 19–20, 23, 25, 27, 44–
    45, 90, 94, 138, 140–141; III 80, 93, 118,
    121, 182, 184–186, 217, 270–274
    opposition to Model Cities housing projects II
    277
    Scottsboro case III 185
National Association of Black Journalists II 96
National Association of Broadcasters II 123
National Association of Colored Women III 167
National Audubon Society VII 215
National Black Political Convention (1972) II 95, 198
National Committee of Negro Churchmen II 95
National Committee to Re-Open the Rosenberg
    Case II 228
National Council of Negro Churchmen (NCNC) II 94
National Council of Mayors VII 258
National Defense and Interstate Highway Act (1956) II
    107
National Defense Highway Act (1956) II 249
National Education Association II 190, II 191
National Environmental Policy Act (NEPA) II 183;
    VII 31, 176, 266, 269,
National Farmers Process Tax Recovery Association III
    159
National Front for the Liberation of Angola (*Frente
    Nacional de Libertação de Angola* or FNLA)
    VI 1, 6, 87, 165
National Guard Act (1903) VIII 301
National Industrial Recovery Act (NIRA, 1933) III
    27–28, 62, 65, 149,154
    Supreme Court ruling III 25
National Intelligence Estimates (NIEs) VI 256–258,
    260
National Labor Relations Act (Wagner Act, 1935) III
    149, 193
National Labor Relations Board (NLRB) II 188; III
    30, 62, 149, 190–191, 193, 195
National Liberation Front (NLF) I 296; II 119, 263–
    264, 266
National liberation movements VI 183–187
National Negro Congress (NNC) III 184
National Organization of Women (NOW) II 78
National Organization for Women v. *Joseph Scheidler*
    (1994) II 223
National Parks Association VII 30
National Pollutant Discharge Elimination System VII
    264
National Prohibition Act (1919) III 200
National Reclamation Act (1902) III 243

National Recovery Administration (NRA, 1933) III
    30, 154
National Security Act (1947) I 5, 7, 64, 69; VI 61
National Security Agency (NSA) I 74; II 230; VI 157
National Security Council (NSC) I 54, 64, 83, 121; VI
    41, 90, 96, 196, 231
National Security Council memorandum 68 (NSC-
    68) I 83–84, 89, 149, 182, 211, 274
National Security Decision Directives (NSDD) VI 13,
    32, 82, 166
National Socialist German Workers' Party (Nazi
    Party) I 35; IV 267; VI 49, 176, 254, 274,
    277; VIII 92, 94, 167
National Union for the Total Independence of Angola
    (*União Nacional para a Independência Total de
    Angola* or UNITA) VI 1–2, 6, 87, 165
National Urban League II 94; III 80, 184
National Water Act of 1974 (Poland) 18
Native Americans VIII 23, 27
    advocate breaching dams VII 221
    and dam income VII 59
    and fishing VII 57, 197, 220
    assimilation of VII 55, 168
    blamed for reducing salmon catch VII 199
    control of resources on reservations VII 166–173
    dam monitering by Columbia River tribes VII
    223
    displacement of VII 27
    environmental damage to land VII 111
    First Salmon ceremony VII 56
    fishing rights of VII 198, 202
    Great Rendezvous at Celilio Falls VII 56
    impact of dams on VII 29, 51–61, 108, 110
    ingenuity of VII 11
    intermarriage with non-Indians VII 169
    loss of rights VII 151
    on Columbia River VII 202
    opposition by non-Indians living on the
    reservations VII 172
    protest movements VII 199
    relocation of burial grounds VII 60
    relationship with U.S. government III 139–146
    reservations of VII 28
    sacred sites endangered by dams VII 25
    treaties VII 56, 222
Native Americans, tribes
    Aymara Indians (Peru) 74
    Cocopah VII 151
    Flathead VII 167, 169–170
    Hopi VII 169
    Hualapai VII 110, 114
    Kootenai VII 167, 171–172
    Muckleshoot VII 191
    Navajo VII 110–111, 114
    Nez Perce VII 51, 55–56, 59
    Pawnee VII 166
    Pend Oreille VII 167
    Pueblo VII 169
    Quecha VII 151
    Salish VII 167, 171–172
    Umatilla VII 51, 55–56, 59
    Warm Springs VII 51, 55–56, 59
    Wyam VII 57
    Yakama VII 51, 55–57, 59
Natural Resources Defense Council VII 31
Naturalization Act (1952) I 74
Nature Conservancy, The VII 216
Naval Disarmament Conference (1921) V 203
Nazi Germany I 108, 135–136, 138, 149, 152, 241,
    255, 266, 274, 288, 293, 301; VIII 167
    administrative system IV 96
    Aryan myth of superiority VIII 204
    and Austria VIII 284
    Brownshirts (1934) I 134
    concentration camp system III 252
    Final Solution III 256
    ideology IV 86
    influence on German army IV 86

mass extinction of Jews III 251
nonaggression pact with Soviet Union I 306
policy toward Jews III 250–257
racial ideology IV 124
support of German population V 210–217
war aims V 210
Nazi-Soviet Non-Aggression Pact (1939) I 107, 110, 136; IV 57, 125; V 224–227; VI 179, 245
Nebraska 181–182
Nehru, Jawaharlal VI 268, 271; VII 126, 130
Nelson, Gaylord Anton VII 123
Nepal, dams in VII 9
Netherlands VI 77, 183, 188, 264; VII 229–230; VIII 137, 246, 285
    antinuclear protests VI 16
    Brussels Treaty I 208
    Department of Public Works and Water Management (Rijkswaterstaat) VII 92
    human rights foreign policy II 102
Neto, Antonio Agostinho VI 1, 165, 265
Nevada, reclamation projects in VII 26
New Alliance Party II 198
New Braunfels River VII 74
New Conservation, The VII 259
New Deal I 241, 301, 306; III 63, 90, 147–155; VI 56, 129, 151, 158; VII 28, 43, 223, 258, 263; VIII 301
    agricultural policies III 156–163
    dam building VII 29, 202
    Great Depression III 60
    programs III 63
New Delhi Summit (1983) VI 268
New England
    diking in VII 277
    reclamation of salt marshes VII 277
    use of wetlands (salt marshes) in VII 275
    wetlands in VII 271
New Federalism II 183, 185
New Hampshire, wildlife refuges in VII 278
New Jersey VII 265
    integrate laboratory procedures into oyster management VII 43
    mosquito-control ditching VII 273
    privitization of oystering VII 47
New Left I 77; II 159–160, 162, 164; VI 25
New Look I 115, 117, 210–215, 266; VI 133, 141
New Mexico VII 181
New Negro movement III 80, 117
New Woman
    birth control III 171
    fashion III 171
    lesbianism III 168
    physical expectations III 170
    Progressive Era (1890–1915) III 165–173
New World Order
    double-standard of II 157
    Persian Gulf crisis II 153
    purpose of II 154
New York
    integrate laboratory procedures into oyster management VII 43
    privitization of oystering in VII 47
New York City VII 256, 265–266
    water problems in VII 261
New Zealand VIII 133, 160–161
    in World War I VIII 117–123, 220, 266
Newbury, Massachusetts VII 277
    wetlands confiscated in VII 278
Newell, Frederick H. VII 26
Newell, Roger VII 48
Newlands, Francis Griffith VII 25–26
Newlands Reclamation Act (1902) VII 25–26, 201
Ngo Dinh Diem I 290, 298; II 97, 119, 266–267; VI 92–99
Ngo Dinh Nhu II 119; VI 94, 96
Nicaragua I 48–49, 51, 53–54, 57, 94, 96, 141; II 56, 58; III 50; VI 4, 44, 57, 61, 64, 68, 131, 190–

196, 221, 231, 236–237, 241, 261, 265–266, 270
    human rights record I 143
    mining Managua harbor VI 190–191
    National Security Decision Directive 17 (NSDD-17) I 50
    Sandinista takeover I 125–126
    Somoza dictators II 103
    Soviet support of guerrillas VI 58, 193
    U.S. arms shipments (1954) I 123
    U.S. policy in VI 190–196, 249
Nicholas II VIII 171, 174–175, 226, 229, 258, 266, 268
Niemöller, Martin IV 188–189
Nile River VII 2–3
Nipomo Dunes VII 178
Nimitz, Chester W. IV 7, 172; V 7
Nine-Power Treaty (1922) IV 258
1960s progressive movements II 159–167
1920s III 174–180
Nineteenth Amendment II 78
Ninth Amendment II 225, II 281
Nitze, Paul H. I 82–83, 86, 149, 191, 211, 274
Nivelle, Robert-Georges VIII 104, 106, 111, 114, 149, 269
Nixon, Richard M. I 40–41, 44–47, 66, 74, 89, 101–102, 104, 140, 159, 306, 317; II 4, 7, 95, 97, 102, 115, 133, 162, 165, 171–172, 197, 209, 256, 257, 260, 280–281; III 48; VI 4, 23–24, 26, 28, 30, 56, 58–59, 61, 91, 96, 162, 206, 231, 256–257, 284
    anti-communist legislation II 131; VI 203
    childhood of II 176
    Committee to Re-Elect the President (CREEP) II 177
    domestic policy II 175–186
    election (1968) VI 85
    Equal Employment Opportunity Commission (EEOC) II 182
    establishes EPA VII 266
    Executive Order 11458 II 183
    Federal Occupational Safety and Health Act (1970) II 192
    foreign policy II 168–174
    goal of Middle East policy I 162
    human rights I 141; VI 200
    loss to John F. Kennedy II 177
    malicious campaign tactics of II 177
    meetings with Brezhnev II 170
    mutual assured destruction (MAD) policy I 169
    pardoned by Gerald R. Ford II 179
    Pentagon Papers II 177
    presidential election (1960) I 188
    psychological analyses of II 181
    reelection campaign (1972) VI 86, 88
    resignation I 292; II 179; VI 87
    signs Great Lakes Water Agreement VII 120
    "Silent Majority" speech II 9
    vetos Federal Water Pollution Control Act Amendments VII 263
    vice president of Eisenhower II 177
    Vietnam I 291; II 173
    War on Poverty II 270
    Watergate I 144, 292; II 176, 185
Nixon administration I 68, 129; II 3–4; VI 35, 199; VII 269
    acceptance of Israel as a nuclear-weapons state I 158
    applies Refuse Act provisions VII 266
    Cambodia I 41–45; VI 60
    Chile I 130
    China VI 38–44, 201, 204
    foreign policy I 141–143; VI 58–59, 85–91, 198–205
    Latin America I 18
    Middle East I 162
    nuclear proliferation policy I 222; VI 18
    Vietnam VI 40, 86, 99, 203

Nixon Doctrine VI 199

Nkotami Accord (1984) VI 5

Nkrumah, Kwame I 110; III 121; VII 237

Nobel Peace Prize III 243
  Martin Luther King Jr. II 19
  Theodore Roosevelt II 99
  Woodrow Wilson II 99

Non-Aligned Movement (NAM) VI 181, 268, 270–271; VII 240

nongovernmental organizations (NGOs) 19, 247–248, 254

Noriega, Manuel VI 225

Nordic Environmental Certificate VII 87

Normandy invasion (June 1944) IV 14; V 10, 12, 15, 17–23, 37, 41, 58, 80, 102, 196

North, Oliver Col. VI 196, 231

North Africa II 144; VII 148; VIII 233
  growth of industry in VII 147
  invasion of V 5, 35

North Atlantic Regional Study (NARS) VII 261

North Atlantic Treaty Organization (NATO) I 35, 107, 120, 124, 151, 154, 160, 168, 170, 175, 182, 196, 198, 213, 222, 254, 277, 283, 296; II 50, 61, 100, 146, 152, 264, 267; IV 30; V 42, 149; VI 8–9, 11, 18–19, 50, 53, 80, 100–102, 105–106, 115, 131, 134–136, 173, 188, 199, 206–207, 209, 215, 217, 267, 271; VII 83
  creation of I 204–209
  involvement in Bosnian conflict II 154
  military strategy in Europe VI 168–174
  withdrawal of France VI 145

North Carolina, oyster management in VII 49

North Dakota VII 31
  dams in VII 29
  Native Americans in VII 29

North Eastern Water Supply Study (NEWS) 261

North Korea I 41, 293; II 37; VI 50, 54, 102, 147, 149–150, 178, 215–217, 219, 252, 261
  cease-fire with U.S. I 275
  invasion of South Korea (1950) I 87, 208; VI 28
  nuclear weapons development I 217, 219, 224, 239

North Sea VII 104, 204–205, 210, 230
  time needed to flush pollution from VII 142
  and World War I VIII 29, 35, 122, 135

North Vietnam I 40–42, 44–46, 290–299; II 4–8, 263; VI 28, 50, 96–97, 178, 201, 203, 285
  conquers South Vietnam (1975) I 142; VI 24
  declares independence I 290
  Gulf of Tonkin incident I 291
  peace agreement signed I 291
  Soviet support VI 246
  U.S. bombing VI 59, 165

Northam, William E. VII 43

Northern Buffalo Fence (NBF) VII 35

Northern Rhodesia VII 237

Northey, Edward VIII 86, 89

Northwest Kansas Groundwater Management District VII 185, 187

Noto v. *U.S.* I 81

Novikov, Nikolai I 178

"Novikov Telegram" II 35

Nuclear Nonproliferation Act (1978) I 223

Nuclear Non-Proliferation Treaty (NPT) I 216, 217–219, 222, 224; VI 30, 33, 104, 106

Nuclear-power plants, regulation of VII 174–180

Nuclear spying I 239, 241–249, 261

Nuclear Test Ban Treaty (1963) II 117–118

Nuclear weapons I 117, 154, 163, 165–172, 216–224, 225–233, 234–241, 249–257
  arms control VI 30–36
  carried by bombers I 4, 6, 8
  debate in House Armed Servies Committee hearings of 1949 I 8
  introduction I 4
  safety of VI 214
  U.S. monopoly I 27–28

Nueces River VII 70

Nuremberg Laws (1936) III 251; IV 137, 140–141; V 117–118

Nuremberg Party Rally (1935) V 140

Nuremberg war-crimes trials (1945–1946) IV 88; V 225

Nyae Nyae conservancy, Namibia VII 38

Nyasaland VII 237

Nye Commission VIII 284

O

Oahe Dam (United States) VII 29, 31

Objectives for Boundary Water Quality (1951) VII 117, 120

Öcalan, Abdullah VII 79

Odendaal Commission into South-West African Affairs VII 239

Office of Equal Opportunity (OEO) II 270–276

Office of Minority Business Enterprise (OMBE) II 183

Office of Strategic Services (OSS) V 146–147

Ogallala Aquifer VII 181–187

Ohio VII 265

Ohio River Valley VII 256

oil pollution VII 147, 265

oil shale VII 22–23

Okavango VII Delta 33, 236

Okavango River VII 236

Oklahoma VII 10, 181–182, 185

Oklahoma Water Resources Board VII 185

Omnibus Rivers and Harbors Act (1965) VII 261

On the Road (Kerouac) II 109

On the Waterfront (movie) II 190

Ontario Water Resources Commission (OWRC) VII 118

Ontario, Canada VII 116–117
  postwar economic boom in VII 119
  rejects water bill VII 119

Open Door policy (1899) II 38, 99, 267

Operations—
  —Anvil (1944) IV 68, 148; V 72, 236, 238, 241
  —Aphrodite V 98
  —Badr (1973) I 316
  —Bagration IV 150
  —Barbarossa (1941) IV 6, 54, 162, 244, 282; V 67, 80, 127, 137, 176, 180–181, 226–234
  —Blücher (1918) VIII 54
  —Citadel V 177–178
  —Clarion V 98–99
  —Cobra (1944) V 2, 129
  —Coronet V 49
  —Dragoon IV 68; V 35–241
  —Duck Hook II 6
  —El Dorado Canyon (1986) VI 234
  —Husky (1943) V 35, 39, 236
  —Ichigo (1944) V 196–198
  —Market Garden (1944) IV 180, 184; V 13, 16, 21–25, 129
  —Michael (1918) VIII 112
  —Olympic V 49
  —Overlord (1944) IV 42, 44, 63, 148–149, 179, 183, 262; V 34, 36, 58, 69, 72, 236
  —Rolling Thunder I 291
  —Roundup IV 210, 213; V 39
  —Sea Lion V 101, 176
  —Shingle IV 44
  —Sledgehammer IV 210, 213
  —Solarium I 272
  —Success (1954) I 126
  —Thunderclap (1945) V 92, 98–99
  —Torch (1942) IV 62, 181, 193, 210, 213, 241; V 35, 39, 82, 131, 176, 179, 233, 236, 251, 258
  —Uranus V 176
  —Urgent Fury (1983) VI 234

Oppenheimer, J. Robert I 29–31, 257; V 50; VI 158

Orange Free State VIII 31

Orange River VII 1–2, 7, 236–237, 240–241

Orange River Project (South Africa) VII 237, 240

Orcí, Arturo VII 158

INDEX

Ordnungspolizei (uniformed police) IV 141
Oregon VII 201, 220–221
    dams in VII 31, 51–61
    population in VII 54
Oregon Fish Commission VII 31, 53
Oregon Railway and Navigation Company VII 57
Oregon Wildlife Federation VII 53
Organization of African Unity (OAU) VII 240
Organization of American States (OAS) I 21, 71, 94,
    98; II 115, 152; III 53; VI 192, 194
    human rights I 146
Organization of Ukrainian Nationalists (OUN) IV 130
Organization of Petroleum Exporting Countries
    (OPEC) VI 107, 268
Orlando, Vittorio VIII 18, 278
Orontes River VII 78–79, 81
Ortega Saavedra, Daniel VI 190, 195
Osborn, Sidney P. VII 153
Ostpolitik (Eastern policy) VI 59, 144, 149, 204, 206–
    212
Ottmaring Valley VII 204, 207
Ottoman Empire VII 77, 81–83, 138; VIII 37, 82, 104,
    133, 172, 178, 208, 211–217, 228, 281
    Arab rebellions VIII 39, 212
    Army VIII 38, 118
    British policy in VIII 168
    economy VIII 215
    Jews in World War I VIII 166
Owen, Wilfred VIII 61, 191
Oyster Restoration Areas VII 49
The Oyster: A Popular Summary of a Scientific Study
    (1891) VII 41
oysters VII 40–50
    decline of in Chesapeake Bay VII 40–50
    diseases VII 46
    natural enemies of VII 41
Özal, Turgut 79

P

Pacific Gas and Electric Corporation (PG&E) VII
    177–178
Pacific Northwest VII 55
    dams in VII 51
    industrialization in VII 51–53
    railroads in VII 52
    water policy in VII 110
Pacific Northwest Development Association VII 53
Pacific Ocean VII 220
    as dumping ground for thermal waste VII 178
    during World War I VIII 31, 33, 72, 133, 137
Pacific Salmon Crisis VII 219
Pacific Southwest Water Plan VII 109
Pahlavi, Mohammad Reza Shah I 70; VI 166, 266
Pakistan I 89, 158; II 85, 172; VI 53, 83, 88, 149, 201,
    214–215, 219, 238
    Baghdad Pact I 161
    nuclear alliance with Libya I 223
    nuclear weapons development I 15, 217, 219, 221,
    223
Palestine I 160, 164, 317; II 144; VI 164, 188; VII 81–
    82, 138, 139; VIII 37, 39–40, 82, 103, 163,
    166, 208, 212–213, 216, 221
    British withdrawal from VI 83
    disenfranchisement in VII 135
    Jewish homeland in VIII 37, 168
    as mandate VIII 166
    water policy in VII 140
Palestinian Authority VII 136
Palestine Liberation Organization (PLO) I 156; VI 54,
    163, 201
Palmer, A. Mitchell III 221–223, 226
Palmer, Joel VII 56
Palmer raids III 221, 223, 234
Pan-African Congress (1919) III 122; VII 239
Panama Canal I 53; II 257; III 243, 247; VI 40, 190
Panama Canal Treaty I 52
Panama Refining Company v. *Ryan* (1935) III 28

Panda (Moscow TV show) VII 23–24
Pan-Slavism VIII 207, 228
Paris Commune (1871) VIII 147
Paris Peace Accords (1973) I 142; VI 222
Paris Peace Conference (1919) VIII 12, 150, 217
Paris Summit (1960) I 276
Parker, Billy VII 56
Parker, Dorothy III 177
Parker River Wildlife Refuge VII 277–278
Parks, Rosa II 140
Pathet Lao VI 141–142
Patriot Party (1994) II 195, 198
Patton, George S. V 2, 23, 44, 125, 127–129, 136;
    VIII 19, 219
    Battle of the Bulge IV 195
    Italian campaign IV 144
    military background IV 193
    Operation Torch IV 193
    reputation IV 192–199
Paul, Marcel VII 97
Peace and Freedom Party II 197
Peace Corps I 24; II 116; VI 140
Peabody Coal Company VII 111
Peace Water Pipeline Project VII 79, 83
Pearl Harbor (1941) I 89, 261; II 99; III 103, 107–
    108, 214–215, V 4, 35, 43, 110, 131–135, 183,
    187–188, 191–192, 195, 229, 258; VI 150
    wetlands takings compared to attack on VII 278
Pearse, Patrick VIII 155–156, 158, 162
Pender, F. G. VII 53, 55
Pennsylvania
    dams in VII 29
    signs Chesapeake Bay 2000 Agreement VII 49
Pennsylvania State University VII 262
Pentagon II 51, 67
Pentagon Papers (1971) II 177; VI 24, 26
People's Liberation Army (PLA) I 268
Pepó, Pal VII 250
perestroika I 14; II 56, 60; VI 114, 116, 245; VII 20
Perkins, Frances III 150, 200, 251
Perot, H. Ross II 194–202
    advantages to his campaign II 198
    election grassroots movement II 195
    hatred of George Bush II 199
    importance of wealth to his campaign II 202
    presidential campaign II 195
Pershing, John J. III 130, 138; V 14, 126; VIII 10–20,
    21–25, 114
    Mexican expedition III 127
    U. S. Punitive Expedition III 129
Pershing II missiles VI 3, 20–21, 35, 101–102, 208, 229,
    232, 236, 263
Persia VIII 31, 35, 41
Persian Gulf VII 77, 147
Persian Gulf War (1990–1991) I 163, 195–196, 199, 217,
    239; VI 58, 61, 100, 173, 235, 250, 266;
    VIII 168
Peru VII 74
Pétain, Philippe IV 276; V 244; VIII 150, 265
Petrograd Soviet VIII 170, 173, 175, 178, 258
Philippines I 51, I 295; VI 77, 80, 149, 188, 194
    Clark Field and Subic Bay I 145
    crucial to U.S. security I 85
    Opium War III 136
Phongolapoort Dam (South Africa) VII 245
Picasso, Pablo III 79
Picq, Charles VIII 71, 234
Pinochet Ugarte, Augusto I 124, 128–129, 141; VI 64
Plan XVI VIII 233–234
Plan XVII VIII 146, 148, 182, 232–238
Planned Parenthood of Missouri v. *Danforth* (1976) II 222
Planned Parenthood of Southeastern Pennsylvania v. *Casey*
    (1992) II 79, 222, 224
plants
    African grasses VII 217
    alfalfa VII 14, 182
    Bermuda grass VII 217
    black mustard VII 217

corn VII 181, 182
    Huachuca water umbel VII 216
    invasion of alien species in the United States VII
      213
    Johnson grass VII 217
    Kearney blue-star VII 216
    Russian Thistles VII 13
    sorghum VII 181–182
    tiszavirág (Tisza flower) VII 252
    winter wheat VII 181
Platt Amendment (1901) III 47
    revocation of, 1934 III 47
Plessy v. *Ferguson* (1896) II 23, 25, 90, 136, 138, 141,
    280, 290
Plum Island VII 277
Plumer, Herbert VIII 219–220, 224
Po River VII 147
Podoba, Juraj VII 103
Point Reyes National Seashore VII 178
Poison Gas VIII 239–244
Pol Pot I 44, 46, 134, 145, 289; VI 83
Poland I 109–110, 112, 152, 259, 271, 294; II 34, 36,
    39, 153; V 30; VI 110, 130, 133–134, 137,
    178, 181, 217, 237, 244–246, 249, 251–252,
    261, 274, 276; VIII 91, 277–278, 280–281,
    284
    aftermath of World War II I 173
    Baruch Plan I 27, 29, 31
    entry into NATO I 207
    environmental activism in VII 17–24
    expatriates VI 170
    German invasion during World War II V 35, 132,
      179; VIII 284
    German occupation during World War I VIII 92–
      98
    impact of pollution on population of VII 18
    independence movement VI 110
    Jews in during World War I VIII 164–167
    martial law in (1981) VII 19
    partition VI 54
    poisoning of waters in VII 18
    postwar elections I 258
    radioactive fallout from Chernobyl VII 18
    reforms I 154
    Soviet invasion of II 32
    strategic importance I 109
    and Warsaw Pact VI 170
    Yalta Agreement (1945) I 301–302, 304
Polaris Submarine VI 11, 75
Polaris Submarine/Sea-Launched Ballistic Missile
    (SLBM) VI 10
Polish Communist Party, Tenth Congress of VII 20
Polish Ecological Club (Polski Klub Ekologiczny, or
    PKE) VII 18
Polish Green Party VII 20
Political parties
    history of II 199
    history of third parties II 199
    voter demographics II 199
Pollution Control Act (1915, Ontario) VII 117
polychlorinated biphenyls (PCBs) VII 147
Pong Dam (India) VII 130
Pope Pius XII IV 36, 38, 191
Popular Unity Coalition (UP) I 123, 127
Populist Party II 3, 86, 199
    aka People's Party II 196
Porter, Eliot VII 113
Portland Dock Commission VII 53
Portland, Oregon VII 52, 197
    importance of VII 53
Portugal VII 240; VIII 31
    colonial rule in Africa VII 236–237; VIII 86, 89
Potsdam Conference (1945) I 239, 263; II 205; III 13;
    VI 155, 267
Potlatch Corporation VII 226
Potsdam Declaration (1945) III 15; V 50–51, 149, 264
Powell, Adam Clayton, Jr. II 197, 274
Powell, Colin II 100

Powell, John Wesley VII 181
Powers, Francis Gary I 66
President's Foreign Intelligence Advisory Board
    (PFIAB) VI 256–257
Pressler Amendment (1985) I 218
Principle International Alert Center VII 248
Progressive Era VII 10, 47, 122, 257, 271, 273
    women in III 197–203
Progressive movement III 204–211; VII 263; VIII
    295, 301
Progressive Party II 195–196, 209; III 177
Prohibition III 174, 198–211
Prussia VIII 71, 184, 257, 278
    military 30, 67
Pryce, E. Morgan VII 55
Public Broadcasting System (PBS) II 125; VII 184
Public Works Administration (PWA, 1933) III 150;
    VII 43
Pueblo Dam (United States) VII 14
Puget Sound VII 188–189, 191, 193–194
Pugwash Conference I 253
Punjab, India VII 133
    agriculture in VII 130
Pure Food and Drug Act (1906) III 243
Pyle, Ernie V 175
Pyramid Lake VII 169

Q

Quadrant Conference (1943) V 236
Quai d'Orsai (French Foreign Office) V 173
Quebec, Canada, opposes water bill VII 120
Quebec Conference (1943) V 239
Quemoy I 275; II 52; VI 103, 181
    Chinese attack I 265–270
    Eisenhower administration I 211, 213
Quinn v. *U.S.* I 80

R

Rába geologic fault line VII 106
Rachel Carson National Wildlife Refuge VII 278
racism II 163; III 213–219
    American IV 217
    and narcotics legislation III 134
Radio Free Europe I 65; VI 133, 135
Railroad Retirement Pension Act (1934) III 28
Rainbow Bridge VII 30
Rainey, Gertrude "Ma" III 82
Rajasthan, India VII 125
    agriculture in VII 130
    rainfall in VII 126
Rajasthan Canal VII 132
Rákosi, Mátyás VI 134, 276
Ramadan War. *See* Yom Kippur War I 314
RAND Corporation I 119; II 65–66
Randolph, A. Philip II 189; III 123, 184, 217
    march on Washington III 219
Rape of Nanking (1937) IV 152–153; V 153, 192
Raritan Bay VII 265
Rasputin, Grigory VIII 258
Rathenau, Walther VIII 140, 166
Rawlinson, Henry VIII 272, 275
Reagan, Ronald I 48, 51–54, 104, 106, 149; II 56–63,
    102, 190, 199–200, 295; III 48; VI 6, 8, 13,
    17, 20, 25, 31, 33, 50, 58, 104, 109, 190–191,
    205, 208, 221–242, 256–257, 261, 270
    anticommunism II 60; VI 228–229
    election platform I 50
    invasion of Grenada II 58
    nuclear arms race I 183
    Reagan Doctrine II 58
    Screen Actors Guild president II 189
    support of anticommunist regimes II 58
    view of Vietnam War I 295
    Strategic Defense Initiative (SDI) I 195–196, 199
Reagan administration VI 17, 36, 57, 133, 221, 225,
    228–235

INDEX

Afghanistan I 10–16; VI 133, 237
Africa policy VI 1–7
aid to contras I 54
arms control VI 19–20, 22
budget deficits I 202
Central America policies I 48–52, 54, 56
defense spending II 57; VI 109, 226
foreign policy VI 57, 61, 236–242
Iran-Contra affair I 54
Latin American I 14
National Security Decision Directive 17 (NSDD-17) I 50
National Security Decision Directives 32, 66, 75 I 196
Nicaragua VI 190–196
nuclear proliferation I 15
Soviet Union I 196; VI 44, 116, 194, 263
zero-zero option (1981) VI 36
Reagan Doctrine VI 44, 186, 221–227
impact on the Soviet Union VI 226
Reaganomics VI 226
Realpolitik I 285; II 169; IV 123
Red Scare I 174; III 221–226, 229; VI 129, 156, 158–159
impact on Sacco and Vanzetti trial III 233
Redmond, John VIII 154–157, 161
Reform Party (1996) II 195–200
Refuse Act (1899) VII 266, 268
Rehnquist, Justice William H. II 224, 281
Regional Center for Ecological Supervision of the Apuseni Mountains VII 250
Reichstag (German parliament) IV 137; V 115, 134, 211; VIII 164, 256
Reinsurance Treaty (1887–1890) VIII 225–226, 249
Remarque, Erich VIII 55, 59, 186, 188, 264
Republic of Vietnam. See South Vietnam
Republic Steel VII 266
Republican Party I 272; II 51, 180, 194–195, 198; III 118, 211
abortion II 79
benefits from school busing II 295
pro-life platforms II 223
reaction to Marshall Plan II 209
Republican National Convention (1952) II 280
United States presidents II 49
Vietnam policy II 266
Reserve Mining case VII 266, 268–269
Resistance movements V 243–247
aid to Allies V 245
forms of sabotage V 247
Germany's response to V 245
impact in France V 244
Vichy France V 247
Resources for the Future VII 259
Reuss, Henry Schoellkopf VII 266
Revolutionary Left Movement. See Movimiento de Izquierda Revolucionaria I 127, 130
Reykjavik Summit (1986) II 61; VI 33, 36, 224, 231
Reynolds v. Sims, 1962 II 139
Rhine Action Plan (1987) VII 230, 232
Rhine Commission (1815) VII 92
Rhine River VII 204, 207, 209–210, 229–235; VIII 24, 280, 282
chemical spill on VII 230
floods on VII 231
pollution of VII 234
Rhine-Main-Danube Canal 104, 204–210
Rhodes, James A. VII 265
Rhodesia VII 239; VIII 86
British immigration to VII 237
colonialists in VII 7
Rhodesian Unilateral Declaration of Independence VII 240
Rhône River VII 92–95, 147
Rhône River Authority VII 93, 96
Ribbentrop, Joachim von V 134
Ribbentrop-Molotov Non-Aggression Pact (1939) V 28, 30, 32

Rich, Willis VII 201
Rift Valley VII 229
Riis, Jacob August III 260
Rio Grande River VII 152
Rio Treaty I 93
riparian ecosystems in the U.S. Southwest VII 211–218
Rivers and Harbors Act (1899) VII 266
Rivers and Harbors Act (1925) VII 52
Roan Selection Trust VII 5
Robarts, John P. VII 118
Roberto, Holden VI 1, 165
Roberts, Justice Owen III 25, 28, 30; V 188
Robertson, William VIII 77, 102–108, 221
Robinson, Bestor VII 112
Robinson, James H. II 44
Rock Around the Clock (1956) II 219
Rock and Roll II 213–219
"British invasion" II 216
commercial aspects II 219
form of rebellion II 219
liberating force II 213
mass marketing of II 216
origin of term II 214
punk trends II 216
revolutionary force II 214
unifying force II 216
Rockefeller, John D. III 271
Rockefeller, Nelson A. III 48; VII 264
Rocky Boy's Reservation VII 172
Rocky Ford VII 15
Rocky Ford Ditch Company VII 13
Rocky Mountains VII 151, 181, 197
Roe v. Wade (1973) II 78, 220–226, 280, 284
Rogue River VII 31, 223
Romania I 110, 294; II 36, 39, 172; V 64; VI 51, 88, 175, 206, 210, 217, 245, 249, 252, 261, 265, 274, 276; VII 248–250, 252–254; VIII 43–44, 46, 93–97, 163, 216, 230, 278
chemical spill in VII 247–255
Department of Waters, Forests, and Environmental Protection VII 248
Environmental Protection Agency VII 248
forest clear-cutting in VII 254
relationship with Soviets I 253
Soviet Domination I 107
U.S. recognizes communist government I 303
Romanian Waters Authority VII 248
Rommel, Erwin V 123–126, 129, 135, 143, 176, 181, 226; VIII 111
legend V 175
Roosevelt, Eleanor III 150, 217, 219
Roosevelt, Franklin D. II 32, 39, 50, 52, 165, 197, 203, 280; III 10–11, 14, 45, 48, 86, 89, 109, 147, 190, 193; IV 173, 210; V 58, 236, 249; VI 8–9, 20, 36, 56–57, 78, 104, 123, 146–147, 158, 205, 254, 267; VII 28, 97, 152, 202
arsenal of democracy III 64
Asia policy IV 254
attitude toward Soviet Union III 13
belief in a cooperative relationship with the Soviet Union I 101
Brain Trust II 210
Casablanca conference (1943) V 252
election of VII 27
Executive Order 8802 (1941) III 219
Executive Order 9066 (1942) III 103–104
Fireside chats III 148, 152
Four Freedoms V 250
Good Neighbor Policy I 125; III 47
Great Depression III 54–60
Inaugural Address (1932) III 152
isolationism V 289–294
Lend Lease Act IV 160
Native American policies III 141–142
New Deal II 47, 271; III 193, 263
New Deal programs III 62–63
Operation Torch (1942) V 251
opinion of Second Front IV 213

INDEX

presidential campaign (1932) III 148
previous war experience V 253
relationship with George C. Marshall V 251
Roosevelt Court II 281
State of the Union Address (1941) II 99
Scottsboro case III 188
Selective Service Act (1940) V 250
support of Great Britain V 250
support of highway building II 106
support of naval reorganization IV 3
Supreme Court III 24
unconditional surrender policy V 270–276
western irrigation VII 25
World War II strategy V 251, 253
Yalta conference V 252, 309–315
Roosevelt, Theodore I 306; II 195, 199, 271–272; III
    208, 211, 240–247, 177; VIII 18, 22, 129,
    205
    appreciation of public image III 242
    Bull Moose Party III 243
    conservation efforts III 243
    Dominican Republic III 247
    establishes federal refuges VII 271, 273
    First Children III 242
    labor disputes III 243
    New Nationalism III 211
    Nobel Peace Prize II 99, 243
    racial prejudices III 246
    role as a family man III 242
    Rough Riders III 241
    signs Newlands Reclamation Act VII 25
    Spanish-American War (1898) III 245
    supports western reclamation VII 26
    Teddy bears III 242
    views on Latin America I 132
Roosevelt (FDR) administration III 46; VI 154
    dam projects VII 25
    national drug policy III 135
    New Deal III 163
    opium trade III 137
    policy toward Jews III 251
    relationship with labor movement II 188
    Soviet sympathizers in VI 61, 154
    spurs Western growth VII 28
    support of Mexican Water Treaty VII 152
    Third World VI 80
    War Refugee Board (WRB) III 253
Roosevelt (TR) administration
    Anti-Trust Act (1890) III 242
    Big Stick diplomacy III 46
    corollary to the Monroe Doctrine III 247
    Department of Commerce and Labor, Bureau of
        Corporations III 242
    foreign policy III 243, 245
    Hepburn Act (1906) III 243, 245
    National Reclamation Act (1902) III 243
    Panama Canal III 243, 247
    Pure Food and Drug Act (1906) III 243
    United States Forestry Service III 243
Roosevelt Corollary (1904) III 46
Roosevelt Dam (United States) VII 214, 216
Root Elihu VIII 298
Rosellini, Albert D. VII 190
Rosenberg, Alfred V 143, 216
Rosenberg, Julius and Ethel I 274; II 131, 227–234; VI
    154, 156, 158, 177
    and Communist Party of the United States of
        America (CPUSA) II 227
    arrest of II 229, 231–232
    execution of II 233
    forged documents II 230
    Freedom of Information Act II 228
    G & R Engineering Company II 229
    martyrdom II 230
    Meeropol, Michael and Robert, sons of II 228
    possible motives for arrest of II 231
    proof of espionage activity II 230
    Soviet nuclear spying I 241, 243, 246–247

Young Communist League II 228
Ross, Bob VII 74
Rostow, Walt W. I 20, 294
    flexible response I 120
Royal Air Force (RAF) I 235; IV 163, 168; V 86, 90,
    93, 95, 124; VIII 55, 194
    attacks on civilians V 87
Royal Air Force (RAF) Mosquitoes V 60
Royal Canadian Navy V 80, 82, 85
Royal Navy (Britain) V 43, 82, 85, 118, 260; VI 75;
    VIII 132
Ruacana Diversion Wier VII 239
Ruckelshaus, William D. VII 263, 266, 268
Rundstedt, Field Marshal Karl Gerd von 125–126, 129
Rupprecht, Prince VIII 179–180, 184, 246, 274
Rural Institute in Puno, Peru VII 74
Rusk, Dean I 160, 294; VI 71, 95–96, 101
Russia VIII 30, 44–45, 48, 69, 71–72, 76, 82, 92–101,
    122, 182, 208–209, 212–213, 245–246, 251–
    252, 256, 277, 281, 299
    alliances before World War I VIII 35, 225–231
    alliances during World War I VIII 11, 212, 223
    anti-semitism VIII 164
    Army during World War I VIII 69, 75, 170–171
    casualties during World War I VIII 125–126, 268
    Crimean War (1853–1856) VIII 33
    Jews in VIII 164, 167
    Provisional government VIII 96, 167, 170–178,
        260, 261
    Socialists VIII 255, 258, 261
    White Army VIII 168
    women in combat during World War I VIII 125,
        129
Russian Federation VI 47, 53–54, 114
    former communists VI 55
Russian Revolution (1917) VI 176; VIII 96, 163, 170,
    211, 221, 261, 268
Russian Civil War (1918–1920) VI 244
Russo-Japanese War (1904–1905) IV 256; VI 40; VIII
    35, 44–45, 73, 75, 226, 228, 247
Russo-Turkish War (1877–1878) VIII 73, 226
Rwanda I 289; II 101, 155; VI 51, 213
    Tutsi population VI 83

S

SA (storm trooper) I 139
Sacco, Nicola and Bartolemo Vanzetti III 228–237;
    VIII 301
    involvement with Italian anarchist groups III 233
    League for Democratic Action III 235
    New England Civil Liberties Union III 235
    protest over verdict III 231
    trial III 231
Sacco-Vanzetti Defense Committee (SVDC) III 234
Sacramento River VII 29, 272
as-Sadat, Anwar I 159, 309, 311–314; II 150; VI 162–
    164, 170
    death (9 October 1981) I 317
    making peace I 317
    objective I 316
    policies I 316
    "year of decision" I 316
St. James Declaration (1942) V 264
Saimaa Lake, Finland VII 90
Saipan
    fall of (1944) V 112
Sakharov, Andrei I 146; II 104
Salish Mountains VII 171
Salmon 2000 Project VII 229–235
Salsedo, Andrea III 229–231
Salt River VII 214, 216
San Antonio River VII 70, 256
San Antonio Riverwalk VII 71
San Antonio Water System (SAWS) 70, 74
San Antonio, Texas VII 69–70, 74–75
    recycling of water in VII 70
San Francisco VII 262

San Francisco Bay VII 178
San Luís Rio Colorado VII 153, 154
San Marcos River VII 70, 74
San Pedro River VII 216
Sandanistas (Nicaragua) I 48–51, 53–54, 94, 96, 125–
        126; II 58; VI 61, 64, 190–191, 193, 237,
        241, 265
    attempting to maintain control of Nicaragua I 56
    Civil Defense Committees VI 192
    removed from power (1990) I 51
    takeover of Nicaragua (1979) I 54, 141
Sand Dunes and Salt Marshes (1913) VII 277
Sanders, Bernard II 197, 201
Sandoz chemical spill VII 229–230, 232
Sanger, Margaret III 17–18, 171
Santa Barbara, California VII 269
    oil platform blowout off of VII 265
Santa Barbara Declaration of Environmental
        Rights VII 267
Sarant, Alfred II 230
Sardar Sarovar project (India) VII 9, 132, 134
Saronic Gulf VII 148
Sarraut, Albert V 116
Satpura Mountains, India VII 125
Saudi Arabia II 153; VI 164–165, 239; VII 79, 81
    Afghan rebels VI 238
    dependence on United States I 162
    fundamentalist movements I 163
    Iraqi bombing of I 195
    Operation Desert Storm I 157
    pan-Arab campaign I 281
    support of United States I 158
Savage Rapids Dam (United States) VII 31
Save the Narmada Movement VII 127
Savimbi, Jonas VI 1–7, 165
Saynbach River VII 230
Scales v. *United States* I 81
Scalia, Anton II 224
Scalia, Antonin II 143
Schechter Poultry Corporation v. *United States* (1935) III
        28
Schecter, Jerrold L. I 243
Schecter, Leona P. I 243
Schelling, Thomas C. I 171
    flexible response I 121
Schlieffen, Alfred von VIII 71, 75, 179–180, 182, 184–
        185, 245–248
Schlieffen Plan VIII 71, 110, 114, 148, 180, 183, 199,
        208, 245–253
Schlesinger, Arthur M., Jr. I 74; VI 56–57, 154
School busing II 292–299
    Boston opposition to II 294
    Charlotte-Mecklenburg School District II 293
    impact on white flight II 294
    integration of public schools II 293
Schmidt, Helmut VII 207
Schutzstaffeln (SS) IV 84, 118, 130, 137, 139; V 58;
        VIII 60, 95
Schutztruppe (protectorate forces) VIII 85, 89
Schuylkill River VII 256
Scopes Trial (1925) III 33, 37
Scopes, John III 32–34, 37, 39
Scotland VIII 134, 203
Scottsboro case III 181, 185
Scottsboro Defense Committee III 188
Sea of Cortez VII 151
Sea of Galilee VII 136
Sea of Japan VII 148
Sea of Marmara VII 79
Seaborg, Glenn T. VII 176
Seattle, Washington VII 188–195, 197
    city council votes for dam removal VII 222
Seattle Post-Intelligencer VII 191
Seattle Times VII 191
Second Anglo-Boer War (1899–1902) VIII 198
Second International (1889) VIII 260
Second London Naval Disarmament Conference (1935–
        1936) V 204, 208

Second National Water Act (1961, Finland) VII 85, 87
Second Naval Conference (1927) V 204
Securities and Exchange Commission (SEC) III 154
Sedition Act III 229
Segregation II 19, 24, 26, 28, 42, 91, 137, 160, 162–163
    public facilities II 138
    U.S. armed forces IV 216–222
Selective Service II 4–5
Selective Service Act (1917) VIII 296
Selective Service Act (1940) V 250
Selway River VII 29
Senate Foreign Relations Committee II 208
Senate Internal Security Subcommittee (SISS) II 131,
        134
Senate Judiciary Committee III 26
Sephuma, Olive VII 243
Serageldin, Ismail VII 280
Serbia VIII 43–45, 47, 76, 95, 106, 162, 208, 212, 216,
        226, 228–229
    invaded by Austria-Hungary VIII 72
    population reduced by World War I VIII 189
Seufert Bros. v. *United States* (1919) VII 57–58
Seventeenth Amendment II 196
Sexual revolution II 235–240
    beginnings of II 238
    Commission on the Status of Women (1961) II
        238
    effects of II 224
    myth of vaginal orgasm II 238
    power vs. sex II 237
Seyhan River VII 79
Shaler, Nathaniel VII 277
Shanghai Commission (1909) III 137
Shanghai Communiqué (1972) II 172–173
Sharpeville Massacre (1960) VII 239–240
Shashe River, Botswana VII 33
Shasta Dam (United States) VII 29
Shatt al Arab VII 77
Sheaffer, John VII 262
Shelley v. *Kraemer* (1948) II 141
Shelley, Mary II 86
Shellfish VII 41–50
Sherman Anti-Trust Act (1890) III 242
Shevardnadze, Eduard VI 116
Showa Restoration V 112
Shriver, Sargent II 271, 275
    War on Poverty involvement II 272
Shultz, George P. VI 231
Sicherheitsdienst der SS (SD, Security Service of the
        SS) V 214, 216
Sicherheitspolizei (German Security Police) IV 141
Sieg River VII 230
Sierra Club VII 27, 30–31, 108, 111–114, 177
    fights Grand Canyon dams VII 110
Sierra Nevada Mountains VII 112, 272
Sigismund Chapel, Wawel Cathedral, Poland VII 18
Silent Spring (Carson) II 183; III 7; VII 86, 160, 162
Silent Valley Project (India) VII 127
Silvermaster, Nathan VI 126
Simsboro Aquifer VII 75
Sinai Peninsula I 308–309, 311–312, 316–317; VII 2,
        135
    demilitarization I 314
    Israeli forces I 313
Sinn Féin VIII 156, 158–159, 161–162
Sister Carrie (Dreiser) II 239
Sit-in movement (1960s) II 27, 160; VI 25
Six-Day War (1967) I 156–157, 159, 162, 308, 314; VI
        107, 163, 171; VII 135, 140
    aftermath I 312
    Gaza Strip I 314
    Golan Heights I 314
    Sinai Peninsula I 314
    West Bank of the Jordan River I 314
Sixth Amendment II 281
Skagit River VII 223
Skawina Aluminum Works VII 18–19
Skoropadsky, Pavlo VIII 99–100

INDEX

Slim, William V 3, 122, 198
Slovak Green Party VII 103
Slovak Union of Nature and Landscape Protectors VII 103
Slovakia VII 248, 250, 252
    dams in VII 100–107
    environmentalists in VII 103
    importance of Gabcikovo dam VII 103
    nuclear reactor at Jaslovské Bohunice VII 103
    nuclear-power plant at Mochovce VII 103
    symbolic importance of Danube VII 102
Smith Act (Alien Registration Act of 1940) I 77, 79, 81; III 11
Smith v. Allwright, 1944 II 141
Smith, Bessie III 79, III 82
Smith, Holland M. "Howlin' Mad" V 297, 299
Smith, Howard Alexander II 208
Smith, Ian VI 2, 83
Smutts, Jan VIII 85–86, 89
Smyrna VIII 214, 217
Smyth Report I 248
Smyth, Henry De Wolf I 247–248
Smythe, William A. VII 151
Snake River 27, 29, 31, 53–54, 196–197, 220, 221, 223–225, 227
    dams on VII 219–228
Social Darwinism III 260; IV 86, 123; VIII 60, 299
Social Democratic Party I 255; VI 20, 207
Social Ecological Movement VII 20
Social Security Act (1935) III 63, 149
Socialism II 34, 60, 160; VIII 254–262
Socialist convention (1913) III 223
Socialist Labor Party II 42
Socialist Party II 196, 199; III 222–223
    Debs, Eugene V. III 221
Socialist Unity Party (SED) VI 118, 121
Soil Conservation and Domestic Allotment Act (1936) III 157
Solidarity VI 110, 237; VII 17, 19, 20
Solzhenitzyn, Aleksandr VI 200
Somalia II 100, 155–156; VI 164, 271
    claim to Ogaden VI 165
    Ethiopian conflict VI 165
    imperialism I 151
    relations with the Soviet Union VI 165
Somoza Debayle, Anastasio I 48–49, 54, 126, 141; III 51; VI 190–191
Somocistas VI 64, 191
Sonoran Desert VII 151–152
    agriculture in VII 152
Sorensen, Ted II 275
Sorenson, Theodore C. II 117
South Africa I 51; VI 1, 2, 4, 6, 50, 54, 87, 136, 178, 215; VII 2, 5, 67, 236–237, 239–241; VIII 31, 160–161, 208
    apartheid VI 13
    Bill of Rights VII 287
    British immigration to VII 237
    inequalities of water supply in VII 284
    intervention in Angola VI 7
    intervention in Mozambique VI 6
    nuclear weapons development I 219–223
    rinderpest epidemic VII 34
    use of water by upper class VII 7
    water policy in VII 286, 287
South African National Defense Force VII 7
South America, introduction of species to the United States from VII 217
South Carolina
    laws on rice dams and flooding VII 272
    rice cultivation in the tidewater zone VII 272
    slaves cleared swamp forests VII 272
South Dakota VII 181
    dams in VII 29
South East Asia Treaty Organization (SEATO) II 52, 264
South Korea I 86–87, 288, 293; II 37; VI 102, 147–149, 217, 263

domino theory I 266
    invaded by North Korea (1950) I 208; VI 28
    invasion of I 184
    nuclear weapons development I 216, 219, 223
    U.S. intervention I 158
South Vietnam I 40–46, 290, 293–299; II 5–8, 263, 266; VI 58–60, 92–99, 101, 138, 140, 201, 203, 284
    aid received from United States I 158; VI 2, 66, 142, 144
    conquered by North Vietnam I 142; VI 222
    declares independence I 290
    Soviet support I 185
Southeast Asia Treaty Organization (SEATO) I 277; VI 203, 287
Southeastern Anatolia Project VII 77, 83
Southern African Hearings for Communities affected by Large Dams VII 242
Southern Baptist Convention III 38
Southern Christian Leadership Conference (SCLC) II 22, 26, 28, 89
Southern Okavango Integrated Water Development Project VII 243
Southern Pacific Railroad VII 151, 155
Southern Rhodesia VII 237, 239
Southern Tenant Farmers' Union (STFU) II 189; III 159
South-West Africa VII 237, 239
South-West African People's Organization (SWAPO) VII 239
Southwest Kansas Groundwater Management District VII 185
Soviet expansionism I 262; II 34–35, 208, 264, 267; III 10
    U.S. fear of II 129, 207
Soviet intervention
    Hungary I 278, 281
    Middle East I 277
Soviet Union I 77, 91; II 9, 56–62, 64–71, 168, 171; III 10; VI 9, 16, 20–21, 32, 35, 49, 106, 115–116, 147, 149, 161, 201, 206, 208, 236, 250–255, 260, 264; VII 55; VIII 94, 97, 99, 277, 285
    aging leadership VI 111
    aid to China V 198
    aid to Mozambique VI 2
    Angola policy VI 41, 43, 165
    annexes Estonia VII 22
    "Aviation Day" I 192
    bomber fleet I 6; VI 50
    casualties in Afghanistan (1979-1989) I 12
    Central Committee II 59
    Central Committee Plenum II 60
    challenge to U.S. dominance in Latin America I 125
    collapse I 11; VI 47, 50, 58, 108, 213, 224, 227, 235, 237; VII 17, 207; VIII 139
    Cominform I 178
    Communist Party VI 244, 247
    cooperation with Nationalist Chinese government I 304
    coup (1991) VI 114
    Cuban Missile Crisis II 116; VI 70–76
    Czechoslovakia (1948) II 130, 133
    defense spending I 197; VI 54; VI 116, 120, 226
    demographics VI 242
    demokratizatiia I 152
    development of wartime economy IV 233
    diplomatic work I 289
    domination of eastern Europe I 258, 260
    domination of other countries I 271
    drain on resources by war in Afghanistan I 13
    East Germany policy VI 115–122, 211
    Eastern Europe as defensive barrier I 303
    economy I 184; II 57, 59; VI 109, 111, 214, 242
    empire VI 243–249
    entry into war against Japan I 301
    espionage network II 130

Estonian contribution to VII 22
fear of the West I 181
first Soviet atomic bomb test I 244
forces in Afghanistan I 13
foreign aid VI 54, 254
gains control of Eastern Europe I 302
glasnost I 152; VI 108–114
government suspicion of citizens I 185
Gross National Product II 60
human rights record II 104; VI 35, 85, 109, 200, 244
Hungarian uprising I 276
ICBM buildup I 190
ICBM development I 189–194
ideology in foreign policy I 148–154
industrialization ideology VII 104
influence in postwar Europe I 174
invasion of Afghanistan (1979) VI 2, 30, 35, 42–44, 66, 68, 116, 162, 165, 237, 241, 246
invasion of Chechnya (1990s) VI 169
invasion of Czechoslovakia (1968) I 11–12; VI 43
invasion of Hungary (1956) I 12
invasion of Manchuria III 15
Iran policy I 11
Jewish emigration VI 43, 200, 257
komitet gosudarstvennoy bezopasnosti (KGB) II 59
leaders I 262
Middle East policy I 160; VI 160–167, 268
military balance VI 168–174
military capabilities II 30, 64
military expenditures I 125
"Molotov Plan" I 178
New Course I 184, 192
New Economic Policy (NEP) VI 113
nonaggression pact with Germany (1939) II 32
nuclear buildup I 230
nuclear capabilities I 213; II 130, 133; VI 35, 215
nuclear testing I 212; VI 49, 173, 177
nuclear weapons development I 184, 241–249; VI 31, 109, 144
nuclear weapons espionage I 239, 241–249
objections to Marshall Plan I 175, 178
participation in war against Japan I 301
perestroika I 152; VI 108–114
Poland V 3
Iran policy I 11
post–Cold War VI 47–55, 219
post–World War II military budgets I 192
postwar foreign policy I 238
postwar recovery I 177; VI 49, 175
Red Army I 181; VI 130–131, 136, 158, 221, 273, 275–276
relationship with China II 169; VI 40, 43–44, 113, 203
relationship with Cuba VI 63–66, 249
relationship with Great Britain V 28–33
relationship with United States V 28–33; VI 55
response to Marshall Plan I 238
response to Strategic Defense Initiative (SDI) I 186
response to U.S. defense spending I 197
response to West Germany admission to NATO I 206
rift with China I 141
role in postwar Poland I 301
Rosenbergs II 227
satellite states II 58
security interests in Eastern Europe II 36
social problems VI 112
Soviet-friendly countries II 103
space program II 64–70
sphere of influence III 11; V 311, 314
Suez Crisis (1956) VI 246
supports Chinese over Quemoy and Matsu I 265
suspicion of the West II 31
technological deficiencies in weaponry I 196
Third World activities I 11; VI 81, 188
threat to Western allies I 4

troops in Afghanistan, narcotic use I 13
U.N. Security Council membership I 300
views of Marshall Plan I 177
war with Finland IV 57
Winter War (1939–1940) V 28
women in World War II V 304, 306
World War II losses II 267
Yalta Agreement (1945) I 300–301
Zond program II 258
Soviet-Egyptian Pact (1955) I 162
Soweto, South Africa VII 7–8
Spaatz, Carl A. "Tooey" V 7, 92
use of bombing V 98–99
Spain VII 149; VIII 18, 277
beach closings in VII 147
cost of Med plan to VII 146
pollution from industrial centers in VII 147
socialism in VIII 254
Spandau prison V 224
Spanish American War (1898) II 99; III 245; VIII 18, 22–23, 198, 296, 301
treatment of African American soldiers IV 217
Spanish Civil War (1936–1939) IV 167, 223–231; VI 154, 176
Nationalists IV 228, 230
Popular Front IV 228
Spanish Influenza III 95; VIII 189
Spee, Maximilian von VIII 132–133, 135
Spock, Dr. Benjamin III 169
Spokane, Portland, and Seattle Railroad VII 59
Sputnik I 182, 188–189, 192, 256; II 47, 64, 70, 257–258, 260
Staatsangehöriger (subjects of the state) IV 140
Staatsschutzkorps (State Protection Corps) V 214
Stalin, Joseph I 31, 35–36, 59, 66, 86, 102, 108–110, 112–113, 149, 151, 263, 288, 305; II 30–41, 49, 52, 68, 132, 156, 169, 193, 210; III 10, 12; IV 210; V 14, 25–26, 35, 41, 44, 46, 50, 54, 107, 109, 131, 136, 149, 151, 177, 194, 224, 226–227; VI 31, 36, 40, 109, 111, 131, 133, 137, 147, 150, 154–156, 158, 161, 175, 178–179, 207, 242, 244, 250–267; VII 22, 97, 104; VIII 97
at Potsdam Conference I 263
attempt to extract base rights from Turkey I 238
Balkans campaign V 71
death VI 181
domestic atrocities I 260–261
"Election Speech" (1946) II 133
expansionist intentions I 262
foreign policy II 36
genocide practices V 166
German invasion of U.S.S.R. IV 233
lack of concern for Western European economies I 176
making trouble II 205
Marshall Plan I 208
Moscow winter offensive, 1941 IV 237
motivation II 36
on retribution for Nazi war crimes V 218
postwar policy toward the United States I 258
postwar settlement I 110
propaganda IV 234, 236
purges VI 244
relationship with Allied leaders V 27
Soviet nuclear weapons development I 183, 245
Soviet recovery from Second World War I 182
speech of 9 February 1946 I 260–261
support of Operation Anvil/Dragoon V 241
and Tito VI 273–281
view of postwar Germany I 252
war with Germany V 229; VI 274
World War II IV 232–237
Yalta Agreement (1945) I 300; V 309–315
Stalin-Hitler nonaggression pact (1939) II 193
"Star Wars." *See* Strategic Defense Initiative
Stegner, Wallace VII 112
Stevens, Isaac VII 56

Stevenson, Adlai E. VI 75
Stevenson, Charles H. VII 46
Stilwell, Joseph W. V 187, 191–199
Stimson, Henry L. I 28, 263; III 104, 109; V 53, 187
Stone, Justice Harlan III 25
Stone, Livingston VII 197
Strategic Air Command (SAC) I 188; VI 263
Strategic Arms Limitation Treaty (SALT I) I 190, 199;
        II 171; VI 30, 35, 41, 43
Strategic Arms Limitation Treaty (SALT II) I 10, 12,
        143, 146, 191; VI 2, 35, 166
    Soviet criticism of VI 43
Strategic Arms Reduction Treaty (START) I 199, 224;
        VI 44
Strategic bombing
    postwar I 4, 6, 8
    postwar role I 5
Strategic bombing in World War II I 3–4
Strategic Defense Initiative (SDI) I 186, 195–196, 199;
        II 58; VI 3, 22, 36, 109, 223, 226, 229, 234,
        239
Streicher, Julius V 224
Strong, Ted VII 61
Student League for Industrial Democracy (SLID) II
        160
Student Nonviolent Coordinating Committee
        (SNCC) II 22, 28, 91, 93, 161; VI 25
Student, Kurt V 14
Students for a Democratic Society (SDS) II 7, 160, 162
Submarines V 255–261; VIII 11, 287–294
    antisubmarine warfare (ASW) V 256
    antiwarship (AWS) operations V 259
    Great Britain V 260
    I-class V 258
    Italy V 261
    Japanese Navy V 258, 261
    Kriegsmarine (German Navy) V 261
    RO-class V 258
    Soviet Union V 261
    United States V 261
    unrestricted warfare VIII 22, 204, 287–294, 296
Suburbia II 249–255, 293–294
    suburban developments II 160
Sudan VII 3
Sudetenland
    Munich Agreement (1938) I 300
Sudetenland crisis (September 1938) IV 125,
        248
Suez Canal VI 10, 80, 270; VII 2, 147; VIII 38, 213
Suez Crisis (1956) I 192, 289; II 52, 148; VI 8, 11, 80–
        81, 106, 130, 133, 135, 160, 188, 209, 270
    U.S. position I 185; VI 270
Sukarno I 110, 273, 277, 283; VI 81, 268
Sulz Valley VII 207
Summerall, Charles VIII 27–28
Sutherland, Justice George III 25
Suzuki, Kantaro III 15
Swampland Grants (1849 and 1850) VII 272
Swann v. Charlotte-Mecklenburg Board of Education
        (1968) II 293, 296
Swaziland VII 236
Sweatt v. Painter, 1950 II 141
Sweden
    offers Poland environmental help VII 20
    opposition to African dams in VII 240
Switzerland VII 229; VIII 110, 235
Syankusule, David VII 242, 246
Sykes-Picot Agreement (1916) VIII 41
Symington, Stuart I 6, 119, 188–189, 217–218
Symington Amendment (1976) I 218
Syngman Rhee VI 147, 150–151
Syria I 159, 308–309; VI 54, 163, 201, 215, 261, 268;
        VII 135, 138, 148–149; VIII 39, 41, 104,
        213, 216
    attacks Israel I 316; VI 161, 163
    conflict with Jordan I 157
    dams in VII 76–84
    deportations to VIII 166

fundamentalist movements I 163
immigration and population problems VII 82
Israeli invasion of Lebanon I 196
Kurdish peasants in VII 82
lack of environmental control in VII 145
limited-aims war I 314
military buildup I 316
nuclear weapons development I 219
pogroms against Armenians VII 82
revolution I 158
Soviet alliance I 161; VI 43
troop separation agreements with Israel I 159
water policy in 76–84
Szolnok, Hungary VII 247, 249, 252

T

Tabqa Dam (Syria) VII 77, 82, 83
Tacoma City Light VII 53
Taft, Robert A. I 272, 285, 306; II 49, 133, 206; VI 56
Taft, William Henry II 199
Taft, William Howard III 208, 211, 244, 247
    Mann Elkins Act (1910) III 245
    narcotics policies III 136
Taft administration
    Mexican Revolution III 126
Taft-Hartley Act (1947) II 133, 188–189, 192
Tailhook Association Conference (1991) II 80
Taisho, Emperor V 111
Taiwan I 86; II 172; VI 38, 53, 106, 150, 214, 219
    Chinese attacks on Quemoy and Matsu I 265–270
    domino theory I 266
    mutual-security treaty with United States I 268
    nuclear weapons development I 216, 219, 223
    U.S. military equipment VI 43
    U.S. intervention I 158
Taiwan Relations Act (1979) VI 44
Taiwan Straits I 119, 168–169
Tamil Nadu, India VII 125–126
    drought in VII 126
Tammany Hall III 260–264
Tanganyika VIII 86–87, 89
Tanks
    Abrams (United States) VI 223, 241
    Bundeswehr Leopard (Germany) VI 174
    Char B (France) IV 240
    JS-1 (U.S.S.R.) IV 245
    KV-1 (U.S.S.R.) IV 239
    M18 Hellcat (United States) IV 251
    M-2 (United States) IV 245
    M-3 Grant (United States) IV 241, 247
    M36 (United States) IV 251
    M-4 (United States) IV 241–243
    M-4 Sherman (United States) IV 239, 241, 247
    M-4A1 (United States) IV 245
    M-4A2 (United States) IV 245
    M-4A3 (United States) IV 245
    M4A3E2 (United States) IV 249
    M-4A3E6 (United States) IV 246
    Mark III (Germany) IV 243
    Mark IV (Germany) IV 243
    Mark V Panther (Germany) IV 241
    Mk V Panther (Germany) IV 239
    Panzerkampfwagen (Pzkw) I (Germany) IV 244
    Panzerkampfwagen (Pzkw) IVG (Germany) IV
        248
    Pzkw II (Germany) IV 244
    Pzkw III (Germany) IV 244
    Pzkw IV (Germany) IV 244, 246, 249
    Pzkw V (Panther) (Germany) IV 244
    Pzkw VI (Tiger) (Germany) IV 244
    role in World War I VIII 14, 51–58, 112, 193–197,
        242
    role in World War II IV 238–251
    Souma (France) IV 240
    T-34 (U.S.S.R) IV 239, 243–245, 247
    Tiger (Germany) IV 241
    Tiger I (Germany) IV 248

INDEX

Whippets VIII 54, 56
Tao, Didian Malisemelo VII 244
TASS VII 23
Taylor, Maxwell D. I 119, 294; VI 95–96
Teal, Joseph N. VII 52
Team B VI 256–263
Teapot Dome investigation (1922) III 178, 180
Teheran Conference (1943) I 110, 259, 288; II 32; V
            46, 72, 236
Tehri Hydro-Electric Project (India) VII 127
Television
        broadcast license II 122
        commercial development II 122
        impact on American society II 121
        information-oriented programming II 126
        noncommercial II 125
        programming II 122
        quiz show scandals II 123
        role in American society II 125
        Vietnam War II 124
        Vietnam War coverage II 125
        viewer demographics, 1980 II 124
        Watergate hearings II 124
Teller, Edward VI 256–257
Tellico Dam (United States) VII 31
Tennessee River VII 26, 28, 31
Tennessee Valley Authority (TVA) I 27–30; III 154;
            VII 1, 27–28, 130
        impact on South VII 28
Tenth Inter-American Conference I 49
Tet Offensive (1968) I 40; II 5; VI 23, 29, 60
Texas VII 181–182, 185
        water management policies in VII 69–75
Texas Groundwater Management District No. 1 VII
            185
Texas Houston Ship Canal VII 265
Thames River VII 234
Thar Desert VII 125
Thartar Canal Project VII 77
Thatcher, Margaret VI 8, 10, 54, 195
        critic of EEC VI 13
        supports United States VI 13
The Dalles Dam (United States) VII 29, 51–61
The Dalles-Celilo Canal VII 52, 56—57
thermal pollution VII 175
Thessaloníki
        construction of sewage works in VII 148
        industry in VII 148
Third World VI 2–3, 35, 43, 55, 61, 63, 65, 68, 77–78,
            80–81, 83, 116, 131, 133, 140, 145, 149, 160,
            163, 186, 221–222, 236; VII 67
        and the Cold War VI 264–272
        beef imports to Europe VII 37
        collapse of communist regimes in VI 239
        effect on global balance of power I 14
        gross national product I 14
        national liberation movements in VI 188
        Soviet influence VI 188
        U.S. interventions I 15
        U.S. policies on I 22; VI 80
        water crisis in VII 286
Third World Liberation Front II 94
Tho, Le Duc I 291
Thompson, Tommy VII 57—59
Three Emperors' League VIII 225–227
Three Mile Island (1979) II 86
Three-Staged Plan for Optimum, Equitable, and
            Reasonable Utilization of the Transboundary
            Watercourses of the Tigris-Euphrates
            Basin VII 79
Tibbets, Paul W. V 50
Tignes, France, riots at VII 99
Tigris River VII 77
Tijuana River VII 152
Tirpitz, Alfred von VIII 29, 31, 34–35, 249
Tisza Club 252
Tisza River, chemical spill on VII 247–255
Title IX (1972) II 77

Tito, Josip Broz I 36, 59, 86, 108–110, 113, 273, 277,
            283; VI 134, 136, 182, 217, 254, 265, 268,
            271, 273–281; VIII 192
Tojo, Hideki I 134; IV 7; V 49, 194, 264
Tonga (Batonka) people VII 5, 239, 242, 245
        effect of dam on VII 4
Tokyo trials (1945–1948) V 263–269
        comparison with Nuremberg trials V 266–267
        dissent of Radhabinod Pal V 267
        International Military Tribunal for the Far East
            (IMTFE) V 266
Torrey Canyon accident (1967) VII 143
Total Strategy White Paper VII 240
Totally Equal Americans VII 172
Townsend, Charles Wendell VII 277
Trading with the Enemy Act (1917) III 223
"Tragedy of the Commons" VII 47, 48, 70, 73
Trans-Jordan VII 81; VIII 166, 214
Treaties—
        —Brest-Litovsk (1918) VIII 95–97, 141, 173, 278
        —Bucharest (1918) VIII 95
        —Dunkirk (1948) I 204
        —Frankfurt (1871) VIII 278
        —Lausanne (1923) VIII 214
        —Locarno (1925) V 116–120
        —London (1913) VIII 212
        —Ouchy (1912) VIII 212
        —Moscow I 107
        —Sevres (1920) VIII 214, 217
        —Versailles (1919). See Versailles Treaty
Treblinka I 138; V 54, 57, 158, 161
Trees
        cottonwoods VII 12, 212, 214, 215
        elms VII 232
        mesquites VII 212
        oaks VII 212, 232
        riparian importance of VII 215
        salt-cedars VII 12, 215, 217
        willows VII 212, 214, 215, 232
Tribal Grazing Lands Policy (TGLP) VII 34
Trident Conference (1943) V 236
Trinity River VII 223
Tripartite Pact (1940) V 294
Triple Alliance VIII 44, 46, 226, 229
Triple Entente VIII 35, 45
Trotsky, Leon VI 179, 274–275; VIII 167
Trout Unlimited VII 31, 213
Trudeau, Pierre E., signs Great Lakes Water Quality
            Agreement VII 120
Truitt, Reginald V. VII 43–44, 47
Truman, Harry S I 28, 35, 65, 69, 109, 113, 148, 159,
            257, 285; II 39, 42, 44, 49–50, 197, 199,
            203–204, 280; III 10–14, 62; V
            46, 98, 106; VI 20, 56, 144, 146–148, 153,
            205, 231, 250, 284
        acceptance of a divided Europe I 264
        adoption of containment policy I 262
        anticommunism VI 155
        appointment of Baruch I 27
        approval of NSC-68 I 182
        at Potsdam Conference I 263
        atomic bombing of Japan I 239
        attitude toward Stalin I 259, 261–263
        containment policy I 274
        Executive Order 10241 II 131
        foreign policy I 58; II 205
        foreign policy links to domestic ideology II 209
        Interim Committee III 15
        Marshall Plan I 176
        response to communism II 130
        restraint in use of nuclear weapons I 235
        service in World War I VIII 192
        Truman Doctrine II 145
        unconditional surrender policy V 275
        veto of Taft-Hartley Act II 188
        views on postwar role of military I 5
Truman administration I 30, 59, 74; II 36; VI 59, 101,
            147, 150, 155, 224

INDEX

acceptence of Soviet nuclear program I 237
accused of abandoning China to communism I 59
aid to China I 60
aid to Taiwan I 266
Baruch Plan I 31
CIA, creation of I 64
Cold War policy I 266
concern about communist influence in Europe I
    174, 176
concern about trade imbalances in Europe I 175
concludes cooperation with Soviets impossible I
    82
containment I 154
containment policy I 272
containment strategy I 183
CPUSA I 79
creation of NSC I 83
defining U.S.-Soviet rivalry I 75
Executive Order 9877 I 5
federal employee loyalty program I 76
foreign policy I 60
future of Europe I 110
Key West Agreement I 5–6
Loyalty Order I 79
McCarran Act I 74
Marshall Plan I 173–179
National Security Act I 7
National Security Council memorandum 68 (NSC
    68) I 211, 274
national-security policy I 77, 210
policy toward Soviet Union I 258–263
reduction in defense spending I 7
Soviet nuclear spying I 242
Taiwan policy I 266
use of nuclear weapons I 215
view of Chinese civil war I 294
views on Guatemala I 129
West Berlin policy I 293
Yalta Agreement (1945) I 301
Truman Doctrine (1947) I 36, 65, 75, 89, 109, 151,
    175–176, 177, 296; II 100, 130, 132, 207–
    210; VI 9, 11, 161, 250, 252, 267
Truscott, Lucian K., Jr.
    Italian campaign IV 146, 149
Truth in Securities Act (1933) III 154
Tunisia VII 149
Turkey I 49, 82, 87, 89, 110, 113, 238, 294; II 144,
    153, 207; VI 161, 244, 250–252, 255; VII
    148–149; VIII 44, 95, 104, 106, 122, 211–
    217, 277
    Armenians deported to VII 82
    Baghdad Pact I 161
    base rights I 288
    civil rights violations I 209
    crucial to U.S. security I 85
    dams in VII 76–84
    environmental control in VII 145
    Jupiter missiles VI 71–75
    Kurds in VII 83
    member of NATO VII 83
    Soviet intervention in I 73, 258
    U.S. aid to resist Soviet influence I 176
    water policy in VII 76–84
    Young Turk revolution VIII 45
Turkish-Iraqi Mixed Economic Commission VII 79
Turner, Frederick Jackson
    frontier thesis II 245
Tuskegee Institute III 268–272

U

U.S. Steel Corporation VII 269; VIII 296
U Thant VI 75
U-2 spy plane incident (1960) I 65–66, 70, 189–190,
    192, 194; II 38, 54, 229, 260; VI 64
U-2 spy plane reconnaissance VI 70–71
U-boats. See *Unterseeboote*
Udall, Morris King VII 109, 114

Udall, Stewart Lee VII 109, 112, 259, 267
Ukraine VI 133, 136, 215, 218, 251; VII 248, 252; VIII
    94, 96–99, 280
    Chernobyl accident in VII 18, 22
    Cossacks VIII 99
    forest clear-cutting in VII 254
    mass executions in VI 251
    nuclear-deterence theory I 231
    pogroms VIII 168–169
    surrender of nuclear weapons to Russian
        Federation I 220
    Ukrainian Insurgent Army (UPA) IV 130
Ulbricht, Walter I 35, 38
    Berlin I 120
Ulster Volunteers VIII 155, 161
Ultra IV 260–264; V 79, 85
    Battle of the Atlantic, 1941–1945 IV 263
    Battle of Britain, 1940 IV 264
    Battle of the Bulge, 1944 IV 264
    contribution to Allied invasion plans IV 262
    North Africa campaign IV 264
    role in D-Day planning IV 261
Umkhonto we Sizwe (MK) VII 239
Unconditional surrender policy V 46, 53, 270–275
    German reaction V 272
    Japanese reaction V 273
Union of Soviet Socialist Republics (U.S.S.R.) *See* Soviet
    Union
Union Pacific Railroad VII 60
United Arab Republic (UAR) I 282; II 147–148
    Soviet ties II 148
United Auto Workers (UAW) II 189; III 191, 194
United Fruit Company I 70, 123, 125–126, 129–130
United Mine Workers II 190–191
United Mine Workers Strike (1902) III 244
United Nations I 29–30, 50, 53, 98, 194, 217, 219–220,
    278, 284, 288–289, 305; II 20, 40, 46, 51,
    53, 61, 71, 87, 100, 115; VI 31, 135–136, 147,
    151, 158, 234, 261; VII 2, 65, 79, 81, 240,
    245; VIII 11
    adopts TVA model VII 1
    agencies working in Latin America I 22
    Atomic Energy Commission I 27, 29
    censure of Soviet Union for invasion of
        Afghanistan I 12
    China seat VI 44, 148
    Council for Namibia VII 241
    creation of II 100, 208
    Economic Commission for Latin America
        (ECLA) I 20
    human rights I 146
    Hungarian uprising (1956) VI 270
    intervention in the Congo II 115
    and Korea VI 146
    nuclear weapons I 28
    Panel on Water VII 286
    Resolution 338 VI 163
    Resolution 339 VI 163
    Resolution 340 VI 163
    response to invasion of South Korea II 37
    Security Council II 100; VI 11, 13, 163, 284
    sets tone on water policy VII 286
    status of Taiwan I 269
    Suez Crisis (1956) VI 80, 270
United Nations Charter II 102
United Nations Development Programme
    (UNDP) VII 7
United Nations Educational, Scientific and Cultural
    Organization (UNESCO) VII 143
United Nations Environmental Program (UNEP) VII
    143, 248
United Nations Food and Agricultural Organization
    (FAO) VII 143
United Nations Special Commission (UNSCOM) I
    239
United Nations War Crimes Commission V 264
United States—
    advisers in Vietnam I 291

INDEX

aid to China V 198
Air Force II 65–66
alliance with Israel I 156
Animal and Plant Health Inspection Service VII 217
anti-German feelings during World War I VIII 296
antinuclear protests VI 16
antiwar movement VI 23–29
Arab oil embargo I 162
arms control VI 30
Army IV 9–12; VI 126, 140, 149, 153, 171; VII 166; VIII 10–17, 20–25, 27, 67, 206, 269
Army Corps of Engineers VII 13, 26–27, 29, 52, 54–55, 57, 59–60, 202, 214, 220–224, 259, 261, 263, 266
Army War College VIII 16
Asia policy IV 253–259
backs Zionist settlements in Israel VII 136
Bill of Rights II 98, 101; VII 170
bipartisanship II 203–212
bombing of Cambodia I 45
bore-hole drilling in VII 66
Bureau of the Budget II 271
Bureau of Land Management VII 216
Bureau of Reclamation 13, 27–29, 110, 112, 202, 216, 259
capitalist economic system of I 184
Children's Bureau, Division of Juvenile Delinquency Service 1960 report II 273
Cold War ideology I 148–154; VI 47–55, 213–220
communist activities in VI 126, 129
Congress VI 56–62, 194, 222, 224, 285–286; VII 59, 175; allies of environmentalists VII 123; appropriated money for dams VII 55; approves Chesapeake Bay oyster-restoration VII 49; approves Flood Control Act of 1944 VII 29; authorizes Hetch Hetchy Dam VII 112; authorizes TVA VII 28; cedes swamplands to states VII 272; creates flood plan VII 273; environmental concerns of VII 256; environmental policy of VII 257; and Fourteen Points VIII 281; funds regional wastewater systems planning VII 262; Indian policy VII 167–168; on thermal pollution VII 175; passes Central Arizona Project bill VII 114; passes laws to promote western settlement VII 26;
Constitution II 98, 101; VI 56, 283–284; Eighteenth Amendment (1919) III 198–200, VIII 295; Fifteenth Amendment (1870) III 270; Fifth Amendment (1791) III 107; Nineteenth Amendment (1919) III 171–172, 206, VIII 295; taking clause, 274; Tenth Amendment (1791) VI 57; Twenty-first Amendment (1933) III 200
Council of Economic Advisors II 271
Cuba policy VI 70–76
dams in VII 14, 25–32, 219–228
Declaration of Independence II 98, 101
decolonization VI 77–83
Defend America Act of 1996 I 196
defense spending I 125, 180–181, 210; II 67; VI 116, 144, 151, 214, 224, 226, 232, 238
Department of Agriculture (USDA) II 84, 271; VII 161
Department of Agriculture, Bureau of Agricultural Economics III 66
Department of Defense I 7; VI 57; VII 216
Department of Housing and Urban Development (HUD) II 112, 277
Department of Justice II 4–5, 45; VII 175, 266
Department of Labor II 271, II 166; VIII 298
Department of the Interior VII 10, 54, 57, 155, 176, 266
diplomacy II 97; VI 106, 158, 188
drug policy III 132–138

economic aid to Latin America I 17–26; III 50
electrical-power production VII 27
environmental movement in VII 31, 256
environmental policy in VII 256–270
Environmental Protection Agency (EPA) VII 220, 258, 264, 268
farm population II 86; VII 187
financial aid to France II 267
first strike theory I 234–240
Fish and Wildlife Service VII 55, 176, 215, 273, 277
fish culture in VII 201
fish hatcheries in VII 202
foreign policy II 3, 35, 97, 101, 103–104, 151, 203–212; III 46, 49; VI 56–62, 87, 106, 150, 188, 254
Forest Service VII 216
Formosa Doctrine I 265, 268
funds to France under Marshall Plan VII 98
General Staff Act (1903) VIII 301
Geological Survey (USGS) VII 26, 182, 277
global objectives II 269
guarentees to Israel military VII 83
gunboat diplomacy VI 270
Haiti III 45
House: Committee on Public Works VII 268; Conservation and Natural Resources Subcommittee VII 266; Government Operations Committee VII 266; hearings on private property takings VII 277; overrides Nixon veto of Water Pollution Act VII 263; Public Works Committee VII 258, 261, 268–269; Rivers and Harbors Subcommittee VII 258; stops Grand Canyon dam VII 109; testimony on water pollution in VII 41; House Armed Services Committee, hearings in 1949 I 6–8
human rights policy I 140–146; II 100
immigrants' influence on Cold War policy I 271, 274
immigration policies III 254
imperialistic tendencies II 31
interventions in: Brazil (1964) I 15; British Guiana (1953–1964) I 15; Chile (1973) I 15, 123–133; Costa Rica (mid 1950s) I 15; Cuba (1906–1909, 1912, 1917–1922) III 47; Dominican Republic (1916, 1965) I 15, 125; Ecuador (1960–1963) I 15; Grenada (1983) VI 44, 237; Guatemala (1954) I 15, 20, 123–133; Haiti (1915, 1990s) I 125; VI 58; Indonesia (1957) I 15; Iran (1953) I 15; Nicaragua (1912, 1926, 1980s) I 125, 129; VI 190–196, 249; Panama (1903) I 125, 129
inasion of alien plant species VII 213
invasion of Cambodia I 40–47; VI 165, 271
isolationism V 288–294
Joint Chiefs of Staff memo 1067 II 40
Joint Logistic Plans Committee II 40
limited-nuclear-war doctrines I 165–172
Lever Act (1917) VIII 301
Middle East VI 61, 162–164
multinational investment in India VII 132
mutual assured destruction (MAD) policy I 169–171
National Advisory Committee for Aeronautics (NACA) VIII 197
National Guard VIII 14, 16, 22–23
National Marine Fisheries Service (NMFS) VII 221, 223
National Park Service VII 60, 112
National Security Agency (NSA) II 65; VI 57, 124
National Security Council II 50
National Security Council memorandum 68 (NSC-68) II 206
and NATO VI 101
National War Labor Board VIII 296, 301
nativism VIII 299

"no-cities doctrine" I 171
Northeastern drought VII 261
nuclear-power plants in VII 174–180
nuclear stockpile I 213–214
nuclear-nonproliferation policy I 216–224
Office of the Coordinator of Inter-American affairs (OCIAA) III 48
Olympic boycott I 10, I 12
opening of Japan IV 256
opium trade III 137
opposition to African dams in VII 240
Pacific Northwest VII 188–195, 196–203: dams in VII 219, 226–228; impact of white settlers upon VII 197; industrial development in VII 198
policy on cleaning Great Lakes VII 116–124
policy makers II 4
power after World War II I 259
Presidential Directive (PD) 59 I 171
property rights in VII 271–279
protest against Soviet invasion of Afghanistan II 102
protocol on nonintervention III 47
Public Health Service (USPHS) VII 162, 164, 259
racism in World War II III 213–219
reaction to Sino-Soviet split II 169
Reclamation Service VII 26
relations with Canada VII 116–124
relations with China II 98, 171; VI 4, 38–45, 88, 201, 203
relations with Great Britain V 28–33; VI 8–14
relations with Mexico VII 151–159
relations with Soviet Union V 28–33; VI 9, 55, 157, 200, 228–235
role in Greek coup of 1967 I 15
role in Jamaica (1976–1980) I 15
Sedition Act (1917) VIII 301
Senate: and treaties VII 153; Commerce Committee VII 268; Environment Subcommittee VII 268; hearings on quality of water sent to Mexico VII 153; Interior Committee VII 258; overrides Nixon veto of Water Pollution Act VII 263; passes Grand Canyon dam bill VII 109; Public Works Committee 258, 261–262; rejects Versailles Treaty VIII 156; Select Committee on National Water Resources VII 258; Subcommittee on Air and Water Pollution VII 261, 264; supports Mexican Water Treaty VII 152
Senate Foreign Relations Committee I 306; II 7, 205; VI 153
Senate Select Committee on Intelligence Activities, 1974 investigation of CIA activites in Chile I 124
social problems VI 144, 187
Soil Conservation Service VII 217
Southeast, wetlands harvest in VII 273
Southwest, riparian ecosystems in VII 211–218
southwestern willow flycatcher 215
Soviet nuclear weapons espionage I 241–249
Space Program II 241–248, 256–259; VI 140
spying on Soviet military capabilities I 190–192
State Department VI 124, 154, 194, 257
strikes against Iraq's nuclear plants I 239
supply of water in 283
support for Slovak dam in 103
support for Taiwan I 266
support of dictators II 103; VI 64
Supreme Court II 19–20, 23–26, 45, 78, 90–91, 136–141, 220, 224, 280–287: abortion issues II 221; Arizona-California water dispute VII 109; gender discrimination II 182; Japanese internment III 103, 105; Kansas-Colorado water dispute VII 13; National Industrial Recovery Act III 149; Native Americans III 140, VII 57, 168, 170;

New Deal III 25; "Roosevelt Court" II 281; Sacco and Vanzetti appeal III 232; segregation II 293; use of Refuse Act VII 266;
Third World VI 61, 80, 188
Trading with the Enemy Act (1917) VIII 299
troop buildup in Vietnam I 291
visit of Ozal to VII 79
War Department VIII 23, 27
War Industries Board VIII 296, 301
water policy in VII 151–159
water pollution in VII 256–270
West: development of VII 26; public-works projects in VII 28; reclamation projects in VII 26; water policy in VII 181–187
wetlands 271–279
Wilsonianism I 205
women in World War I VIII 130, 296, 298; in World War II V 303–304
World War II economic gain III 64
World War I VIII 125, 177, 191, 204, 223, 287, 295–302 ; casualties 125, 268
United States Employment Service VIII 301
United States Fish Commission (USFC) VII 201
United States Military Academy, West Point VIII 16, 22
United States v. Winans (1905) VII 57
United Steelworkers Union VII 267
United Towns Organization VII 143
Universalism I 284–289
University of California Japanese American Evacuation and Resettlement Study (1942–1946) V 186
University of Chicago VII 262
University of Idaho VII 225
University of Maryland VII 48
University of Oregon VII 60
University of Washington VII 60, 202
Untermenschen (subhumans) IV 86, 99, 131
Unterseeboote (U-boats) V 2, 79–83, 135; VIII 106, 134–135, 138, 196, 223, 287–294, 296
bases in World War I VIII 219
technology V 83
Type IX V 80
Type VII V 79, V 80
Type VIIC V 83
Upper Colorado River Storage Project VII 30
Upper Stillwater Dam (United States) VII 31
Urban political bosses III 259–265
Uruguay
communist guerrilla movements I 125
in War of the Triple Alliance I 125
military coups I 26
reduction of U.S. military aid I 141
Utah VII 31, 112

V

Vaal River VII 7–8, 240–241
Vance, Cyrus R. I 143, 145; VI 42, 263
Vandenberg, Arthur I 306, 203, 205, 207–208
Vandenberg, Hoyt Sanford I 6, 236
Van der Kloof Dam (South Africa) VII 243
Van Devanter, Justice Willis III 25, 27, 31
Vanishing Air (1970) VII 269
Vanzetti, Bartolomeo III 229–238
Vargha, Janos VII 101
Vatican VIII 208–209
V-E Day IV 62; V 60
Velsicol Chemical Company VII 162–165
Velvet Divorce (1992) VII 100
Velvet Revolution (1989) VII 101
Venereal Disease VIII 128
Venona Project I 242–243; 247; VI 123, 126, 154, 156
Ventura, Jesse II 199, 201
Vernichtungskrieg (war of annihilation) IV 88, 141
Versailles Treaty (1919) I 255, 285, 293, 300; II 99, 145; III 99, 180; IV 17–18, 86, 164, 266–

273; V 148, 202, 292; VI 176; VIII 20, 58, 95–96, 156, 166, 173, 207, 264, 277–285, 295, 298–299

Article 231, War Guilt Clause IV 267; VIII 280, 282, 284

impact on German economy IV 269

impact on World War II IV 267

Vichy France IV 275–280

anti-Semitism IV 277, 280

cooperation with Nazis IV 276, 278

National Renewal IV 276

Statut des juifs (Statute on the Jews) IV 277

support of the *Wehrmacht* (German Army) IV 277

Victoria, Queen of England VIII 30, 32, 35

Vienna Declaration I 253

Viet Minh V 146–148; VI 106

Vietcong I 40–42, 296–297; VI 93, 96

attacks on U.S. bases (1965) I 291

begins war with South Vietnam I 290

Vietnam I 41, 46, 50, 54, 82, 87, 89, 273, 290–294, 298–299; II 3–5, 7–10, 40, 173, 269; VI 32, 50, 59, 64, 80–81, 98, 101, 107, 201, 203, 229, 261, 270–272; VIII 35, 193

as a colony of France I 290

Buddhist dissidents VI 92

French withdrawal from I 213; II 266; VI 102, 106

imperialism I 151

peace agreement with France I 290, 297

seventeenth parallel division II 267; VI 98

U.S. bombing of I 183

U.S. military buildup I 183; VI 96

Vietnam War (ended 1975) I 40, 44–45, 89, 101, 140, 142, 144, 290–299; II 3–10, 97, 177, 180, 224, 257, 260, 263–265, 273; VI 8, 23–29, 33, 38, 56–57, 61, 85, 88, 98–99, 103, 138–145, 173, 185, 202, 222, 266, 283–285; VIII 60, 188, 266

comparison to Soviet invasion of Afghanistan I 14

domino theory I 266, I 297–298

doves II 263

folly of U.S. militarism I 183

Gulf of Tonkin Resolution I 291

hawks II 263

impact on Republican and Democratic concensus II 208

impact on U.S. domestic programs II 270; VI 185, 202

labor movement support of II 193

number of casualties I 291

Operation Duck Hook II 6

Operation Flaming Dart I 291

Operation Rolling Thunder I 291

reasons for U.S. involvement I 292, 295, 297–298

result of containment policy II 265

result of French colonial system II 267

television coverage II 124–125; VI 145

Tet Offensive II 9, 180, 275

U.S. troop buildup I 291

U.S. troops leave I 291

Vietminh I 290

Vietnamization VI 99

Villa, Francisco "Pancho" III 125–130; VIII 16, 18, 22

Villard, Henry VII 57

A Vindication of the Rights of Women (Mary Wollstonecraft) II 74

Virginia

liberalizes oyster-leasing laws VII 42

oyster industry in VII 40–50

privitization of oystering VII 47

signs Chesapeake Bay 2000 Agreement VII 49

Vistula River VII 18, 20

Volksgemeinschaft (people's community) IV 80, 83

Volstead Act (1919) III 200

Volta River VII 2, 4

Volta River Project VII 4

Volunteers in Service to America (VISTA) II 272, 276

Voting Rights Act (1965) II 26, 91, 162–163, 165, 283

W

Wagner Act (1935) II 188; III 27–31, 63, 66, 149, 190

Walesa, Lech VI 110; VII 20

Wallace, George C. II 180, 197, 199, 273, 281

Wallace, Henry A. I 31, 148, 287; II 197, 207, 209; III 159, 162

Pete Seeger and the Weavers II 214

presidential race (1948) II 211

Waller, Thomas Wright "Fats" III 79

Wannsee Conference (1942) IV 139; V 161

War of Attrition (1970) I 308, 316

War of 1812 VII 116

War of the Triple Alliance (1864–1870) I 125

War on Poverty II 270– 279; VI 141

counter-assault to II 277

reasons for failure of II 271

War Powers Resolution (1973) VI 58, 61, 195, 222, 283–287

War Refugees Board (WRB) III 253, 256

War Relocation Administration (WRA) III 102

Warhol, Andy II 216

Warm Springs Reservation VII 56, 60

Warne, William E. VII 55

Warren, Earl II 90, 136, 138, 142, 180, 280–291, 296

Warsaw Pact I 102, 154, 206, 256; II 60–61; VI 50, 110, 118, 121, 130–131, 168–170, 177, 184, 207–208, 235, 249, 267, 271

withdrawal of Hungary I 185

Warsaw Treaty Organization (WTO) I 154

Wasco County-Dalles City Museum Commission VII 60

Washington VII 201, 220

dams in VII 27, 31, 198

farmers opposed dam breaching VII 226

nuclear weapon development in VII 55

Pollution Control Commission (PCC) VII 193–194

population in VII 54

Washington, Booker T. III 117, 120, 267–274

comparison to W. E. B. Du Bois III 271

Tuskegee experiment III 123

Tuskegee Institute III 268

Washington, D.C. 261, 269

Washington, George VII 29; VIII 230

Washington Conference (1943) IV 144

Washington Naval Conference (1921–1922) IV 2; V 103, 204–205, 207–208; VI 30; VIII 298

Washington State Pollution Control Commission VII 189, 193

Washington State Sports Council VII 53

water

"prior appropriation" law VII 109

as a commodity VII 280–288

as resource VI 2

extraction of VII 62–68

importance of VII 76

Islamic law on VII 83

recycling of VII 70

sand abstraction VII 63, 66

supply of VII 280–288

use by upper class in South Afirca VII 7

Water Manifesto, The VII 283, 317–332

Water Pollution Control Act VII 123, 268,

Water Pollution Control Act Amendments VII 259, 263

Water Quality Act (1965) VII 123, 175, 261

Water Quality Improvement Act (1970) VII 174, 176

Water Resources Planning Act (1965) VII 259

Water Resources Research Act (1964) VII 259

Water Rights Court VII 88

Water Wasteland (1971) VII 265, 268

Water Workers and Distributors Union of Baja California VII 159

Watergate scandal I 47, 90, 291–292; II 176, 185, 257, 278; VI 24, 85, 87–88, 90, 124, 204

Watts riots II 257, 276; VI 141

Webster v. *Reproductive Health Services* (1989) II 222

Wedemeyer, Albert Coady V 42–43, 126, 149, 280
Wehrmacht (German Army) IV 19, 24, 85–86, 88, 108,
        125, 130, 141, 167, 230, 277; V 37, 96, 104,
        106, 118, 125–126, 132, 135, 153, 179, 211,
        219, 226, 229, 232, 244, 272, 275, 282–283;
        VIII 92
    Case Yellow IV 282
    early victories V 213
    Hitler's ideology V 137–144
    Manstein Plan IV 107
    mechanized warfare IV 282
    myth IV 286
    opinion of guerrilla warfare IV 93, 101
    panzer divisions IV 284
    reputation IV 281, 287
    role in war atrocities IV 85–94
    Tank Forces development IV 106
    utilization of tanks IV 283
    weapons development IV 105
Weimar Republic IV 270; V 115, 210–211; VI 176;
        VIII 144, 284–285
Weinberger, Caspar W. VI 2, 21, 221–222, 229, 231
Welles, Orson III 237
Wells, Sumner V 58
Weltpolitik VIII 31, 44, 249, 266
West Berlin I 194, 288, 293; VI 147–149
    Soviet blockade (1948) I 238
West Caprivi Game Reserve VII 35
West Germany I 113, 154; VI 101, 103, 121, 168–169,
        201, 204, 206–212
    aid received from U.S. I 158
    antinuclear protests VI 16
    emigration VI 118
    entry into NATO I 206
    joins NATO I 108
    military I 255
    Minister of Federal Transportation VII 207
    nuclear proliferation I 223
    nuclear weapons development I 222
    opposition to African dams in VII 240
    postwar economy I 174
    relations with Poland VI 211
    relations with the Soviet Union VI 211
    Social Democrats I 36
Western Desert Project (Egypt) VII 2
Western Ghats VII 125
Western Kansas Groundwater Management District No.
        1 VII 185
Westmoreland, William C. I 291; II 5
    Vietnam War policy I 299
wetlands VII 271–279
    as private property VII 272
    scientific understanding VII 273
Wheeler, Burton K. II 209; III 26
white flight II 250, 292–293
    in Boston II 298
White, Walter II 44; III 218
    march on Washington III 219
White Panther Party II 95
Whitehouse, Joseph VII 171
Whittier, John Greenleaf VII 275
Wild and Scenic Rivers Act (1968) VII 31
Wilderness Act (1964) VII 31
Wilderness Society VII 30, 112, 258
William II 24, 29–31, 35, 72, 97, 152, 184, 209, 213,
        226, 229, 252, 257, 282
Wilson, Edward O. VII 234–235
Wilson, Henry Hughes VIII 77, 108, 237
Wilson, Woodrow I 88, 151, 285; II 8, 46, 145, 156,
        199; III 25, 55, 98–99, 175, 208, 211, 223,
        244; VI 57, 77, 188; VIII 11–12, 16–18, 22,
        96, 204, 228, 261, 277–278, 281–282, 295,
        298–299
    flu epidemic III 100
    foreign policy III 46
    Fourteen Points (1918) II 99, 101, 152; III 99,
        175; VI 106; VIII 20, 298
    idealism VIII 280

Mexican Revolution III 124, 128–129
    model of human rights I 145
    New Freedom III 211
    Nobel Peace Prize II 99
    Paris Peace Conference (1919) II 264
    World War I VIII 289, 291, 296
Wilson administration
    first national antinarcotic law III 135
    Mexican Revolution III 126
    Red Scare III 221
Wilson Dam (United States) VII 26
Wilsonianism I 19, 204–207, 304
Wind River Reservation VII 170
Window of vulnerability I 189–191
Winter War (1939–1940) I 108
Winters Doctrine VII 172–173
Winters v. *United States* (1908) VII 168, 172
Wisconsin VII 122, 264, 267
    pollution control in VII 264
Wisconsin State Committee on Water Pollution VII
        122
Wohlstetter, Albert J. I 213, II 65
Wollstonecraft, Mary II 74
Wolman, Abel VII 47
Women's Air Force Service Pilots (WASPs) V 303
Women's Army Corps (WAC) V 303
Women's movement II 162, 165
    and Prohibition III 198
    Progressive Era III 165–173
    and World War I VIII 124–130, 296, 298
Woodstock II 257
Woodstock Dam (South Africa) VII 243
Woodwell, George M. VII 262
Woolf, Virginia VIII 130
Workers World Party II 197
Works Progress Administration (WPA), 1935 III 150,
        163
World Bank I 20, 22, 124, 145; VI 120; VII 5, 7–8, 62,
        83, 130, 132, 146, 241, 280, 287
    Resettlement Policy VII 244
    sets tone on water policy VII 286
World Bank Inspection Panel VII 8, 9
World Commission on Dams VII 9, 127, 130, 133, 242
    report of (2000) VII 317–332
World Commission on Water for the Twenty-First
        Century 286
World Health Organization (WHO) VII 143, 253
World Jewish Congress III 256; V 58
World War I (1914–1918) I 88, 112, 149, 284, 286; III
        210, 223, 229, 244; VI 57, 176, 178, 267; VII
        82
    African Americans III 268; IV 218; VIII 298,
        301
    airplanes VIII 115, 193–197
    Anglo-German naval rivalry VIII 29–36
    causes I 205
    chemical warfare VIII 239–244
    combat tactics VIII 109–116
    East Africa VIII 84–90
    Eastern Front VIII 49, 60, 79, 91, 94, 110, 114,
        125, 182, 240, 242, 252
    firepower and mobility VIII 109–116
    gender roles VIII 124–130
    impact on American business in Mexico III 128
    impact on Jews VIII 163–169
    impact on U.S. isolationism V 289; VIII 295–302
    Lost Generation VIII 186–192
    mass mobilization III 19
    Middle East VIII 37–42, 60
    military innovations VIII 193–197
    motivations of soldiers VIII 59–64, 263–269
    Ottoman Empire VIII 117–123
    New Women III 168, 172
    prewar alliances VIII 225–231
    religion VIII 202–210
    Socialists in Europe VIII 254–262
    Western Front VIII 11–13, 16–19, 21, 24, 27–28,
        39, 51, 56–57, 59, 61, 77–79, 90, 96, 102,

INDEX

104, 106, 108–110, 112, 114, 117, 122, 177, 179–185, 187–188, 195, 197, 208, 221, 264, 272–273, 276, 282
  women in VIII 296, 298
World War II (1939–1945) I 61, 91; III 11, 50, 250–257; VI 8, 27, 31, 36, 49, 77, 79, 126, 146, 179, 267; VII 27, 29, 53, 69, 90, 93, 109, 152, 168, 174, 188, 199, 202, 204, 236–237, 257, 263–264, 273, 278, 287
  African American contributions IV 221
  Allies V 27–33; VI 169
  Anglo-American alliance IV 208
  Axis powers V 62–67
  Balkans V 68–78
  Catholic Church VIII 209
  effect on Great Depression III 63
  homefront segregation IV 218
  impact on Civil Rights movement IV 220
  impact on colonial powers VI 183
  Japanese internment III 102–109
  Kyushu invasion III 13
  Okinawa III 15
  Operation Olympic III 14
  Operation Overlord II 39
  Pacific theater III 13, 214; VI 254
  Pearl Harbor III 214–215
  relationship of Great Britain and U.S. II 31
  resistance movements V 243–247
  role of tanks IV 238–251
  Soviet casualties II 38
  strategy: IV 104–128; Allied V 19–26; Anglo-American disputes V 34–40; Anglo-Americn relations V 41–47; atomic bomb V 48–55; Axis V 62–67; Balkans 68–78; bomber offensive V 86–100; Eastern Front IV 53–60; Italian campaign IV 143–150; Operation Barbarossa V 226–234; Operation Dragoon V 235–242; unconditional surrender V 270–277; Yalta conference V 309–316
  submarines V 255–261
  Teheran Conference (1943) II 32
  threat of Japanese invasion III 108
  Tokyo trials (1945–1948) V 263–269
  unconditional surrender policy V 270–276
  U.S. combat effectiveness V 278–286
  U.S. Marine Corps V 295–301
  War Plan Orange III 108
  women's roles V 302–308; VIII 130
  Yalta Conference (1945) II 39
World's Fair, Chicago (1933) III 2
World's Fair, New York (1939) II 122
World's Fair, St. Louis (1904) III 242
World Water Commission VII 280, 281
World Water Forum (2000) VII 286
World Wildlife Fund (WWF) VII 107

X

Xhosa VII 67, 242

Y

Yakama Reservation VII 60
Yakovlev, Aleksandr N. I 104, 152
Yalta Conference (1945) I 73, 110, 252, 254, 256–257, 259, 273, 285, 288, 300–307; II 39, 205, 211; V 32, 75, 88, 252, 309–315; VI 126, 153, 158, 267
  "betraying" east European countries I 59
  criticism of I 302, 306
  "Declaration of Liberated Europe" I 300
  Far East I 303–304

German war reparations I 300
  Poland V 310–311
  Stalin's promise of elections I 151
  United Nations V 310, 314
Yamamoto, Isoroku IV 2, 6
Yamashita, Tomoyuki
  trial of V 265
Yarmuk River VII 78, 81
Yasui, Minoru V 188–189
Yasui v. *U.S.* (1943) V 188
Yates v. *United States* (1957) I 81; II 281
Yatskov, Anatoli II 230
Year of Eating Bones VII 242
Yellow Sea VII 148
Yeltsin, Boris VI 113–114
Yemen VIII 39, 41, 212
  assasination of Ahmad I 282
  civil war (1962) II 150
  pan-Arab campaign I 281
  revolution I 158
Yom Kippur War (1973) I 162, 222, 308–317; VI 41, 43, 107, 161, 163, 166, 171, 204, 268
Yosemite National Park VII 112
Young Lords II 94, 197
Young Plan, 1929 IV 270
Young Turks VIII 37, 45, 211
Yugoslavia I 36, 108, 273, 277, 294; II 154, 156; VI 134, 136, 175, 181, 217, 219, 226–227, 243–244, 265, 271, 273–275, 277; VII 248–249, 252–254
  collectivization VI 274
  NATO in VI 219
  "non-aligned" movement I 283
  Soviet domination until 1948 I 107; VI 54
  U.S. aid I 86
Yuma County Water Users Association (YCWUA) VII 154
Yuma Valley VII 151, 155

Z

Zahniser, Howard VII 112
Zaire VI 81
  support for FNLA and UNITA VI 1
Zambezi VII 5
Zambezi River VII 1–2, 4, 236–237, 239
Zambezi River Authority VII 245
Zambezi Valley Development Fund VII 245
Zambia 1, 4, 236–237, 239
  as British colony 4
  copper mines in 5
Zapata, Emilano III 125, 127, 129–130
Zeppelins VIII 200
Zhou En-Lai II 168, 172; VI 43
Zimbabwe VII 1, 4–5, 66, 236–237
  as British colony VII 4
  black nationalist movement in VII 9
  eviction of blacks from traditional homelands VII 8
  water extraction in VII 63
Zimbabwe African National Union (ZANU) VII 239
Zimbabwe African People's Organization (ZAPU) VII 239
Zimbabwe Electricity Supply Authority (ZESA) VII 7
Zimmermann Telegram VIII 296
Zimmerwald Conference (1915) VIII 256, 259, 261
Zionism VIII 41, 168, 208
Zola, Emile VIII 147
Zwick, David R. VII 268

Index

INDEX